Children's
Literature
Review

Guide to Gale Literary Criticism Series

For criticism on	Consult these Gale series
Authors now living or who died after December 31, 1959	*CONTEMPORARY LITERARY CRITICISM (CLC)*
Authors who died between 1900 and 1959	*TWENTIETH-CENTURY LITERARY CRITICISM (TCLC)*
Authors who died between 1800 and 1899	*NINETEENTH-CENTURY LITERATURE CRITICISM (NCLC)*
Authors who died between 1400 and 1799	*LITERATURE CRITICISM FROM 1400 TO 1800 (LC)* *SHAKESPEAREAN CRITICISM (SC)*
Authors who died before 1400	*CLASSICAL AND MEDIEVAL LITERATURE CRITICISM (CMLC)*
Authors of books for children and young adults	*CHILDREN'S LITERATURE REVIEW (CLR)*
Dramatists	*DRAMA CRITICISM (DC)*
Poets	*POETRY CRITICISM (PC)*
Short story writers	*SHORT STORY CRITICISM (SSC)*
Black writers of the past two hundred years	*BLACK LITERATURE CRITICISM (BLC)*
Hispanic writers of the late nineteenth and twentieth centuries	*HISPANIC LITERATURE CRITICISM (HLC)*
Native North American writers and orators of the eighteenth, nineteenth, and twentieth centuries	*NATIVE NORTH AMERICAN LITERATURE (NNAL)*
Major authors from the Renaissance to the present	*WORLD LITERATURE CRITICISM, 1500 TO THE PRESENT (WLC)*

ISSN 0362-4145

volume 50

Children's Literature Review

Excerpts from Reviews,
Criticism, and Commentary
on Books for Children
and Young People

Deborah J. Morad
Editor

GALE

DETROIT · LONDON

STAFF

Deborah J. Morad, *Editor*

Cindy Buck, Sheryl Ciccarelli, Sara Constantakis, Mary Gillis, Catherine Goldstein, Sharon Gunton, Alan Hedblad,
Melissa Hill, Motoko Fujishiro Huthwaite, Arlene Johnson, Paul Loeber, Carolyn C. March, Thomas McMahon,
Adele Sarkissian, Martha Urbiel, Kathleen L. Witman, *Contributing Editors*

Karen Uchic, *Technical Training Specialist*

Joyce Nakamura, *Managing Editor*

Susan M. Trosky, *Permissions Manager*
Edna Hedblad, Michele Lonoconus, *Permissions Associates*

Victoria B. Cariappa, *Research Manager*
Corrine A. Stocker, *Project Coordinator*
Barbara J. McNeil, Andrew Guy Malonis, Gary J. Oudersluys, Maureen Richards, *Research Specialists*
Jeffrey D. Daniels, Tamara C. Nott, Tracie A. Richardson, Cheryl D. Warnock, *Research Associates*
Phyllis P. Blackman, *Research Assistant*

Mary Beth Trimper, *Production Director*
Deborah Milliken, *Production Assistant*

Barb Yarrow, *Graphic Services Supervisor*
Christine O'Bryan, *Desktop Publisher*
Randy Bassett, *Image Database Supervisor*
Robert Duncan, Michael Logusz, *Imaging Specialists*
Pamela A. Reed, *Imaging Coordinator*

Library of Congress Catalog Card Number 76-643301
ISBN 0-7876-2078-5
ISSN 0362-4145
Printed in the United States of America

10 9 8 7 6 5 4 3 2 1

Contents

Preface   vii
Acknowledgements   xi

Preface

Literature for children and young adults has evolved into both a respected branch of creative writing and a successful industry. Currently, books for young readers are considered among the most popular segments of publishing. Criticism of juvenile literature is instrumental in recording the literary or artistic development of the creators of children's books as well as the trends and controversies that result from changing values or attitudes about young people and their literature. Designed to provide a permanent, accessible record of this ongoing scholarship, *Children's Literature Review (CLR)* presents parents, teachers, and librarians—those responsible for bringing children and books together—with the opportunity to make informed choices when selecting reading materials for the young. In addition, *CLR* provides researchers of children's literature with easy access to a wide variety of critical information from English-language sources in the field. Users will find balanced overviews of the careers of the authors and illustrators of the books that children and young adults are reading; these entries, which contain excerpts from published criticism in books and periodicals, assist users by sparking ideas for papers and assignments and suggesting supplementary and classroom reading. Ann L. Kalkhoff, president and editor of *Children's Book Review Service Inc.*, writes that "*CLR* has filled a gap in the field of children's books, and it is one series that will never lose its validity or importance."

Scope of the Series

Each volume of *CLR* profiles the careers of a selection of authors and illustrators of books for children and young adults from preschool through high school. Author lists in each volume reflect:

- an international scope

- representation of authors of all eras

- the variety of genres covered by children's and/or YA literature: picture books, fiction, nonfiction, poetry, folklore, and drama

Although the focus of the series is on authors new to *CLR*, entries will be updated as the need arises.

Organization of This Book

An entry consists of the following elements: author heading, author portrait, author introduction, excerpts of criticism (each preceded by a bibliographical citation), and illustrations, when available.

- The **Author Heading** consists of the author's name followed by birth and death dates. The portion of the name outside the parentheses denotes the form under which the author is most frequently published. If the majority of the author's works for children were written under a pseudonym, the pseudonym will be listed in the author heading and the real name given on the first line of the author introduction. Also located at the beginning of the introduction are any other pseudonyms used by the author in writing for children and any name variations, including transliterated forms for authors whose languages use nonroman alphabets. Uncertainty as to a birth or death date is indicated by question marks.

- An **Author Portrait** is included when available.

- The **Author Introduction** contains information designed to introduce an author to *CLR* users by presenting an overview of the author's themes and styles, biographical facts that relate to the author's literary career or critical responses to the author's works, and information about major awards and prizes the author has received. The introduction begins by identifying the nationality of the author and by listing the genres in which s/he has written for children and young adults. Introductions also list a group of representative titles for which the author or illustrator being profiled is best known; this section, which begins with the words "major works include," follows the genre line of the introduction. For seminal figures, a listing of major works about the author follows when appropriate, highlighting important biographies about the author or illustrator that are not excerpted in the entry. The centered heading "Introduction" announces the body of the text.

- **Criticism** is located in three sections: **Author's Commentary** (when available), **General Commentary** (when available), and **Title Commentary** (commentary on specific titles).

  - The **Author's Commentary** presents background material written by the author or by an interviewer. This commentary may cover a specific work or several works. Author's commentary on more than one work appears after the author introduction, while commentary on an individual book follows the title entry heading.

  - The **General Commentary** consists of critical excerpts that consider more than one work by the author or illustrator being profiled. General commentary is preceded by the critic's name in boldface type or, in the case of unsigned criticism, by the title of the journal. *CLR* also features entries that emphasize general criticism on the oeuvre of an author or illustrator. When appropriate, a selection of reviews is included to supplement the general commentary.

  - The **Title Commentary** begins with the title entry headings, which precede the criticism on a title and cite publication information on the work being reviewed. Title headings list the title of the work as it appeared in its first English-language edition. The first English-language publication date of each work (unless otherwise noted) is listed in parentheses following the title. Differing U.S. and British titles follow the publication date within the parentheses. When a work is written by an individual other than the one being profiled, as is the case when illustrators are featured, the parenthetical material following the title cites the author of the work before listing its publication date.

    Entries in each title commentary section consist of critical excerpts on the author's individual works, arranged chronologically by publication date. The entries generally contain two to seven reviews per title, depending on the stature of the book and the amount of criticism it has generated. The editors select titles that reflect the entire scope of the author's literary contribution, covering each genre and subject. An effort is made to reprint criticism that represents the full range of each title's reception, from the year of its initial publication to current assessments. Thus, the reader is provided with a record of the author's critical history. Publication information (such as publisher names and book prices) and parenthetical numerical references (such as footnotes or page and line references to specific editions of works) have been deleted at the discretion of the editors to provide smoother reading of the text.

- Centered headings introduce each section, in which criticism is arranged chronologically; beginning with Volume 35, each excerpt is preceded by a boldface source heading for easier access by readers. Within the text, titles by authors being profiled are also highlighted in boldface type.

- Selected excerpts are preceded by **Explanatory Annotations,** which provide information on the critic or work of criticism to enhance the reader's understanding of the excerpt.

- A complete **Bibliographical Citation** designed to facilitate the location of the original book or article precedes each piece of criticism.

- Numerous **Illustrations** are featured in *CLR*. For entries on illustrators, an effort has been made to include illustrations that reflect the characteristics discussed in the criticism. Entries on authors who do not illustrate their own works may also include photographs and other illustrative material pertinent to their careers.

Special Features: Entries on Illustrators

Entries on authors who are also illustrators will occasionally feature commentary on selected works illustrated but not written by the author being profiled. These works are strongly associated with the illustrator and have received critical acclaim for their art. By including critical comment on works of this type, the editors wish to provide a more complete representation of the artist's career. Criticism on these works has been chosen to stress artistic, rather than literary, contributions. Title entry headings for works illustrated by the author being profiled are arranged chronologically within the entry by date of publication and include notes identifying the author of the illustrated work. In order to provide easier access for users, all titles illustrated by the subject of the entry are boldfaced.

CLR also includes entries on prominent illustrators who have contributed to the field of children's literature. These entries are designed to represent the development of the illustrator as an artist rather than as a literary stylist. The illustrator's section is organized like that of an author, with two exceptions: the introduction presents an overview of the illustrator's styles and techniques rather than outlining his or her literary background, and the commentary written by the illustrator on his or her works is called "illustrator's commentary" rather than "author's commentary." All titles of books containing illustrations by the artist being profiled are highlighted in boldface type.

Other Features: Acknowledgments, Indexes

- The **Acknowledgments** section, which immediately follows the preface, lists the sources from which material has been reprinted in the volume. It does not, however, list every book or periodical consulted for the volume.

- The **Cumulative Index to Authors** lists all of the authors who have appeared in *CLR* with cross-references to the biographical, autobiographical, and literary criticism series published by Gale Research. A full listing of the series titles appears before the first page of the indexes of this volume.

- The **Cumulative Index to Nationalities** lists authors alphabetically under their respective nationalities. Author names are followed by the volume number(s) in which they appear.

- The **Cumulative Index to Titles** lists titles covered in *CLR* followed by the volume and page number where criticism begins.

A Note to the Reader

CLR is one of several critical references sources in the Literature Criticism Series published by Gale Research. When writing papers, students who quote directly from any volume in the Literature Criticism Series may use the following general forms to footnote reprinted criticism. The first example pertains to material drawn from periodicals, the second to material reprinted from books.

[1]T. S. Eliot, "John Donne," *The Nation and the Athenaeum,* 33 (9 June 1923), 321-32; excerpted and reprinted in *Literature Criticism from 1400 to 1800,* Vol. 10, ed. James E. Person, Jr. (Detroit: Gale Research, 1989), pp. 28-9.

[1]Henry Brooke, *Leslie Brooke and Johnny Crow* (Frederick Warne, 1982); excerpted and reprinted in *Children's Literature Review,* Vol. 20, ed. Gerard J. Senick (Detroit: Gale Research, 1990), p. 47.

Suggestions Are Welcome

In response to various suggestions, several features have been added to *CLR* since the beginning of the series, including author entries on retellers of traditional literature as well as those who have been the first to record oral tales and other folklore; entries on prominent illustrators featuring commentary on their styles and techniques; entries on authors whose works are considered controversial; occasional entries devoted to criticism on a single work or a series of works; sections in author introductions that list major works by and about the author or illustrator being profiled; explanatory notes that provide information on the critic or work of criticism to enhance the usefulness of the excerpt; more extensive illustrative material, such as holographs of manuscript pages and photographs of people and places pertinent to the careers of the authors and artists; a cumulative nationality index for easy access to authors by nationality; and occasional guest essays written specifically for *CLR* by prominent critics on subjects of their choice.

Readers who wish to suggest authors to appear in future volumes, or who have other suggestions, are cordially invited to contact the editor. By mail: Editor, *Children's Literature Review,* Gale Research, 27500 Drake Road, Farmington Hills, MI 48331-3535; by telephone: (800) 347-GALE; by fax: (248) 699-8065.

Acknowledgments

The editors wish to thank the copyright holders of the excerpted criticism included in this volume and the permissions managers of many book and magazine publishing companies for assisting us in securing reproduction rights. We are also grateful to the staffs of the Detroit Public Library, the Library of Congress, the University of Detroit Mercy Library, Wayne State University Purdy/Kresge Library Complex, and the University of Michigan Libraries for making their resources available to us. Following is a list of the copyright holders who have granted us permission to reproduce material in this volume of **CLR**. Every effort has been made to trace copyright, but if omissions have been made, please let us know.

COPYRIGHTED EXCERPTS IN *CLR*, VOLUME 50, WERE REPRODUCED FROM THE FOLLOWING PERIODICALS:

The ALAN Review, v. 21, Spring, 1994. Reproduced by permission.—*America,* v. 133, December 6, 1975. © 1975. All rights reserved. Reproduced with permission of America Press, Inc., 106 West 56th Street, New York, NY 10019.—*American Artist,* v. 43, May, 1979. Reproduced by permission.—*Appraisal: Science Books for Young People,* v. 23, Spring, 1990. Copyright © 1990 by the Children's Science Book Review Committee. Both reproduced by permission.—*Best Sellers,* v. 25, May 15, 1965; v. 30, July 1, 1970. Copyright 1965, 1970, by the University of Scranton. Both reproduced by permission.—*Booklist,* v. 66, December 1, 1969; v. 70, February 15, 1974; v. 71, January 1, 1975; v. 73, November 1, 1976; v. 73, April 1, 1977; v. 73, April 15, 1977; v. 73, May 15, 1977; v. 74, October 15, 1977; v. 75, March 15, 1979; v. 76, November 15, 1979; v. 76, April 1, 1980; v. 76, May 1, 1980; v. 77, October 1, 1980; v. 78, September 1, 1981; v. 78, October 1, 1981; v. 78, December 1, 1981; v. 78, April 1, 1982; v. 79, September 1, 1982; v. 79, October 15, 1982; v. 80, September 1, 1983; v. 81, January 15, 1985; v. 82, November 1, 1985; v. 83, April 15, 1986; v. 83, October 1, 1986; 83, October 15, 1986; v. 84, October 15, 1987; v. 86, September 1, 1989; v. 86, October 15, 1989; v. 87, September 1, 1990; v. 87, November 15, 1990; v. 88, July, 1991; v. 88, September 15, 1991; v. 88, December 15, 1991; v. 88, April 15, 1992; v. 88, July, 1992; v. 89, May 15, 1993; v. 90, October 1, 1993; v. 91, September 15, 1994; v. 91, November 1, 1994; v. 92, September 15, 1995; v. 92, October 15, 1995; v. 92, March 1, 1996; v. 92, April 1, 1996; v. 93, September 1, 1996; v. 93, October 1, 1996; v. 93, November 15, 1996; v. 94, September 1, 1997; v. 94, November 1, 1997. Copyright © 1969, 1974, 1975, 1976, 1977, 1979, 1980, 1981, 1982, 1983, 1985, 1986, 1987, 1989, 1990, 1991, 1992, 1993, 1994, 1995, 1996, 1997 by the American Library Association. All reproduced by permission. —*The Booklist,* v. 66, January 15, 1970; v. 66, February 1, 1970; v. 67, November 15, 1970; v. 68, June 15, 1972; v. 70, October 15, 1973; v. 70, February 15, 1974; v. 71, September 1, 1974; v. 71, March 1, 1975; v. 72, September 15, 1975; v. 72, October 15, 1975; v. 72, December 15, 1975; v. 72, April 1, 1976. Copyright © 1970, 1972, 1973, 1974, 1975, 1976 by the American Library Association. All reproduced by permission.—*The Booklist and Subscription Books Bulletin,* v. 61, June 15, 1965; v. 64, September 15, 1967; v. 64, July 15, 1968; v. 65, February 15, 1969. Copyright © 1965, 1967, 1968, 1969 by the American Library Association. All reproduced by permission.—*Books for Your Children,* v. 4, Spring, 1969. © *Books for your Children* 1969. Reproduced by permission.—*Bulletin of the Center for Children's Books,* v. XVIII, March, 1965; v. XVIII, July, 1965; v. 19, May, 1966; v. 19, July-August, 1966; v. 20, September, 1966; v. 21, November, 1967; v. 22, March, 1969; v. 22, July-August, 1969; v. 23, November, 1969; v. 24, April, 1971; v. 24, May, 1971; v. 25, June, 1972; v. 26, September, 1972; v. 26, February, 1973; v. 27, November, 1973; v. 28, October, 1974; v. 28, April, 1975; v. 28, June, 1975; v. 29, January, 1976; v. 29, March, 1976; v. 30, January, 1977; v. 30, March, 1977; v. 31, October, 1977; v. 31, November, 1977; v. 31, June, 1978; v. 32, July-August, 1979; v. 33, June, 1980; v. 34, February, 1981; v. 35, December, 1981; v. 35, January, 1982; v. 35, March, 1982; v. 35, June, 1982; v. 35, July-August, 1982; v. 36, September, 1982; v. 36, April, 1983; v. 38, October, 1984; v. 38, April, 1985; v. 38, June, 1985; v. 38, July, 1985; v. 39, November, 1985; v. 40, November, 1986; v. 40, December, 1986; v. 40, February, 1987; v. 40, March, 1987; v. 40, May, 1987; v. 40, June, 1987; v. 41, September, 1987; v. 42, January, 1989; v. 43, October, 1989; v. 43, November, 1989; v. 44, November, 1990; v. 44, March, 1991; v. 45, January, 1992; v. 45, February, 1992. Copyright © 1965, 1966, 1967, 1969, 1971, 1972, 1973, 1974, 1975, 1976, 1977, 1978, 1979, 1980, 1981, 1982, 1983, 1984, 1985, 1986, 1987, 1989, 1990, 1991, 1992 by The University of Chicago. All reproduced by permission./ v. 46, September, 1992; v. 46, June, 1993; v. 47, November, 1993. Copyright © 1992, 1993 by The Board of Trustees of the University of Illinois. All reproduced by permission./ v. XIV, July-August, 1961; v. XVI, September, 1962. Copyright © 1961, renewed 1989; copyright © 1962, renewed 1990 by The University of Chicago. Both reproduced by permission.—*Catholic Library World,* v. 48, December, 1976; v. 52, December, 1980. Both reproduced by permission.—*Childhood Education,* v. 43, October, 1966; v. 51, April-May, 1975. Copyright © 1966, 1975 by the Association. Both reproduced by permission of the Association for Childhood Education International, 11501 Georgia Avenue, Suite 315, Wheaton, MD.—*Children's Book News,* v. 3, January-February, 1968; v. 3, September-October, 1968. Both reproduced by permission.—*Children's Book Review,* v. I,

XLIII, October 1, 1975; v. XLIII, October 15, 1975; v. XLIV, March 1, 1976; v. XLIV, July 1, 1976; v. XLIV, September 1, 1976; v. XLV, February 1, 1977; v. XLV, September 15, 1977; v. XLVI, February 1, 1978; v. XLVII, March 15, 1979; v. XLIV, September 1, 1979; v. XLVII, November 15, 1979; v. XLVII, April 1, 1980; v. XLVIII, June 15, 1980; v. XLVIII, November 15, 1980; v. XLIX, August 15, 1981; v. XLIX, November 15, 1981; v. L, July 15, 1982; v. LI, February 15, 1983; v. LI, May 1, 1983; v. LIII, May 15, 1985; v. LV, January 1, 1987; v. LV, April 1, 1987; v. LV, July 15, 1987; v. LVI, March 1, 1988; v. LVI, July 15, 1988; v. LVII, November 1, 1989; v. LIX, April 1, 1991; v. LIX, July 15, 1991; v. LX, February 1, 1992; v. LXI, December 15, 1993; v. LXIII, August 15, 1995; v. LXIII, October 1, 1995; v. LXVI, January 1, 1998. Copyright © 1968, 1969, 1970, 1971, 1972, 1973, 1974, 1975, 1976, 1977, 1978, 1979, 1980, 1981, 1982, 1983, 1985, 1987, 1988, 1989, 1991, 1992, 1993, 1995, 1998 The Kirkus Service, Inc. All rights reserved. All reproduced by permission of the publisher, *Kirkus Reviews* and Kirkus Associates, L.P.—*Kirkus' Service,* v. XXXV, July 1, 1967; v. XXXV, July 15, 1967; v. XXXVI, February 15, 1968; v. XXXVI, April 15, 1968; v. XXXVI, June 15, 1968; v. XXXVI, October 15, 1968. Copyright © 1967, 1968 The Kirkus Service, Inc. All rights reserved. All reproduced by permission of the publisher, *Kirkus' Service* and Kirkus Associates, L.P.—*Learning,* v. 5, January, 1977. Reproduced by permission of The Education Center, Inc.—*Library Journal,* v. 90, July, 1965 for a review of "The X-Factor" by Dorothy S. Jones; v. 93, June 15, 1968 for a review of "Robin Hood of Sherwood Forest" by Mary I. Purucker. Copyright © 1965, 1968 by Reed Publishing, USA, Division of Reed Holdings, Inc. Both reproduced by permission of the respective authors.—*The Lion and the Unicorn,* v. 16, December, 1992. © 1992. Reproduced by permission of The Johns Hopkins University Press.— *Multicultural Review,* v. 1, July, 1992. Reproduced by permission of Greenwood Publishing Group, Inc., Westport, CT. —*The New York Times Book Review,* June 13, 1965; January 31, 1971; October 3, 1971; November 17, 1974; January 25, 1976; July 2, 1978; January 31, 1982; January 2, 1983; May 1, 1983; November 4, 1984; May 26, 1985; May 8, 1988; December 25, 1988; May 19, 1991; May 22, 1994; November 10, 1996. Copyright © 1965, 1971, 1974, 1976, 1978, 1982, 1983, 1984, 1985, 1988, 1991, 1994, 1996 by The New York Times Company. All reproduced by permission./ May 26, 1935; November 2, 1941; April 23, 1944; July 13, 1947; August 22, 1948; November 11, 1951; January 10, 1954; August 29, 1954; November 18, 1956; January 5, 1958; December 14, 1958; January 18, 1959; January 31, 1960; May 20, 1962. Copyright 1935, renewed 1963; copyright 1941, renewed 1969; copyright 1944, renewed 1972; copyright 1947, renewed 1975; copyright 1948, renewed 1976; copyright 1951, renewed 1979; copyright 1954, renewed 1982; copyright © 1956, renewed 1984; copyright © 1958, renewed 1986; copyright © 1959, renewed 1987; copyright © 1960, renewed 1988; copyright © 1962, renewed 1990 by The New York Times Company. All reproduced by permission.—*Publishers Weekly,* v. 189, May 30, 1966; v. 191, April 17, 1967; v. 195, April 14, 1969; v. 198, August 31, 1970; v. 202, July 17, 1972; v. 204, October 29, 1973; v. 205, April 15, 1974; v. 206, December 2, 1974; v. 206, December 30, 1974; v. 207, May 19, 1975; v. 213, May 1, 1978; v. 217, March 14, 1980; v. 219, March 13, 1981; v. 219, June 5, 1981; v. 226, November 2, 1984; v. 227, June 7, 1985. Copyright © 1966, 1967, 1969, 1970, 1972, 1973, 1974, 1975, 1978, 1980, 1981, 1984, 1985 by Xerox Corporation. All reproduced from *Publishers Weekly,* published by R. R. Bowker Company, a Xerox company, by permission./ v. 230, August 22, 1986; v. 231, April 10, 1987; v. 234, July 29, 1988; v. 239, January 1, 1992; v. 239, June 22, 1992; v. 241, August 8, 1994; v. 242, September 25, 1995; v. 243, February 12, 1996; v. 243, February 19, 1996; v. 243, September 16, 1996; v. 244, July 7, 1997. Copyright 1986, 1987, 1988, 1992, 1994, 1995, 1996, 1997 by Reed Publishing USA. All reproduced from *Publishers Weekly,* published by the Bowker Magazine Group of Cahners Publishing Co., a division of Reed Publishing USA.—*The Reading Teacher,* v. 50, October, 1996. Reproduced by permission. —*Reading Time,* v. 37, May, 1993. Reproduced by permission.—*The Saturday Review,* v. XXXVIII, December 17, 1955; v. LIV, February 20, 1971. © 1979, General Media Communications, Inc. Both reproduced by permission of *The Saturday Review.*—*The Saturday Review of Literature,* v. XXVII, April 15, 1944; v. XXXI, October 16, 1948. © 1979, General Media Communications, Inc. Both reproduced by permission of *The Saturday Review.*—*The School Librarian,* v. 14, March, 1966; v. 14, July, 1966; v.15, July, 1967; v. 16, March, 1968; v. 16, July, 1968; v. 17, March, 1969; v. 17, December, 1969; v. 18, June, 1970; v. 20, September, 1972; v. 21, December, 1973; v. 24, March, 1976; v. 24, December, 1976; v. 25, December, 1977. All reproduced by permission.—*School Library Journal,* v. 13, January, 1967; v. 14, September, 1967; v. 14, November, 1967; v. 15, November 15, 1968; v. 16, October, 1969; v. 16, May 15, 1970; v. 17, September, 1970; v. 17, December, 1970; v. 17, February 15, 1971; v. 18, December, 1971; v. 19, September, 1972; v. 19, October, 1972; v. 20, September 15, 1973; v. 20, November, 1973; v. 20, March, 1974, v. 20, May 15, 1974; v. 21, September 15, 1974; v. 21, April, 1975; v. 21, May, 1975; v. 22, December, 1975; v. 22, February, 1976; v. 23, December, 1976; v. 24, September, 1977; v. 25, March, 1979; v. 26, November, 1979; v. 26, April, 1980; v. 26, May, 1980; v. 27, December, 1980; v. 27, April, 1981; v. 28, December, 1981; v. 28, May, 1982; v. 29, January, 1983; v. 29, March, 1983; v. 29, May, 1983; v. 30, January, 1984; v. 31, January, 1985; v. 31, February, 1985; v. 31, April, 1985; v. 32, September, 1985; v. 32, October, 1985; v. 33, October, 1986; v. 33, November, 1986; v. 33, March, 1987; v. 33, April, 1987; v. 34, June-July, 1987, v. 34, November, 1987; v. 34, May, 1988; v. 35, November, 1988; v. 35, September, 1989; v. 35, October, 1989; v. 36, October, 1990; v. 37, February, 1991; v. 37, April, 1991; v. 37, October, 1991; v. 38, February, 1992; v. 38, June, 1992; v. 38, September, 1992; v. 39, May, 1993; v. 39, September, 1993; v. 40, May, 1994; v. 40, December, 1994; v. 41, October, 1995; v. 42, March, 1996; v. 42, June, 1996; v. 42, October, 1996. Copyright © 1967, 1968, 1969, 1970, 1971, 1972, 1973, 1974, 1975, 1976, 1977, 1979, 1980, 1981,

COPYRIGHTED EXCERPTS IN *CLR*, VOLUME 50, WERE REPRODUCED FROM THE FOLLOWING BOOKS OR PAMPHLETS:

ILLUSTRATIONS APPEARING IN *CLR*, VOLUME 50, WERE REPRODUCED FROM THE FOLLOWING SOURCES:

PHOTOGRAPHS APPEARING IN *CLR*, VOLUME 50, WERE REPRODUCED FROM THE FOLLOWING SOURCES:

Children's Literature Review

Candy Dawson Boyd

1946-

(Born Marguerite Dawson Boyd) African-American author of fiction and picture books.

Major works include *Circle of Gold* (1984), *Breadsticks and Blessing Places* (1985; published as *Forever Friends*, 1986), *Charlie Pippin* (1987), *Chevrolet Saturdays* (1993), *Fall Secrets* (1994).

INTRODUCTION

Recognized for her books about contemporary children growing up in loving and supportive African-American families, Boyd brings a positive message of hope and renewal to her stories. Writing primarily for middle graders and young adults, she is celebrated for her sensitive portrayal of emotions and family relationships common to young readers of all ethnic backgrounds. Boyd is also praised for her "direct and down to earth" prose and for her depictions of dynamic but very human characters struggling with everyday problems in ordinary settings—at home, in school, and in the community. Boyd's stories offer an alternative to stereotypical literature that portrays black neighborhoods filled with gangs, violence, drugs, and fatherless children. Her protagonists are intelligent and curious children who gain support and hope from strong, loving families that also can be, inversely, problematic in and of themselves. Although the children confront injustices, loss, grief, and frustration at home and in society, they also feel comforted by the laughter and compassion of their family environment. Like Charlie's embittered father in *Charlie Pippin,* adults in Boyd's fictional world often display a cynicism towards life that idealistic children struggle to understand. Denise M. Wilms observed that "Charlie's family is black, but their relationships and emotional pain reach beyond color, and the story's impact won't quickly fade." Addressing universal themes—friendship, striving for excellence, broken dreams, death—Boyd's books affirm her respect for children's emotions and her determination to create readings that speak to a multicultural audience. Boyd admits that helping children, or giving them a "safe place to go" is her "biggest reward for writing."

Biographical Information

Born and raised in Chicago, Illinois, Boyd confessed that, growing up, she had no desire to become a children's writer or a teacher. "I didn't particularly like kids," she recalled, "and the thought of spending all day with them! . . . " Instead, Boyd dreamed of becoming a jazz singer, but was deterred when she joined the high school junior choir and discovered she was tone deaf.

She later attended Northeastern Illinois State University, where she pursued an acting career. Although Boyd received leading roles in plays and encouragement from teachers, she says that racial attitudes interfered with the possibility of a successful career. During her college years, Boyd became active in many social causes, particularly the civil rights movement. She sent food and clothing to African Americans in the South, established the Negro History Club at her school, and created a coffee shop where speakers could lead discussions on contemporary issues. Eventually, these activities superseded her schoolwork. Boyd quit college and worked for a year as a field staff organizer with Dr. Martin Luther King, Jr.'s Southern Christian Leadership Conference. Emotionally devastated by the deaths of movement leaders such as Medgar Evers, the Kennedys, and Dr. Martin Luther King, Jr., she returned to college to pursue a degree in education. Boyd continued to participate in the civil rights movement with activist Jesse Jackson in the teacher's division of Operation PUSH (People United to Save Humanity).

After college, Boyd worked for several years as an elementary school teacher in her own predominately black Chicago neighborhood. She pursued her social ideals in the classroom—actively fighting racism, organizing marches to beautify the neighborhood, and demanding that the black national anthem be played in schools. "I was a militant teacher," she explained. "I knew that being black and poor meant life was going to be a lot harder for my students, and I wanted them to have as much opportunity as possible."

In 1971, Boyd moved to Berkeley, California, where she taught a multi-ethnic classroom of students. Seeking reading materials for her students, she found a disturbing lack of children's books for the diverse cultural backgrounds that comprised her classroom. Boyd admits that the scarcity of multicultural readings prompted her to become a writer. "I got absolutely enraged when I went out and I looked at the atrocity of the books out there. . . . I wanted material, good books, strong books, books that had very interesting characters and ordinary stories. But I never saw children of color in realistic fiction depicted as children whose culture, embedded within them as a part of who they were, came out in ways that were ordinary and regular. That enraged me and I decided to become a writer." After completing her doctorate in education, she began teaching at St. Mary's College of California. She spent the first two years of her career as a writer reading all of the books written for children in the Berkeley Public Library. In 1984, she published her first novel, the award-winning *Circle of Gold.*

Major Works

Boyd's writings are embellished with the stories of her ancestors and neighbors. Drawing from her own childhood experiences, Boyd creates works that ultimately show how a family survives and prevails despite setbacks and hardships. In *Circle of Gold,* young Mattie Benson suffers from the loss of her father, who has died prior to the opening of the story. To support Mattie and her twin brother, Mattie's mother works long hours in a factory and manages the apartment building where they live. Sensing that her mother is tired and unhappy, Mattie desires to buy her an expensive gold pin for Mother's Day, hoping to regain the family cohesiveness lost after her father's death.

Boyd's second published work, *Breadsticks and Blessing Places,* hits closer to home. Largely based on her own experience, *Breadsticks* served as a goodbye to the childhood friend who died when Boyd was in fourth grade. Boyd spent two years conducting research on grief as experienced by children. She related: "I learned that children grieve deeply over a long period of time and that the rituals that adults use at wakes and funerals don't work for children." *Breadsticks* tells the story of Toni, a twelve-year-old girl from an upwardly mobile African American family. Afraid of dissappointing her parents, who want to send her to a prestigious prep school, Toni struggles to learn math so she may pass the

entrance examination. However, she is unable to maintain her concentration when her best friend Susan is killed by a drunk driver. Overwhelmed by grief and depression, Toni is helped through her slow and painful route to recovery by her friend Mattie, who, in losing her father, shares an emotional bond with Toni. Zena Sutherland commented that "Boyd deals fully and candidly with a child's reaction to the death of a close friend as well as to other aspects of the maturation process that are universal."

In *Charlie Pippin,* Boyd once again explores family relationships that have become troubled. Charlie Pippin is a hard-working and resourceful eleven-year-old black girl who, despite her good intentions, has difficulty following her school's disciplinary code. At home, she has a distant relationship with her stern, authoritarian father, a Vietnam veteran who is embittered and unwilling to discuss his experience. Hoping to better understand her father, Charlie chooses to write her social studies report on the Vietnam War. In her research, Charlie uncovers a newspaper clipping about her father and two of his close friends who were killed in action during the war. She learns of her father's heroism from her mother and grandparents, and of his dreams of becoming a painter before the war. Trying to bring the family closer together, Charlie prompts her father to honestly confront the ghosts of his past.

In a similar vein, Boyd bridges the gap between stepfather and stepson in *Chevrolet Saturdays.* The life of Joey Davis is thrown in turmoil after his parents' divorce and his mother's remarriage. The hard-working, energetic fifth-grader becomes lazy and self-centered—getting into trouble at school, neglecting his schoolwork, and alienating his stepfather, Mr. Johnson. As Mr. Johnson tries to comfort Joey, Boyd emphasizes the healing power of family unity and compassion. Boyd's optimism shines through in these "nice" characters, who Sheilamae O'Hara observes are "people who make mistakes, but who care about doing the right thing." In *Fall Secrets,* school becomes, as Boyd described, "a major part of what happens to the child." Young Jessie is bombarded by the pressures of starting middle school, making new friends, and keeping her grades up while pursuing her interest in drama. But Boyd also presents deeper issues about color and race, which surface in Jessie's jealousy of her lighter-skinned, fair-haired sister, Cass.

Awards

Circle of Gold was named a Notable Children's Trade Book in the Field of Social Studies by the National Council for the Social Studies and the Children's Book Council in 1984, and a Coretta Scott King Honor Book by the American Library Association in 1985. *Breadsticks and Blessing Places* was selected for the Children's Books of the Year List by the Child Study Children's Book Committee at Bank Street College.

TITLE COMMENTARY

📖 *CIRCLE OF GOLD* (1984)

Jeanette L. Sidley

SOURCE: A review of *Circle of Gold,* in *Social Education,* Vol. 49, No. 4, April, 1985, p. 329.

Mattie wants to buy her unhappy mother a special gift for Mother's Day, hoping to regain the love and unity shared by the family before the death of her father. Despite her best efforts, problems at school and at home become overwhelming. Finally, Mattie learns the meaning of love and understanding through a simple miracle. A sensitive, poignant story of contemporary family life.

📖 *BREADSTICKS AND BLESSING PLACES* (1985)

Publishers Weekly

SOURCE: A review of *Breadsticks and Blessing Places,* in *Publishers Weekly,* Vol. 227, No. 23, June 7, 1985, p. 81.

A black educator, Boyd has gained insights into young people in situations like those she dramatizes in this novel. Toni Douglas, 12, frets over her difficulties, keeping up with a hard course in math. She's afraid to disappoint her parents who insist that blacks must excel scholastically to succeed in today's world. The girl's studious friend Mattie helps her but Toni would rather frolic with carefree Susie, whose life seems rich and glamorous. Then Susie is killed by a speeding automobile. Toni suffers severe emotional trauma and her recovery is slow. At length, however, she shows signs of maturing; while still saddened by the loss, Toni is gaining perspective and viewing her future hopefully. Readers don't have to be black to become involved with Boyd's very human characters.

Zena Sutherland

SOURCE: A review of *Breadsticks and Blessing Places,* in *Bulletin of the Center for Children's Books,* Vol. 38, No. 11, July, 1985, p. 202.

Toni is twelve, black, plump, member of a loving family, a student at an all-black school in Chicago who hopes to improve her mathematics performance enough to pass a test that will enable her to be admitted to a special school, the King Academy. She's doing make-up work in math but loses her concentration and her interest when one of her two best friends is killed by a drunken driver. The title refers to two of the things that are associated with Toni's bereavement; several friends help her work out her grief and anger. The book ends

with Toni admitted to the King Academy. Boyd deals fully and candidly with a child's reaction to the death of a close friend as well as to other aspects of the maturation process that are universal. The tempo lags occasionally but the writing on the whole has good pace and Toni's story is written with insight and compassion.

Gerry Larson

SOURCE: A review of *Breadsticks and Blessing Places,* in *School Library Journal,* Vol. 32, No. 1, September, 1985, p. 142.

Boyd's novel is a reprieve from the gang violence, broken homes and despair of many urban, adolescent novels. Sixth-grader Toni Douglas is the sheltered daughter in an upwardly-mobile black family. Throughout the book, she is learning to cope—with parental and academic pressure to get into King Academy, with an unexpected new teacher, with the onset of menstruation, with two friends who don't get along, with the realization that friend Susan is a shoplifter and with Susan's death. And yet, although the novel's outcome is upbeat and wholesome, the narrative is lackluster. Boyd crowds her story about growing up on Chicago's South Side with too many adolescent themes and a mixed bag of predictable characters. Toni's myriad concerns obscure rather than define her character. When her customary reserve and reliability give way to angry outbursts and rebellious behavior, she is tolerated and understood by stable parents and sincere friends—an enviable but unsuspenseful situation. Finally, Toni's grief and anxiety are neatly dispelled when she conducts her own farewell ceremony for Susan and then is accepted into King Academy. Young adult readers who are expecting real family tension, inner turmoil over puberty, emotional growing pains and conflicting desires to conform and to be independent may find Toni a role model but not a soul mate. Nonetheless, this novel's positive perspective may attract junior high readers tired of crisis-laden, victimized, lonely teenage characters.

Denise M. Wilms

SOURCE: A review of *Breadsticks and Blessing Places,* in *Booklist,* Vol. 82, No. 5, November 1, 1985, p. 402.

A young black girl, Toni Douglas, faces the challenges of adolescence with no more than the usual trepidation until her best friend Susan is killed by a drunken driver. Stunned, Toni is unable to come to terms with her grief. She finds the funeral dissatisfying, is angry with classmates and friends who go on as if nothing has happened, and begins to flounder in her schoolwork. Her parents worry not only because Toni seems stymied in her grief, but because she's soon to face entrance examinations for King Academy, a top-notch, college prep public school. Toni's depression does indeed threaten to overwhelm her until another good friend, Mattie, who has lost her father, helps Toni find a way to put Susan's memory in its proper place. Boyd's story is well conceived. Although its central focus is how Toni comes to terms with Susan's death, there are other significant threads, as well as the clear intent of portraying a warm, loving, well-adjusted black family. Exposition is occasionally stiff, but characterization and plotting are excellent. Boyd has integrated themes about the complexities of friendship and the striving for excellence into a remarkably cohesive story that offers much to think about as Toni works out the changes and challenges in her life. Yet the novel's style is direct and down-to-earth and well within the reach of a general rather than a special audience. The accent is on the positive, and that is good to see.

Marian Rafal

SOURCE: A review of *Breadsticks and Blessing Places,* in *Voice of Youth Advocates,* Vol. 8, No. 5, February, 1986, pp. 382-83.

Twelve-year-old Toni feels pressure on all sides: her parents dream of sending her to King Prep School, but Toni doesn't know if she wants to change schools. Moreover, how is acceptance to the prestigious school even possible if she is failing sixth grade math? On top of that, Toni's two best friends, Mattie and Susan, can barely tolerate each other. Just as Toni begins to make progress with her math skills and Mattie and Susan reach an uneasy truce, Susan is tragically killed by a drunk driver. Young Mattie is unable to cope with this loss and rejects all efforts of comfort, pulling away from those near her. This story of a young black girl's first loss is marred by stilted writing and a lack of character development.

CHARLIE PIPPIN (1987)

Jerry Flack

SOURCE: A review of *Charlie Pippin,* in *School Library Journal,* Vol. 33, No. 7, April, 1987, p. 92.

On one front, this is a novel about a sixth-grade girl's social studies project and her inability to get along with her father, but on another level it is about the much larger issue of dreams shattered and lost. In it, Boyd examines the perceptions that young people may have of the Vietnam War, as well as the impact that the war and the homefront divisiveness of the war era continue to have on families, especially those in which there are veterans. Chartreuse "Charlie" Pippin is an 11-year-old black girl living in Berkeley, California. Not much seems to go right for her. She is a hardworking, successful businesswoman cut from the same delightful, rebellious cloth as her grandmother, but her entrepreneurial skills cause her problems with both her father and school authorities. Her decision to learn about the Vietnam War as a school report only leads to further conflict with her father, who refuses to discuss the war. The domestic resolution is in keeping with the larger issue of the war:

it is not so much a peace settlement as a cease fire. Charlie and her friends are finely drawn. Some of the adult characters, however, are perilously close to becoming stereotypes, especially the father and school principal, both of whom seem unusually stern and inflexible. On the whole, *Charlie Pippin* is a good novel about vital people and important issues.

Kirkus Reviews

SOURCE: A review of *Charlie Pippin,* in *Kirkus Reviews,* Vol. LV, No. 7, April 1, 1987, p. 550.

As a character study of a girl trying to understand the Vietnam War and what it did to her father, this has problems but is worth reading.

Chartreuse ("Charlie") Pippin is a pretty black sixth grader in Berkeley. She decides to study the war to try to answer some of her own questions. Why does her mother accept her father's rigid attitudes, saying that he lost his dreams? Why do her father and uncle, both vets, feel so differently from each other? What was the war about, anyway? Unfortunately, the answers she gets are confusing. If her father had lost his dream of being a painter when he returned from Vietnam 16 years before, why is there a painting he did of her as a toddler? Her determination to sneak around authority gives this some amusing moments, but it makes the book as tense as the unhappy relationship between father and daughter that is supposedly healed as she pays tribute to his lost comrades in arms.

There are many issues here—the racism of the Vietnam War, nuclear war, and family tension. Father-daughter relationships make a good theme, but the things that both Charlie and her father learn are not expressed in a way that a child can really understand. This might have been better as a YA novel; yet the characters and situations seem real, and the questions the book addresses are important and not well-represented in books for children.

Publishers Weekly

SOURCE: A review of *Charlie Pippin,* in *Publishers Weekly,* Vol. 231, No. 14, April 10, 1987, p. 96.

Chartreuse (Charlie) is convinced that her authoritarian father hates her because he always yells at her. So, she is shocked to learn from her grandmother, Mama Bliss, that Mr. Pippin was a "rebel" too at her age. For a class project, Charlie elects to study the Vietnam War, which her father always refuses to discuss with her. More surprises come when Charlie finds out that Mr. Pippin was a war hero. Despite her father's antagonism, Charlie researches the Vietnam War and nuclear weapons. Along the way, she learns that individuals—including children—can make a difference if they speak out. At the story's emotional ending, Charlie makes peace with her father, and he makes peace with his ghosts from the war. A strong black protagonist makes this a rare YA book; the finesse with which Boyd ties its many themes into a very moving, unified whole turns this into a stellar offering.

Denise M. Wilms

SOURCE: A review of *Charlie Pippin,* in *Booklist,* Vol. 83, No. 16, April 15, 1987, p. 1282.

Boyd's involving novel explores the relationship between a girl and her father as she tries to find out what the war in Vietnam was about and why it embittered her father. Charlie's dad is a stern, hardworking man who is strict with his daughters and essentially uncommunicative; it's left to Charlie's mother to ease the rough spots and keep the family together. A school project on war and peace motivates Charlie to investigate the Vietnam War, but her angry father refuses to talk about the subject. When she also becomes interested in the peace and no-nukes movements, he sourly keeps her at a distance, even when her speech for an oratory contest takes her to a district-level competition. But Charlie's interest in her subject is unquenchable, especially when she discovers an old news clip that reveals her father was a decorated hero and lost two of his best friends in tragic, harrowing circumstances during the war. When Charlie's Uncle Ben, who also fought in Vietnam, invites her to fly to Washington, D.C., with him for a weekend, Charlie knows she has to go despite the fact that her father has refused permission. She schemes her way out of the house to join her uncle, visits the Vietnam memorial, and returns with rubbings of the names of her father's two beloved friends; these treasured tokens become the catalyst for a moving reconciliation between Charlie and her father. Boyd's story probes sensitive issues with remarkable balance. While the story's theme is decidedly antiwar, it presents an affecting portrayal, from a child's standpoint, of the anger, concerns, and painful emotional wounds that many returned veterans still bear. Charlie's family is black, but their relationships and emotional pain reach beyond color, and the story's impact won't quickly fade.

Zena Sutherland

SOURCE: A review of *Charlie Pippin,* in *Bulletin of the Center for Children's Books,* Vol. 40, No. 9, May, 1987, p. 163.

Charlie (Chartreuse) Pippin is eleven, jealous of her older sister Sienna, baffled by her father's stern intransigence. She's black and bright; she's often in trouble at school (and that makes even more trouble at home) because she sets up businesses in school. Charlie wonders why her father is so angry, why he is irked by her school project, which entails a study of the Vietnam War in which he served. This is a story in which potential exceeds performance: although marred by awkward

stylistic lapses, it has good pace and flow. It never quite loses a quality of fragmentation, and it is used by the author as a vehicle for statements about war in general, the Vietnam War in particular, and the threat of nuclear war. Charlie, despite her mercenary flouting of school rules (and several instances of lying) is a rather engaging and certainly lively character. A little more revision, a little less didacticism, and this could be an even better story about a black family than it is.

Jane Van Wiemokly

SOURCE: A review of *Charlie Pippin,* in *Voice of Youth Advocates,* Vol. 10, No. 4, October, 1987, p. 196.

Eleven year old Charlie (short for Chartreuse) has trouble at school and at home. There's a Discipline Code at school, of which Charlie always seems to run afoul. She believes that her teacher, Mrs. Hayamoto, dislikes her. Worst of all, she thinks that her father doesn't love her as much as her older sister. To compensate, she tries to learn more about her extremely strict Vietnam veteran father in order to understand his often rigid outlook on life. Charlie gets herself appointed to the War and Peace committee for a school assignment and begins to study the Vietnam war, her father's involvement in it, and his resulting broken dreams.

On the positive side, Charlie is very self-motivated and enterprising, selling anything from pencils to self-made origami objects to Halloween face painting services. She's a real "businesswoman," showing pluck and effort in whatever she attempts. Unfortunately, Charlie also is the kind of person who gets into trouble or does the wrong thing, whether from disobedience or out of nervousness or simply from making the wrong decision. Despite her father's outbursts, Charlie's Black family life is stable and portrayed positively as loving and caring. Unobtrusively the reader will learn some facts about the Vietnam war, as well as how one family copes with its results.

CHEVROLET SATURDAYS (1993)

Marilyn Long Graham

SOURCE: A review of *Chevrolet Saturdays,* in *School Library Journal,* Vol. 39, No. 5, May, 1993, p. 103.

The divorce of his parents and his mother's remarriage throw fifth grader Joey into a self-centered, one-track state of mind. He refuses to accept his stepfather, whom he calls "Mr. Johnson," and thinks constantly about his father returning home. His school work suffers and his relationship with his mother becomes strained. Finally, when his stepfather goes to school to talk to the principal on his behalf, Joey sees the light. Their relationship improves—until the boy carelessly allows Mr. Johnson's dog to run away. In the end, Joey shows maturity, problems are resolved, and a strong friendship begins to develop between him and his stepfather. Joey and his pals are likable and believable; his parents, stepfather, and pharmacist-friend Doc are hardworking African-Americans who have overcome major hurdles in their lives. All are skillfully drawn and integrated into a convincing, contemporary story. The story's pace is slow at first, but quickens as Joey begins to find that life is more than his own selfish desires. A good novel that speaks to the large audience of children with stepfamilies.

Sheilamae O'Hara

SOURCE: A review of *Chevrolet Saturdays,* in *Booklist,* Vol. 89, No. 18, May 15, 1993, p. 1686.

Joey Davis has felt like a displaced person since his parents divorced. When his mother marries Mr. Johnson Joey finds it impossible to accept the fact that they form a family. He wants his parents to love each other and live together again. The story has few surprises. Boy rejects kindly stepfather; real father distances himself; stepfather is establishing relationship when boy's carelessness alienates stepfather; boy makes amends, and new family ties are formed. All of the principal characters are nice people, people who make mistakes, but who care about doing the right thing. That and the fact that the family is a normal, hardworking black family outweigh the predictable plot.

Roger Sutton

SOURCE: A review of *Chevrolet Saturdays,* in *Bulletin of the Center for Children's Books,* Vol. 46, No. 10, June, 1993, p. 309.

While Joey doesn't find his new stepfather Mr. Johnson "a bad man or even a mean one," he wants his own dad back, and the anxiety about his parents' divorce and his mother's remarriage is causing Joey some trouble in school, not helped by his hostile new fifth-grade teacher. This adjustment-to-divorce story covers all the bases in a way that's predictable but still sympathetic, as Joey grows to trust his stepfather via a series of Saturdays spent working with Mr. Johnson in his remodeling business. Mr. Johnson is a perfect role model, strict yet paternal, but his frequent sermons sound too much like the author talking to her readers with an earnestness that sometimes distracts from the fictional focus. Still, the African-American cast is a lively one, and Joey's school problems will strike a responsive chord among readers frustrated when their best efforts never seem to be quite good enough.

Frances Bradburn

SOURCE: A review of *Chevrolet Saturdays,* in *Wilson Library Bulletin,* Vol. 68, No. 5, January, 1994, p. 119.

The family is the most important, yet sometimes the most destructive, human unit a person ever encounters. How we develop as adults depends much on how we have dealt with our adolescence. Oftentimes, children and teens overcome horrible circumstances with the help of only one caring individual. At other times, young people struggle painfully through their maturation process in spite of parents who are caring and self-sacrificing.

Divorce or death often plays a part in this development. In Candy Dawson Boyd's latest book, *Chevrolet Saturdays,* the divorce of Joey's parents and his mother's subsequent remarriage, as well as his father's decision to seek a promotion that forces him to move to Chicago, bring change to the boy's personality. He goes from being a model student to a lackadaisical one with a great deal of help from an unhappy, burned-out sixth-grade teacher. His reputation turns from good kid to school troublemaker. He even shoplifts a package of unappetizing cupcakes from a corner store, a spontaneous action that he himself doesn't understand. All this he blames on his parents' divorce.

His mother's new husband realizes Joey's unhappiness and gently tries to soothe the boy's obvious misery. "Mr. Johnson" understands his craving for family. He himself had been shuffled from foster home to foster home, finally even stealing a car, before a social worker rescued him, providing the loving, stable nurturing he needed to become a successful adult.

Boyd comprehends the impact of divorce on children, an impact that can only be lessened, not obliterated, when separated parents such as Joey's put their children's needs above their differences and create healthy, albeit new, environments for them. She also understands how one teacher can destroy all the good teaching of the past and how educational labels can change completely a child's perception of himself. Most of all, she helps middle readers of all races and ethnic backgrounds understand how challenging it is to be an African American in a white world.

FALL SECRETS (1994)

Publishers Weekly

SOURCE: A review of *Fall Secrets,* in *Publishers Weekly,* Vol. 241, No. 32, August 8, 1994, p. 440.

Jessie, a well-intentioned African American girl, seems to have more than a sixth grader's fair share of worries. She is adjusting to a new performing arts school, where she is under pressure to get good grades—and land choice roles in various productions. She feels inferior to her lighter-skinned, straight-haired older sister, a cheerleader who hopes to be a doctor. She is also haunted by memories of the recent fires that destroyed her family's Oakland, Calif., home and almost killed her father. And she is burdened by a "secret" involving an apparently devastating incident that occurred two years earlier. Each of the three classmates Jessie is grouped with has a secret of her own, too—all of which (including Jessie's) are alluded to with such tedious frequency that by the time they're revealed they are almost anticlimactic: Jessie, for example, was told she was "funny looking" and "a terrible letdown" by a teacher who had previously taught the older sister. Information on several key figures in African American history is neatly woven into Boyd's story. Unfortunately, some frayed ends show in needless repetitions and in dialogue that doesn't always ring true.

Ilene Cooper

SOURCE: A review of *Fall Secrets,* in *Booklist,* Vol. 91, No. 2, September 15, 1994, p. 135.

Jessie Williams has a lot on her mind. She's started at a middle school focused on the performing arts, where she can persue her dream of becoming an actress, but it's hard to do drama and keep her grades up. Making friends at a new school can be dicey, too, and Jessie is also worried about her grandmother's Parkinson's disease, her father's wobbly business, and her sister's problems with her boyfriend. Jessie also occasionally flashes back to the Oakland fires, a year earlier, that almost destroyed her home. Clearly, this book has way too much going on, and it lacks some badly needed humor to leaven it. There's a stiffness here that not only cripples the plot, but also affects the characters. But Jessie's major worry is one rarely touched on, and its the main thing that makes the book interesting. Jessie is dark-skinned like her mother, but her sister, Cass, is light-skinned and has straight hair. And despite Jess' talents, she is jealous and thinks she's not as good as Cass. There is continuous dialogue throughout about color, what it means, and what people let it mean, particularly within the African American community. The attractive cover will pull readers in; the honest discussion will strike a responsive chord.

Marie Orlando

SOURCE: A review of *Fall Secrets,* in *School Library Journal,* Vol. 40, No. 12, December, 1994, p. 104.

As Jessie Williams enters the Oakland Performing Arts Middle School, she must deal with pressure to perform academically, her jealousy toward her older sister, Cass, and the difficulties of working in a small group at school. The girls who make up the "Fours" all have hidden problems that affect their group dynamics, but they manage to work cohesively on class projects, including performing at a local home for senior citizens. Always in the background are the devastating effects of the Oakland/Berkeley fire that both traumatized and mobilized the whole community. Bolstered by her loving family and a boy at school who makes her feel special, Jessie is able to confront her own insecurities. Despite workmanlike writing, stilted dialogue, and some heavy-handed messages, there are some interesting things happening here. The characters are well drawn and, while

readers may question the girls' need for secrecy about their problems, they will recognize the pressures of adolescence and exult in Jessie's determination to forge a new relationship with Cass, who's been having her own problems, and her growing pride in her African American heritage.

DADDY, DADDY, BE THERE (1995)

Kirkus Reviews

SOURCE: A review of *Daddy, Daddy, Be There,* in *Kirkus Reviews,* Vol. LXIII, No. 16, August 15, 1995, p. 1185.

A touching ode to the need of children to have their fathers involved in all aspects of their lives. Boyd eloquently sings the wish of the title, penning it into every page of the lilting text, a child's plea for the father's presence at solo recitals, ball games, at difficult times and glorious ones. Mentioned are moments that are wistful and frightening, "when my questions need your ears . . . during the hard times when the money goes, during the saxophone-blowing-blues nights." Articulating feelings that many children would have trouble putting into words, this is a book for all families, including fathers who want to reassure their offspring that they will always be close by with their love. In powerful, dream-like images, [Floyd] Cooper includes families of all ethnicities, giving this fine marriage of pictures and words a universal appeal.

Publishers Weekly

SOURCE: A review of *Daddy, Daddy, Be There,* in *Publishers Weekly,* Vol. 242, No. 39, September 25, 1995, pp. 56-57.

Boyd's image-laden narrative makes a passionate appeal to "Daddy" to "be there" to share the small and significant incidents in a child's life and—more incisively—to right the wrongs, some of which have been created by Daddy himself. The words of the book's title introduce—and end—just about every page of this belabored text, in which the narrator's entreaties range from hopeful ("Hug Mama and smile at her / On Tuesdays and in the grocery store") to plaintive ("Daddy, Daddy, / Be there, / Not only on weekends or across telephone lines, / Not only during commercials or between innings") to almost pathetic begging ("I saw you push Mama / And take another drink / And turn the television up, / Then leave, slam the door shut. / I feel the holler, the push, the door slammed. / Please stop. Stop, please. Please. Stop. / Make home safe"). Though cloying, Boyd's poetic plea strikes deep notes that will ring true for many children and parents, and may be useful as a starting point for needed dialogue Featuring kids and adults of various ethnicities, [Floyd] Cooper's intentionally hazy, brown-toned illustrations reinforce the text's unfettered emotional content.

The Reading Teacher

SOURCE: A review of *Daddy, Daddy, Be There,* in *The Reading Teacher,* Vol. 50, No. 2, October, 1996, p. 155.

Candy Dawson Boyd's expressive text is perfectly complemented by Floyd Cooper's drawings in **Daddy, Daddy Be There,** an emotionally charged picture book that reveals the importance of father's relationships with their children. Boyd's well-chosen words and Cooper's captivating muted-color illustrations give life to the inner voices of children. An array of life's experiences are featured that vividly portray a father's significant role and the need for bonding between father and child.

A DIFFERENT BEAT (1996)

Hazel Rochman

SOURCE: A review of *A Different Beat,* in *Booklist,* Vol. 93, No. 6, November 15, 1996, p. 586.

On the cover two African American girls scowl at each other. One is dark skinned, the other lighter; and issues of ethnic identity and self-esteem, competition, and friendship are at the heart of this candid contemporary story, a sequel to **Fall Secrets** (1994). Hurt by a teacher's racism, sixth-grader Jessie worries that some people don't like her dark skin. She knows that a lot of whites reject her, and some black people, too—does her own father? Her rivalry with a classmate at her performing arts middle school focuses on the girls' view of their blackness as well as on their artistic gifts. The story is too didactic, and some characters function too much as therapists. But Jessie's home and school are drawn with warmth and wit. Through individual people Boyd dramatizes the rich diversity within the African American community. She confronts issues long ignored in middle-grade fiction. Young girls will recognize Jessie's hurt and anger and her struggle to accept who she is.

Additional coverage of Boyd's life and career is contained in the following sources published by Gale Research: *Black Writers,* Vol. 2; *Junior DISCovering Authors;* and *Something About the Author,* Vol. 72.

Barbara Corcoran

1911-

(Also writes as Gail Hamilton and Paige Dixon) American author of fiction and plays.

Major works include *A Dance to Still Music* (1974), *The Clown* (1975), *Making It* (1980), *The Potato Kid* (1989), *Stay Tuned* (1991)

INTRODUCTION

Although Corcoran has written mysteries, romances, and historical fiction, she is celebrated for her realistic young adult novels that focus on the physical and emotional problems of adolescence. With a sure touch born of her own experiences and an instinctive sympathy for the loneliness and challenge of this time of life, she creates young protagonists—typically females—who struggle to attain independence, forge an identity, and understand human weakness while discovering their own strengths in the process. Although her secondary characters often lack depth, she is widely praised for skill in developing sympathetic, realistic, and fully three-dimensional main protagonists who often suffer from a condition that causes them duress, such as a learning disability, deafness, terminal illness, chronic shyness, minority status, estranged parents, or family break-up. Through adventures and physical ordeals, her characters are able to grow and reach a new level of maturity—becoming self-sufficient and accepting others and themselves. When not creating perceptive young adult characters, Corcoran also deals with the issue of animal welfare through wildlife books. Likewise, she often includes animals in her young adult novels as a source of love and focus in the lives of her protagonists. Corcoran's well-paced and engrossing stories have won her many loyal readers over the past thirty years. Reviewers recognize her as a thoroughly professional writer who makes the crafting of "highly readable novels that combine vivid, sensitive characterizations with engaging story lines" look easy. Jean Fritz commented on one of the major messages of Corcoran's works: "'Trust life,'" she says, 'Go into the world. There'll be good people out there as well as bad. There'll be help.' She handles her theme like a prism, holding it up to catch the light at different angles, turning it this way and that so that each book is a fresh expereince and variation of the pattern."

Biographical Information

Born in Hamilton, Massachusetts, Corcoran was the only child of John Gilbert and Anna (Tuck) Corcoran. Many of her later writings were drawn from early childhood experiences, including time spent with her father, who

was a physician and music lover; adventures at a nearby New Hampshire camp; and her struggle with an illness that left her temporarily deaf. When once asked where she got her ideas for writing, she replied: "The answer is not so much that you go looking for ideas . . . it's more likely that they are already stored away in your memory. Sometimes they may be things that happened to you, or stories you have heard about other people's experiences." Particularly influential, however, was her parents' divorce when she was in the seventh grade. "The children of a broken home always suffer. . ." she once professed, "more than the adults realize." Corcoran's understanding of the plight of the child of divorced parents has brought depth and sincerity to many of her novels. After her parents separated, she and her mother moved to North Beverly, Massachusetts, where she attended high school. At her father's wish, she later enrolled at Wellesley College where she wrote and published a few poems.

After graduating with a BA in 1933, she turned to play writing until the Great Depression compelled her to find a job. Although she still attended as many plays as she could in Boston, she took a job writing history text books for the Works Progress Administration Writers Project. She also worked behind the scenes as a stage manager for two local summer stock theater companies. This first-hand experience, she admitted, taught her more about playwriting than she would ever have picked up at the Yale School of Drama, where she wished to pursue graduate studies but her father had refused to finance. When World War II commenced, one of her plays was produced and several of her short stories were sold. As with so many Americans at the time, Corcoran's life changed completely. She postponed her writing career to volunteer as a plane spotter and to work as an electronics inspector at an Ipswich factory taken over by the U.S. Navy. Her health suffered, however, from a year of forty-eight-hour weeks and she was forced to resign. After her recovery, she moved to Washington, D.C., and found a tight-security job helping to break codes for the Army Signal Corps.

Corcoran's first postwar job as advertising manager for a small chain of New England stores helped her get back in the habit of writing: she created newspaper ads and penned two weekly columns about the stores' wares. She also began publishing magazine stories again, but she still felt restless. "It seemed to me," she commented, "that I was on a track going nowhere." With her mother and many of her theater friends in California, she decided to move to Los Angeles where writing "was not only acceptable but praiseworthy." She worked for a celebrity informative service for eight years, but continued to write at night and published occasional magazine pieces. Getting a film script accepted, however, turned out to be very difficult, so she abandoned her efforts to find a niche in the Hollywood entertainment industry.

In 1954, she relocated to Missoula, Montana, a place she fell in love with while visiting, and decided to pursue a master's degree at the University of Montana with an eye toward teaching college English. Back in academia for the first time in twenty-one years, she completely immersed herself in writing and shifted from plays to fiction. She went through a string of jobs in Los Angeles, Santa Barbara, Cincinnati, and Covington, Kentucky. Eventually, the long-coveted university job came through and she spent five years teaching English at the University of Colorado in Boulder. Without a doctorate, though, she was forced to leave and later accepted an offer at Palomar College, a junior college in California where, in spite of a heavy teaching load, she began writing *Sam* (1967). When *Sam* was accepted for publication by *Athenaeum*, Corcoran began writing three more novels over the next two years. These also were sold for publication; however, with her health at risk from the teaching and writing workload, she decided to quit teaching to write full-time. She returned to Montana, a familiar setting for many of her books and a place she long considered home. In Montana, she kept up her prolific output, which now stands at more than eighty books in many genres—realistic fiction, mystery, romance, historical romance, wildlife tales, and many short stories, essays, and plays.

Major Works

Corcoran's debut novel, *Sam*, introduces one of the major themes of her writing: a young protagonist with only one parent encounters an unfamiliar situation or place and develops, often through a relationship with an animal, a better understanding of self and others. Fifteen-year-old Sam, who has been home-schooled by her anti-social father on a Montana island, experiences profound culture shock when she enters high school for the first time. Sam's training of an Irish wolfhound, given to her by her uncle, becomes a focal point in her troubled life. Even with first-novel flaws, *Sam* has been a long-time favorite with readers who enjoy seeing how Sam learns to make choices in the midst of cultural conflict and inevitable change.

Corcoran's own childhood and her year of teaching at a private girls' school were important sources for *This Is a Recording* (1971). With her parents on the verge of divorce, fourteen-year-old Marianne is sent to Montana to live with her grandmother, a former actress. Marianne faces several conflicts during her journey from the city to the country—a barn burning, a hunting accident, and her own feelings about her parents' breakup. Reviewers have praised the realistic depiction of the effect of divorce on teenage children and commended the novel's fast-moving plot. Typically regarded by reviewers as Corcoran's best novel, *A Dance to Still Music* is emblematic of her basic theme: the capacity of a young protagonist to bear adversity with spirit and increasing self-knowledge. Fourteen-year-old Margaret recently becomes deaf from a severe illness and feels unsupported by her mother who has moves the family to Florida from Maine. Margaret runs away, intending to return to Maine, but gets no farther than the front porch of a house inhabited by Josie, an older woman whose quiet presence helps Margaret find a way to accept her disability and go forward with her life. Corcoran drew from her own experience with temporary deafness while writing *A Dance to Still Music*. "I used my memory of the mastoid days to re-create what it feels like to suddenly be deaf," revealed Corcoran. "It seemed to me that the deaf got a lot less sympathy than, for instance, the blind. People got tired of repeating, of having to raise their voices, of being misunderstood, and they were often impatient, or worse, behaved as if the deaf person were not there. *A Dance to Still Music* remains my favorite of my own books." Like *A Dance to Still Music*, *Axe-Time, Sword-Time* (1976) introduces Elinor, an eighteen-year-old girl with a learning disability who takes a job in a wartime factory as her parents are about to divorce. Corcoran brought her wartime experiences to bear on this novel, re-creating details from her job as a Navy electronics inspector that lend a compelling authenticity to the book. In a similar vein, Corcoran culls information from her European travels to create *The Clown*. Set in the former Soviet Union, *The Clown* is a Cold War tale of defection and suspense. Lisa, an orphan fluent in Russian, travels to Moscow with her aunt and uncle as a translator. During the journey she meets a young Russian clown who is trying to escape to the

West. Lisa helps him defect by giving him her uncle's passport. While Zena Sutherland remarked that "the details of the planning and execution of the escape are intriguing," other reviewers have noted that Corcoran does not solve the problem of the stranded uncle.

Making It is based on actual incidents that occurred in Missoula, Montana. Seventeen-year-old Sissy, one of six children of a Colorado minister, moves to Los Angeles to live with her older sister Charlotte while attending UCLA on a scholarship. To her dismay, Sissy learns that the sister she once idolized finances her high living by working as a prostitute and drug dealer. Sissy's apprehension is compounded by grief when Charlotte is murdered. After the publication of *Making It,* for a brief time Corcoran churned out adult romances whose heroines all find adventure, intrigue, and ultimately love. She also began a mystery trilogy. In *You're Allegro Dead* (1981), Corcoran introduces Stella and Kim, twelve-year-old sleuths sent to a revival of Camp Allegro by their mothers who attended the camp as children themselves. At camp, the typical summertime activities become frightening and dangerous when someone throws rocks at Stella and takes a shot at Kim. In *A Watery Grave* (1982), the two friends are guests in the New England home of the Farleys on the anniversary of their son's drug-related death. Stella and Kim solve the mystery of another death, though not before more violence permeates this suspenseful tale. Stella and Kim find suspense and mystery once again at Camp Allegro during a winter holiday in *Mystery on Ice* (1985), the third book in the mystery series.

Shifting focus and theme, Corcoran's works in the 1980s and early 1990s concentrate on contemporary teenage problems. In *The Potato Kid* fourteen-year-old Ellis is looking forward to an exciting summer of horseback riding until her mother takes in a needy ten-year-old girl named Lilac for the summer, expecting Ellis to look after her. This is an inauspicious beginning to the girls' relationship, but a friendship is eventually ignited when Lilac's mother refuses to take her back. Ellis has a riding accident, and her grandfather suffers a heart attack. Lilac's adoption by Ellis's grandparents ends a story noted for its authentic characters and heartwarming appeal. *Stay Tuned* is set in a cheap, crime-ridden New York City hotel where sixteen-year-old Stevie lives with her father. Stevie's neighbors, thirteen-year-old Eddie and his little sister Fawn, have been left alone after the recent death of their grandmother. Unhappy with her living arrangment, Stevie takes Eddie and Fawn with her to live with relatives in New Hampshire. En route they meet Alex, an eighteen-year-old who has left home after a disagreement with his father. The four end up at a campsite in Maine where Alex teaches them survival skills while allowing them to make their own decisions. Through the course of their journey, all four have the opportunity to grow in understanding of others as well as themselves. Like so many of Corcoran's books, *Stay Tuned* earned accolades as an "engrossing story" with sympathetic characters that any young reader might like to know.

TITLE COMMENTARY

SAM (1967)

Kirkus Service

SOURCE: A review of *Sam,* in *Kirkus Service,* Vol. XXXV, No. 38, July 15, 1967, p. 815.

Growing up as a slowly sharpening awareness of the layered complexity of life and ultimately as engagement—"We can't keep out of it. . . . We're people. We're stuck with it"—in the first juvenile by an author who writes with spare, precise suggestiveness. The story of Sam ("a foolish name for a fifteen-year-old girl") builds quietly from her first glimpse of an Irish wolfhound and the defection of foolish, fond Uncle Everett to Las Vegas; as a reward for not disclosing his intended departure (her first hard choice), Uncle Everett gives her a wolf-hound, Cormac, whose training and showing become the focal point of a variously troubled existence. Sam lives on an island in Montana, a retreat for her cynical father and sometimes prison for her ingenuous mother; tutored at home, she is self-conscious and uncertain—*but* "I cannot grow up like Rima the Bird Girl"—in her first encounter with the high school syndrome. Suddenly she is someone, and Sam suspects it is because she hasn't told on the two big wheels who hit her and ran in an auto accident; but one of the boys didn't want to run, and as his guilt assumes distasteful, demeaning forms, Sam decides that he must be forced to confess, at whatever cost to her social acceptance. The third choice is the hardest: Uncle Everett returns, laden with gifts and debts; feeling for him despite his weakness ("He is our uncle" and "I would never have had Cormac at all without him"), she determines to sell the now-very-valuable dog to help him. The violent death of Uncle Everett that forestalls the sacrifice is the only faintly contrived note, but the decision has been made, and the reader is convinced that Sam meant what she said, and understands why. A sub-plot involving the romance of the attractive music teacher will be less comprehensible to youngsters, but it hardly matters. Sam is a magnificently realized character in a novel whose maturity is inherent, whose concerns are moral in the most fundamental sense. For the reader undeterred by the circumspect establishment of situation, it offers many levels of response.

Zena Sutherland

SOURCE: A review of *Sam,* in *Bulletin of the Center for Children's Books,* Vol. 21, No. 3, November, 1967, p. 39.

Sam and her brother were used to the isolation of the island on which they lived; their father had always felt that being involved with other people only brought trouble. But Sam was fifteen; she wanted to be with her peers. When she did have a chance to test her father's theories, it looked as though he were right: the boys at school were tough, the girls snobbish; her uncle was a weak man and a gambler, his wife a foolish and helpless woman. Yet Sam found, after her uncle's death, that she never regretted the protective affection she'd given him, that even if her father were right about people she was one of them and couldn't avoid her commitment as a human being. With good characterization and writing style, and with a balanced treatment of facets of Sam's life, the book will appeal especially to those readers who are interested in dogs, since a good portion of the story is devoted to Sam's dog, their participation in a dog show, and plans for attending future shows.

Nancy Young Orr

SOURCE: A review of *Sam,* in *School Library Journal,* Vol. 14, No. 3, November, 1967, p. 74.

Sam, a 15-year-old girl, begins her junior year in high school, attending public school for the first time; until now she and her brother have been tutored by their cynical father at their Montana island home. The half-year of her life described here is a time of testing her father's distrust of people against her first independent contacts with the world. There are experiences at school, her first dance and a brush with the "in crowd," a hit-and-run accident with Sam as the victim, and intermittent visits by weak, gambling Uncle Everett. His gift of an Irish wolfhound and Sam's training and showing of the prize dog are the focus for the story's divergent elements. Sam's uncertain eagerness to face life and to understand other people in spite of their weaknesses give the story some strength, but the author almost stacks the deck in favor of the father's misanthropic philosophy. There are a number of improbable events in which secondary characters emerge as exaggerated, stereotyped examples of human frailty. Sam develops the courage to face new people and experiences, but for no logical reason—the book does not provide the necessary balance of feeling for any joy in life or goodness in people; Sam's changing views of her father—from initial hero-worship to near-pity at the end—are not realistically portrayed nor does the plot prepare readers for the emotional about-face.

Marilyn Gardner

SOURCE: "The Facts About Teen-Age Fiction," in *The Christian Science Monitor,* November 2, 1967, p. B11.

Ask today's teens what they'd most like improved in their relationships with adults, and the answer would undoubtedly be understanding and respect. Ask parents and teachers the same question about teens and the response would probably be similar. Yet it is precisely these two qualities which often seem the most difficult to engender between the two groups. The solution? More and better communication, which sounds simple enough in theory but which too often proves more difficult in practice.

Small wonder, then, that problems of communication, understanding, and respect should figure so importantly in several new books for younger teens. Fictional fare for this group is becoming steadily more palatable, and the four selections here are generally indicative of the trend.

The most impressive offering is *Sam,* a magnificently drawn portrait of a 15-year-old girl with a boy's name, a strange background, and a lot to learn about life. Everything about Barbara Corcoran's first book is unusual, from its highly individual group of characters and their island setting in Montana to the complex situations they must resolve.

Educated at home by her anti-social rancher-miner father, Sam finds herself the product of a totally different world when she finally enters school as a junior. She attends her first football game and first dance, rides her first bicycle, and is confronted for the first time with alien customs, social values, and questions of right and wrong. At the same time a valuable dog, the gift of an irresponsible uncle, temporarily brings other problems. Life suddenly becomes a series of important choices and decisions: a reexamination of her parents' strange values, for one thing, and searching answers to questions of Who is right? and What is most important? The result is a mature, wise, and well-developed story, as individual and appealing as Sam herself.

SASHA, MY FRIEND (1969)

Kirkus Reviews

SOURCE: A review of *Sasha, My Friend,* in *Kirkus Reviews,* Vol. XXXVII, No. 15, August 1, 1969, p. 783.

"You couldn't really expect anything in Montana to be like California"—and Hallie, who has an "apricot-colored party dress" tucked-away and "never liked blue jeans at home" is appalled at the rugged isolation of the Christmas tree farm prescribed for her father after his injury in the accident that killed her mother. On page 110 she's still despondent—this despite the accession of Sasha, an orphaned wolf cub. His loss (in a malicious neighbor's trap) is overshadowed by the simultaneous illness of her father, forcing Hallie to manage the Christmas tree harvest alone. Thanks to the good neighborliness of the poor, intrepid Penneys, of squatter Black Thunder and of the rough-and-ready loggers, plus her own new-found pluck and stamina, she pulls through, becoming a true Montanan in the process. It's a long time a-coming and Hallie, at fourteen, is a self-pitying clod with no claim on the reader's sympathy.

Ethel L. Heins

SOURCE: A review of *Sasha, My Friend,* in *The Horn Book Magazine,* Vol. XLV, No. 5, October, 1969, pp. 540-41.

It was difficult for Hallie at fifteen to keep from wallowing in a sea of bitter self-pity. The automobile accident that had taken her mother's life had left her father recovering all too slowly from severe injuries. The doctor urgently advised him to leave the smog and the tension of Los Angeles and go to his boyhood home in Montana, where he had inherited the family's vast Christmas-tree farm. Young and fun-loving, Hallie was inconsolable at leaving the comfortable southern California life—the friends, the beach parties, the constant excitement—to live in a trailer at the edge of a remote forest. Schooling was to be by correspondence course; friends were to consist only of Birdie, the strange crippled girl, and Black Thunder, the elderly Indian. And when she longed for a dog to comfort her loneliness, there came into her life a beautiful white motherless wolf pup, who everyone warned would be impossible to raise and tame. The themes are not new to children's books: a girl's painful adjustment to wilderness living and a fierce attachment to an unconventional pet. But the author, who lives in Montana by preference, writes with conviction as she tells an absorbing story set against the austere beauty of her adopted state.

Cherie Zarookian

SOURCE: A review of *Sasha, My Friend,* in *School Library Journal,* Vol. 16, No. 2, October, 1969, p. 148.

An unusually good girl's story of adventure, courage, adaptation to a wilderness life, and love for a pet white wolf. After her mother is killed in an auto accident, Hallie goes with her convalescing father to his Christmas tree farm in Montana. Deprived of her Los Angeles home, friends, and way of life, lacking even the familiarity of school attendance to ease her loneliness, Hallie makes her own life in a small house trailer; she learns to cook, ice skate, and shoot, and makes friends with a crippled girl and an old Indian. All this is saved from being trite and goody-goody by a very plain, straightforward, unsentimental style that results in an extremely moving and sensitive story.

The Booklist

SOURCE: A review of *Sasha, My Friend,* in *The Booklist,* Vol. 66, No. 11, February 1, 1970, pp. 667, 669.

After her mother's death teen-age Hallie and her father move from Los Angeles to northwestern Montana for his health. Living in a trailer on a Christmas tree farm and isolated from school, Hallie is homesick, desolate, and unprepared for wilderness living but, as she learns to cope, acquires an orphaned wolf cub for company, and experiences the friendship and helpfulness of neighbors, she begins to regard the place as home. A well-paced, enjoyable story, believable because Hallie's adjustment does not come too suddenly or easily.

THE LONG JOURNEY (1970)

Kirkus Reviews

SOURCE: A review of *The Long Journey,* in *Kirkus Reviews,* Vol. XXXVIII, No. 13, July 1, 1970, pp. 687-88.

Hawkins Dry Diggings once was just another Montana mining town; now it's a ghost town and a long way from Butte for a girl of thirteen alone on horseback. During her chiaroscuro trip to Uncle Arthur's for advice about Grandfather's failing vision, Laurie's eyes are wide open for a lot of reasons: ever since her parents died when she was three she's had only correspondence courses, *National Geographic,* boxes of old books, and Grandfather's protective cynicism to teach her about the world. What she knows is the land, well enough to subsist on it, while steering clear of towns and people who'd pluck her away from home and into an orphanage. (Grandfather's biggest bugaboo is institutions.) What she doesn't know about is bathtubs, telephones, revolving doors, cream sauces, fluffy living . . . and the other "civilized" appurtenances she encounters when contingencies like a howling storm and a bullet wound bring her suspectingly into contact with other ways and awaken some dormant propensities. Darker still is Laurie's fearsome meeting with a crazed itinerant devil-sort who reinforces Grandfather's pronouncements confusingly, because the friendlier helpful folks seem to belie them. At once wise and innocent, Laurie's not an ambiguity: she's just ambivalent—uncertainly steeling herself against what she's been warned against, but experiencing new directions with a guarded interest and rightful pride. Every bit as firm a character as *Sam,* she marshalls resources to cope with things she hasn't any categories for—brooding sometimes, singing sometimes, mulling over Sylvia Plath, pretty wretched by the end of the road until the sunny upswinging at Uncle Arthur's. This is no formula melodrama despite pat predictables and the happy compromise that promises the best for Laurie of both worlds: part of its charm is the confluence of opposites that aren't really, and again like *Sam* it grips and gives on more than one dimension.

Susan Stanton

SOURCE: A review of *The Long Journey,* in *School Library Journal,* Vol. 17, No. 1, September, 1970, p. 114.

A tense adventure story set in Montana. Thirteen-year-old Laurie lives with her grandfather in a deserted mining town. Because the old man is going blind, Laurie must ride her horse to Butte to get advice from her Uncle Arthur. Her isolated life has made her fear towns, roads, and strangers, and her trip is made more difficult by trying to avoid all these. On the way, she does meet many people, some mean, some helpful; a wandering madman who pursues her provides a constant threat of terror in the story. But, at last, Laurie does reach Uncle Arthur, and help is obtained for Grandpa. Equally important is the fact that the girl's journey has greatly broadened her knowledge of people, material comforts, and the possibilities for intellectual growth open to her. The story is fast-paced, with believable characters; the Montana setting is very evocatively portrayed.

Sheryl B. Andrews

SOURCE: A review of *The Long Journey,* in *The Horn Book Magazine,* Vol. XLVI, No. 5, October, 1970, p. 478.

When thirteen-year-old Laurie's grandfather, Peter Bent, finally has to come to terms with his worsening cataract condition, his granddaughter must travel across Montana on horseback to get help from her Uncle Arthur in Butte. Raised by her grandfather in a deserted old mining town and instilled by him with an unreasoning fear of "'institutions'"—orphan asylums in particular—Laurie sets off on her horse Hook, determined to avoid contact with any person in authority. Eventually, though, she discovers the truth in something that Emily Kimball, a retired schoolteacher who shelters her during a heavy hail storm, tells her about people: "'Time and again they'll let you down, but by and large you have to trust them.'" The strength of the book lies in the presentation of this central philosophy, as the author simply and clearly portrays the characters—both good and bad—that Laurie meets on her long journey to Butte and to her new self. The story is weakened, however, by the melodramatic treatment of the villain, "Old Hell-and-Damnation Hastings," who suggests the mad itinerant preacher in Davis Grubb's *The Night of the Hunter.* And one cannot help but wonder at the sheer number of adventures that the girl faces on her way: She is haunted throughout the story by the preacher, finds and releases a frantic colt tangled in barbed wire, is shot in the arm by a rancher, gets caught in a small forest fire, and rescues a three-year-old girl from a cliff ledge. Still, the author of *Sasha, My Friend* and *A Row of Tigers* has created another very enjoyable adventure story.

Marjorie Barr Spector

SOURCE: A review of *The Long Journey,* in *The New York Times Book Review,* January 31, 1971, p. 26.

Laurie James is an adolescent becoming acquainted with—not sex and drugs—bathtubs, elevators, towns and people. It's not always easy to believe in her background but it's worth the effort.

Raised for most of her 13 years by a hermit-like grandfather in a Montana ghost town, Laurie has had a lopsided education. *National Geographic,* her dead father's books and correspondence school lessons were her contacts with the world until she has to ride across state seeking help for her grandfather's blindness. Her jour-

ney might be humorous to some, but to her it is a constant and serious education in life.

Her grandfather, disquieted by the foolishness of the human race, taught benign misanthropy to Laurie—who finally has a chance to measure his teaching by her own experience. Whether struggling with the mysteries of a bathtub spigot or racing into the night to evade a half-mad itinerant preacher, she pits her own good sense against the unfamiliar and generally comes out on top. Finally, when she must choose between isolation and civilization, her decision is as honest and thoughtful as this book about her journey.

A STAR TO THE NORTH (with Bradford Angier, 1970)

Virginia Haviland

SOURCE: A review of *A Star to the North,* in *The Horn Book Magazine,* Vol. XLVII, No. 1, February, 1971, p. 55.

Intolerable incompatibility with a too-busy, autocratic father and a self-centered stepmother sends Kimberly, fourteen, and Nathaniel, sixteen, off on an escape to Uncle Seth and his cabin in the Canadian northwoods. Their rare and generous brother-sister relationship adds warmth to the story. Nathaniel accepts Kimberly's surprise appearance on the journey and Kimberly endures increasing hardships as they cover the final lap of their journey by canoe through perilous white water. Both of them face disillusionment at their destination when Uncle Seth's affair with a woman precludes hospitality. The human factors and the travel details—there is a brilliantly described shooting of the rapids when Kimberly's sprained ankle makes portage impossible—raise the book above many such accounts of adventure. At the end of the story, parental relationships are not improved, but are faced squarely, while a maturing point of view enriches the character study.

Mary B. Mason

SOURCE: A review of *A Star to the North,* in *School Library Journal,* Vol. 17, No. 4, February 15, 1971, p. 55.

A partially successful story of wilderness survival. Seeking to escape the stifling life in Southern California as well as parental dictatorialness, Nathaniel takes off for British Columbia where he hopes to spend the summer with his "backwoods" uncle. He is intercepted by his 14-year-old sister, also a fugitive, and together they begin a long canoe journey. They acquire a dog, encounter numerous hazards and predicaments (wild waters, damaged canoe, injuries, unfriendly animals) but experience the satisfaction of learning to cope. At the end of the journey they are faced with the most difficult obstacle of all: the fact that their uncle is not prepared to take them in. But, by now, Kimberly is ready to accept the family peace offering, a year in Switzerland, and a place is found for Nat. Though the plot is only average in interest and execution, the brother-sister relationship is well handled, and real feeling is conveyed for wilderness life.

Zena Sutherland

SOURCE: A review of *A Star to the North*, in *Saturday Review*, Vol. LIV, No. 8, February 20, 1971, p. 31.

A sixteenth birthday was special, wrote Grandmother, enclosing a check for $500. Nathaniel knew just what to do with it: go North. Last summer he had helped his uncle, a college dropout, build a cabin in Canada, and that was the life for him. He pitied his sister Kimberly, stuck in the plush conformity of Malibu Beach and aching to escape with him, but he never dreamed he'd find her sneaking off the train at the end of his journey. No outdoorswoman, Kimberly slows the plan for a rapid trip by canoe and portage to the cabin, but she's courageous and determined, and Nathaniel is impressed. Both are resourceful in coping with obstacles and dangers. The story has pace and suspense, the dialogue and characterization are consistently acute, and the setting is appealing.

Zena Sutherland

SOURCE: A review of *A Star to the North*, in *Bulletin of the Center for Children's Books*, Vol. 24, No. 8, April, 1971, pp. 120-21.

The Canadian wilderness is the setting for a vigorous tale of two young people coping with unexpected problems on a runaway journey. Kimberly, fourteen, had followed her older brother when she learned that he was going off to the woods to visit a young uncle he'd helped the summer before. So there she was—and what could Nathaniel do but take her along on his planned canoe trip to Uncle Seth's remote cabin? Staunch and determined, the two learn to accept each other's inadequacies in amiable fashion, arriving at the cabin to find their polarization fixed. (Uncle Seth, it appears, has shacked up with a woman and is not at all enchanted to see them.) Kimberly has learned that roughing it is not for her, and departs. Nathaniel is just as sure that the simple life is for him; although disappointed in Seth, he arranges for a cabin of his own. The wilderness journey has a felicity of detail that is appealing, the plot is sound and nicely developed, there is action and excitement in the young people's adventures, and the brother-sister relationship is drawn with perception.

THIS IS A RECORDING (1971)

Kirkus Reviews

SOURCE: A review of *This Is a Recording*, in *Kirkus Reviews*, Vol. XXXIX, No. 13, July 1, 1971, pp. 681-82.

"My family gave me this tape recorder as a propitiation for their sins, especially the sin of going off to Europe without me and dumping me on my grandmother in the wilds of Montana. . . . The world will little note nor long remember what I say here, but I will one day transcribe this tape into the written word, and when I am old, I will read it with bitterness and rue"—an author's prerogative. Far better, however, to enter laughing and indulgently elevate one eyebrow now and then ("It gives you a look of skepticism and superiority and absolute mastery of the situation"). In Marianne's case the problem is adaptation and at fourteen she's full of somehow coexisting incongruities: she's just finished *Portnoy's Complaint* and she signs herself E. Pluribus Unum in an anti-pollution letter to a Montana editor, but her teeth alas are "solid braces" and she has this throwback attachment to a security blanket in the form of a gunbelt; she also has the kind of pride that goeth before a fall, as she says (and then does—with an audience— from a horse). New York's St. Regis is her Eloisian stopover between Boston and Missoula ("my father has a pathological preoccupation with credit cards"); and like all Barbara Corcoran's unconventionally heroic types (individuals, rather), she tests her own elasticity before embracing Montana's disparities. Marianne almost caves in when the burdens grow too heavy for her round shoulders . . . in which connection—"if any parent ever hears these words, let me implore you not to nag at your children to stand up straight. It does not work." She's a sturdy seriocomic performer who sounds, at her refreshing best, thoroughly spontaneous; an entertaining if variously imperfect recording . . . say the flip side of *Sam,* and play it again.

Georgess McHargue

SOURCE: A review of *This Is a Recording*, in *The New York Times Book Review*, October 3, 1971, p. 8.

"There was a poor young boy who left his country home/ And came to the city to seek employment," recounts the grand old W. C. Fields number, and everyone knows what traps and trials await youthful innocence in the sinful city. Nearly as prominent in folk tradition is the urban easterner-gone-west.

Newest addition to the westward procession is 14-year-old Marianne Temple. Arriving by air in Missoula, Mont., Marianne faces the unknown with a tape recorder, a gunbelt (albeit a toy one) and a large load of resentment at being thus packed off to visit a grandmother she hasn't seen since she was 2.

Like every dude since Balboa, Marianne is confounded by the West. Grandmother Katherine Carter turns out to be a retired actress. Her house is not "like the one in *Bonanza,*" but a gabled Victorian residence full of antiques where she dines each evening with candlelight and wine. Katherine's hired hand is a college-bound native American named Oliver Everybodylooksat, a kindly and self-reliant individual neither wild-eyed nor picturesque.

Marianne's months in Montana are packed with enough action to satisfy any TV fan. They center on a conflict between Oliver and a bigoted under-sheriff (more Bull Connor than Bat Masterson), and include a barn-burning, false arrest and a dramatic hunting accident.

Counterpoint to these events is Marianne's slowly unfolding realization that her parents are planning a divorce. The spectrum of her reactions nicely complements her growing affection for Katherine and friendship with Oliver, so that in the end her departure is as unwilling as had been her arrival. Though the story does not pretend to offer any great depth of insight into personalities and situations, the narrator's voice (Marianne's) has made the most of a brisk and lively surface.

However, one reservation must be registered. For a with-it kid like Marianne, some initial tenderfoot-type gaffes are just plain incredible. No one who writes outraged letters-to-the-editor about pollution (signed E Pluribus Unum) can convincingly make remarks like "I didn't know Indians went to college."

Caviling aside, this is an exceptionally readable story and possesses one further shining, if negative, virtue. For once in fiction the non-equestrian tenderfoot stays that way to the end, instead of winning the junior trophy in the local rodeo during the last chapter.

Virginia Haviland

SOURCE: A review of *This Is a Recording,* in *The Horn Book Magazine,* Vol. XLVII, No. 6, December, 1971, pp. 619-20.

A tape recorder registers Marianne's account of a school year in a small Montana community. "Abandoned" by her parents who are travelling to Europe, she lives with her widowed grandmother, a former actress. A somewhat sophisticated tenth-grader from an Eastern city, Marianne is curiously addicted to TV Westerns; because of her awkwardness and tactlessness, she encounters misery and every kind of adjustment problem. After having painfully survived disasters at school and in the woods, she eventually gains the friendship and respect of two Indian boys and of her own wise grandmother. In the course of her development, Marianne learns much about the destruction of wildlife and about discrimination against Indians. As a heroine, she engages the reader less readily than do those of the author's previous Western stories, although the overall conception and the style of the story are excellent. The small line drawings provided as chapter headings make the volume attractive.

Cherie Zarookian

SOURCE: A review of *This Is a Recording,* in *School Library Journal,* Vol. 18, No. 4, December, 1971, p. 63.

Another superior, fast-moving novel with a Montana setting by the author of *Sasha, My Friend* and *The Long Journey.* Boston-bred Marianne, a clever 14-year-old with a lively sense of the ridiculous, is sent to Montana to live with her independent, ex-actress grandmother while her parents decide what to do about their failing marriage. In Montana, Marianne meets Indians Oliver Everybodylooksat and his brother Dougie Three Toes, and gains knowledge from them of wildlife, ecology, and conservation. She also learns about coping with mocking classmates, a bully, and a corrupt assistant sheriff. Told in the first person as a tape-recorded diary, this is not just another city-girl-matures-in-the-country-and-begins-to-love-nature story. The tone is generally whimsical, characterizations are vivid, there's plenty of action, and Marianne's wry, humorous and insightful observations spark interest throughout.

A TRICK OF LIGHT (1972)

Kirkus Reviews

SOURCE: A review of *A Trick of Light,* in *Kirkus Reviews,* Vol. XL, No. 3, February 1, 1972, p. 135.

Within the improbable framework, this is a comfortable and unassuming story of a girl's learning to "let go" of her more independent twin brother. At the outset, the accomplishments (listed rather than demonstrated) of Cass' parents almost invite resentment: their father teaches high school math and woodworking and an adult cabinet-making class, makes and sells early American reproductions, and plays the banjo; Muth runs the post office, does needlepoint, braids rugs to sell, plays the piano, and raises apples, vegetables, flowers, goats, sheep, hens, peacocks and six children—with enough leftover energy to name her daughters Rosalind, Ophelia and Cassandra. Then there's the twins' winter overnight in a nearby summer camp, all so they can go on looking for their wounded dog Bingo in the morning—however convenient a set-up for their close interaction, less reasonable (and less considerate of their unnotified parents) than sleeping at home. But once they're dug in at the camp, the twins' thwarted stabs at communication are quietly authentic; Cass' later fall through the ice carries readers right along into the "menacing" pool, and Bingo's ultimate death brings the story to a convincing close as it brings the twins uncloyingly (and unpossessively) together.

Ethel L. Heins

SOURCE: A review of *A Trick of Light,* in *The Horn Book Magazine,* Vol. LXVIII, No. 3, June, 1972, p. 267.

Stories about young adolescents need not deal with shattering human problems to be either credible or significant; and since every age has its own anxieties, a well-written, convincing, honest book needs no justification.

Cassandra and her twin brother Paige had always been inseparable, like two halves of a whole person. But lately Paige had seemed different: interested in ham radio, football, and his own friends. Cassandra felt resentful, excluded, betrayed. Then one day, their beloved dog—the one bond that still held firm between them—was struck by a car and, gravely injured, had run off alone into the snowy woods. Diffidently at first, brother and sister set out to search; but the two-day-long ordeal, with its inevitable sorrow at the end, opened new insights and led to new understanding.

The Booklist

SOURCE: A review of *A Trick of Light,* in *The Booklist,* Vol. 68, No. 20, June 15, 1972, p. 908.

Since Cassandra and her twin brother Paige have always been very close, Cassandra cannot understand why Paige recently seems to be developing interests and friendships that do not include her. Not until their dog is hit by a car and the twins spend two days together searching for the injured animal in the New Hampshire woods does Cassandra begin to understand that the changes in their relationship are a necessary if painful part of growing up. Although the theme is stressed rather heavily at the end and the mild profanity seems unessential, the story sustains interest throughout and the portrayal of Cassandra is both sympathetic and realistic.

Zena Sutherland

SOURCE: A review of *A Trick of Light,* in *Bulletin of the Center for Children's Books,* Vol. 26, No. 6, February, 1973, p. 88.

There comes a time when brothers and sisters, however close they have been as small children, acquire other interests and drift away. Cassandra resented the fact that this had happened to her twin brother Paige, and her resentment was all the stronger because to her Paige was still the most important person in the world. She takes a step toward maturity and emotional independence when she and Paige spend the night alone in a camp that is closed for the winter and she has a chance to talk to him and to see that he does still care for her. They are in the camp because they have been looking for their dog (hurt by a car) whose tracks are in the woods. It has grown late and they have decided to stay there to get an early start the next morning—but are not concerned with the parents who do not know where they are. The dog is found, badly hurt but alive, but he dies at the vet's. Cassandra, when her twin tells her, gently suggests that he visit his friend: she now understands that their drifting apart is inevitable and she is charitable enough to make it easier for Paige. The relationship is seen with perceptive sensitivity, the writing style is competent, but this aspect of the story and the situation of isolation that brings it into focus do not ever quite blend.

DON'T SLAM THE DOOR WHEN YOU GO (1972)

Kirkus Reviews

SOURCE: A review of *Don't Slam the Door When You Go,* in *Kirkus Reviews,* Vol. XL, No. 13, July 1, 1972, p. 728.

Wishing all the time that her parents cared enough to come after her, but sure that they'd rather be touring Europe than bringing up their "menopause baby," 17 year-old Judith runs away from her Florida home and joins two friends in a cross-country drive to a Montana ghost town they've picked out from a map. But living off the land entails unforeseen difficulties and in the end Judith (whose real interest is in ancient civilizations) is happy to be found by her 37 year-old sister, a nun whom she hasn't seen in 15 years but who seems to really want Judith to share her Los Angeles apartment (and maybe even take some classes at UCLA). Sister Angelica, a "new nun" who turns up in a pink linen suit, is merely a less familiar stereotype than Eric the vegetarian commune leader Judith loves briefly, or Edmund the 10 year-old drug orphan she befriends, or Hap the gun-boarding, hippie-hating barber who exposes Eric's moral emptiness by shaving his head and beard one midnight at gunpoint. For Judith, then, a sober search for self among the facades of a too resolutely modern day Western.

Publishers Weekly

SOURCE: A review of *Don't Slam the Door When You Go,* in *Publishers Weekly,* Vol. 202, No. 3, July 17, 1972, p. 122.

A highly sophisticated story about Judith, Lil, and Flower, with a dash of young love and sex deftly handled. The three teen-age girls, alienated from their parents, leave home and drive to a ghost town, Plunketville, Montana, to try their luck at living "off nature" in the wilds. The climax comes when rabid right-wingers attack the girls and their friends who are trying to set up a commune. The conclusion is a surprise but wholly logical. Realistic and satisfying, with a full quota of drama and suspense.

Diane Gersoni-Stavn

SOURCE: A review of *Don't Slam the Door When You Go,* in *School Library Journal,* Vol. 19, No. 2, October, 1972, p. 117.

Barbara Corcoran's latest is certainly not her best—it's a preachy story of three teen-age girls who run away to Montana, rough it for a while, meet up with hippies, hippie-haters, a tough waif, and a tender-hearted sheriff and finally make their separate, believable decisions about dropping back in. The chief protagonist is intelligent, studious Judith; her sister travelers are flirtatious, popular Flower and conservative horsy Lily. One interesting, gratifyingly realistic twist is that the boy Judith yens for doesn't fall for her beautiful soul but instead succumbs to Flower's more obvious charms. It's also refreshing to encounter a fictional 10-year-old who curses like real 10-year-old boys. And, Corcoran does her usual good job of describing the Montana landscape. Still, the story is laden with obtrusive messages—it's good to live your own life while remaining tolerant of other life styles: it's bad to be materialistic and to take drugs, etc.—and most of the characters are stereotypes.

ALL THE SUMMER VOICES (1973)

Kirkus Reviews

SOURCE: A review of *All the Summer Voices,* in *Kirkus Reviews,* Vol. XLI, No. 13, July 1, 1973, p. 691.

Fourteen in 1910, David has a summer job working beside grown men in the shipyard, along with other responsibilities he takes over from his unreliable father, who drinks too much and makes only a spotty living. But the painful father-son friction is eased a bit when Papa is talked into buying a used Model T to replace the aging horse that draws his taxi, and the two achieve at least a temporary rapport after David is accidentally knocked unconscious and into the water at a ship launching and Dad fishes him out. Another voice in David's summer choir is that of his mother's father, who helps care for the horse and, more important, helps David to recognize his father's virtues and to partially understand his drinking. An occasional tight lip would have made David's mother—a totally supportive, uncomplaining wife—more believably sub-seraphic; with David himself, however—both understandably resentful and youthfully self-righteous—it is easy to empathize, and the textures of life in 1910 Essex, Massachusetts, are an integral, enriching part of his story.

The Booklist

SOURCE: A review of *All the Summer Voices,* in *The Booklist,* Vol. 70, No. 4, October 15, 1973, p. 290.

Against a wonderfully mellow Essex, Massachusetts backdrop Corcoran relates the experiences of young David O'Brien's summer of 1910. The story revolves around David's mixed feelings toward his father, whose occasional drinking bouts and irresponsibility irritate the industrious boy. David's frustration with his father's ways leads him to upstage Mr. O'Brien, first by attending to his horse-drawn taxi service and favoring a partnership in a model-T taxi, and then by saving the family's aging horse, pledged by his father to a sly trader in remuneration for an accident caused by the Ford. It is David's maternal grandfather who contributes most to the boy's gradual understanding of his father and to his realization that money, while important, is not everything. Corco-

ran's richly flavored New England setting and her perceptively wrought interplay of family feelings place this high on the list of titles exploring adolescent growth.

Publishers Weekly

SOURCE: A review of *All the Summer Voices,* in *Publishers Weekly,* Vol. 204, No. 18, October 29, 1973, p. 36.

It's the summer of 1910 and young David is proud to be working at the shipyard in Essex, Massachusetts. But the boy has problems: his father is irresponsible, given to drinking too much at times. His brother Andrew is sailing with the Gloucester fishing fleet, set to be a real "highliner," the captain who brings back the biggest catch. Though David is a hard worker and a good boy, he isn't treated as an adult at home, as Andrew is. During a worrisome season, Mr. O'Brien's Ford auto bucks and kills the horse pulling the rig of Old Harry, the scissors grinder. David is desolate when he finds that his father has promised to give Harry the family horse, the boy's beloved Lady, in payment. Using his wits, David manages to keep Lady in the family and to earn his father's respect. This is an engrossing novel of a bygone time and grand entertainment.

Jean C. Thomson

SOURCE: A review of *All the Summer Voices,* in *School Library Journal,* Vol. 20, No. 3, November, 1973, p. 48.

Set in the port of Essex, Massachusetts around 1910, this is a weak tale about a boy who learns to respect his father despite his failings. Fearing that the family will end up in the Poor House if the old man doesn't stop drinking, David works hard at his grueling summer job in the shipyard and fills in for Papa when he's too drunk to meet his commitments. The boy's self-righteousness gets on his father's nerves, and the two clash repeatedly, while Mother tries to mediate. David and his father are reconciled when Dad helps save a neighbor's life and rescues David from drowning. This contrived solution shows David that he's a loving father and a brave man. David gets the point (and readers won't miss it either): don't judge the complex world of adults too harshly. David doesn't talk to people his own age; instead he deals with adult problems and listens to adult pronouncements. Action is submerged in the history of the time or town or needlessly interrupted to produce a story that's not as interesting as its locale.

THE WINDS OF TIME (1973)

The Booklist

SOURCE: A review of *The Winds of Time,* in *The Booklist,* Vol. 70, No. 12, February 15, 1974, pp. 654-55.

With her mother reentering a mental hospital and her divorced father off painting somewhere, Gail is packed up by a steely-willed social worker to go and live with her hated Uncle Chad. An automobile accident on their journey to his home in North Dakota gives Gail the opportunity to escape and she finds herself on the Partridge family estate where its two residents, the aging Mr. Sonny and his ninety-six-year-old mother welcome her with no questions asked. The unlikely circumstances that allow Gail to encounter and then live with the Partridges mar the book's credibility, and the story as a whole lacks the artistry of Corcoran's perceptive adolescent study in *All the Summer Voices;* but Gail's newly discovered happiness, though patly found, will satisfy unsophisticated readers.

Kirkus Reviews

SOURCE: A review of *The Winds of Time,* in *Kirkus Reviews,* Vol. XLII, No. 5, March 1, 1974, p. 243.

Deserted by her father five years ago when she was eight, alone now since her mother was taken off to a mental hospital, and terrified of being sent to Dakota to live with mean, "wicked" Uncle Chad, Gail trusts no one and has no patience with adult attention to "the past." Her early musings on the difficulty of living "now" are annoyingly managed and unconvincing, but after Chad, with a court order, fetches her West and she runs away from his car after a highway accident en route, Gail finds herself wanted and sheltered in an isolated dream-come-true household that is beautifully believable. Stumbling into an abandoned pool she is met by two dogs (Basenjis) named Isis and Osiris and rescued by Sonny Partridge, an old man with a lopsided face (one side paralyzed from a stroke) who lives with his ninety-year-old mother in their enormous, unmodernized (even to electricity) family home. Sonny, a marvelous plain cook, makes his home in the pantry, his mother (who reads Tarot cards) sleeps in the kitchen, and there is even a young naturalist, Christopher (nineteen or so), who comes and goes and chats with Gail about his eco-study of the area as they sit high in a tree, hiding from Uncle Chad and the sheriff. The vague theme of appreciating the past is never really worked in (or worked out) and Corcoran is not above such narrative tricks as terrifying Gail (and her readers) with her characters' unconventional entrances—Sonny at the pool, Christopher through a bedroom window during a windy night, etc. But it's no wonder that Gail opens up to this family, and when at last her artist father arrives from Hawaii in answer to her postcard, occasioning a party with Sonny's chokecherry wine and candles in the long-unused ballroom, who wouldn't second his toast "To the Partridges, and to all the lovely miracles of life?"

Publishers Weekly

SOURCE: A review of *The Winds of Time,* in *Publishers Weekly,* Vol. 205, No. 15, April 15, 1974, p. 52.

The author's exquisite prose is complemented by Miller's equally inspired pictures. A bow to a more leisurely past, the story concerns 13-year-old Gail. Her father has defected and her mother is in a mental institution, so she is made a ward of her Uncle Chad, a man she dislikes and distrusts. On their way to his place, Gail escapes and comes to a huge, primitive dwelling in a remote spot. Here live Sonny Partridge, an elderly man, and his nonagenarian mother. They take the girl into a household where she meets Christopher, a young naturalist. Gail is charmed by these people and falls more in love daily with old times, old ways. The story is moving and convincing and we have the joy of Gail's reunion with her father, who arrives to take care of her and to salute her temporary family.

School Library Journal

SOURCE: A review of *The Winds of Time,* in *School Library Journal,* Vol. 20, No. 10, May 15, 1974, p. 69.

Gail, an embittered, distrustful 13-year-old, is completely changed by her exposure to a strangely innocent, otherworldly family *in The Winds of Time* by Barbara Corcoran. After Gail's mother has been admitted to a mental hospital, the social worker arranges for Gail to live with her Uncle Chad, whom she despises. When her insensitive and drunken uncle skids off a mountain road in a snowstorm and is knocked unconscious, Gail, thinking only of escape, dashes off into the woods. In a tree-encircled hollow she discovers an enormous old house inhabited by a bright-eyed, doll-like lady and a strange man with a twisted face—90-year-old Mrs. Partridge and her elderly son. Gail is readily (and without question) accepted into this household and is safely secreted in a valley where people, animals, and nature form one harmonious ecosystem. Marred by a pat ending, this slight mystery with Gothic overtones is stronger in atmosphere and characterization than in plot.

Marilyn Sachs

SOURCE: "Mementos from the Past," in *The New York Times Book Review,* November 17, 1974, p. 40.

The Winds of Time by Barbara Corcoran has more of a manufactured feel than any of the [other titles under review]. It is a strictly gothic tale about a runaway city girl who stumbles her way during a blizzard to an old gabled, turreted house in the wilds of North Dakota. The house is inhabited by an old man and his mother who have shut their doors against the present and live on the memories of their past. There is a wicked uncle, a stupid sheriff, a handsome teenage boy who is all for ecology, and an artist father who rides to the rescue at the end on a motorcycle.

📖 *A DANCE TO STILL MUSIC* (1974)

Kirkus Reviews

SOURCE: A review of *A Dance to Still Music,* in *Kirkus Reviews,* Vol. XLII, No. 14, July 15, 1974, p. 742.

Another Corcoran runaway finds an idyllic haven, this time with Josie, who cleans motel rooms by day and enjoys the tropical delights of the Florida Keys in her shipshape houseboat. While Josie is an impossible, but nonetheless highly attractive, paragon of quiet maturity and unselfish acceptance, Margaret, the runaway fourteen-year-old, is a bundle of frustration and rebellion. Newly deaf, Margaret is struggling against the unfamiliar isolation of her condition and against the label "handicapped" which has cut her off from friends, her guilt stricken mother, and her love of music. The houseboat, where the two nurse an injured faun, study the local marine life and enjoy each other's home cooking, is merely the stage for Margaret's gradual adjustment. It might be argued that her succesful resistance against attending a regular school for the deaf presents all such institutions in an unfairly negative way. However, for the hearing person, Margaret is a reliable guide to the problems of a handicap that is less well understood—and often less sympathetically treated—than blindness. And as always, Corcoran's gentle, supportive solutions have a convincing grace that compensates for their circumscribed reality.

The Booklist

SOURCE: A review of *A Dance to Still Music,* in *The Booklist,* Vol. 71, No. 1, September 1, 1974, p. 39.

Though Key West, Florida, presents a radically different setting, the plot elements here bear strong resemblance to the author's recent *The Winds of Time.* A troubled adolescent—Margaret—exits from her unhappy home situation and gains peace and perspective through gentle, uninquiring outsiders. Since an ear infection has left her deaf, Margaret insists on not speaking, for fear she'll talk too loud, and she angrily rejects the prospect of being sent to a special school by her mother and soon-to-be stepfather. Her solution is to run, and in doing so she encounters Josie, a perceptive widow living alone on a houseboat. While staying with Josie, Margaret slowly emerges from her shell, and when her newly married mother turns up, wins parental approval of plans to attend an inviting university workshop on communication for the profoundly deaf. Corcoran's portrayal of Margaret is not always smooth in its execution and so the girl fails to elicit the sympathy one might expect on the part of a reader. But there is enough reality in Margaret's plight to sustain interest, particularly for those who might find the book therapeutic.

Carole Sebastian

SOURCE: A review of *A Dance to Still Music,* in *School Library Journal,* Vol. 99, No. 16, September 15, 1974, p. 101.

An earache leads to deafness for 14-year-old Margaret. Unable to adjust to her handicap, she feels like an albatross around her waitress-mother's neck. (Her father disappeared at Margaret's birth.) Although a former honor student, the girl rejects going to a school for the deaf which she believes would only teach handicrafts. Her mother's impending marriage makes school for the deaf a definite possibility and causes Margaret to run away. On the road she helps an injured deer which leads to a friendship with Josie, a widow who lives on a houseboat, and an eventual coming to terms with her deafness. A low-keyed and realistic novel, this is better suited to teenage readers than Joanne Greenberg's *In This Sign,* an adult novel which also treats the plight of the deaf person.

Jean Fritz

SOURCE: A review of *A Dance to Still Music,* in *The New York Times Book Review,* November 17, 1974, p. 8.

Not all desperate teen-age runaways have the good fortune to run straight into the arms of exactly the right person to help them. Barbara Corcoran's heroines generally do. With a lesser author, this could be simply slick plotting, but with Barbara Corcoran the very fortuitousness is, I think, part of the message at the core of her writing. "Trust life," she says. "Go into the world. There'll be good people out there as well as bad. There'll be help." She handles her theme like a prism, holding it up to catch the light at different angles, turning it this way and that so that each book is a fresh experience and a variation of the pattern.

In this book the heroine is closed off from the world by deafness. Fourteen-year-old Margaret, after a severe illness, is trying in a bitter way to accept her handicap but not to overcome it. Recently uprooted from her home in Maine, she lives with her waitress mother in Key West, Fla., where she neither knows nor cares to know anyone. She won't even talk for she knows that deaf people are apt to sound strange. So she lives an aimless life until she learns that she is to go to a school for the deaf and her mother is to be married to a retired Navy man.

With the idea of hitchhiking back to Maine, Margaret hides in a pick-up truck until the truck accidentally hits and wounds a fawn. Generally there is a wild animal in Barbara Corcoran's books; indeed her stories are played out on the thin line between wilderness and civilization, and the intertwining of the two adds depth to her theme. It is now that Margaret meets Josie, the lucky, made-to-order person, who takes Margaret and the fawn aboard her houseboat and gradually brings them to the point of re-entering their worlds. One of Barbara Corcoran's most gripping stories.

Charity Chang

SOURCE: "'The Perilous Gard' and Others," in *Children's Literature: Annual of the Modern Language Association Seminar on Children's Literature and the Children's Literature Association,* Vol. 4, 1975, pp. 199-203.

Childhood, especially the growing-up years, is sometimes characterized by loneliness and uncertainty, a groping toward being, becoming. The themes of alienation and self-discovery appear with frequency in contemporary fiction. In *A Dance to Still Music* these themes are paramount and handled by Barbara Corcoran with finesse. Key West, Florida, provides the setting for the story of Margaret, a deeply sensitive and intelligent deaf girl of fourteen who lives with her restless and somewhat self-pitying mother, Maggie. The purpose of *A Dance to Still Music* is not ordinary entertainment, certainly not light amusement. This is a haunting story, one with suspenseful plot, undergirded with bold, fast-paced mental actions to which much of the physical is only incidental. The characters are vivid, real, sometimes Steinbeckian. Margaret's special loneliness is acute, and somewhat beyond Maggie's comprehension. The giant steps taken by Margaret in her determination not to impede her mother's future help her to find her own. The love and protectiveness she gives to sustain the life of a wounded deer comes back to fulfill her own life in unsuspected ways, from unsuspected sources. In the hands of a less gifted writer Margaret's story could have been maudlin; instead it is a "dance to still music," a celebration of life. Such a story needs few illustrations. Those conceived and provided by Charles Robinson, however, provide a very correct complementary touch.

📖 *MEET ME AT TAMERLANE'S TOMB* (1975)

Kirkus Reviews

SOURCE: A review of *Meet Me at Tamerlane's Tomb,* in *Kirkus Reviews,* Vol. XLIII, No. 4, February 15, 1975, p. 181.

Barbara Corcoran stoops to foreign intrigue when fat, fourteen-year-old Hardy Harlow visits Samarkand with her family and falls "hopelessly, unrequitedly, nauseatingly, marvelously in love" with Paul, her sister's drummer boyfriend. More attentive though is Mr. Kemel, a Turk who sometimes wears western clothes and limps and sometimes lurks around dressed as a Moslem. Kemel, it turns out, wants Hardy to take a smuggled necklace of purported sentimental value to his daughter when the Harlows fly to Moscow; Paul says Kemel is a dope smuggler and of course he's right but Kemel is so insistent that he kidnaps Hardy's younger brother Andrew in

order to win her compliance. It's all improbable, cliched and silly and a long way from the comfortable ambience the author can wrap us in when she stays closer to home.

The Booklist

SOURCE: A review of *Meet Me at Tamerlane's Tomb,* in *The Booklist,* Vol. 21, No. 13, March 1, 1975, pp. 689-90.

The Russian town of Samarkand provides a unique setting for this topical suspense yarn. While the Harlow family visits Samarkand, 14-year-old Hardy and her brother increasingly distrust Mr. Kemel, a Turkish gentleman who hovers about the family. Paul, a genial musician friend who dates Hardy's sister Penny, fuels their distrust, and the effusive Mr. Popov, who entertains their professor father, doesn't quite fit his role either. Drug traffic directed by Kemel proves to be the secret, and Hardy and her brother manage to trip up Kemel's connection. Corcoran's writing is smooth, and an underlying theme of Hardy's coming to grips with her inferiority complex strengthens the story, though the characterization of the credulous Mrs. Harlow is unconvincing. And of course Hardy and Andrew are remarkably level-headed under fire. Light, literate, if not particularly memorable mystery.

School Library Journal

SOURCE: A review of *Meet Me at Tamerlane's Tomb,* in *School Library Journal,* Vol. 21, No. 9, May, 1975, p. 70.

The heroine of *Meet Me at Tamerlane's Tomb* by Barbara Corcoran is fat, 14-year-old Hardy, the ugly duckling of a glamorous family. Vacationing in exotic Samarkand in the Soviet Union with her family—college-professor father who teaches Russian, languorous mother, sophisticated older sister, and smart younger brother Andrew—Hardy is almost tricked into becoming courier for Mr. Kemel, a Turkish hashish smuggler. With the help of her sister's boyfriend with whom she has fallen in love, Hardy turns Mr. Kemel over to the grateful Soviet authorities. A near miss, this attempt at humorous junior-grade espionage never quite jells.

America

SOURCE: A review of *Meet Me at Tamerlane's Tomb,* in *America,* Vol. 133, No. 18, December 6, 1975, p. 404.

Samarkand! Hardy is romantic enough to enjoy her family's visit to the ancient city of the conqueror Tamerlane (now part of the Soviet Union), but her most romantic thoughts are centered on Paul, a drummer in the hotel band, though his are very obviously on Hardy's older sister, Penny. Hardy should have reserved her interest for Mr. Kemel, whom she and her young brother, Andrew, encounter quite often. When Andrew is kidnapped by Kemel and his crew, Hardy has to overcome her fears and face up to this smart talker with his horrible ultimatum. Credible and very readable, with good background not overemphasized, for girls 10-13.

📖 *THE CLOWN* (1975; also published as *I Wish You Love,* 1977)

Kirkus Reviews

SOURCE: A review of *The Clown,* in *Kirkus Reviews,* Vol. XLIII, No. 13, July 1, 1975, p. 717.

Corcoran has refined the blend of intrigue and romance first attempted in the trivial *Meet Me at Tamerlane's Tomb,* but this is still without the body or, oddly, the bouquet of her earlier home-grown daydreams. Here orphaned Liza, almost seventeen, falls instantly in love with a (Soviet) Georgian clown performing in Moscow. The clown is nervous; Liza follows him and finds a KGB agent also on his tail, about to arrest him for having applied for an exit visa to Israel. But Liza, a late U.S. consul's daughter, knows her way around, and—without a hitch though you're sure there has to be one by page 188—smuggles him (with inept, obnoxious Uncle George's passport) to Copenhagen, where the friendly housekeeping couple she lives with there help her to accept his leaving for a circus career in the States. Smooth, well managed escapism.

Denise M. Wilms

SOURCE: A review of *The Clown,* in *The Booklist,* Vol. 72, No. 2, September 15, 1975, p. 163.

The author's fluid writing and knack for characterization raise this topical story above the level of dimestore suspense drama. The setting is Moscow, and the unlikely plot involves 16-year-old Liza Parke, who capably schemes to smuggle an about-to-be-arrested Jewish circus clown out of the country. The operation, carried out by posing the clown as her visiting uncle, goes off without a hitch; Corcoran holds back from cliff-hanging suspense by opting to structure the conclusion around the breakup of the emotional ties that have sprung up between Liza and her clown. He is offered a lucrative job with a circus in the States while Liza remains in Copenhagen to finish school. Though the story easily carries readers along, secondary characters often serve to project a negative image of prevailing conditions in present-day Russia: governmental personnel are stone-faced and abrupt, underlings are often characterized as victims, and Liza's periodic registration of irritation at or distaste for various aspects of official status quo imply a cold war attitude on the part of the author.

Virginia Haviland

SOURCE: A review of *The Clown,* in *The Horn Book Magazine,* Vol. LI, No. 5, October, 1975, pp. 461-62.

Deriving background detail from the tourist's Moscow, the author has built up an international adventure, in which sixteen-year-old Liza saves a clown from the KGB by getting him to Copenhagen. The clown, a Georgian Jew, has applied for an exit visa but is fearful of being sent to a mental hospital. Unfortunately, the motivation behind the intrigue is unconvincing: Liza is attracted to the clown by his kind, anxious look and by his brilliant performance in the ring. But the situations and details are plausibly worked out. Because of Liza's earlier stay in Europe with her father, a diplomat, she speaks Russian and is familiar with Moscow and Copenhagen. She is visiting Moscow with her aunt and uncle, when her aunt is suddenly called home to the United States. Uncle George, a photographer, is too absent-minded to miss his passport, which Liza uses for the clown, or to note that Liza has arranged a picture-taking engagement for him at the same time he is scheduled to fly to Denmark. The remaining arrangements are carefully plotted—the securing of clothes, money, a watch, and a camera to make the clown look like Uncle George. A successful, fast-moving tale with a background and an atmosphere that are convincing enough.

Zena Sutherland

SOURCE: A review of *The Clown,* in *Bulletin of the Center for Children's Books,* Vol. 29, No. 5, January, 1976, p. 75.

A fast-paced adventure story has a strong plot, an unusual setting, sympathetic characters strongly drawn, suspense, love interest and a vigorous writing style. The orphaned daughter of an American diplomat, Liza is in Moscow with a tiresome aunt and uncle who need her help, since she has lived there and speaks some Russian. Aunt May is called home, and Liza uses her uncle's passport and clothes to smuggle out of the country a Russian clown who is in danger for political reasons. Having seen Grigol in a performance, Liza had followed him, learned that he was in peril, and offered her help. The details of the planning and execution of the escape are intriguing and convincing, and the end of the story is satisfying but not pat. A doughty and believable heroine, a cracking good book.

📖 *AXE-TIME, SWORD-TIME* (1976)

Kirkus Reviews

SOURCE: A review of *Axe-Time, Sword-Time,* in *Kirkus Reviews,* Vol. XLIV, No. 5, March 1, 1976, p. 260.

Like many Corcoran heroines Elinor has a physical handicap, in this case brain damage from a childhood accident that has prevented her from learning to read and spell. There are other problems too: her doctor father's decision to leave home coinciding with the outbreak of World War II which sends both Elinor's only brother and her highschool sweetheart off to the service. Ironically, it is the War which opens up a job inspecting electronics components and frees Elinor from her Mother's determination to keep her in school. Elinor's shyness turns small successes, like learning the charts for civil defense plane spotting, into moving victories; at other times her reserved gentility may create considerable social distance between her and the reader, just as it colors her relationship with the factory girls she supervises at the plant. For many, Elinor's personal difficulties may be less interesting than her typical Forties teenager pastimes, and Corcoran handles this background well, sharing the young people's enthusiasm for jazz as well as Elinor's nervousness about checking into a ski resort with her Jewish-sounding last name. Elinor can't match the energy level of her English-based counterpart in Judith Kerr's *The Other Way Round* (1975); her softspoken manner makes a lesser though still agreeable impression.

Denise M. Wilms

SOURCE: A review of *Axe-Time, Sword-Time,* in *The Booklist,* Vol. 72, No. 15, April 1, 1976, p. 1111.

Her shallow mother is the source of much tension in Elinor's life: Mrs. Golden refuses to recognize the nature of Elinor's reading disability and despite her poor high school record, continues to push her toward college. Her father, an anesthesiologist, realizes that the childhood head injury Elinor suffered is responsible, but in these early 1940s little is known about treating such disorders. Still, Elinor knows she is not stupid and at 18 is moved to declare independence from her mother's pretenses and overprotectiveness. She starts by attending a Hampton Beach dance she knows her mother would disapprove of; later she helps her English teacher spot planes, again against her mother's wishes. It is while learning plane types that she discovers tracing their form helps fix them in her mind; the technique holds out promise for her rehabilitation. After her parents separate, Elinor continues to see her father; it is the quiet disapproval of Elsa Braun, the German refugee he has been seeing, which prompts Elinor to seek out the job she lands as an inspector in a navy defense plant. Buoyed by her competency there and by the knowledge that career options are open to her, she finds the future more promising. A liberal sprinkling of well-known names makes Corcoran's re-creation of the times a little too studied, but Elinor's evolution is credible, and the look at what a learning disability meant at a time when little was understood about it is thought-provoking.

Ann A. Flowers

SOURCE: A review of *Axe-Time, Sword-Time,* in *The Horn Book Magazine,* Vol. LII, No. 3, June, 1976, pp. 294-95.

Thirty-five years ago, much less was known about learning disabilities and brain-damaged children than is known now. Eighteen-year-old Elinor Golden had suffered great difficulty in reading and writing since early childhood when she was hit on the head with a golf ball. Little help or understanding had been offered; her mother, coldly ambitious for her, refused to admit Elinor's disabilities while her teachers were unsympathetic. Only her doctor-father, her brother, and her friend Jed gave support. Against a background of family disunity—her mother and father were getting a divorce—Elinor's struggles to control her own life and to contribute to the war effort were certainly commendable. Elinor's rebellion against her mother took the form of finding war work inspecting secret electronic equipment in a factory. She proved to be remarkably competent and was given more responsibility, thus starting on her way to independence. In spite of a slightly unfocused feeling, owing, perhaps, to the author's inclusion of autobiographical elements, Elinor's passage into adulthood is well-presented and believable.

James Norsworthy

SOURCE: A review of *Axe-Time, Sword-Time,* in *Catholic Library World,* Vol. 48, No. 5, December, 1976, p. 234.

Just before World War II begins, Elinor, an 18-year-old with a reading disability problem, tries to cope with her personal problems and those of her family and friends. A powerful novel in the Corcoran tradition that involves the hurt of divorce, unrealistic parental ambitions for their children and the attitudes of people before wars begin. Highly recommended for girls grades 6 and up.

THE FARAWAY ISLAND (1977)

Kirkus Reviews

SOURCE: A review of *The Faraway Island,* in *Kirkus Reviews,* Vol. XLV, No. 3, February 1, 1977, pp. 97-98.

This begins with fourteen-year-old Lynn bumbling about in an agony of shyness, and Corcoran's sympathy not only with her but, by extension, with such adolescent pains in general, is almost as heavy-handed. Then Lynn, fearful of entering a foreign school, is sent to Grandmother on Nantucket while the rest of the family spends a Fulbright year in Belgium. But the local kids' intolerance of off-islanders scares Lynn away from enrolling there as well, and so, guiltily, she goes on deceiving Grandmother about her daily whereabouts—all the while worrying, too, about the old woman's memory lapses and Mr. and Mrs. Small's attempts to push her into an institution. The characterization of this busybody couple is also a bit overdone, and throughout the visit Lynn and Grandmother don't take readers beyond the level of tepid insights. But unlike most authors Corcoran is better at happy endings than at problems. As Lynn naturally sheds her clumsiness in this more accepting home, the good vibrations that emanate from a new young doctor who reassures Grandmother, from a new boy on the island who helps Lynn brave the new school, and even from Cyrano, her adopted black sheep, are as warming as ever.

Booklist

SOURCE: A review of *The Faraway Island,* in *Booklist,* Vol. 73, No. 15, April 1, 1977, p. 1165.

While a year in Belgium might seem exciting to many teenagers, 13-year-old Lynn, who is painfully self-conscious and shy, is terrified to learn of her father's Fulbright lectureship and resultant family travel plans. Her father, the most empathetic parent, arranges a compromise: Lynn will spend the year with her grandmother on Nantucket Island. But Nantucket, too, is a strange place. Though Lynn has visited there in earlier summers, she knows none of the year-round residents. Her beloved, understanding grandmother has grown older and is now often forgetful. The circumstances, combined with her own shyness, make it easy for her not to enroll in school and thus to become even more fearful of being found out. As the year goes by and Lynn becomes more aware of and concerned about her grandmother's fears and problems, she learns that she is stronger and more self-sufficient than she had believed herself to be. The characterizations of Lynn and her grandmother are quite well done; the parallels of changes in adolescence and old age are interestingly apparent; and a sense of place is well established. Background characters (especially Lynn's family) tend to be flat and unbelievably stereotyped, but that is a minor distraction in this very quiet novel.

Mary M. Burns

SOURCE: A review of *The Faraway Island,* in *The Horn Book Magazine,* Vol. LIII, No. 4, August, 1977, pp. 438-39.

Unlike her family, Lynn was terrified by unfamiliar places, situations, and people. Consequently, when her father announced that they would be living in Belgium during the term of his appointment as a Fulbright lecturer in geography, she failed to join in the general rejoicing. Sympathizing with her discomfort, he suggested that she spend the year, instead, on Nantucket with her grandmother. Unfortunately, the alternative proved almost as difficult: Grandmother Linley had become forgetful and less agile, causing gossip among meddling townspeople, and the few teenagers Lynn met were markedly unfriendly. To circumvent her problems, Lynn began skipping school, avoiding direct questions, and pretending that she had come merely for a short visit. Only when the near disastrous consequences of her deception forced Lynn to face and eventually to conquer her fears was the

situation resolved. More enjoyable for its evocation of setting, brief vignettes of local inhabitants, and ingenuity of plot than for its depth of characterization, Lynn's story is a light, smoothly structured novel, reassuring in its conclusion.

Zena Sutherland

SOURCE: A review of *The Faraway Island,* in *Bulletin of the Center for Children's Books,* Vol. 31, No. 2, October, 1977, p. 31.

Shy and timid, adolescent Lynn is apprehensive about going to school in Brussels for a year when her father gets a Fulbright grant. The alternative is to live with her grandmother on Nantucket, so Lynn goes to the island, only to find her grandmother has become vague and forgetful at times. She also finds the local girls unfriendly, so she decides she will stay out of school when the term begins, but not tell Grandmother. She makes a pet out of a black lamb she buys from a neighbor, but doesn't tell Grandmother. Increasingly concerned about the forgetfulness, Lynn resents one couple's officious interference and the suggestion that the solution is a rest home. She does make one friend, a boy, and she realizes that she must enrol in school, that she must get a doctor to see her grandmother. The book has a quiet tone and sedate pace, a strong evocation of the island setting, and variable depth of characterization; while there is no strong story line, Corcoran does picture a credible change in Lynn as she assumes responsibility and gains self-confidence.

📖 *HEY, THAT'S MY SOUL YOU'RE STOMPING ON* (1978)

Zena Sutherland

SOURCE: A review of *Hey, That's My Soul You're Stomping On,* in *Bulletin of the Center for Children's Books,* Vol. 37, No. 10, June, 1978, pp. 156-57.

"Rachel knew exactly how her father felt. Smothered." She also knew that she was being sent to visit her grandparents because her parents were having bitter quarrels. Sixteen, she arrives at a modest Palm Springs motel to find that the residents are all, like her grandparents, elderly people. The one friend she makes is the beautiful Ariadne, staying at another motel with a fashion-plate mother. Rachel hasn't expected to be so involved with all her grandparents' friends, but she's deeply concerned about them and about Ariadne, who proves to be emotionally disturbed. So she learns about caring—and by the time her dependent mother is in Reno, Rachel volunteers to be with her. She still judges her parents, but she can accept them and accept the responsibility that love entails. A familiar theme, but Corcoran has given it a fresh slant. The characters are strongly drawn, the narrative smooth, and Rachel's reactions and fears emerge naturally via letters to an only brother in Europe.

Mary M. Burns

SOURCE: A review of *Hey, That's My Soul You're Stomping On,* in *The Horn Book Magazine,* Vol. LIV, No. 3, June, 1978, p. 282.

Pained by the growing incompatibility between her parents, sixteen-year-old Rachel Douglas elects to pay an extended visit to her maternal grandparents until her mother and father reach a decision about their futures. She is convinced that people should expect little sympathy—even from their children—for self-imposed dilemmas. But gradually, through the quiet wisdom of her grandparents and her observations of the other elderly vacationers at the comfortable but unfashionable Palm Springs resort motel, she acquires a tolerance for human failings and the understanding that concern for one's parents, however burdensome it may sometimes be, is not lightly dismissed. Her final decision—to provide her distraught mother with the companionship she needs—is reinforced by her brief encounter with two physically and psychologically scarred young people whose lives contrast sharply with the remembered security of her own childhood. Written in a taut, brittle style, the story conveys the effects of divorce upon a family, while simultaneously suggesting the tensions which precipitate it. Because the characters are particularly well-drawn, the novel combines several motifs, such as the abused child and the problems of aging, into a coherent whole without shifting its central focus from the constant inner struggle between self-preservation and concern for others.

"ME AND YOU AND A DOG NAMED BLUE" (1979)

Pat Harrington

SOURCE: A review of *"Me and You and a Dog Named Blue,"* in *School Library Journal,* Vol. 20, No. 7, March, 1979, pp. 136-37.

Fifteen-year-old Maggie's ambition is to train for a women's pro baseball team in Cincinnati. Meanwhile, she stretches her disabled dad's Army pension to buy groceries. Borrowing an irresistible, pale blue Jaguar makes her the protege of flamboyant CoCo Rainbolt, sometime folksinger for captive audiences in jails. CoCo, a beaut of a meddler, breeds Kerry Blue terriers and plans to work Maggie into the act. Railroaded into a kennel job instead of cooking at the Clam Shack, Maggie bounces between other people's conflicting expectations for her until she balks at both game plans and chooses her own direction. The author juggles three scenarios: life with a flawed father on the seashore, a baseball career, and dog raising. Father is an irritable mix of literary allusions and down-to-earth know how whose disability is poorly developed: at one time, it confines him to the house; at another point, it poses no problem on a boat. The heedless dilettante CoCo is one of many clichés in a ramshackle structure. The book's only surprise is that Maggie tolerates such inept interference chapter after chapter.

Denise M. Wilms

SOURCE: A review of *"Me and You and a Dog Named Blue,"* in *Booklist,* Vol. 75, No. 14, March 15, 1979, p. 1153.

Corcoran's writing always flows and her contemporary stories make enjoyable reading. This latest explores the problems of Maggie Clarke, 15 and unsure of her future except that she wants baseball to be a part of it. That dream nearly takes a backseat role in her involvement with CoCo Rainbolt, a wealthy socialite with a social worker bent, who takes Maggie forcefully under her wing. CoCo, Maggie, and her father are all three fresh characters, and the abrasive dynamics of the Maggie-CoCo relationship are well spun out. It's also nice, in terms of craft, to see that Maggie's baseball penchant and status as the local team's only female player aren't overplayed, and that her father is allotted considerable dimension as a prickly, independent sort. Practiced and likable.

Kirkus Reviews

SOURCE: A review of *"Me and You and a Dog Named Blue,"* in *Kirkus Reviews,* Vol. XLVII, No. 6, March 15, 1979, p. 331.

Motherless Maggie is content to play on her high-school baseball team, work at Mr. Sullivan's clam shack, and dream of a career in pro ball—but then, having yielded to the temptation to "try out" a beautiful Jaguar left invitingly on a beach, Maggie is taken over by the car's fabulously wealthy owner CoCo Rainbolt, a do-gooder who sings to prisoners and such. Instead of pressing charges on the car "theft," CoCo takes up with Maggie and her father—but plans the outings her way; gives Maggie a dog—but continues to give her orders on its care; and offers her protege a job in her kennels, which Maggie's beguiled father forces her to take. Maggie goes along because an upcoming dog show tour will take her to Ohio where she secretly plans to split and join a women's ball team; but finally CoCo goes too far and Maggie, giving up her dream, is on the verge of widening her sights. Maggie's disabled, beer-drinking father is nicely drawn, but Corcoran is as heavy-handed with CoCo, who runs most of this show, as CoCo is with everyone else; and the conflict among the three makes for a fairly thin plot. Nevertheless Maggie's baseball interest combined with her likable good sense gives this a limited, topical appeal.

Ann A. Flowers

SOURCE: A review of *"Me and You and a Dog Named Blue,"* in *The Horn Book Magazine,* Vol. LV, No. 3, June, 1979, p. 300.

The dog was a pedigreed Kerry Blue terrier, a gift to Maggie Clarke from wealthy CoCo Rainbolt—all the more surprising because fifteen-year-old Maggie had seen the woman's Jaguar and "borrowed" it, and only Co-Co's patronizing interest saved her from serious trouble with the police. Maggie was really a decent, likable girl and a remarkable athlete, a star on the high school baseball team. Living with her widowed father, a disabled veteran, was difficult; not only was money tight, but he was demanding and unpredictable, and Maggie began to feel the necessity of escape. In addition, bossy, insensitive CoCo was trying to run her life. Maggie was coerced into taking a job in CoCo's kennels, but when her interference caused Blue's death, the girl was able to make a declaration of independence. The book has many ambiguities and dimensions; the reader never fully understands CoCo's puzzling character or motivation (nor does Maggie), there is no definite resolution of the problem of Maggie's future, and some characters appear without apparent reason. But it is this very uncertainty that gives the book the feeling of a piece of real, ongoing life.

RISING DAMP (1980)

Mary I. Purucker

SOURCE: A review of *Rising Damp*, in *School Library Journal*, Vol. 26, No. 8, April, 1980, pp. 121-22.

Shallow, soap opera parents, selfishly intent on their own lives, pack their sometimes troublesome daughter, Hope, off to Ireland with her mother's assistant, Eileen Helding. Eileen becomes entranced with Paddy Malone, who owns the cottage, and Hope is infatuated with a gypsy lad, Kol, who convinces her that he wants to go to the "U.S. of America" with her. After giving him $500, Hope never sees him again although she waits on the beach for him until after dark and is nearly overtaken by the tide. Kol leaves a note for her that his uncle stole the money from him but that he will pay it back. The characters are stick-figures, but the most unappealing thing about this book is the author's use of thieving gypsies who turn out to be just as bad as expected!

Denise M. Wilms

SOURCE: A review of *Rising Damp*, in *Booklist*, Vol. 76, No. 15, April 1, 1980, p. 1124.

Hope's affluent, self-absorbed parents regard her as an unfathomable burden, and when she refuses to accept summer camp, they shuffle her off to Ireland in the company of Eileen, a woman just jilted in a love affair. That opening provides Corcoran opportunity to explore the friction between two people who know virtually nothing about each other. Hope, the spoiled, selfish, and significantly neglected child, keeps Eileen at arm's length and tries to manipulate circumstances to her own advantage. Eileen, for her part, gives Hope plenty of room to move, without giving up her own single-minded plans to stay in the secluded countryside where her grandmother

once lived. Hope's subsequent involvement with a gypsy youth (the least well characterized relationship in the novel) counts as a breakthrough in her defensive barrier building. The first genuine reaching out she has allowed herself proves pivotal in her coming to terms with and respecting Eileen. By the month's end, the two have a genuine liking for and understanding of each other, and Hope is ready to face her homelife on more mature terms. Corcoran is adept at verbal portraiture; her personalities are facilely and professionally sketched. The resulting story moves briskly, making this another tidy, absorbing novel from a most practiced, prolific writer.

Kirkus Reviews

SOURCE: A review of *Rising Damp*, in *Kirkus Reviews*, Vol. XLVIII, No. 12, June 15, 1980, pp. 783-84.

Like so many of Corcoran's heroines, 15-year-old Hope is the more-or-less castoff kid of respectable but indifferent parents; hers are totally involved in their separate careers and consider her a troublesome nuisance to be tucked away at camps and boarding schools. And like so many of Corcoran's novels, this takes its heroine to foreign soil for a bittersweet encounter and an ultimately reinforcing experience. Here Hope is sent off for a summer month in a thatched-roof Irish cottage, in the care of her mother's assistant Eileen who has just been jilted by the man she'd hoped to share the cottage with. Neither traveler is happy with the situation; but Eileen is pleasantly distracted by the attentions of their charming, widowed Irish landlord, and Hope meets Kol, a gypsy boy who suggests returning to America with her . . . but first he'll need her $500.00 for the air fare. Hope hands it over and makes plans to meet Kol, but next day the gypsies vanish—and Kol with them. Hope, abandoned again, hates herself for having trusted. Kol is cleared in the end, when he sneaks back with partial repayment, the promise of more, and a note explaining that his uncles had found and taken the money. Meanwhile, though, cold messages from Hope's parents plus her evident misery over Kol's seeming betrayal win Eileen's sympathy for the undemonstrative young girl. The real outcome of the episode, then, is a bond between the two women, who now decide to leave the cottage and spend the remainder of their month in Dublin. Like most of Corcoran's characters these are none too rounded. (Kol's behavior, especially when he's found not guilty, is inexplicable.) But she brings the principals together with her usual good grace, and the Irish background contributes the usual overlay of travelogue romance.

Alice Virginia Dodd

SOURCE: A review of *Rising Damp*, in *Catholic Library World*, Vol. 52, No. 5, December, 1980, p. 237.

Corcoran has given girls grades 7-9 a fast-paced story of a fifteen-year-old girl who is really disliked by her parents and for good reason. Hope is smart, spoiled, sneaky and rude. When she gets home from boarding school, her Mother packs her off to a cottage on the west coast of Ireland with an unsuspecting university colleague. The beautiful and often forlorn Connemara countryside is the background to Hope's encounter with a handsome gypsy boy and Eileen's friendship with a local Irish gentleman. Because of Eileen's sensitivity and concern for this defiant, locked-into-herself girl, when a near catastrophe occurs her kindness and wisdom form a key into that lock. Highly recommended.

THE PERSON IN THE POTTING SHED (1980)

Barbara Elleman

SOURCE: A review of *The Person in the Potting Shed,* in *Booklist,* Vol. 77, No. 3, October 1, 1980, p. 207.

Dorothy and her brother Franklin join their recently remarried mother in a rented, run-down Louisiana plantation house that is also occupied by its eccentric owner, her smooth-talking brother, an overly devoted servant, and an alcoholic, semideranged gardener named François. From the time of their arrival Dorothy and Franklin sense something wrong, but not until they discover the gardener sprawled in the potting shed with a bashed-in head are their suspicions confirmed. The body disappears, other clues surface, and the two children eventually unravel a mystery that is imbedded in relationships begun years ago. This fast-moving mystery succeeds, despite lightweight plot and character portrayals, because of its suspenseful scenes and eerie atmosphere.

Kirkus Reviews

SOURCE: A review of *The Person in the Potting Shed,* in *Kirkus Reviews,* Vol. XLVIII, No. 22, November 15, 1980, p. 1464.

A breath of a mystery (113 skimpy pages) in very complicated, PG-rated circumstances, but okay for kids receptive to lots of plot and little internal development. Dorothy and slightly younger brother Franklin (both presumably, if ambiguously, in their early teens), whose father died 18 months back, are staying at a decaying Louisiana plantation, Belle Rêve, with their mother and her new English husband, Ian, who's as uncomfortable with them as they are with him. Still more disconcerting to Dorothy and Franklin, though, are the odd sorts who populate Belle Rêve: uncommunicative owner Eva Du-Pré; her witchy mother Jasmine; their testy servant Felicité; drunken old gardener François, and Eva's brother Arthur, who keeps appearing unexpectedly but seems to be the only "normal" person around. The only really solid citizens it turns out, however, are black teenager Justin and his grandfather—for Dorothy and Franklin find François lying inert; don't believe, thereafter, that he's gone to visit a sister; trace his wooden chest to a dug-up field—where Franklin, looking inside, finds the

body; and then, when the chest disappears, have to suffer Ian's wrath ("You've been wanting to humiliate me ever since we met") before they can prove to him and the police that they are right—which also enables scholarly Ian to prove his mettle to them. The explanation for François' death and its coverup? Jasmine and he were once lovers; she was accidentally responsible for his death; Felicité, to protect her, tried to make it look as if he'd gone away; Arthur, to keep the kids from finding out the whole "sordid little story," made the body disappear—because, sit tight, he's François' and Jasmine's illegitimate child! Actually, it's even more complicated than that, but Corcoran is a practiced storyteller who makes everything perfectly clear; what she doesn't do is give any of it—including the stepfather situation—any substance.

Virginia Haviland

SOURCE: A review of *The Person in the Potting Shed,* in *The Horn Book Magazine,* Vol. LVI, No. 6, December, 1980, p. 640.

A mystery story steeped in the atmosphere of its Louisiana bayou setting. Dorothy and Franklin arrive from their boarding schools to spend the summer with their mother and new stepfather Ian, a visiting professor of architecture at Tulane University. They are all interested in the estate Belle Rêve, part of which they are renting; it had once been a plantation with a tradition of French civilization and culture. Now the place presents a complex of genuinely baffling questions. Eva DuPré, descendant of the early owners, works in a bookshop and lives in another part of the great house. Her brother Arthur, a tennis instructor, comes and goes, as does their mother, a senile woman confined to a nearby rest home. Other characters include Felicité, the housekeeper, and the often drunk gardener François. All of them seem to flit about and vanish without explanations. Dorothy and Franklin, trying to adjust to their stepfather and to the unfamiliar surroundings, become aware of frightening things—screams in the night, a strange intruder, and the disappearance of François. Ignoring Ian's skepticism, they pursue clues, ultimately solving a mystery rooted in a long-ago love affair and thus winning their stepfather's respect.

School Library Journal

SOURCE: A review of *The Person in the Potting Shed,* in *School Library Journal,* Vol. 27, No. 4, December, 1980, p. 72.

In **The Person in the Potting Shed** Barbara Corcoran has created an intriguing plot within the confines of an unusual setting. Their new stepfather Ian is an expert on Southern architecture, but for Dorothy and Franklin the Belle Reve plantation in Louisiana where they will be spending the summer is only a moldy, creepy bunch of buildings. The odd surroundings come complete with a mad old woman, a drunken gardener and decadent owners. It doesn't take Dorothy and Franklin long to discover strange things going on (including a disappearing corpse), linked with an ill-fated love affair from long ago. The misunderstanding between stepparent and children is comfortably handled, and the air of mystery is as thick as moss on the bayou.

Margaret Mary Ptacek

SOURCE: A review of *The Person in the Potting Shed,* in *Voice of Youth Advocates,* Vol. 4, No. 1, April, 1981.

Dorothy and Franklin are two preteens with several adjustments to make. First, they haven't seen each other or their mother in 15 months; second, they have a new stepfather; and third, they are forced to spend their summer on an old plantation in New Orleans. This is a strange environment compared to their New England home. They attempt to make the best of things by exploring the area. The owner of the plantation doesn't appreciate this especially after they discover a body. Corcoran has woven together a pleasant mystery using believable characters and a plausible plot. It is a step above most YS mysteries, containing suspense without being melodramatic. The children are not "super snoops" but normal curious children. The parents are genuine without a cardboard or sickening quality. The subplot of the children's adjustment and "vice versa" to their stepfather may be very useful in an open ended discussion focussing on this area.

MAKING IT (1980)

Zena Sutherland

SOURCE: A review of *Making It,* in *Bulletin of the Center for Children's Books,* Vol. 34, No. 6, February, 1981, p. 109.

"I did love her, more than anyone. She was my ideal," Sissy says, describing her older sister Charlotte, the beautiful Charlotte who was the family pet, who was expected to become important, maybe even famous someday. When Sissy, who tells the story, receives a scholarship to UCLA she is thrilled in part because Charlotte is in Los Angeles; from a poor parsonage family, Sissy has been able to accept the scholarship only because parents of a friend have insisted that she share an apartment, rent-free. Sissy is a sensible, stable girl, a good influence on their daughter. Sissy is indeed stable, and rather conservative, and she is horrified when she realizes that her sister's beautiful clothes and handsome apartment come from her earnings as a call girl and a drug dealer. She's also cautious and conventional in her relationship with Marty, with whom she's in love; it's Marty who helps her face the tragedy of Charlotte's murder. Despite the serious issues the story explores, it is not morbid or somber; the first part of the book is a smooth blend of material about Charlotte, about Sissy's relationships with her parents, and about Sissy's college plans, and the last part has the development of the love affair with Marty to balance the sad story of Charlotte.

Ann A. Flowers

SOURCE: A review of *Making It,* in *The Horn Book Magazine,* Vol. LVII, No. 2, April, 1981, pp. 195-96.

Sylvia Duncan, a quiet, shy, seventeen-year-old from Fort Lewis, Colorado, has always adored her beautiful older sister Charlotte. Sylvia's parents are of no help to her; her father, a clergyman, has more or less abdicated his family responsibility, and she is no favorite of her domineering mother, who prefers Charlotte and her retarded younger brother Harvey. A fine student, Sylvia goes to U.C.L.A. after graduation from high school. Also living in Los Angeles is Charlotte, always vague about her movements; Sylvia finds out, to her horror, that her sister is actually a high-priced call girl and a dealer in drugs. Sylvia has her own problems; she has fallen in love and against her rather straight-laced background is forced to deal with her feelings about sex and love. Ultimately, Charlotte is murdered because of her drug connections, and Sylvia has started to make her own decisions. Although seen only through her sister's eyes, Charlotte is well characterized; her belief that she can get away with anything and that the end justifies the means is clearly contrasted with Sylvia's standards. The theme of rebellion against parental values is played out against a broad tapestry of many lives—so many, in fact, that one feels the author was not quite sure whose story she was telling. Thus, the book gives a realistic but slightly unfocused picture of modern life with all its complications. A straightforward style adds verisimilitude to a contemporary story.

Jack Forman

SOURCE: A review of *Making It,* in *School Library Journal,* Vol. 27, No. 8, April, 1981, p. 138.

Sylvia, the narrator, is a high-school senior in a small Colorado town; she has an older sister, supposedly away at college, of whom great things are expected by her stand-offish minister father and bitter, guilt-ridden mother. (This slightly macabre family also includes a retarded younger brother and Sylvia's twin, who died because he was not vaccinated against diptheria.) With the help of a classmate's rich parents, Sylvia decides to attend UCLA, where she gradually learns that her older sibling has quit school to become a prostitute and drug dealer. At UCLA, Sylvia also meets her first love—Marty Ross—a pre-med student who, readers are constantly reminded, is gentle, caring and understanding. Marty helps Sylvia through the tragedy of her sister's murder at the hands of jealous drug dealers. Corcoran has created a morality soap opera with an imporbable plot, didactic statements and predictable stereotypes. Marty is a laughable paragon and Sylvia is every inch the contemporary female rejecting the unhappy models of her parents and her sister's perverted values and drearily learning to become her own person. There's more to a story than a message. *Making It* doesn't make the grade.

Kirkus Reviews

SOURCE: A review of *Making It,* in *Kirkus Reviews,* Vol. XLIX, No. 16, August 15, 1981, p. 1010.

The old cliché of the preacher's daughter who goes wrong is acted out here, without a spark of individuality, by Sissy's beautiful older sister Charlotte—who leaves her drab Colorado home for Smith College and learns from an aunt back East that her pious mother had an abortion in her teens. (Mother's present long-suffering image is enhanced by the retarded son she's now devoted to and the dead one, Sissy's twin, who succumbed to diphtheria at eight.) Resentful of her family's grim values and hand-me-down clothes, Charlotte leaves school for a life that brings her the expensive duds and satin sheets she's always wanted. She also buys. clothes for the adoring Sissy—but when Sissy enters UCLA, with a scholarship and further help from a friend's family, she begins seeing her sister, and is literally sick (for days) on discovering that Charlotte is a call girl and, more recently, a drug dealer. Sissy participates in a little intrigue to help her sister when Charlotte's dealing brings her up against the mob, but Charlotte's greed gets the better of her and she's killed, stabbed in the back, while attempting to flee to Hawaii. It's all a blow to Sissy . . . but meanwhile she's acquired a loving pre-med student, who stands by her and proposes marriage when it's over. (This being a modern romance, Sissy, who's not yet 18, answers that she needs time on her own first.) In short, the stereotypes grow less and less credible as the story drags on to its melodramatic, then sappy, conclusion.

YOU'RE ALLEGRO DEAD (1981)

Denise M. Wilms

SOURCE: A review of *You're Allegro Dead,* in *Booklist,* Vol. 78, No. 3, October 1, 1981, p. 233.

Stella and Kim suspect something strange might be afoot at Camp Allegro, and their concern intensifies after someone throws rocks at Kim and after they stumble on a stranger beneath Point House porch after dark. The camp director won't take the girls' concern seriously; but they sleuth on, eventually uncovering a bank robber who used the empty camp facilities as a refuge till it reopened. This doesn't keep readers on edge as much as they might like, but it has its gritty moments, mainly in the realistic way the girls' encounters with the mystery figure are handled. A subplot involving their dislike of a fellow camper adds interest but finishes on an artificial note. This is not Corcoran at her best, but her practiced

hand still keeps readers intrigued where others might easily fail.

Kirkus Reviews

SOURCE: A review of *You're Allegro Dead,* in *Kirkus Reviews,* Vol. XLIX, No. 22, November 15, 1981, p. 1407.

Stella's mother and her old camp chums have the idea of starting up a camp like the one *they* went to—"a good old-fashioned all-around camp for normal girls"—and Stella and best-friend Kim, both 12, are roped in: a pretty good starting point for a return to the old rah-rah camp days that turns into the thinnest, dumbest sort of mystery. With nary a character who can be so much as characterized—apart from nasty show-off Nicole (saddled with a "monstrous" mother)—even the daily doings fall flat. But there aren't many of those: mostly we're meant to wonder who left a *recent* silver dollar under the boat-house, who stole a bag of flour, who threw rocks at Stella, etc.—who's hanging around and trying to protect his turf. Turns out to be a local bank robber, whose reasons for not taking flight are no more convincing than his presence in the story to start with. Meanwhile the fun that could have been gotten from putting today's young females in a camp set up to their mothers' taste is almost totally dissipated.

Zena Sutherland

SOURCE: A review of *You're Allegro Dead,* in *Bulletin of the Center for Children's Books,* Vol. 35, No. 5, January, 1982, pp. 83-4.

Kim and Stella, twelve, aren't enthralled when they are sent off to Camp Allegro, just re-opened through the support of loyal former campers like Stella's mother. They soon find that they have a similar loyalty, although their camp experiences are often spoiled by the machinations of attention-getting, self-centered Nicole. The latter seems the cause of several unpleasant experiences, but surely it isn't Nicole who throws rocks at Stella and who shoots at Kim, hitting her leg with shotgun pellets? The investigation that follows vindicates some of Stella's suspicions that had been dismissed by the camp director, leads to the discovery of a bank robber (a rather contrived aspect of the story) and shows that Nicole isn't all bad. Good style, adequate characterization, believable situation, not so believable plot development.

Celia H. Morris

SOURCE: A review of *You're Allegro Dead,* in *The Horn Book Magazine,* Vol. LVIII, No. 1, February, 1982, p. 41.

Stella and her best friend Kim are not sure they will enjoy going to the summer camp Stella's mother attended years before and so often praised. But almost immediately, mysterious happenings make Camp Allegro more of an experience than the routine of riding, hiking, and swimming the twelve-year-olds had expected. The author skillfully plants many clues and makes a number of characters, both adult and juvenile, seem culpable. Credibility is slightly stretched when the camp director, an old Allegro alumna herself, is so single-mindedly concerned with avoiding trouble at the newly reopened camp that she refuses to believe the girls' report of witnessing a man fleeing from under the main building late one night. But the director's disbelief makes more plausible the girls' reluctance to tell of an even more frightening event—the kidnapping of Stella; and the almost palpable tension mounts while the girls await the return of a sympathetic counselor. In the final dramatic scene Kim and Stella (aided appropriately by the counselor) act with youthful impetuousness and naïveté but also with courage. And the reader trying to put all the puzzle pieces together will be pleased that the clues lead to the most logical solution.

📖 *CHILD OF THE MORNING* (1982)

Barbara Baker

SOURCE: A review of *Child of the Morning,* in *Children's Book Review Service,* Vol. 10, No. 12, Spring, 1982, p. 116.

Susan begins to suffer blackouts and headaches after suffering a concussion in a volleyball game. She resists advice about seeking medical help and refuses to admit that her problem might be serious. Helping with a summer stock theater group opens new career horizons and finally brings her epilepsy to the fore. This brief (112 pages) novel features a cast of cardboard characters and little time for plot strands to develop; the epilepsy message is strident. The last chapter crams months of medical episodes (which should be important to readers who care about Susan) into a few pages. Not one of Corcoran's best.

Stephanie Zvirin

SOURCE: A review of *Child of the Morning,* in *Booklist,* Vol. 78, No. 15, April 1, 1982, p. 1014.

After a volleyball accident leaves her subject to recurrent blackouts over which she has no control, and friends and family question her capabilities, Susan manages to find solace in dancing and in her girl-Friday activities with a summer-stock theater—all the while hoping her episodes will disappear. But the spells worsen, and her joy at the opportunity to dance in front of a live audience is spoiled when she blacks out on stage and is told she has epilepsy. Corcoran does not probe the physical and emotional consequences of the disease as fully as Girion did in *A Handful of Stars,* and her characters and plot are merely sketched; but there's a gentle tone about

her writing that brings Susan, her environment, and her problem into a fine, soft focus while it draws readers into the story.

Zena Sutherland

SOURCE: A review of *Child of the Morning,* in *Bulletin of the Center for Children's Books,* Vol. 35, No. 10, June, 1982, p. 184.

The family doctor said it was nothing to worry about, but Susan and her parents were baffled by the fact that she had had brief spells of unconsciousness ever since she'd had a head injury during a school volleyball game. Sometimes, when this happened, she'd fall. Nobody in her small town would give her a summer job but she did get one, part time, as odd-job girl for a summer theater group; later she was asked to dance in one production. Her performance was fine, although it ended in a blackout. By this time there was a new doctor in town, and he recognized her seizures as epileptic. After a worrisome series of drugs produced only adverse side effects, the right drug for Susan was isolated, and the book ends with Susan at last feeling that her condition can be controlled, and that the future can hold a career in dance for her. Although the parental apathy and medical inertia strain credulity a bit, the story is otherwise nicely crafted, with strong minor characters, good pace, and the theatrical milieu that adds appeal.

Bill Erbes

SOURCE: A review of *Child of the Morning,* in *School Library Journal,* Vol. 29, No. 5, January, 1983, p. 83.

Susan has Symptomatic Epilepsy that has not been diagnosed and is not being treated. All Susan knows is that ever since she got a concussion while playing volleyball, she has been subject to brief spells of blacking out or fainting. Hiding these spells as best she can and refusing to believe something is seriously wrong, Susan takes a job with a summer theater group. Jobs such as poster-hanging and scenery painting lead to positions with more responsibility, and Susan is eventually given a small but important dancing role in a production of *The Tempest.* It is only after Susan has a seizure during a performance that proper medical treatment is secured. This short novel presents a sensitive yet objective view of epilepsy. The diagnosis and successful treatment take only 13 pages, probably a simplification, but the point still is made that epilepsy can be treated and need not be as frightening as its reputation.

📖 *A WATERY GRAVE* (1982)

Kirkus Reviews

SOURCE: A review of *A Watery Grave,* in *Kirkus Reviews,* Vol. L, No. 14, July 15, 1982, p. 798.

A family called Farley moves into a nearby house equipped with pool and tennis court, and best friends Kim and Stella hear hints of mystery and tragedy. With both sets of parents on a Bermuda vacation and their college-girl sitter in hospital for an appendectomy, Kim and Stella soon find themselves "camping" in the Farleys' guest house. They hear of a Farley son who died of a drug overdose at a fraternity party. Now, a year later, four of the dead boy's friends are Farley guests, and Mr. Farley is determined to learn how the accident occurred. He is sure (correctly) that his son never took drugs. One of the four guests, about to talk, is found stabbed to death in the pool; a Farley child, a junior eccentric, is kidnapped; and Kim and Stella, who are pretty much ignored, do some spying which helps the local police pinpoint the two guilty guests. The snooping also gets Kim nearly drowned in the pool by an unseen night-time assailant—a violent warning, police conclude, rather than attempted murder. Corcoran takes a stab at distributing suspicion, but the only surprise is which one of the guilty couple actually carried out the murder. Corcoran keys this to the undemanding mystery reader, but the writing, characterization, motivation, and setting are so mechanical and simplified as to be implausible, and there is none of the exotic ambience that saves other such Corcoran mysteries. Routine stuff, for addicts who prefer it that way.

Zena Sutherland

SOURCE: A review of *A Watery Grave*, in *Bulletin of the Center for Children's Books*, Vol. 36, No. 1, September, 1982, p. 6.

Adolescents Kim and Stella are staying in the guest cottage of their new neighbors, the Farleys, because their parents are all on a trip and the young woman who was to stay with them has had an emergency appendectomy. They find Mr. Farley gruffly amicable, his wife nervous and vague, and their four invited guests (friends of a son who had died of a drug overdose—although not a drug user—exactly a year before) suspicious and defensive. One of the four is murdered, and Kim and Stella provide the police with several clues but also do some sleuthing on their own. Due in large part to their perspicacity, the mystery is solved, although both Stella and a young Farley are victims of violence in the process. The characterization is minimal, and the plot too dependent on coincidence to lend credence to its development. While readers may enjoy the suspense and action, they may feel the lack of the logic that is one of the criteria of better-structured mystery stories.

Denise M. Wilms

SOURCE: A review of *A Watery Grave*, in *Booklist*, Vol. 79, No. 1, September 1, 1982, p. 40.

Stella and Kim, the friends who weathered mystery and adventure at Camp Allegro in *You're Allegro Dead*, find more of the same here, although this time the setting is local. At the heart of it are the Farleys, a new family still in shock over the sudden death by drugs of their son the year before. When Mr. Farley assembles his son's closest friends for a death-anniversary meeting, another death occurs; and Stella and Kim, as houseguests of the Farleys, are too close for the murderer's comfort. The story flows easily from Corcoran's practiced hand, with plenty of smooth dialogue and the attractive, affluent surroundings of a small New England town. Just "who done it" or why isn't precisely clear till near the finish, which means suspense holds nicely in this proficient, easily consumed tale.

STRIKE! (1983)

Zena Sutherland

SOURCE: A review of *Strike!* in *Bulletin of the Center for Children's Books*, Vol. 36, No. 8, April, 1983, p. 146.

At first, when the teachers in his high school went on strike to protest the censorious campaign by the town's Committee for a Balanced Curriculum, which involved removing books (and even one attempt to burn books) Barry was sympathetic but uninvolved. He doted on one pretty teacher who was an activist, and he also tended to react negatively to the conservatism of his bullying father. However, participation forced him to think seriously about the issues, and soon Barry found that he felt strongly about the right to read. The story builds to a logical climax, and Barry is deeply pleased when both of his parents rally to join the cause in which he has come to believe. This has a message, but it's not a book in which the message gets in the way of the story, for Corcoran so carefully integrates her characters and their beliefs with their actions and reactions that the plot flows naturally. A thoughtful approach to a current problem blends smoothly with a perceptive study of an adolescent and his problems.

Ilene Cooper

SOURCE: A review of *Strike!* in *Booklist*, Vol. 78, No. 15, April 1, 1983, p. 1031.

Fifteen-year-old Barry gets along just fine with his mother, but his relationship with his business executive father is a different story. A major bone of contention is Barry's desire to take shop courses in his pursuit of a carpentry career while his father wants him in Harvard striving for an M.B.A. In the midst of this hostility comes another provocation. The teachers at Madison High go on strike and while Barry's sympathies lie with the strikers (especially the kind, attractive Mrs. Cronin), his father sits on the school board opposed to the strike. Money is not the only issue; certain townspeople are removing textbooks and materials from the school, and the censorship issue becomes part of the fray. Barry must decide whether to shatter the already fragile relationship between his father and himself and actively support the strike. Corcoran is at her best when describing Barry's personal relationships. She is least successful with drawing the many supporting characters who are stereotypical, either Bad or Good. And the episode in which the chief Moral Majority type seemingly hires a thug to beat up the leader in the strike is melodramatic. Junior high students will probably respond well to the parental problem Corcoran describes, but for discussion of censorship issues, they'd be better off reading Hentoff's *Day They Came to Arrest the Book.*

Robert Unsworth

SOURCE: A review of *Strike!* in *School Library Journal,* Vol. 29, No. 9, May, 1983, p. 80.

When the teachers decide to strike over the issue of book censorship, it places a heavy strain on the already poor relationship between high schooler Barry and his father, who is a member of the school board. Barry supports the teachers and readers can accurately predict the rest. Teacher strikes and censorship are two explosively emotional issues but Corcoran does nothing more than the drearily predictable with both. There is almost no discussion of the issues. The members of the censorship committee as well as Barry's father are wildly overdrawn caricatures. Towards the end of the story there's an actual book burning, a riot and a fist fight between Barry and his dad but it's unlikely that any readers will stick with the novel that long.

Kirkus Reviews

SOURCE: A review of *Strike!* in *Kirkus Reviews,* Vol. LI, No. 9, May 1, 1983, pp. 527-28.

Another high-school book censorship novel, with a personal focus on 16-year-old Barry's uneasy relationship with his rigid lawyer father, who is on the school board. The town is torn up when the teachers go on strike with two demands: a pay raise and protection from the Committee for a Balanced Curriculum, which is removing "immoral" books (including a standard dictionary) from the classrooms and libraries. From a combination of conviction, circumstance, and a crush on a teacher, Barry finds himself in the student group supporting the strike. Shady Mr. Durham, a member of the repressive committee and a former state legislator, hires local "riffraff" to pack a school board hearing and then to beat up a teacher leader. Barry and his father come to blows when the father quits the school board and Barry accuses him of giving in to pressure; but then, at the Committee's public book-burning, Barry is beaten up by the "riffraff" and his father gently carries him off to the doctor. Turns out Dad quit the board when they wouldn't accept his compromise proposal—no raise for the teachers but condemnation of the committee—so that's okay.

Corcoran's stereotyped depiction of the censorship fight hasn't the force or intelligence of Hentoff's *Day They Came to Arrest the Book;* and though she provides more of a conventional story in Barry and his father, it's just that, a conventional story.

THE WOMAN IN YOUR LIFE (1984)

Ethel R. Twichell

SOURCE: A review of *The Woman in Your Life,* in *The Horn Book Magazine,* Vol. LX, No. 5, September-October, 1984, pp. 595-96.

Finding in Aaron the burly strength and love of the outdoors that she remembers in her dead father, Monty blindly centers her life on the young man, who disappears when she is caught helping him smuggle drugs across the Mexican border. Naïve and isolated from her much-married mother, Monty is an inevitable victim in the disaster and, with her convent education, an unlikely candidate for the term she must serve in prison. Although the girl's prison experiences, told in her journal entries which alternate with a third-person narrative, seem less harsh than one might expect, her despair at Aaron's desertion is convincingly portrayed. Monty is confronted by a formidable array of prostitutes, forgers, and shoplifters, but their initial antagonism later turns to friendship. Her eventual departure from prison and her future success are never in doubt in the slickly told story, yet the bizarre cast of characters and the look into prison life offer a certain fascination. Lively rather than profound, glib rather than thoughtful, the book's pace and sense of timely detail should nevertheless have an appeal for teenaged audiences.

Publishers Weekly

SOURCE: A review of *The Woman in Your Life,* in *Publishers Weekly,* Vol. 226, No. 18, November 2, 1984, p. 78.

Corcoran's reputation rests solidly on novels that readers sense are based on situations that excite her compassion for people as well as her acute perceptions of influences on them. This story is about Anne Byington Montgomery. "I'm Monty. In this place I'm FX 10375."

"This place" is euphemistically called a federal correctional facility. The text alternates with passages from Monty's journal to trace the path taking her to prison when she meets and falls for Aaron Helding. He's a fellow student at the college in Montana where Monty is making good grades until she begins spending most of her time with the brawny Paul Bunyan type whose "Babe" Monty willingly becomes. Her concerned friend Paula fails to persuade Monty that "macho is out," for the man convinces her that he is the only person who has cared for her since her father's death.

Monty tops Bunyan's Babe in oxlike obedience to Aaron. He takes her to Mexico where he stashes drugs in his van and orders her to drive it across the border while he walks to the American side. No one, Aaron assures Monty, will suspect her. She's arrested and sentenced to three years, refusing to incriminate her lover.

Doing time, Monty gradually forms relationships with other women prisoners and officers, who teach her valuable lessons. She realizes also that Paula is a real friend, the one person who communicates with her from the outside, offering moral support and a chance for a new start. Monty can, eventually, see Aaron as he is, eager to use anyone like her, who had lacked self-respect and common sense.

Corcoran's descriptions of Monty's barren childhood as the daughter of a much-marrying, frivolous mother add conviction to the story readers will find hard to forget.

Christine Denk

SOURCE: A review of *The Woman in Your Life,* in *School Library Journal,* Vol. 31, No. 6, February, 1985, p. 82.

As her mother marries and remarries, 18-year-old Monty is shunted from nursery school to camp to convent school. Feeling unwanted and unloved makes her particularly susceptible to Aaron, a forestry student whom she meets at the University of Montana. He asks for help in a mysterious "get rich quick" scheme. Thrilled that he needs her, and longing for a chance to prove her love, she travels with Aaron to Mexico, where he buys mescaline to smuggle across the border. She is caught and sent to prison; her silence ensures his freedom, and she never hears from him again. Gradually Monty realizes that she was used as a result of her low self-esteem. In prison, she finally finds the loving family she has longed for: wise, tough Susie, known as "mother," and "grandfather," a murderer who helps her through the rough times. There is no pat ending here. Monty isn't sure what she'll do with her life, but she does leave prison with new-found courage to face her future. Well-paced, with high interest, *The Woman in Your Life* offers possibilities as a hi/lo book and as a subject for book talks.

📖 *I AM THE UNIVERSE* (also published as *Who Am I Anyway?,* 1986)

Publishers Weekly

SOURCE: A review of *I Am the Universe,* in *Publishers Weekly,* Vol. 230, No. 8, August 22, 1986, p. 100.

Narrator Kit Esterly's first problem is the paper she has to write for her eight-grade English class on who she is. But she doesn't *know* who she is. Added to that are her mother's incessant headaches that turn out to be caused by a brain tumor, the disappearance of her younger brother Daniel's cat, preschooler Terry's demands for attention and teenage Andy's goofy behavior when he starts dating. Being the "sensible" one, Kit has to hold the family together while her mother is in the hospital. The strain takes its toll, and a tension-releasing prank lands her in police custody. But, ultimately, everything works out, and Mrs. Esterly returns home, her health—and Kit's happiness—restored. Corcoran (*Face the Music,* etc.) has beautifully captured a preteen's teetering between childish blunders and adult insights. A delightful character, Kit is a heroine despite herself. Like many 12-year-olds, she's funny when at her most serious, with wisecracks that come straight from the heart.

Cindy Darling Codell

SOURCE: A review of *I Am the Universe,* in *School Library Journal,* Vol. 33, No. 2, October, 1986, pp. 171-72.

Corcoran's portrayal of a normal family holding together under stress is skillfully done. Kit's mother is operated on for a brain tumor, and the task of holding the family together falls to Kit. Her older brother seems like a stranger now that he is starting to date. Daniel, a genius, is failing third grade; her younger sister seems to need more and more attention. Kit is struggling with a theme entitled, "Who Am I?" This first-person narration is psychologically revealing, as Kit begins to learn more about herself and her strengths. Characterizations are excellent. The Esterly parents are wise and warm. Siblings, while they have moments of conflict, are kind and decent to each other. These strong characterizations also allow Corcoran to prick stereotypical thinking. An author imagined to be old turns out to be young and bumbling. A housewife fails at cooking, but a vagabond ex-war photographer flourishes in the kitchen. An auto accident produces a friend, not a lawsuit. Simple language ensures a wide readership, but the intellectual content is there for those who wish to pursue it.

Denise M. Wilms

SOURCE: A review of *I Am the Universe,* in *Booklist,* Vol. 83, No. 3, October 1, 1986, pp. 268-69.

Assigned to write a paper on who she is, 12-year-old Katherine stews over the question but finds no sure answer until she and her family weather the crisis of her mother's hospitalization and successful brain surgery. With her mother ill and her father preoccupied, Katherine and her older brother assume responsibility for the day-to-day household operation. They hit on bribery as a way of inspiring their younger brother, Daniel, to work up to his third-grade potential. Heretofore he's been flunking, even though his IQ is 140. Katherine works on her writing, attracting the attention of a visiting author and getting her story published in a local newspaper. However, the pressures of coping push her to a night of petty vandalism—hurling eggs at random targets. With news that her mother is going to get well, Katherine begins to relax and to enjoy learning who she is: "I am the popper of corn, the baker of bread, the writer of stories. I am the daughter, the sister, the friend. I am Katherine." The story moves quickly and smoothly because of a deft first-person narration. There is little contrivance and, though the story's emotional peaks are few, readers looking for light contemporary drama will find this effective.

Roger Sutton

SOURCE: A review of *I Am the Universe*, in *Bulletin of the Center for Children's Books*, Vol. 40, No. 4, December, 1986, p. 64.

A daunting title for an engaging story about a thirteen-year-old girl who, in the space of a few weeks, is confronted with too much: Kit's mother's frequent, agonizing headaches have been diagnosed as symptoms of a brain tumor, compounding and magnifying Kit's usual problems with school and family, and her growing awareness of herself as a writer. This is a lot for an author, much less a thirteen-year-old, to handle, but Corcoran weaves the various plot strands with ease, and Kit's slightly caustic—though heartfelt—narration keeps the tone light. There are a few mis-steps (Kit being picked up by the cops for egg-throwing) where the characters act like psychological profiles, but on the whole, Kit and her family—especially her eccentrically gifted little brother—are warmly and carefully drawn. Give this one to Anastasia Krupnik fans who are looking for something a little "older."

Beth Wheeler Dean

SOURCE: A review of *I Am the Universe*, in *Voice of Youth Advocates*, Vol. 9, No. 5, December, 1986, p. 214.

Katharine Esterly is almost 13 years old and wants to be a writer. Kit, as she is called, sees her life as revolving around the members of her family. Her older brother's girlfriends, her younger brother's school problems, and her little sister's constant craving for attention are compounded by the entire family's worry over Kit's mother and her increasingly severe headaches. When Mrs. Ramer, Kit's English teacher, assigns a theme on the subject "Who Am I" for a class competition, Kit finds herself worrying about whether she can do her best work with this particular subject. Kit feels that there is no "her" outside of her connection with her family and her attention to their needs. When the cause of her mother's headaches is diagnosed as a brain tumor requiring dangerous surgery, the entire family reacts to the stress and anxiety.

This is not a dark book. There is a warmth throughout generated by the caring of this family for each other and the people their lives touch. Kit grows through her feelings of uncertainty and fear. Nothing changes in Kit but her perception of herself, but that's a big step and one to be proud of. The first person narrative leaves you wishing you knew more about the other characters. The book leaves you with a smile. It is the story of a family that might in different days have been called normal. Now we would call them lucky. Buy this book. It may not be the best you have ever read, but it definitely feels good.

YOU PUT UP WITH ME, I'LL PUT UP WITH YOU (1987)

Kirkus Reviews

SOURCE: A review of *You Put Up with Me, I'll Put Up with You*, in *Kirkus Reviews*, Vol. LV, No. 1, January 1, 1987, pp. 55-6.

When Kelly's widowed mother decides to join two old friends and their children in a house she's inherited and start a restaurant with them, only-child Kelly takes a while to adjust.

Almost a teen-ager, Kelly also imagines herself on the verge of establishing an identity for herself in her exclusive school; her negative attitude toward the move gets her off to a rough start with new roommate Esther, involved in trying out to be a high-school cheerleader, and with almost everyone else in her new extended family. Kelly and Rhonda, an overly dramatic girl next door, have a minor adventure trailing a figure Rhonda is sure is involved in a drug ring, only to find that it's just Alexander, a boy who's another occupant of the house. In fact, all the characters Kelly first views as enemies prove similarly benign, and by the end an unreasonably large number of conflicts have been resolved.

Although Corcoran's theme is commonplace and her characters predictable, plot details are original enough to hold the interest of those young people who empathize with Kelly's problems.

Zena Sutherland

SOURCE: A review of *You Put Up with Me, I'll Put Up with You*, in *Bulletin of the Center for Children's Books*, Vol. 40, No. 7, March, 1987, pp. 123-24.

The only child of a widowed mother, Kelly is content with her life and beginning to adjust to a new junior high school. She is upset and sulky when her mother announces they're moving again, this time to share with two other women (and assorted progeny) the house inherited from a grandparent. The three women are going to refurbish a deserted schoolhouse and open a restaurant. Corcoran uses Kelly's resistance to every aspect of change as the main theme in the story; minor plot lines include coping with a "weird" friend's behavior, having a crush on an older boy, and learning to accept the sixteen-year-old cheerleader, Esther, with whom she's been forced to share a bedroom. This isn't as cohesive as most of Corcoran's books, but there are no false notes, and the writing style is smooth. Some character exaggeration and an uneven pace weaken the story.

Judy Butler

SOURCE: A review of *You Put Up with Me, I'll Put Up with You,* in *School Library Journal,* Vol. 33, No. 7, March, 1987, p. 169.

Interesting characters act and react toward one another at a pleasant pace and in a sufficiently detailed New England setting to create an enjoyable reading experience for teens. Kelly's mother decides to return to her old home town and open up a restaurant with two friends, one divorced and the other a widow like herself. Kelly, a seventh grader, is faced not only with the prospect of changing schools and making new friends, but, worst of all, adjusting to living with three mothers and four other children. She sets out determined to hate the entire arrangement and everyone involved. Gradually, as she gets to know not only the four children but two colorful townspeople, she begins to understand that her own sarcastic, sometimes spoiled attitude toward change limits her understanding of people. Humor, mystery, and a sympathetic but realistic analysis of a young girl's feelings, fears, and self-discoveries are combined in this creative and highly readable story.

Wendy Gaal

SOURCE: A review of *You Put Up with Me, I'll Put Up with You,* in *Voice of Youth Advocates,* Vol. 10, No. 1, April, 1987, p. 30.

Twelve-year-old Kelly, an only child, is unhappy in the small, private school she has attended since her father's death. Then she is cast as Mercutio in the school's production of *Romeo and Juliet.* This, she believes, will give her an opportunity to demonstrate her talent and earn deserved recognition from her aloof classmates. Then her mother informs Kelly that they are moving to the house that they inherited from Kelly's grandmother. There, in a small, rural, seaside community, Kelly's mother and two friends plan to open a restaurant. Worse still, the three women and their families will share the house. Predictably, Kelly has difficulties with these arrangements and even attempts to thwart her mother's attempts to establish the restaurant. However, Kelly is basically "a good kid" and is slowly drawn into the caring environment of her new extended family and the small insular community. Most importantly, she learns to compromise and to look beyond the surface of appearances.

This is a pleasant coming-of-age novel that will appeal to young female readers. A small mysterious subplot and several colorful, eccentric characters enliven the quiet plot. References to Madonna. The Talking Heads, and contemporary television programs plant the story firmly in the present.

THE HIDEAWAY (1987)

Kirkus Reviews

SOURCE: A review of *The Hideaway,* in *Kirkus Reviews,* Vol. LV, No. 13, July 15, 1987, p. 1068.

An unusually well-written "problem" novel that is much more.

Fifteen-year-old Tom runs away from a training school where he's been placed for four months until his court hearing. Though he's supposed to have seriously injured a man in an automobile accident, Tom wasn't driving. His older "sometime friend" Buddy, who is to enter Yale in the fall, was—and ran away from the scene. Tom, who had given Buddy the keys to his mother's new Audi and who was as drunk as Buddy as he rode in the seat beside him, has protected him. Tom's mother, recently divorced from his stepfather, has refused to have Tom wait out the time to his hearing in her house. Though Tom has never been in trouble before, his stepfather's new wife says one child—Tom's 13-year-old half-sister Shelly—is enough. As he spends days hiding in an abandoned theatre, Tom comes to see that loyalty and hero worship can be misplaced and that "a person has to learn to take consequences."

Tom is not, as in so many novels for children, a puppet hero, but he is convincingly revealed as a real boy caught at a critical moment who needs to find enough good in himself to choose to live out the rest of his life. The story, quietly moving in its depiction of helpless parents, the devotion of a sister, a boy's nearly giving up on himself, and, especially, Tom and Buddy's bitter yet compassionate wheelchair-bound victim, is an elegant achievement.

Zena Sutherland

SOURCE: A review of *The Hideaway,* in *Bulletin of the Center for Children's Books,* Vol. 41, No. 1, September, 1987, p. 5.

Sent to a reform school because he had accepted the blame for injuring a man when driving while intoxicated, 15-year-old Tom has run away. He had never told the authorities that his friend Buddy had been the driver; now he wants desperately to find Buddy and clear his own name. Hiding out in an empty summer theater, Tom gets in touch with his supportive young half-sister, and he gets help from an elderly man, Harv, who is not inquisitive or judgmental; both of them help Tom solve his problem, especially after the long-sought meeting with Buddy proves that he's completely contemptuous and callous. This has good characterization, a competent writing style, and a modicum of suspense; it is weakened by a plethora of small contrivances of plot and small stylistic errors.

Stephanie Zvirin

SOURCE: A review of *The Hideaway,* in *Booklist,* Vol. 84, No. 4, October 15, 1987, p. 384.

Certain that Buddy Peterson doesn't realize his predicament, Tom Eaton runs away from the security facility where he has been awaiting judgment to find Buddy and straighten matters out so Tom doesn't have to take the drunk-driving rap alone. After all, he wasn't really at the wheel, although that is not what he told the police. It was 18-year-old Buddy who drove the Eaton car into an oncoming vehicle, crippling its driver. With the help of his sister and a septuagenarian fisherman with whom he hides out, Tom confronts his friend, only to find his loyalty has been sadly misplaced. Tom's younger sister comes off by far the smarter of the two teens, and while the whole story lacks depth, it is always nice to see a victim turned into a survivor. Corcoran manages it in easily digestible fashion.

Robert E. Unsworth

SOURCE: A review of *The Hideaway,* in *School Library Journal,* Vol. 34, No. 3, November, 1987, p. 114.

Just how far does loyalty to a friend go? Tom, 15, thinks it goes very far, even to the point of covering up for a friend who drove a car that was involved in a DWI accident that leaves a man permanently paralyzed. One night, Tom borrowed a car and let his friend Buddy (no subtlety here) drive when he knew that he himself was too drunk. Buddy fled the scene of the accident and denied any involvement. Tom is sent to a juvenile detention center to await disposition of the charges. He runs from the camp and heads home, in the mistaken belief that when he confronts Buddy, Buddy will admit to his role in the accident. It is here that the story, which is set along the northern Massachusetts coast just north of Boston, begins. With the help of his younger sister, an old man, and the accident victim himself, Tom is made to realize that his friendship with Buddy should know some boundaries; by novel's end readers can believe that someplace down the line Buddy gets his come-uppance. The story is implausible. Can readers believe that Tom is so naive? Can they accept the notion that his parents, even if divorced and with new mates, never bothered to visit him in the several months he was in detention? Is Tom's sister, an eighth grader, really more intelligent and caring than her parents? The story fails because readers can't see Tom taking so long to come around to realizing that Buddy will never admit his guilt.

THE SKY IS FALLING (1988)

Kirkus Reviews

SOURCE: A review of *The Sky Is Falling,* in *Kirkus Reviews,* Vol. LVI, No. 14, July 15, 1988, p. 1057.

When 14-year-old Annah's father loses his job as a bank president during the Depression, her family must sell their beloved Victorian house in Boston and split up to find work. Annah leaves private school, dancing lessons, and friends to live with Aunt Edna, a spunky young widow roughing it in a cabin on a frozen lake in New Hampshire. There, Annah learns several survival skills, from snowshoeing and woodchopping to making friends and dealing with enemies among the roughnecks at the public school, who regard her as "summer people." She puts her own problems in perspective when she meets Dodie, a poverty-stricken, abused girl who needs her friendship. The story ends with a personal sacrifice that signals a new maturity for Annah. Everyone grows in this book: brother Herb goes from romanticizing his poverty to working for social causes; Annah's mother reacts at first with fainting spells, but later learns to sell real estate. Corcoran, a much-experienced author, has a gift for perceptive portrayal of a young girl's insights and reactions; she suggests that growth brought by experience makes a better person.

Publishers Weekly

SOURCE: A review of *The Sky Is Falling,* in *Publishers Weekly,* Vol. 234, No. 5, July 29, 1988, p. 233.

Readers are unlikely to be attracted to this book by its cover, which features a murky montage of sullen, disproportionate figures looming against a forbidding landscape. That's too bad, for this work is every bit as engrossing as the author's last two, *The Hideaway* and *I Am the Universe.* Just after Annah's 14th birthday in 1931, all her family's money is lost in the stock market, her father is fired, and she is sent away from her comfortably affluent home in a Boston suburb to live with her aunt in a lakefront cottage in rural New Hampshire. Taunted as a "summer person" by her new schoolmates, Annah befriends Dodie, also an outcast, but at the opposite end of the social scale. As their friendship develops, Annah learns some important lessons about poverty and self-sacrifice, just as Dodie learns that being proud doesn't preclude accepting charity. Corcoran warmly evokes the Depression era in telling detail—Moxie sodas, marcelled hair—while making some timeless observations about loving relationships and the common thread that unites people regardless of social distinctions.

Andrea Davidson

SOURCE: A review of *The Sky Is Falling,* in *Voice of Youth Advocates,* Vol. 11, No. 4, October, 1988, p. 181.

When Annah's banker father loses his job, Annah's family is forced to split up. Every member of the family feels the effects of the Depression in a different way—Annah's mother learns that she has a flair for selling real estate in Florida, Annah grows up a lot living with Aunt Edna in New Hampshire and unselfishly helping a poor friend and her little blind brother, and Annah's brother Herb cheerfully drops out of college to find work wherever he can. The uncorrected proof I saw had good cover artwork and kept me interested in Annah's plight, as the story is told through her eyes. Annah at 14 having to accept her Uncle Herb jumping out of a window and her father losing his job and making money shoveling snow will give the reader a fairly good idea of what life was like for a once affluent family during the Depression. The tragedies seem more surface treated than in depth, but the characters are sympathetic, even though everything turns out all right for Annah's family. A good introduction to life during the Depression for younger teens or reluctant teen readers.

Zena Sutherland

SOURCE: A review of *The Sky Is Falling,* in *Bulletin of the Center for Children's Books,* Vol. 42, No. 7, January, 1989, p. 118.

It did seem to Annah that what happened to her family in 1931 was equivalent to the disaster of the title. Dad lost his job and went to Chicago to look for work, Mother joined her parents in Florida, brother Herb had to drop out of college, and Annah was sent to live with Aunt Edna in an isolated cabin in rural New Hampshire. Bullied by intransigent classmate Mabel, Annah feels an outsider until she makes friends with another newcomer, Dodie. Dodie is victimized by her brutal stepfather, is the protector of her blind brother, and is eventually separated from her alcoholic mother—all of which seems on the heavy-handed side. Annah, whose character seems to strengthen on a diet of adversity, gives up her chance to live with the former family servant she loves in order to let Dodie take her place, a circumstance that makes the servant seem peculiarly hospitable. Convincing as a story of the Depression era, the novel is marred by immoderacy (the plight of Dodie, the viciousness of Mabel) but is, as is usually true of Corcoran's work, capably written.

📖 *THE POTATO KID* (1989)

Roger Sutton

SOURCE: A review of *The Potato Kid,* in *Bulletin of the Center for Children's Books,* Vol. 43, No. 3, November, 1989, p. 53.

Ellis, fourteen, had her summer all planned, and especially looked forward to a month away from home working as a stable girl. But the arrival of Lilac, courtesy of a church DO-GOOD project, changes every-

thing. Lilac is from the impoverished potato growing region in northern Maine and Ellis, it seems, is expected to devote her summer to taking charge of the sulky, neglected child. Neither Ellis (the narrator) nor Lilac is particularly likeable; it's a credit to Corcoran's skill that she makes us care for them nonetheless. The growing—and grudging—respect that develops between the two is realistically halting, and while there's a bit of a fairytale finale, readers will be happy that unwanted Lilac finds a home at last.

Kirkus Reviews

SOURCE: A review of *The Potato Kid,* in *Kirkus Reviews,* Vol. LVII, No. 21, November 1, 1989, p. 1590.

When Mom—a do-gooder who delegates the actual work of her philanthropic projects to others—announces that the family is taking in a needy child for the summer, daughter Ellis, 14, is dismayed; she's sure her own plans will be forfeited.

And so they are, but not as she expects. Mom plans to park ten-year-old Lilac with Dad's parents, but then Gramps has a heart attack, and Ellis—with some help from her older sister and younger brother—becomes chief caretaker for this self-possessed waif from the potato fields of northern Maine. Everyone's so upset by Gramps' hospitalization that no one pays much attention to Lilac; her history comes out belatedly. Her novelist-to-be dad died four years ago; her overworked Mom is about to marry again and hopes Lilac will be adopted. Believably, even these revelations don't immediately dispel the antagonism between Ellis (with her legitimate grievance) and Lilac (with her natural response to it); it takes a couple of extra twists to the lively plot to make them friends.

Corcoran, author of 60+ books, holds attention. There's much that rings true here, especially the family too centered on its own middle-class preoccupations to be sensitive to the needs of a young outsider. The book would be stronger, however, if we knew how they got that way; Mom, especially, has no excuse but inherited snobbishness for her non-contributions to her own family as well as to Lilac. The outcome—Lilac will stay with the grandparents after all—is not wholly plausible. Still, warm-hearted and entertaining.

Elizabeth S. Watson

SOURCE: A review of *The Potato Kid,* in *The Horn Book Magazine,* Vol. LXVI, No. 1, January-February, 1990, p. 62.

Lilac Kingsmith comes to a Down East town from the potato country of northern Maine to stay for the summer with the Worthington family. It's clear from the first that this visit is not Lilac's idea of a good time. She arrives frightened and belligerent, but gutsy; by supper-time she has already tried to run away, but then agrees to stay on a trial basis. Fourteen-year-old Ellis Worthington, the narrator, is equally unenthusiastic, since it falls to her to watch over the younger girl. As the summer progresses, relationships develop and impressions change, and the two girls learn about mutual respect and about humanity. The story is played out among three generations, with the grandparents and children the most fully developed characters. A nicely handled horsey background, two interesting and refreshingly—if at times grudgingly—nice heroines, and a subtle exploration of values combine in a first-class story.

Jean Kaufman

SOURCE: A review of *The Potato Kid,* in *Voice of Youth Advocates,* Vol. 12, No. 6, February, 1990, p. 342.

When Ellis' mother volunteers to host a needy child for the summer, most of the burden of caring for ten year old Lilac falls to 14 year old Ellis. Ellis had planned to spend the summer horse-back riding and in August she was going to be a stable girl at an equestrian center. Lilac's arrival and the mild heart attack of Ellis' grandfather change all those plans. Ellis is asked to "keep an eye on Lilac," but Lilac is sneaky and unfriendly so the two girls don't get along. Through several small mishaps, Ellis begins to appreciate how different Lilac's life has been, but it takes two major problems for them to become friends.

The first problem comes in a letter from Lilac's mother telling Lilac that she should "get herself adopted" since the mother has remarried and there is no space for Lilac. The second problem is a riding accident in which Ellis falls and breaks her leg. The family rallies to cope with these problems. They comfort and help Ellis during her recuperative period and Ellis' grandparents decide to adopt Lilac. The two girls are brought together in solving these problems and begin to be friends.

This is a smoothly written and heartwarming family story. The main character Ellis is like any normal 14 year old girl—loving, jealous, hard-working, lazy, kind, selfish, conscientious, and sorry for herself all at different times in the book. Readers will relate well to Ellis' emotions and frustrations over the change in her summer plans. The information on the plight of the small farmer is smoothly if sparsely integrated into the story. Some might call the ending unrealistic but I call it hopeful. It is what one always hopes will happen—that people will care enough to help those in need. Delightful—upbeat.

📖 *ANNIE'S MONSTER* (1990)

Katharine Bruner

SOURCE: A review of *Annie's Monster,* in *School Library Journal,* Vol. 36, No. 10, October, 1990, pp. 113-14.

Annie MacDougal, 13, is the oldest of four children. Their father is an austere, Oxford-educated parish priest; their mother, much younger, is a former hippie. When Flanagan, a huge Irish wolfhound pup, joins the family, he changes their lives. On a romp through the untended local arboretum, he leads Annie to a sick homeless woman who had been dismissed from an overcrowded mental hospital. She shares her secret with her brother Robert, who seeks help from Father Ben, the young curate whom kids adore but whose street-smart ideas constantly shock adults. Mrs. MacDougal also comes to the rescue and finally even Annie's father proves to be an ally. Meanwhile Flanagan, by his monstrous size alone, frightens the villagers, precipitating vicious front-page news stories and an argument at a town meeting. Corcoran's story, written in a brisk upbeat style, successfully continues her trademark theme of consideration for people in adverse circumstances, buffeted by a generally uncomprehending public. Even though peripheral characters are superficially stereotyped, the main personalities come across as solid and singularly attractive. Readers, even reluctant ones, will find enjoyment here.

Carolyn K. Jenks

SOURCE: A review of *Annie's Monster,* in *The Horn Book Magazine,* Vol. LXVI, No. 6, November-December, 1990, p. 742.

Annie's monster is an Irish wolfhound named Flanagan, whose size and exuberance have frightened some of the people in the small New England town where they live. When the dog leads her to the hiding place of a mentally ill woman, Annie must decide what to do. Cora has been turned out of the state hospital and has run away from an inadequate halfway house, and good-hearted Annie is afraid that her stern father, an Episcopalian priest, will send her back. Annie's father and Benny, the young curate, are forever arguing about the extent of the church's social responsibility; now Cora's situation brings out the true character of many of the townspeople. Benny arranges to have Cora stay at his house, but ignorance causes his neighbors to fear Cora, just as it has caused others to fear Annie's large dog. Father Dougal MacDougal's staid conservatism shifts as he watches people's reactions, and he is moved to investigate the conditions at the state hospital. Annie, too, grows and changes; she learns to take charge of her big affectionate dog and to take charge of herself as she discovers her own talents and worth.

Catherine D. Moorhead

SOURCE: A review of *Annie's Monster,* in *Voice of Youth Advocates,* Vol. 13, No. 5, December, 1990, pp. 278-79.

This story should have been titled, "Annie's Monsters." All at once, 13-year-old Annie has to deal with the monsters of prejudice, mental illness, homelessness, plus antagonism towards teenagers. Annie's mom is an ex-hippie and much more realistic about life than her father who is the Episcopalian minister in the small Maine town in which the MacDougal family lives. Father's stock answer to most of the problems of Annie and her three younger siblings is, "pray," while Mom sits down, really listens, and helps them think through their problems.

Annie has just been offered a year old Irish wolfhound named Flanagan and she is taking the advice of both parents. But will Father give the final approval, no matter how hard she prays? She is ecstatic when Father decides she may keep Flanagan. Some of the thrill goes quickly when the cranky next-door neighbors and mothers of young children down the block are anything but ecstatic at the size of the dog. Within days they notify the newspaper that Flanagan is a menace and go so far as to bring charges against him as a danger to the townspeople. Annie really feels the antagonism toward teenagers when she talks with the newspaper editor and attends the town council meeting to defend Flanagan.

On one of their daily walks through the woods, Annie and Flanagan find Cora, a bedraggled, homeless woman living in an abandoned shed in a local park. Cora is obviously mentally ill, having been put out of one institution after another. As the weather turns cold and rainy, Annie worries about Cora, who has sworn Annie to secrecy about her hideout. Annie is torn, should she break her promise to Cora and get help for her or should she honor Cora's wishes and perhaps watch her die during the winter. Unable to stand the responsibility any more, Annie tells her favorite brother Robert and almost immediately her father's assistant Ben has arranged for Cora to stay at his house while he is on vacation. Neither Ben nor Annie ever dream they would have so much opposition from neighbors who are so fearful of someone with a mental illness living close to them.

In typical Corcoran style, the author has realistically brought together different kinds of people and social problems of today. Most of the problems are taken care of with surprising ease and rapidity, such as Father's complete about-face on social issues and the finding of a permanent home for Cora. There are some loose ends which could do with a bit more resolution. Why is so much made of brother Malcolm's tennis defeat and why is the one-eyed little girl ever introduced in the story? All in all, however, it is a splendid novel with a sensitive, caring heroine with whom most middle American teenage girls will be able to empathize.

STAY TUNED (1991)

Ruth Ann Smith

SOURCE: A review of *Stay Tuned,* in *Bulletin of the Center for Children's Books,* Vol. 44, No. 7, March, 1991, p. 162.

"Stevie huddled on the narrow cot with her feet pulled up under her, the baseball bat held tight in her hand. She thought she heard a rat, but it was a huge cockroach that scuttled across the floor." What's a nice Iowa farm girl doing in a dangerous New York city rooming house? Fending off rats, prostitutes, and drug pushers, waiting for her father to come home with a job, Stevie worries about the abandoned children next door. When her father gets a job in Alaska and sends Stevie off to New Hampshire to live with unknown relatives, she decides to take the two kids, Eddie, a Jewish kid from Brooklyn, and his young half-sister, Fawn, along. When their train tickets are stolen and the kids are dumped off in the middle of nowhere, they happen to stumble on Alex, who agrees to take them to his hideout, an abandoned summer camp. Corcoran writes with a tough realism that mitigates the too-fortunate happenstances in the story. The adults are evenly divided between the indifferent or cruel and the kind. Stevie's father, selfishly absorbed in his new life in Alaska, is unwilling to have her join him. Helpful adults (including a nice librarian, and an elderly lady who eventually adopts them) are present but not overwhelming, leaving the children to overcome their personal demons. Eddie, in particular, must face his fear of the wilderness and his understandable distrust of authority. His conversations with his dead grandmother, held as if over the radio, provide a gauge of his changing emotional state. While the happy ending is somewhat predictable, it is not overly sweet. This is a natural for a book talk.

Gerry Larson

SOURCE: A review of *Stay Tuned,* in *School Library Journal,* Vol. 37, No. 4, April, 1991, p. 118.

Despite convenient plot twists, unlikely circumstances, and surprising self-confidence shown by the homeless main characters, Corcoran infuses warmth into the conclusion of her novel. When Stevie's father, a bankrupt Iowa farmer, takes a job in Alaska, he hastily arranges for her to live with his estranged brother, and drops her off at Penn Station to make her way to New Hampshire alone. While staying in a run-down New York City hotel, she meets Eddie, 12, and his little sister, Fawn, who have been deserted by their mother. With her living expenses, Stevie purchases tickets for Eddie and Fawn, and the trio head north. Once they escape the city, the children's odyssey is one stroke of good luck and one sympathetic adult after another. Eddie and Stevie are wise beyond their years: tolerant of the flaws in others and assertive and endearing when necessary. Eddie amuses the others with his imaginary radio broadcasts and derives emotional strength from his private exchanges with his beloved deceased grandmother. The backgrounds, demeanor, language, and values of these kids seem unlike those of homeless youth. Although the fairy tale ending may raise a cynical eyebrow, Corcoran's characters are likable, and readers who favor happy endings will overlook the book's implausibilities.

Kirkus Reviews

SOURCE: A review of *Stay Tuned,* in *Kirkus Reviews,* Vol. LIX, No. 7, April 1, 1991, p. 469.

An Iowa farm foreclosure, abandoned children, a flea-bag SRO hotel in N.Y.C., small-town anti-Semitism, the death of a parent—yes, all these elements *can* coexist in one novel, albeit unsuccessfully.

After her mother dies, Stevie's father takes her from their farm to New York. He's looking for work, and finds it—in Alaska. Stevie can't go along, so her father hastily arranges for her to live with his estranged brother in New Hampshire. At Penn Station, someone steals her ticket and money—and also her uncle's address. Fortunately, streetwise Eddie and his little sister are with her; they were in the next room at the hotel, and she is newly devoted to them. There is more good fortune ahead: all three are temporarily adopted, first by a teen-age would-be boat-builder and later by a kindly librarian.

Nothing adds up in this story of coincidences, overloaded plotting, and shifting points of view (Stevie's is dropped early on, and Eddie's takes the story to its close). Far-fetched and ultimately pointless.

Margaret Galloway

SOURCE: A review of *Stay Tuned,* in *Voice of Youth Advocates,* Vol. 14, No. 2, June, 1991, p. 94.

Once again we have three "abandoned" children making their way to a safe haven in a New England setting. Stevie, 16, isn't happy in the cheap New York hotel in which her father chooses to live until he finds a job. The only thing of interest is a brother and sister next door who seem to have no adult on board. What makes them interesting is the radio broadcasts the brother pretends for his sister's entertainment. Stevie's father takes a job in Alaska, and the kids next door are left alone. These two circumstances provide for a good plot shift. Stevie takes a chance and brings Eddie, 13, and Fawn, 8, the brother and sister, along to her relatives in New Hampshire. Alas, because of a mix-up with tickets, they end up in Maine with a 17-year-old boat-builder named Alec. Their life at the abandoned camp is at once exciting, soul-searching, frightening and wondrous.

The title of the book refers to the radio broadcasts Eddie delivers to his deceased grandmother; and in many ways this is Eddie's story. It is often through his eyes that we see the affection and understanding developing among the young people and the adults who take them in. This story does not have the lyrical quality or the perceptive characterization of Voigt's *Dicey's Song*. It is, however, a good read for reluctant patrons because the story line is still an attractive one to teenagers. There are few stories that are as engrossing as surviving on your own or with friends.

FAMILY SECRETS (1992)

Publishers Weekly

SOURCE: A review of *Family Secrets,* in *Publishers Weekly,* Vol. 239, No. 1, January 1, 1992, p. 56.

The prolific Corcoran *(Stay Tuned; The Potato Kid)* tackles adoption in her latest work. When 14-year-old Tracy moves with her family to a small Massachusetts town, she receives shocking news: the people she knows as Mom and Dad are not her biological parents. (The couple recently learned that Tracy's birth mother has died, thereby releasing them from the legal agreement that prohibited disclosing their secret.) Stunned, the girl worries that her relationship with her three siblings will be altered but is soon reassured that their ties are stronger than she realized. Pivotal in the events here is David, a 17-year-old neighbor who lost his family in a boating accident and has since put his life on hold. Tracy, however, shines the brightest as a compassionate yet very real teenager who is thoroughly deserving and appreciative of the love bestowed upon her. The climax involving a pyromaniac is somewhat predictable, but the upbeat resolution is suitably gratifying.

Barbara Chatton

SOURCE: A review of *Family Secrets,* in *School Library Journal,* Vol. 38, No. 2, February, 1992, p. 85.

When 13-year-old Tracy moves with her family to the small town in Massachusetts where her father grew up, she learns that she is actually the child of a schoolmate of her father's. As she struggles to find herself in a new town, with new friends, and with a new understanding of her place in her family, she meets David, an older boy who carries an even heavier burden. His parents and sister drowned in a boating accident and he is grieving while trying to care for his mentally disturbed uncle, who may be responsible for local arsons. The book is brief, suspenseful (David's uncle seems to be particularly violent towards Tracy and may be stalking her), sentimental, and includes some quirky characters. The story wraps up neatly when a fire at David's house frees him from his uncle, and Tracy is given a tape made by her mother just before her death that reconciles the girl to her adopted family and her mother's decision to give her away. Philippa Pearce's *The Way to Sattin Shore* and Nina Bawden's *The Outside Child* handle the emotion and suspense of this kind of situation in a stronger manner, but Corcoran's book will appeal to readers who like a mildly suspenseful family story and a satisfying, if unrealistic, conclusion.

Kirkus Reviews

SOURCE: A review of *Family Secrets,* in *Kirkus Reviews,* Vol. LX, No. 3, February 1, 1992, p. 181.

The "secret" comes out only a few pages into this story when Tracy, second daughter of the Stewart family, learns that she was adopted as a baby, a truth now revealed because her birth mother has died. The title's "family" refers not only to Tracy's ongoing reassessment of the word's meaning as she meets the people related to her birth mother, but to the Stewarts' move from Cambridge to Tracy's father's hometown on Massachusetts' North Shore. While still adjusting to her new knowledge, Tracy meets David, whose entire family was tragically killed the year before, and also other residents who look out for each other in small-town style. Tracy's ideas and definitions evolve right to the book's last line: "even if your real family isn't there, friends can be a kind of family too." Unfortunately, that sentence rings as hollow as others found in various crucial scenes, infusing the story with trivializing sentiment rather than with genuine reflection on familial love.

Judy Fink

SOURCE: A review of *Family Secrets,* in *Voice of Youth Advocates,* Vol. 15, No. 2, June, 1992, pp. 92-93.

Shortly after her family's move to a small coastal town north of Boston where her father grew up, Tracy learns that she is adopted. Tracy's birthmother was a high school friend of her father's and swore him and his wife to silence until her death or Tracy's 18th birthday. She died of cancer a few weeks before Tracy's family's move. All this comes as quite a shock to Tracy, who has often felt isolated from her family because her physical characteristics are so different. Now she knows why. The three other kids in the family take the news easily and without any questions or doubt that Tracy is their sister, blood relative or not. Tracy wants to know more about Felicia Shaw, her birthmother, but learns little more than that Felicia was an ambitious but self-centered singer, and that she resembles her birthmother.

A second story line involves an older teenager, David, who has a family secret of his own: his parents and younger sister were killed in a boating accident and he is left with the burden of caring for his mentally ill uncle, who sees Tracy and thinks she is Felicia Shaw, whom he idolized.

Tracy's search for information about her birthmother is relatively easy, and in this sense, *Family Secrets* is unlike most other novels about adoption. Her birthmother did not want a child, but had enough of a sense of responsibility, obligation, and even curiosity to find a way for Tracy to know something about her background, through a posthumously delivered tape. This provides a feeling of completion and reinforces Tracy's sense of belonging in the family she was raised in. As for David, Tracy hopes that he will see that his friends in the community will stand by him, functioning as a kind of family.

This is an involving and fast read, with elements of romance and suspense tied in with the theme of family being the people who care about you. Some of the characterizations could have been stronger, particularly the adults. Tracy's parents are understanding, but play very small roles. It seems strange for the family to move to this town without having first told Tracy about her adoption. That in itself, although the catalyst for the entire book, is an unsettling element nonetheless.

Tracy is satisfied with her family and with her adoption. Similar feelings are expressed by the children and adults interviewed for Maxine B. Rosenberg's *Growing Up Adopted.* In both books, the question "what if I'd stayed with my birthmother?" comes up but there is also the realization that the family that raised them is theirs.

WOLF AT THE DOOR (1993)

Susan Oliver

SOURCE: A review of *Wolf at the Door,* in *School Library Journal,* Vol. 39, No. 9, September, 1993, pp. 228-29.

It's hard being such a responsible person and it's hard being the only fully drawn character in a novel, but Lee McDougall survives and even blossoms in Corcoran's latest offering. Her father has lost his job, and so the family is moving, again. This time they're relocating to a wild piece of land they own and have used for camping; a wealthy (and famous) grandmother has bought a house and had it delivered as a gift for Lee's mother. Lee is miserable about the whole deal, until she and her mother rescue a mistreated wolf from a roadside zoo, supplying the girl with both a confidant and a commitment. While she is rehabilitating the animal, her younger and considerably more flamboyant sister is weaseling her way into the local theater group and debate is heating up in the community about the new family who has a pet wolf. By the book's finale, Lee has acquired four more wolves, a definite sense of herself, and a plan for her future as a result of her relationship with and understanding of wildlife. The wolves create a wonderful presence, and they are more compelling than the human characters. (Acknowledgments and a bibliography hint at extensive research.) This is less powerful but more accessible than *The Cry of the Wolf* by Melvin Burgess; together they create a dynamic picture of the first animal to bond with humans.

Chris Sherman

SOURCE: A review of *Wolf at the Door,* in *Booklist,* Vol. 90, No. 3, October 1, 1993, p. 330.

Thirteen-year-old Lee McDougall has always lived in the shadow of her beautiful and talented younger sister, Savannah, who was named after their grandmother, a renowned actress. The girls' father's decision to move the family from Missoula to a more remote area of

Montana makes Lee feel even more unimportant. She finds herself drawn to an abused yearling wolf her mother rescued from a roadside zoo, and her life assumes new focus when she's given four additional wolves to care for. When Savannah's success in a local theater group inspires a visit from their grandmother, Lee is surprised to find that her once indomitable Nonny is aging. She's further dismayed when Nonny confides that she wants to take Savannah back to Los Angeles. Neighbors' vicious opposition to harboring the wolves eventually unites the sisters and draws the attention of a philanthropist who funds the McDougals' wolf refuge. Corcoran's briskly paced story offers wonderful information about wolves as well as a very sympathetic character in Lee.

Deborah Stevenson

SOURCE: A review of *Wolf at the Door,* in *Bulletin of the Center for Children's Books,* Vol. 47, No. 3, November, 1993, pp. 77-8.

Lee isn't happy about her family's move to rural Montana or her younger sister Savannah's burgeoning amateur stage career, but she's enthusiastic about her acquisition of a wolf (saved from a local one-man "zoo") and then of four more (their owner is leaving for Europe). Lee is fascinated with the wolves, particularly poor mistreated Ruthie, to whom she confides her fears and frustrations. The wolves become the center of local controversy, however, with a neighboring rancher threatening them and, ultimately, succeeding in poisoning Lee's beloved Ruthie. Although some of the events are over-dramatic (the violent end of Ruthie's former owner, the serendipitous acquisition of the other wolves), Corcoran successfully blends some diverse plot elements here. The wolves are compelling but realistically distant and skittish (readers hoping for extensive and anthropomorphic lupine characterization should look elsewhere), and the family dynamics between parents, sisters, and visiting grandmother are subtle and telling, enriching the story without distracting from its focus. The wolves will appeal to young naturalists, who will also enjoy the more complicated human story in which they figure. A reading list of books about wolves is appended.

Cynthia Beatty Brown

SOURCE: A review of *Wolf at the Door,* in *Voice of Youth Advocates,* Vol. 16, No. 5, December, 1993, p. 288.

Lee McDougall's little sister Savannah, named after their famous actress grandmother, is beautiful and talented. She knows what she wants to do with her life: follow in the footsteps of her grandmother and become an actress. Lee is less certain of her future, but she knows she doesn't want to live in Savannah's shadow. After years of moving frequently because of her father's duties with the army, Lee and the family move one last time to a small house in the woods near Flathead Lake in Montana. While Savannah gets involved with the local theater group, Lee and her mother stumble across a so-called "zoo" with a nearly starved wolf. Lee's mother is a biologist and both she and Lee decide to rescue the wolf from the pitiful excuse of a zoo. The wolf, now named Ruthie, gives Lee a purpose to her new life in the woods. Savannah and many of the neighbors are afraid of wolves and don't want them around. Some of the neighbors even take matters into their own hands after Lee is unexpectedly given four more wolves to take care of. Property is damaged and the wolves are fed poisonous meat. All of the wolves are rescued from the meat except for Ruthie; the best efforts of the local vet are not successful in saving her. Throughout this summer in the woods, Lee has learned a lot about wolves and has come to realize that her life ambition will include working with wolves, to help preserve them from extinction and to educate people that they are not vicious wild beasts to be afraid of. The author educates us in wolf behavior, while letting us get to know the entire McDougall family.

Additional coverage of Corcoran's life and career is contained in the following sources published by Gale Research: *Authors and Artists for Young Adults,* Vol. 14; *Contemporary Authors New Revision Series,* Vol. 48; *Contemporary Literary Criticism,* Vol. 17; *Dictionary of Literary Biography,* Vol. 52; *Junior DISCovering Authors, Something About the Author,* Vol. 77; and *Something About the Author Autobiography Series,* Vol. 20.

Holling C(lancy) Holling
1900-1973

American author and illustrator of fiction and picture books.

Major works include *The Book of Indians* (1935), *Paddle-to-the-Sea* (1941), *Tree in the Trail* (1942), *Seabird* (1948), *Minn of the Mississippi* (1951), *Pagoo* (1957).

INTRODUCTION

With his unique talent for combining factual information with storytelling, Holling, a gifted naturalist, illustrator, and author, is widely recognized for creating an entertaining body of literature that is also educational. His books have a timeless appeal for young adults and children through the middle grades. Critics praise his ability to transfer his first-hand experience of nature into stories that come alive and excite the reader's imagination. Holling moves his readers with vivid images and a vibrant text that blends authentic and exact details of natural science, geography, and history, with compelling, dramatic fiction. Sharing equal importance with the text are Holling's beautiful illustrations—praised for their accuracy, artistry, an even opulence; they often carry the story forward, reflecting the narrator's viewpoint, and embellish information in the text. Holling writes of the subjects from nature and history that captured his imagination since his boyhood—Native American legends and lore, and life in the outdoors, especially animal and marine life. The factual material of his stories often provides a background for demonstrating the development of social and moral values over time and for dramatizing the influence of change on our way of life. "Although the action part of my stories is fabricated," he once explained, "I have always tried to make the atmosphere surrounding them completely authentic." His animal characters struggle for security, endure hardships, experience pleasure, and interpret life—mirroring human existence. Perhaps Holling's greatest contribution to children's literature is his creation of the "geo-history," as critics have dubbed his amalgam of geography, science, history, and fiction. With *Paddle-to-the-Sea,* the form won instant acclaim for "presenting geography in a fresh, original, imaginative way," and that remains true more than fifty years later.

Biographical Information

Born and raised on his family's farm in Holling Corners, Michigan, Holling grew up fascinated by the mysteries of nature around him. Avidly curious and precocious, he was drawing authentic pictures of animals by the age of three and composing verses by the time he was five. After attending high school in Michigan, he graduated from the

Art Institute of Chicago in 1923, having spent one year of his study with etcher Ralph M. Pierson in New Mexico. At the Chicago Museum of Natural History, Holling studied taxidermy from 1923 to 1926, and studied privately with anthropologist Ralph Linton. In 1925, he married Lucille Webster, a fellow art student who would also become his artistic collaborator for several works, including *The Book of Indians, The Book of Cowboys* (1936), *Little Buffalo Boy* (1939), and *Pagoo.* The following year he and his wife accepted one-year teaching positions on New York University's first University World Cruise. Holling later worked in advertising as an artist and copywriter before concentrating on writing and illustrating books. During his early career, he wrote several books on Indians of the American West before publishing his most well-known book, *Paddle-to-the-Sea,* in 1941. Holling and his wife made their home in Pasadena, California, until his death in 1973.

Major Works

The Book of Indians presents a wealth of facts about North American Indians, explaining how they are grouped by their habitat—the people of the Forest, the Plains, the Desert, and the Sea—and describing their homes, customs, and modes of travel. These details are enlivened with stories that cover one hundred years of change in the lives of Indian children, their families, and friends. In *Paddle-to-the-Sea,* an Indian boy carves a miniature canoe with a paddler inside, and on the canoe he inscribes the message, "Please put me back in water." In the spring the little canoe begins its journey in Lake Nipigon, Canada, and travels eastward through the Great Lakes and the St. Lawrence River to the Atlantic Ocean. After four years of exciting and suspenseful adventures— threats from a forest fire, a sawmill, and even Niagara Falls, among many others—Paddle reaches the great Ocean and makes his way toward France. A reviewer for the *Christian Science Monitor* wrote, "Traveling with Paddle by story and pictures is good fun . . . and is a fascinating way to learn geography."

Tree in the Trail reveals the changing pattern of life on the Great Plains through the story of a single tree. A struggling cottonwood sapling is first found in 1610 by an Indian boy destined to become a great Medicine Man who would foretell that the tree would travel from its hill. Under the protection of other Indians, the tree grows and matures. During more than 200 years of life, it becomes a peace tree where fighting men establish a truce, a "talking tree" where travelers leave messages, and a medicine tree that saves lives, including that of a young man named Jed who is making his first trip on the Santa Fe Trail. After the tree is hit by a lightning bolt and finally felled by a tornado, Jed builds an ox yoke from the tree's wood and discovers Indian, French, and American ammunition—a link with history—buried in the tree's trunk. Taking the yoke with him, Jed makes the journey to Santa Fe, where he meets a descendant of the Medicine Man who had predicted the tree's fate.

Similar to the canoe voyage in *Paddle-to-the-Sea, Seabird* chronicles the travels of a wooden seagull through time and progressive changes in navigation. In 1832, fourteen-year-old Ezra Brown carves a sea gull from a walrus tusk during his first trip aboard a New Bedford whaler and carries the bird wherever he goes. The Seabird journeys around the globe with four generations of Brown's family: Ezra's son aboard a clipper ship to the Orient, his grandson on the first steamship across the Atlantic, and finally his great-grandson on an airship through space. In *Minn of the Mississippi,* Minn is a tough, three-legged snapping turtle who begins life in the Minnesota headwaters of the Mississippi River. Over the next twenty-five years, Minn is carried 2,500 miles down the Mississippi to the Gulf of Mexico, often in danger of being killed or captured, but always managing to get free. Minn's journey follows the story of the mighty river itself—its history and romance. "Minn's story—" noted a reviewer for the *Chicago Sunday Tribune*, "the river's story are of equal fascination as the author weaves them together in this beautiful book." Holling collaborated with his wife on *Pagoo* (short for "Pagurus"), the lighthearted story of a hermit crab and

other marine creatures who live along the beaches and tide pools of the seashore. Pagoo grows from an egg the size of a pencil dot and goes through a multitude of changes and moltings as he frantically searches for an empty shell in which to fit himself and escape from a host of enemies. The underlying symbolism of this story was an important consideration for Holling. He wanted young adults to understand the uncomfortable process of growing up, explaining that he wished to "make children aware of this concept. . . , this urge in a minute living thing to change and search, somehow aware that his body is developing into the precise shape that will fit a shell he will find someday."

Awards

Paddle-to-the-Sea was named a Caldecott Honor Book in 1942 and received the Lewis Carroll Shelf Award in 1962. *Seabird* won the Commonwealth Club of California Literature Award in 1948 and was named a Newbery Honor Book in 1949. *Minn of the Mississippi* received the Boys' Club Junior Book Award in 1951 and a Newbery Honor Book citation in 1952. In 1961, Holling and his wife received the Southern California Council on Literature for Children Award for *Pagoo*.

GENERAL COMMENTARY

Irvin L. Ramsey

SOURCE: "Holling C. Holling: Author and Illustrator," in *Authors and Illustrators of Children's Books: Writings on Their Lives and Works,* R. R. Bower Company, 1972, pp. 209-16.

[The following excerpt is from an essay originally published in Elementary English *in February, 1954.]*

It has been said that an author or an artist who turns his talents toward literature for children doesn't have to know much. Holling C. Holling as an author-illustrator has certainly produced some writings and illustrations that refute such a statement. He has provided children with books that are filled with beauty—beauty that is natural and real, beauty that is rich in understandings of the past and the present, beauty that points youngsters toward the future, and that holds enjoyment and pleasure for the young reader. In other words, Holling C. Holling has the ability to portray the deep-down beauty of a river, a lake, a freighter, or a lonely tree on the Great Plains in such a way that he leads his reader to enjoy, appreciate, and understand them beyond mere factual understanding.

Mr. Holling's books are not hastily prepared or stereotyped. Only through much research, thought, and observation could he have written his books. In the Foreword to *The Book of Indians* Mr. Holling makes it clear to his readers that he is concerned with authenticity and that children need authentic materials to read. He states:

> As a boy, I wanted to know all about Indians. How did they really live? Did they always have horses? Did they always wear war-bonnets? How did they make those arrowpoints that Grandfather found in the fields? There were thousands of questions in my mind, and very few answers in the books I had.

> In later years I began to look for the answers in many places. I am still asking questions. In all parts of the country scientists are digging in the earth, writing about what they have found, and the things they find and the books they write are being stored in museums and libraries. Mrs. Holling and I have visited these museums and libraries and have talked with the scientists them-selves. Besides that we have lived with Indians. In the northern forests we paddled their birchbark canoes, and slept in their wickiups. We rode our horses beside theirs across the great plains and camped in their teepees in the mountains. In the desert they made us feel at home in their pueblos. We have fished with them in the surf of the Pacific Ocean. This book is the result of some of that hunting, riding, camping and research.

In his acknowledgment in *Minn of the Mississippi,* Mr. Holling further indicates the intent with which he writes:

> This is a book about a river, and a turtle in it. I thought that I knew the river well; but long residence in southern California tends to drain the memory of sustained wetness such as is found in rivers. As for turtles—hadn't I caught bushels of them in Grandfather's woodlot pond? Yet that was long ago. How long I didn't realize until, on a visit to Michigan, this book was begun. Much had been forgotten, and much I really had never known. Once again I must begin a brooding activity—"research." Once more I must go to school to rivers—and to turtles . . .

It is difficult to classify Mr. Holling's books. This seems due to the fact that he has combined the techniques of fiction with many areas of information into single books that portray a total pattern of life. Perhaps this is the most distinguishing characteristic of Mr. Holling's writings. This combination indicates that this author has not based his works solely on child interests but has also concerned himself with writing for children in terms of how they learn and develop.

Mr. Holling is an author who trusts children with big ideas. He has recognized child curiosities and child interests. He has attempted to satisfy these curiosities and interests in a meaningful way. Sometimes he achieves this effect through descriptions of natural phenomena; sometimes through historical description; sometimes through industrial explanations. For example, he tells in *Seabird* about glaciers and the beginning of an iceberg in this way:

From Paddle-to-the-Sea, *written and illustrated by Holling Clancy Holling.*

The flying Gull crosses frozen rivers of glaciers—gigantic icicles laid along the valleys. Moving inch by inch to the sea, they ended in ice walls towering up from the water . . .

. . . An ice-chunk big as a hill split off from the walls and dropped into the sea. It sank and heaved upward again, a white mountain gushing foam. Thunders of its falling rolled for miles. Mad waves lashed the cliffs, rushed to sea tossing ice cakes, and lost themselves in the gray veil of a summer snowstorm. Yet even this birth of a floating iceberg . . .

If one were inclined to present children with isolated geographical, scientific, historical, and social facts, he would find it difficult to defend his position against children who have traveled with Minn, Paddle, Seabird, Peter and Barbara Ann, and Buffalo-Calf. Children who are familiar with these books and have lived with the characters in them would see no value in rigorous drills and memory exercises devoted to learning such dull unrelated statements as: the source of the river is the place where the river begins; the mouth of a river is the place where the river empties into a larger body of water; upstream is toward the source of the river; an iceberg is a floating piece of ice that has broken off from a glacier; Jamestown was settled in 1607; the Santa Fe trail started at St. Louis, Missouri and ended at Santa Fe, New Mexico; a turtle is a reptile that is cold-blooded and has a toothless beak and a bony shell which protects the body, the head, and the limbs. With Holling, his young readers have come to know that information achieves life qualities not because they are facts which make a difference in daily life.

This author has consistently concerned himself with the concept of change and its influence upon our way of life; he has presented backgrounds for the development of social and moral values. Yet, it would be unfair criticism to say that he has been dogmatic in his presentations; he has dealt with problems in settings that are real and genuinely reflective of locales. Unfortunately, many children need the good counsel offered to Peter and Barbara Ann by Idaho Ike in *The Book of Cowboys:*

"People in the East think sometimes that all a cowboy does is ride around on buckin' broncs, shootin' all over the place with sixguns and rifles!" said Idaho Ike . . . "But nowadays there's no need for guns out here most of the time. Of course, when you're in rattlesnake country, a revolver comes in handy and sometimes a coyote or wolf that's been killin' stock needs attendin' to. But today a cowpuncher could ride most all the time and never need any kind of a gun. . . . "

[The] boy of the bayou also has his problems:

"Ah hate tuttles—" muttered the boy softly. Then he shrieked "TUTTLES! . . . AH HATE TUTTLES! AH HATE! AH HATE! AH HATE! . . . "

Minn sank quickly, but now came a torrent of blows. . . .

Then it was over. The pole jerked upward, the bayou settled to shadowy calm, but the voice snarled on—"Ah hate everything! . . . Call me pore white trash. Call *me* white trash! Whut if Pappy hain't got no money! He got cricks in th' back. Cain't do nothin' but sleep—an' whup me. . . . But *they* ain't got no right. *They* ain't got th' say of *me.* Jes' wait. Jes' wait till Ah git a MILLION DOLLARS! . . ."

Mr. Holling has been imaginative as he has selected and developed plots that have simplicity, child-likeness, and a strong sense of reality. Would it be difficult to find a boy with a turtle; or a boy with a carving; or a boy with a favorite tree; or a boy with a bow and arrow; or a boy with a cowboy suit?

Though there is a similarity in the plots of his books, Mr. Holling has not been repetitious or monotonous. He has developed plots in such a way that his characters meet life situations related to and consistent with the locales in which they find themselves. His plots have adventure, sincerity, authenticity, and appeal. In all his stories his characters grow and live through struggle for security, they endure hardships, they sense pleasure, and they interpret life. Mr. Holling has maintained a balance among these basic needs and has woven them into true pictures that provide children with literature commensurate with their interests, needs, and capabilities.

Mr. Holling's books are beautifully illustrated, especially *Seabird, Paddle-to-the-Sea, Tree in the Trail,* and *Minn of the Mississippi.* Mrs. Holling is also an artist and has contributed much to the illustrations. . . .

In their illustrations, the Hollings have effectively used deep dark colors that illustrate so well the moods of their stories. The formats of all their books are large and their illustrations are large full-page illustrations that in *Paddle-to-the-Sea, Seabird,* and *Tree in the Trail* illustrate one single page of writing; in *Minn of the Mississippi* there is a full-page illustration for every two or three pages of writing.

In the illustrations one finds the same fullness and completeness, as well as exactness, that is so manifest in the writings. They are not just pictures that specifically illustrate a point; they have depth and meaning that go beyond mere usefulness or immediacy. When one looks at Holling's pictures, he sees more than just a turtle in a river or a whaling boat at sea; he sees life that is complex, both dependent and independent, and he sees life that is ongoing. These illustrations have more than color, more than design, and more than specific interpretations. Mr. Holling knows that his illustrations must be true to the content and he also knows that an illustration should be good art.

Mr. Holling has employed the technique of further providing the reader with scientific and historical technicalities through the use of black-and-white diagrams and illustrations in the wide margins. This technique may be questionable; for some readers the books may appear to be cluttered with so much detail that they seem to be text-bookish. It does seem plausible though that here is a provision for the more advanced reader who is interested in greater detail than that given in the story. Too, it is a provision for adults, and there are adults who could profit from and enjoy these books.

Mr. Holling realizes that children no longer need to be crammed with namby-pamby stories. He realizes that they are capable of developing deep understandings of the realities of their natural-social world. He has provided them with literature rich in those things which lead to appreciation and interpretation of life.

Virginia Kirkus' Service

SOURCE: A review of *The Book of Cowboys* and *The Book of Indians,* in *Virginia Kirkus' Service,* Vol. XXV, No. 16, August 15, 1962, p. 759.

[Holling's *The Book of Cowboys* and *The Book of Indians*] back in 1934 and 1935 became immediately and deservedly popular. Later Holling's name was better established on literary grounds through his *Seabird, Minn of the Mississippi, Pagoo,* etc. But his *Cowboys* and *Indians* filled a niche nobody has rivalled. Although he has chosen to put his factual information in the guise of stories, the facts are there. What cowboys were really like, what they wore, what they do, on the ranches, at rodeos and so on, is reasonably familiar but not the why of their clothes and their way of life. Sometimes Holling describes the West today; sometimes its earlier days . . . This is perhaps more true of *Indians* for he tells might-be-true stories, spanning 100 years, of Indian children in the different regions:—the forests and lakes, the plains, the deserts and mesas, the rivers and the sea coast. And through these stories—and the lovely marginal drawings, one learns about the life of these Indians before the days of reservations. We welcome the availability of these two volumes.

Barbara Bader

SOURCE: "Of the American Indian," in *American Picturebooks from "Noah's Ark" to "The Beast Within,"* Macmillan Publishing Company, Inc., 1976, pp. 410-13.

"As a boy," Holling begins, "I wanted to know all about Indians," and [in *The Book of Indians,* written by Holling and illustrated in collaboration with his wife Lucille] woven into the activities and adventures of his fictional children, a boy and a girl from each of the four major regions, are the relevant particulars and more; like a genre painter, Holling omits nothing from the scene. Under a platform attached to the wickiup, the family dogs—"of which there were many"—snooze: "There was always a scrap of meat to be hoped for, because the

cooking fire was just a few feet away and a clay pot was forever simmering on the red coals." Far from being a distraction, the details are the very stuff of the story. Holling was an artist-illustrator before he was a writer—an artist-observer, storing up data aboard Great Lakes freighters or among the Southwest Indians, and, in the taxidermy department at the Field Museum, a transcriber of appearances. In writing as in drawing, he made a complete and meticulous record.

In *The Book of Indians,* the one balances the other, not in space but in weight—for the many words it takes to describe how, for instance, a wickiup was constructed would be incomprehensible without the marginal illustrations. On the other hand, the display of arrowheads, some of flaked flint, some of bone ground sharp, would be just so much decorative filler without the explanation of their differences.

Recognition of the Hollings' scrupulousness came from the most exacting quarters. The Indian Service's Education Division deemed *The Book of Indians* "one of the few books for children about Indians which we can wholeheartedly recommend" and "almost unique [in] having no misstatements, either in the text or in the pictures."

The Book of Cowboys (1936) followed in the same vein, and then there began the quartet of 'geo-histories' covering the United States from the Midwest eastward and westward—*Paddle-to-the-Sea* (1941) and *Tree in the Trail* (1942); from north to south—*Minn of the Mississippi* (1951); and around the circumference—*Seabird* (1948): all big books bounteously illustrated, swathes of geography and history spiraling around a fixed center like a double helix around an atom.

In *Paddle-to-the-Sea* the focal point is the tiny wooden canoe-and-Indian set out by an Indian boy in the Canadian wilderness, carried by the melting snow into a stream which empties into Lake Superior and then transported, by lake currents and chance storms, by freighter and motorboat, through the Great Lakes and the St. Lawrence "and on at last to the sea," the Indian boy's very hope for him. It is a story very similar to an Iroquois legend, Holling learned later, and Paddle-to-the-Sea is one of those inanimate figures that, like the Steadfast Tin Soldier, quickly take on life; the words "Please put me back in the water" are carved on his bottom, and you find yourself hoping for him—hoping too that someone will save him from the sawmill's looming buzzsaw, that something will sweep him out from his prison under the dock, that somehow he'll survive fire and ice and Niagara Falls.

A great, great deal happens, the course of events carefully charted, the encroachments duly explained and incorporated into the story. At every opening is the big color picture putting Paddle into position for his next move and with it the marginal drawings that suggest how he got there. The big pictures themselves have a kind of magical realism, what is meant when art is taken as a lens on life. In reality, light is never so even, air so clear, colors so strong, contours so pronounced, everything so *present:* it is a thoroughly conventionalized rendering, realer than real, of a sort once common in commercial art and, in Photo-Realism, resurgent today. But it is not only what children at a certain age consider art to be, it is highly satisfactory as illustration.

Holling was to become smoother and slicker in *Tree in the Trail,* and in *Minn* more of a painter, immersed in light and shade, in both cases with a certain loss of integrity whatever the gain—in *Minn*—in terms of sheer dazzlement. At the same time, however, and not to be discounted, the marginal drawings sharpen and multiply until they approximate a pictorial encyclopedia.

Dorothy Butler

SOURCE: "Reading Begins at Home," in *The Horn Book Magazine,* Vol. LIX, No. 5, October, 1983, pp. 551.

By this time you will have a "chapter" book underway . . . a book like Holling Clancy Holling's *Paddle to the Sea;* or should I say *Paddle to the Sea* with *Tree in the Trail* to follow, for wherever will we find another two such books? Can you imagine a family of New Zealand children thousands of miles away from the Great Lakes or the Santa Fe Trail, their lives taken over for the whole of one summer by the fate of a tiny carved canoe and of a small cottonwood tree? I noted, as I consulted them, that both books have the same child's name in the front, with "Christmas, 1960" inscribed below it. This boy must have just turned six, but everyone in the family, from his eldest sister of thirteen down, was captivated by first one book and then the other. You will certainly need more than one copy each of these two; the youngsters will want to pore over the whole-page pictures and the meticulous black-and-white sketches and diagrams in the margins. We acquired *Seabird* during the next year. The same old magic was seen to abide within its expansive pages with, this time, the story of sail leading in the end to steam—a theme to enchant the child whose forebears braved the longest journey in the world in wooden sailing ships to settle in the Antipodes.

Sadly, all of these titles are now out of print in an English edition and so not readily available in my country. Our own old copies I guard jealously for grandchildren and other young friends.

TITLE COMMENTARY

📖 *THE BOOK OF INDIANS* (with wife Lucille Holling, 1935)

Anne T. Eaton

SOURCE: A review of *The Book of Indians,* in *The New York Times Book Review,* May 26, 1935, p. 10.

A book which fills a need. Here in one volume is descriptive material and stories about types of Indians living in different kinds of country. The first chapter explains these divisions and tells why "The Forest Indians," "The People of the Plains," "The People of the Desert" and "The People of the Sea" were given these names. There is a chapter about the home life of each type of Indian, followed by two chapters relating their adventures. There are six full-page illustrations in color, full of characteristic detail and many marginal drawings. The information seems to be authentic and the stories are lively and interesting.

Unfortunately Mr. Holling in his effort to give vividness to his writing has sacrificed dignity and atmosphere by putting a remarkable lingo into the mouths of his Indians, which is evidently meant to correspond to the white man's slang and colloquial speech. This detracts from the convincing quality of the tales. We may not know exactly how the Indians talked among themselves, but one feels quite sure that their speech was not like this: "Listen, Wolverene; your son, who has seen eight Summers, calls himself a man! Split-my-moccasins! If he catches anything bigger than a rabbit this trip the village won't hold him! Get going, chipmunk, and catch this bundle. And don't get it wet!" And a little later, "Skin-me-for-a-badger, we've forgotten our breakfast! What do you bet I get a muskellonge before we reach the portage?"

In spite of this blemish the book will be popular and useful. It pleases children from 7 to 10 and will be extremely helpful to teachers.

May Lamberton Becker

SOURCE: A review of *The Book of Indians,* in *The New York Herald Tribune Books,* August 4, 1935, p. 7.

The man who made this book wanted to know "all about Indians" when he was a boy, so he says in its foreword; when he grew older he set to work to find out all he could in museums and libraries and by living along with Indians themselves. The result, as anyone can see, is the book he would have liked to own when he was a boy.

Its chief attraction is the pictures. These are spirited in design, quite brilliant in color, and conscientious in detail. Besides color pictures at intervals there are on every page, serving as ornamental margins and also as explanatory comment on the text, drawings in brown of all sorts of Indian utensils and weapons, domestic animals, clothing and houses: of the last-named there are several floor plans. The whole makes a sort of continuous picture-story.

The text is not so moving. It is a series of stories introducing Indian children at different points and places in Indian history. The first four episodes take place, long before the coming of the white man, in the Great Forests where Otter-Tall and his girl-cousin Flying-Squir-

From Paddle-to-the-Sea, *written and illustrated by Holling Clancy Holling.*

rel live; the marginal drawings show their village of basket huts and an Indian in process of weaving one out of green saplings. Mink-Woman and the children make corn-husk dolls and skin clothing, Otter-Tall and his friends play on the ice games they have handed on to us; the life of the tribe goes on around them. The fifth chapter moves to the plains country where Buffalo-Calf lives with his mother: a great fall hunt sets out, three hundred warriors and several hundred dogs dragging travois poles to carry the gear for two or three months of wandering. A hundred years pass and the white man has come: a teepee once made of seven skins now takes twenty, but Rides Away-Tinkling and her mother still prepare and sew the skins in the ancient fashion. Her father gives up the bow and arrow when he gets a magic tube from the trader, but goes back to the earlier method when the tube blows up on him. Now the scene shifts to deserts and mesas, and there are stories first of a boy who lived in the cliff-dwellers' city in Mesa Verde Park when that was in its prime, and then of a girl whose home was on the mesa years after, Indians of Northern regions close the book. It has much miscellaneous information about widely distributed tribes and gives a general idea of a pre-Columbian America that does not often get into a child's book. Young visitors to Indian collections at the museums of New York or elsewhere will like these pictures and stories.

PADDLE-TO-THE-SEA (1941)

Alice M. Jordan

SOURCE: A review of *Paddle-to-the-Sea,* in *The Horn Book Magazine,* Vol. XVII, No. 5, September, 1941, pp. 357-58.

A superbly illustrated book full of color and showing fine creative ability. Paddle-to-the-Sea is a little person in a canoe, carved by an Indian boy, set on a snow bank, north of the Great Lakes, to follow his course through the different water ways to the ocean. This is geography of the best kind, made vivid by the power of imagination. The little figure which slips past the beaver dams and logging camps of the North to ride the currents of the Great Lakes and the mighty Niagara, seems to come alive through his stupendous journey. We follow his passage to the dip net on the Grand Banks in real suspense. The artist-author knows by experience the life of the men along the route, as well as the appearance of forests, great docks, rapids and steamers. This is his most important book, so far.

Alice Monroe

SOURCE: A review of *Paddle-to-the-Sea,* in *Library Journal,* Vol. 66, No. 15, September 1, 1941, p. 736.

A large informational picture book of the Great Lakes and the St. Lawrence. An Indian boy set a toy canoe on a hill near Lake Nipigon, Canada, in order that the spring thaws might carry it to the river, the river to Lake Superior, and eventually the St. Lawrence take it to the sea. Much description of the natural and industrial aspects of the country is brought in through the hazards of the trip. The canoe's journey is used to show the flow of currents and of traffic, and each occurrence is made to seem plausible. The numerous full-page illustrations in color and the margin decorations in black and white are good. There are also diagrams of a sawmill, a freighter, the canal locks at the Soo, and Niagara Falls.

Anne T. Eaton

SOURCE: "Down to the Sea," in *The New York Times Book Review,* November 2, 1941, pp. 28, 30.

Up in the Nipegon country North of the Great Lakes, an Indian boy carved a little figure in a canoe a foot long and started his "Paddle Person" on a journey through the different waterways across the Great Lakes and down the St. Lawrence to the ocean. Full page pictures in rich, beautiful colors accompanied by a clear, effective text make the reader feel that he is actually sharing the journey. There is suspense, for the little carved figure has many narrow escapes; by the time a dip net picks him up off the Grand Banks he almost seems to have come alive and to have accomplished his dangerous journey through a fine determination of his own.

Here is geography presented with freshness and originality and imagination. *Paddle-to-the-Sea* will appeal to a wide range in age, younger children respond to the idea of the small canoe making its long voyage to the sea, older readers are delighted with the fine sweep of country the book shows them, the snowy hills, the brooks and beaver ponds, the logs breaking up, northern marshes with their wild life, storms on the lakes, Detroit factories, Niagara, the St. Lawrence. A book that school and public libraries will want to add to their shelves and one that children will enjoy owning that they may look again and again at the pictures whose interest it will be difficult to exhaust.

Florence Bethune Sloan

SOURCE: "Forward with Books!" in *The Christian Science Monitor,* November 3, 1941, p. 11.

Paddle-to-the-Sea, written and illustrated by Holling C. Holling, one of the most beautiful books of the year, tells of the travels made by a figure of an Indian in a canoe. A young Indian boy carved the figure, christened it Paddle-to-the-sea and set it on a melting snow bank, one spring day in the Nipigon country of the Great Lakes. As the boy sent the little figure on its way he said: "I have learned in school that when the snow in our Nipigon country melts, the waters flow to that river. The river flows into the Great Lakes, the biggest lakes in the world. . . . You will go with the water and you will have adventures that I would like to have."

The travels and the amazing things he experienced are vividly described in word and picture. An illuminated map traces the journey of the figurine from the cabin near Lake Nipigon through the Great Lakes to the sea. Mr. Holling's pictures, which are beautifully reproduced, have a remarkable quality—bringing out in a most unusual way the beauty of the scenes. Traveling with Paddle by story and pictures is good fun for nine to twelve-year-olds and is a fascinating way to learn geography.

Terry Borton

SOURCE: "The Teachings of 'Paddle-to-the-Sea,'" in *Learning*, Vol. 5, No. 5, January, 1977, pp. 26-30.

The lamb had been perfectly seasoned; the wine was light and plentiful. Mercifully, the dinner conversation was no longer about education, but flowed easily from politics to pollution.

The woman next to me said, "The trouble is that pollution's been going on so long. Why, I remember a book back in third grade that had stuff about pollution in it. All about a little canoe going through the Great Lakes."

Another guest picked up on her remark. "I remember that book! He got stuck in some garbage under a pier!"

Somewhere in the back of my brain a memory neuron fired. "Was it *Paddle-to-the-Sea?*" I asked.

Suddenly the table was ababble with memories and nostalgia. Six of the eight of us had read *Paddle* as children, and we all had vivid recollections of it. As I listened to the talk, I was, in spite of myself, thinking education again. There we were, a group of adults who had read and forgotten thousands of textbooks, and yet we all remembered so much information from this one story we had read 30 years ago. What classroom teacher, I wondered, could hope to have a lesson remembered with so much energy and detail? Who was this author? What did he do that had such an impact on us? Could I, and other teachers, learn enough from his approach so that years from now our students would still remember what we were trying to teach?

"You know," said our host, "I think I've still got that book down in a trunk somewhere in the basement. I'll go see."

The talk at the table continued.

"Sure I remember! A little Indian boy carved a model of a canoe with an Indian in it, and named him 'Paddle-to-the-Sea.' He started him on a river in Canada, and Paddle went all the way down through the Great Lakes to the ocean."

"Right! And there were those great pictures. The forest fire! Remember the fire? And the sawmill! Paddle got stuck in a log going right into the saw blade. Remember that picture?"

"And little pictures, too. Don't forget all those little pictures down the margins, showing how the water flowed in the locks—that kind of thing."

Our host returned, having found his copy of *Paddle*, binding broken and pictures marred, with his name scrawled in the corners. As I turned the pages, with the others looking over my shoulder, I remembered my childhood love for this book, and I realized that we had not remembered its lessons by accident. *Paddle*'s author was a teacher who had known exactly what he was doing. . . .

Collaborating with his wife, Lucille, [he] wrote a series of "geo-historical" books describing different areas of the country. *Paddle-to-the-Sea* was one of the most successful, selling more than 250,000 hardcover copies, and becoming a classic that still is available in most children's bookstores and libraries. Like all of Holling's books, it was clearly instructional and was characterized by the traits that readers remember so well: a compelling story, dramatic full-page color illustrations, and marginal sketches accompanied by explanatory lettering. These three elements comprised Holling's teaching method.

"The idea for the story of *Paddle* came from a carving that a little Indian boy gave Holling," Lucille Holling told me over the phone. "The carving wasn't of a canoe, but Holling was so impressed with it that he said, 'I'll make a carving the vehicle for a story about a boy who wanted to see the world but couldn't leave home.' Holling always used some insignificant thing as the central character for his stories. He didn't want something important or beautiful in itself; he wanted it to be important because of what happened to it in his imagination."

And so Paddle, the crudely carved alter ego of an Indian boy, set out to fulfill the boy's dream of traveling half a continent to the sea. The story is in the ancient picaresque tradition of the Everyman hero on the journey of life, and Paddle has plenty of close shaves and perilous adventures. But for Holling, the story of Paddle's four-year journey was primarily a way to explore the geography and history of the region. "The action part of my stories is fabricated," he said in a 1955 interview in *The Horn Book*, "but I have always tried to make the atmosphere surrounding them authentic."

Holling's combination of fabricated action and authentic atmosphere is a powerful way to help children remember and understand, because it reaches back to the primal means of learning through which vast amounts of man's culture was transmitted for generations. Perhaps intimidated by the razzmatazz of television, teachers lately have been neglecting the use of storytelling for instructional purposes. But to use this ancient teaching method in their own classrooms teachers do not have to possess TV's glamour or Holling's gift for the written word. What we teachers need is Holling's insight into the relationship between narrative action and factual information. . . .

Each full-page color illustration in *Paddle* captures a moment from a specific chapter. Aside from their often dramatic subject matter, these pictures were striking because of their shifts in perspective. Early in the book, we see paddle in the foreground, sitting on a snow-covered hill that is the starting point for his journey. With the landscape stretching below him, Paddle dominates the wilderness, as he must have dominated the vision of the boy who made him and sent him on his quest for the sea. But later, tossed among the beaches of Lake Michigan, Paddle lies small and forgotten amid the gunk of an industrial society. Caught in the forest fire, he is an almost indistinguishable silhouette against the holocaust. Swept along with the freighter traffic of the locks, he disappears from the pictures entirely.

In the written story, Paddle looms large as the central character. The pictures remind us that the only thing making him important in the real world is that we have come to care what happens to him. Lucille Holling remembers a discussion during the painting of these pictures: "Holling would say, 'I'll make the children hunt for him.' He wanted them to be involved with Paddle's fate." And because Holling's readers are little people who must make their way in a world of giants, they *are* involved.

The teaching power of Holling's pictures came not so much from his technical artistic proficiency as from his insight into the life of children and from the way he used images to evoke feeling. . . .

Holling used story line and large color illustrations to capture the child's imagination and bring it into dramatic interaction with the geography and history of the Great Lakes region. Much more additional information about that region was supplied by intricate drawings in the margins of Holling's text. Although he was criticized by reviewers for cluttering his books with detail, these compact little lessons fascinated his readers, who studied the drawings avidly to learn more about what was happening to Paddle. Readers received this information quickly and easily—literally, as an aside.

Though Holling's purpose in these marginal notes was clearly didactic, he often presented the information in a unique teaching form. Using a method that he learned from the Indians, Holling drew sketches that forced the shapes of unfamiliar geographic features into familiar natural forms. The Great Lakes drainage system became bowls on a hillside; Lake St. Clair became the heart of industry; Lake Superior, a wolf's head. This technique of forced visual metaphor is the basic component of many training courses in creativity and memory; it is a powerful mnemonic device. And, like Holling's other

teaching methods, its use does not require specialized talent—a visual association merely has to be forced on some subject matter, and the more far-fetched the better. . . .

When Holling was a young boy, he was frustrated when he couldn't find books that would tell him about the owls, the people, the rivers and the mountains he was interested in. At the age of ten he took a vow to write books for children when he grew up. But Holling became more than an author and illustrator: he cultivated a remarkable talent for teaching. He believed that to make learning last, the instruction needed to become part of what a child had already felt and experienced. His great insight was into the ways that a child's personal feelings can be combined with intellectual understanding through action and art. He developed a method of teaching that was so simple anyone could use it, yet so compelling that his work deeply touched the children who saw it. Combining adventure, beauty and precise detail, his books taught with a force that showered sparks into the minds of his young readers.

Thirty years later, the fires still glow.

TREE IN THE TRAIL (1942)

May Lamberton Becker

SOURCE: A review of *Tree in the Trail,* in *The New York Herald Tribune Books,* December 13, 1942, p. 10.

In shape, size and general arrangement this valuable picture-story book corresponds to Mr. Holling's striking success of last year, *Paddle-to-the-Sea,* and like that reminds us that he made some time ago one of the best color books about Indians—and one about cowboys—that young boys have had. It has more of a story than last season's tale of a toy canoe set to float through the Great Lakes chain and the St. Lawrence to the Atlantic Ocean, its passage marked by large pictures glowing with color. This time the hero of the story stays put for the first part of the book, being a cottonwood tree on the great plains of the Southwest, saved as a sapling in 1610 by a young Indian who became a great Medicine Man and foretold that this tree would some day travel from its hill. In its long life—over 160 years—its reputation as a Peace Tree, a place of truce, is firmly established; it becomes a "talking tree" to whose trunk messages are fixed by passing travelers. Its strange shape suggests, to one such journeyer, that of a Suffering Madonna; more than once it saves a life, and when it saves Jed, a young man making his first trip on the Santa Fe trail, he takes it under his special care. When a twister brings down the dead tree's ancient frame, Jed, setting out to construct a yoke from the center of its trunk, finds embedded stone arrowheads, steel silvers, iron points and a century-old ball from a smooth-bore—"ancient history coming to light" which the reader has seen happen earlier in the book. The yoke, whose story has gone abroad, becomes an object of veneration by all Indian tribes: it makes the journey to Santa Fe, where a descendant of the original Medicine Man runs through the tree's history and bids Jed keep it always.

The care with which all this is documented by pictures gives it exceptional usefulness. Besides the large color plates, every important detail in the story appears in small pencil studies on the wide margins of facing pages.

Booklist

SOURCE: A review of Tree in the Trail, in Booklist, Vol. 39, No. 9, January 15, 1943, p. 205.

The story of a cottonwood tree that watched the pageant of history on the Santa Fe trail where it stood, a landmark to travelers and a peace-medicine tree to Indians, for over 200 years. Similar in format to Paddle-to-the-Sea but less satisfactory. Both text and page seem overloaded and there is little unity between facing pages—the large colored illustrations require distance for fullest appreciation whereas the marginal drawings on the opposite pages invite closer scrutiny.

SEABIRD (1948)

Virginia Kirkus' Bookshop Service

SOURCE: A review of Seabird, in Virginia Kirkus' Bookshop Service, Vol. XVI, No. 16, August 15, 1948, pp. 398-99.

Once again, in slimly fictionized form, Holling has conveyed a substantial slice of history, in gorgeous, opulent, colorful, informational fashion, if a wee bit overstuffed. Seabird, carved out of ivory by a cabin boy, Ezra Brown, back in 1832, acts as a peg on which to hang the story of four generations of seafaring Browns. Fascinating details of whaling ships make the early part of the book a delight, but it tends to get rotund and stuffy in the later sections. However, the author's vivid, full color illustrations, and detailed decorative sketches are worth the price. A handsome job indeed, definitely deserving a place as supplementary reading for upper grades, and good merchandise for the holiday market. With a little more ease and humor, a little less pageant-of-history feeling, this would have been one of the outstanding juveniles of the year.

Ellen Lewis Buell

SOURCE: A review of Seabird, in The New York Times Book Review, August 22, 1948, p. 17.

Centered around the ivory figure of a sea gull this new story by the author-artist of Paddle-to-the-Sea and Tree in the Trail is a saga in miniature, of a family of American seafarers. Ezra Brown carved Seabird from a walrus tusk during his first trip aboard a New Bedford whaler. Later the bird became the mascot of Ezra's son's clipper ship on its trips to the Orient. When Ezra's son's son captained his first steamship across the Atlantic Seabird went too, and when Ken Brown, Ezra's great-grandson, piloted his airship through space Seabird soared higher than a live bird above the sea. Thus readers of the middle years will find here an outline of nearly a century and a quarter of the development of navigation, told in appealingly human terms. The prose is evocative, exciting to the imagination. The full-page illustrations are academic in style but lush in color. Together with informational marginal drawings they contain just about everything a boy would want to see on the subject.

Frances C. Darling

SOURCE: "Stories with Pictures Are Fun," in The Christian Science Monitor, September 14, 1948, p. 11.

Seabird, by Holling C. Holling, is a beautiful book in every sense of the word—full-page, strikingly lovely illustrations in color; marginal drawings, accurate in detail and decorative in effect; and a good story that covers American adventures in sea and air over a span of four generations. What more can we wish?

The "Seabird" is an ivory gull, carved by young Ezra when he was Ship's Boy on an old-time whaling vessel. The loveliest, it seems to me, of all the fine pictures is the one in which Ezra sees the real gull, flying high amid the snowflakes. The boy is solitary in the crow's-nest; he and the gull are two shadowy figures against the wintry sky.

Wherever Ezra goes, he carries the seabird which he carved. Clippers take the place of old whaling ships, and then Ezra's son and grandson grow up in the age of steam and oil and then, as the years pass by, Ezra's great-grandson is born into the age of airplanes, and still the "Seabird" is carried with them all.

"The old men shall dream dreams and the young men shall see visions," and this book gives us a hint of the dreams and visions that have gone into the growth of our country, her ships and their cargoes. The other day I watched a boy of twelve turning the pages. Slowly, slowly, he studied the little sketches, brooding over the big pictures. "This," he said, "is a book I shall like for a very long time."

I could wish that the bits of information, lettered beside the little sketches, were printed more clearly. As it is they look well on the page and keep the feeling of old ship logs with their fine annotations, but they are not easily read, and they are an important part of a fine book.

Margaret C. Ernst

SOURCE: A review of Seabird, in The New York Herald Tribune Books, November 21, 1948, p. 8.

Seabird is an entrancing and beautiful book for anybody, from the age of eight on, who cares about the sea and ships. This book does for the sea what Mr. Holling did for the Great Lakes in *Paddle-to-the-Sea* and for the Southwest in *Tree in the Trail,* and does it superbly by text and illustration. The pictures are so much a part of the story that you cannot consider them separately. Every alternate page is a dramatic and beautiful colored illustration, and every page of text is enriched with elegant, accurate marginal drawings showing with architectural deftness how a whaleship is rigged, the tools of the whalemen, the way a clipper is built, how an anchor grips the sea bottom.

And while the reader learns so much about the sea, the ships that ride it, the whales the harpooners killed, he is told, too, a fine story of a sailing family and of their mascot Seabird. Ezra Brown, fourteen, and cabin boy on a New Bedford whaler, sees from his crow's nest lookout, an ivory gull, soaring up and over an iceberg just in time to save the ship from crashing. Ezra fashions a seabird for himself out of walrus ivory, with coral eyes and amber beak, a good luck talisman that flies with four generations of Brown men. There is Ezra himself who becomes captain of a clipper; his red-haired son Nate who captains the Half-Way, a vessel combining sail and steam; his son James, designer of vast steamers, and finally Ken, today, sailing the skies, with Seabird in the cabin of his plane.

Though the brief story covers four generations, it has a unity built on the character of the men and boys of the Brown family.

📖 *MINN OF THE MISSISSIPPI* (1951)

Virginia Kirkus' Bookshop Service

SOURCE: A review of *Minn of Mississippi,* in *Virginia Kirkus' Bookshop Service,* Vol. XIX, No. 18, September 15, 1951, pp. 530-31.

Mr. Holling's interests and subjects follow as desultory a path as the Mississippi, but he can certainly be forgiven, for this new lovely picture book, bursting with legend, history, natural science, convincing personalities and even a few wise saws, has such a bountiful collection of loving detail and good story, that it is bound to keep the reader happy and busy for some time. In the career of Minn, a snapping turtle, as she is carried, often against her will, down the Mississippi, the author has revealed the fabulous life of the great river,—the busy cities, wild bayous, lonely and lovely regions, all kinds of men and boats, and always-present reminders of the past in the magical underwater life of which Minn is a part, relics of bygone civilizations, and the course of the river as it meanders, rushes and rips down its two thousand five hundred miles. The illustrations—black and white sketches and full-page, full-color illustrations by the author—are stunning in characteristically authentic

detail and luxurious use of color. Rich fare for libraries *and* good merchandise, a memorable successor to *Seabird.*

Ethel C. Ince

SOURCE: A review of *Minn of Mississippi,* in *The Christian Science Monitor,* October 4, 1951, p. 15.

A fascinating panorama of the whole Mississippi Valley unfolds, in story and pictures, in *Minn of the Mississippi,* by Holling Clancy Holling, as a small turtle, born in the Minnesota headwaters, travels down the great river and—after twenty-five summers of varied experiences, interspersed with struggle and drama—finds herself in the bayous south of New Orleans. This is another of Mr. Holling's expansive, yet detailed, regional panoramas of the North American scene, with beautiful accurate marginal drawings as well as full-page pictures.

Louise S. Bechtel

SOURCE: A review of *Minn of the Mississippi,* in *The New York Herald Tribune Books,* November 11, 1951, p. 4.

A snapping turtle takes a journey of 2,500 miles, from the headwaters of our greatest river down to the Gulf of Mexico. He does it in a gorgeous, big picture book (8 1/2 by 11 inches) with twenty full color pages and about 150 marginal sketches. It is not for the picture-book age, but for intelligent readers of about ten to twelve, and also for Mr. Holling's wide following, younger and older.

The text combines story, nature study, geography, history, human-interest stories. The author's mind ranges along the course of the great river as would that of an alert curious child. He tells how log rafts are built, how the fur-traders used to pack their pelts, the workings of dams and locks, the meaning of river names, all the kinds of river boats from then to now, etc. Such facts are carefully pictured in the margins, whose rich content includes many small maps, and some beautiful sketches. The end is dramatic for the turtle, by now very old, and equally so for its look into the mind of a Cajun boy: he is partly bitter at the lot of his people, but mostly glad of his freedom to work. Men at work have been no small part of the whole exciting journey.

This children's picture epic of the heart of America follows the well-loved *Paddle to the Sea* (Great Lakes), *The Tree in the Trail* (Sante Fe) and *Sea Bird* (Atlantic Coast.) The four titles offer our boys and girls a unique vision of their country, each focussing first on the wildlife Mr. Holling knows so well, but spreading wide into the works of men and the sweep of history. They make a special, intellectually valid contribution to modern children's books. Imaginative teachers could make fine use of them all. But first they belong in the home library, to be pored over and enjoyed at leisure.

Young and old will share the new book with equal delight in its variety of facts, its stories of "the River of Dreams," and the contrasting dramas on all the brilliant big color pages. Congratulations and thanks to Mr. Holling.

Marian Rayburn Brown

SOURCE: "A Turtle Takes a Trip," in *The New York Times Book Review,* November 11, 1951, p. 30.

In Minnesota a snapping turtle digs upward from the white egg buried in the sand and wobbles down to the Mississippi. She moves seaward, hibernating during the long winters, bumped and rolled along by the spring floods. Caught and imprisoned by a shantyboat owner, strung on a pole by two boys, dug out of winter quarters by turtle hunters, Minn always manages to get free. By the time she reaches the Gulf the reader has been introduced to the historical background and romance of the Mississippi as well as to present-day life along its banks.

Here is a rare combination of science, geography, history and fiction. Full-page illustrations and marginal drawings of birds, maps, boats and prehistoric animals add to its interest.

Bertha E. Mahoney-Miller

SOURCE: A review of *Minn of Mississippi,* in *The Horn Book Magazine,* Vol. XXVII, No. 6, December, 1951, p. 411.

A book really packed with thoroughly interesting information about the river—its history and character along its 2552 miles—and about turtles, the snapping turtle Minn in particular. The marginal drawings in black and white are wonderfully enlightening, and the full-page pictures in color often beautiful. In format this follows the pattern of *Paddle-to-the-Sea* and *Sea Bird,* and is the fourth title in the group. I for one long to see the rich talents of this author-artist break the bounds of this set pattern. *Rocky Billy*—I have never forgotten that first book of the Rocky Mountain goat, so alive and so free.

📖 *PAGOO* **(with wife Lucille Holling, 1957)**

Virginia Kirkus' Service

SOURCE: A review of *Pagoo,* in *Virginia Kirkus' Service,* Vol. XXV, No. 16, August 15, 1957, p. 585.

Holling Clancy Holling, who wrote *Sea Bird* and *Minn of the Mississippi,* etc., adds another opulently illustrated, richly researched account of the life of a hermit crab to his earlier triumphs. The little Pagurus, ("Pagoo", for short) of whom he writes, lives in Tide Pool Town. The life cycle of the little hermit crab is dangerous

From Pagoo, *written and illustrated by Holling Clancy Holling with wife Lucille Holling.*

indeed. "Old Instinct" aids the plucky little crustacean as he molts, and wanders homeless through sea caves and grottoes until he finds a home in "Travelling Towers". Pagoo enjoyed his penthouse apartment in a pink barnacle atop a starfish until a hungry Sculpin devours his dream home. Only a chase by other hermit crabs could have made Pagoo venture into Deep Hole, where an Octopus lay in wait. Strangely enough, Pagoo is saved from the tentacle of the Octopus by a Moray Eel. Illustrations by the author and Lucille Webster Holling, twenty full pages in color and a myriad of black and white drawings, are superb. Those in color have jewel-like tones, while the marginal black and whites are more scientific and anatomical. A handsome contribution for the child whose current interest is life beneath the sea.

H. Seymour Fowler and Lauretta G. McCusker

SOURCE: A review of *Pagoo,* in *Library Journal,* Vol. 82, No. 22, December 15, 1957, p. 3247.

A richly illustrated account of the life cycle of the hermit crab and other marine invertebrates. Although it is scientifically accurate, some biologists might reject the book because of its continuous use of anthropormorphism in describing lower animal forms. However, this personification helps arouse the young readers' interest in Pagoo. Black-and-white drawings add information as well as interest, and the sparkling, sea-green illustrations are captivating. Pronunciation given for scientific words. For intermediate grades, but good remedial material in junior high, too.

Margaret Sherwood Libby

SOURCE: A review of *Pagoo,* in *The New York Herald Tribune Books,* December 22, 1957, p. 7.

No one who has ever crouched fascinated over a tide pool, peering into its depths and shallows, can fail to be amazed and delighted by the beautiful pictures of those iridescent wonderlands the Hollings have pictured in *Pagoo,* the life-history of Pagurus, a hermit crab. The twenty full-color illustrations are like color photographs, fairly glimmering with the curious, luminous beauty of sunlight filtered through water. They have been drawn from Pagoo's point of view so the small rock, the starfish, the anemone loom huge and menacing. The margins of every page are filled with beautiful, soft gray drawings of the other denizens of Pagoo's world. These drawings are as informational as the text, for they are done with care and accuracy and are frequently labeled with the creature's name or explanations of his habits.

The text tells the life history of one hermit crab from the time he was hatched from "an egg the size of a pencil dot" until, after many changes, moultings and discovering new shells to live in as well as lucky escapes from a multitude of enemies, he mated and another little Pagarus "found his place in the endless rocking rhythms of the sea." The account is excellent, dramatic yet factually true. Our only reservation is in regard to the device of the "old Pal," who "hisses" at Pagoo, "Scoot, protect that bare half of yours." The account is so good that this seems unnecessary and confuses the conception of instinct. Children would read it just as eagerly, and the same humorous turn of phrase could be used if Pagoo just sensed the need for protection. This is a book for younger children and one that will be enjoyed in families and by individual youngsters between nine and twelve who spend their holidays at the shore.

Phyllis Fenner

SOURCE: "A Crab's Life Isn't Easy," in *The New York Times Book Review,* January 5, 1958, p. 22.

"Little Pagurus—Pagoo for short—would grow into a two-fisted Hermit Crab—if he could make it. . . . Pagoo's chances of growing up were not very good." Pagoo, we learn from Mr. Holling, was as tiny as a pencil dot and glassy-surfaced so as to be almost invisible in an ocean full of dangers. His only other protection was his instinct, "a wonderful guardian for one so young who had not had time to learn things." The ocean was "one huge kettle of food" and Pagoo was lucky to eat and not be eaten. He grew, kicked off his first shell, grew some more, and with each molting became larger and larger until he was entirely covered with armor.

Mr. Holling's information about Pagoo and other marine creatures who live along the beaches and in the tide pools is presented in lively and humorous fashion. Twenty full-color plates and beautiful, detailed marginal drawings on every page complement the text and make this a book to treasure.

Bulletin of the Center for Children's Books

SOURCE: A review of *Pagoo,* in *Bulletin of the Center for Children's Books,* Vol. 11, No. 7, March, 1958, p. 70.

Using the same pattern as his *Minn of the Mississippi,* the author describes and pictures the life of a hermit crab from the hatching of the egg to maturity. The illustrations, both full page color and black and white marginal drawings, are excellent and give the book its real value. The text is, unfortunately, irritatingly coy in tone and Pagoo is so highly personified that he loses his reality as a hermit crab.

Additional coverage of Holling's life and career is contained in the following sources published by Gale Research: *Major Authors and Illustrators for Children and Young Adults;* and *Something About the Author,* Vol. 15.

Trina Schart Hyman

1939-

American illustrator of picture books.

Major works include *King Stork* (adapted from story by Howard Pyle, 1973), *Snow White* (adapted from story by the Grimm Brothers; translated from German by Paul Heins, 1974), *Rapunzel* (retold by Barbara Rogasky from story by the Grimm Brothers, 1982), *Saint George and the Dragon*: *A Golden Legend Adapted from Edmund Spenser's Faerie Queen* (adapted by Margaret Hodges, 1984), *The Fortune-Tellers* (written by Lloyd Alexander, 1992), *Bearskin* (adapted from story by Howard Pyle, 1997).

INTRODUCTION

A highly regarded illustrator of scores of picture books and poetry collections for preschool and primary graders, Hyman is best known for her work with folklore and fairy tales. Praised by Christine C. Behr as "the gifted creator of many of the most beautiful princesses, gallant knights, gruesome monsters, and frightful hags ever to grace the pages of a picture book," Hyman has provided pictures for such classic stories as the works of the Grimm Brothers, J. M. Barrie's *A Christmas Carol* (1983), Geoffrey Chaucer's *The Canterbury Tales* (1988), and Mark Twain's *A Connecticut Yankee in King Arthur's Court* (1988) as well as tales of Jewish and European folklore from Czechoslovakia, England, Germany, Ireland, the Middle East, Norway, and other areas of the world. She has teamed with many of the most celebrated of contemporary children's authors to produce a body of work that has garnered her a host of honors. Reviewers applaud her illustrations for their blending of realism, fantasy, and humor, and her expressive, romanticized depictions of the human character and body. In a review of Eric Kimmel's adaptation of *Iron John* by the Grimm Brothers, Carolyn Phelan paid tribute to Hyman's "sensitivity to the expressiveness of the human form," adding that "the characters reveal their hearts and minds in the illustrations as clearly as in the text." Deeply interested in the human drama, Hyman strived to create characters that revealed their deeper, inner selves. "People," she explained, "—and this includes monsters and other fantastic creatures—are endlessly fascinating to me as subject matter. Facial expressions, body language, gestures of both action and repose can express a wealth of information. . . . The story within the story can nearly always be found in my illustrations." Hyman often frames her illustrations in richly figured borders that go beyond literal decoration to evoke deeper meanings of the stories. Her pictures for Margaret Hodges' *Saint George and the Dragon,* for which she received the Caldecott Medal in 1985, were deemed "uniquely suited to this outrageously romantic and appealing legend" by a reviewer for *School Library Journal.* A critic

for *The Horn Book Magazine* further praised her skill at getting inside the skin of time, character, and place, explaining, "the artist is more faithful to the poet's concept than the adapter, for in the margins surrounding the texts are found angels, spirits, and witches embodying Spenser's eerie world of fantasy and spiritual conflict." In her artwork, Hyman aims to uncover the magic hidden in everyday life. "One of the nicest things about being an artist is the ability to see things a little differently. . . ," she explained in her acceptance speech for the Caldecott Medal, "perhaps a little more imaginatively than most other people do. To be able to see the possibilities in things . . . to see what it is that makes that thing inherently itself. And then, sometimes, to go beyond the surface of the thing and see what it is that the thing wishes to become: the cities that live in clouds, the landscapes that become human bodies, the human face that becomes an animal, the tree that becomes a woman."

Biographical Information

Hyman grew up in a rural area about twenty miles north of Philadelphia, Pennsylvania. She was a shy child with a vivid imagination. Speaking of her childhood as she accepted the Caldecott Medal, she recounted, "It was quite clear to me that everything in the world was under a spell of enchantment, and that the most ordinary objects had secret lives of their own. Everything—the wind, the trees, coffee cups, toothbrushes—had a soul, a spirit. It therefore seemed the most natural and believable thing in the world that stones and birds should speak or that a frog should turn into a prince." Hyman's parents were very understanding, taking her fantasies in stride and never chiding her for her timid nature.

Hyman came into her own after she graduated from high school and began taking art classes. For the first time she was surrounded by other artists who "ate, lived, and dreamed art." "It was as though I had been living all my life in a strange country where I could never fit in," she commented. Hyman attended the Philadelphia Museum College of Art and later studied in Boston and Stockholm, Sweden. She also married during these years, and while she and her husband were living in Sweden, she got her first illustrating job. In 1963, one of Hyman's friends became art director for adult books at Little, Brown Publishing. As a favor, she offered Hyman an illustrating job. Helen Jones, the children's book editor, saw Hyman's work and offered her another book to do. Jones later became Hyman's beloved mentor.

Over the next few years, Hyman had a baby and some time later divorced her husband. She also purchased a farmhouse and moved to the country, where her home became a haven for other artists. She served as art director for *Cricket* magazine from 1972 to 1979, where she made valuable contacts with a large group of writers and illustrators. She continues her work as an illustrator, as well as a writer and illustrator of her own books, including *The Enchanted Forest* (1984), in her quest, as Christine Behr puts it, for "the perfect integration of text and artwork."

Major Works

Hyman first received widespread recognition for her work with the 1973 publication of *King Stork,* a fairy tale by Howard Pyle. Her illustrations, for which she received the *Boston Globe-Horn Book* award, were somewhat controversial, including a depiction of a table carved with a couple embracing amorously, which she defended as "a symbol of Life." A year later, Hyman received special critical attention for her adaptations of *Snow White* and its successor, *Sleeping Beauty.* In both books, Hyman aimed for a pictorial narrative, where all the characters (even the minor ones) came alive. Hugh Crago claimed that "in this series of rich, somber painting, where careful and often significant background detail never overwhelms the drama of foreground events, the longing, devotion, hatred, and fear . . . are given full reign as never before in a version for young viewers." The rich illustrations in *Rapunzel* also received critical praise for

their ability to convey a range of emotion; however, many reviewers considered the decorative borders surrounding each page as too restrictive. Her elaborate borders worked to better effect in *Saint George and the Dragon,* creating the illusion that the reader views each page through a window. A reviewer in *Bulletin of the Center for Children's Books* remarked, "At her romantic best, Hyman illustrates this classic tale . . . with paintings of a marvelously fierce dragon, an impeccable knight, a dazzlingly lovely Princess Una. Notable for their color and composition, the illustrations are framed by borders that often have a Tiffany look." She used a similar border technique in *Little Red Riding Hood,* a favorite childhood story that she both retold and illustrated. Recognizing the allure of Hyman's vivid details, Janet French remarked, "Each page of text is enclosed in a border of intricate design; paired with it is a full-page watercolor illustration overflowing with the sort of minutely observed details that children love. These pages delight the eye."

Writing about a later work, Lloyd Alexander's *The Fortune-Tellers* (1992), *School Library Journal* contributor Linda Boyles commended Hyman's "masterful" pictures, noting the interplay between the "expressive figures" and a West African landscape with "colors so rich and clear that they invite readers to touch the fabrics and breathe the air." Howard Pyle's original American story *Bearskin,* about a lost baby found and nurtured by a she-bear, combines elements from many classic folktales. Using a multi-ethnic cast of characters drawn in india ink and acrylics, Hyman brings the long ago and far away into a contemporary context, making "this neverland" as Carolyn Phelan expressed, "seem so real."

Awards

In 1968, Hyman received the *Boston Globe-Horn Book* honor for *All in Free but Janey* and, in 1978, for *On to Widecombe Fair.* In 1970, *The Pumpkin Giant* (retold by Ellen Green) was selected one of the American Institute of Graphic Artists "Children's Books." *King Stork* received the *Boston Globe-Horn Book* award for illustration in 1973. Hyman's own version of *Little Red Riding Hood* received the Golden Kite Award for Illustration and the Parents' Choice Award for Illustration in 1983, as well as the Caldecott Honor Book designation from the American Library Association in 1984. In addition to the 1984 Caldecott Medal, *Saint George and the Dragon* was cited by the *New York Times* as one of the Best Illustrated Books of the Year. Hyman received the Dorothy Canfield Fisher Award for *A Castle in the Attic* in 1987 and Golden Kite honors for *Canterbury Tales* in 1988 and *The Fortune-Tellers* in 1992. In 1990, *Hershel and the Hanukkah Goblins* was designated a Caldecott Honor Book by the American Library Association. Hyman herself received awards from Keene State College (New Hampshire), the School of Library and Information Science of Drexel University, and the Free Library of Philadelphia for her body of work.

ILLUSTRATOR'S COMMENTARY

[The following is Hyman's acceptance speech for the Caldecott Medal awarded to her by the American Library Association in 1985 for her illustrations in Saint George and the Dragon.*]*

Trina Schart Hyman

SOURCE: "Caldecott Medal Acceptance," in *The Horn Book Magazine,* Vol. LXI, No. 4, July-August, 1985, pp. 410-21.

I have waited a long time for this moment—ten years, to be exact. And now, I am so happy to be able to take this wonderful opportunity to tell all of you how deeply sorry I am and how much I regret the carving on the witches' table and the inscription on the tombstone. Not because I didn't mean every line of them—but simply because I'm sick to death of being asked to explain and apologize. Gotcha!

It has occurred to me, in a few weak moments since January fourth, that one of the reasons *Saint George and the Dragon* may have been selected for the Caldecott Medal is that it's the cleanest, most innocent, least likely-to-offend book I've ever illustrated. And if that's so—well, it wasn't my fault! I just draw what the story tells me to draw; this one happened to be pure in heart; that's all. Although once you've established a reputation, it seems to follow you around. Shortly after *Saint George* was published my friend Cyndy Szekeres called me up and said, "Oh, Trina, you devil dog, you! How sneaky and clever you were to make that apple tree a sexy naked woman reaching out for George!"

"What are you talking about, Cyndy? *What* naked woman?!"

"Come *on,* Trina! The *apple* tree!—you know—the one George is sleeping under! It's a nude woman, upside down! Terrific!"

Well, that apple tree on page twenty-two happens to live in my back yard, and if there's a naked lady in it, *I* never knew she was there. But when I hung up the phone, I realized that I was already mentally composing a letter of explanation and apology to answer the flood of outraged letters from parents and teachers and the Dallas Public Library. Happily, Cyndy is the only one who has ever seen the naked lady. And don't ask me to point it out to you, because I still can't see it!

I know what she means, though. One of the nicest things about being an artist is the ability to see things a little differently, a little more carefully, perhaps a little more imaginatively, than most other people do. To be able to see the possibilities in things; to see the magic in them, to see what it is that makes that thing inherently itself. And then, sometimes, to go beyond the surface of the

thing and see what it is that the thing wishes to become: the cities that live in clouds, the landscapes that become sleeping bodies, the human face that becomes an animal, the tree that becomes a woman.

When I was a child, it was easy for me to see these transformations—the hidden souls of everyday things. At any moment the sky could produce a long-lost fairy-tale city; a chair would leer at me with the face of a demon; a leaf turned into an insect and hopped away; my sister turned to look at me with the face of a cat; or an apple tree changed, with the light, into a beautiful woman. It never occurred to me to disbelieve anything that I read in Grimms' fairy tales or in the Greek and Norse myths that I loved so much. It was quite clear to me that everything in the world was under a spell of enchantment, and that the most ordinary objects had secret lives of their own. Everything—the wind, the trees, coffee cups, toothbrushes—had a soul, a spirit. It therefore seemed the most natural and believable thing in the world that stones and birds should speak or that a frog should turn into a prince. My mother and father never discouraged this point of view—as a matter of fact I think they were rather tickled by what they called my "vivid imagination," and they had the good sense to take my fantasies in stride. If I mentioned that there was an angel on the roof, my father would agree that there probably had been. The year I became Little Red Riding Hood, my mother sewed me a very beautiful little red cape with a hood and usually remembered to call me Little Red Riding Hood rather than Trina. When I had to get a vaccination at the doctor's and was about to throw a fit at the sight of the needle, my mother told me not to worry—it was just like Sleeping Beauty being pricked by the spindle. And so I calmly took the shot in the arm and then proceeded to fall into a deep sleep that lasted for a hundred years!

We believed in fairies in my family. We believed in the power and magic and mystery that exists in nature, anyway. After all, if angels are living in the heavens, why shouldn't fairies be hiding in the forest or trolls in the earth? It is easy to see these things once you know they are there. And for me it has always been easier to draw a picture of what I've seen rather than to try to explain it with words. I drew a lot—I think I was born drawing. I drew because I needed to as well as for the sheer joy of it. And because I loved to draw—because I was an artist—I learned to look very carefully at things. I learned to watch closely and to remember what I had seen. I learned to look for those things that were hiding or waiting to emerge as well as at the outward appearances of things.

Of course, when you go to school, they do their best to knock it all out of you. Most of the grown-up world, it seems, is in a conspiracy to teach us to disbelieve in the magic we see so easily as a child—to deny the existence of those powerful images we see with our hearts rather than with our minds. So school was an unhappy and difficult time for me. A socially backward kid whose only attributes are a "vivid imagination" and a need to draw pictures all day long was not exactly appreciated in the public school system of Cheltenham Township, Pennsylvania. I was a further pain in the neck because in first grade I preferred reading Edith Hamilton's *Mythology* to following the fascinating saga of Dick and Jane and Spot, line by bumbling line. No one had ever told my parents that it wasn't cool to teach your kid to read books at a decidedly preschool age, and I was made to suffer in subtle ways for their innocent mistake. However, I was stubborn, and I was tough with the peculiar kind of toughness that timid children learn to develop. And the Brothers Grimm were strong—stronger than Dick and Jane, and stronger than my grade-school teachers.

Eventually, I learned to shut up about the angels and to do my real drawings at home, where they wouldn't be subjected to embarrassing questions. I learned to survive, and the fairies and angels survived with me. I have to look a little harder for them now, but I know they are still there because they have always been there. And one very good thing came out of those school years when I was a stranger in a strange land. It was always very clear to me—and to everyone else, too—exactly what I would do when I grew up. I would be an artist, and I would be the sort of artist who made pictures that told stories. It wasn't until the seventh grade that I learned about the word *illustrator,* but when I heard it, I knew that that was me.

I can't say that I've never wavered from that chosen course. I've always secretly wanted to be a ballet dancer, and once I wanted to be an organist. More realistically, I've always longed to be the sort of artist who simply paints pictures—big, mysterious, grown-up paintings on canvas—with oil paint. But I can't. I can't because there are too many stories in the world, too many books waiting to be illustrated, and not enough time to illustrate them all or to learn how to do it well enough. Besides, I have this consuming, fatal passion for books—the books themselves, the way they look and smell, the feel of them, and of course the stories that they have to tell. When I'm upset or depressed or unhappy, I go to a bookstore for comfort, the way other people go to a church or to a therapist. Books and illustrations are a part of me: They're not just what I do; they're what I *am.*

Twenty-five years ago, when I was just starting out as a children's book illustrator, I used to trot across the Boston Common at least once a month with my portfolio to show my latest efforts to Helen Jones, the children's book editor at Little, Brown and Company. Helen Jones was a tough, clear-eyed, no-nonsense Yankee lady. She was a feminist before we had even started using the word. She was smart, opinionated, had a wicked sense of humor, and did not suffer fools gladly. She cared deeply about children's books and knew everything there was to know about publishing them. I was terrified of her, and I fell in love with her at first sight. I badgered her with my portfolio until she finally gave me a book to do—a collection of Christmas stories and poems by Ruth Sawyer called *Joy to the World.* It was the start of a long—and for me tremendously enriching and happy association. It was Helen who gave me my first book of fairy tales to illustrate and who was brave enough to publish a story I'd written called *How Six Found Christmas.* She gave me the chance to try my hand at illustrating every sort of children's book—picture books, young adult novels, mystery stories, folk tales. She also initiated me into the terrors of speaking before large groups of people. At Helen's insistence the first time I agreed to speak—and draw—was to a group of over one thousand grade-school children in John Hancock Hall in Boston. I guess she figured if I could survive that, I could speak anywhere! She took me to my first ALA convention and my first Newbery-Caldecott Awards dinner in 1964. She taught me almost everything I know about how children's books are made—how they are produced, marketed, and sold.

When Helen Jones died in 1973, I had one page left to do on a book I had begun at her suggestion. That book was *King Stork* by Howard Pyle. I finished the job, and then I fell apart. I honestly did not know how I was going to continue my work without her guidance and support. But I did, of course—I did because I had to and because she would have been furious with me if I hadn't. The subsequent books that I did for Little, Brown under Emilie McLeod and John Keller were *Snow White* and *Sleeping Beauty*—the kind of lavish picture-book fairy tales that Helen might have trusted me with by then if she had been alive. After that, my association with Little, Brown became sporadic. Things there had changed, as they were changing everywhere. I began working with various other publishers; I was involved with *Cricket* magazine and going through several interesting life crises, both personal and professional. During one of the most severe and frightening of these professional life crises, it was Kate and John Briggs and Holiday House who picked me up, dusted me off, and set me back on my feet again. It was they who helped me renew my faith in myself as an illustrator. It was they who suggested that I take the plunge and do that autobiographical picture book—*Little Red Riding Hood.* At that point I was even beginning to notice the fairies again.

Then, one day in the spring of 1983 I got a call from an assistant editor at Little, Brown and Company named Karen Klockner. They had a manuscript by Margaret Hodges—a retelling of "Saint George and the Dragon." Would I be interested in illustrating it? Well, sure—I would take a look at it. And from that first look I was hooked. Wow! It was good. It was better than good; it was extraordinary. "Okay, Helen," I muttered. "I'll do it." Later on that summer, I got another phone call—this time from Margaret Hodges. She and her husband were just off to England for a month—would it be possible for them to come to Lyme on their way back to meet me and talk about the book?

Now, there is an old, unwritten, but very sensible rule

From Saint George and the Dragon, *retold by Margaret Hodges. Illustrated by Trina Schart Hyman.*

in children's book publishing that says you must never let the author and illustrator meet, at least not until after the book is on its way to the printer. It's a good rule because authors and illustrators almost never agree on how a book should be illustrated and, besides, they usually hate each other on first sight anyway. But I wanted to meet Margaret Hodges. I wanted to meet the woman who had crafted this extraordinary bit of prose, and I knew that I also needed her help. I had lots of questions about *Saint George and the Dragon*—the most important one being, what period of history should I set this story in? As usual, with any book that has even the vaguest historical reference, there are piles of reference work to do because you've got to be careful about particulars. And in this instance we had Edmund Spenser, who was an Elizabethan, to deal with as well as George himself, whom nobody can seem to pin down to a particular period, never mind agree that he existed at all. So I told Margaret Hodges that I would be delighted to meet her and her husband and to please look for any kind of visual reference material on George that I could use for the book.

A month later, when I saw Margaret and Fletcher Hodg-

es walking up my driveway, something magical happened to the landscape. I swear that the light changed. The trees became enchanted princesses; the clouds became castles; and the fairies came out of the flowers. It was a case of love at first sight, again. You can see this scene for yourselves on the back of the jacket for *Saint George.*

We decided during lunch to put our George in his own, vague, pre-Arthurian time, and not in Mr. Spenser's Elizabethan period. We decided that perhaps I could use Spenser's bits about the little sailors and their voyage to bring in something Elizabethan. Or that maybe I should make a parallel to the main story in the borders of the pages, using Elizabethan children doing a George and the Dragon Mummers' play. I had already decided to make this book my own version of an illuminated manuscript, with decorative, lavishly illustrated page borders. Amazingly, it turned out that we agreed completely on how this book should look. In other words Margaret said, "You do exactly what you think is best, Trina, and I'll like it!" Wonder of wonders! We spent the rest of the afternoon talking about fairies—Margaret believes in them, too. Fletcher and my friend

Barbara talked about books. New friends, new beginnings, and an exciting new book to work on! Life can be kind.

Later on that summer there was a conference with Karen Klockner and Bob Lowe. Bob has been the art director for children's books at Little, Brown for as long as I have been doing books for them. We are the only two left who remember how it was in the old days with Helen Jones. While Helen was teaching me how to be an illustrator, Bob was teaching me how to talk to printers. It was good to be working with him again.

It was also good to work with Karen, who looks like a fairy-tale princess and who instantly displayed the qualities I admire most in an editor—the sensitivity and intelligence to leave me alone with the job and the confidence to say, "Call me if you need me."

To be left alone with the job is very important to me. I came into this world alone, and I'll go out of it alone, and each book I do is the same kind of birth and maybe the same kind of death, on a smaller scale. I don't do sketches, or preliminaries. I think about it, instead. I think about the story and about what it means and about how it can be brought to life in pictures. I think about the characters and what makes them tick and where they're coming from and where they might be going to. Who *are* these people? What do they like to eat for breakfast? How do they react in a situation that's *outside* this story? What are they *really* thinking while this story is happening to them? I think about the landscape. Where is this taking place? What time of year is it? What was the weather like? Was the sky in the fourth century the same as the sky we see now? Obviously, it wasn't. What was it like, then? Were the stars brighter, the light more pure, the colors clearer? What was this dragon like? *Were* there dragons? Of course there were. They still exist somewhere, I bet. So, what did he look like? What did *he* eat for breakfast?

I think about all this a lot. I think about it so much that eventually I start to dream about it. And when my dreams start to become the dreams of the characters in the book, when their reality becomes a part of my subconscious, when I can live in their landscape, when I put on the little red cape with a hood and tie the red ribbons under my chin, then I know what to do with my pictures.

When I'm halfway into a book, the people who know and love me best always say things like, "You haven't been *listening* to me. I told you last week that the oil burner sounded weird!" Or, "What do you mean, you're not coming to my fiftieth birthday party! I told you about it months ago!" Or, "Hey, Trina, the bugs are only four months late. I'm going to shoot myself tomorrow, in case you're interested!" Or, *"Trina!* I *told* you about this person! He's very important to me! Where have you *been?"* Well, I've been in the book. That's where I live now, and it's hard for me to come out of it. I know that there's another world out there, going on about its business, but *my* world is right here with George and his valiant old horse and Una and the dwarf and the

lamb and the donkey. And, wow! The dragon is right there, waiting for them! Hey, I know you can't hear it or see it or smell it or feel it the way I can, but wait for it! Wait a few days and I'll show you. I'll help you to see it the way it really happened!

Look. There are the fairies: They're listening, waiting. Fairies always know how the story will turn out. They stole George when he was a tiny baby. His mom left him in a field, just the way some moms today leave their babies in the car when they're shopping in the supermarket. So the fairies took him, and the fairy queen brought him up to be a warrior—strong and clean-limbed and pure-hearted and totally committed. And then she turned him free and said, "Go for it."

At just about the same time, here comes Una, looking for a hero to kill the dragon that's been destroying her father's kingdom. She's a very strong, self-confident, independent young woman. My research into fourth-century England told me that women were brought up that way. They hadn't invented the word *feminist* then, but they didn't have to. Women were expected to be self-sufficient and strong. Who else was going to run the kingdom when Daddy and Big Brother and the rest of the men-folk were off fighting wars? We haven't come such a long way, baby.

Una travels with the dwarf. I figured he was probably the household astrologer: a servant and at the same time a wise and learned man. Maybe he is a Jew or an Armenian or an Arab. Someone who was a cripple—an outsider: an observer, a visionary who was left behind by the Romans because he was too embarrassing or too clever to be taken back to Rome as a slave. I think that Una's mother, the queen, asked him to go along on this journey—to look after Una and, more important, to bring back a true report of what happened. She knows that Una is a dedicated and save-the-world idealist; but she also knows about sixteen-year-old girls. Una takes her pet lamb along, too—obviously for symbolic reasons. I guessed that she started out on her journey as soon as the roads were passable—maybe sometime in March. It took her about three months to reach the west coast of England to meet George just as he is riding out into the world for the first time. He is wearing a suit of chain mail that the fairies fashioned for him and a breastplate of cast-off Roman armor. He is bearing the sword that men will call Excalibur in some future time. His shield comes from the grave of an ancient hero and bears the symbol that the flag of England is based upon—the red cross.

The fairies are watching them. They know the beginning and the end of this story, but they're curious anyhow, which is one of the best things about fairies. They also know that they are at this time engaged in their own great and perhaps final battle with the angels of the new religion. The angels of Christianity are taking over in the battle for people's hearts and minds. So the fairies have sent their own changeling, their sweetest, most powerful hero, to do the dragon job—who will succeed in his quest and be called forever a saint on the Christian calendar.

It is one of the fairies' last, greatest jokes on the world. But Una and George know nothing about this and neither does the dragon. What is the dragon thinking through all this?

The dragon isn't evil or wicked. He isn't anything but an animal. What he's thinking about most is food and maybe a little stalking and hunting, and then he just wants to be left alone. Maybe he's irritable because he hasn't found a female dragon to mate with in the past hundred years or so. Who knows? The dragon is a nuisance, and he's terrifying, like most of the primal forces in nature, and so he has to die.

Every morning, unless the temperature is lower than ten degrees below zero, I take the same two-mile walk with the dogs. We go down to the river and then past Bernard Tullar's farm and back up the hill to our own road and then home. The landscape of our upper Connecticut River Valley is very like the west country of England and Wales—all sharp little grassy hills and wooded valleys and rocky fields. One misty morning in March, when I was taking this walk and thinking about what the dragon was thinking, I heard him coming towards me, across Bernard's cow pasture. I heard him first, like the sound of distant thunder, and then I saw him—I saw the huge shape of the dragon appear on the crest of the hill. And before I even had the chance to be frightened, he was gone.

A few days later, I got to the page where George kills the dragon. As I usually do, I read the text on that page over again for the thirty-seventh time, and then I read it five more times, just to make sure I'd got it right. And then I realized I couldn't do it. I often say "I can't do it" when all I really mean is that this is going to be very difficult. But this was different. How on earth was I going to show George—somehow having got between the dragon's huge jaws, stabbing his sword up through the roof of the monster's mouth and piercing his brain? Do you know what this would *look* like, *really?* Can you imagine the blood, the ghastliness, the *violence* of that scene? You think the carving on the witches' table was bad? I was horrified at the thought of what I had to do, and worse than that, I was stymied. I paced the floor for an hour, and then I made a desperate, unprecedented decision. I called Margaret Hodges. This was the only time in my entire professional career when I knew I was truly beaten—I had to call the author to ask what I should do. "Margaret, I wonder if you can help me. I'm just about to start on the spread where George kills the dragon, and I can't do it. I mean, I can't draw it. The whole thing is physically impossible, and, besides that, it's disgusting and gross."

"Oh, dear," said Margaret, "I do see what you mean! Well, Trina, why don't you just forget about all that and draw the scene *after* George has killed the dragon. That will be just as dramatic, and maybe it is the best solution."

I love you, Margaret Hodges. You're not just a vivid imagination—you're clever as well! It took me nine months to complete the illustrations for *Saint George and the Dragon.* I learned a lot during those months. I learned about herb-lore and ancient roses and wild flowers, when I decided to decorate my borders with whatever grew in the fields and hedgerows of fourth-century England. I learned that the Romans named England "Alba," for the many wild white roses that grew there. I learned that the ancient Celts and Britons were terrific weavers and dyers and metal-smiths. I learned that the richest and most valued color in those days was red—so I gave my angels red wings. I learned a lot about lizards and dinosaurs and other strange and wonderful reptiles. I leaned about pre-Norman conquest sailing craft and pre-Arthurian armor and weapons. I learned that Winston Churchill wrote the best stuff about prehistoric England and that Arthur Rackham drew the best dragons in the world.

I learned that I could give everything I have—all of whatever talent and skill and craft and thought and love and guts and vision I possess to yet another picture book. And that when it was all finished and done with, it still wasn't good enough. I wish I could have done it better. I wish I could have made you *see* the dragon the way I saw him that morning on the hillside. I can see the fairies, but I still haven't learned how to draw them the way they really are. Not yet. Maybe next time. But now it's time to stop and time to say thank you.

Thank you, Mimi, for giving me my first fairy tales and for allowing me to believe in them.

Thank you, Helen Jones. I wish you were here.

Thank you, dear Barbara, for putting up with me through *Saint George,* and all the other books, too. And for taking all those beautiful slides of my pictures.

Thank you, Patricia McMahon, for keeping the dragons at bay.

Thank you, Karen Klockner, for being wise and understanding and sensible and courageous.

Thank you, Bob Lowe, for being there when I needed you, during the work on this book and the seventeen others that came before it. It's been a long time, and it seems that we're both good survivors.

Thank you, Margaret Hodges, for giving me a story so good that even after I'd read the same paragraph four hundred times in a row, the words shone just as pure and clean as if they'd been written with air and fire and stone.

And thank you, librarians and members of the American Library Association for awarding the Caldecott Medal to *Saint George and the Dragon.* You couldn't have given me a nicer surprise.

GENERAL COMMENTARY

Michael Patrick Hearn

SOURCE: "The 'Ubiquitous' Trina Schart Hyman," in *American Artist,* Vol. 43, No. 442, May, 1979, pp. 36-43, 96-7.

Howard Pyle, N.C. Wyeth, and Arthur Rackham were all great storytellers. The classic illustrators depicted primarily the drama within the texts they embellished. Within this tradition works Trina Schart Hyman, one of the most admired and controversial of American picture book artists. She has admitted, "As an artist and an illustrator, I would like to be able to draw heroes, villains, beautiful women, plucky children, noble steeds, primeval forests, weather, sunlight, stars. Everything!" As one of the most prolific of contemporary illustrators, she has been called on to draw nearly every subject. Her seemingly inexhaustible productivity has inspired at least one reviewer to call her "that ubiquitous Trina Schart Hyman." Yet her apparently unlimited dexterity does not suggest any carelessness on her part. Her *Snow White* and *The Sleeping Beauty* exemplify current pictorial storytelling at its finest.

Her technical virtuosity did not spring forth suddenly, like Athena from the head of Zeus. Her craft was mastered over many years of study and hard work. As a child growing up in Wyncote, Pennsylvania, Diane Katrina Schart enjoyed the pictures of Jessie Willcox Smith and Fritz Kredel and at twelve thought of being an illustrator like them. While in high school, where she illustrated her class yearbook and other such ephemera, she took Saturday morning drawing classes in Philadelphia. She eventually studied under Henry C. Pitz, the great defender of the Brandywine tradition in American popular art. This celebrated artist-author introduced his students to the master illustrators of the past, to Rackham, Dulac, Pyle, and Wyeth. . . .

Her strongest supporter [in the publishing world] was Helen Jones of Little, Brown, the editor who had worked with Robert Lawson on *Ben and Me* and most of his other books for children. As Hyman now acknowledges, it was Ms. Jones "who *really* taught me most of what I know about children's books." Much of her training also relied on unorthodox experimentation. Once while working on the overlays for a three-color preseparated picture book, Hyman had trouble making the ink stick to the acetate. By accident she dipped her brush in some gin, and the color miraculously affixed to the slick surface. "I used a half bottle of gin on that book," she explains. The only question the art director had was, "Why do the drawings smell like a martini?"

Hyman supplemented her income from books by submitting illustrations to various textbook companies. This work was often parochial and generally uninspired (she drew her first *Snow White* for one of these anthologies, and "it was pretty bad, too"). Despite rigid editorial control, this experience proved to be valuable professional training. She was given everything to draw, from tractors to fairy princesses, and this "bread and butter" work came in handy now that she had a daughter to support. Her marriage had failed (she was divorced in 1967), and she and Katrin retired to New Hampshire. Once she moved to the country, she started getting frequent calls from publishers. One prominent editor who had said six years before, "Come back when you know how to draw," now told her, "I'm very familiar with your work. Why didn't you show me your drawings before?" Hyman did not bother to keep in touch with that editor.

Although she now illustrated as many as ten books a year. Hyman did not receive wide recognition for her art until the publication of her edition of Howard Pyle's fairy tale *King Stork.* This picture book was a love letter to the "Grand Old Man" of American book illustration. "I've decided that my most favorite book is Howard Pyle's *The Wonder Clock* [from which *King Stork* was taken]," the artist recently explained, "because it has everything: good stories, amusing poems, a solid design, lively decoration, beautiful drawing, and a masterful blend of fantasy and reality. . . . It satisfies my soul." She also recognized the latent eroticism in Pyle's classic tale which did not amuse all children's book specialists. The revealing decolletage of the beautiful, evil princess irritated those who felt it inappropriate. Others took offense that a young artist should dare to reillustrate the great Howard Pyle, and they also objected to a detail on the witch's carved dining table. Concerned with a recent Supreme Court ruling on obscenity, several librarians wrote Hyman asking why she included a couple embracing amorously on this piece of furniture. Hyman replied that it would have been inappropriate for so powerful a sorceress "to sit down at a pristine, formica-covered, Danish modern table, every night!" She intended the carving to show the procession of Death to Life, Life to Death. "I chose a skeleton as a symbol of Death, and an embracing couple as a symbol of Life," she further explained. "If the embrace is a carnal one, that is because carnal love is the root of all Life. . . . And if you think *that* side of the table is shocking, you should be glad you can't see the other side, where the carvings symbolize War and Taxes!" Her critics were charmed by her reply, and one asked if she might one day be blessed with seeing the other side of the infamous table.

Her reputation as "a daring, 'naughty,' deliberately trouble-making illustrator" did not end with *King Stork.* Recently she instigated a furor by putting the name of an irresponsible reviewing service on a tombstone with the legend "A Nasty Soul Is Its Own Reward." This notation was only an inconspicuous detail in a graveyard scene, but it did not pass the intrepid eye of at least one reviewer who wrote a vehement editorial in a library journal on this illustrator's lack of professionalism. The illustrator was applauded by her fellow artists because they, too, had been the defenseless targets of unsympathetic "critics." "I always work for kids first," she has said. "I care about their feelings and their opinions far more than I care about the opinions of grown-ups, who so often distort the clearest and most innocent of images with their clouded and suspicious eyes." Nonetheless, her editors now thoroughly scrutinize every one of her designs. . . .

[Although she is the art director for *Cricket*] Trina Schart Hyman's principal occupation remains children's book illustration. The popularity of *King Stork* afforded her the luxury of her first major full-color picture book, *Snow White.* She had grown weary of separating all her color work, and she wanted to try a book fully executed in the more direct method of ink with acrylic washes. Choosing *Snow White* as her subject was risky. Nancy Ekholm Burkert's cool, elegant interpretation of the classic tale had recently appeared, and Maurice Sendak intended to include Snow White and her wicked stepmother in his collection *The Juniper Tree and Other Tales from Grimm.* Hyman was not discouraged by the competition; she had waited 15 years to attempt such a picture book and she was certain she could breathe new life into the old standard. She turned not to Walt Disney, but back to the original version, recently translated by Paul Heins, then editor of *The Horn Book Magazine.* She was not afraid, even if Hollywood had been, to show her heroine strangled by the witch's corset and drugged by the enchanted comb. Her moving *Snow White* revealed the darker side of fairy tale.

She followed this popular book with a lighter, more energetic sequel, *The Sleeping Beauty.* In the new book she boldly retold this story herself. She had both written and illustrated only one other book, the holiday fable *How Six Found Christmas.* Although her setting for *The Sleeping Beauty* is the French court, she chose for her story not the classic original by Charles Perrault with its anti-climactic cannibalism but the later more refined version by the Brothers Grimm.

All the vivid action of the story is apparent in her rough pencil "dummy," in which she worked out each scene as it would appear in the finished book. Except for this mock-up, she rarely bothers with preliminary drawings. She works directly on her illustration board in pencil, then reworks the design in ink, and if it is for a full-color picture book, it is finished in acrylic. For *The Sleeping Beauty,* she altered her technique slightly by replacing lamp black with sepia ink and by lightening her color. "It was appropriate in *Snow White* to be heavy and psychologically dark and deep," Hyman explains. "This is, appropriately, a lighter kind of story, and although I'd never try to stiffle my own tendencies to human insight and drama, I'd like this book to be less 'heavy' than *Snow White,* and more fun, humanistic, and romantic. Warmer, I guess." Her purpose was to have the pictures "be like a kind of dream that's remembered sometimes at good moments."

Once Hyman had set the mood she proceeded to the cast. She is one of a few contemporary illustrators who have mastered the art of sustaining character throughout a story. She treats each principal with a psychological depth rare in children's book illustration. Of the King she wrote: "One of those powerful, shrewd, but emotionally unstable types . . . who is at his best on the battlefield and during the hunt, and at his worst in subtle situations. He is a bearish bull of a man, great at drinking parties, with a lion's mane of red hair." Of the Queen: "Equally as powerful as the King, only in a different way—she *had* to be powerful to live with this guy all this time and still hold her own. She's got your basic inner strength, and she's stubborn and subtle." Of the Princess: "Her beauty is not so much a question of classic bone-structure, it's more sheer health, energy, and intelligence. This is just as Briar Rose should be. . . . After all, she *is* partly her father's daughter." Careful not to betray her characters by careless history, Hyman does considerable research to authenticate her settings. Realizing that royalty in the 15th century were often illiterate, she has a monk write the invitations to the baby's christening. As a full century passes in the course of the story, her prince is properly dressed in the height of fashion at the 16th-century French court. Her accuracy is even evident in her horses: shaggy, small-hooved ponies, as used in the country, are the mounts for the Sleeping Beauty's court, an enormous, heavy-footed war steed for the prince.

Technically she does not employ models, but Hyman often relies on her family and friends for prototypes of her characters. Her daughter Katrin was the original for Snow White, and another artist, Nancie West Swanberg, inspired the wicked step-mother. The artist herself and even her former husband have made their appearance, as two of the seven dwarfs. The Sleeping Beauty herself was modeled on a friend of Katrin's who died in a car accident while the book was in production. *The Sleeping Beauty* is dedicated to her memory.

Perhaps Hyman's greatest strength as an artist lies in her drama. Too few illustrators have a sense of tension; too many picture books rely on static decoration which may appeal to an adult's sensibilities but which rarely arrest a child's attention. What this artist admires in the illustrations of N.C. Wyeth also applies to her own work. A picture should deal "with romance and drama, good and evil, adventure and conflict—and most of all with making someone want to know the story. . . . Illustration should transport you, grab you, take your mind away and make you use your imagination. It should enchant you and put you in some other place and time." Clearly her *Sleeping Beauty* succeeds in all these desires. The book is beautifully paced; even the front matter reflects the story's theme by showing the castle passing through the four seasons. Hyman depicts nearly everything suggested by the text, from the powerfully delineated burning of the spinning wheels to the dormant flies clustered on the sleeping cook's apron. She shows no mercy in her terrifying wall of thorns, entwined with the bodies of dead and dying suitors. Her great technical virtuosity would mean nothing if she did not inspire the reader to ask, "What is happening? What happened before, to make this happen now? And what will happen afterward?"

The popularity of *Snow White* and *The Sleeping Beauty* has allowed her to choose only those manuscripts that most appeal to her. Now accepting fewer assignments, she is able to devote more time to an individual title. She is presently writing and illustrating a picture book based upon her life in New Hampshire, and she has begun work on a new edition of Hans Christian Andersen's *The Snow Queen,* the one story above all others she has wanted to illustrate. Certainly no fairy tale is more suited to her special talents than Gerda's search for her friend Kay in the realms of the ice maiden. Undoubtedly *The Snow Queen* will continue the grand tradition of illustration she has already carried on in her *Snow White* and *The Sleeping Beauty*.

Jill P. May

SOURCE: "Illustration as Interpretation: Trina Hyman's Folk Tales," in *Children's Literature Association Quarterly,* Vol. 10, No. 3, Fall, 1985, pp. 127-31.

As a child, Trina Schart Hyman lived in the world of fairies and witches, princesses and queens. In her autobiography [*Self-Portrait*], she speaks of her early play with her younger sister: "Mostly we loved fairies. They were more real to us than anything we could really see." Hyman's comment is reminiscent of Sigmund Freud's idea [stated in *Delusion and Dream*] that at play the child "behaves like an imaginative writer, in that he creates a world of his own or, more truly, he arranges the things of his world and orders it in a new way that pleases him better . . . [H]e takes his play very seriously and expends a great deal of emotion on it."

In her work as an illustrator, Hyman is not afraid to reach back into such childhood fantasies, in order to create a romantic world of happily-ever-after stories; nor is she afraid to evoke and reinterpret the work of other illustrators who have influenced her, or to use the faces of friends and family members in her pictures. In a sense her pictures order the old tales she illustrates in a new way. Her art is an eclectic, emotional medium that creates a new understanding of the real world by reinterpreting the elements of old world folklife. Particularly in her visual interpretations of folk tales, Hyman creates her own personal drama.

Hyman's versions of the Grimm tales can evoke a deep response from the viewer because her personal interpretations of them unveil the universal conflicts of fidelity, trust, envy, and pride the tales contain; indirectly, they all deal with the Oedipal struggles lodged in the family. She interprets two of the tales, *Snow White* and *Rapunzel,* in Freudian terms; and her *Snow White* also contains Christian symbols which indirectly bring new significance to the tale's early roots. A third tale, *Little Red Riding Hood,* is Hyman's return journey to her own early fantasy world. These three books, when viewed as a progressive journey by the artist back to her own childhood world of play, reveal much about the artist and her interpretative skills.

Snow White the first of Hyman's versions of fairy tales, was created while Hyman and her daughter were living with the artist Nancie West Swanberg and Nancie's twin daughters. Nancie became the model for the queen; Katrin, Trina's daughter, became the young princess. Hyman's steady, helpful, protective neighbor Hugh made his first appearance in this story; he was the huntsman. The dwarves were modelled on people who had influenced Hyman, including Hyman's father, Katrin's father, Paul Heins, Konrad Lorenz (and even Hyman herself). She once confessed, "My *Snow White* . . . is a very symbolic and personal story, and I really did put my own heart into those pictures." The need to include so much of her personal life in her art is closely related to Freud's explanation [stated in *Delusion and Dream*] of dream as being "rarely the representation—one might say, the staging—of a single thought, but generally of a number of them, a web of thoughts." At times however, Hyman's book contains material that seems to deal less with her own adult world than with the adolescent world of her daughter, Katrin, who was twelve years old when Hyman created *Snow White*. Perhaps more important, it addresses the real possibility that a child without familial protection will be vulnerable to the adults around her.

Hyman has depicted Snow White's stepmother, the new queen, as a striking beauty with calm, cold eyes. While the queen is beautiful in outward appearance, there is nothing in Hyman's presentation of her to suggest that she is concerned about any other human being alive. Her magical mirror is appropriately surrounded with demonic images who solemnly leer at her. By the second illustration, Hyman makes it clear that this vain woman's concern is that her beauty will wane while that of her stepdaughter blossoms. When the stepmother is next pictured, she is disguising herself as an old peddler in front of her magic mirror. Her eyes are sadly troubled; the demonic images framing her mirror look on in surprise, or with apparent foreknowledge of her demise. From this point on, the stepmother is shown wearing masks of either age and poverty or agony and despair. As her obsession with her failing beauty increases, the gilded demonic images which encircle her mirror grow more grotesque. When she is last pictured, she is in her finest clothing. Yet, though she has contrived to look young and beautiful, her glacial stare and facial distortion clearly show that the queen's obsessions for youth and beauty, for life in this sphere, have driven her to insanity. Her rage against youth and death has caused her destruction. The potency of this psychological message of the tale is further demonstrated in the last illustration. The mirror is now peacefully reflecting the new queen. Joining the young queen's image are two wizened figures, one a man and one a woman, and the faces of future childen. At the bottom of the mirror Hyman has placed outstretched hands in the sacrificial position reminiscent of Christ's suffering on the cross. Combined, the images point to the salvation of the innocent and the rebirth of the virtuous.

In fact, Hyman's illustrations imply that this story deals

with the struggles between superstition and Christianity throughout. In the end, Hyman shows that the powers of the occult die in favor of Christianity. The story of Christian struggle against evil powers begins when the first queen, a serene dark-haired beauty, is pictured gazing outward, towards nature and God's world. There are two things on the stool before her: books, and a vase holding holly. Since books were usually prepared by religious men, there is little doubt that they would contain Christian sentiments. Further, the queen has wished for a child "as white as snow, as red as blood, and as dark as ebony." The traditional Christmas carol "The Holly and the Ivy" tells us that the holly's flower is white, its berry is "as red as any blood" and that the leaves are "as sharp as any thorn," but it also reassures us that "Of all the trees within the wood, the holly bears the crown." Thus, in Hyman's first illustration for *Snow White,* we see visual reference to God's saving power, to the importance of the sacrifice of human innocence in God's overall scheme, and to the idea that a girl child could be born as fair and as pure as the Christ Child who saved all Christians. The only clearly defined visual image accompanying the text on one side of this double page spread is a three part triptych consisting of the mother Mary and her child surrounded by two saints. Hyman again clearly alludes to the similarities between *Snow White* and the Christmas story.

Hyman's young princess is beautiful, and she is also naive and trusting. Like Eve in the garden of Eden, she has no real understanding of evil or sin. She is humankind regenerated, oblivious of original sin. After each of her three trials against evil, she regains her youth and her innocence. It is the third trial, that of the apple, which assures Snow White's own survival against paganism and demonstrates her significance as a woman able to free herself from the curse of the earlier apple. In this way, Hyman's interpretation shows that there is a need among women to find a savior who is female, and who will break the association with evil women inherit from the Old Testament story of Eve.

Like the serpent in the garden, the witch offers Snow White the apple of knowledge. Snow White accepts the red half, symbolic of death, and she bites into it. Unlike Eve, however, she does not swallow the fruit, and thus does not truly die; Paul Heins's translation for Hyman's illustrated version reads, "Because of the jolting, the piece of poisoned apple was dislodged from her throat. And not long after, she opened her eyes, raised the lid of the coffin, sat up, and was alive again." Unlike Adam, furthermore, Hyman's prince is not greeted by a worldly woman. Snow White is shown gazing into the eyes of the prince with a look of unequivocal innocence. Her recovery is greeted with surprise, much as a miracle would be, by the prince's servants; but the young man is shown kneeling at the young woman's side with a look of concern and endearment. The coffin in which Snow White is seated contains a purple cushion; the Christian color of salvation clearly suggests that she transcends the world of the dead.

Hyman's story has concentrated upon the conflict between good and evil, upon the struggle between folklife and religion. Her story is only indirectly concerned with the young prince and his relationship with his new bride. The love story is depicted in only two scenes, and both of these occur before the princess returns to the ordered world found within castle walls. Her prince, like those found on the pages of Arthurian legend, wanders into the forest and seeks out adventure. Much like any knight-errant on a quest, he is willing to marry his soul to a vision, to a woman with whom he is unable to physically relate, in trade for an idealistic dream of perfection. This interpretation corresponds to the early French idea of courtly love, as expressed in Christine de Pisan's argument that ". . . a goodly number [of knights] have loved faithfully and wholly who never lay with [their ladies], nor ever deceived or were deceived; and whose principal purpose in loving was to render their conduct more worthy." Like the early tales of chivalry, Hyman's interpretation conveys the idea that the adventure is more noteworthy than the adventurer.

The second folktale Hyman illustrated, *The Sleeping Beauty,* is much less personal than *Snow White* or the books that come later. The young woman she modeled Sleeping Beauty after was Katrin's best friend, and her interpretation of the story does not focus on familial concerns of loyalty or independence. Instead of concentrating upon either the parents' fears and their need to protect their daughter, or on the young girl's struggle to free herself from constant parental supervision, Hyman focused upon the questing prince. His story lacks the personal intensity of *Snow White.* Much of the time he is shown wandering; his face is rarely in view. The entire book seems to be a transitional one. The book is taller and thinner than her other three folktales; the fact that Hyman chose not to give the artwork similar dimensions to *Snow White* indicates that she did not link this book to her larger scheme of visual interpretation.

When Trina Hyman visited Purdue University in 1979, she expressed concern about the traditional placement of text over illustration. Her favorite book artist was Howard Pyle, who separated pictures from text while maintaining a unity of design and story. Hyman acknowledged, however, that his books contained lengthy stories and were decorated rather than retold. She admitted that she liked the idea of Nancy Ekholm Burkert's complete separation of text and illustration in her version of *Snow White* because it appealed to the graphic artist's desire to be considered a creator of pictorial works of art; but she felt that the separation from text was too stark and that Burkert's interpretation of the story would be lost. Concerning the use of the castle arches around the text of her *Sleeping Beauty* she commented, "It works better than *Snow White*'s textual layout, I suppose, but it's not right." Hyman was trying to find a format which would help her in the telling of the story. She wanted text, story, and design to vigorously reinforce each other and combine to create a total graphic effect.

By the time Hyman was ready to illustrate *Rapunzel* she

had discovered a graphic artist whose total book design fitted her needs. The Russian illustrator of folktales Bilibin did not interpret texts, but he did extend the folk roots of the tales through textual and illustration borders. Folk art motifs, familiar Russian floral and animal life, and the ideals of peasant life were reflected in his stylistic borders. Concerning her discovery of Bilibin, Hyman wrote, "It was shortly after I was at Purdue, I think— I picked up a whole series of the paperback versions printed in Russia. I couldn't wait to try out my own version of his absolutely splendid disregard for 'clean design', and his exquisite color. . . ." Although Bilibin's design cannot be termed clean, it can be described as complete. Furthermore, his use of folk design and of flora in the borders reinforces the folkloric mood of the stories.

Hyman's *Rapunzel* contains all the graphic richness found in the patterned design of Bilibin. Her borders evoke something of faerie as well as down-to-earth reflections of nature. In addition, Hyman's borders do more than describe the scene; they are interpretative in quality, and they reflect the underlying meaning of the story. The husband and wife, for instance, are surrounded with folk print patterns which depict their world as bright, cluttered, and cheery. By contrast the borders surrounding the scenes while Rapunzel is in the tower hint at deeper emotions. The first scene between Rapunzel and the prince is bordered with bricks and brass hinges, and suggests that the girl is securely isolated from the world. Once the prince becomes a steady visitor to the tower, the borders again reflect the early folk patterns, only this time the motif is hearts and flowers—love in bloom— and the colors are in the delicate life-giving ones of spring: yellows, greens, and pinks. When the witch discovers Rapunzel's secret, the borders become dark, devoid of reflection, binding, until the final scene, which shows the prince and Rapunzel returning to his home with their two children. Once again the borders are those used in the first scenes of Rapunzel's parents, and once again an orderly pattern surrounds a highly romantic scene. In Rapunzel, Hyman's format had jelled, and she obviously was aware of it. Both *Rapunzel* and *Little Red Riding Hood* are similar in size to *Snow White.*

Rapunzel also marks Hyman's return to the expression of her own life experiences. By now Katrin was a young woman, ready to leave home. Hyman was facing a personal conflict much like the one faced by the witch in *Rapunzel:* a personal desire to hold onto her young daughter opposed to an overwhelming need to let go so that this young woman could determine her own happiness. Hyman has said that Rapunzel is no one she knows, yet there are strong facial and physical similarities between the dark-haired young heroine of *Snow White* and the blonde maiden in *Rapunzel,* and there are romantic similarities between Rapunzel's prince and Katrin's ice skating partner depicted in Hyman's *Self-Portrait.* Freud, discussing the interpretative qualities of "dream-work" [in *The Interpretation of Dreams*], notes: "These commonly reveal themselves as a complex of thoughts and memories of the most intricate possible construction. . . .

[A]ll these things are dream-material, not the representation of intellectual activity in the dream." And Hyman had earlier written, "When I am troubled, or unhappy, I go to my drawing board and try to work it off."

The story itself has some similarities to *Snow White.* It is the desire for forbidden food (in this case the rapunzel lettuce) which causes the woman's ill health. Unlike Snow White, Rapunzel's mother eats the lettuce; once she has gained knowledge of earthly sweetness, she loses sight of what is right, and will do anything to gain more. The lettuce causes the woman to lose her natural innocence. She will endure and suffer disgrace in order to satisfy her newly discovered physical pleasures. In the end, she faces pain through the birthing process much as Eve did, and she loses the seed of her sins, Rapunzel.

Rapunzel is not poorly treated by the witch. In fact, one of Hyman's most lush and peaceful scenes shows the young girl sitting at the feet of the old woman in an apple garden surrounded by brier roses, hollyhock, lilies, and birds. The young girl is leaning forward, intently listening to the older woman. Her face shines with love and trust. The old woman seems gentle in her regard for the girl. She returns the girl's stare with equal love. Nevertheless, this woman is fearful of the young girl's beauty, not out of a sense of jealousy toward the blossoming of womanhood, but because she fears losing Rapunzel to the world of mankind forever. Hyman does not concentrate upon the older woman's anxieties, however, and does not show the old woman's face again until she is seen with the prince in the tower. This time the witch displays the animalistic rage and power seen on the faces of mothers who wish to protect their young from the enemy. Yet the prince is not Rapunzel's enemy; he is her lover. And it is this very love which drives the witch to act against both man and woman. In her rage of jealousy she determines that if Rapunzel is not to be totally hers, she is not to be anyone's. Once again the Oedipal struggle is fully developed, and Hyman has shown it in its entirety. In the end the witch is depicted alone with her thoughts while the two young lovers are free to turn their backs on Rapunzel's filial devotion and to enter their own orderly world. Hyman's story begins with a man and a woman at peace with their lives and surrounded by nature, and it ends with another man and a woman entering that natural world together.

Rapunzel and the prince are visual representations of folkloric culture. The prince, Hyman wrote, was wearing a version of a Russian nobleman's hunting gear. Folklorists who study folk costume suggest that such attire is an outward badge of group identity, dictated by community tradition. Folklorist Don Yoder has further refined the theory [in *Folklore and Folklife*] stating that folklore costumes also show the individual's relationship to his culture, and that peasant costume reflects the fashions of the upperclass.

The young Rapunzel has loosely bound blonde hair tied

in ribbons. Her white and red checked apron is similar to her mother's, but her clothes in the early illustrations cannot be defined as cultural representations. Once locked into the tower, however, Rapunzel is more symbolically dressed. Her hair, now kept in one long braid, can be seen wrapped around her head in the fashion of Swiss or German maids. She continues to wear the checked apron, which now falls over a printed brown and gold skirt, and Hyman has added some Liechtenstein traits. Her blouse is pale, loosely bound and low cut. Tied over it is a red jerkin. While her hair is no longer entwined with red ribbons, her blouse is. When the prince first sees Rapunzel, she is barefoot (and soon she will also be pregnant). She is a gentle, earthy girl whose folk costume shows her peasant heritage. She wears her clothes much as one would wear a uniform. There is little change in her appearance from day to day. When she is discovered by her prince at the end of the tale, she is using her apron as a blanket for her two small children. As a girl of peasant stock, she demonstrates that her dress is not simply a reflection of traditional fashion but is utilitarian, and can be changed to fit a new status in the world. Thus, Hyman's Rapunzel has stepped out of the märchen and into the real world of the German peasant.

Rapunzel's prince is not dressed in typical European clothes. He does not, for example, wear a loosely fitting shirt and pants, sturdy socks, wooden shoes, or a weather-beaten work hat. A Cossack, the prince wears leather boots with engrained trim, a patterned tunic girded at the waist, and a fur-lined hat more fitting a huntsman in the mountain hills. His richly patterned and ornate armbands further define his costume. His pants are stylishly tucked into his boots, and his curly hair is carefully styled. The prince, in a painfully color-coordinated costume, is no lower class peasant. It is very clear that these two young people come from different cultures and different backgrounds.

It is while wandering "like a homeless beggar in the forest" and eating berries that the prince's cavalier attitude changes. Unable to see and unable to control his destiny, the prince must be saved by a virtuous damsel. When he finds Rapunzel, she restores his sight and his honor. Hyman shows that the prince is dependent upon the girl's redemption in her last full-page illustration. Ragged and weary, the prince is kneeling at the feet of his beloved. Only his boots remain intact. Yet, he clearly chooses not to step out of the artificial world of the costumed huntsman, and holds tightly to the threads of his past, unable to see another way. When Rapunzel restores his sight through her love, she frees him from this past. Now that he can see, he can be at peace with nature and return with her to his castle where he will resume his courtly life. Hyman's final scene of the prince and Rapunzel is misty and rosy. Ahead are the gentle sloping hills of civilization; behind are the barren forests of despair.

Hyman's *Little Red Riding Hood* represents the completion of a personal journey for her. She had freed herself from the burden of protecting Katrin by allowing her to seek her own goals. Now she could return to her own childhood and deal once more, and much more directly, with her own fantasy world. Her favorite book, she remembers in *Self-Portrait*, was *Little Red Riding Hood*, and her favorite game was playing Little Red Riding Hood. At the end of each day her father returned home to become the huntsman. The cover jacket of her autobiography further demonstrates that with *Little Red Riding Hood* Hyman has returned home to her Pennsylvania childhood. On the front of the dust jacket the adult artist is seen. As the eye moves left to the back cover one sees a white or blank space: it works as a wall would, separating the present from the past. Red Riding Hood peers timidly from behind that wall, accompanied by a large dog named Sam. It is significant that the story in *Little Red Riding Hood* is both retold and illustrated by Hyman. As she explains, "This is *my* story, you see." Once more, a comment by Freud [in *Delusion and Dream*] throws light on Hyman's work; concerning childhood fantasies, he wrote, "In some people a recollection of their favorite fairy tales takes the place of the memories of their own childhood: they have made the fairy tales into screen-memories."

The format of *Little Red Riding Hood* is similar to *Rapunzel*. The borders reflect motifs of Pennsylvania Dutch folk art, common garden plants and insects, and quaint wallpaper. The mood in the borders is both pleasant and kitschy; it is wholesomely reassuring. Hyman's early childhood backyard has been blown up to become a child's play world, a place of romantic adventure. Hyman herself describes the scene of the tale in her autobiography, when she calls her childhood home a place with "open grassy fields, some dense patches of woods, hidden rocky streams, and just a few old houses. . . ." However, this is a return visit to the childhood fantasies by an adult, and so the characters do not evolve from Hyman's childhood alone. The mother is Hyman's, as is the grandmother, although, the latter, Hyman admits, looks a lot like Hugh O'Donnell's wife. The hunts man is O'Donnell, Hyman's New Hampshire neighbor who had earlier appeared as the huntsman in *Snow White*. Thus, *Little Red Riding Hood* is also a tribute to Hyman's adult world in the New Hampshire woods.

Little Red Riding Hood again deals with the parent/child struggle. The child's struggle against her adoration and blind trust of her father is symbolized by Little Red Riding Hood's encounter with the symbolic wolf. The replacement of trust in the father to trust in a new male protector is clearly shown with the hunter's arrival. Hyman's wolf is a marvelous character. He is majestic in his stature. In the first two full-page scenes when he meets Little Red Riding Hood he is as tall as she, and he is definitely a beast. Yet, though his paws are large, his expression seems kind and his stance implies protectiveness. Little Red Riding Hood's face is first filled with anxiety, but in the second scene she seems to greet the wolf's friendship with guarded trust. There is something exciting about this overpowering beast, with his protective male aura that causes the little heroine to throw caution to the wind and embrace the unknown. In the final scene of this initial encounter, Little Red Riding Hood disregards her mother's advice in favor of the wolf's suggestion to relax and enjoy nature. The wolf is not in the large illustration, but he runs on in the right hand border, drawing his drama towards grandmother's house.

The wolf can't be bothered with charming the grandmother or with playing games. We see him standing upright at the door, taller than a wolf, and posed more like a human. Describing his encounter with grandmother, Hyman simply writes, "He ran straight to the bed, and without even saying a good-morning, he ate up the poor old grandmother in one gulp." Then, however, he dresses in disguise so that he can play psychological games with Red Riding Hood.

When Red Riding Hood enters grandmother's cottage, she is apprehensive, and she is even more uncertain when she stands next to grandmother's bed. Obviously she doesn't recognize the wolf, but she doesn't see her grandmother either. In the final of the three scenes depicting the second encounter with the wolf, Red Riding Hood has her face turned away from the viewer once again, but her stance leaves no doubt about her terror and disillusionment. The wolf takes on a most animalistic expression as he springs from the bed to eat up poor Little Red Riding Hood. He is all animal now, no longer covering up his deceitful scheme. His only interest in Little Red Riding Hood is in consuming her. Much like a cat with its prey, he has had the fun of playing with his catch, and now he wants only his just dessert. Later, however, when the huntsman finds him fast asleep, his fat belly protrudes and his paws curl comically out of his nightie.

The huntsman is also depicted in three full page scenes. When first seen, his face is turned towards grandmother's house. His weapons are clearly depicted; on his shoulder he carries a gun, and strapped to his belt is a hunting knife. He makes no pretense of being a civilized man. Rather, he look like a rugged frontiersman who thinks of the woods as his own uncivilized home. In the next scene he stands over the wolf, his face full of anger and suspicion. Finally, we see him holding Little Red Riding Hood, and shaking grandmother's hand. His expression is commonplace. He seems neither surprised at the adventure's outcome nor overly happy to be a hero. Red Riding Hood leans on the huntsman's shoulder. Her expression is full of the terrifying knowledge that she has been tricked by false flattery. Her trust and admiration go to the hunter, a simple forthright man.

In the end, Little Red Riding Hood stays to celebrate with her grandmother and then returns home, walking through the woods alone. She is aware of the deceitful nature of others and capable of handing new encounters on her own.

Freud called storytellers "valuable allies," worthy of respect. He comments [in *Delusion and Dream*], "In psychological insights, indeed, they are far ahead of us ordinary people, because they draw from the sources that have not been made accessible to science. . . . What is called chance by the outside world resolves itself, as we know it, into laws; also, what we call arbitrariness in psychic life is based on laws that are present but dimly surmised." Trina Hyman's story interpretations reflect such laws. Of her own life Hyman writes [in *Self-Portrait*], "Everything that I have told you is, of course, a fairy tale. Life is magical, after all. Nothing is safe and everything changes." Hyman's own interpretations of oral literature draw upon her own memories and her own fantasies to show that fairy tales can be as magical (and as meaningful) as life itself.

TITLE COMMENTARY

📖   ***ALL IN FREE BUT JANEY*** **(written by Elizabeth Johnson, 1968)**

Kirkus Reviews

SOURCE: A review of *All in Free but Janey*, in *Kirkus Reviews*, Vol. XXXVI, No. 14, July 15, 1968, p. 759.

"Once a little girl named Janey liked to play Hide and Seek. She was not very good at hiding and she was not very good at seeking. But she was very good at finding fleecy castles in the clouds and goblin faces in the dark." This, on the last page, precisely recapitulates the story and suggests why it will have little appeal for kids: nobody likes an all-time loser or a child who doesn't play the game. As drawn—light olive, blue, black— there are knights hiding in the clouds, gnomes to seek under the porch. They might be worth finding if it would get you anywhere.

Diane Farrell

SOURCE: A review of *All in Free but Janey,* in *The Horn Book Magazine*, Vol. XLIV, No. 5, October, 1968, pp. 553-54.

Author and artist have accomplished a rare and difficult feat—to give substance in words and pictures to a remembered experience of childhood in terms that today's children will appreciate and understand. Janey was a little girl who "liked to play Hide and Seek. She was not very good at hiding and she was not very good at seeking. But she was very good at finding fleecy castles in the clouds and goblin faces in the dark." The magic and mystery of Janey's inner world are unfolded in the illustrations. Gnomes and brownies troop under the front porch, and knights go riding across the sky. Lacy, delicate leaf prints are spattered over solid lines and color just as Janey's fantasies overlay the solid world of house and garden, tree and telegraph pole. Sharp eyes can discern the laughing faces of hiding children. Every imaginative child will sympathize with Janey; even the

From King Stork, *written by Howard Pyle. Illustrated by Trina Schart Hyman.*

matter-of-fact ones will enjoy her adventures. A distinguished book.

HOW SIX FOUND CHRISTMAS (1969)

Marilyn R. Singer

SOURCE: "Inside the Vacuum of Reverence," in *School Library Journal,* Vol. 16, No. 2, October, 1969, p. 168-71.

A subtle, entertaining statement of the foregoing can be found in Trina Schart Hyman's slim but meaningful book, *How Six Found Christmas.* A solitary little girl hears that there is such a thing as Christmas but doesn't know what that is. She goes into the Great Snow Forest to look for one, and along the way meets some birds and animals who join her in the search, each wanting to know Christmas in his own way: the cat by feel, the dog by smell, etc. They come across a beautiful glistening green bottle lying in the snow, and the girl feels that this must be it. She takes the bottle home, fills it with berries and pine, and because of its beauty, this is Christmas for her. The illustrations, in black, olive and red, depict a very appealing, wistful little girl. Her extremely poor, shabby clothes and home, however, produce a

rather morbid effect that is intrusive. Depicting the girl in this way seems to weaken the author's message—"Christmas is not only where you find it; it's what you make of it"—since such an impoverished character has little choice in the matter. The spare text uses accumulative repetition to build to the denouement. The writing itself has a quiet dignity that at times is poetic, almost biblical in tone.

Zena Sutherland

SOURCE: A review of *How Six Found Christmas,* in *Bulletin of the Center for Children's Books,* Vol. 23, No. 3, November, 1969, p. 47.

"Once upon a time there was a little girl who had never heard about Christmas and therefore did not know what it was," this brief tale begins. The child goes hunting for a Christmas; each of the five she meets (cat, dog, fox, hawk, and mockingbird) joins her, sharing her ignorance and her curiosity. They find a green bottle in the snow, and the little girl, who thinks it very beautiful, decides that this is a Christmas, so she takes it home and fills it with pine and berries. "And lo! It was Christmas!" the story ends. The illustrations are quite delightful, the characterful animals set against a series of lovely scenes of snowy woods. The story is weak: slight of plot, too sophisticated in dialogue for the read-aloud audience, and the ending—despite the alluring idea that a bit of beauty is Christmas—anticlimactic.

Ruth P. Bull

SOURCE: A review of *How Six Found Christmas,* in *Booklist,* Vol. 66, No. 7, December 1, 1969, p. 458.

A charming, short adventure tale for small children describes the quest of a little girl, a cat, dog, hawk, fox, and mockingbird who are unfamiliar with Christmas but curious to know what it is. When they come upon an old green bottle half buried in the snow, each of them, for different reasons, decides this gleaming object must be a Christmas and the little girl takes the bottle home and fills it with branches of red berries and pine. The story, appealingly illustrated in black, red, and green, which has a rather nebulous connection with traditional Christmas, is described by the author as "a little fable about the senses and about what is important to different people."

KING STORK (adapted from story by Howard Pyle, 1973)

Paul Heins

SOURCE: A review of *King Stork,* in *The Horn Book Magazine,* Vol. XLIX, No. 4, August, 1973, p. 373.

Choosing a storyteller's favorite from the twenty-four stories of *The Wonder Clock,* the artist pays homage to a great and famous illustrator. Originally illustrated with four black-and-white line drawings, the story has been transformed into a picture-story book in full color, consisting almost entirely of doublespreads with rectangular white inserts, which contain the judiciously displayed text. Never high-keyed, the color ranges from the pastel to the somber, with occasional chiaroscuro effects; the line drawings, which superbly characterize the attitudes and the motions of the human characters, are just as effective with the monstrous and the grotesque. More exuberant than Pyle's marvelously Durer-like drawings, the new pictures give the story a fresh twentieth-century flavor that is decidedly in keeping with the vigor of the text.

Margery Fisher

SOURCE: A review of *King Stork,* in *Growing Point,* Vol. 13, No. 9, April, 1975, p. 2613.

Howard Pyle's version, originally in *The Wonder Clock,* emphasises the romantic aspect of the Grimms' tale of the drummer who wins a witch princess and gains authority over her with the help of the King of the Storks, whom he has helped with the traditional generosity of a questing hero. The pictures echo the mood of the re-telling, with a renaissance setting and costume and with a great deal of decorative detail all carried out in a low-keyed range of colour; the sinister power of the princess is suggested by an emphatic use of darkness and shadow.

The Junior Bookshelf

SOURCE: A review of *King Stork,* in *The Junior Bookshelf,* Vol. 39, No. 3, June, 1975, pp. 173-74.

King Stork . . . is coloured by a slightly incongruous sophistication. Howard Pyle's story, which draws on a number of folk-tale originals and dovetails them in characteristic fashion, has disturbing undertones, and these are picked out in the new illustrations. These have a strength and a sensuality which may suit today's children, but perhaps not in nursery school! Here is an artist to watch, with some apprehension.

☐ *GREEDY MARIANI AND OTHER FOLK-TALES OF THE ANTILLES* (compiled by **Dorothy Sharp Carter, 1974)**

Booklist

SOURCE: A review of *Greedy Mariani and Other Folktales of the Antilles,* in *Booklist,* Vol. 70, No. 12, February 15, 1974, p. 654.

Twenty colorful and highly tellable folktales from the group of islands which include Jamaica, Haiti, Cuba, Puerto Rico, and the Dominican Republic. One finds among these stories a few familiar faces and variants of timeless themes—a wily Jamaican Annancy, a Montser-

rat Brer Rabbit, a classic fool named Juan Bobo, and the doctor who made a deal with Death, as also related in Asbjornsen's Norwegian tale "The boy with the beer keg." Less familiar stories include "How the moonfish came to be," which recounts the moon's irresponsible gambol in the Caribbean Sea, and the title story about a woman who, for sheer turpitude, deserves the fatal blow she receives from a Haitian-style zombie. Regardless of the reader's familiarity with various elements in the tales, he will find the writing always clever, quick-paced, and full of rich, ethnic flavor. Hyman's fine line drawings are evocative, humorous, and often helpfully literal.

Beryl Robinson

SOURCE: A review of *Greedy Mariani and Other Folktales of the Antilles,* in *The Horn Book Magazine,* Vol. L, No. 3, June, 1974, pp. 275-76.

The twenty tales in this entertaining collection of folklore from Haiti, Jamaica, Cuba, Puerto Rico, and islands of the Lesser Antilles were selected from a number of published sources and have been retold with flair. Many of the stories are variants of familiar themes that appear in other cultures; however, in form, setting, nuances of expression, and general style, they reflect the social and natural conditions of the islands. There are trickster tales, in which both Brer Rabbit and Annancy figure prominently; there are how and why stories; and tales sly with irony. While many are light-hearted, the title story is a grisly one, in which Mariani's insatiable desire for money leads her to a fatal confrontation with a zombie. Strong black-and-white illustrations do justice to the varying moods and settings of the tales.

Zena Sutherland

SOURCE: A review of *Greedy Mariani and Other Folktales of the Antilles,* in *Bulletin of the Center for Children's Books,* Vol. 28, No. 2, October, 1974, p. 25.

One of the most delightful collections of folktales to appear in a long, long time, these stories from the West Indies are illustrated with black and white drawings that are handsome and dramatic. The stories are entertaining in themselves, but they are made delectable by the adapter's style, which captures to perfection the conversational tone of the oral tradition, extracts every ounce of humor from the stories, and handles deftly the use of other languages in dialogue.

☐ *SNOW WHITE* (adapted from story by the **Grimm Brothers; translated from German by Paul Heins, 1974)**

Diane Farrell

SOURCE: A review of *Snow White,* in *The Horn Book Magazine,* Vol. LI, No. 1, February, 1975, pp. 36-37.

In this version of the familiar tale, the artist and translator have produced a true picture book. The language of the translation is idiomatic, direct, and graceful. And the pictures interpret the story as thoroughly and carefully as does the text, adding depth and dimension to the characters, which are visually memorable. Snow White is not cloyingly sweet nor is she a vapid beauty, but a lively, pretty child, who grows into a grave and beautiful woman. The dwarfs are sober and kind, misshapen but not grotesque; each is distinctively characterized. The prince has a rough strength and sensitivity. The Queen is no witch, but a flesh-and-blood woman, tormented by fear, jealousy, and rage; a beautiful woman, with features distorted by passions, whose evil uncomfortably recalls the darkness of our own natures.

The forces of darkness war visibly with the forces of light on pages where flickering candle flames strive to dispel the gloom of castle and cottage, and only chance rays of light penetrate the blackness of the forest. The illustrator's characteristic line is visible, but the vigorous imagination of the full-color double-spreads surpasses that of all her previous work. A myriad of small details enrich the drawings and enlarge upon the text: the modest garb of Snow White's mother contrasted with the clinging, décolleté gowns of the Queen; the mandrake roots hanging on the wall; the full moon that marks the Queen madness; the demons, framing the magic mirror, whose faces change with the Queen's moods; the dwarfs' furnishings—each wooden chair elaborately and individually carved, each goblet unique, each square of the quilt on Snow White's bed distinct.

This edition of *Snow White* will be loved by all who fall under the spell of its illustrations. They are passionate pictures which expose the basic human conflicts that give the tale its timeless, universal appeal.

📖 MAGIC IN THE MIST (written by Margaret M. Kimmel, 1975)

Anita Silvey

SOURCE: A review of *Magic in the Mist,* in *The Horn Book Magazine,* Vol. LI, No. 2, April, 1975, pp. 139-40.

"Once, when mountains sang and people listened, when Cader Idris was covered by snow and Plynlimon was hidden by fog, there lived in west Wales a boy named Thomas." Studying to be a wizard, young Thomas could not even keep his hut warm with his incantations, so he had few companions, "for even the creatures of the bog liked a bit of warmth." But with his solitary friend, a toad Jeremy who "had learned to listen to the wind," he discovered a dragon and, clutching it to him in order not to break the spell, returned home. In a special moment, the dragon kindled a fire, which warmed "the hut and those in it." The lilt and rhythm of the storytelling transform this sensitive and gentle tale into a beautiful picture-book text. In fact, it is rare in contemporary picture books to find an author so attuned to the sound of language, to phrasing, and to cadence. The illustrator accentuates the subtle mood of the text, giving a concrete feeling of place but never interfering with the sense of mystery and magic.

Mary Sue Horvat

SOURCE: A review of *Magic in the Mist,* in *School Library Journal,* Vol. 21, No. 8, April, 1975, p. 46.

A young boy living alone in a shack in Wales aspires to become a wizard. Thomas tries spell after spell in his cold, dark dwelling but cannot even light a fire. The boy and his frog companion go out in the marsh where they find magic—a baby dragon which breathes on Thomas' fire, warming the room and everyone's hearts. Hyman's pen-and-ink drawings effectively convey the chill starkness of marshlands and bogs, but since the pictures are difficult to see clearly from a distance this poetic story is best read to small groups.

📖 ON TO WIDECOMBE FAIR (written by Patricia Gauch, 1978)

Selma G. Lanes

SOURCE: A review of *On to Widecombe Fair,* in *The New York Times Book Review,* July 2, 1978, p. 11.

There is an infectious lilt to the language of Patricia Lee Gauch's story adaptation of an English folk song, and Trina Schart Hyman has given the loose-jointed tale a grandiose—probably Caldecott Medal-contending—graphic production. Sketching on location at Widecombe in Devon, the artist recreates the village with its overpowering church tower, the lay of the surrounding moors; and she provides loving, close-up vignettes of local flora, fauna and architecture. In addition, she presents us with a septet of memorable country bumpkins, each individualized with rafish charm. Yet the ultimate effect of her busy alternating full-color and black-and-white spreads is of a surfeit—overblown action and detail almost smothering the frail narrative. This latter concerns seven ne'er-do-wells who kill an old gray mare when, drunkenly, they all attempt to ride her at once, en route home from the Widecombe Fair. One wishes for slightly more story and less pictorial splendor, seductive as each separate bit of art work is.

Paul Heins

SOURCE: A review of *On to Widecombe Fair,* in *The Horn Book Magazine,* Vol. LV, No. 5, October, 1978, pp. 506-07.

The story, an expanded version of the English folk song printed at the end of the book, tells how seven men of Devon borrowed an old gray mare to carry them to Widecombe Fair. The mare died on the way home and returned to haunt the moor, bearing all of the burdensome riders on her back. In the song the narrative, told in the manner of a ballad and kept to a minimum, is overwhelmed by a rollicking refrain, which lists by name the seven riders of the old mare. From these verbal hints the illustrator has created a picture book that does full justice to her talents. Not only does she devise scenes that suggest the activity and the verve of Caldecott, but she also demonstrates her skill in depicting vitally individual comic characters. In pairs of pages that alternate full color and black and white, the pictures are at once exuberant and quietly evocative of the English landscape. As in Howard Pyle's work, the book is carefully designed to allow for a subtle interplay between pictures and text, and the composition of the pages allows for a variety of vignettes, which add to the aura of abundance and good humor generated by the book.

The Junior Bookshelf

SOURCE: A review of *On to Widecombe Fair,* in *The Junior Bookshelf,* Vol. 44, No. 1, February, 1980, p. 17.

Trina Schart Hyman has visited Widecombe to some effect, and she and the author make **On to Widecombe Fair** a real song of praise to Glorious Devon. The artist is as much at ease with the landscape as with the physical peculiarities of Tom Pearse and his disreputable neighbours. The book has been carefully designed, a little in the Caldecott tradition. The story is told in prose, and at the end comes the poem with its musical setting. A nice one this.

THE NIGHT JOURNEY (written by Kathryn Lasky, 1981)

Zena Sutherland

SOURCE: A review of *The Night Journey,* in *Bulletin of the Center for Children's Books,* Vol. 35, No. 4, December, 1981, p. 72.

Like Leonard Fisher's *A Russian Farewell* this describes the escape of a Jewish family from the persecutions and pogroms of Tsarist Russia. The story is illustrated with black and white drawings, strong in line and composition, realistic in approach, but romantic in feeling; it is told as a story-within-a-story, as thirteen-year-old Rachel learns, bit by bit, what her great-grandmother went through as a child. The two parts of the story are deftly woven together, with the contemporary scenes having enough humor and characterization to give them substance but not so much that they detract from the drama of Nana Sashie's exciting tale.

Ethel L. Heins

SOURCE: A review of *The Night Journey,* in *The Horn Book Magazine,* Vol. LVIII, No. 2, April, 1982, pp. 166-67.

In her first novel the author of *The Weaver's Gift* and other nonfiction tells a story that spans four generations of an American Jewish family and firmly links their Old World background with their New World lives. Bored by school, Rachel becomes interested in talking with her over-protected great-grandmother Nana Sashie. But her parents and her grandmother are all fearful that stirring ancient memories will distress the aged woman; so with youthful stubbornness and the instinctive understanding of the old that is often evident in the young, Rachel begins to pay clandestine visits to Nana Sashie's room. Gradually her reminiscences take shape, and her story unfolds—of czarist Russia with its horrifying pogroms and of her own family's daring hairsbreadth escape to freedom in 1900, following a plan the nine-year-old Sashie herself had devised. Comparatively little fiction about this phase of Jewish history has been written for children, and the author has dealt skillfully with her plot. But while she writes her factual books in a clean, straightforward manner, her fictional style wants chastening; for her writing is marred by an excess of emotion and by repetitious, ornate metaphors. The rather heavy black-and-white drawings convey a definite sense of time, place, mood, and characters.

SELF-PORTRAIT: TRINA SCHART HYMAN (1981)

Betsy Hearne

SOURCE: A review of *Self-Portrait: Trina Schart Hyman,* in *Booklist,* Vol. 78, No. 7, December 1, 1981, p. 498.

Hyman's imaginative blend of graphics and description joins pieces of her childhood, artistic development, and mature life with a vivid honesty that will liberate readers who have suffered through too many tedious adulatory juvenile biographies. On motherhood: "I had visions of a shy little pink-fairy daughter who would stand by my drawing board and keep me company. . . . I never saw a more stubborn, aggressive, opinionated baby in my whole life." The drawings show Hyman's characteristically skillful draftsmanship along with strong color, composition, and general book design. A warm, first-person narrative by someone adept at cross-hatching the real and the magical.

Marilyn Kaye

SOURCE: A review of *Self-Portrait: Trina Schart Hyman,* in *The New York Times Book Review,* January 31, 1982, p. 27.

This is the third in a series about children's book illustrators, who present reflections on their life and their art in words and pictures. In a conversational, yet frequently eloquent fashion, Trina Schart Hyman guides the reader through the various ups and downs of her personal and professional life. A speculative tone is evident throughout, generated by a thoughtful sensitivity that stops short of intensity or self-indulgence. More than the first two works in the series (by Margot Zemach and Erik Blegvad), Miss Hyman's self-portrait is personal and introspective.

While the illustrations have the distinctive, romantic quality present in much of Miss Hyman's work, particularly her fairy tales, the imaginative, intricate portraits of friends and settings display a vivid, robust richness that suggests real life rather than fantasy. There is an abundance of illustration here, and more text than in the two previous books. It is unfortunate that the standardized size of these editions results in a somewhat cramped and clutered format, which doesn't display Miss Hyman's artistry in the best possible light.

For the adult who is interested in the personal factors that affect and direct a creative spirit, there is much here. But it would be difficult to determine to what extent young readers will be able to draw connections between the artist's musings and her work. Yet even if read on a superficial level, this warmly intimate state-of-the-art book is satisfying, if for no other reason than that the talent and character of its subject-creator are attractive.

Gregory Maguire

SOURCE: A review of *Self-Portrait: Trina Schart Hyman,* in *The Horn Book Magazine,* Vol. LVIII, No. 1, February, 1982, p. 65.

The artist has produced an abbreviated autobiography, as rich, colorful, and distinctive as the drawings for which she is so well known. Telling the story of her development as an artist in ten chapters (with titles such as **"The Farm," "Little Red Riding Hood," "My Father and the Museum"**), she selects episodes and images which are small-scale and readily comprehensible; the casual prose style is similarly encouraging. If the book were not intended as an autobiography, the pages might have seemed overcrowded with text and art—there are fifty-three drawings—but a life story is necessarily full of constantly changing images, scenes, and characters, and the ultimate effect is festive. The artist has never used color more expressively; the brightly remembered fields of her early childhood in Pennsylvania and the pink chill of an autumn semester spent in drawing out of doors are rendered in evocative light acrylic washes overlaid with darker strokes of color pencil. Visual and textual references to the story of Red Riding Hood, an early favorite, crop up repeatedly and underscore the author's remark that "life is magical, after all."

Zena Sutherland

SOURCE: A review of *Self-Portrait: Trina Schart Hyman,* in *Bulletin of the Center for Children's Books,* Vol. 35, No. 7, March, 1982, p. 131.

Like the two earlier books in the publisher's series of autobiographies of artists, this is brief, candid, informal, and profusely illustrated by the author/artist's work. Hyman's sense of humor is as evident in her writing as in her drawing as she describes her childhood, her marriage while an art student, the year she and her husband spent in Sweden, where she had her first commission: illustrating a children's book at the behest of editor Astrid Lindgren. Hyman returned to the United States where she had a daughter, moved from Boston to New York, was divorced, and moved to the New Hampshire countryside where she still lives. Interspersed throughout the personal material are facts about books and other assignments on which Trina Hyman worked. A lively and informative book, this should interest fans of all ages.

RAPUNZEL **(retold by Barbara Rogasky from story by the Grimm Brothers, 1982)**

Patricia Dooley

SOURCE: A review of *Rapunzel,* in *School Library Journal,* Vol. 28, No. 9, May, 1982, p. 62.

This faithful but lively retelling offers answers to some questions begged by the original: How did Rapunzel first get into the doorless tower? (It *has* a door, later sealed up by the witch.) How does the witch get herself and Rapunzel out of the tower after she has cut off the girl's hair? (She uses the ladder Rapunzel has secretly been making.) How does Rapunzel happen to bear the Prince twins before they get back to civilization? (A neat sidestep explains, "by that time, they had married.") Some of Hyman's familiar specialities—a dark forest, abundant flowing tresses (even more abundant than usual, given the story), a strong- and competent-looking Prince—appear again to advantage. This Rapunzel is born to a peasant family, and there is a pleasantly cluttered cottage interior; the garden of the witch is a lovely flower-bright place, and the witch is a gaunt but human old woman. Most engaging of all are the lovely borders and vignettes on every page, filled with fruits, flowers, small landscapes and decorative patterns. The highly organized layout and borders, attractive in themselves, enhance Hyman's art by imposing a kind of discipline on her romantic style: the straight lines and regular patterns set off the curves and flowing lines alongside them.

Zena Sutherland

SOURCE: A review of *Rapunzel,* in *Bulletin of the Center for Children's Books,* Vol. 35, No. 11, July-August, 1982, pp. 206-07.

Framed in borders that have delicate floral or geometric patterns, Hyman's pictures are distinctive for their composition, draughtsmanship, restrained use of color, and fidelity of detail. Romantic and often mysterious, they are most appropriate for the familiar folktale about the beautiful girl whose lover climbs her rope of golden hair and whose cruel treatment by a possessive witch ends when Rapunzel, her prince, and their infant twins are united. The style of the adaptation is undistinguished but adequate.

Kenneth Marantz

SOURCE: A review of *Rapunzel,* in *The New York Times Book Review,* January 2, 1983, p. 19.

[Barbara Rogasky] produces several sentences describing the evil witch and her power to produce nightmares. When her prince sees the witch ascend Rapunzel's hair, he says matter-of-factly, "So that's how it's done." And, probably in anticipation of some potential censor, she interjects a comment in passing about a marriage in the tower that would legitimize the birth of Rapunzel's twins. Even the nobility of character, generally a hallmark of fairy tales, is altered à la modern psychology when Rapunzel's father is made to cry out "Don't hurt me!" or the prince falls from the tower cringing in fear before the wicked witch. Miss Ash has

him leap through the window in grief at losing his beloved. . . .

Trina Schart Hyman . . . creates a naturalistic setting for Miss Rogasky's version. The dark brown pages establish the story's melodrama. In decorative frames of several sizes the many scenes add information and extend the emotions generated by the text. Action is suggested by gestures and by such devices as falling leaves and swirling scarves. Further realism is produced by changing the prince from a beardless stalwart into a haggard, bearded, kneeling figure at the story's end.

LITTLE RED RIDING HOOD (adapted from story by the Grimm Brothers, 1983)

Kirkus Reviews

SOURCE: A review of *Little Red Riding Hood,* in *Kirkus Reviews,* Vol. LI, No. 4, February 15, 1983, p. 181.

The illustrations are schmaltzy, the book's design is gingham-and-posies old-fashioned, the whole production plays

From Comus, *adapted by Margaret Hodges from story by John Milton. Illustrated by Trina Schart Hyman.*

to an American-frontier-nostalgia sensibility (at variance with the fantastical aspects of the tale)—but the story is far more distinctly and firmly pictured than in Lisbeth Zwerger's vaporous *Little Red Cap.* Though the book is a hokey historical reconstruction, that is, it does at least provide a lot to look at (furnishings, patterns, provender); and though the figures are stagey rustics, they do have a semblance of personality. The telling is plain—meaning both undistinguished *and* free of literary flourishes.

Janet French

SOURCE: A review of *Little Red Riding Hood,* in *School Library Journal,* Vol. 29, No. 7, March, 1983, p. 162.

Versions of *Little Red Riding Hood* presently available provide for both the purists and the romantics among us. Harriet Pincus has illustrated the Harcourt edition with droll, semi-naive drawings perfectly suited to the folk origin of her unadorned text. Hyman's book, on the other hand, is more elaborate. Its appeal, as one would expect, lies in her richly colored illustrations. Each page of text is enclosed in a border of intricate design; paired with it is a full-page watercolor illustration overflowing with the sort of minutely-observed details that children love. These pages delight the eye. The modest elaboration of the text neither enhances nor hinders enjoyment of the story with one regrettable exception. The dramatic peak of the traditional telling is forged in that quartet of repeated observations: "Oh Grandmother, what big . . . you have!" In this edition, the sense of the observations is unchanged, but the parallel structure is gone and, with it, much of the drama and suspense.

Kate M. Flanagan

SOURCE: A review of *Little Red Riding Hood,* in *The Horn Book Magazine,* Vol. LIX, No. 2, April, 1983, pp. 159-60.

Trina Schart Hyman's retelling basically follows the Grimm story, although the text has been fleshed out with some extraneous details (for instance, the little girl is called Elisabeth). Unfortunately, the alteration of the familiar exchange between the girl and the wolf in the grandmother's bed lacks the drama and rhythm of the original, and the retelling's concluding lines weaken the story's ending. The illustrations seem to be a labor of love; richly colored paintings of the forest teem with exquisitely detailed plant and animal life, and the interior scenes, awash with atmospheric light, are beautifully composed and executed. From the white birch trees to Grandmother's rustic cabin and the huntsman's Yankee features, the watercolors are infused with a New England flavor. The visual impact of the full-page paintings are hampered, however, by the elaborate borders rigidly framing the text on opposite pages; the borders, containing decorative patterned friezes, small still lifes, or related scenes, are quite lovely in themselves but overpower the book's design.

Kenneth Marantz

SOURCE: A review of *Little Red Riding Hood,* in *The New York Times Book Review,* May 1, 1983, p. 30.

The story of Little Red Riding Hood's misadventures with a wolf as she brings a basket of goodies to her ailing granny is among the most recited of all Grimms' tales. Its popularity and apparent simplicity have made for frequent visual interpretations. Here are the two most recent. . . .

Trina Schart Hyman creates a waif-like, tousled-haired 6-year-old in bulky high-laced shoes. Hers is an innocent world of kittens, flowers and a wolf that at first meeting looks like a large friendly dog. Full-page scenes are completely developed in opaque colors and framed. Text pages are similarly framed and include pictorial vignettes that enhance the narrative. They all combine to create a stable, comfortable world that is disturbed by an alien force, the sharp-toothed wolf.

Lisbeth Zwerger's 9-year-old is more self-assured and her wolf represents a subtler form of sinister evil. Coyly flirtatious in the forest, oddly graceful while struggling into grandma's nightgown, he is all the aggressor as he tenses his muscles to jump on Red Cap when she draws the bed's curtains. There are about half the number of illustrations in Miss Zwerger's version and each full-page watercolor painting spares us all but the essential characters and props; backgrounds are warm, amorphous grays so our attention is fully fixed upon the figures.

Where Mrs. Hyman's youngster fails to share the goodies in her basket with the hunter, Miss Zwerger's older, more socially conscious girl serves both grandma and their rescuer. While Mrs. Hyman only writes about killing the wolf and then cutting him open, Miss Zwerger shows the open belly of the live wolf (albeit bloodless) as the victims are pulled out. Each version, from the points of view of a younger and older child, is consistent, and each integrates artistic imagination and sound psychological insight.

📖 ***SAINT GEORGE AND THE DRAGON: A GOLDEN LEGEND ADAPTED FROM EDMUND SPENSER'S FAERIE QUEEN* (retold by Margaret Hodges, 1984)**

Zena Sutherland

SOURCE: A review of *Saint George and the Dragon,* in *Bulletin of the Center for Children's Books,* Vol. 38, No. 2, October, 1984, p. 27.

At her romantic best, Hyman illustrates this classic tale, adapted from Edmund Spenser's *Faerie Queene,* with paintings of a marvelously fierce dragon, an impeccably heroic knight, a dazzlingly lovely Princess Una. Notable for their color and composition, the illustrations are framed by borders that often have a Tiffany look. The adaptation by Hodges is capable, simplifying Spenserian language but not abandoning it altogether as she retells the dramatic story of the gallant Red Cross Knight who fought the dragon, won a princess, and became the patron saint of England.

Rosalie Byard

SOURCE: A review of *Saint George and the Dragon,* in *The New York Times Book Review,* November 4, 1984, p. 22.

The most famous literary version of St. George is the Red Cross Knight in Book I of Edmund Spenser's 16th-century epic poem, "The Faerie Queene," a patriotic, religious and moral allegory that is, above all, an extraordinarily inventive and entertaining story.

The description of the knight's three-day battle with the dragon is the heart of this new illustrated adaptation in which Margaret Hodges offers a faithful translation of Spenser's detailed account of the knight's mortal struggle with the ghastly brass-scaled, fire-belching dragon and his hideous, taloned tail. She even includes one of Spenser's most delightful touches—the child who, when the struggle is over, can't resist touching the dead dragon's talon, to the terror of his chiding mother.

On the surface, the story of the Red Cross Knight would seem ideal for a picture book, with its color and romance and the glorious set piece of the battle. But it seems a pity to have compressed the rich multiplicity of Spenser into so few pages that the beginning and the ending, leading up to and away from the dragon read more like a synopsis than a story.

Miss Hodges's collaboration with Trina Schart Hyman is visually lovely. The pictures resemble illuminated manuscript. Each page of text is framed with geometric borders decorated with beautifully detailed drawings of English flowers combined with motifs that both evoke the Middle Ages and refer to images in Spenser—angels, satyrs, mandrake roots, unicorns and the shield of St. George.

One of the most subtle and charming details is the border repetition of little ships under sail, a reference also used in the text as Spenser's metaphor for both his own storytelling and the knight's quest as a voyage. Facing the pages of text are full-page pictures that spill over the border frames. The dragon in full action virtually bursts off the page.

Paul Heins

SOURCE: A review of *Saint George and the Dragon,* in *The Horn Book Magazine,* Vol. LX, No. 6, November-December, 1984, p. 767.

Since the adapter has simplified Spenser's allegorical

narrative to conform to the simple pattern of a traditional story, the Knight of the Red Cross is no longer a symbol of holiness, but—as Saint George—he remains the stalwart champion of Una and the slayer of the dragon. The various adventures and trials of Una and the knight are omitted save for the battle with the monster. Full justice is done to the details of the struggle as they are found in Canto 11 of Book I in Spenser's epic romance; and the adapter's narrative style, which incorporates many of the poet's images, is smooth and graceful. In contrast with the full-page, full-color illustrations, which are dramatic or festive, the pages of text are framed with borders filled with a variety of decorative motifs and vignettes. If anything, the artist is more faithful to the poet's concept than the adapter, for in the margins surrounding the texts are found angels, spirits, and witches embodying Spenser's eerie world of fantasy and spiritual conflict.

Janice M. Del Negro

SOURCE: A review of *Saint George and the Dragon,* in *School Library Journal,* Vol. 31, No. 5, January, 1985, p. 76.

Hodges capably retells the legend of St. George and the Dragon, a popular and well-known fragment from Spenser's *Fairie Queen.* She has made it a coherent, palatable story suitable for a wide range of ages. The action is fast-paced and immediate—George, the Red Cross Knight, sent questing by the Queen of Fairies, accompanies the princess Una back to her father's kingdom to slay the dragon that besets it or to die in the attempt. After the traditional three attempts he succeeds, and everyone lives happily ever after. This retelling is more than adequate, and Hyman's illustrations are uniquely suited to this outrageously romantic and appealing legend. Fairies and unicorns interwine with cross-emblazoned shields and red-winged angels in the borders. The paintings are richly colored, lush, detailed and dramatic. Hyman's dragon is appropriately ferocious; her hero is appropriately brave; and her princess—bless her—is a red-head, not a blond. This is a beautifully crafted book, a fine combination of author and illustrator.

A CHILD'S CHRISTMAS IN WALES (adapted from story by Dylan Thomas, 1985)

Peggy Forehand

SOURCE: A review of *A Child's Christmas in Wales,* in *School Library Journal,* Vol. 32, No. 2, October, 1985, p. 192.

Thomas' poignant yet hilariously real story of a special holiday as a child in Wales is certainly one of the most read-aloud stories of Christmas. Hyman has sparkled the pages of Thomas' timeless narrative with pen-and-ink drawings with vibrant washes, alternating them with black-and-white sketches. The unmistakable Hyman characterizations, so full of warm expressions and the detail of the early 20th-century rooms are exquisite. Hyman so aptly portrays Thomas' humor in her depiction of the fire brigade's arrival amidst smoke, only to have Miss Prothero inquire of them, "Would you like anything to read?" The scenes selected for illustration highlight Thomas' boyishness and the warmth of his family with more charm and sharper detail than Ardizonne's version of the same title. This Christmas treasure of both Hyman's illustrations and Thomas' eloquent prose will draw readers into the world of Wales. A book to delight both children and parents.

Bulletin of the Center for Children's Books

SOURCE: A review of *A Child's Christmas in Wales*, in *Bulletin of the Center for Children's Books*, Vol. 39, No. 3, November, 1985, pp. 58-59.

With a picture on every page and with double-page spreads that are illustrated alternately in full color and in black and white, this is an edition of a Christmas story that should be particularly enjoyed by children. The lyric writing of poet Thomas is not always easy reading for children, but most readers will find it worth any effort to enjoy this contemporary classic. At its best when read aloud (at its very best when read aloud as recorded by Sir Richard Burton for a first hearing) this is made even more enjoyable by the romanticized realism and competent draughtsmanship of a major children's book artist.

Mary M. Burns

SOURCE: A review of *A Child's Christmas in Wales*, in *The Horn Book Magazine*, Vol. LXI, No. 6, November-December, 1985, p. 722.

Established as one of the classic Christmas stories, Dylan Thomas's remembrance of his childhood in Wales is remarkable not as a nostalgic decoration to be dusted off for the holidays but as a work with evocative imagery, magnetic language, and an enduringly youthful perspective. The setting and characters are so vividly evoked that it is not difficult to understand the story's attraction for illustrators. Yet there is ample scope for interpretation because the story is as much a celebration of universal experience as it is a recollection of a particular time and place. In 1980 Edward Ardizzone cast the story in a picture book format, emphasizing the biographical aspects of the work by the depicting central character with blind, curly hair. In contrast, this new version is an illustrated story because of its format and the scale of its drawings. More detailed than those of Ardizzone, Hyman's pictures are representational in style, more literal yet not simply photographic renditions. . . Hyman is particularly successful with interesting characters and with animals. She has elected to present the manuscript not so much as a biography but as a distinct entity. Rooted in the American tradition of illustration

as a medium for storytelling, the pictures are a series of vignettes filled with background details which expand the text and at the same time link one pictorial episode with the next. The whole is viewed as a story within a story, for the frontispiece and copyright page drawings, showing an old man and a child walking together, suggest that the succeeding pages are indeed the recollection of times past transmitted by one generation to another. Quite likely, older readers will be more attracted to this newer interpretation because of its size, shape, overall design, and the wonderful melange of details in each illustration. Hyman's illustrations make this book one with general audience appeal at Christmas—or anytime.

CAT POEMS (compiled by Myra Cohn Livingston, 1987)

Cynthia K. Dobrez

SOURCE: A review of *Cat Poems*, in *School Library Journal*, Vol. 33, No. 8, May, 1987, p. 89.

This successful collaboration from Livingston and Hyman provides a selection of 19 cat poems by noted poets Eve Merriam, John Ciardi, Karla Kuskin, and others. Six poems were commissioned for this book; the others appear in previously published works, a few of which are out of print. Two of the poems also appear in Lee Bennett Hopkins' anthology, *I Am the Cat*. Varied styles, rhymes, meters, and moods are executed in the poems about the habits and adventures of cats. Hyman's deft pencil drawings animate the mischievous antics of the felines, creatively contained within simple brown ink borders. Her drawings are as fluid in movement as a cat. Cat lovers who enjoyed following the cats throughout Hyman's *Little Red Riding Hood* will delight in their full treatment here.

Betsy Hearne

SOURCE: A review of *Cat Poems*, in *Bulletin of the Center for Children's Books*, Vol. 40, No. 10, June, 1987, pp. 191-92.

A natural for cat lovers, this is a wry combination of verse and illustration. The best example is John Ciardi's "The Cat Heard the Cat-bird," which plays with readers' perceptions of a bird before and after the appearance of its predator ("—What bird, dear?/I don't see any cat-bird here"). Meanwhile, in the full-page black-and-white drawing opposite sits a wickedly smiling feline with two feathers sailing past its fat stomach. The feathers, with Hyman's inimitable artistic mischief, precisely echo the curves in the cat's tail and the shades of its patchy fur. Valerie Worth, X.J. Kennedy, and William Jay Smith are among the popular poets contributing to the nineteen selections here, but Jean Cocteau puts in a surprise appearance, and there are strong entries from J. Patrick Lewis ("A Tomcat Is") and Rosalie Moore ("Cat-alog"), as well.

Ann A. Flowers

SOURCE: A review of *Cat Poems,* in *The Horn Book Magazine,* Vol. LXIII, No. 4, July-August, 1987, p. 480.

Something about cats inspires cat-lovers to write and other cat-lovers to read vast numbers of poems about the beloved animals. Cats, looking utterly superior and unconcerned the entire time, seem to be able to wring poetry from the greatest poets down to the merest corner scribbler. This collection of nineteen poems has some unfamiliar ones—for example, a translation of Jean Cocteau's "Cat"—and many old favorites, such as "Catalog" by Rosalie Moore ("Cats sleep fat and walk thin") and T. S. Eliot's "The Song of the Jellicles." Especially enjoyable are Trina Schart Hyman's affectionate illustrations of fat cats, thin cats, lost cats, purring cats, alley cats, sleeping cats, silly cats rolling in catnip, dancing cats, all kinds of cats in all their mysterious allure. A neat, very satisfactory treat for the cat-lover.

CANTERBURY TALES (adapted by Barbara Cohen from tales by Geoffrey Chaucer, 1988)

Helen Byrne Gregory

SOURCE: A review of *Canterbury Tales,* in *School Library Journal,* Vol. 35, No. 3, November, 1988, p. 110.

Cohen has chosen wisely to adapt four stories from Chaucer's masterpiece for children with an overview of the pilgrimage, whetting the appetite for the real thing. She doesn't bowdlerize as Farjeon and McCaughrean, who included more stories, had to. Cohen's choices: "The Nun's Priest's Tale" (Chauntecleer), "The Pardoner's Tale" (revelers in search of death), "The Wife of Bath's Tale" (variant of Sir Gawain and the Loathly Lady), and "The Franklin's Tale" (honor, fidelity, and generosity). She has given equal importance and depth to the tellers and to the tales. Her language, as always, is clear and fine. Hyman's glowing watercolors, bordered in gold, illuminate the tales. She has not painted the characters in flat, medieval style, but has given them the depth that the tales do, bringing them to life, dressed precisely as Chaucer described them, captured in a medieval frame, as Chaucer had framed them in the pilgrimage. Enjoy this impressive blend of talent.

Mary M. Burns

SOURCE: A review of *Canterbury Tales,* in *The Horn Book Magazine,* Vol. LXV, No. 2, March-April, 1989, pp. 214-15.

Adaptations and variants of familiar or famous or obscure tales abound. Some add to our appreciation of the original; many do not. Now, at last, comes an adaptation which deserves to be celebrated, for it is an incredible achievement. Handsomely illustrated, it is not a slick eye-catcher but rather a gorgeous book, lovingly

produced with respect for and understanding of the source. Certainly, Geoffrey Chaucer is the foundation of our English literary heritage, but his language is not the discourse of the eighties. Barbara Cohen has by some alchemy managed to retell four of the Canterbury Tales in prose that sings of its source and yet makes the reader or listener aware that many of the comments applicable to Chaucer's times are equally pertinent for our own. Take, for example, this litmus test for assessing one's companions from "The Wife of Bath's Tale": "I think poverty is a pair of spectacles through which a man can recognize his true friends." Or consider this description of the Pardoner which recalls recent scandals in television evangelism: "He could get more silver out of poor people in one day than an honest country parson could earn in two months." Trina Schart Hyman's illustrations are equally authoritative—as if her participation in this book was predestined. Her portraits of the selected narrators are in the grand tradition, for she captures the nuances of the personalities as if they were as familiar as neighbors. Costumes and settings are meticulously executed yet, like the text, are readily understood by a contemporary audience. The excellent introduction is a model of precision and scholarship without pedantry. Barbara Cohen's apologia strikes exactly the right note of one humble before so great a task: "The highest hope I have for this version is that it will lead some of its readers to the original." If this book can't do that, nothing can. Yet, those for whom the original will always seem too forbidding will have gained much from this glimpse into a work which might otherwise have been denied them. The book certainly belongs in every library serving junior high and high school students; those teaching introductory college courses should also consider it carefully, for it reads aloud smoothly and enticingly.

HERSHEL AND THE HANUKKAH GOBLINS (written by Eric A. Kimmel, 1989)

Ilene Cooper

SOURCE: A review of *Hershel and the Hanukkah Goblins,* in *Booklist,* Vol. 86, No. 1, September 1, 1989, p. 77.

Set somewhere in Eastern Europe in the nineteenth century, this new story about Hanukkah introduces Hershel of Ostropol, a wanderer, who is anxious to spend the holiday in the next village. Hershel is looking forward to delicious potato latkes and bright candles. Instead, he finds a group of cowering residents who can't celebrate Hanukkah because of the goblins that haunt the synagogue. Only when the king of the goblins himself lights the candles on the eighth night of Hanukkah will the spell be broken. Hershel informs the rabbi that he'll take care of the goblin problem, and so sets out to trick the creatures and reclaim the holiday. Echoing the works of I. B. Singer (though not approaching their artistry), this is a story whose essentials—cleverness, bravery, and other worldly happenings—always attract readers. Using dark wintry colors, Hyman creates an appropriately gloomy landscape for what could be a truly chilling story. Certainly, the king of the goblins, when he appears, is a hellish figure. The rest of the goblins, in keeping with some of the story's lighter moments, are more cartoonlike, and their benign countenance detracts from the dread as Hershel eliminates his foes one by one. (Goblins five, six, and seven are never seen, perhaps to keep the book a tidy length). Hyman's human characters, however, are strongly delineated, as always, and the story as a whole is a fresh addition to holiday shelves.

Betsy Hearne

SOURCE: A review of *Hershel and the Hanukkah Goblins,* in *Bulletin of the Center for Children's Books,* Vol. 43, No. 2, October, 1989, p. 36.

Billed as an original story, this is built with familiar folk motifs in Jewish traditional garb. Hershel agrees to spend eight nights of Hanukkah in a haunted old synagogue to rid the village of goblins. He fools the first, tiny goblin by crushing a hard-boiled egg that looks like a rock; the second, larger goblin by tempting him with a bottle of pickles into which the greedy goblin stuffs his hand and gets stuck; and the third, by a clever gambling ruse with the dreidel. We don't find out exactly how Hershel survives the other four devilish visitors, but the eighth night brings the frightful King of Goblins, whom Hershel tricks into lighting the candles himself by pretending it's too dark to see. Thus the spell is broken and the spirit of Hanukkah triumphs. Well, after all, the Maccabees must have used a few tricks of their own—there are only so many ways to outmaneuver an opponent. This will provide relief from the boring, candy-coated read-alouds that so often comprise holiday fare and will fit companionably with haunted castle variants. Hyman is at her best with windswept landscapes, dark interiors, close portraiture, and imaginatively wicked creatures. Both art and history are charged with energy.

School Library Journal

SOURCE: A review of *Hershel and the Hanukkah Goblins,* in *School Library Journal,* Vol. 35, No. 14, October, 1989, p. 42.

An original Hanukkah story that first appeared in *Cricket Magazine.* Hershel comes upon a village on the first night of Hanukkah, but not a single menorah nor candle does he see. He learns that the villagers' synagogue is beset by goblins who break dreidels, blow out Hanukkah candles, and throw latkes on the floor. In order to defeat them, Hershel must spend eight nights in the synagogue, lighting the candles each night. And, by means of trickery familiar to readers of folktales, he does outwit the goblins. The illustrations are dramatically rendered in Hyman's familiar full-color art; she creates fearsome goblins and inserts comic details throughout. However, some of the details may seem rushed over: she shows a less well known *Hanukkiah* rather than the more familiar rounded menorah, and although Hanukkah candles

may not be used for any purpose other than a symbolic one, it is clear in several places that Hershel is using the light to see. For those who can put these difficulties aside, this is a rip-roaring good story that succeeds on more levels than it fails. A note from the author explaining the true rules of the dreidel game (which Hershel has manipulated to his own ends), the significance of the menorah, and a short history of Hanukkah is appended.

Hanna B. Zeiger

SOURCE: A review of *Hershel and the Hanukkah Goblins,* in *The Horn Book Magazine,* Vol. LXVI, No. 1, January-February, 1990, pp. 52-53.

There are old Yiddish folk tales about Hershel Ostropolier, a wanderer and storyteller who was totally irreverent and unawed by authority; Eric Kimmel has written an original story in this tradition. Hershel of Ostropol undertakes to rid a village of the goblins that are haunting an old synagogue, preventing the villagers from celebrating Hanukkah. Hershel is warned by the rabbi that in order to break the goblins' power he must spend eight nights in the synagogue, lighting the candles in the menorah each night; on the last night, the king of the goblins must light the candles himself. Provisioned with hard-boiled eggs and a jar of pickles—the villagers have no potato latkes to give him—Hershel meets a goblin on each of the first seven nights and outwits them all. On the last night, when the king of the goblins appears, Hershel pretends not to see or believe in the "monstrous shape filling the doorway," claiming that it is just one of the village boys trying to scare him. Tricked because of his pride into lighting the ritual candles and breaking the spell, the king, in his fury, creates a whirlwind that destroys the synagogue, leaving only Hershel and the menorah and the gleaming lights of Hanukkah in the village below. Trina Schart Hyman's goblins are humorously loathsome, yet she manages to convey a sense of awe and fear when the king of the goblins looms up in the open door of the synagogue. Above all, her illustrations capture the humor and earthy, peasant quality of Hershel, who can look at a monster that makes his blood turn to water and quip, "'I know you're not Queen Esther.'" This book is welcome both as a Hanukkah story and as a trickster tale.

THE KITCHEN KNIGHT: A TALE OF KING ARTHUR (retold by Margaret Hodges from story by Sir Thomas Mallory, 1990)

Betsy Hearne

SOURCE: A review of *The Kitchen Knight: A Tale of King Arthur,* in *Bulletin of the Center for Children's Books,* Vol. 44, No. 3, November, 1990, pp. 62-63.

Margaret Hodges, experienced in adapting classics such as *Saint George and the Dragon,* which was excerpted from Spenser's *Faerie Queene* and also illustrated by Trina Schart Hyman, has made a resounding version of this medieval tale from Malory's *Le Morte d'Arthur*. The kitchen knight is really King Arthur's nephew in humble disguise, come to win his spurs by challenging every strong knight that comes down the pike—the black one, the blue one, and, finally, the red one. The beautiful Linesse, whose sister Linette first scorned the kitchen knight's ragged appearance, is his prize, but she's imprisoned in a tower. Ours not to question the royal rules of chivalry, though constant testing by physical thumps does seem increasingly archaic from this distance. However, Hyman's paintings convey great dignity on the whole affair. Her portraiture is stronger than ever. The monolithic weight of war horses, armor, shields, and battle-field morality is balanced by graceful lines and a sly glint in the expressions of the outspoken Linette. The borders here are appropriately plain, with the graphic narrative furthered, instead, by miniature insets that detail action happening somewhere other than in the full-page scenes. This frame within a frame composition achieves a kind of "meanwhile" storytelling effect appropriate to the tale within a tale.

Julie Corsaro

SOURCE: A review of *The Kitchen Knight: A Tale of King Arthur,* in *Booklist,* Vol. 87, No. 6, November 15, 1990, p. 660.

When a proud lady requests a knight to fight for her sister, the adventure is granted to a handsome stranger who has spent the previous year scrubbing pots and pans in King Arthur's kitchen. Although the damsel is disgusted ("Out of the wind. The smell of your clothes offends me"), the Kitchen Knight proves his courage and strength during their journey to the Castle Perilous by soundly defeating several powerful adversaries. Even after his true identity is revealed and he triumphs over the evil Red Knight, Sir Gareth must still win Lady Linesse (which, of course, he does). There are some motivation problems in Hodges' restrained adaptation, but her retention of the basic story, emphasis on the knight's heroic deeds rather than his bloodline, and elimination of much of the bawdiness are successful. The dramatic sweep of Hyman's lusty paintings, with their rich details and colors, is enhanced by the occasional placement of a small portrait within a large double-page spread, allowing the viewer to see both the central drama and a reaction shot (for example, the battle and the prisoner watching from her tower). In addition, Hyman uses a less defined line than usual to create a more impressionistic effect. A beautifully illustrated medieval story that concludes with a fascinating source note.

Carolyn K. Jenks

SOURCE: A review of *The Kitchen Knight: A Tale of King Arthur,* in *The Horn Book Magazine,* Vol. LXVII, No. 1, January-February, 1991, p. 77.

This fine retelling of "The Tale of Sir Gareth of Orkney" from Malory's *Le Morte d'Arthur* is full of mystery and action. Gareth, the nephew of Arthur, appears at Arthur's court but will not reveal his identity until he has been there for a year. During that time he works and eats in the kitchen while readying himself to do knightly deeds. He does not have an easy time of it: Sir Kay the steward is rude to him, and proud Linette, whose cause Gareth is championing, judges him on his kitchen-boy appearances and spurns him repeatedly. Arthur and Lancelot continue to believe in him, however, and he overcomes the Knight of the Red Plain. Hyman's boldly colored illustrations are in the same style as those in Hodges's *Saint George and the Dragon;* in this book, however, the layout is different. The borders are plain, and sections of text are framed within the full-page picture. The artist also uses insets as windows on her characters; for example, a close-up portrait of the perilous Red Knight is superimposed on a sweeping scene of his army emerging from the turreted castle to do battle with Gareth. This lesser-known tale will be of interest to those who follow the legends of King Arthur.

📖 *THE FORTUNE-TELLERS* (written by Lloyd Alexander, 1992)

Publishers Weekly

SOURCE: A review of *The Fortune-Tellers,* in *Publishers Weekly,* Vol. 48, No. 28, June 22, 1992, p. 61.

The hands of fate deftly propel this original folktale. A seedy fortune-teller profits from gullible and sometimes desperate villagers who seek predictions for a rosier future. One unhappy carpenter takes to heart the seer's hardly helpful advice—"Rich you will surely be, on one condition: that you earn large sums of money"—and looks forward to a prosperous life. Most surprising to the craftsman, he ends up in the right place at the right time and the prediction comes true. Alexander's chipper text has a jaunty and infectious "just so" tone. Amazing coincidences fuse the plot elements, but the story's logic remains intact, successfully suspending the reader's disbelief. Hyman's acrylic, ink and crayon illustrations capture the landscape and people of West Africa in vivid detail. Indigenous plants and animals—including comically placed lizards—dot each scene, and the villagers' lushly textured apparel is spectacular. Especially opulent are spreads featuring the fortune-teller's cluttered quarters and the market stalls with their baskets and pottery.

Hazel Rochman

SOURCE: A review of *The Fortune-Tellers,* in *Booklist,* Vol. 88, No. 21, July, 1992, p. 1938.

Alexander's rags-to-riches story combines universal elements of the trickster character and the cumulative disaster tale. Hyman's pictures set it all in a vibrant community in Cameroon, West Africa. An old fortune-teller assures a young carpenter he'll be rich (if he earns large sums of money), he'll be famous (once he becomes well known), etc. Then the old man disappears; the people think he's been transformed into the carpenter, who quickly takes on the fortune-teller's role, learns the portentous babble, and becomes rich, famous, and happy. Meanwhile, we discover what really happened to the old man: he fell out of the window, had a series of accidents, and disappeared without a trace.

The energetic, brilliantly colored paintings are packed with people and objects that swirl around the main characters. Bathed in golden light, the carpenter's dreams of wealth, power, and romance look pale beside the magical daily life of the community. You can look and look at these pictures and see ever more detail of patterns and textures in foods, creatures, carvings, basketware, and, above all, the woven patterned cloths worn by everyone in gorgeous combinations. For the last part of the story—the bad fortune that happens as easily as the good—the packed pictures empty out to a view of wide savanna and the old man falling from the sky like Icarus, lost without a trace. With its ups and downs, this is a funny, playful story that evokes the irony of the human condition.

Betsy Hearne

SOURCE: A review of *The Fortune-Tellers,* in *Bulletin of the Center for Children's Books,* Vol. 46, No. 1, September, 1992, pp. 4-5.

The problem with this book is that there's so much to look at you won't want to put it down. If you're lucky, somebody will read it to you so that you can listen to the resounding story while you look; if you're clever, in fact, you'll *make* someone read it to you while you look (slowly, look again, read it one more time); and if you're generous, you'll give kids the same experience. The title page opens on a vivid market scene in Cameroon, where a carpenter sets out for his day's work. "Will I be hammering and sawing the rest of my days?" he asks himself. No, says a fortune-teller whom he consults. "Rich you will surely be . . . on one condition: that you earn large sums of money. . . . You shall wed your true love . . . if you find her and she agrees. And you shall be happy as any in the world if you can avoid being miserable." We should all have such prophesies—and turn them into the same satisfying life as the carpenter's. As for the fortune-teller? Ask the runaway ox, the lion, the hornets, and the giant eagle, all of whom affect his fate beyond the wildest possibilities of prediction, an irony that should not escape sharp observers old or young. The trickster's hand is hidden here; it is the author's, and a clever tale he has turned, proving as adept at a picture book text as he is at complex fantasy series. What lends the words special significance is the contemporary West African setting that Trina Schart Hyman has peopled with a witty cast of individualized men, women, and children. Each double spread bursts with action in the form of physical posture and facial expression. Hyman's linework has always been powerful, but

the colors, patterns, and textures here seem freshly energetic and profoundly warm-hearted. The scenic detail is rich without becoming cluttered; equatorial chameleons, it turns out, are just as entertaining as European fairies. In the form of a funny story, this offers children a vital new world through which to wander.

Linda Boyles

SOURCE: A review of *The Fortune-Tellers,* in *School Library Journal,* Vol. 38, No. 9, September, 1992, p. 196.

A young carpenter, tired of hammering and sawing, seeks out a fortune-teller to see what his future holds. The cagey old prophet promises him a rosy future—well, maybe. "'Rich you will surely be,'" says the fortune-teller, if "'you earn large sums of money.'" Moreover, "'You shall wed your true love . . . if you find her and she agrees. And you shall be happy as any in the world if you can avoid being miserable.'" Pleased with these promising, if ambiguous, predictions, the carpenter leaves, only to get halfway home and decide he has more questions to ask. But the fortune-teller has mysteriously vanished, leaving the carpenter in the quirky hand of fate where, in typical Alexander fashion, his life takes a surprising and humorous turn. The story's warm and witty tone is reinforced by Hyman's masterful illustrations. Expressive figures are dynamically placed against a West African landscape, in colors so rich and clear that they invite readers to touch the fabrics and breathe the air. Visual details—carved wooden stools, traditional cloth patterns, signs in French—add an authenticity to the story (which is actually set in Cameroon), while touches of humor in postures and expressions underscore Alexander's gentle wit. These illustrations are obviously a labor of love. Vibrant with life and good humor, this is a supremely satisfying creation.

📖 *IRON JOHN* **(adapted by Eric A. Kimmel from story by Grimm Brothers, 1994)**

Carolyn Phelan

SOURCE: A review of *Iron John,* in *Booklist,* Vol. 91, No. 5, November 1, 1994, p. 498.

Adapted from the Grimms' fairy tale "Iron John" also known as "Iron Hans," this tells of young Prince Walter, who lives in the forest protected by a wild man (actually a king living under an ancient curse). When he grows to manhood, Walter takes a position as a gardener in a nearby castle and falls in love with Elsa the garden girl, a good-hearted servant. Three times Walter returns to the forest, where Iron John gives him rich clothing to wear to a ball, fine jousting armor for a tournament, and gilded battle armor for rescuing the king. Finally, Iron John's spell is broken, and when Elsa's tears heal Walter's battle wounds, Walter takes her for his wife, and they leave for Iron John's kingdom. Abridged and, as the afterword explains, somewhat changed from the Grimms' tale, Kimmel's dramatic narrative flows from scene to scene with a clear sense of adventure and romance and an underlying sense of mystery. Hyman's beautifully composed illustrations (her first in oil paints for a picture book, according to the jacket notes) are notable for their rich colors and subtle interplay of light and darkness. Her distinctive linear style is softened somewhat yet loses none of its sensitivity to the expressiveness of the human form. The characters reveal their hearts and minds in the illustrations as clearly as in the text. A fine, dramatic retelling.

Susan Scheps

SOURCE: A review of *Iron John,* in *School Library Journal,* Vol. 40, No. 12, December, 1994, p. 97-98.

In this altered version of the well-known tale, Kimmel has combined elements of the original plot and the Cinderella story. He has omitted the introduction to the tale, which describes the wild man's capture, and begins the story as the young prince (named Walter) frees his father's prized possession and then, fearing his wrath, runs away with Iron John, who raises him. When Walter is grown, he is sent out into the world and volunteers to serve a king. After winning the hearts of the *three* princesses at a masked ball and beating all challenges at the king's tournament, the young man is wounded while slaying a band of robber knights who have carried off the princesses. Only the tears of his beloved (here a garden maid named Elsa) save him. He is never reunited with his parents, but returns to Iron John's kingdom. Hyman has illustrated the tale in full- and one-third page, muted oil paintings peopled with characters whose lovely faces are familiar echoes of many of her earlier folktale illustrations. Her forest is dark and eerie by night, a fern-filled grotto by day; her palace garden a charming composite of color; her wild man appropriately wizened and hoary. Alas, the captivating romanticism of the pictures cannot compensate for the lack of cohesiveness and requisite fairy-tale elements. In contrast, each part of the original Grimm tale contributes something to the whole.

THE ADVENTURES OF HERSHEL OF OSTROPOL (retold by Eric A. Kimmel, 1995)

Kirkus Reviews

SOURCE: A review of *The Adventures of Hershel of Ostropol,* in *Kirkus Reviews,* Vol. LXIII, No. 19, October 1, 1995, p. 1431.

Ten tales about the legendary Jewish trickster Hershel, including stories in which he outwits his own family, a bandit who tries to rob him, a local rabbi, an angel, and a count, and one in which he is outwitted by another trickster but gets revenge. Kimmel makes each of Hershel's escapades an ingenious delight, short enough to

hold the attention of young children but clever enough for their older siblings. Hyman's wonderful black-and-white pictures leave readers wanting more. Kimmel's retelling aptly captures the ethnic origins of the collection, detailed in a foreword, and a last chapter, "Hershel's Sayings," is a treat.

Hazel Rochman

SOURCE: A review of *The Adventures of Hershel of Ostropol,* in *Booklist,* Vol. 92, No. 4, October 15, 1995, p. 405.

"It's no disgrace to be poor, but it's no great honor either." Funny and humane, Kimmel's 10 Yiddish folktales about the trickster Hershel are rooted in the *shtetl* village community of the nineteenth-century Ukraine. Kimmel says that Hershel was a real character, a wandering beggar, who endeared himself to the common folk by making the pompous and arrogant look foolish. The joy and wit of these stories never denies the daily struggle with poverty and homelessness ("Times were bad. Hershel's family was starving"). As in the Caldecott Honor Book *Hershel and the Hanukkah Goblins,* Hyman's wild, beautifully detailed drawings (in black-and-white above the title of each story, in riotous color on the jacket) capture Hershel's farcical interchange with the village creatures and characters, including the miser, the bandit, and the rabbi. With their wry idiom, these are stories for telling across generations. Kimmel points out that—like Coyote, Anansi, and B'rer Rabbit—this trickster belongs to all of us.

COMUS (retold by Margaret Hodges from story by John Milton, 1996)

Publishers Weekly

SOURCE: A review of *Comus,* in *Publishers Weekly,* Vol. 243, No. 8, February 19, 1996, p. 215.

Milton's "A Mask. Presented at Ludlow Castle," itself based on the ancient English folktale "Childe Roland," makes an odd choice for adaptation into a picture book, even on the heels of Hodges's and Hyman's collaborations *St. George and the Dragon* and *The Kitchen Knight.* In masques, after all, the characters stand around and declaim, briefly act or more likely dance, and then declaim again—the charms of which don't translate in this stiffly paced retelling. The protagonists, at least, are children, here named Alice, John and Thomas. Separated from her brothers in a dark wood, Alice is ensnared by Comus, a sorcerer who is the offspring of Circe and Bacchus. She resists his proffered drink—which would turn her into a half-beast like all his followers—and is rescued by her brothers, with the magic aid of a Good Spirit and the local river nymph. This deus ex machina plot, typical of masques, is cleansed of Milton's thematic obsession with Alice's virginity and possible loss of it, although a few of Hyman's paintings suggest the sexual undertones. Hyman compensates in part for the brittle narration by cleverly suggesting a stage with curtain-opening imps, also furnishing a deeply gloomy and haunted wood, a horrifically comic mob of monsters and the bright dawn of a happy ending. This volume may give a taste of 17th-century English pageantry and appeal to parents seeking adaptations of classic works, but it is probably too mannered to kindle much enthusiasm in young readers.

Margaret A. Chang

SOURCE: A review of *Comus,* in *School Library Journal,* Vol. 42, No. 3, March, 1996, p. 196.

John Milton's 1634 masque, originally written in blank verse and based on the ancient English folktale, "Childe Roland," has been recast as a picture book. Goblins pull aside a curtain on the title and dedication pages, suggesting that the events that follow happen on stage. Milton's plot is the template as two brothers rescue their lost sister from the clutches of an evil magician, Comus. Supernatural help comes from a Good Spirit disguised as a shepherd and from a gentle nymph of the River Severn. Comus captures humans with a drink that turns them into beasts. The wild scene showing these debauched monsters feasting recalls Puritan Milton's distrust of aristocratic excess. Hyman's illustrations are compelling, from the dark opening scenes in the forest, where children will enjoy spotting nasty creatures lurking among the trees, to the climactic fight between the brothers and Comus. The last page, with its note explaining the story's provenance, shows the actors taking a curtain call. Unfortunately, the conventions of the masque hobble plot development. The denouement comes too quickly and without preparation. "Childe Roland" works better as a story; adults may want to invite children to compare the two. With its dramatic illustrations, this book could serve as an introduction to Milton and his times for older students, while entertaining younger readers with its tale of elemental conflict between vulnerable children and powerful evil.

Janice Del Negro

SOURCE: A review of *Comus,* in *Booklist,* Vol. 92, No. 13, March 1, 1996, p. 1182.

In accessible, beautiful language, Hodges retells John Milton's "Masque at Ludlow Castle," a tale of the eternal battle between good and evil. Innocent, young Alice is kidnapped by the evil magician Comus, but she resists his enchantment long enough for her spirited brothers, aided by an angel and a sympathetic water nymph, to come to her rescue. In the hands of artist Hyman, the story becomes a visual battle between light and dark, with moody, effective watercolors reflecting the intensely romantic mood of the text. The faces of the characters are beautifully rendered: Hyman's villains are truly evil, and her forces of good glow—first in the darkness

From The Golem, *retold by Barbara Rogasky. Illustrated by Trina Schart Hyman.*

of the deep woods, then in the smoky, candlelit hall of the evil magician. Hodges includes a brief source note with enough information to lead eager readers to the original tale and other versions.

THE GOLEM: A VERSION (retold by Barbara Rogasky, 1996)

Susan Scheps

SOURCE: A review of *The Golem,* in *School Library Journal,* Vol. 93, No. 3, October, 1996, p. 126.

Like Isaac Bashevis Singer, Rogasky has novelized the legend of the golem—a monster created of clay—who, under the guidance of the chief rabbi of Prague, rescued the Jews from persecution by anti-Semitic Christians in the late 16th century. Rogasky's strong storytelling skills are evident as she first recounts anecdotes relating the rabbi's problem-solving skills, and then tells of a priest whose hatred of the Jews caused him to murder a Christian child in order to implicate the Jewish community in her death and spread the Blood Libel. The rabbi's solution to this vicious crime results in the capture and imprisonment of the evil priest and an end to the wrongful accusations. Hyman's colorful, fairy tale-like illustrations bring the story to life. The artist has included enough humorous detail in several of her painted scenes to lighten the heaviness of the major theme. In contrast, Uri Shulevitz's black-and-white illustrations perfectly capture the more somber tone of Singer's *Golem*. While the legend is adult-oriented by virtue of both its concept and historical roots, Rogasky and Singer both recount it on a child's level. The peculiar nature of the tale and its unusual setting will probably prevent its universal appeal. The book will be best appreciated in Jewish secular schools and in homes where its historical context is familiar.

Hazel Rochman

SOURCE: A review of *The Golem*, in *Booklist*, Vol. 42, No. 10, October 1, 1996, p. 335.

Rogasky tells . . . [in the Jewish legend of the Golem] in 13 expansive chapters with a colloquial warmth and a Yiddish idiom ("Why? Who knows why?") that makes you read it aloud. There's terror when the Poles come after the Jews, especially when they accuse the Jews of killing children to drink the blood, a lie used for centuries to fuel anti-Semitism. In a foreshadowing of the Holocaust, the evil priest Thaddeus, being led away to prison, curses the Jews ("I will return and you will not recognize me . . . I will tell the same lies . . . You will burn, burn as if in the ovens of hell"); a picture of the gates of Auschwitz ends the chapter. Some of the plotting and counterplotting gets convoluted. But the terror is framed by the rabbi's wise control and by uproarious episodes of domestic farce when the golem takes his household orders literally. Hyman's illustrations in shades of brown and blue, some tall and full-page, some small and unframed, reveal the ordinary and the mysterious in the ghetto community. From the rabbi in his library among his piles of books to the golem rampaging through the streets of Prague, there is a depth of perspective, an expressive sense of character, and an exquisite detail of line. Both author and illustrator provide endnotes about sources in Jewish Mysticism and history.

BEARSKIN (adapted from story by Howard Pyle, 1997)

Publishers Weekly

SOURCE: A review of *Bearskin*, in *Publishers Weekly*, Vol. 244, No. 27, July 7, 1997, p. 67.

Decidedly American and far sunnier than the Grimms' tale of the same name, this is the first of Pyle's original tales in *The Wonder Clock* (published in 1887). A king casts the miller's son into the wilderness to avert a wise man's prophecy that the boy will one day marry the king's daughter. The miller's son is then raised by a bear, and though he is loved, he yearns for his own kind. With the help of his wits and some gifts from the bear, he slays a dragon and, of course, marries the princess. No European prince or peasant, Bearskin speaks with the no-nonsense dialect of a true American, even when about to fight the dragon: "Just go in back of the bushes yonder, and leave it with me to talk the matter over with Master Dragon." Hyman (*St. George and the Dragon*) paints him as Native American in appearance, and indeed populates the book with a pointedly multiracial cast: most of the royal types and peasants look European, while all the wise and understanding characters do not (e.g., the princess and the chief forester's clever wife are of African descent). Hyman proves her mastery with paintings that range from the bountiful picture of the chief forester's kitchen, ducks, rabbit and chili peppers hanging from the rafters, dogs at his feet, wife advising him with wooden spoon in hand; to the sweet picture of baby Bearskin drifting like Moses on the river; to the manly Bearskin assuming St. George's stance as he charges into the three-headed dragon. Hyman infuses these memorable characters with just the right visual touches of humor and intelligence to meet the standards of Pyle's classic American tale.

Ann A. Flowers

SOURCE: A review of *Bearskin*, in *The Horn Book Magazine*, Vol. LXXIII, No. 5, September-October, 1997, p. 588.

"Bearskin," the first story in Howard Pyle's book of literary fairy tales, *The Wonder Clock*, is an agreeable tale incorporating several familiar mythic and folkloric elements. As the result of a wise man's prediction that a miner's baby will marry the princess, her father the king orders the baby's death, but the child is set adrift in a basket by a compassionate huntsman. Found and nurtured by a she-bear, Bearskin grows to be immensely brave and strong. He rescues his princess from a dragon and manages, by guile, to marry her. Howard Pyle was one of the greatest and most famous of nineteenth-century American children's illustrators, but his illustrations for "Bearskin," though striking, are few and rather stilted. Hyman's many lively paintings not only add a sense of the progression of the tale and provide remarkably clear characterization but also seem to marry Pyle's mannered and rather archaic literary style to a more contemporary context. Hyman has chosen to present her characters multi-ethnically—Bearskin himself is clearly of Asian origin, the princess has a black mother and a white father, and even the she-bear has a very human aspect. Although this could have seemed like p.c. overload, the world we are shown is a place of such harmony and unity that anyone would be happy to dwell in it.

Carolyn Phelan

SOURCE: A review of *Bearskin* in *Booklist*, Vol. 94, No. 5, November 1, 1997, p. 468.

From Howard Pyle's classic collection *The Wonder Clock* comes this original story, which combines elements from many traditional tales. Ordered by his king to kill an infant, a huntsman kills a small animal and brings back its heart. The baby boy is laid in a basket and set adrift on a river. A bear finds him, suckles him, and raises him into a strong, handsome lad called Bearskin, who goes to work for the king's swineherd. The bear has magical powers and can grant his foundling's wishes for a horse, fine clothes, and a suit of armor. Brave and clever, Bearskin kills a dragon who threatens the countryside and the princess, outwits the wicked steward who tricks the king, and wins the heart and hand of the princess. With Pyle's colorful language left intact, the story reads aloud well, and the addition of illustrations makes it accessible to younger children than those who might pick up *The Wonder Clock*. Using india ink and acrylic paints, Hyman has made a series of pictures as spirited and good-hearted as the tale. The line is fluid and graceful, the content is dramatic and sometimes humorous, the landscapes are achingly lovely, and the scenes are filled with lively details and individualized characters. The artwork opens a window on a long-ago-and-far-away land with a multicultural cast of characters, a concept that works beautifully. Hyman's magic lies in making this neverland so real. An intriguing new edition of a fine, original fairy tale.

Additional coverage of Hyman's life and career is contained in the following sources published by Gale Research: *Contemporary Authors,* Vols. 49-52; *Dictionary of Literary Biography,* Vol. 61; *Major Authors and Illustrators for Children and Young Adults;* **and** *Something About the Author,* Vol. 95.

Jean Lee Latham

1902-1995

(Also wrote as Janice Gard and Julian Lee) American author of fiction, nonfiction, plays, poetry, and retellings.

Major works include *Carry On, Mr. Bowditch* (1955), *Trail Blazer of the Seas* (1956), *This Dear-Bought Land* (1957), *Drake, the Man They Called a Pirate* (1960), *Rachel Carson: Who Loved the Sea* (1973).

INTRODUCTION

Latham is best known for her biographies for primary and middle graders. She wrote more than twenty biographies profiling doctors, inventors, explorers and scientists. Latham has been applauded for her skill at blending fictionalized characters, dialogue, and incidents with the factual information about her subjects to form a compelling, suspense-filled narrative appealing to young readers, especially boys. With this technique, she was able to successfully incorporate a great deal of the often technical information associated with her subjects while sustaining the interest of readers. She explained her technique in her acceptance speech for the Newbery Award for *Carry On, Mr. Bowditch*: "There are about one dozen imaginary characters in the story; on the other hand, there are about four dozen historical characters who, whenever they touch the life of Nathaniel Bowditch, are handled with accuracy as to time, place, and personality." Most of Latham's subjects are American men who overcame enormous obstacles to make significant contributions to their profession. Recognizing the fun and appeal of Latham's works, Ellen Lewis Buell once remarked that Latham "has a knack of making people of the past seem very much alive."

Biographical Information

Latham was born in Buckhannon, West Virginia, the second of four children. She once related that she had early training as a storyteller: "I had to wash the dishes. I found that if I told stories my just-younger brother, George, would dry the dishes. Sometimes if the story was interesting enough, George would wash *and* dry the dishes. . . . " She graduated from West Virginia Wesleyan College in 1925 and after taking additional course work in drama at Ithaca Conservatory (now Ithaca College) she went on to earn a Master of Arts from Cornell University. She served as editor-in-chief from 1930 to 1936 for Dramatic Publishing Company in Chicago and published a number of adult plays and radio dramas. During World War II, Latham postponed writing to study electronics, eventually working for the U.S. Signal Corps Inspectors Agency where she trained women inspectors.

She earned the Silver Wreath, a civilian award from the U.S. War Department, for her efforts. She returned to writing after the war and produced her first juvenile biography in 1953. In addition to writing, Latham enjoyed "any kind of fun that is in motion . . . ," particularly bicycling, dancing, swimming, and hiking and attempted to "try something new at least every six months." She died in 1995 at the age of 93.

Major Works

Carry On, Mr. Bowditch details the life of Nathaniel Bowditch, a mathematician and astronomer, who before the age of thirty had written *The New American Practical Navigator*, still used as the standard authority on navigation. In order to learn more about the subject, Latham read junior-high level books on mathematics, astronomy, and sailing and conducted research in Bowditch's native Mississippi, reading astronomers logs and diaries of his contemporaries. As a result, Mary Silva Cosgrave concluded that the biography "is a living, dramatic story of an inspiring man, little known outside of maritime circles." On a similar note, *Trail Blazer of the*

Seas profiles Matthew Maury, another man who made significant contributions to navigation. Limited in mobility because of a leg injury, Maury worked in the Depot of Charts and Instruments where he conceived of scientifically planned sailing directions that charted wind and ocean currents to improve the safety of sea travel. *This Dear-Bought Land* is a fictionalized account of the Jamestown settlement as seen through the eyes of fifteen-year-old David Warren. When Warren's father, an investor, is killed the night before he is to sail to Virginia, Warren defies Captain John Smith by going in his father's place as a regular seaman. *Drake, The Man They Called A Pirate* chronicles the adventures of Sir Francis Drake, who, before the age of seventeen, was captain of his own ship. Seeing the need to secure England's naval power, he raided Spanish vessels and conquered the Spanish Armada. *Rachel Carson: Who Loved the Sea* tells about marine biologist Rachel Carson who combined her love of science and her writing ability to produce popular science books. Balancing Carson's personal history and her scientific accomplishments, Latham's book explores the difficulties experienced by women entering a field dominated by men, and touches on contemporary issues, such as pollution and conservation.

Awards

Latham received the Newbery Medal and IBBY Honor Award for *Carry On, Mr. Bowditch* in 1956 and the Boys' Clubs of America Junior Book Award for *Trail Blazer of the Seas* in 1957.

AUTHOR'S COMMENTARY

[The following is Latham's acceptance speech for the Newbery Medal for Carry On, Mr. Bowditch, *which she delivered at a meeting of the American Library Association in Miami, Florida, on June 19, 1956..]*

Jean Lee Latham

SOURCE: "Newbery Acceptance Speech," in *The Horn Book Magazine*, Vol. XXXII, No. 4, August, 1956, pp. 283-92.

I remember once when a six-year-old pal of mine watched me finish typing the manuscript of a book. He said, "Now, Deanie, what'll you do? Send it away and get a cover on it?" I told him that was a consummation devoutly to be wished. Writing is supposed to be a very solitudinous occupation. But the process of reaching your reader with your story—that's quite a cooperative enterprise. So I'd like to thank all those who had a part in the process of "getting a cover on the book" of *Carry On, Mr. Bowditch:*

Mary Silva Cosgrave for many things—but especially for the suggestion of the title—which I think was sheer inspiration; John O'Hara Cosgrave for the illustrations which do so much to bring the world of the story to life. Editor and artist—they played a vital part in "getting the cover on the book."

Then, after the cover *was* on the book, so many people have cooperated in helping *Carry On, Mr. Bowditch* to reach its reader: the publisher in his marketing of it, the reviewers in their comments. And of course no one group does more to keep a book in the hands of the readers than the librarians. So to them, and especially to the Children's Library Association of the American Library Association, and *very* especially to the committee who selected the book for the Newbery Award, my warmest thank-you's.

And now I'd like to talk for a bit about the preliminary time spent with a book, before it is ready to "send it away to get a cover on it."

Every time I read a good book on the subject of writing I remember my first target practice with a rifle. I remember that, after I had fired about ten rounds, I asked my teacher, "How many times did I hit the bull's-eye?"

He chuckled. "Bull's-eye? You only hit the backstop twice!"

Very meekly I asked, "What's my score?"

"Oh, you don't get any score for just hitting the backstop. But cheer up! If you can't hit the the backstop, you'll never hit the bull's-eye."

The backstop of that target always reminds me of the background of a story. And teachers of writing say, over and over again, each in his own words: "Stay in your own back yard; write what you know about; the plot is only the skeleton; you must flesh the bones with reality."

Of course, when I began writing, it was a long time before I believed those wise words. As many young writers before me, and many who will come after me, I wrote of things I knew nothing about because I thought they were "interesting." I wrote dozens of little gems that could never hit the bull's-eye because I was missing the backstop.

Finally I learned better. I learned that I must stay in my own back yard, or, if I departed from it, I must take the trouble to become back-yard familiar with the world of my story.

For instance—the background of *Carry On, Mr. Bowditch*. It's the world of Salem in the late seventeen hundreds, the world of the sea in the days of square-riggers.

My back yard was West Virginia. My nautical experience consisted of two canoe rides and one trip on a ferryboat across the Chesapeake Bay. I've always been glad they did not build that Chesapeake Bay bridge sooner. I might not have had *any* maritime background.

A great many people have asked me why I chose to write about Nathaniel Bowditch. Sometimes they even say *why in the world* did I choose to write about him!

It seems to me a writer has a personal Geiger counter that, on occasion, says to him: *Dig here for treasure.* The most unexpected things may cause that personal Geiger counter to signal that a story lies buried. I remember what started me writing the best-known of my plays—*Old Doc.* I was reading a table of statistics on the average income and the life expectancy of the general practitioner. *Carry On, Mr. Bowditch* started when I read the introduction to a book published by the United States Naval Department, Hydrographic Office. I was reading the introduction because there did not seem to be anything else in the book that I could understand. The book had been written more than one hundred and fifty years ago by a man not yet thirty. That was enough to pique my interest. I found a few more facts about Nathaniel Bowditch: that once the undersized, undernourished son in a poverty-stricken home had to leave school when he was ten; that he spent nine years in the near-slavery of an indentured apprentice. That was the boy who, before he was thirty, wrote *The American Practical Navigator,* which is still "the sailor's Bible" all over the world. There *had* to be a story there; I wanted to tell it.

I knew I was going to spend a long time on background. I did. There were some little matters such as mathematics, astronomy, and seamanship. I had to start at junior-high level, with books like *How to Have Fun With Arithmetic,* and *A Boy's First Book of the Stars,* and work up to celestial navigation.

Navigation was just one part of it; background is a way of life; I had to know how people lived, what happened to them, and, most important of all, how they felt about what happened.

But my personal Geiger counter said: *Dig here for treasure.* I dug.

Sometimes people ask, "What do you mean by fictionized biography? Is it true?" The facts of a man's life, insofar as they are known, are handled with accuracy. But the facts I had about Nathaniel Bowditch would not have filled twenty pages of typing. The manuscript ran two hundred and twenty pages. I had to flesh the bones with reality.

I invented characters, conversations, and incidents to bring those facts to life. It is a fact that Nathaniel Bowditch taught the man who sailed before the mast. I invented all the men of the crews who sailed on those five voyages with him, except Captain Prince and one cabin boy.

About Nat's sister, Lizza, I had one fact; she died when Nat was seventeen. The biographer said, "The two had been close together, so her death went hard with the boy." There are twenty-seven scenes in the book between Nat and Lizza, scenes full of what they said and did and dreamed about in those days. That is what I mean by fictionized biography.

There are about one dozen imaginary characters in the story; on the other hand, there are about four dozen historical characters who, whenever they touch the life of Nathaniel Bowditch, are handled with accuracy as to time, place, and personality.

So I did spend quite a bit of time on background. When I had finished my research, my notes would have filled ten books the size of *Carry On, Mr. Bowditch.* Speaking in terms of my target practice, I had learned to hit the backstop. But, of course, I did not have any score. I still had to tell the story.

To do that, I must forget the attitude of the researcher and become the storyteller, with my mind, like all Gaul, divided into three parts. With every sentence, every scene, and every chapter, I must be thinking of three things at the same time.

One part of me lived his days with Nathaniel Bowditch. Since it was his story, I crawled into his mind and stayed there, seeing his world through his eyes. I lived in the here-and-now with him, unable to see around the corner to the next day, even to the next hour.

Yet, the second part of me *could* see around the corner—the days and months and years ahead—to the final scene. I was as completely divided by two as that soldier I heard of who was waiting to go over the top. He looked down at his shaking knees. He muttered, "Go ahead and shake. If you knew where I'm taking you, you'd shake harder than that." Part of me was feeling nothing but the hope or fear of one moment with Nathaniel Bowditch; another part of me was thinking—sometimes happily, sometimes regretfully—"If you knew where I'm taking you . . ."

And the third part of me was thinking of my reader. For I knew my story would not happen on paper; it would happen first in my imagination and then in the imagination of my reader. All that would be on paper would be just enough to make the story live for him. So I thought of my reader.

Before I think of one reader in particular, I always remember three things I believe about readers in general:

First: Storytellers may come from every state in the Union, but my reader is from Missouri; I can't tell him anything. I must show him. If I want him to believe anything about my character, I must prove it in terms of what my character says and does and dreams about.

Second: This matter of happy endings. It's axiomatic

that most readers like happy endings. But—what is much more important, I believe—is that readers like the story to end as soon as it "gets happy," as soon as all problems are solved. My reader likes suspense. If I am to hold him, I must overlap the end of one problem with the beginning of another, until the final scene of the story.

Third: Writing for my reader is rather like going on a picnic. Both operations take a bit of planning.

When a mother promises her son a picnic, she must not just hop in the car and ride off to admire the scenery. Sooner or later he says, "Where's the sandwiches?" It's hard to divert his attention.

She may try: "Isn't the lake blue today?" (Where's the sandwiches?) "Oh, look at that beautiful tree!" (Where's the sandwiches?) "Come on, dear, let's try to see pictures in the clouds!" (*Where's the sandwiches?*)

When I promise my reader a story, I must not forget what a story is; I must not plunge into the middle of my first inspiration and swim off through a sea of words. Sooner or later my reader says, "What happened?" It's hard to divert his attention, too.

I may try: "Isn't that a neat metaphor?" (What happened?) "Did you notice that simile?" (What happened?) "Let's read this paragraph aloud and notice the rhythm!" (*What happened?*)

However, my reader is not interested primarily in plot. He is interested in what happens because he is interested in the character it happens to. No incident has any place in the story unless it has an emotional impact on the character—and on the reader. He wants the sandwich of fiction—one layer of incident between two layers of emotion.

He likes to live with the character his anticipation of some impending event; to live with him through what happens; to live with him through the aftermath, as he picks himself up and starts on again toward the next event that promises or threatens.

When I had remembered these three things that I believe about readers in general—that they like suspense, that they want to *see* the story happen and, most important of all, they want to *feel* the story happen—then I was ready to think of my particular reader.

I knew I must think of him, so that the story that happened between us—in my imagination and his—would be like lasting friendship, based on what goes without saying. I must not bewilder him with something he could not understand; I must not bore him by explaining something that he did understand. So I must know my reader, respect him, and appreciate him.

Carry On, Mr. Bowditch was aimed at a specific reader—the adolescent boy.

I was lucky enough to have two younger brothers. I began spinning yarns long before I began writing. There was a very practical reason back of my first stories: I had to wash the dishes. I found that if I told stories my just-younger brother, George, would dry the dishes. Sometimes, if the story was interesting enough, George would wash *and* dry the dishes, too, without noticing what he was doing.

But don't think I wasn't working! You see, George was going to grow up to be an engineer. Did you ever try to keep a budding engineer interested in a story? It's excellent training. I learned very young not to get enthralled with my vocabulary. George was strictly a what-happened type of listener. I could either tell a good story or I could do my own dishes.

I learned a lot about boys that way, and I've learned a lot from them. They are excellent critics; they keep your feet on the floor.

I remember when I was in college and my younger brother, Frank, was still in grade school. There was a little group in college who took my writing very seriously. Of course I basked in their approval. I almost forgot my early training under a budding engineer. I'm afraid I even indulged in purple passages.

During vacation, one of that admiring group surprised me with a visit. She drove into town, found my neighborhood, and asked directions of a gang of boys playing sandlot baseball.

"Do you know where Jean Lee Latham lives?" She admitted later she probably said it in hushed tones.

One grubby little fellow answered, "That's Frank Latham's sister." He pointed with his thumb. "Her house is right over there, by Frank's pup tent."

As my brothers grew up, I had two nephews to keep my feet on the floor. And I've always been lucky enough to have friends with a son or two.

When I wrote my first fictionized biography, *The Story of Eli Whitney,* I had two excellent critics: Michael O'Mara, aged nine, and Connie Anderson, aged ten. They were younger than the reader the book was aimed at, but I knew they read in advance of their years.

We spent all one Saturday on the final draft of the book. That is, I had *thought* it was the final draft. I remember I fed them well, too; lunch, then homemade cookies and milkshakes.

I knew the book had possibilities when Michael started explaining things to me, as if I had had nothing whatever to do with it.

The story opens in 1775, just before the beginning of the Revolutionary War, when Eli Whitney was a boy. I was reading a passage where Eli's friend, Hiram Wedge, the peddler, is telling the boy of the threat of war. Hiram says:

> There's a silversmith in Boston I want to talk to. He knows what's coming. He tried to tell me, but I was too busy peddling my wares to listen.

Michael, aged nine, pointed his finger at me. "And do you want to know who that silversmith is, Deanie? Well, I'll tell you! That's Paul Revere! You just wait and see!"

Later I was reading the scene where young Eli gets a letter from Hiram Wedge. The letter is dated Boston, April 18, 1775.

> Dear Eli
>
> I promised to let you know what the silversmith said. He wasn't home when I got here tonight. They said he was out on an errand . . .

Michael stopped me again. "See, Deanie? I told you that was Paul Revere! And do you want to know where he is? He is riding to warn the people that the British are coming! You just wait and see!"

When we finished the book, they said they liked it fine. But I had learned long ago to get the full benefit out of a reader-critic. There is one question that is Open Sesame to his helpfulness. I plied them with more cookies and milkshakes. I said, "Now, I need your help. I have to cut this much out of the book." I held up about fifty pages. *"What can come out?"*

They sipped and munched; they pondered. Then, without looking at the manuscript, they reviewed the entire book, suggesting what could come out. What did they choose? The flashbacks, all the flashbacks, and nothing but the flashbacks!

They would say, "Remember when he was *here?* So you don't have to go back to when he was *there,* do you?" Or, "Remember when *this* was happening? So you don't have to go back to when *that* happened, do you?"

Every blessed flashback.

I thanked them. When they had departed, full of cookies, milkshakes and good works, I started rewriting the book. Ever since then I've written these biographies in chronological order.

Sometimes adults have told me that *Carry On, Mr. Bowditch* is not a juvenile book. They seem to mean it for a compliment.

One friend of mine, a writer himself, got quite wrought up about it. He pounded the table. "This is *not* a juvenile book!"

I said, "There aren't any words in it that I could not

have understood at twelve."

He bristled. "Oh, I'd have understood them, too."

"There aren't any emotions I could not have sympathized with. I believe I knew more, and felt more, and understood more, than some grownups realized."

He sighed and looked soulful. "So did I!"

I grinned at him. "What makes you think *we* were so special?"

Some people who are familiar with my adult radio plays ask me if I don't find it a bore to "write for children." No. There is nothing boring about writing for the adolescent when you believe he knows more, and feels more, and understands more, than some grownups realize. And the most challenging thing about him is this: His dreams are outsized.

When I think of the juvenile reader, I always remember Salomon de la Selva's brief poem "Measure:"

> In a tiny pool
> You could jump over,
> I saw reflected
> All of the sky.
>
> I wondered: How
> Should one rightly measure
> This lovely water,
> By the earth that holds it?
> By the heaven it holds?

I hope I never forget the magnificent sweep of the imagination and dreams of youth; I hope I never forget that, when a boy comes only to a man's shoulder, his dreams are tall!

Tall as the dreams of Nathaniel Bowditch: even when he was a half-pint bit of humanity, his dreams reached the sky. Through all the hardship and heartbreak, he kept those dreams. When he died, they said this of him:

> As long as ships shall sail, the needle point to the north, and the stars go through their wonted courses in the heavens, his name will be revered as one who helped his fellow-men in time of need, who was and is a guide to them over the pathless ocean.

I'm glad that one day, four years ago, I picked up a book and read the introduction. I'm glad my personal Geiger counter said: *Dig here for treasure.*

Jean Lee Latham

SOURCE: "With the Help of My Reader," in *The Writer*, Vol. 75, No. 12, December, 1962, pp. 19-20, 46.

The question I hear most often from fellow writers is,

"How do you make your biographies move so swiftly?" Sometimes they add, "And why?"

Why? Because I *have* to!

Pacing a story is a matter of covering a given time span in a given number of pages. For instance: If a manuscript of two hundred pages covers a time span of one month, the story may move at covered-wagon speed. The author may spend about seven pages on each day. And, since he will doubtless skip some days, he may spend even more time on certain scenes.

If that manuscript covers a time span of one year, the story must move more swiftly—perhaps at stagecoach speed. The stopping places are farther apart and the intervening time between scenes must be covered more swiftly.

If that manuscript covers a time span of many years, then the problem of pacing the story becomes acute. That is the problem I face in my fictionalized biographies. That is why they must move so swiftly.

Of course one may summarize a man's life in four paragraphs of fine print. But I do not like to summarize. I like to tell the story of a life in dramatic scenes so that my reader can see it happen. Moreover, my readers have told me in no uncertain terms that they like the story to be told in chronological order, without flashbacks. So I must cover the life of a man from some moment in his boyhood to some peak in his career, with a time span of at least thirty years. Yet I must not skimp on the development of a scene that my readers will enjoy. Therefore, I must move swiftly over intervening time. I know I must "light running on the first page and run scared to the end."

How? I do it with the help of my reader. The relation between us must be like lasting friendship—based on "what goes without saying." I depend on my reader to read between the lines. With his help I can make very swift transitions. If I give him the right transition line he jumps without a bit of trouble from one scene to another. Not only that, but sometimes he can jump from the *climax* of one scene to the *middle* of the next one.

Here are examples from two of my books:

Young Man in A Hurry: The Story of Cyrus W. Field covers thirty-one years, from 1835 to 1866. Here are some transitions which begin on page 59. By that point in the story the "young man in a hurry" has begun his career with a salary of one hundred dollars a year, has risen to be a junior partner in a firm, weathered a bankruptcy that was not of his doing, has made his fortune before he is thirty-five. He has retired to "take it easy"—he thinks. But he meets Mr. Gisborne, a telegraph engineer. Mr. Gisborne has attempted to build an overland telegraph line across Newfoundland and a submarine cable from Newfoundland to Nova Scotia. His company has failed. He tries to interest Cyrus in raising money to continue to work.

Cyrus is not too much interested. He puts off Mr. Gisborne with a promise to "think about it" and goes home. He is living near Gramercy Park. Two of his neighbors are his brother Dudley, a famous lawyer, and Peter Cooper, financier and philanthropist.

That night Cyrus studies a globe of the world. Suddenly he is on fire with an idea: Why not raise money to lay a cable across the Atlantic Ocean? Since he is a "man in a hurry" he wastes no time. He writes letters to two experts to get their opinions on the feasibility of the idea. Then . . .

> When he had finished his letters he was too excited to sleep. Cold as it was he went out to walk. If only Peter Cooper were awake—but Mr. Cooper's house was dark. Maybe Dudley—yes, a light burned in Dudley's library.
>
> "A cable clear across the Atlantic?" Dudley stared. "Have you the faintest idea what it would cost?"

Those six words, "a light burned in Dudley's library," are all the clue my reader needs to move to the middle of the next scene. He knows that Cyrus will stop at Dudley's house, climb the steps, stamp off the snow, and knock on the door. He knows that Dudley will open the door, ask what Cyrus is doing out so late, get an answer, invite Cyrus in, help him out of his overcoat, and take him into the library. My reader even knows what Cyrus is going to say to Dudley. So I may skip all that. I allow one line of space to indicate a break, and jump to the middle of the next scene, with Dudley's answer.

That scene continues to its climax. Cyrus manages to get Dudley interested in the legal aspects of the problem. Then there is another transition:

> . . . Cyrus got up. "Tomorrow I'll see if Peter Cooper will listen."
>
> "So," Mr. Cooper said, "Mr. Gisborne's company failed after only forty miles of line were built? That's not much of a recommendation, is it, Cyrus?"

The words, "Tomorrow I'll see if Peter Cooper will listen," make the transition. My reader knows the next important point of call. He does not have to follow Cyrus out of Dudley's library, wait for him to put on his overcoat and pick up his hat, open the door, say good night, walk down the street to his home, enter, go to his bedroom, undress, go to bed, go to sleep, wake up, wash, shave, dress, eat breakfast, and go to Mr. Cooper's house. My reader even knows what Cyrus is going to say to Mr. Cooper. Again I allow one line of space to indicate a break, and jump to the middle of the next scene, with Mr. Cooper's answer.

Drake: The Man They Called a Pirate covers thirty-three years from 1555 to 1588. The story begins when Drake, a boy of ten, decides to leave home so that his father will have "one less mouth to feed." He dreams of becoming a great mariner. So he wants to find a great mariner to apprentice himself to. He tells his younger brother Johnny of his secret plan. He says he will go as soon as he finds the right ship—one with a master mariner.

"I'll ask around. The sailors are used to me asking questions. They won't catch on to anything."

"A master mariner, eh?" The sailor stared across the water. "Best mariner that's in the Medway right now? I'd say old Adam Tanner . . . "

Again my reader has his clue. He knows that the next morning Drake will board a ship in the Medway River, fall into conversation with a sailor, and gradually work it around to his question. Again I allow one line of space to indicate a break, and jump to the middle of the next scene, with the sailor's answer.

The scene between Drake and the sailor continues. Then there is another transition:

" . . . That Tanner's the meanest old devil that ever walked a deck. But, man alive, he's a mariner! I've heard men say . . . "

Ten minutes later Fran stood on the wharf by the little coaster.

The words, "But, man alive, he's a mariner!" are the clue. The scene does not continue through all that the sailor says of Adam Tanner. It ends with suspension periods: "I've heard men say . . . " Again I allow the line of space to indicate a break, and jump to the moment when the boy goes to Adam Tanner's little coaster, the *Sally*.

Now I take time to develop a scene—to introduce Adam's crew, especially Pedro. He will be important throughout much of the story. I take time for Fran's meeting with Adam. I think it will interest my reader.

(Recently I received letters from a group of fifth-graders. Their teacher had read *Drake* to them. What favorite scenes did they mention? A moment in this coming scene when Adam knocks Fran across the deck; a moment, much later in the story, when Fran and Pedro meet again after they had been separated for years.)

The scene on the *Sally* reaches a climax with Adam's refusal to take the boy as an apprentice:

"No, I won't sign you on! Get off my ship and stay off! I catch you around here again, I'll keelrake you!" And Adam strode forward to bellow at his men. "Pedro! Carey! Bear a hand! We're going out in the morning!"

Fran stood a moment, studying the *Sally*. He looked longest at some cargo, lashed to the deck and covered with a tarpaulin. He nodded to himself, saluted Adam Tanner's back, and left the ship.

At dawn the *Sally* went out with the turn of the tide.

Again my reader has his clue, "He looked longest at some cargo." He knows the boy will come aboard the *Sally* that night. He knows where he will hide. There is no need to go into detail about the rest of that day and that night. The reader knows what has happened. He even has the pleasure of knowing more about the situation than some of the characters in the story. He has read between the lines.

GENERAL COMMENTARY

Mary Silva Cosgrave

SOURCE: "Jean Lee Latham Wins Newbery Medal," in *Library Journal*, Vol. 81, No. 6, March 15, 1956, pp. 738-39, 747.

Jean Lee Latham started writing at such an early age that by the time she was ten years old she felt she had written herself out. When she reported this gloomy thought to her mother, she was comforted with these words, "I believe that happens to writers all the time, Jeanie. When it does, they just go live some more." This is exactly what Jeanie has done, with boundless energy, ever since.

Born in Buckhannon, West Virginia, Jeanie attended public schools there and in Elkin and received her B. A. degree from West Virginia Wesleyan College. Never satisfied with doing one thing at a time, Jean ran a linotype machine for the county newspaper during her college days. At Ithaca Conservatory (now Ithaca College) she taught drama and academic subjects while working for her degree in drama. And it seemed only natural for her to continue with her teaching at Ithaca Conservatory while studying for her M.A. degree at Cornell University.

Shortly after leaving Cornell, Jean Lee Latham was called to Chicago for a conference with the Dramatic Publishing Company. The weekend conference stretched into a six-year term as editor in chief, during which she wrote her own plays and radio shows in the evenings and over weekends.

She resigned as editor in 1936 and devoted her full time to freelance play and radio writing. It wasn't long, however, before she acquired for herself another completely engaging occupation. The switch, this time, was to technical electronics under the U. S. Signal Corps Inspection Agency. "This, by the way, was the one time in my life

I didn't do two things at a time! I ate, slept, and studied electronics," she recalls. This concentration resulted in her being appointed civilian in charge of the National Training Program for Signal Corps Inspectors, and somewhere along the line, she was awarded the Silver Wreath.

After VJ Day she reconverted to her peacetime occupation of writing, exploring this time a new field—narrative writing. In December 1951 she began research on a fictionized biography for children, and by September of 1952 this exuberant author had done the necessary research and written two books. Of course, at the same time, there were a few other activities underway: publicity director for the St. Petersburg, Fla., Red Cross Campaign; librarian for ten weeks at the Warm Springs Foundation in Georgia; and Gray Lady at the Veterans' Administration Hospital in St. Petersburg.

Her first children's book, *The Story of Eli Whitney*, was published in 1953, followed in 1954 by *Medals for Morse*, both Aladdin Books. On August 30, 1955, Houghton Mifflin published *Carry on, Mr. Bowditch*, for which Jean Lee Latham has been awarded the 1956 Newbery Medal.

Asked frequently why she chose to write about inventors, scientists, or human calculating machines, Miss Latham's blue eyes sparkle as she answers, "They chose me!" She admits, however, that some credit is due to her brother George, who, as an incipient engineer during their childhood, was a critical listener to her repertory of stories. Further, he agreed with her contention that scientists and mathematicians are human and interesting. *Carry on, Mr. Bowditch* did, however, take its author far "out of my own back yard. My nautical background consisted of two canoe rides and one trip on the Chesapeake Bay ferry. Starting at a junior high school level, I worked up by degrees, in mathematics, astronomy, and sailing."

Research took Miss Latham to Salem, Marblehead, and Boston, while her reading ranged from Mr. Bowditch's journals to modern books on navigation. Her biography of Mr. Bowditch is a living, dramatic story of an inspiring man, little known outside of maritime circles. Apprenticed at the age of 12 to a ship chandler, Nathaniel Bowditch sold marlinespikes, belaying pins, hemp rope, and kept the books for the chandlery until he was 21. Night after night in his attic room he filled notebooks with everything he could learn about ships and the sea, mathematics, and astronomy. When his apprentice days were over, he went to sea and astounded everyone with his knowledge of navigation. Before he was 30, Mr. Bowditch had written *The American Practical Navigator*, an amazing book when he wrote it and from that time on a standard text in the U.S. Naval Academy.

While she was writing *Carry on, Mr. Bowditch*, Miss Latham lived in a trailer in St. Petersburg, Florida. She soon found herself, with standing room only, forced to move to an apartment nearby. Her next book, *Trail Blazer of the Seas*, a biography of the American hy-

drographer Matthew Fontaine Maury is scheduled for fall 1956 publication by Houghton Mifflin.

Miss Latham manages to find time in her busy life for swimming, dancing, bicycle riding, and always, "something new." Her latest venture has been a course in Elementary Piloting and Small Boat Handling under the U.S. Power Squadron. She also has to her credit several published plays, radio plays produced on all the major networks, and a three-act stage play, "Old Doc," presented on the Kraft Television Theatre. It goes without saying that Jean Lee Latham, like Nathaniel Bowditch, will never be becalmed.

Ellen Fulton

SOURCE: "Jean Lee Latham," in *The Horn Book Magazine*, Vol. XXXII, No. 4, August, 1956, pp. 293-99.

To every thing there is a season,
and a time to every purpose under the heaven:

The opening verses of the third chapter of Ecclesiastes are the favorite Bible passage of Jean Lee Latham. The clear-cut statements please her, for they fit her way of life. Her days, her activities, her achievements all fall into their proper seasons. She goes through life purposefully, with her feet on the ground, leaving the past behind her, living intensely in the present, and feeling "at home to the future."

a time to build up

"How about having coffee outside under the trees?" suggested Jean.

From her trailer where we had been chatting over generous portions of scrambled eggs and bacon, it was merely two steps down to the shadowed coolness of the lawn. Jean brought along a manuscript from the desk that filled one entire end of the trailer.

"This," she said, "is Nathaniel Bowditch at the age of six when the story begins," and she read aloud the first dramatic chapter.

During the summer of the following year when I was in Nova Scotia, a prepublication copy of *Carry On, Mr. Bowditch* was delivered to our rural mailbox. I read it through that night. Appropriately enough, the sound of surf breaking on the beach below our cottage accompanied my reading. I could not even wait until morning to write to Jean about my enthusiasm, pride and delight in her book.

a time to be born

My regret is that I never knew "Miss Winnie," Jean's mother. It has been said of her that she could do anything she determined to do. She grew to maturity with a heart damaged by a childhood illness. The family doctor told her she never should risk bearing a child. But Miss Winnie gave birth to four. Of the strong, energetic, talented quartet, Jean was the second, arriving April 19, 1902, in Buckhannon, West Virginia. As Jean says, "We really split into two camps: Julie and George, the mathematics teacher and the engineer; Frank and I, the writers."

Miss Winnie's understanding of children must have been unusual. She guided them with a "hands off" policy, realizing that what seemed most important to them at the moment should be considered as important to their development. Her children shared in the responsibilities of the home, each having appointed tasks and being expected to perform them. But they were never nagged or driven to do them. If Jean was preoccupied in writing a play and her dish-washing chore remained undone, there was no complaint from Miss Winnie. The dishes waited. The task was done when Jean's writing urge had been satisfied. Jean admits that she still keeps house that way.

a time to plant

Watching Jean conduct her seminars on "You as a Writer of Fiction" during the spring of 1954 at Craft Village in St. Petersburg, Florida, I was impressed by her teaching ability. With clarity she explained various phases of fiction writing; with pungent humor she emphasized many commonplace directions; with patience and understanding she dealt explicitly with countless details. She added to her teaching the dignity of the importance of being not only a good writer but a meticulously expert writer.

Her teaching experience began in 1926 after she had received her B.A. (1925) from West Virginia Wesleyan College and while she was taking a postgraduate course there. She continued teaching while a student of Drama at Ithaca Conservatory where she received the degree of Bachelor of Oral English in 1928, and while working at Cornell University for her Master of Arts, which was awarded in 1930.

From Cornell she went to Chicago as Editor-in-chief of the Dramatic Publishing Company. After six years, as she puts it, she "stopped working and started merely writing."

a time of war

In response to the nation's call for civilian workers in National Defense, Jean switched to a new field, that of electronics, taking a special training course, in 1942, at West Virginia Institute of Technology in Montgomery.

Her first assignment was to Signal Corps Inspection at the Crosley Plant, Cincinnati, where she was promptly given the job of writing inspection procedures on a new piece of equipment. By the end of the year she had been called to National Headquarters of the Signal Corps Inspection Agency, Dayton, Ohio. The following spring she was assigned to handle the training program of Signal Corps Inspectors in the Newark, New Jersey, region. In 1944 she was given the double job of continuing that assignment and writing and supervising the training course for the advanced training of women inspectors. Since Signal Corps Inspection jumped from 90 men in peacetime to 6,000 in wartime, with a continually shifting personnel, and since the courses were conducted in far-separated centers, it meant considerable commuting between Dayton, Chicago, Philadelphia, New York and Newark.

and a time of peace

She resigned in 1945 and came to St. Petersburg to reconvert to peacetime production—writing. It was "good weather and solitude" she sought in Florida and found both, although at times the solitude, essential to a writer, has to be insured by the cut-off switch on her telephone and the understanding of friends and neighbors.

A characteristic of Jean's is doing two things at a time. For a while, in 1949, she was Publicity Director for the American Red Cross Fund campaign in Pinellas County, Florida. For five years she worked as a volunteer Gray Lady in the psychiatric department of the Veterans Administration Hospital at Bay Pines, Florida. In 1951 she was substitute librarian at Warm Springs Foundation.

Since 1952 she has produced five books. *The Story of Eli Whitney* was published in 1953 and *Medals for Morse* in 1954. The latter has been translated into German. *Carry On, Mr. Bowditch* was published in 1955 and was chosen as an April 1956 selection of the Junior Literary Guild. This autumn *Trail Blazer of the Seas* will come out. *This Dear-Bought Land* is scheduled for publication in 1957.

a time to gather stones together

"Stones" in Jean's case might be symbolic of honors. During her career she has been the recipient of a number of them, including election to Phi Kappa Phi (Cornell University) and to Zeta Phi Eta (Northwestern University). She was awarded the War Department's Silver Wreath for work during the War. In May 1956 she received the honorary degree of Doctor of Letters from West Virginia Wesleyan College, and in June '56 the Newbery Medal.

a time to cast away stones

"Stones" are also symbolic of nonessentials in Jean's way of life. Once, when I asked her what she would like me to bring her from Nova Scotia, she said, "If I can't wear it out or eat it up, I don't want it." She glanced around her book-crowded trailer and I understood. Her needs were reduced to essentials there. And I began to call her Jeanie David Thoreau. Like Thoreau she chose to be unencumbered by nonessentials, thereby gaining more freedom for her consuming passion for writing. When she moved into an apartment, the same simple standards were maintained. Although she now has more space, most of it is used for spreading out writing paraphernalia.

a time to seek

Jean says her zest for living and her delight in experiencing new things is an "inherited trait." These adventures have ranged from operating a linotype machine for the Buckhannon *Delta* during her last two years in college to her latest adventure, taking a course in Elementary Piloting and Small Boat Handling under the U. S. Power Squadron Training Program at St. Petersburg.

a time to speak

Jean says it shocked some of their neighbors in Elkins, West Virginia, when they learned that she was a drama student at Ithaca Conservatory, but she had a champion in Miss Winnie.

When one dear neighbor said, "Mrs. Latham, if Jean goes on the stage, what will God think?" Miss Winnie answered, "I don't believe God would have put the love of make-believe in people if He didn't expect part of them to act."

The neighbors never had to bear the shock of seeing Jean on the stage, but they might have read her stage plays or listened to her radio dramas. The stage plays include: *The Blue Teapot, Old Doc, Gray Bread, Señor Freedom, The Nightmare.* Among her important radio dramas was a juvenile historical serial in 140 episodes on the Lewis and Clark Expedition. There were many other half-hour shows for First Nighter, Grand Central Station, and other programs.

Jean is in demand as guest speaker for radio and other occasions. When she consents to give such programs, she puts into the preparation of script or speech the same meticulous work for effectiveness that she puts into her books. Thoroughness and perfection are her standards. These standards are hers by inheritance and by training.

In late May 1956, she received a request from the Library of Congress to record *Carry On, Mr. Bowditch* for Talking Books for the Blind. Jean gave her consent and asked to try out as recorder herself. She submitted a tape recording of two scenes from the book to The American Printing House for the Blind, Louisville, Kentucky, with the result that she received an invitation from them to make the recording and went to Louisville to do it.

Jean, dramatist, actor and author combined in this instance to contribute another literary item to the specialized department of the Library of Congress.

a time to keep silence

Jean's energy is tremendous; her achievements are varied and numerous; her capacity for making and keeping friends is a glowing, rich, warm attribute. To what objective will she turn her energies next? her friends ask. Jean doesn't say. Whatever it will be, it will be absorbing and friends will watch her build up more successes in creative writing. She may have even now a purpose in mind. She will find the right season for it.

TITLE COMMENTARY

📖 *MEDALS FOR MORSE, ARTIST AND INVENTOR* (1954)

Virginia Kirkus' Service

SOURCE: A review of *Medals for Morse, Artist and Inventor,* in *Virginia Kirkus' Service,* Vol. XXII, No. 14, July 15, 1954, p. 439.

There is a certain light touch (perhaps a finger on a telegraph key?) to this biography of Samuel F. B. Morse, painter and inventor, but the vital facts of his life are present in adequate detail. Boyhood experiences in school and college set the scene for the development of his character—independent and unconventional—and his ambition—to be a great painter of Americana. As he studies in Europe, struggles at home and lives, through the death of his wife, there is warmth to the story. Though the sense of frustration, through the years it took him to succeed with the telegraph, is glossed over by a casual style, the portrait of him is at least companionable if not deep. Douglas Gorsline's pictures have a stipped effect.

Helen Perdue

SOURCE: A review of *Medals for Morse, Artist and Inventor,* in *Library Journal,* Vol. 80, No. 2, January 15, 1955, p. 191.

This new "American Heritage" book portraying so sympathetically yet accurately the dreams, trials, heart-breaks, and successes of Morse fills a need in the saga of world communication. The philosophy behind the oft-repeated phrases: "Go on and finish it," and "What are friends for?" is especially important in the lives of children today. An addition to any biography collection that can be read and enjoyed by readers from grade 5 through junior high. Excellent illustrations by Douglas Gorsline.

📖 *CARRY ON, MR. BOWDITCH* (1955)

Virginia Kirkus' Service

SOURCE: A review of *Carry On, Mr. Bowditch,* in *Virginia Kirkus' Service,* Vol. XXIII, No. 18, September 15, 1955, p. 706.

A readable biography of the man who was scarcely out of his teens before he had written the authoritative book on navigation still used at Annapolis takes Nathaniel Bowditch from a childhood in Salem through a good part of a successful seafaring career. Though Nat was apprenticed to a ships' chandler when he was twelve and was of slight stature, these two drawbacks only served to spur him on. He read Latin and Newton at night. When his apprenticeship was finished he went to sea and began astounding captains with an extraordinary navigation ability that got their ships out of stringent circumstances—a monsoon in Manila and a three day fog outside of Salem. While the drama of these events is the main substance of the book, some profitable attention is paid to Nat's methods of studying, his conviction that he could explain navigation clearly, and the important principles he followed. Nice drawings by John O'Hara Cosgrave II.

Jennie D. Lindquist

SOURCE: A review of *Carry On, Mr. Bowditch,* in *The Horn Book Magazine,* Vol. XXXI, No. 5, October, 1955, p. 368.

A fictionized biography of Nathaniel Bowditch, a born mathematician who grew up in Salem; was taken out of school and apprenticed to a ship chandler when he was twelve; read and studied by himself; and when he finally went to sea astonished everyone by his ability to apply his knowledge to navigation. Miss Latham has highlighted the incidents in his life that are particularly appealing to young people, and included so much natural, lively conversation that this is a swift-moving book. And it is also a good picture of the man who, before he was thirty, wrote *The American Practical Navigator,* still a standard guide in the U.S. Naval Academy.

Booklist

SOURCE: A review of *Carry On, Mr. Bowditch,* in *Booklist,* Vol. 52, No. 4, October 15, 1955, p. 82.

An animated narrative biography which successfully brings to life Nathaniel Bowditch, mathematician and astronomer, who before the age of thirty had written *The New American Practical Navigator* still used today as the standard authority on navigation. Although his formal schooling ended at the age of ten, Bowditch continued to study incessantly throughout a nine-year apprenticeship to a Salem ship chandler—even teaching himself Latin in order to read Newton's *Principia*—and afterwards learned, practiced, and taught practical navigation during a successful seafaring career. Bowditch's perseverance, methods of study, and success should inspire today's young people. Enhancing illustrations of Salem and sailing vessels.

New York Herald Tribune Books

SOURCE: A review of *Carry On, Mr. Bowditch,* in *New York Herald Tribune Book Review,* November 13, 1955, p. 8.

The intriguing title of this biographical novel about the *Practical Navigator* might well epitomize the whole trend of Nathaniel Bowditch's life. From early boyhood he was forced to carry on in situations not of his own choosing and was able to turn them into valuable experiences.

Because of his family's poverty he had to relinquish his dreams of going to Harvard and become an apprentice in a Salem ship chandlery. During the long period of indenture he studied navigation, even learning Latin in order to read Newton's *Principia*. When later he went to sea, he continued his studies and won the support of the crew by patiently explaining the secrets of navigation. His scientific mind and wizardry at mathematics enabled him to discover a new way to work lunars. Furthermore, his thorough checking of Moore's *Practical Navigator* revealed more than 8,000 errors in this important tool for seamen. His study and these valuable experiences resulted in the writing of his *American Practical Navigator* before he was thirty. His personal reward was an honorary degree from Harvard for his contributions to seamanship.

The author of this book merits special commendation for her writing ability. She has created out of a mass of involved, technical material a living, dramatic story, which will hold the interest of most young people. It reads like a lively sea yarn, yet does not skimp on the mathematical and navigation data. In fact, Bowditch's own simple explanation to his unlettered crew could not have been any more lucid than Miss Latham's account of the discoveries of this "human calculating machine." Special commendation is due also to John O'Hara Cosgrave 2d, the illustrator, for his delicate black-and-white drawings of old Salem and the ships of other days.

Helen Perdue

SOURCE: A review of *Carry On, Mr. Bowditch,* in *Library Journal,* Vol. 80, No. 20, November 15, 1955, p. 2646.

Delightful, interesting, and inspiring biography of a rather obscure yet important figure in the maritime history of our country. How he accomplished his life's ambitions will interest boys and most girls of 10-15. The oft-repeated phrase "you can do anything with mathematics" and the emphasis on accuracy will please teachers of that subject. Illustrations, rich in detail, by John O'Hara Cosgrave II add authenticity and value. Excellent format. Recommended for purchase in all libraries.

Zena Sutherland

SOURCE: A review of *Carry On, Mr. Bowditch,* in *Bulletin of the Center for Children's Books,* Vol. IX, No. 4, December, 1955, p. 50.

An absorbing account of the life of Nathaniel Bowditch, author of *The American Practical Navigator* that is still a standard text in the U.S. Naval Academy. Nat's short stature was considered a serious handicap to his ambition to become a sailor, and when, at the age of twelve, he was apprenticed to a ship's chandler for nine years, even Nat was inclined to despair of ever completing his education or becoming a ship's captain. However, through the help and encouragement of friends who recognized his unusual mathematical ability, he educated himself and, after his apprenticeship was served, earned a place as second mate on a vessel. From there on his rise was rapid as captains began to realize that he not only had the ability to handle a ship, but could teach even the dullest of the sailors to do navigation. The fictionalized account makes good reading as a sea story as well as biography, and the book could be used as supplementary reading in mathematics classes.

Norma Rathbun

SOURCE: A review of *Carry On Mr. Bowditch,* in *Saturday Review,* Vol. XXXVIII, No. 51, December 17, 1955, p. 35.

The romance of old Salem, sailing ships, the adventures and legends of the sea, and the perseverance and integrity of a boy are skilfully combined in this very readable biography. Readers from nine on will find this a thrilling and challenging story of a mathematical genius who fought the handicaps of physical smallness, poverty, and superstitions and wrote the *American Practical Navigator.*

Graphic, authentic illustrations by John O'Hara Cosgrave II in double-spread black-and-white drawings and chapter headings add greatly to the historical detail of the book.

TRAIL BLAZER OF THE SEAS (1956)

Virginia Kirkus' Service

SOURCE: A review of *Trail Blazer of the Seas,* in *Virginia Kirkus' Service,* Vol. XXIV, No. 18, September 15, 1956, pp. 707-08.

The *Trail Blazer of the Seas* was Matthew Maury, a Tennessee boy who despite strong family opposition, entered the Navy in the early 1800's and went on to become one of its most valuable servants. His story, steeped in the annals of navigation, responsible sea route control, weather analysis and so forth, shows the seriousness and forethought of Jean Lee Latham's *Carry On, Mr. Bowditch,* the biography that won the Newbery Award for 1956. Rather than exposition, most of the text is on-the-scene narration, but conversations and characterizations have been planned with close attention to authentic detail and the material that emerges—on young Mat's training as a midshipman, the trip around the Horn that convinced him of the need for planned sea traffic, his later work with the department of charts and instrument, his controversial advocating of Southern sea repair stations—will absorb and delight anyone with an interest. Handsome prints by Victor Mays, many of which illustrate the implements with which Maury worked, supplement the story.

Virginia Haviland

SOURCE: A review of *Trail Blazer of the Seas,* in *The Horn Book Magazine,* Vol. XXXII, No. 5, October, 1956, p. 365.

Matthew Fontaine Maury's thirty years in the United States Navy—from his service as midshipman begun in 1825 to his final position as a Commander—were filled not with battles against enemy ships but with warfare against ignorance and reactionary ideas about naval training and scientific knowledge of winds and currents at sea. Lieutenant Maury was the human gadfly whose persistent stinging proved it was possible to chart sea lanes and give out advantageous sailing directions. Thus, as an oceanographer, he founded a new science of the physical geography of the sea, for which he received many honors from abroad but only belated attention at home. Miss Latham treats the vast amount of detail she has found through research in an easy conversational style, using quotations from letters, sample charts, and figures to make her story vivid. Teen-age boys should find it as absorbing as her Newbery Medal-winning *Carry On, Mr. Bowditch,* particularly the account of Maury's early years at sea.

The Booklist and Subscription Books Bulletin

SOURCE: A review of *Trail Blazer of the Seas,* in *The Booklist and Subscription Books Bulletin,* Vol. 53, No. 5, November 1, 1956, p. 126.

An absorbing fictioned biography of Matthew Maury, nineteenth-century American naval officer and hydrographer, by the author of *Carry On, Mr. Bowditch.* The expert narration lends a sense of immediacy to the account of Maury's life and achievements, clarity to the explanation of his work, and reality to the inspiring and perceptive portrait of a man who all his life fought for his ideas against bitter opposition.

New York Herald Tribune Book Review

SOURCE: A review of *Trail Blazer of the Seas,* in *New York Herald Tribune Book Review,* November 18, 1956, p. 12.

Matthew Fontaine Maury was a fighter, "if you're for something you've got to fight even if you know you'll be licked." He was destined to fight all his life against odds for his ideas. Beginning as a boy he had to fight to get into the navy. As he gained experience and knew the slowness of navigation in the early eighteen hundreds ideas for all sorts of improvements came to him. Jean Latham dramatizes his struggle to get his wind and current charts made and their conclusions accepted. The reader rushes ahead as full of interest in these achievement as in a battle at sea. It is the technique used successfully in the Newbery Prize-winning *Carry On, Mr. Bowditch.* In her Newbery acceptance speech Mrs. Latham said it was being "back yard familiar" with the world of her story before she proceeded to "flesh the bones with reality." It is no small achievement to do this with a fairly uneventful life whose chief interest lies in blazing trails, a Naval Academy, separate lanes for East and West bound shipping—apparently not quite achieved in 1956—an Atlantic cable, a weather bureau. We like Victor Mays' dark and strong black and white pictures, especially those of sailing vessels.

Learned T. Bulman

SOURCE: "Mapping the Oceans," in *The New York Times Book Review,* November 18, 1956, pp. 16, 20.

In the early Eighteen Hundreds many problems beset those who sailed the high seas. Gales, storms, calms and generally uncertain weather conditions too often meant doom.

Dedicated to the Navy as a youth and chairbound to the Depot of Charts and Instruments because of a leg injury, Matthew Fontaine Maury conceived of scientifically planned sailing directions for ships—and spent six heartbreaking years proving their safety. He measured the depth of the ocean bottom, planned sea lanes to avoid collision and instigated the Brussels Conference on Ocean Meteorology in 1853. He received the highest honors the governments of the world had to bestow, only to be temporarily retired as an incompetent! For three years he doggedly kept on with his work and was finally reinstated as commander.

Another fine biography by Newbery Award winner Jean Latham, this does not seize the reader's interest as quickly as did *Carry On Mr. Bowditch,* but, once caught, one enjoys it to the end.

Zena Sutherland

SOURCE: A review of *Trail Blazer of the Seas,* in *Bulletin of the Center for Children's Books,* Vol. X, No. 4, December, 1956, p. 52.

In a style similar to that of her *Carry On, Mr. Bowditch,* the author presents the life of Matthew Fontaine Maury and his contribution to the development of navigation through his charting of wind and ocean currents

and his work for a naval academy. Although the style is highly fictionalized, the facts of Maury's life are accurate, and his personality as shown here agrees with descriptions of him given in more scholarly biographies. The style is quite readable, and the book will be enjoyed as a good story in addition to being interesting biography.

THIS DEAR-BOUGHT LAND (1957)

Virginia Kirkus' Service

SOURCE: A review of *This Dear-Bought Land,* in *Virginia Kirkus' Service,* Vol. XXV, No. 3, February 1, 1957, p. 80.

A fictionalized account of the Jamestown venture (and a third book from the author of the Newbery prize winning *Carry On, Mr. Bowditch*) becomes the story of young David Warren, a weak, undersized boy who is taken aboard the *Susan Constant* as a common sailor when his father, a prominent investor in the London Company, is killed. It is David's determination that leads him to the fo'c'stle rather than the officers' quarters where his father's friend, Wingfield, would have had him. Learning seamanship the hard way, David also comes in contact with Smith, is both repelled and fascinated by the man's daring and becomes an eager witness to the events of the next months. Smith's commitment for attempted mutiny, the upsets caused by his inclusion in the council, the disastrous Indian attacks and the more beneficial negotiations with them—all are familiar. But seen through David's eyes and following his own passage from boyhood to manhood, they take on a creditable vitality and the climax—the last minute arrival of Lord De la Warr and the supply ships when all had been thought lost—is realistic. A polished narrative that shows careful research and a good sense of the issues involved.

Helouise P. Mailloux

SOURCE: A review of *This Dear-Bought Land,* in *The Horn Book Magazine,* Vol. 33, No. 2, April, 1957, p. 140.

The settlement of Virginia, and especially the part which Captain John Smith played in it, as seen through the eyes of fifteen-year-old David Warren. The circumstances which put David on the voyage are somewhat far-fetched, as is his reason for sailing before the mast rather than as a gentleman. But the story as a whole is credible and well told; it is primarily one of ordeal—trial by weather, Indians, illness, fatigue, ignorance, hunger, traitorous companions, homesickness—but it is never melodramatic.

The Booklist and Subscription Books Bulletin

SOURCE: A review of *This Dear-Bought Land,* in *The Booklist and Subscription Books Bulletin,* Vol. 53, No. 16, April 15, 1957, p. 434.

When his father, an investor in the London Company, was killed on the eve of his departure to Virginia, undersized David Warren, fifteen, went in his stead, sailing not as a gentleman but as a common seaman in defiance of Captain John Smith who maintained the venture was not one for women and children. Skillful, vivid narration gives vitality and a sense of immediacy to the absorbingly detailed story of David's experiences and growth to manhood, of the founding of Jamestown, and of John Smith, whose courage, vision, and resourcefulness played an important role in the development of both boy and colony.

George H. Favre

SOURCE: A review of *This Dear-Bought Land*, in *Christian Science Monitor*, May 9, 1957, p. 11.

The story of Jamestown, of Captain John Smith and Pocahontas, of Chief Powhatan, and of all the nameless colonizers who fought to keep a tenuous toe-hold on the American continent has been told many times. Sometimes this telling is romantic and gallant, sometimes impersonally historic, sometimes tragic. Jean Lee Latham has rewritten the Jamestown epic in a powerful way. A twelve-year-old or an adult can hardly fail to respond to the courage, determination, foolhardiness, and sometimes criminal weakness of its characters.

There is much that is inspiring in the Jamestown story and much that is horrifying. The young reader who picks up this book should be a well-balanced and thoughtful individual, who can see through the misery and horror of one of history's great moments, and pick out the fine and brave qualities that made the effort worthwhile. Following young David Warren's career, as right-hand man to Captain John Smith, in this fine book should make that not a difficult task.

New York Herald Tribune Book Review

SOURCE: A review of *This Dear-Bought Land*, in *New York Herald Tribune Book Review*, May 12, 1957, p. 29.

Four seventeenth-century boys are setting sail in books to Jamestown from London this year of the 350th anniversary of the founding of that colony. . . .

Their stories told by four different authors, Marion Nesbitt, Miriam E. Mason, Lavinia Dobler and Jean Lee Latham, are planned to interest readers about the age of the young heroes. They all cover about the same period of Jamestown's history, from the sailing in December 1606 to the arrival of Lord Delaware. Jean Lee Latham's *This Dear-Bought Land* is by far the best of them all. It is written with the zest one gives a favorite subject, is dramatic and paints a vivid picture of the desperate venture.

She also offers very ingenious suggestions in explanation

of the early silence of Captain John Smith about many incidents which he reported in his later years. David Warren, hurt and insulted by Captain John Smith, the first time he meets him, reluctantly grows to admire him. Thus the readers gain an understanding picture of the thorny and indomitable character. David's story begins dramatically with a hold-up and murder. There is a deft use of Christmas carols, first in his English home before the tragedy and again when he and Captain John Smith are in Powhatan's power, threatened with death. As David struggles to become a strong and helpful man, his love for the colony grows until he can echo Smith's words: "It has been my hawk, my hounds, my wife, my child, the whole of my content, this dear-bought land."

Zena Sutherland

SOURCE: A review of *This Dear-Bought Land*, in *Bulletin of the Center for Children's Books*, Vol. X, No. 10, June, 1957, p. 131.

In a more fictionalized style, but with the same competent, forceful writing that characterized her biographies of Bowditch and Maury, the author tells of the early days of the Jamestown settlement from its founding to the arrival of Lord Delaware just as the colonists were about to give up and return to England. The story is told as it happens to fifteen-year-old David Warren, son of an investor in the London Company, who, when his father died, took his place, but insisted on sailing before the mast rather than as a passenger. Through David the reader comes to know the men who built the Jamestown colony, in all their strengths and weaknesses, and, like David, will alternate between hate and admiration for John Smith—with admiration winning through in the end. An excellent piece of historical fiction to give young people of this generation an understanding of the quality of men who founded the early colonies.

YOUNG MAN IN A HURRY: THE STORY OF CYRUS W. FIELD (1958)

Virginia Kirkus' Service

SOURCE: A review of *Young Man in a Hurry: The Story of Cyrus W. Field*, in *Virginia Kirkus' Service*, Vol. XXVI, No. 13, July 1, 1958, p. 464.

Jean Lee Latham, whose **Carry On, Mr. Bowditch** won the 1955 Newbery award, achieves in this biography of Cyrus Field a picture not only of a phenomenal man, but of a period marked by possibility and challenge. Field, by thirty, was—in the world's terms—a highly successful man. But it was not until the middle of the nineteenth century that he struck upon a program which was commensurate with his ability, for it was then that he undertook the job of laying a cable which would run beneath the Atlantic Ocean from Newfoundland to Ireland. Such a means of sending messages would be invaluable in times of war and emergency, but it demanded of its pioneers infinite patience and courage. After years of repeated failure and frustration, the cable was laid, and as the biography closes, Field speculates on the possibility of achieving the same end in the Pacific. Well written and documented, this is a substantial contribution to the library of American lives.

Margaret Warren Brown

SOURCE: A review of *Young Man in a Hurry: The Story of Cyrus W. Field,* in *The Horn Book Magazine,* Vol. XXXIV, No. 5, October, 1958, pp. 390-91.

At fifteen, Cyrus Field was earning $50 a *year* as an errand boy. Twenty years later he was able to retire with an honest fortune. The extraordinary qualities of character which made this possible were later responsible for the laying of the first trans-Atlantic cable. It took thirteen years of one heartbreaking failure after another. Desperately seasick on each trip, Field crossed the Atlantic seventy-four times in his efforts to raise the colossal sums necessary and to keep the project going. The story is powerfully written, and intensely exciting. The solving of the numerous apparently unsolvable problems involved in the manufacture and laying of thousands of miles of cable becomes spellbinding. Drama and suspense reach a great climax on the deck of the *Great Eastern,* largest ship afloat in 1866, when with Field we finally see the cable successfully laid. A magnificent book.

The Booklist and Subscription Books Bulletin

SOURCE: A review of *Young Man in a Hurry: The Story of Cyrus W. Field,* in *The Booklist and Subscription Books Bulletin,* Vol. 55, No. 3, October 1, 1958, p. 80.

A lively narrative biography of Cyrus W. Field the American capitalist who made a fortune and attained an important position in the business world before the age of thirty-five and, after a brief retirement, devoted nearly 13 years to projecting and promoting the laying of the first Atlantic cable. Although this is less outstanding than the author's earlier books, Field's faith and dogged determination are clearly revealed and the frustrations, failures, and final success in laying the cable are engrossingly detailed.

Carolyn W. Field

SOURCE: A review of *Young Man in a Hurry: The Story of Cyrus W. Field,* in *Library Journal,* Vol. 83, No. 20, November 15, 1958, p. 3307.

A story that never minimizes hard work and long hours is the basis for this fast-moving yet vivid picture of Field and his years of struggle to get the Atlantic cable laid. Boys and girls in 6th-10th grades will relive his

heartbreaking failures and final success and should close the book filled with admiration for the great men of vision who never give up. Good paper, excellent print, and fine black-and-white illustrations, by Victor Mays.

Howard Boston

SOURCE: "He Linked Two Worlds," in *The New York Times Book Review,* January 18, 1959, p. 28.

In most history textbooks only passing reference is made to Cyrus W. Field. No reader of Jean Lee Latham's latest fictionalized biography will ever be disposed to dismiss the enterprising Field so briefly. This lively and convincing book brings the man most responsible for the Atlantic Cable unforgettably to life.

We meet 15-year-old Cyrus in 1835 when he arrives in New York City to become an errand boy in a dry-goods store, and we follow his rise in the business world. The account really takes off, though, when Field throws himself into the project of tying the Old and New Worlds with a submarine cable. The staggering problems he tackles—and the heartbreaking setbacks he receives—make absorbing reading.

Laying underseas cable and sending messages through it are highly technical operations, but Miss Latham makes them not only crystal clear but exciting. A cable splicing in mid-Atlantic becomes as dramatic an achievement as a delicate surgical operation. Readers of this fast-moving, conversation-packed biography will be genuinely impressed with Field's integrity and perserverance.

DRAKE, THE MAN THEY CALLED A PIRATE (1960)

Virginia Kirkus' Service

SOURCE: A review of *Drake, The Man They Called a Pirate,* in *Virginia Kirkus' Service,* Vol. 28, No. 3, February 1, 1960, p. 96.

Hero or pirate? This is the question not only history but his contemporaries asked of Francis Drake. According to this text, the bold Englishman, servant to Queen Elizabeth, was every inch the patriot. Shrewd, fearless, and enterprising, the young man, who, before reaching the age of seventeen, was captain of his own ship, recognized the menace of the Spaniards to England and foresaw that England's destiny lay in securing their naval power. In his capacity of self-elected protector of England's rights against Spain, often the tactics that he used were unorthodox. Alone, he and the men of his ship raided Spanish vessels and harried the Spanish fleet in the Caribbean. But this he did in order to cut off supplies from Philip. The author, winner of the 1955 Newbery Award, stresses the fact that he refused to kill women, children or unarmed men. Sir Francis Drake's life was one of colorful achievement and this biography does much to convey the richness of event and atmosphere which was the portion of one of Elizabeth's most celebrated knights.

Zena Sutherland

SOURCE: A review of *Drake, the Man They Called a Pirate,* in *Bulletin of the Center for Children's Books,* Vol. XIII, No. 11, July-August, 1960, p. 178.

Exciting and informative, an excellent biography of Sir Frances Drake. As vivid as any picaresque fiction is the story of Drake's colorful career in one of history's most colorful epochs. The action at sea is vividly described, and the Elizabethan background lends drama; Drake himself is a strong character. The book concludes with the conquest of the Invincible Armada, a fitting climax to the long years of Drake's remorseless enmity toward Spain.

Virginia Haviland

SOURCE: A review of *Drake, The Man They Called a Pirate,* in *The Horn Book Magazine,* Vol. XXXVI, No. 4, August, 1960, p. 301.

A full biography which reads like historical fiction as it covers its hero's voyages from the precocious age of ten through his one-man war on Spain in the Caribbean and around the world, to the climax of his career vanquishing the Armada. Heavily conversational but without earlier speech and salty language, the book lacks period flavor, yet gives a clear account of Drake's genius as a mariner and the historical background of his adventuring.

MAN OF THE MONITOR: THE STORY OF JOHN ERICSSON (1962)

Learned T. Bulman

SOURCE: A review of *Man of the Monitor: The Story of John Ericsson,* in *The New York Times Book Review,* May 20, 1962, p. 30.

On March 9, 1862, two iron-clad sea monsters fought in deadly combat off the Virginia coast. One of these, the Monitor, was the invention of Swedish-American John Ericsson—in every way a successful failure.

At 13, mechanical-minded Ericsson was in charge of a 600-man crew on the Göteborg-Stockholm locks. At 23, an officer in the Swedish Army, he was sent by royal order to England to study mechanics and work on several of his own inventions. In the next thirty-five years, first in England, then in the United States, he suffered humiliation and bankruptcy. Naval and military officials

saw no need for change; state and national governments were tight-fisted and short-sighted. Although he had perfected a caloric engine, screw propellor, special devices for cannon, a steam fire-engine and many other essential inventions, it took the armor-plated Monitor to finally bring him some fame and fortune.

As she did with Nathaniel Bowditch and Matthew Maury, Jean Lee Latham has made an impressive figure of a nearly forgotten man. Again she stops at a focal point—the battle of the Monitor and the Merrimac; Ericsson died twenty-seven years later. Again one misses a chronology. But, like all of her fictionised biographies, this is fast-paced, informative reading.

The Booklist and Subscription Books Bulletin

SOURCE: A review of *Man of the Monitor: The Story of John Ericsson,* in *The Booklist and Subscription Books Bulletin,* Vol. 58, No. 21, July 1, 1962, p. 761.

An animated fictionized biography of John Ericsson, the nineteenth-century Swedish-American engineer and inventor who designed the ironclad warship, the *Monitor.* Covering Ericsson's life from the age of eight to his designing of the *Monitor* and its successful encounter with the *Merrimac,* the narrative presentation shows the development of Ericsson's ingenious mechanical ability, traces his career as an inventor, engineer, and soldier, and describes his important achievements. For younger readers than is Burnett's *Captain John Ericsson.*

Margaret Sherwood Libby

SOURCE: A review of *Man of the Monitor: The Story of John Ericsson,* in *New York Herald Tribune,* July 1, 1962, p. 9.

The second biography of John Ericsson to appear in a year is told almost entirely in dialogue. This and the decorative black and white pictures of Leonard Everett Fisher make it more alluring to the average 12-year-old than the more sober narrative of Constance Bueil Burnett, *Captain John Ericsson.* Having attracted the young readers Miss Latham, like a competent craftsman, tries to hold their interest by squeezing as much excitement as possible out of the many frustrations of her hero's life: She is less successful in this than in her Newbery prize-winning life of Nathaniel Bowditch or even in *This Dear-Bought Land,* the fictionalized life of Captain John Smith. Perhaps this is because all her characters talk alike, in a pleasantly ordinary modern speech. Whatever the reason, a less vivid picture of the ever-optimistic inventor of the "Monitor" is given here than in Mrs. Burnett's book, but those who are deterred by the other book's more mature approach will find the same tale of endless gallant new starts after sickening failures, often due to no fault of Ericsson's inventions.

Zena Sutherland

SOURCE: A review of *Man of the Monitor: The Story of John Ericsson,* in *Bulletin of the Center for Children's Books,* Vol. XVI, No. 1, September, 1962, p. 10.

A very good biography, somewhat simpler in style and vocabulary, and with more dialogue than Burnett's *Captain John Ericsson,* which devotes more attention to the years preceding Ericsson's residence in England. Smoothly-written and lively in style, this book is excellent for a younger audience than the Burnett book; it has value not only as a biography but also as a good book of the Civil War period.

RETREAT TO GLORY: THE STORY OF SAM HOUSTON (1965)

Virginia Kirkus' Service

SOURCE: A review of *Retreat to Glory: The Story of Sam Houston,* in *Virginia Kirkus' Service,* Vol. XXXIII, No. 6, March 15, 1965, p. 318.

The book is probably intended as a biography cum fictionalized dialogue of Houston. However, since the dramatization is heavy, and the historical details have been played up according to their effectiveness with respect to the total narrative, the book's value is as an exciting adventure based on actual events. The most vivid part of the book occurs during Houston's leadership of the rebel armies against Mexico. The vastness of Texas and the complexity of varying events throughout the state is made quite clear. This is an outstandingly realistic portrayal of a war. Houston's oft repeated battlecry, when it comes, is strong and fresh in its impact. The opening of the book, which deals with young Sam as a mischievous little boy, seems rather foolish, but once it reaches the time in his adolescence when he joined an Indian tribe it becomes a compelling drama of a hero who seems more than human. The book continues through Houston's career as Governor and U.S. Senator, a period when he was ridiculed and glorified in turn. His integrity seems noble (even when he was a drunk) and his courtship has a heavily romantic glow. It is an exciting pageant dealing with a great man, born to be a legend.

Best Sellers

SOURCE: A review of *Retreat to Glory: The Story of Sam Houston,* in *Best Sellers,* Vol. 25, No. 4, May 15, 1965, p. 99.

In this story of Sam Houston history is made to live again by the author. Conversations may be pure imagination, but they do not distort historical fact; rather, they help to make the facts more meaningful for the young reader. In this day we need more biographies of great men who have sacrificed their lives for noble principles of patriotism. Here is the life of a great patriot, a man who cared little for self and money and a great name. Young readers will find it difficult to lay aside this volume as they follow young Sam from the family farm in Virginia through his career as an adopted Indian, a schoolteacher, a regular of the U. S. Army and, finally, through his days as governor in Texas. His was a life that was shrouded by sorrow and condemnation, but he did have years of brightness. It is a life of a man all young readers should meet, since it is the life of an essentially good man, a brave man who followed the highest principles.

Lon Tinkle

SOURCE: A review of *Retreat to Glory: The Story of Sam Houston,* in *The New York Times Book Review,* June 13, 1965, p. 24.

Jean Lee Latham makes Sam Houston a believable and very human hero. Tallest of the Texans, Old Sam remains Texas's most colorful figure. But his career had national significance, touching the fate of the Indians in the nation, the Mexican War that added our southwest quarter to the union, the Civil War and, of course, the evolution of Texas from Mexican province to independent republic to American statehood.

The private personality behind this flamboyant public figure is as interesting as the career. With impressively swift pace, Miss Latham, who knows what to omit or merely suggest, does not skimp Sam's character at all. It is clear why as a boy, bored with country school and storekeeping in Tennessee, he ran off to live with the neighboring Cherokees. It is clear why he later became Andy Jackson's protégé, clear how his courage and personal sense of honor dominated the major events in his life: among them the tragedy of his first marriage, his heroic role in the Battle of San Jacinto and his resignation as Texas's Governor when he could not approve secession. This superior account makes both man and history clear and absorbing.

The Booklist and Subscription Books Bulletin

SOURCE: A review of *Retreat to Glory: The Story of Sam Houston,* in *The Booklist and Subscription Books Bulletin,* Vol. 61, No. 20, June 15, 1965, p. 996.

A highly fictionalized biography that retains all the more glamorous elements of the legends which have grown up around Houston's name and yet succeeds in giving Houston a dignity and stature which he deserved. The author resorts so frequently to fictionalization in attributing conversation, thoughts, and feelings to Houston that the book would qualify equally well as historical fiction or biography, and many boys will read it simply as a good story. Houston's weaknesses are not glossed over but are explained in a manner that shows sympathetic understanding rather than disapproval. A worthy addition to library collections of materials about historical characters.

Zena Sutherland

SOURCE: A review of *Retreat to Glory: The Story of Sam Houston,* in *Bulletin of the Center for Children's Books,* Vol. XVIII, No. 11, July, 1965, p. 164.

An unusually vivid biography, in which the subject is approached with objectivity rather than with adulation, with the result that the candid portrayal of Houston seems that of a real and fallible person. And all the more a real hero. The emphasis is on Houston's military and political involvement in Texas as it changed from Mexican Texas to an independent republic to a state of the Union. Famed for his physical courage, Houston is even more impressive for his moral courage and integrity, especially when—knowing that he would be deposed from the position of Governor—he refused to sign an oath of allegiance to the Confederacy. And there the book ends, with Houston's wife saying that never had she been as proud as at that moment.

📖 ANCHOR'S AWEIGH: THE STORY OF DAVID GLASGOW FARRAGUT (1968)

Raymond W. Barber

SOURCE: A review of *Anchor's Aweigh: The Story of David Glasgow Farragut,* in *School Library Journal,* Vol. 15, No. 3, November, 1968, p. 120.

A vivid picture of the U.S. Navy from 1810 through 1869 and a less skillful, fictionized depiction of David Farragut who gained fame in the Civil War naval battles of New Orleans and Mobile Bay. During his career, Farragut witnessed the decline of the sailing ship, the rise of steam power, and the advent of the iron-clad ship. Despite the addition of much fictionized dialogue, Farragut is seen solely as a Navy man and never comes across as a believable human being. The historical background is interesting but as a biography, this falls flat.

Sidney D. Long

SOURCE: A review of *Anchor's Aweigh: The Story of David Glasgow Farragut,* in *The Horn Book Magazine,* Vol. 44, No. 6, December, 1968, p. 704.

The early naval career of David Glasgow Farragut as presented in the biography has the flavor of a Gilbert and Sullivan libretto: nine-year-old Midshipman Farragut being fitted for his uniform and longing for real orders; ten-year-old Midshipman Farragut aboard the *Essex,* fiercely determined to act as big as anyone, to shout as loud, to be as brave. But the image of the small boy playing midshipman fades rapidly after he receives—at the age of twelve—command of a prize ship captured by the *Essex.* From this episode on, the reader is filled with a growing admiration for David Farragut, both as an officer and as a person. The author depicts a man who is plagued by disappointment and delay in his career and whose personal life was often marked with sorrow. Even the Civil War, which was to make him the most noted naval figure of his time, forced him to choose between his home and his country, and marked the passing of the beautiful sailing ships he loved. The biography—written with sincerity and humor—ends with David Farragut a national hero and an international personage.

The Booklist and Subscription Books Bulletin

SOURCE: A review of *Anchor's Aweigh: The Story of David Glasgow Farragut,* in *The Booklist and Subscription Books Bulletin,* Vol. 65, No. 12, February 15, 1969, p. 660.

A well-known biographer skillfully re-creates the character and personality of a famed American naval hero in a lively narrative account replete with authentically drawn scenes of marine warfare and life aboard sailing vessels. Incidents of Farragut's personal life are included but major focus is on his service with the U.S. Navy which began during the War of 1812 at age ten and was climaxed by his action in Mobile Bay as admiral in the Union Navy. The book is illustrated with small drawings of ships and maps.

📖 FAR VOYAGER: THE STORY OF JAMES COOK (1970)

Kirkus Reviews

SOURCE: A review of *Far Voyager: The Story of James Cook,* in *Kirkus Reviews,* Vol. XXXVIII, No. 9, May 1, 1970, p. 507.

"You're going to go far." Shoulders squared and mind alert ('brains-above-his-station,' they call it), the young James Cook follows his star . . . right out of biography into the heady gambits of historical fiction. Quick ciphering turns a "lubber" into a tutor, correspondence with a sea-struck boy serves as the courtship of his pretty cousin, a kraut rebellion is reversed by offering it only to the officers, gentleman botanist Banks faces humiliation if he crosses the master of the *Endeavor.* And when Cook announced that not home but *Terra Incognita Australis* was their destination, "Nobody complained; nobody lost his nerve." But, the fact is that, thanks to the sauerkraut and other anti-scorbutics, nobody got scurvy—only the Captain's laconic instructions, cook Thompson's jaunty "Aye, aye sir" and the officers' gulps are of the author's devising. So with this whole venture, composed of dramatic scenes, vigorous

dialogue, colorful personalities—it's eminently readable, not unreliable, just somewhat flushed (and in the case of his wife, affected: "There are some things [like danger] a man doesn't tell a woman"). But closer to the course of his career than, say, *South Sea Shilling,* a fictionalization that some libraries are still classifying as biography.

Margaret Shepherd

SOURCE: A review of *Far Voyager: The Story of James Cook,* in *Best Sellers,* Vol. 30, No. 7, July 1, 1970, p. 145.

It was predicted that James Cook would go far because he had "brains above his station." Indeed, he had. Although he was born the son of a laborer, he rose to the rank of Captain of the Royal Navy. He surveyed the coasts of Tahiti, New Zealand, Australia, and western North America and discovered the Sandwich Islands.

A gripping tale of the sea and of the men who challenged it. Clear, succcinct explanations of nautical terms and elementary navigation blend in with the natural tempo and flavor of the story.

Mary M. Burns

SOURCE: A review of *Far Voyager: The Story of James Cook,* in *The Horn Book Magazine,* Vol. XLVI, No. 4, August, 1970, pp. 400-01.

Thoroughly conversant with the equipment, traditions, and living conditions aboard eighteenth-century sailing ships, the author has written Cook's story with the flair and pace of a first-rate adventure yarn set against the background of the Seven Years' War and the American Revolution. By the dictates of eighteenth-century English society, James Cook, son of a day laborer, should never have become a naval officer, a privileged position usually reserved for the sons of the gentry. Indeed, he should probably have never even been an able seaman, for he was eighteen when he first set forth as apprentice on a Whitby collier. His metamorphosis from seaman to commissioned officer in His Majesty's Navy is substantial material in itself for an engrossing narrative. His exploits as one of history's greatest navigators and explorers add dramatic tension as well. Today's young reader for whom the world has already become too small should find it illuminating to consider an era—merely two centuries ago—when much of the Pacific Ocean was unknown. By demonstrating the magnitude of Cook's accomplishments during his Pacific explorations, the biography presents him as no casual thrill seeker but rather as a meticulous and dedicated scientist. Respected for his knowledge and humanitarianism, Cook nevertheless was separated by his visionary genius from ordinary friendships and the full companionship of his wife and family—a subtheme to which the author gives sympathetic attention. His death in 1779, due in part to the Hawaiians mistaking him for the man-god "Lono," is the stuff of tragedy, and the author

makes of it a dramatic yet dignified conclusion to her narrative.

RACHEL CARSON: WHO LOVED THE SEA (1973)

Elizabeth L. Miller

SOURCE: A review of *Rachel Carson: Who Loved the Sea,* in *School Library Journal,* Vol. 20, No. 1, September, 1973, p. 70.

This short career-biography tells about scientist Rachel Carson's girlhood and clearly explains the difficulties of entering a field dominated by men. Because her knowledge of marine biology was coupled with an ability to write well, she was assigned to prepare scripts for a radio program, "Romance under the Waters": these articles became the nucleus for her notable books about the sea. *Silent Spring,* which grew out of her battle against the careless use of dangerous chemicals, aroused the conscience of the nation. For older readers, a lengthier, more complete title about Carson is Philip Sterling's *Sea and Earth: the Life of Rachel Carson.* Latham's book, in a large print format, will be useful for third graders who know about ecology and conservation as well as for visually handicapped older readers.

Zena Sutherland

SOURCE: A review of *Rachel Carson: Who Loved the Sea,* in *Bulletin of the Center for Children's Books,* Vol. 27, No. 3, November, 1973, p. 46.

Although the first part of this biography dwells rather tediously on Carson's childhood, it is better written than most series biographies for younger readers, and the treatment is otherwise balanced. The book describes Rachel Carson's early determination to be a writer, her love affair with science, and her decision to combine her scientific career with her writing ability to produce some of the finest of contemporary popular science books. The personal material tends to be superficial, so that the reader learns how Rachel Carson took care of young relatives rather than what sort of person she was; however, the book does give the most pertinent facts about a subject who is important because of what she accomplished, and it touches on the topical issue of pollution.

ELIZABETH BLACKWELL, PIONEER WOMAN DOCTOR (1975)

Judith Goldberger

SOURCE: A review of *Elizabeth Blackwell, Pioneer Woman Doctor,* in *The Booklist,* Vol. 72, No. 8, December 15, 1975, p. 579.

A clearly written, if unexciting, biography of the first

woman doctor in the U.S. Blackwell's personal struggles for recognition and her important role in furthering the cause of women in medicine are outlined here. The text is occasionally condescending and oversimplifies both the doctor and her life. However, at this grade level, little is offered on the subject at present.

Charlotte Ladd

SOURCE: A review of *Elizabeth Blackwell, Pioneer Woman Doctor,* in *School Library Journal,* Vol. 22, No. 6, February, 1976, p. 40.

After 72 titles, the Discovery series has a sameness in format and style which certainly begins to pall. Latham does not impart any of the excitement of Blackwell's achievement (she was the first woman doctor in the U.S.), and the stilted short sentences give a dull interpretation of one woman's stubborn struggle in the face of great opposition from the masculine world of medicine. Skip this.

Felissa L. Cohen

SOURCE: A review of *Elizabeth Blackwell, Pioneer Woman Doctor,* in *Science Books & Films* Vol. XII, No. 1, May, 1976, p. 43.

This is one of the better biographies of Elizabeth Blackwell. It begins when she was eight years old and follows the Blackwell family in their move from Bristol, England, to America. Woven into the first chapter is the belief of Mr. Blackwell that his daughters should have the same education as his sons—"girls are thinking creatures, too." Latham, by giving details on Blackwell's early life, allows the young reader to see her develop and makes her seem to have real depth. Latham follows her struggle to enter medical school, earn her diploma and begin her internship and describes her setback when she loses one eye. Her interactions with such notable figures as Florence Nightingale, Marie Zakrzewska, her sister Emily Blackwell, and Rebecca Cole (the first black woman doctor) are chronicled. Her hard work to attain her goals, her beliefs about health and preventative medicine and her support by the Quakers are detailed. Her later years in England are handled in much less detail, and a child might have difficulty in determining the time frame of the last chapter. The illustrations are pertinent and well done, the information is accurate and the story is clearly told. An excellent addition to school or public libraries.

> Additional coverage of Latham's life and career is contained in the following sources published by Gale Research: *Major Authors and Illustrators for Children and Young Adults;* and *Something About the Author,* Vol. 68.

Ann McGovern (Scheiner)

1930-

American author of fiction, nonfiction, poetry, picture books, and retellings; editor.

Major works include *Too Much Noise* (1967), *If You Sailed on the Mayflower* (1969), *Sharks* (1976; revised and reprinted with new illustrations as *Questions and Answers about Sharks,* 1995), *Night Dive* (1984), *Swimming with Sea Lions and Other Adventures in the Galápagos Islands* (1992), *Playing with Penguins and Other Adventures in Antarctica* (1994), and *The Lady in the Box* (1997).

INTRODUCTION

McGovern has written over fifty books for primary and middle graders, ranging from histories and biographies to humorous picture books, folklore, and poetry. She is particularly well-known for her science books based on her experiences scuba diving in waters all over the world. These underwater stories, such as *The Desert Beneath the Sea* (1991), co-authored by "Shark Lady" Eugenie Clark, and *Playing with Penguins and Other Adventures in Antarctica* have garnered her praise for their skillful interweaving of factual information about sea creatures, the marine biologists who study them, and explorations of exotic places within a story narrated by a young protagonist. Reviewers have said her books are "an appealing addition to the science shelf"; others have recognized the educational value of McGovern's works, favoring books such as *Questions and Answers about Sharks* over beginning science textbooks. In a similar vein, reviewers have commended McGovern's histories and biographies for their "light and lively" style and "fresh," "fascinating" approach to factual and historical material. Using simple, declarative sentences and a child-oriented question-and-answer structure, McGovern creates history books that convey to young readers little known facts of daily life in colonial America, on the frontier, and in a Native American village. "Because history bored me so much when I was in elementary school," McGovern explained, "my goal was to make our past exciting for children." A reviewer for *Publishers Weekly* noted *If You Sailed on the Mayflower* as "a history book that spells pure fun." Her newest book in the "If You . . . " series is *If You Lived 100 Years Ago* (1999).

McGovern's biographies focus on women in history who displayed courage, intelligence, and compassion in their struggle against social injustices. These books explore the lives of women such as Harriet Tubman, Eugenie Clark, and Deborah Sampson, a young woman who fought in the Revolutionary War not so much out of patriotism as from a yearning for the adventure denied her because of her sex and poverty. McGovern explained that in *Wanted Dead or Alive: The Story of Harriet Tubman,* "I

chose a woman in history whom black and white girls could admire. I like to write books about heroines for today's society." In all of her works, McGovern endeavored to dispel stereotypes and sensationalism about her subject matter with truth and knowledge. *If You Lived with the Sioux Indians* (1974), for example, emphasizes the peaceable nature of the Sioux nation. Likewise, *Questions and Answers about Sharks* was intended to deflate popular fears of shark attack and to "tell the truth about these amazing creatures," McGovern revealed. "I learned that out of hundreds of known species of sharks, only a handful have ever attacked any humans." Commending McGovern's ability to attract young readers to the wonders of science, Clarence Truesdall praised *Down Under, Down Under: Diving Adventures on the Great Coral Reef* (1989) as "one of the best books of its kind," a "valuable acquisition" for school libraries and classrooms, and "one of those rare books which can hold its own against television."

Biographical Information

The daughter of an elementary teacher and a bacteriologist, McGovern was born in Manhattan, NY. After her father's death when she was five, her relationship with her mother became strained and she began to escape into books and poetry, reading and writing about more exciting places and more loving families at a very early age. "My mother became very strange after my father died," she explained. "I felt unwanted and unloved. . . . Because of my sad childhood, I became a writer, a reader, a dreamer, a survivor, a lover of the arts, and a traveler." As a child, she also developed a stutter, which made her shy and withdrawn in school. McGovern began working at age fourteen, taking jobs such as folding socks at a children's clothing store, shelving books at the library, and later modeling clothes for catalogues. She eventually attended University of New Mexico for one year before she married her English professor and had a son, Peter. A year later, she divorced and she and Peter moved back to New York City where she took a job stamping and dating galley proofs in the production department of Western Publishing, publishers of Little Golden Books. She began writing children's books after overhearing an editor at Western Publishing say she needed a book on Roy Rogers; that evening McGovern researched and wrote the book, presenting it to the editor the next day. In 1955, her first book, *Roy Rogers and the Mountain Lion,* was published and she was taken out of the production department and made an editor, writing Little Golden Books from television shows. Another chance encounter, this time with a childhood friend, illustrator Nola Langner, led to their collaboration on several picture books, including *Little Wolf* (1965), *Half a Kingdom,* (1977), and *Stone Soup* (1968; reprinted, 1986). She also collaborated with Ezra Jack Keats on *Zoo, Where Are You?* (1964), and later worked for Scholastic and as a freelance writer. In 1961, she traveled to Mexico, her first vacation and first time out of the country. From her trip she developed an interest in history and travel and began writing such books as *If You Lived in Colonial Times* (1964) and *If You Grew Up With Abraham Lincoln* (1966). In 1970, she married Martin Scheiner, and their travels together all around the world inspired several books with a scientific edge, including *Down Under, Down Under: Diving Adventures on the Great Barrier Reef,* and *The Desert Beneath the Sea.* McGovern has visited all seven continents, seen seven total eclipses, attended a Sultan's birthday party in Malaysia, watched orangutans in Borneo, ridden on an elephant to photograph tigers in India, viewed huge Kodomo dragons in Indonesia, gone scuba diving among sharks in the Great Barrier Reef, and was among the first Americans ever to scuba dive in China. "I can't believe," McGovern commented, "that the sad, shy, stuttering child I once was grew up to become a happy adult with fifty books published."

Major Works

Reflecting on her career as a writer, McGovern once wrote, "I realize [my books] reflect my life in three ways: ideas that I strongly believe in; desire for knowledge (I never finished college); [and] exciting personal experiences." Her folktale *Stone Soup* has become a classic, as has *Too Much Noise,* of which a reviewer for *Horn Book Magazine* stated, "Small children will love the peasant humor, the rhythmic repetition, the absurd logic, and the tongue-in-cheek illustrations." Written in a question-and-answer format from a child's perspective, her history books are informal enough to attract even reluctant readers yet are full of accurate details about daily life in earlier eras—what children wore, what they ate, what types of houses they lived in. "In my historical books," she explained, "I try to ferret out the truth; even though the truth may not be popular. I think it important to tell it like it was; to show, for example, that the Pilgrims got seasick on the Mayflower and threw up like ordinary folk." *If You Grew Up with Abraham Lincoln* (1966) follows Lincoln from his rural childhood to his adult career as a lawyer in a small town to his years as a politician in the nation's capital, answering questions about frontier life in the mid-nineteenth century. Likewise, *If You Sailed on the Mayflower* uses a child-oriented approach and simple text to present information on the Pilgrims, their voyage on the Mayflower, and their first year at Plymouth, asking questions such as "Did children go to school?," "Would you have had any fun on the *Mayflower?*," and "What kind of furniture did the Pilgrims have?" *If You Lived with the Sioux Indians* asks questions concerning the daily life of a young Sioux Indian in the 1800s such as "What kind of house would you live in?" and "What was the Sioux religion?," and provides information to help dispel stereotypes about Native Americans ("The Sioux Indians did not have red skin. No Indians did.")

McGovern also used a question-and-answer format for *Questions and Answers about Sharks,* which many reviewers regarded as a readable presentation of scientific facts about these myth-plagued creatures. As with her earlier histories, her numerous books on the sea, its inhabitants, and those who study underwater life were intended to educate in an entertaining manner, often relaying information within a fictional story narrated by a young protagonist. In *Night Dive,* a twelve-year-old girl describes her participation in a scientific expedition with a diving party that includes her mother, a marine biologist, in search of a rare fish. Despite its fictional framework, *Night Dive* has received recognition for its clear, succinct explanations of scuba diving techniques, scientific methods of gathering information, and presentation of marine flora and fauna. Commending McGovern's choice to use a fictional device to present scientific information, Denise M. Wilms stated that "the narrative allows for a bit of dramatic tension without compromising the book's factual display." Several of McGovern's science-adventure books, including *Night Dive,* are illustrated with her own photographs of underwater life or those taken by her husband or her son, James Scheiner. In *Swimming with Sea Lions and Other Adventures in the Galápagos Island,* McGovern implements a diary format in which a young girl is the author of a journal narrating a trip with Grandma to the Galápagos Islands. The journal also contains excerpts from Grandma's diary that provide more detailed scientific information on the animal and sea creatures they encounter. She uses the same writing technique in *Playing with Sea Lions*. McGovern's fascination with sharks spawned *Shark Lady: True Adventures of Eugenie Clark* (1978) and *Adventures of the Shark Lady: Eugenie Clark Around the World* (1998), two biographies on pioneering marine biologist and friend, Eugenie Clark. Clark collaborated with McGovern on *The Desert Beneath the Sea*, which explores garden eels, lion fish, octopi with horns, long-nosed sea moths, and other creatures that inhabit the sandy bottom beneath the Caribbean Sea. McGovern's simple prose, comprised of declarative sentences filled with accurate scientific information, prompted many reviewers to recommend her underwater books for budding young marine biologists as well as for older reluctant readers interested in marine photography and exotic locales.

On a different note, McGovern's latest picture book, *The Lady in the Box*, tells the story of a homeless woman and two children who help her. Recognized for its "direct, disarming prose," *School Library Journal* commented, "A modern morality tale that never strays too far from the stark reality of homelessness while portraying the generosity and concern of two children for a stranger. . . . A poignant selection that addresses the possibility for compassion in society."

Awards

Stone Soup was honored with an IRA Children's Choice Award and named a Notable Children's Trade Book. McGovern received the Scholastic Book Services' Lucky Book Club Four-Leaf Clover Award in 1972 and was named author of the year by the Club in 1974. She also received Outstanding Science Trade Book awards from the National Science Teachers Association for *Sharks* (*Questions and Answers about Sharks*) in 1976, for *Shark Lady: True Adventures of Eugenie Clark* in 1977, for *Night Dive* in 1984, and for *Swimming with Sea Lions and Other Adventures in the Galápagos Islands* in 1992.

TITLE COMMENTARY

Zena Sutherland

SOURCE: A review of *Why It's a Holiday*, in *Bulletin of the Center for Children's Books*, Vol. XIV, No. 11, July-August, 1961, p. 178.

Short sentences and few difficult words, pedestrian illustrations; illustrations are rather confusing in those cases where several scenes run together on a page, as they do in the section on New Year's Day, where a medieval and a modern scene look as though they might be one picture. Chiefly devoted to legal holidays, with one section for special religious holidays and another called "Other special days"; Christmas is, of course, listed as a legal

holiday, but there may well be non-Christian religious groups who will disagree with the statement that "Christmas is the best holiday of the year. For it means something special all over the world." Some of the days in which children have great interest, such as Hallowe'en or Valentine's Day, are given just a few sentences, whereas Election Day and Veteran's Day are several times that length.

WHY IT'S A HOLIDAY (1960)

Virginia Kirkus' Service

SOURCE: A review of *Why It's a Holiday* in *Virginia Kirkus' Service*, Vol. XXVIII, No. 15, August 1, 1960, p. 619.

To children just beginning to read, holidays are of paramount importance for it is at this time that the adult calendar assumes meaning in their lives. Here is a list of holidays—New Year's Day, Lincoln's Birthday, Washington's Birthday, Independence Day, Labor Day, Columbus Day, Veteran's Day, Thanksgiving, Christmas, Rosh Hashanah, Yom Kippur, Succoth, Hanukkah, Passover, Valentine's Day, Arbor Day, Flag Day, Halloween, United Nations Day. The background and festivities of each occasion [are] described in simple terms which provide the child with a miscellany of historical and cultural data. Illustrated by Dagmar Wilson, this is recommended for classroom libraries.

THE STORY OF CHRISTOPHER COLUMBUS (1962)

Martin Goldberg

SOURCE: "Searching for Columbus," in *Multicultural Review*, Vol. 1, No. 3, July, 1992, pp. 10-12.

Ann McGovern's *Story of Christopher Columbus* is recommended for a child doing a report. Chock-full of information, it provides a good background on the explorer beginning with his apprenticeship as a midshipman and emphasizing his first voyage. An interesting three-page essay entitled "How Do We Know About Columbus" informs the reader of what is and isn't known about the explorer, as well as how we have obtained such information.

WHO HAS A SECRET? (1964)

Virginia Kirkus' Service

SOURCE: A review of *Who Has a Secret*, in *Virginia Kirkus' Service*, Vol. XXXII, No. 3, February 1, 1964, p. 104.

The kind of secret illustrated in the beginning (e.g., the ground has a secret; the picture shows mice crowded every which way in tunnels with an occasional snake trying to pass) is vastly different from the type depicted in the major portion of the book (e.g., fall has a secret; the secret is Halloween). The first ones are more effective; there is a notable humor in the discovery of these which is replaced by a guessing technique in the later ones. The carefully drawn, breezy illustrations, in which the artist has cleverly combined pencil and color, are directed to a young audience that will enjoy them. A near strong success by the author of *Why It's a Holiday*.

Zena Sutherland

SOURCE: A review of *Who Has a Secret?* in *Bulletin of the Center for Children's Books,* Vol. XVIII, No. 7, March, 1965, pp. 106-07.

A picture book with a slight text, simply written; the illustrations are soft in execution, partly realistic, partly stylized. The book has a repeated pattern of two double-page spreads: the first shows, for example, a boy kneeling near a pond—"The pond had a secret"—and the second spread shows the fish in the pond. Again, two rabbits— "The rabbits have a secret"—and in the next double-page spread, an all-over pattern of rabbits. The concept is appealing: in simple, everyday things there are wonders not immediately visible; the fact that some of the secrets seem a little artificial weakens the impact, however. For example, the attractive page showing children trimming a Christmas tree follows the sentence "Winter has a secret." Here the secret is not an intrinsic quality as is the plant that grows from the seed that has a secret.

ZOO, WHERE ARE YOU? (1964)

Virginia Kirkus' Service

SOURCE: A review of *Zoo, Where Are You?* in *Virginia Kirkus' Service,* Vol. XXXII, No. 17, September 1, 1964, p. 892.

The strength of this book lies in Caldecott Medal winner Keats' color swirled illustrations. The story provides some night scenes that enable the artist to present some effective silhouette work. The book follows Josh, a little boy who sets out to collect animals for a projected zoo. He always returns with junk instead—and so it is finally a junk zoo. His day and night trips are spurred by the near-fantasy animals he never manages to bag. There is some recognition value here for the impetuous collector but it is the sort of story that can exist only in conjunction with these particular pictures.

Virginia Haviland

SOURCE: A review of *Zoo, Where Are You?* in *The Horn Book Magazine,* Vol. XLI, No. 1, February, 1965, p. 42.

Living in a zoo-less town, Josh wants a zoo of his own and, equipped with proper catching and carrying equipment, sets off to collect an assortment of creatures. Small children who would delight in seeing a zoo materialize will be quite satisfied with Josh's accumulation, instead, of what he calls "junk." In the striking full-color collage illustrations with varied textured effects there are a sunny-yellow morning background, blues and lavender in the afternoon, and at night extraordinary skies of marbled papers in deep purples and greens. A fresh and childlike picture book.

IF YOU LIVED IN COLONIAL TIMES (1964; reprinted, 1966)

Publishers Weekly

SOURCE: A review of *If You Lived in Colonial Times,* in *Publishers Weekly,* Vol. 189, No. 22, May 30, 1966, p. 88.

A well-known writer and a well-known artist combine their talents to answer in words and pictures the questions small children ask about the old days—from "Did the children have to worry about table manners?" to "What games did they play?"

Zena Sutherland

SOURCE: A review of *If You Lived in Colonial Times,* in *Bulletin of the Center for Children's Books,* Vol. 19, No. 11, July-August, 1966, p. 181.

A book that gives a great deal of information and is nicely appropriate to the capability of the beginning reader: short topics, simple style, large print; the illustrations are plentiful, attractive, and often humorous. The running text is divided into short topics, each headed by a question; for example, "Did children have to worry about table manners?" or "How did people get the news?" Through the answers to such questions, the young reader can get a good picture of daily life in the colonial period; much of the text is directly concerned with the activities or living habits of colonial children, but some of the book gives basic information about colonial industry, or administration, or communication.

LITTLE WOLF (1965)

Virginia Kirkus' Service

SOURCE: A review of *Little Wolf,* in *Virginia Kirkus' Service,* Vol. XXXIII, No. 19, October 1, 1965, p. 1037.

Despite the bigger bluster of his name, Little Wolf has a certain kinship with Chipmunk, of *Chipmunk in the Forest;* both were more chicken than brave. Little Wolf at least was not afraid; he just didn't like the idea of hunting and preferred to help the animals. When he did some first aid on the chief's son, the tribe at last recognized his special potential—"You will be a mighty healer some day." The idea of the tribe responding to a cute, lovable, passive type may not seem very plausible, but it's a pleasant thought. The brown and white stylized drawings are interesting and appropriate.

Roseanne H. Harrington

SOURCE: A review of *Little Wolf,* in *Childhood Education,* Vol. 43, No. 2, October, 1966, pp. 96, 98.

Little Wolf's family and tribe are scornful of him, for he goes into the woods only to learn about animals, plants and herbs, never to hunt. The only animals he brings back are those in need of his restorative skills. Goaded by his father's insistence that he must hunt, he takes his bow and arrow into the woods, only to reject again the concept of destruction. On his way home he comes upon Brave Bear, young son of the chief and already an accomplished hunter. To Brave Bear's surprise, Little Wolf's peculiar talents solve an urgent problem. Upon the boy's return, Little Wolf's father concedes that the art of healing may be as essential to the tribe's welfare as the art of hunting. Illustrations in a rich, earthy brown blend well with the rhythmical cadence of the words.

THE QUESTION AND ANSWER BOOK ABOUT THE HUMAN BODY (1965)

Virginia Kirkus' Service

SOURCE: A review of *The Question and Answer Book About the Human Body,* in *Virginia Kirkus' Service,* Vol. XXXIII, No. 20, October 15, 1965, p. 1080.

The Believe-It-Or-Not question and answer approach to human biology employed in this book takes into account the balmy sense of wonder that younger children bring to information about how we all work (i.e., "Can you swallow standing on your head?" "Do people who can wiggle their ears hear better?" "What is an itch?"). The brief, direct answers also take into consideration the short attention span, the need to know fast. The big, labelled, diagrammatic cross sections of various organs supply the necessary visual detail. Bones, muscles, skin, senses, nervous system, digestion and circulation are given this catechism coverage and it comes up more exciting than beginning textbooks in biology and hygiene.

Science Books: A Quarterly Review

SOURCE: A review of *The Question and Answer Book About the Human Body,* in *Science Books: A Quarterly Review,* Vol. 1, No. 3, December, 1965, pp. 166-67.

Factually, there is nothing wrong with the contents of this addition to the question-and-answer books for young people. However, it is a disorganized series of illustrat-

ed answers to questions that the author wanted to answer, not necessarily what the reader would logically ask. It is made somewhat more useful by means of the analytical index. However, the lack of a systematic approach will result in the acquisition of disjointed information—not an undersanding of human anatomy and physiology. . . .

IF YOU GREW UP WITH ABRAHAM LINCOLN (1966)

Zena Sutherland

SOURCE: A review of *If You Grew Up with Abraham Lincoln,* in *Bulletin of the Center for Children's Books,* Vol. 20, No. 1, September, 1966, p. 15.

Like the author's . . . *If You Lived in Colonial Times;* a simply written and delightfully illustrated book that describes the day-to-day aspects of frontier living; here the book adds some information and some anecdotes about Lincoln. Where would you live? What kind of house would you live in? What was the furniture like? Incorporated into the answers to these and other questions are some facts about how Abe Lincoln (and other boys) dressed, what his chores were, what his frontier cabin was like. The text moves from the Kentucky frontier to New Salem, then to Springfield; thus the author has an excellent opportunity to describe country life, the small town, and the larger town.

Irene Davis

SOURCE: A review of *If You Grew Up with Abraham Lincoln,* in *School Library Journal,* Vol. 13, No. 5, January, 1967, p. 329.

The basic concept of history is made meaningful to young students through the many well-chosen details of daily life in the time of Lincoln. This sense of sequence in time, an important social studies concept, is also developed by detailing the changes which developed during the span of Lincoln's life. Simple vocabulary and uncomplicated sentence structure make for easy reading. Informative, sometimes amusing illustrations on every page and readable type combine to produce inviting format for this grade level.

TOO MUCH NOISE (1967)

Virginia Kirkus' Service

SOURCE: A review of *Too Much Noise,* in *Virginia Kirkus' Service,* Vol. XXXV, No. 6, March 15, 1967, p. 335.

The story is as old as shhh . . . : *a little noise* may seem *too much noise* but when you add *a lot of noise* and then take it away, *a little noise* seems *a quiet noise.* Old Peter complains to the wise man of the village: "My house makes too much noise. My bed creaks. My floor squeaks. The wind blows the leaves fall on the roof. *Swish. Swish.* My tea kettle whistles. *Hiss. Hiss.*" Following the wise man's advice, he gets first a cow ("Moo. MOO"), then a donkey ("HEE-Haw"), a sheep ("Baa. Baa"), a hen ("Cluck. Cluck"), and a dog and a cat ("Woof. Woof . . . Mee-ow. Mee-ow") until . . . "I am going crazy," says Peter. And the wise man replies, "Let the cow go . . . the donkey go . . . the sheep go . . . the hen go . . . the dog and the cat go." Now only the bed creaked . . . the floor squeaked . . . the leaves fell . . . the tea kettle whistled . . . "Ah. Oh," said Peter. "How quiet my house is." A simple repetitive tale, equally suitable for noisy participation and for settling down to "a very quiet dream."

Publishers Weekly

SOURCE: A review of *Too Much Noise,* in *Publishers Weekly,* Vol. 191, No. 16, April 17, 1967, p. 58.

This is a funny book, a very funny book, a book about two men who will seem very familiar to TV watchers, for the farmer who is being driven up the wall by noises looks like the Pepperidge Farm farmer, and the village wise man who tells him what to do about noises is the spitting image of Groucho Marx. Together, they introduce children to a lot of animals, to a lot of noises, and to a bushel-basket of laughs.

Ethel L. Heins

SOURCE: A review of *Too Much Noise,* in *The Horn Book Magazine,* Vol. XLIII, No. 3, June, 1967, p. 337.

In her own version of an old folk tale, the author tells of Peter, an old man who found his house too noisy: the bed creaked, the floor squeaked, the leaves blew off the trees onto the roof, and even the teakettle whistled. When Peter complained, the village wise man ordered him to bring into the house a cow, a donkey, a sheep, a cat, and a dog. Only when the din became predictably unbearable and Peter was ordered to turn all of the animals out again was he able to appreciate the peace and quiet of his home. Small children will enjoy the peasant humor, the rhythmic repetition, the absurd logic, and the tongue-in-cheek illustrations, in which the wise man looks like a bearded Groucho Marx.

The Booklist and Subscription Books Bulletin

SOURCE: A review of *Too Much Noise,* in *The Booklist and Subscription Books Bulletin,* Vol. 64, No. 2, September 15, 1967, p. 130.

The too crowded house of a familiar old tale becomes a too noisy house in this entertaining picture-book story. Bothered by the noises in his house, an old man follows the advice of the village wise man by first ac-

quiring and then getting rid of a cow, donkey, sheep, hen, dog, and cat. Only then can he appreciate how quiet his house is. The simplicity and straightforwardness of the folktale are evident in both the telling of the cumulative story and in the amusing colored illustrations.

ROBIN HOOD OF SHERWOOD FOREST
(retold by McGovern, 1968)

Kirkus Service

SOURCE: A review of *Robin Hood of Sherwood Forest,* in *Kirkus Service,* Vol. XXXVI, No. 8, April 15, 1968, pp. 463-64.

The merry band returns in modern spelling, a somewhat eased vocabulary and enormously suggestive charcoal lines and smudges, deflating the overblown rich, assuring the innocent poor, and winning the hearts of good people everywhere. Tricked into shooting one of the king's deer, Robin Hood resorts to a life that proves crime does pay, also earns the absolute loyalty of his men: ablest archer Will Stutely; seven-foot-plus Little John; never-lasting Friar Tuck. The Sheriff of Nottingham is tricked and mistreated; Allan-a-Dale sings for his supper, wins his true love; Maid Marion arrives as a boy, turns to forestry (and Robin Hood to husbandry) soon enough. Romping, roguish and always in the right, the poor man's champion is pardoned and enlisted by Richard the Lion-Hearted, last seen on his way to London. Sherwood Forest has been trimmed without raising problems of conservation: "thee" and "thou" in the dialogue, modern forms in the narrative. With a sense of continuity and wholeness, the high spirit that was Lincoln green for similarly spirited younger children.

Mary I. Purucker

SOURCE: A review of *Robin Hood of Sherwood Forest,* in *Library Journal,* Vol. 93, No. 12, June 15, 1968, p. 2541.

This telling loses steadily in comparison with other versions, particularly those by Howard Pyle and J. Walker McSpadden. Spilka's black-and-white illustrations are rough, spirited, and full of humor, but the text is filled with cliches and trite similes; in addition, the author's clumsy attempts to write in olde English and, at the same time, to simplify are unsuccessful. Pyle's own shortened version is still simpler, more vigorous, and truer to the story tradition of the loftily motivated thief as hero. And slow readers will find little here to induce them to less reluctance; the Dolch version remains their best aid.

The Booklist and Subscription Books Bulletin

SOURCE: A review of *Robin Hood of Sherwood Forest,* in *The Booklist and Subscription Books Bulletin,* Vol. 64, No. 22, July 15, 1968, p. 1287.

While lacking the rich, historical background and distinctive period flavor of Howard Pyle's Robin Hood, these 10 episodes told in simple, direct modern language effectively capture the gallant spirit and gay camaraderie of Robin Hood and his Sherwood Forest cohorts. The book begins with Robin Hood's banishment for shooting the king's deer and ends with the band's pledge of service to Richard the Lion-Hearted; in between are some of the most popular tales about Allan-a-Dale, Little John, Friar Tuck, and Robin's running battle with the sheriff of Nottingham.

BLACK IS BEAUTIFUL (1969)

Publishers Weekly

SOURCE: A review of *Black Is Beautiful,* in *Publishers Weekly,* Vol. 195, No. 15, April 14, 1969, p. 97.

Black Is Beautiful—we mean this book, not the concept itself—is absurd. And destructive. It's absurd because children (if the book was done for children) are not the ones that have to be told. There's not a child alive who was born with the birth defect of a prejudice. That's a blemish they acquire from their old folks. It's destructive because in its straining to prove black is beautiful ("wet stones and shells on the sand") it separates, or laboriously attempts to separate, black from white. Which is not the hope men of good will hope for, is it?

Zena Sutherland

SOURCE: A review of *Black Is Beautiful,* in *Bulletin of the Center for Children's Books,* Vol. 22, No. 11, July-August, 1969, p. 179.

A series of photographs (some competent compositions, some hazy shots of children) accompanies a text in which a few poetic lines on each page reiterate the message of the title. "Zig-zag of lightning. Thunder crack; Stormy sky; the clouds turn black. Black is beautiful." Or, "Puppies in a window. A tankful of fish. Bright ribbons in black hair. Black is everywhere. Black is beautiful." The text is slight, the repeated asseveration that being black is beautiful—a welcome message but rather flimsily based on the prevalence of black in objects around us.

STONE SOUP (retold by McGovern, 1968; published with new illustrations by Winslow P. Pels, 1986)

Ilene Cooper

SOURCE: A review of *Stone Soup,* in *Booklist,* Vol. 83, No. 4, October 15, 1986, pp. 354-55.

A tired and hungry young man knocks at an old woman's door, but she refuses his request for a meal. He asks her for a stone, setting the familiar circumstances in motion. There are many versions of this old favorite, and it is the pictures that differentiate the various retellings; these are intriguing. Here, the old woman usually appears alone on one page, while the boy sits, lounges, juggles, and watches on the opposite side. Both are heavily caricatured, with the woman's greed as apparent as the boy's pleasure. The neatly bordered pictures are executed in deep hues that capture the folkloric feel of the story. The only false note is the ending: the boy appears to believe in his magic stone, after readers have been led to think he was perpetrating a joke. Libraries not having individual copies of this story will find McGovern's rendition worth consideration.

Luann Toth

SOURCE: A review of *Stone Soup,* in *School Library Journal,* Vol. 33, No. 3, November, 1986, p. 80.

An "easy-to-read retelling" of a traditional folktale. While it is considerably shorter than Marcia Brown's *Stone Soup* and is written in short, declarative sentences, it is also a lackluster retelling that is repetitious and downright tedious to read. It's a bit like being served a big bowl of stone soup *without* the benefit of meat, vegetables, or any spice. There are only two characters: a young man who is hungry and an old woman who learns about *Stone Soup.* The elaborate, detailed pastel drawings are evocative, but the perspective is sometimes askew. The old woman looms tall in some drawings while appearing frail and petite in others. The facial expressions often border on the grotesque. Stick to the original.

Betsy Hearne

SOURCE: A review of *Stone Soup,* in *Bulletin of the Center for Children's Books,* Vol. 40, No. 6, February, 1987, pp. 112-13.

Intended as an easy-to-read book, this suffers the consequences of jerky prose, but McGovern does try to turn the repetition to rhythmic advantage once the story is underway. At any rate, the humor of a poor lad boiling a rock and fooling a stingy woman into adding vegetables to the water is irresistible, and the pictures, though oddly sinister in color and expression, are skillfully drafted and composed. An audio-tape cassette is available with the book.

Pauline Davey Zeece

SOURCE: "I Can Do It—We Can Do It Together," in *Day Care and Early Education,* Vol. 22, No. 2, Winter, 1994, pp. 34-7.

Hungry and alone, a young man walks through a village. He approaches a little old lady to ask for something to eat. She does not want to give him food, but her curiosity allows her to share a simple round gray stone. And that is the beginning of stone soup. Into the pot go additional ingredients gained with gentle persuasion: sweet yellow onions; long, thin carrots, juicy beef bones, a bit of pepper, a handful of salt, and finally butter and barley. The soup becomes a meal fit for a king, and so they dined together. There are many lessons about sharing and cooperating to be learned from this classic story. Children love reading about and creating their own stone soup (but don't forget to remove the stone before serving!).

HEE HAW (1969)

Kirkus Reviews

SOURCE: A review of *Hee Haw*, in *Kirkus Reviews,* Vol. XXXVII, No. 18, September 15, 1969, p. 992.

The donkey has the last laugh here (*hee-haw*) and maybe he deserves it but when Showalter told and Ungerer illustrated *The Donkey Ride* (1967) they made much more fun of the man and boy taking advice from everyone as they take a donkey to market. Altogether there's less of a satirical sting and the pictures, particularly, are filled with ornamental details that don't point up the story like Ungerer's peasant types.

Booklist

SOURCE: A review of *Hee Haw*, in *Booklist*, Vol. 66, No. 10, January 15, 1970, p. 621.

Another version of the fable told by La Fontaine . . . about the man and the boy with the donkey who, by trying to please everyone please no one, not even themselves. In the present picture-book story, adapted from Aesop, the sprightly text and the caricature-like colored illustrations bring out the personality of the characters and the humor of the situation. Libraries will probably want both versions.

IF YOU SAILED ON THE MAYFLOWER (1970)

Publishers Weekly

SOURCE: A review of *If You Sailed on the Mayflower,* in *Publishers Weekly,* Vol. 198, No. 9, August 31, 1970, p. 280.

For a history book that spells pure fun, try Ann McGovern's question and answer book about the *Mayflower* and the Pilgrims' first year in America. There is a wealth of little-known facts here, presented in such a light and lively style that younger readers will never think of this as history reading.

Booklist

SOURCE: A review of *If You Sailed on the Mayflower,* in *Booklist,* Vol. 67, No. 6, November 15, 1970, p. 270.

A question-and-answer approach is used to impart information on the Pilgrims, the *Mayflower,* the voyage to the New World, the first year at Plymouth, and the Thanksgiving celebration. Many details of everyday life of special interest to children are given in answer to such child-oriented questions as "Did children go to school?" and "Would you have had any fun on the *Mayflower?*" Abundant illustrations, many humorous, and a simple, chatty text. No index, but the table of contents lists the questions that are answered in the book.

Sharon M. Karmazin

SOURCE: A review of *If You Sailed on the Mayflower,* in *School Library Journal,* Vol. 96, No. 4, February 15, 1971, p. 48.

Using a question and answer format, the author has detailed the Pilgrims' voyage on the *Mayflower,* their landing at Plymouth and their first year. Although the book is full of factual material, it is written in a simple style, suitable for young readers. Brown illustrations, generous in number, elucidate the text and are often humorous. Readable type and appealing format make this book a good choice for both school and public libraries, for younger children and older reluctant readers.

Zena Sutherland

SOURCE: A review of *If You Sailed on the Mayflower,* in *Bulletin of the Center for Children's Books,* Vol. 24, No. 9, May, 1971, pp. 140-41.

A great deal of information is given with simple informality in a text with question-and-answer format, the illustrations leavened by humor. The book covers all the familiar material about the Pilgrims' first year, but focuses on topics ("What kind of ship was the Mayflower?", "What kind of furniture did the Pilgrims have?", "Were there special jobs for boys and girls?") although the arrangement is basically chronological. The type is large, with questions printed in brown and the text in black; a cutaway drawing of the ship precedes the text.

IF YOU LIVED WITH THE CIRCUS (1972)

Kirkus Reviews

SOURCE: A review of *If You Lived with the Circus,* in *Kirkus Reviews,* Vol. XL, No. 6, March 15, 1972, p. 331.

Beatrice Schenk de Regnier's 1964 *Circus* leads in verbal and photographic "dizzy razzle-dazzle" and Laura Sootin's *Let's Go to a Circus* (1960) in backstage particulars, but this briskly accessible question and answer session has its place somewhere between the two. There is some annoying writing down ("Guess who are the teachers at the College of Clowns. Other Clowns!") and some less than stunning revelations (about hard work, danger, strict rules) along with more esoteric information (the difference between a funambulist, equilibrist, and aerialist), some silly questions ("Are clowns always funny?" "Would you make a good animal trainer?") along with the more practical ("How do you put on clown make-up;" "How do you get to be a clown?")—but on balance this attractively designed walkaround, with its lively black-and-red drawings and its list of "special circus words," should draw a reasonable crowd.

Zena Sutherland

SOURCE: A review of *If You Lived with the Circus,* in *Bulletin of the Center for Children's Books,* Vol. 26, No. 1, September, 1972, p. 11.

The question-and-answer format is often the kiss of death for an informational book, but here the questions are those a child might ask and are coached in informal, conversational style. The answers to such questions as "How do you put on clown makeup?," "Could you play with the wild animals?" or "How old do you have to be to perform in the circus?" are generous, giving in toto a broad picture of day-to-day life for circus performers and their children, and including information about training, safety, makeup, et cetera.

Phyllis Yuill

SOURCE: A review of *If You Lived with the Circus,* in *School Library Journal,* Vol. 17, No. 1, September, 1972, p. 69.

In a question-answer format similar to her previous history books (*If You Sailed on the Mayflower,* 1970; . . . *Lived in Colonial Times,* 1966; . . .) the author here gives children the inside story of life with the circus. Readers and listeners will learn that playing "Stars and Stripes Forever" warns performers of impending disaster, that there is a College of Clowns in Florida, that of all circus animals camels have the worst breath, that snakes get milk baths, and much more. Although there is no index, a table of contents lists the questions answered in the text and a glossary of circus terms concludes the book. Lively black-and-red drawings effectively capture the spirit of the circus and make this an attractive addition to library collections of circus books.

SCRAM, KID! (1974)

Kirkus Reviews

SOURCE: A review of *Scram, Kid!* in *Kirkus Reviews,* Vol. XLII, No. 21, November 1, 1974, p. 1145.

"In the city, where Joe lives, there are different things to do on different Saturday mornings in the park"—and Langner indicates the variety by superimposing a white square depicting the main action onto shaded pages, sometimes divided into frames, that show other real and imagined goings-on. The story is far simpler than the format—it's about how none of the boys playing baseball will let Joe join them, and how, after some yelling back and forth ("Go jump in the lake . . . Get lost. . . . Make like a drum and beat it"), he wanders off and finds another kid to sail a boat with—and Langner's casual thick-pencil drawings have an unassuming, down-to-earth humor that fits the everyday situation and saves the whole from looking overdone. Her unpretty kids' telling postures and expressions, the moms and babies, lovers, and umbrella carts in the background, and Joe's picture fantasy of the baseballers' dunking in shower, sink, and toilet bowl when he shouts, "Go soak your head!"—all help to make this a more pleasurable park outing than most.

Publishers Weekly

SOURCE: A review of *Scram, Kid!* in *Publishers Weekly,* Vol. 206, No. 26, December 30, 1974, pp. 100-01.

In a city park, kids looking for fun and games can find plenty of both: but not young Joe. More than anything else, he wants to get into a baseball game, but the answers he gets to his pleas to let him in the game are "Scram, kid!" and other, even more impolite suggestions. Every time he's rejected, he imagines his adversaries in various humiliating circumstances: "Go soak your head!" Joe hears, and envisions all the ballplayers lined up, waiting to stick their heads in a toilet. At last, Joe finds the best possible way to spend the day, and not in a dream, but with a friend. The "real" sequences are in the talented Ms. Langner's black-and-white sketches; the dream fulfillments, in sepia. Ann McGovern's story should be cherished by every boy and girl who has ever been rejected, which would seem to exclude nobody.

Booklist

SOURCE: A review of *Scram, Kid!* in *Booklist,* Vol. 71, No. 9, January 1, 1975, pp. 461-62.

The mix of reality and humorous fantasy in the illustrations should induce young readers or listeners to sympathize with Joe, who tries to enter a baseball game at the park but is repeatedly rebuffed with the dictum "Scram, kid." Rather than being crushed at the response, he displays a healthy resiliency. "Go fly a kite," he mutters, or later, "Go soak your head," and with each response comes a literal daydream of the ballplayers' comeuppance. Joe's sure sense of himself is refreshing, and it is no surprise when he finally joins a friendly stranger about to sail his boat. The pencilled drawings have some sloppy line work that is bothersome, but the depiction of Joe and the park activities works well enough.

Zena Sutherland

SOURCE: A review of *Scram, Kid!* in *Bulletin of the Center for Children's Books,* Vol. 28, No. 8, April, 1975, p. 134.

There were other things one could do on Saturday but Joe really wanted to play baseball. Every time he tried to get in the game, he was rebuffed; every time he was rebuffed, he had dreams of vengeance. Finally, disgruntled, he asked a boy if he could help sail his boat. Result: instant friendship, happy Saturday. The illustrations show Joe's imaginary ventures in a different color; on many pages there are many small, separate scenes of activity. The style is casual and direct, the illustrations frowsty-attractive, the familiarity of the situation appealing, but the plot is slight and on some pages the distinction between the real and the imaginary is not quite clear.

Doris Noble

SOURCE: A review of *Scram, Kid!* in *Childhood Education,* Vol. 51, No. 6, April-May, 1975, p. 328.

Having nothing to do at home, Joe goes to the park and tries to join in a game there, but the "big kids" will not let him join their baseball game. Then Joe fantasizes his anger—telling them "to make like a drum and beat it," "go fly a kite." Many children have experienced this kind of rejection and Joe shows them how to deal with the situation in a constructive manner, by finding other children in the park with whom to play.

📖 IF YOU LIVED WITH THE SIOUX INDIANS (1974)

Kirkus Reviews

SOURCE: A review of *If You Lived with the Sioux Indians,* in *Kirkus Reviews,* Vol. XLII, No. 74, December 15, 1974, p. 1309.

What kind of house would you live in? Did boys and girls learn the same things? What were good manners? Could anyone become an Indian chief? Questions and answers about everyday life, full of browsable specifics and pleasantly laid out, in an uncrowded format with full-page black-and-white drawings that make for a sympathetic impression of the people and culture. However, the text manages only a superficial glimpse; McGovern is pat where uncertainty might be wiser (the name redskin came from their red war paint?), the manners come off as stranger than they might with more explanation, and the name Sioux itself is never questioned or its origin mentioned.

Hayden E. Atwood

SOURCE: A review of *If You Lived with the Sioux Indians,* in *School Library Journal,* Vol. 21, No. 8, April, 1975, p. 56.

In what might better be called *A Catechism of Sioux Indian Instruction,* McGovern asks a wide range of questions concerning the daily life of a young Sioux Indian in the 1800's: e.g., " . . . what kind of house would you live in?"; "How did the Sioux hunt buffalo?"; "What was the Sioux religion?"; and, "Who owned Sioux land?" The answers are concise and enlightening, although sometimes bland, and the generally helpful black-and-white illustrations are not always captioned. The book is most valuable in helping to dispel myths about Native Americans ("The Sioux Indians did not have red skin. No Indians did."), and it is broader in coverage than Sonia Bleeker's *The Sioux Indians: Hunters & Warriors of the Plains.*

Zena Sutherland

SOURCE: A review of *If You Lived with the Sioux Indians,* in *Bulletin of the Center for Children's Books,* Vol. 28, No. 10, June, 1975, p. 163.

Using the question and answer format of her earlier books, McGovern gives a multifaceted picture of Sioux life in the 1880's. The text describes buffalo hunting, marriage customs, housing and tools, clothing, recreation, battles, travel, and food; it goes into considerable detail about the care and training of children and the ritual ceremonies at which they were accepted as adults. The book is profusely illustrated, very informative, and sympathetic toward the Indians in their relationship with white people; both the vocabulary and the concepts are appropriate for the primary grades reader.

📖 THE SECRET SOLDIER: THE STORY OF DEBORAH SAMPSON (1975)

Kirkus Reviews

SOURCE: A review of *The Secret Soldier: The Story of Deborah Sampson,* in *Kirkus Reviews,* Vol. XLIII, No. 20, October 15, 1975, p. 1190.

McGovern doesn't say but this is doubtless based on the first-person writings and lectures in which Deborah Sampson publicized her successful career as Robert Shurtliff, Continental soldier. Here we move deliberately from Deborah's trials as a poor orphan determined to get an education, through some bulletins on the progress of the war, and on to Deborah's army stint which ended (after discovery by a doctor) with her appearing before General Paterson in lace and ribbons—"This lovely young lady in her pink gown? Robert Shurtliff, the young soldier?" The dialogue throughout is more tedious than revealing—"Why aren't you thinking about getting married, child, like girls are supposed to do?" On the sluggish side, but an adequate, thorough testimonial to one of the most appealing heroines of the Revolution.

Cyrisse Jaffee

SOURCE: A review of *The Secret Soldier: The Story of Deborah Sampson,* in *School Library Journal,* Vol. 22, No. 4, December, 1975, p. 53.

Although occasionally dry in the telling, this is nevertheless a valuable, timely biography of Deborah Sampson who, disguised as a boy, fought for one and a half years in the Continental army until her true identity was discovered (Deborah then became a wife and mother but still continued to defy convention by traveling and lecturing). History and biography are carefully integrated as readers follow Deborah from childhood to young adulthood, paralleling the young nation's fight for freedom with Deborah's own desire for independence and selfhood. The simply written, clear account, complemented by Grifalconi's line drawings, is for younger readers than Cheney's excellent *The Incredible Deborah, a Story Based on the Life of Deborah Sampson.*

Zena Sutherland

SOURCE: A review of *The Secret Soldier: The Story of Deborah Sampson,* in *Bulletin of the Center for Children's Books,* Vol. 29, No. 7, March, 1976, pp. 114-15.

Although the first two chapters of this biography are rather heavily fictionalized, it is on the whole a capably written book, objective in tone. Deborah Sampson Gannett's story (described for older readers and in greater detail by Cora Cheney in *The Incredible Deborah*) is exciting as adventure, appealing because of the protagonist's departure from a conventional sex role, and timely because of the current emphasis on the revolutionary period in American history. This describes very simply—with adequate background information about colonial dissent and rebellion—Deborah's successful plan to pose as a man and join the Continental Army, her service as a soldier, the discovery that she was a female after she was wounded, and her career as a lecturer in later years, after she had married and her children were grown.

📖 *SHARKS* (1976; revised with new illustrations and reprinted as *Questions and Answers about Sharks,* 1995)

Barbara Elleman

SOURCE: A review of *Sharks,* in *Booklist,* Vol. 73, No. 5, November 1, 1976, p. 410.

Using a question-and-answer format, McGovern covers a wide range of information about sharks. Readers will discover facts such as what sharks look like, where they live, who their friends and enemies are, how often they eat, and when, where, and why they attack. The material is presented in a readable, straightforward manner with obvious intent to dispel much of the sensationalism attached to this fad fish; the quiet image is carried over in black line drawings which create a mood rather than supply graphic description.

Diane Holzheimer

SOURCE: A review of *Sharks,* in *School Library Journal,* Vol. 23, No. 4, December, 1976, p. 50.

Middle graders will learn much about these fascinating and mysterious creatures here. The large print, question-and-answer format is appealing and the detailed line drawings on every other page are distinctive. Though covering less information than Zim's *Sharks* which is for slightly older readers, this is still a worthwhile purchase, especially given the continued *Jaws* mania.

Zena Sutherland

SOURCE: A review of *Sharks,* in *Bulletin of the Center for Children's Books,* Vol. 30, No. 5, January, 1977, pp. 77-78.

McGovern uses the question-and-answer format that is familiar to readers of her earlier books, with such queries as "What sharks are most dangerous?" "What is the biggest shark?" "How does a mother shark care for her pups?" and "Do sharks have friends?" The answers give a great deal of information, although they provide no facts about mating or longevity. The illustrations are subdued, occasionally blending the watery outlines with the water itself so that the pictures are not quite clear. Not comprehensive, but a good introduction, this is simply written and makes clear the fact that scientists do not yet know all the answers.

Kirkus Reviews

SOURCE: A review of *Sharks,* in *Kirkus Reviews,* Vol. XLIV, No. 17, September 1, 1979, p. 978.

"When do sharks attack people? . . . What do sharks' teeth look like? . . . Do sharks have friends?" The question-and-answer format of the author's *If You Lived . . .* books works well with this subject, where to pose a question is to create suspense. Of course McGovern uses the device flexibly—the question "How do sharks find their food?" elicits two pages on the animal's different senses—but as usual it keeps things flowing for readers who are discouraged by tighter looking pages. McGovern merely skims her subject, but to her credit she doesn't exploit its ferocity. . . . Equally unsensational are Tinkelman's black line drawings which have a quiet, rippled, underwater look.

THE UNDERWATER WORLD OF THE CORAL REEF (1976)

Barbara Elleman

SOURCE: A review of *The Underwater World of the Coral Reef,* in *Booklist,* Vol. 73, No. 18, May 15, 1977, p. 1421.

In areas where ocean waters are warm and clear and the sea floor lies less than 300 feet below the surface, vibrant-colored, magical-looking coral reefs slowly and silently grow. With lucid text, the author of *Sharks* describes the exotic undersea world, building of reefs, inhabitants (both night and day), scenes at feeding time, dangers that prevail, interdependence of various plants and animals, and reasons for the variety of color. McGovern, a scuba diver, concludes her narrative with brief remarks about divers who come to explore. Full-color photographs introduce young readers to intriguing species such as barracuda, squirrelfish, foureye butterfly fish, and vase sponges.

Margaret Bush

SOURCE: A review of *The Underwater World of the Coral Reef,* in *School Library Journal,* Vol. 24, No. 1, September, 1977, p. 132.

Physical characteristics of coral reefs and the animals living in them are briefly and simply surveyed. The text—all in short sentences—is saved from monotony by the author's attention to finding interesting details and by her writing style which manages to stay lively throughout. The numerous color photographs are sometimes a bit muddy, but there is a very helpful distribution map showing the location of coral reefs around the world.

HALF A KINGDOM: AN ICELANDIC FOLK-TALE (1977)

Barbara Elleman

SOURCE: A review of *Half a Kingdom: An Icelandic Folktale,* in *Booklist,* Vol. 73, No. 16, April 15, 1977, pp. 1267-68.

Half the kingdom is the reward offered to the one who can find the missing prince—stolen away by the troll sisters. Everyone searches "far and wide" except for the peasant girl Signy, who looks "near and narrow" and finds the prince bewitched and asleep in a cave. With the help of a couple of singing swans, the two outwit the trolls and Signy accompanies the prince back to the king where she collects her reward, marries the prince, and lives happily ever after. McGovern modernizes this Icelandic tale with sprightly humor—"I don't know whether I *want* to be found," says the prince. Langner's pencil drawings, a mixture of careful and uncontrolled line-work, depict malevolent trolls, sleek swans, and a plucky Signy against a darkly somber, wintry background.

Ann A. Flowers

SOURCE: A review of *Half a Kingdom: An Icelandic Folktale,* in *The Horn Book Magazine,* Vol. LIII, No. 3, June, 1977, pp. 305-06.

In this tale, no imprisoned princess awaits deliverance by a noble prince. Prince Lini is captured by troll maidens and is rescued by a Signy, a poor peasant girl with strong ideas of equality. After the reward of half the kingdom is offered for the return of the prince, the strongest and wisest men search without success. But Signy, capable and shrewd, finds Prince Lini, outwits the troll maidens, and institutes a new regime in her half of the kingdom—with more work for the rich and more help for the poor. The girl's fine, sturdy character and the overtones of social justice produce a slightly unconventional but believable example of the variety found in folk tales. Strong black-and-white drawings set forth the cold, snowy landscape and portray the personalities of Signy and of the hideous troll maidens.

Allene Stuart Phy

SOURCE: A review of *Half a Kingdom: An Icelandic Folktale,* in *School Library Journal,* Vol. 24, No. 1, September, 1977, p. 111.

In this retelling of an old Icelandic adventure, a prince mysteriously disappears into the fog one morning and is held captive by amorous trolls, before being rescued by a spirited peasant girl with a social conscience and skill at playing checkers. Earning the hand of the prince and half his father's kingdom, the lass establishes a new welfare system and shares adventures with the prince for the rest of their happy days. The feminist line of McGovern's narrative never becomes preachy, and both the telling and the illustrations are leavened with touches of humor.

Zena Sutherland

SOURCE: A review of *Half a Kingdom: An Icelandic Folktale,* in *Bulletin of the Center for Children's Books,* Vol. 31, No. 3, November, 1977, p. 50.

A story based on an Icelandic folktale is illustrated with vigorous but overly busy black and white drawings. Prince Lini, the beloved son of a wealthy, selfish king disappears in a fog while riding through the forest: his father offers half his kingdom to whoever can bring him back. Signy, a poor peasant girl, uses her knowledge of the forest and finds Lini in a cave, captive of two trolls who, via magic words and singing swans, can put him into an enchanted sleep. Signy learns the magic words, wakes Lini, she and he think of a way to outwit the trolls, and the story ends with betrothal and agreement that with their half of the kingdom the two will apportion their wealth to help the poor. The practical Signy is an attractive protagonist, and the story has many of the familiar folktale ingredients, but there's an absence of the cadence of oral tradition in this retelling.

Margery Fisher

SOURCE: A review *Half a Kingdom: An Icelandic Folktale,* in *Growing Point,* Vol. 16, No. 9, April, 1978, p. 3293.

An Icelandic folk-tale is the basis for a picture-book whose illustrations, conceived in a flat, formalised style in black, white and grey, with human figures like stone images, give an impression of a cold, remote, anonymous land. Here a prince kidnapped by trolls is rescued by Signy, "a poor peasant girl" who helps him to discover how to break their power and who supports his determination to help the poor against royal policy. The unusual juxtaposition of politics and magic and the extended text mark this as a book for older children intrigued by traditional motifs rather than for the very young.

FEELING MAD, FEELING SAD, FEELING BAD, FEELING GLAD (1977)

Kirkus Reviews

SOURCE: A review of *Feeling Mad, Sad, Bad, Glad,* in *Kirkus Reviews,* Vol. XLVI, No. 3, February 1, 1978, p. 103.

"I fell and dropped my candy/and banged my knee/and tore my jeans./My friend called me a cry baby./*Cry baby. Cry baby.*/Just wait till the same thing happens to her./ Oh. My knee hurts!" If that's a poem, then Dr. Spock, or maybe Haim Ginott, is the modern Homer. McGovern provides 19 such expressions of the four feelings listed in the title, many of them simply statements of the situations that aroused them. "I wish I could touch the stars," is the essence of one entry, and others state that "My friend moved away," "There is nothing nice about today," "I'm not ready for sleep," or (under glad) "I slip-slop slosh through the mud. . . . I like mud, I am mud." It's easy to recognize the feelings so revealed—and Wurmfeld's staged photos of real children leave no question as to which ones are being conveyed—but their presentation here is too flat to wring more than one or two flickers of responding emotion from the lot.

SHARK LADY: TRUE ADVENTURES OF EUGENIE CLARK (1978)

Zena Sutherland

SOURCE: A review of *Shark Lady: True Adventures of Eugenie Clark,* in *Bulletin of the Center for Children's Books,* Vol. 32, No. 11, July-August, 1979, p. 196.

Fascinated by the aquarium when she was a child, Eugenie Clark never wavered in her desire to become an ichthyologist, and after obtaining her doctorate, she became director of a marine laboratory, a noted author, and a professor of zoology. While her biography is written simply, it describes a rewarding career, and it should appeal to readers because of the exciting underwater research Clark has done, particularly in investigating the habits of sharks. A list of Clark's books is included, but no photographs; the black and white pictures are—for the most part—informative and dramatic.

LITTLE WHALE (1979)

Dorothy M. Martinez

SOURCE: A review of *Little Whale,* in *School Library Journal,* Vol. 26, No. 3, November, 1979, p. 67.

Told in simple sentences that abound with factual information, this picture book traces the birth and growth of *Little Whale,* who exemplifies the characteristics and habits of the great humpback. The flowing blue-and-green double-page illustrations take readers into the watery realm inhabited by these awesome mammals. Following her migration northward, and subsequent return, the little leviathan, now mature after five years, answers the call of a male. McGovern ends with an ecological warning of the danger still existing for whales, hunted for their oil. A glossary of whale words rounds out this valuable addition for any collection.

Barbara Elleman

SOURCE: A review of *Little Whale,* in *Booklist,* Vol. 76, No. 6, November 15, 1979, p. 506.

One of the 80 different kinds of whales in the world, the humpback gets its name, according to McGovern, from a small fin on the back. Physical descriptions and behavioral characteristics of this great mammal of the sea are clearly and succinctly presented in smooth narrative that young whale buffs will find fascinating and easy to read. McGovern follows the life of one particular humpback from the time of its birth to adulthood and includes material on its enemies, food, water acrobatics, migration, and association with humans. Full-color art rendered mainly in deep sea blues and greens depicts the creatures in their watery environment. An author's note comments on the possible extinction of whales. Glossary appended.

Kirkus Reviews

SOURCE: A review of *Little Whale,* in *Kirkus Reviews,* Vol. XLVII, No. 22, November 15, 1979, p. 1329.

Little Whale (a humpback) drinks milk from her mother, practices taking care of herself, flips out of the water when feeling playful, encounters a scuba diver and later a whaling ship, migrates to colder waters with her pod ("How do whales find their way . . . ? No one knows for sure. But year after year whales return to the same place"), and—a sudden year later—finds a mate of her own. McGovern switches back and forth, not at all smoothly, between Little Whale's representative experiences and man's uncertain knowledge of humpback life. ("Father whale sings a low song underwater. . . . The sea is full of the songs of humpback whales. . . . Some scientists say that only male whales sing." Later, "Father whale sings a song underwater. His song may mean, 'Time to go.'"). The personalizing device is so indifferently used here that it would probably have been better to drop it altogether—unless you consider Little Whale's feminine gender some sort of plus. As it stands, with an appended anti-whaling note, this will serve where coverage of the humpback whale is a desideratum in itself.

MR. SKINNER'S SKINNY HOUSE (1980)

Publishers Weekly

SOURCE: A review of *Mr. Skinner's Skinny House,* in *Publishers Weekly,* Vol. 217, No. 10, March 14, 1980, p. 75.

Everything fits in McGovern's disarming and original comedy. The book's format is tall and skinny and Gerberg's zippy cartoons, in cheerful colors, fittingly elongated. Mr. Skinner loves the narrowest house he finds at "1½ Bedford Street" (just like one where the author once lived in Greenwich Village). Mr. Skinner is happy with his skinny dachshund and pet snake who enjoy his oboe music. But, in time, he needs human company. Unfortunately, all his roomies turn out to be too big for the slim house. Then Mr. Skinner meets Ms. Thinner who not only fits his dear house but plays the clarinet. And so they marry and make beautiful music together. Inspired touches in the telling and illustrations throughout the book make it most endearing as well as very funny.

Kirkus Reviews

SOURCE: A review of *Mr. Skinner's Skinny House,* in *Kirkus Reviews,* Vol. XLVII, No. 7, April 1, 1980, p. 436.

Everything in skinny Mr. Skinner's skinny house at 1½ Bedford Street is skinny—his oboe, his giraffe picture, the spaghetti he cooks, the pot he cooks it in. Even the snowman in his garden is skinny. For pets to keep him company, he buys a dachshund and a snake—and lively companions they are, as they caper through the skinny pages. Still lonely, however, Mr. Skinner invites first one, then another friend or relative to share his house—but each in turn finds it too small for his or her activities. (The actor, for example, can't rehearse in his Pinocchio costume: his nose keeps bumping into the wall.) McGovern and Gerberg make clever fun of all the

comings and goings, and a nifty fit of the inevitable solution—clarinetist Ms. Thinner, who pops up in the nick of time and to whom Mr. Skinner proposes "when the new moon was a thin slice in the dark sky." The wedding party is a ball, and the whole enterprise represents vertical living at its sprightliest—with a sound structure and plenty of space at the top for all those high spirits.

Nancy Palmer

SOURCE: A review of *Mr. Skinner's Skinny House,* in *School Library Journal,* Vol. 26, No. 9, May, 1980, p. 60.

Mr. Skinner is a skinny man who moves into a skinny house where he hangs skinny pictures (giraffes, of course), cooks skinny spaghetti, and plays a skinny oboe. When he grows lonely, he buys a long dog and a thin snake and invites a succession of friends and relatives to live with him. But the house is too narrow for a signmaker, an actor who wears a long nose for his Pinocchio role, and a rock band whose "vibes" are awful when each member has to play on a different floor. Mr. Skinner's narrow escape from solitude comes in the form of the lovely Ms. Thinner. It's true skinny love, and they all live happily in their little skinny house. The idea of an exceedingly narrow abode, and the problems it causes for those of the non-skinny persuasion, will appeal to children, although the story here could use a little fattening up. The book's tallish, narrow format is a good frame for the colorful, often clever illustrations. Their cartoony line, however, tends to give *everything* a skinny look, lessening the effect of the thin items.

Barbara Elleman

SOURCE: A review of *Mr. Skinner's Skinny House,* in *Booklist,* Vol. 76, No. 17, May 1, 1980, p. 1295.

In this modern, romantic fairy tale a skinny Mr. Skinner moves into a narrow house and searches for the right someone to share his new residence. Though his dachshund, Hot Dog, and pet snake, Slinky, are good companions, he longs for a true friend to share his slim strands of spaghetti, his thinly flaming fireplace, and the music from his slender oboe. His cousin, the signmaker, finds the house too confining; his aunt lacks room for all her plants; his actor-friend needs more rehearsal space; and the Asparagus Stalks rock group think the vibes are awful. In despair, Mr. Skinner decides to sell until he meets Ms. Thinner, who plays the clarinet, and the two live happily ever after. The cartoon-style drawings burst with energy and rainbow-pad colors that emphasize the lighthearted humor.

Zena Sutherland

SOURCE: A review of *Mr. Skinner's Skinny House,* in *Bulletin of the Center for Children's Books,* Vol. 33, No. 10, June, 1980, p. 195.

Vigorous, cartoon style line drawings add an appropriately ludicrous note to a tall tale in a tall, thin book about a thin man in a thin house. Mr. Skinner's succession of tenants found the house too narrow, and he was lonely despite his thin dachshund and his pet snake. About to sell his home, he ran into the lovely Ms. Thinner, just as skinny as he. Rapport! Duets! (A thin oboe and a thin clarinet.) Love, and a wedding. Not substantial, but fun; the story is simply written, and the exaggerated humor children enjoy is echoed in the pictures. For example, Mr. Skinner holds the middle of his snake, while the top, weaving above his head, helps put things on high shelves.

Celia H. Morris

SOURCE: A review of *Mr. Skinner's Skinny House,* in *The Horn Book Magazine,* Vol. LVI, No. 3, June, 1980, p. 288.

Mr. Skinner was a skinny man who moved into 11/2 Bedford Street, the narrowest house in the city. There he played his skinny oboe, cooked narrow spaghetti in a narrow pot, and made a thin snowman standing sideways in his garden. But he was lonely and decided, "'This house . . . won't do for one alone.'" First he added two pets, "Hot Dog, a long dog, and Slinky, a thin snake"; then a succession of would-be housemates—from his cousin Sue, a sign maker whose signs were too wide, to the Asparagus Stalks, a rock group whose "vibes were awful." But just as he was about to give up, he "bumped right into the skinniest woman he had ever seen"—Ms. Thinner, a clarinet player. A wedding ensued, and the couple settled down to make music in the narrow house in which "even their shadows fit." Cheerfully colored line drawings add their own touches of nonsense, just right for the zany book—with a tall, skinny format, of course.

NICHOLAS BENTLEY STONINGPOT III (1982)

Barbara Elleman

SOURCE: A review of *Nicholas Bentley Stoningpot III,* in *Booklist,* Vol. 79, No. 4, October 15, 1982, p. 314.

Bored with his life of traipsing around a yacht with his wealthy parents, preppy-looking Nicholas Bentley Stoningpot III longs for adventure. When a storm capsizes the vessel overnight, Nicky drifts onto an isolated island, where he enjoys himself immensely. He makes friends with a monkey, builds a house, and concocts plates, a toothbrush, and other needed items from objects found in trunks washed ashore. From time to time, ships sail by, but Nicky happily staves off rescue by donning the costumes of a pirate, an old lady, and even a wild beast. Someday, Nicky thinks, he'll go back to the real world. ("But not yet. Not for a long, long time.") This clever story should catch the fancies of young Robinson Crusoes and inspire dreams and conver-

sation about their own would-be island adventures. With aplomb, de Paola smoothly transforms Nicky from a snob complete with blazer and Izod T-shirt to a scruffy islander and gives life to the hideaway with splashes of bright flowers and beguiling animals. Pictures keep even pace with the story, creating a well-balanced flow between graphics and text, and the final-page silhouette yields a comfortable security.

Ann A. Flowers

SOURCE: A review of *Nicholas Bentley Stoningpot III,* in *The Horn Book Magazine,* Vol. LIX, No. 1, February, 1983, p. 39.

In an amusing fanciful tale Nicholas Bentley Stoningpot III was a poor little rich boy with an alligator even on his pillowcase and parents preoccupied with their social life. One day the beautiful cruise ship on which they were passengers sank in a storm, and Nicholas was cast ashore on a desert island—the perfect island with parrots, goats, a friendly monkey, a sandy beach, plenty of coconuts and fish, and lots of interesting flotsam and jetsam. Nicholas was so happy there, he used a succession of disguises (as an old lady or a pirate, for example) to fool possible rescuers, and he determined not to leave until he was good and ready. Children would probably envy his blissful life—free of parents, school, and boredom. The illustrations show a lush tropical setting as well as Nicholas changed from a prim "preppy" to a pleasing free spirit.

Katharyn F. Crabbe

SOURCE: A review of *Nicholas Bentley Stoningpot III,* in *School Library Journal,* Vol. 30, No. 5, January, 1984, p. 66.

This poor little rich boy fantasy is thematically concerned with the desire of children to be free of the constraints adults put on them and to be the center of their worlds. Shipbound Nicholas is bored with adult conversation, adult food, adult elegance. When a great storm swamps the boat, Nicky washes up on an island where there are no adults to ignore him, to make him go to bed or to make him eat things he doesn't like. He builds a house, gathers food and cultivates friends (a monkey and two goats). Nicky foils various rescue attempts but the text keeps open the possibility that Nicky will return to his family someday but "Not yet. Not for a long, long time." DePaola's illustrations, a mixture of watercolor and tempera, are invaluable in establishing the mood and extending the meaning of the text. On the yacht, the colors are generally clear and light, but a great deal of white shows the emptiness that surrounds Nicky. A double-page storm scene in which the colors are all grayed and the adults (who had been flamboyant and individualized on deck) are reduced to standardized cogs in the lifeboat divides the book in half. On the island, the colors are once again clear, but the white space shrinks, the designs often run all the way to the edges and the colors increase in intensity. In the last design, which confirms Nicky's alienation from his family, a silhouetted Nicky, his monkey and two goats, flanked by palm trees, watch the moon rise over the sea. The peacefulness and completeness of the scene reflect the nature of Nicky's quest better than anything else in the book.

The Horn Book Magazine

SOURCE: A review of *Nicholas Bentley Stoningpot III*, in *The Horn Book Magazine*, Vol. LXIX, No. 2, March-April, 1993, pp. 230-31.

The amusing, fanciful tale of a poor little rich boy happily cast ashore on a desert island when his cruise ship sinks in a storm. Also washed ashore are interesting bits of flotsam and jetsam, which keep him occupied and provide him with disguises to fool possible rescuers—for he is determined not to leave until he is good and ready.

📖 NIGHT DIVE (1984)

Denise M. Wilms

SOURCE: A review of *Night Dive,* in *Booklist,* Vol. 81, No. 10, January 15, 1985, p. 719.

A 12-year-old girl's first-person narrative describes the excitement and wonder of nighttime scuba diving. She is part of the adventure with her mother, a marine biologist who is hoping to view a special type of parrot fish that sleeps in a cocoon. As the dive gets under way, readers are presented with much information on both diving procedure and the marine flora and fauna that the divers encounter. Excellent color photographs expand the narrative's reality. McGovern's choice to use a fictional device to present scientific information works well here because the narrative allows for a bit of dramatic tension without compromising the book's factual display. Attractive and pleasingly designed, this is an appealing addition to the science shelf.

Christine Lisiecki

SOURCE: A review of *Night Dive,* in *School Library Journal,* Vol. 31, No. 6, February, 1985, p. 77.

Through the discoveries of a 12-year-old girl on her first nighttime scuba dive, readers learn about the different ocean creatures that are active at night. As the book is written in a conversational style rather than as straight facts, readers—including reluctant ones—will learn information in an enjoyable way. Beautiful full-color photos of the various creatures the girl sees are included; however, they are often several pages from the textual description. Some information on scuba diving, including a labeled photo of scuba gear, is included. The book

itself is brief and is not comprehensive, but it will peak children's interest in scuba diving and ocean life. A good addition to an oceanography or water sports collection.

Zena Sutherland

SOURCE: A review of *Night Dive,* in *Bulletin of the Center for Children's Books,* Vol. 38, No. 8, April, 1985, p. 152.

Having the story of experiencing night-diving told by a fictional girl of twelve gives this exciting book an appealing informality and immediacy; the subject may draw an even broader audience than that indicated. Beautiful color photographs show some of the creatures visible at night in the warm Caribbean waters; the narrator, who has had scuba lessons and whose mother, a marine biologist, is one of the diving party, is candid about her fears, ebullient when she gets over them, and sensible about safety precautions. McGovern uses no more fictionalization than is necessary to make the framework of the text convincing.

📖 EGGS ON YOUR NOSE (1987)

Alice Cronin

SOURCE: A review of *Eggs on Your Nose,* in *School Library Journal,* Vol. 33, No. 10, June-July, 1987, p. 86.

In the sing-song style of Dr. Seuss, P. D. Eastman, and other pioneers of the easy reader, McGovern has created some "fluff and fun" celebrating a toddler's messy eating habits with fried eggs. Chambliss' colorful cartoon-like illustrations support the silly mood and action of the slight text. It may seem strange to see a toddler having the time of his life with two to three dozen eggs, but preschoolers and beginning readers will love the exaggerated humor.

📖 DOWN UNDER, DOWN UNDER: DIVING ADVENTURES ON THE GREAT BARRIER REEF (1989)

Susan H. Williamson

SOURCE: A review of *Down Under, Down Under: Diving Adventures on the Great Barrier Reef,* in *School Library Journal,* Vol. 35, No. 13, September, 1989, p. 266.

Despite attractive, color photographs, **Down Under, Down Under** has several major flaws. McGovern tells the adventure through the first-person narrative of a fictitious girl whose marine biologist mother takes her on a ten-day diving cruise on the Australian Great Barrier Reef. While it's hard to believe that a 12 year old would participate in the complex, and often dangerous, dives described, the girl in the pictures contributes to this feeling of doubts since she looks like an adult. Too many activities and too much information are jammed into this slim volume, and as a result, neither is fully developed. The narrative also lacks organization at times; information often seems out of place. Those with an interest in marine biology or diving will be attracted by the vibrant cover photo, and browsers will enjoy the illustrations. However, not enough information is given to make this useful for research.

Betsy Hearne

SOURCE: A review of *Down Under, Down Under: Diving Adventures on the Great Barrier Reef,* in *Bulletin of the Center for Children's Books,* Vol. 43, No. 2, October, 1989, p. 38.

Although the information and photography in this non-fiction are involving, the voice is a puzzle. The first-person narrator is not the author but a 12-year-old girl recounting her experiences diving around the Great Barrier Reef off the Australian coast, and the effect doesn't always forward the facts: "I could watch the darling clown fish for hours." The implied-journal style leads to some abrupt transitions ("Would they [potato cods] slurp in my arm like a vacuum cleaner? I can't figure out Captain Chris") and false build-up of suspense ("Is one shipwreck worth the risks? . . . One bite and you're dead in five minutes. . . . Its spines are full of venom, too . . . "). The final chapter, "Getting Ready for a Dive," would have set the stage much more clearly at the beginning of the book. Diving enthusiasts will enjoy browsing through the clearly reproduced, vivid underwater photographs, but a straightforward informational tone would have improved the text.

Phillis Wilson

SOURCE: A review of *Down Under, Down Under: Diving Adventures on the Great Barrier Reef,* in *Booklist,* Vol. 86, No. 4, October 15, 1989, p. 459.

The world at the bottom of the sea has held a fascination for humans since earliest times. . . . McGovern's account of diving adventures on the Great Barrier Reef [is captivating]. As she did in *Night Dive,* the author constructs an engrossing narrative supposedly told by a 12-year-old girl, already an accomplished diver. She recounts the events of a 10-day dive with numerous full-color photos on nearly every page. The dialogue is believable, and the encounters with shipwrecks and underwater "monsters" are vividly described. An unusual approach that works.

Tippen McDaniel

SOURCE: A review of *Down Under, Down Under: Diving Adventures on the Great Barrier Reef,* in *Appraisal: Science Books for Young People,* Vol. 23, No. 2, Spring, 1990, p. 43.

A twelve-year-old girl, a junior certified diver, tells of her experiences on a dive boat with her mother, eighteen other divers and a crew of five. Her mother is a marine biologist and explores the coral reef as one of her professional activities.

At various times in her underwater adventure the youngster swims inches away from gray reef sharks; is surrounded by poisonous sea snakes; pats a 200-pound potato cod; and watches the clown fish which live in large sea anemones. The most exciting part of the trip is the exploration of the sunken "ghost ship", where fish are said to be as big as cars.

As readers become engaged in this underwater adventure, they learn about the development of the reef and the various sea life it hosts. They also learn about the damage done to this living structure by people who collect coral from it.

The first-person narrative is a wonderful way for young people to learn about underwater life. This experience is enhanced by the outstanding color photographs.

Ann McGovern, herself an experienced diver, has written other books about underwater life, including *Night Dive,* in which the diver is also a young girl. Readers seeking broader role models for young women will be pleased that the young diver and the oceanographer are female. The inclusion of a simple line map would have been helpful to the reader in locating the Great Barrier Reef. For those children wanting more information on the Reef, there are *The Underwater World of the Coral Reef* by McGovern and *A Walk on the Great Barrier Reef* by Caroline Arnold.

Clarence Truesdall

SOURCE: A review of *Down Under, Down Under: Diving Adventures on the Great Barrier Reef,* in *Appraisal: Science Books for Young People,* Vol. 23, No. 2, Spring, 1990, pp. 43-4.

Reading this book, and becoming enraptured with the beautiful photographs, is the next best thing to scuba diving in the "warm waters of the Great Barrier Reef of Australia." Now you get the title, yes? Buy the book and go diving "down under" with a twelve-year-old girl, experiencing this wonderful world through the words of an enthusiastic child. Technically reliable, competently photographed, and engagingly written, here is one of the best books of its kind.

An excellent choice as a gift for a child, and certainly a valuable acquisition for your school or classroom library. This is one of those rare books which can hold its own against television. Illustrations are beautiful, underwater, full-color photographs, and all are enough to give any young reader a vicarious experience down under, "down under." One of the best juvenile books available on scuba diving.

DESERT BENEATH THE SEA (with Eugenie Clark, 1991)

Kirkus Reviews

SOURCE: A review of *The Desert Beneath the Sea,* in *Kirkus Reviews,* Vol. LIX, No. 14, July 15, 1991, p. 933.

Author McGovern teams up with marine biologist Clark ("the shark lady") to scuba dive in the Caribbean and record the strange, beautiful creatures that inhabit the shallow, sandy-bottomed "desert beneath the sea." Despite the tedious "You are there" technique ("You look carefully at this desert beneath the sea. You see a small pointed pebble"), the resulting text is fairly exciting. Phillips's watercolor art is serviceable but doesn't capture the topic's grandeur—one longs for a photo of the eel garden (hundreds of eels swaying in the current, their tails anchored in a hole in the sandy floor), or of the strange new microscopic species nicknamed the "jumping grains of sand." Still, a vivid first-hand account of a working scientist. Both common and scientific names of animals are given in a pronouncing index, but there are no size references.

Patricia Manning

SOURCE: A review of *The Desert Beneath the Sea,* in *School Library Journal,* Vol. 37, No. 10, October, 1991, p. 140.

McGovern and Clark have banded together to produce an interesting array of windows on the creatures inhabiting the "desert" beneath the sea—open sand areas providing an exposed habitat at best. Readers, meet such rare creatures as the horned sand octopus, the long-nosed sea moth, and the jawfish, as well as more populous beings, including garden eels, tilefish, and a symbiotic odd couple—the shrimp and the goby. The book also investigates the scientific procedures used by marine biologists, and explains how data accrued can be analyzed in the lab and integrated with previous knowledge to produce new and exciting configurations. It is heavily illustrated with Phillips's colorful watercolor-and-pencil drawings. While the book does not provide in-depth material, it does give insight into the scientific process, the place of serendipity in investigation, a look at some particularly fascinating marine creatures, and—most importantly—at a cooperative effort between two women in widely divergent professions, whose interest and skills have been blended seamlessly for readers' edification and inspiration.

Sheilamae O'Hara

SOURCE: A review of *The Desert Beneath the Sea,* in *Booklist,* Vol. 88, No. 8, December 15, 1991, p. 767.

McGovern, an author of children's books, and marine biologist Clark describe the wondrous creatures they studied during scuba-diving forays—an octopus with horns, garden eels that look as if they have been planted in the sand, lionfish that have poison-tipped dorsal fins, and many more fascinating sea denizens. The authors write clearly but never condescendingly and do not hesitate to use large words when they are the best ones. Phillips' illustrations often surround the text like a sea around an island. His fish burrow, undulate, jump, and mate, but his pictures are not large enough in many cases to do justice to his subjects. An index gives the common and scientific names for the creatures described and provides a pronunciation guide, a boon for the nonscientist who is reading aloud, but a glossary would have been welcome to define unfamiliar terms like *symbiotic* and *anemone.* The collaborators make their careers sound so fascinating that children could easily aspire to be writers or marine biologists or underwater photographers after reading the book. Suggested as an introduction to science for an adult to peruse with a child or two, or for older children to read by themselves.

David L. Feigenbaum

SOURCE: A review of *The Desert Beneath the Sea,* in *Science Books & Films,* Vol. 28, No. 2, March, 1992, p. 53.

The Desert Beneath the Sea is coauthored by an experienced writer of children's books (McGovern) and a noted marine biologist (Clark), resulting in a novel presention on the work of real-life marine biologists in the field. The young reader is first invited to suppose he or she were asked along on a scuba diving research trip to study the reclusive animals of the ocean's shallow, sandy bottom. This realistic chapter illustrates how Dr. Eugenie Clark and her assistants go about observing the behavior of the sand tile fish, and readers can see the kinds of tasks they would be asked to perform if included on the trip. From there, however, the book takes a more typical approach, lightly discussing the behavior of various fish and invertebrates found in this plain environment. Most of the species discussed are little known outside of science—the razorfish, feather starfish, sand perch and Moses sole, for example—because creatures of the sand are not colorful and rarely written about. A chapter titled "Slinky Garden Eels" is particularly well done as an example of the mysteries of the sea. The scientists observe these fish with time-lapse photography and tagging, and the questions that still remain unanswered are clearly spelled out. The book goes off on a bit of a tangent as you get to the back and the subject is not high tech, nevertheless, it is well illustrated throughout with colorful drawings and is accurately done. It reminds me most of some of the Cousteau documentaries, and probably will work best when read (and explained) by an adult to an inquisitive child. I think libraries can use more books like this.

SWIMMING WITH SEA LIONS AND OTHER ADVENTURES IN THE GALAPAGOS ISLANDS (1992)

Kathryn P. Jennings

SOURCE: A review of *Swimming with Sea Lions and Other Adventures in the Galapagos Islands,* in *Bulletin of the Center for Children's Books,* Vol. 45, No. 6, February, 1992, p. 163.

In a follow-up (with the same attendant flaws and strengths) to **Down Under, Down Under,** an anonymous girl is the author of a diary chronicling a trip with Grandma to the Galápagos Islands. The description of the boat tour around the islands is fascinating, as are the accompanying color photographs of the unusual Galápagos animals. On the other hand, the fictional elements of the story don't have enough follow-through and leave the reader dangling—what is the narrator's name and age? (She looks about ten.) Why doesn't she mention any of the other passengers? Why are there no pictures of her and Grandma together? Some of the language the diarist uses is not that of a ten-year-old ("Wonder of wonders" and "the dismal bellowing of the sea lions"). Excerpts from Grandma's diary become an informal glossary, providing more detailed facts about the animals. For the most part, the narrator's enthusiasm and the great quantities of information slipped into the diary entries will serve nicely as an introduction to the unique Galápagos Islands.

Karen Hutt

SOURCE: A review of *Swimming with Sea Lions and Other Adventures in the Galápagos Islands,* in *Booklist,* Vol. 88, No. 16, April 15, 1992, p. 1526.

A two-week exploration of the Galápagos Islands is described through small photographs and short diary entries, written by an unnamed child who refers to McGovern as "Grandma." Focusing on the exotic animal life and the scenery, the narrative varies from a chatty, at times stilted tone to a drier, more factual one. A wealth of information about the Galápagos Islands is incorporated into the text, but the work lacks cohesiveness, and while the full-color photos show the beauty and unusual animal life of the islands, they are too small to be effective. Additional information presented in "Grandma's Notes" at the end of the diary entries is well written and easy to use because it is organized by date, but the absence of an index will frustrate researchers. For large collections or those where Darwin's work in the Galápagos is of particular interest.

Doris Gove

SOURCE: A review of *Swimming with Sea Lions and Other Adventures in the Galápagos Islands,* in *Science Books & Films,* Vol. 28, No. 4, May, 1992, p. 111.

This book is written as a diary of a child about 10 years old during a two-week trip with Grandma around the Galápagos Islands. With exclamation points, emotional responses, and words like "adorable" to describe fur seals, the text captures a child's point of view convincingly enough for my seven-year-old consultant. It also offers information about the Galápagos' variety of animals and plants, the history of the islands, and the efforts to preserve the fragile habitats. Not many children's books can get away with footnotes. This one does, partly by not calling them that, but mostly by making them interesting. The notes are added by Grandma and explain the geological origin of the islands (to go along with the diary entry about walking on lava), Charles Darwin's discoveries and his theory of evolution, and the courtship of boobies, frigate birds, and sea lions. The illustrations look like tourists' snapshots and match the diary format of the text. One photograph seems to be mislabeled—a chick with webbed feet is identified as a frigate bird chick, which, according to Grandma's notes, does not have webbed feet. Otherwise, the information is excellent. My consultant and I learned that the cold Humboldt current allows penguins to live on the equator, that a mail barrel in Post Office Bay since 1787 is still used; that frigate birds cannot land in the water because they are not as waterproof as other seabirds, and that some grandmas like to scuba dive with hammerhead sharks. Humor and unusual use of color and design help make this book excellent. I recommend it for school, library, and home use.

Frances E. Millhouser

SOURCE: A review of *Swimming with Sea Lions and Other Adventures in the Galápagos Islands,* in *School Library Journal,* Vol. 38, No. 6, June, 1992, p. 134.

This is a personal account of a trip to the Galápagos Islands rather than an introduction to the area's scientific aspects. Written as a day-by-day journal of a boy's vacation with his grandmother, it is accompanied by small, rather dark, full-color photographs arranged in a diary/scrapbook format. As such, this is a browsing item, rather than a resource for reports. McGovern includes not only the enjoyable and thrilling discoveries possible in such a place, but also such miseries as walking through sticky, muddy goo and being bitten by fire ants. The style of writing combines adult terminology and point of view with childlike expressions. On one page, the woods are described as smelling good, "like spices," and the opuntia cactus trees as being "taller than four people standing on each other's shoulders." Yet, on other pages readers find such descriptions as "ten adorable young sea lions" or a penguin who "was so cute."

Kelly A. Ault

SOURCE: A review of *Swimming with Sea Lions and Other Adventures in the Galápagos Islands,* in *The Horn Book Guide to Children's and Young Adult Books,* Vol. III, No. 2, Fall, 1992, p. 301.

The giddy excitement of a young girl on her first trip to the Galapagos Islands is captured in diary format, but the overabundance of exclamation points is annoying. She visits ten islands, each with its own distinctive inhabitants. Sea lions, giant tortoises, flamingos, and iguanas are all explored in the photographs and text, with elaborations on some aspects of the islands and their creatures at the end of the book.

 *THE LADY IN THE BOX* (1997)

Ilene Cooper

SOURCE: "Finding Room at the Inn," in *Booklist,* Vol. 94, No. 1, September 1, 1997, p. 138.

[An affecting story brings] home the message that Christmas must be shared to be truly experienced.

In McGovern's story, there is [a] cardboard box at Christmastime. . . positioned in front of the Circle Deli, where the heat comes through the vents. Its occupant, old Dorrie, is helped by Ben and his sister, Lizzie, who bring her food and clothing. When the deli owner insists that Dorrie move, the children's mother gets involved, leading to a slightly better situation for Dorrie and the children's involvement in a homeless shelter. . . . [T]his book predilections for helping the less fortunate and has a reasonableness about how much people can help the homeless better their lives. The art here, too, is very strong. Oil paintings, thickly layered at times, demand attention. Several scenes are powdered with snow, adding a beauty that reflects a real-life snowy city scene.

[This book becomes a modern parable] about reaching out to those who can find no room at the inn.

Additional coverage of McGovern's life and career is contained in the following sources, published by Gale Research: *Contemporary Authors New Revision Series,* Vol. 44; *Major Authors and Illustrators for Children and Young Adults; Something About the Author,* Vol. 70; and *Something About the Author Autobiography Series,* Vol. 17.

Andre Norton

1912-

(Also writes as Andrew North and Allen Weston, a joint pseudonym; born as Alice Mary Norton) American author of fiction.

Major works include *Star Man's Son, 2250 A.D.* (1952), *The Beast Master* (1959), *Catseye* (1961), *Witch World* (1964), *Iron Cage* (1974).

INTRODUCTION

One of the first women to break into the male domain of science fiction, Norton has become perhaps the most popular American writer of "science fantasy," a genre in which elements of science fiction are combined with supernatural events to form a complex universe. Norton's particular audience is young adult—although she also writes for adults—and many of her books feature young protagonists, frequently outcasts or misfits seeking a place in society, who attempt to discover their own identities while battling for a just cause. As Norton's protagonists are initiated into the adult world, they learn such life lessons as accepting responsibility for their own actions, choosing thoughtfully between good and evil, forgoing self-pity and caring for others, or finding satisfying and productive work that brings them into their proper place in the community. Norton's fiction is highly respected for its emphasis on character and action that is often lacking in hard core science fiction. Her heroes and heroines not only face physical challenges, but ethical ones and characteristically grow "in wisdom, knowledge, and virtue under stress," Sandra Miesel explained. Readers are enticed by Norton's depictions of telepathic animals which, endowed with human-like intelligence and sensitivity, play a central role in her stories. Her books are full of such sentient creatures: dolphins, horses, and birds, but most of all cats, for which she has a personal fondness. She has written more than 150 books, turning out three books a year at her most productive and writing sixty-five titles in science fiction alone. She also has published twelve works of historical fiction, thirty-two fantasy novels, and more than fifteen miscellaneous other works, not including the many science fiction and fantasy collections she has edited.

Despite her prolific output, public popularity (several of her books have sold more than one million copies), and consistently positive critical reception, Norton has not received all the recognition to which she may be entitled. Much of her work has traditionally been lumped into the juvenile fiction grab bag, although significant numbers of adults count themselves as devoted Norton fans. Moreover, there is some critical debate as to whether Norton developed her talent over the long years of her career. Some see no significant evolution of themes

or techniques from her early works to her later ones; others marvel at her perceptions of human complexity and her ability to tell a fresh story, however familiar its theme. Norton herself has never aspired to be anything other than, as she once admitted, a "very staid teller of old-fashioned stories with firm plots and morals," and in that there is unanimous agreement that she succeeds admirably. Many of her works have lasting impact, remaining in print decades after their first publication. The enduring impression instilled by her fiction prompted a reviewer for *Library Journal* to regard Norton as "one of the first women sf/fantasy writers with the selling clout to match the Asimovs and the Heinleins."

Biographical Information

Norton was born as Alice Mary in Cleveland, Ohio, the second daughter of Adalbert Freely and Bertha Stemm Norton. Twenty years younger than her sister, Norton was raised as an only child in a household that treasured not only books and reading but history, especially the family's ancestry as early American colonists and one of Ohio's early pioneer families. In this environment, Norton found that writing came easily to her. She wrote her first novel in high school, and after honing her craft and making several revisions, she published it ten years later as *Ralestone Luck* (1938). Initially, Norton did not intend to pursue a writing career. In 1930, she enrolled in Western Reserve University hoping to become a history teacher. The Great Depression, however, forced her to leave college two years later to find work. She eventually landed a job with the Cleveland Public Library where she spent twenty years, mainly as a children's librarian, excepting a one-year leave in 1941 when she opened a bookshop of her own in Maryland. She also began taking night courses in creative writing at Western Reserve. Although she had an interest in science fiction, at the time, the genre consisted predominately of short stories, for which she had little enthusiasm. Instead, she began penning historical novels and adventures. Her first published work, *The Prince Commands* (1934), was a trademark of the four books she would turn out in her first decade of writing: escapist reading, though solidly researched, that featured a juvenile male protagonist. During this period, she legally changed her name to Andre, having been advised that male readers of historical adventure books would be less likely to pick up a volume by an obviously female author. The publication of *The Sword Is Drawn* (1944) was a turning point in Norton's literary career. This book introduced a series of others about the Dutch resistance in World War II. The series won her an award from the Dutch government for its authenticity and also established the first of her devoted readers—both male and female—who for more than fifty years have been eager for a new Norton title.

Norton's career as a librarian ended when she was diagnosed with agoraphobia, a condition that seriously limited her mobility for decades. Ironically, her illness spawned her profession as a popular science fiction writer. From 1950 to 1958, she was a reader for Gnome Press and edited science fiction anthologies for World Publishing. Meanwhile, she discovered that the science fiction market had developed far beyond the short story genre. Making good use of her own writing credentials and her contacts in publishing, Norton sold her first science fiction book, *Star Man's Son, 2250 A.D.,* to Harcourt Brace in 1952. Marketed initially as a juvenile book, *Star Man's Son* sold well enough for Ace Paperbacks to reissue it as an adult novel two years later, and the book has sold over one million copies over the years. By the late 1950s, Norton quit her publishing jobs to write full time. Ill health continued to plague her, however, and in 1966 she moved to Florida with her beloved cats to make her home in a gentler climate.

Major Works

The historical novel *Scarface* (1948) is one of the four books that Norton wrote as a beginning writer equipped with the research skills of a librarian. Set in the pirate stronghold of Tortuga, it follows the adventures of a

cabin boy called Scarface, the only name he has ever known. While his sadistic overlord, the infamous Captain Cheap, sometimes hints at a mystery in the boy's past, Scarface is primarily interested in escaping his oppressive situation aboard the ship Black Flag. An opportunity for escape arrives when Cheap decides to attack Bridgetown, governed by Sir Robert Scarlett. The courageous governor helps Scarface discover his true identity, but not before the boy's own courage is challenged to the hilt.

Although many of her novels are regarded as works in a series, Norton primarily writes stand-alone stories, readable as sequels or sets because of their common heroes, villains, and complex settings. In *Star Man's Son, 2250 A.D.,* Norton introduces a common theme— the journey toward maturity and self-discovery. This first book of the "Star" series chronicles the descendants of the survivors of a nuclear war on a distant planet as they try to create a new life for themselves. Fors, a young mutant boy, is spurned from his tribe, the Puma Clan, because his mother is one of the Plains people. Accompanied by a telepathic cat named Lura, Fors secretly leaves to search for a lost city that is rumored to be free of radiation. Fors's journey leads him through perilous landscapes devastated by atomic warfare, into violent encounters with the Beast Things (horrific creatures whose exposure to radiation masks their origins as human beings), and to friendship with the prince of a previously unknown tribe. Fors is constantly tested, not only in terms of physical strength and mental agility, but ethically. He, of course, passes his tests, although not without great effort, and emerges stronger and more mature, having discovered his own self-worth.

The relationship between Norton's protagonists and their supernaturally endowed animal friends is usually an alliance between equals, one to which each party brings crucial talents and resources. Besides sharing the ability to communicate telepathically, Fors and Lura are united in their alien status, and indeed, Fors feels that he has more in common with his feline friend than with his own people. In *Catseye,* the young protagonist, Troy Horan, pursues liberty with the help of a band of nonhuman friends: a kinkajou, a hawk, a fox, and two of Norton's ubiquitous cats. Norton's animals also have many of the same capabilities as their human friends. Hosten Storm is the only human member of a scouting team in *The Beast Master.* His compatriots—an eagle, a meerkat, and a dune cat—display high levels of human skill and sensitivity. Furthermore, Norton often gives her animal characters a political agency that most authors would typically reserve for human beings. In *Iron Cage,* for example, bears band together to resist tyrannical human efforts to dominate animals by caging them and using them for experiments. In a similar vein, animals band together in *Breed to Come* (1972) to head off possible re-colonization of Earth by humans who would destroy the planet's resources. Sandra Miesel once commented that "repressive groups threaten the freedom and most especially the integrity of living beings. Norton has a visceral horror of such external control or compulsion of any sort. Persons should be free in body, inviolate in spirit."

Norton's concern with the excesses of uncontrolled science and malevolent progress also informs her science fantasy novels. Armed with telepathy, one of Norton's favorite devices, the witches of *Witch World* fend off the Kolder invaders, mechanized villains from a parallel universe. These industrialized villains are often the repository for much of what Norton finds wrong with the "civilized" world. Recognizing Norton's antipathy towards technology, Rick Brooks commented that "Norton consistently views the future as one where the complexity of science and technology have reduced the value of the individual." Norton's villains are often countered by talismans, magic, and the rhythms of the natural world. A *Times Literary Supplement* critic explained that "power [in Norton's works] is generated by the obedience to the nature of things, by stones that have lain in earth or other talismanic objects." The witches in the "Witch World" series possess magical abilities that stem from their strong connections to the land, to being somehow plugged into a collective unconscious, and from their awareness of an intrinsic order of the cosmos. Furthermore, with the "Witch World" books female characters became increasingly more important, and she has written about active, intelligent heroines in many of her novels, including *Forerunner Foray* (1973). Her female protagonist, Ziantha, is a highly skilled sensitive. Ziantha's talents are challenged by the inexorable lure of a strange green stone, leading her back through time into the mysterious Forerunner world. This adventure in time travel, lost identity, and vengeful enemies is vintage Norton, combining the imaginative possibilities of both science fiction and fantasy. Through magic, mystical quests, and strange worlds and creatures, Norton celebrates the bonds that connect humanity to nature and the cosmic order. Perhaps the most noteworthy of Norton's accomplishments is summed up by Rick Brooks: "the chief value of Andre Norton's fiction may lie not in entertainment or social commentary, but in her re-enchanting us with her creations that renew our linkages to life."

Awards

Norton has won many awards in each genre in which she writes, beginning with an award from the Dutch government in 1946 for *The Sword Is Drawn*. Individual works garnered Hugo Award nominations, and *The Elvenbane* won a Science Fiction Book Club Reader's Award in 1991. In addition, several of her books were named Junior Literary Guild and Science Fiction Book Club selections. *Bullard of the Space Patrol* earned the Boys Clubs of America Medal in 1951. Several of Norton's awards and honors have recognized her lifetime achievement as a major science fiction and fantasy writer, including the Phoenix Award in 1976; the Gandalf Master of Fantasy Award in 1977; the Andre Norton Award, established by the Women Writers of Science Fiction, 1978; the Balrog Fantasy Award in 1979; the

Nebula Grand Master Award from the Science Fiction Writers of America and the Jules Verne Award, both in 1984; and the Second Stage Lensman Award in 1987.

AUTHOR'S COMMENTARY

Andre Norton

SOURCE: "Science Fiction," in *Growing Point,* Vol. 3, No. 1, May, 1964, pp. 320-22.

Science-fiction, with two sub-divisions, known in the United States as 'space-opera' (action-adventure) and 'sword and sorcery,' has had devoted and vocal followers since the nineteen-twenties. There are innumerable 'fanzines' published with infinite labour and personal expense by readers, reviewing (often more dramatically than the professionals) the books and stories published, discussing plots and characters in absorbed detail. There is no more devoted reader.

During an earlier period, story plots depended upon the invention of some 'gadget,' holding interest by the machine itself. Now the focus has shifted to the characters. The machine may still exist, but it is how it is used by—or uses—people that is important. There are, in reality, three types of popular science-fiction. The first, which gave a name to the whole genus, is the tale based on some scientific fact, real or imaginary, the action developing, either directly or indirectly, from that fact and its influence on those involved. The second is the 'space-opera,' the fast-moving adventure which is classed as science-fiction because the hero uses a space ship in place of a trusty steed, a blaster instead of a sword or pistol; or because the background is on an alien world. But the core of the story is action. Finally, the 'sword and sorcery' tale is more closely allied to fantasy in that 'magic' may be invoked by the hero or villain as an aid to the strong right sword or blaster arm. This has a close affinity to the fairy tale or the heroic saga and may rise to heights of excellent writing. But, while many books may be at once assigned to such categories, others are a combination. Space opera may have a scientific germ, or may take on the swash-buckling of sword and sorcery.

There are several differences between British and American teenage science-fiction which are apparent at sampling. First, the background. For some years galactic exploration, and not solar system voyaging, has interested American writers. A plot dealing with a visit to the Moon or any of our sister planets would be dated, unless the accent were on the characters, as is true of those books by Robert Heinlein. But the background holds no wonder any more; real space probing is catching up too fast. Second, the age of the hero. This is a point where most American and British adventure stories differ. Our readers from ten years up do not care, in this field, to read about characters of their own age or only a few years older. The ideal hero for the teenage or 'young people's' book ranges in age from sixteen to twenty, with accent on the eighteen to twenty grouping. Since a space man needs years of training, this obstacle must be overcome by giving the young hero some quirk of background to explain his ability to take positive action at an early age. An unusual physical or mental attribute, an older relative already involved, can furnish this. Only recently has the idea of a heroine broken into what has been a very masculine field. But several books have now taken this step—notably, *A Wrinkle in Time* by Madeleine L'Engle (winner of the Newbery Medal) and *Podkayne of Mars* by Robert Heinlein.

As a practitioner of the adventure school, my own preoccupation has always been with action. However, this does not mean that character development is not important to me—it is, very much so. Most of my stories are born out of the speculation 'What if? . . .' Wide general reading in many fields provides not only the research necessary for the background (you use the customs of the Sea Dyaks of Borneo, with minor changes, to enrich the presentation of an alien race) but for these 'jump-off' ideas. For example: Research for a western novel uncovered a statement that the importation of horses and the quick adoption of that animal by the Plains Indians delayed European expansion for about a hundred years, since it inaugurated the effective irregular cavalry of such fighting tribes as the Comanches. From this was born *Sioux Spaceman,* in which an Amerindian of the future uses horses to release a downtrodden native tribe on another world. Sometimes one transposes history from the past to the future. My *Star Guard* is really the Anabasis retold on another planet. Beam Piper used the Sepoy Rebellion with high success in *Uller Uprising.*

Or, in contrast to this using our history, one can visualise 'If-Worlds' with infinite possibilities. These are founded on that most intriguing idea that from any major historical decision two possibility worlds then exist in parallel time. Suppose it would be possible to cross from one of these worlds to another, as Blake Walker does in *Crossroads of Time,* to be hunted through the ruined New York existing because of a Nazi victory in the Battle of Britain; or to face, as does the hero of *Star Gate,* the person he himself would be if history in *his* world had taken a different turn.

I have been occupied for some time with the thought that, with our sharp turn in the early nineteenth century to dependence on machines, we may have thrown aside a potentially more important alliance with the forces of nature. This idea has provided me with basis for several books concerning future companionship between man and animal, not on a master-servant level, but as equals of different gifts; and of struggles between machine-based civilisations and nature-inclined cultures.

There are no boundaries on the imagination in science-fiction. 'What if' guesses may lead down many trials, different, exciting, and profitable. In the United States

such schools as the Massachusetts Institution of Technology have recognised the value of this creative speculation. Many of the inventions now integral parts of modern life were first envisioned by science-fiction writers of earlier generations. Who now denies the exactitude of the prophecies of H. G. Wells and Jules Verne? Our forefathers exercised such dreaming in the creation of the unseen worlds of ghosts and fairy tales. We speak of Esper, not magic; of space ships, not flying carpet—only to see much come true. There is always a need for the stretching of the imagination, to find possible answers for the 'What ifs.' And those who write and read science-fiction seem, with some justice, to have discovered roads into probable and not impossible futures.

GENERAL COMMENTARY

Doreen Norman

SOURCE: "Science Fiction," in *Books for Your Children,* Vol. 4, No. 3, Spring, 1969, pp. 14-16.

[W]ith Andre Norton the imagination soars. This writer sets her books out in the galaxy far from the solar system and the results show that she is one of the supreme artists in SF writing. *Star Rangers,* her second science fiction book, clearly demonstrates a feeling that other life forms are not necessarily hostile or evil because they are strange or different. Humanoid beings and the lizard-like Zachathans are stranded on an unknown planet and face the dangers of a potential tyranny together so that they can establish a new life.

In the books which follow this theme is strongly interwoven with the development of telepathy and communication between man and animal. Although Andre Norton's heroes travel in space the journey and scientific details are not important. The story of *Catseye* is only taken up after Troy Horan has been deported from his own planet during a galactic war and is already living as a refugee on the planet Korwar. Whilst Andre Norton is completely readable, her work rises at times almost to the poetic. To journey through her books is a revelation of what a creative imagination can do within the medium of young people's science fiction.

Margery Fisher

SOURCE: A review of *Saragasso of Space, Plague Ship,* and *Postmarked the Stars,* in *Growing Point,* Vol. 18, No. 6, March, 1980, pp. 3651-52.

Evolution is a powerful element in all André Norton's space-novels, whether as the motive force of the plot, as metaphor or as a speculative theme (for instance, in *Breed to Come*). In a general sense, I feel that it is the idea of change in human society, personality and circumstance which makes her books so much more satisfying than those in which ingenious hardware and way-out alien races exist for their own sake. She is second to none in inventing strange landscapes and machines, but what seems to interest her most is the way men (projected into the future but always discernibly Terran) respond to change. She rejuvenates the traditional situations of the adventure story—chase and capture, the testing of national loyalty, courage and physical skills—by sending her characters voyaging with new maps.

New maps and old traditions and, linking these, the preoccupations of our own time. The three books now reprinted, space-adventures vigorous and well-paced, were published in America in 1955, 1956 and 1969 respectively (with Gollancz's hardback editions as late as 1970 and 1971) but the theme of human greed which runs through them is as topical as one could wish now. The villains of *Sargasso of Space* are wreckers (but of sky, not sea) who have reclaimed a Forerunner installation on a remote planet to continue centuries of looting of crashed air-ships. In *Plague Ship* the Free Traders (representing enterprise of the best kind) triumph finally over the clever sabotage of richer and Government-supported trading rivals. In *Postmarked the Stars,* the responsibility for ecological change and the corrupt secret designs of a charitable trust are themes that will strike home to readers of the present. Accomplished story-telling and due attention to character preclude any touch of didacticism in the three books, yet they *do* reflect the ills of the world most forcefully.

This is a trilogy, though each book is self-contained. The link is the Free Trader *Solar Queen* and its crew, with apprentice Dale Thorson as the central character. Each voyage of this star-trader begins with a simple assignment and proceeds through surprise and danger to unexpected new openings. The planet Limbo, bought in an auction as a speculation and at first sight unprofitable, brings a reward for the defeat of the pirates in the form of a contract to trade on Sargol, a planet rich in gems and perfumes, and though, in *Plague Ship,* the circumvention of Inter-Solar calls forth dangerously unorthodox actions from the Free Traders, their new contract to deliver mails (in *Postmarked the Stars*), designed to move them from the centre of the galactic world for a time, ends in the defeat of a serious threat to the whole of that world. The narrative pattern of the books, then, is an expanding one; each begins in a muted, practical ordinariness and gradually gathers momentum, tension and novelty. Continuity is provided by the *Solar Queen* and her crew, which remains the same for the three books. In this crew Dale Thorson is central but he is not in the obvious sense a hero; rather he is there for readers to identify with, as a learner, a young person developing through experience. As such, he is in a way a less positive character than the sober, remote Captain Jellico or the cheerful African astrogator Rip Shannon. What matters is that Dale learns, from his mistakes and from the occasional moments of intuition which help him to interpret events and avoid danger. He is introduced as an apprentice cargo-master, and if at the end

of the third book he is fully qualified and employed, it is as much a matter of luck as of capability. He does learn his trade, certainly. He also grows in tolerance. It is no accident that he learns to work with a crew of mixed races or that he finds a way to communicate with the brach, a bear-like animal enabled through accidental radiation to recover, partially, an earlier existence as a race of *homo sapiens.* It is through Dale Thorson most of all that André Norton expresses once more her conviction that Man, to survive, must learn to accept difference and change, in his fellows and his circumstances. These vigorous and extremely stimulating adventure-stories offer, in their own way, a blue-print for the future.

TITLE COMMENTARY

📖   *THE SWORD IS DRAWN* (first volume of "Swords" trilogy, 1944)

Mary Gould Davis

SOURCE: "Lorens Goes to War," in *The Saturday Review,* Vol. XXVII, No. 16, April 15, 1944, p. 75.

Here is a story that is plotted and written like a modern novel. It has all the elements that older boys and girls seek in their leisure reading. It has characters with whom they can identify themselves. It is a story of this war. It moves swiftly, surely, from one scene to another in the world conflict. Beginning in Holland at the time of the German occupation and when the hero—Lorens van Norreys—is eighteen, the action takes him first to England in one of the now famous little fishing boats that smuggle Dutch patriots to the English coast and then to the Dutch East Indies where he is caught in the Japanese invasion. He crashes in a plane in Australia and, after long months in a hospital, goes to America. Then to England and to Holland—via parachute.

Lorens had made up his mind to get the famous "Flowers of Orange" necklace that his grandfather had given into his care. It lay now in a safe in the old van Norreys house near Rotterdam. To go there is almost certain death, but Lorens goes. His descent at night, the slow emergence of the familiar landmarks, the house that is the headquarters of the Gestapo with its grim, silent mistress and the strange little serving girl; all this is the essence of romance and adventure. Who Kaatje really was is never explained. But much must be left unfinished in a book telling of Axis-dominated countries.

What troubles this reviewer about this story is its conscious effort to further international friendship. We are told that an exchange of letters between college students of various countries started in 1938 has created a "correspondence" friendship between Lorens in Holland and Lawrence in America. Each section of the story is headed with an extract of a letter from Lorens to Lawrence.

Lawrence is told the secret word with which Lorens has sealed the safe in the old house in Rotterdam. And yet, the American boy does not appear as a character in the story. We are told nothing about him. As the action grows swifter, more dramatic, this friendship seems less and less important. It has no meaning in connection with the stirring events that make up the action of the story. One has a feeling that the letters are "dragged in," that the book would be stronger and clearer without them.

Anne T. Eaton

SOURCE: A review of *The Sword Is Drawn*, in *The New York Times Book Review*, April 23, 1944, p. 23.

In Holland, in June, 1940, 18-year-old Lorens Van Norreys, heir to an ancient firm of jewel merchants, is summoned to his dying grandfather. Just before Lorens escapes to England he follows the old man's last directions and leaves the Flowers of Orange—a priceless family necklace—in a safe that can be opened only after two years, and then only by one word. For this word he chooses one that he and a "foreign pen friend" have in common, thus sharing his secret with this friend.

At intervals in the course of the dangerous adventures on which Lorens embarks he manages to communicate with his pen friend in America. Sixty thousand such "pen-friendships" existed among young people throughout the pre-war world, and this fact deepens the reality of Lorens' escape from Rotterdam, the days when he fought the Japs in Java and finally his return to Holland in an attempt to reclaim the necklace and use it to help the Netherlands Royal Air Force in England.

The book is well written and without heroics. Wash and charcoal drawings vividly illustrate the incidents of the tale and catch the strength of Lorens' character.

ROGUE REYNARD (1947)

Alice M. Jordan

SOURCE: A review of *Rogue Reynard*, in *The Horn Book Magazine*, Vol. XVI, No. 4, July, 1947, p. 263.

The old Beast Saga has a new and fresh appearance in the sixteen chapters of this well-made book. Each section is short and uncomplicated enough to hold interest and the sorry experiences of the different animals, rather than the clever tricks of crafty Reynard, enlist the reader's sympathy. Laura Bannon's humorous line drawings enter fully into the spirit of the animal actors.

Ellen Lewis Buell

SOURCE: A review of *Rogue Reynard*, in *The New York Times Book Review*, July 13, 1947, p. 25.

From Aesop to Uncle Remus Brer Fox has been a prime favorite among story-tellers. It was in the Middle Ages, however, that he reached the height of his popularity in the great cycle of tales, "Reynard the Fox." In her adaptation of this beast epic André Norton has gone back to its original spirit, leaving the political and religious implications which came later to the scholars.

Perhaps Reynard is painted a little darker here than he was by the peasants who had a fellow sympathy for guile triumphing over brute force. Even so, readers of 8 to 12 will chuckle as he outwits the messengers sent to fetch him to King Lion's court. Bruin Bear, Chief Herald Hare, even Duke Tybalt, the cat, learn to their pain the depths of his iniquity, and it remained for Squire Hound to bring him to ultimate and fitting justice.

The stories are artfully bound together, retold in a prose which has just enough of the archaic to give it the proper flavor, and Laura Bannon's drawings, though essentially modern, suggest the vigor, richness and humor of the Middle Ages.

SCARFACE (1948)

Virginia Kirkus' Bookshop Service

SOURCE: A review of *Scarface*, in *Virginia Kirkus' Bookshop Service*, Vol. XVI, No. 17, September 1, 1948, p. 439.

Well-sustained, action-packed pirate yarn which should provide good material to bridge that gap for the boys emerging from the comic book stage. Pirates, lost gentry, boarded ships, a captive cabin boy—ingredients for a story of Capt. Cheap pirate lord of Tortuga, who conceived the plan to raid Barbados, stronghold of Sir Robert Scarlett, whose wife and infant son he had captured years before. A sea battle and a dramatic ending resolve identities, and Justin Blade, young Scarface, emerges as the long lost young Scarlett. Straight adventure—well done.

The Saturday Review

SOURCE: A review of *Scarface*, in *The Saturday Review*, Vol. XXXI, No. 42, October 16, 1948, p. 36.

This is an exciting story of the pirates of Tortuga when Sir Robert Scarlett was the English governor of Bridgetown in the Barbados. Scarface, who had been brought up as a pirate under the notorious Captain Cheap, helps Major Cocklyn when he is taken prisoner on Cheap's pirate ship and goes with him to Bridgetown. There he is given the Queen's Pardon, but later he is caught again by Cheap and, when the pirates are defeated in a thrilling battle, condemned to death. In a final dramatic scene, Cheap reveals that Scarface is Sir Robert's own son, taken as a baby from a scuttled British ship.

Older readers will compare this well-written and -plotted story with Howard Pyle. It has humor and atmosphere and action that never falter. Even the minor characters are sharply drawn. It is "strong meat." There is no softening of the brutality and coarseness of the "men from the sea." To older boys and girls and to adults it will probably emerge as one of the outstanding adventure stories of the year. It is an attractive looking book with full-page drawings and chapter headings done in black and white.

HUON OF THE HORN (1951)

Virginia Kirkus' Bookshop Service

SOURCE: A review of *Huon of the Horn,* in *Virginia Kirkus' Bookshop Service,* Vol. XIX, No. 21, November 1, 1951, p. 632.

An unusual though circumscribed item, this translation of the 1534 English version of the romance of Huon of Bordeaux, included in the cycle of the Charlemagne Saga. With relaxed sentence structure which nevertheless retains some of the archaic flavor of the Lord Berners translation, the several legends of the hero who became a friend of the King of the Fairies and later ruler of Fairyland is told in brief episodes. Actually, in spite of a profusion of serpents, elves and magic props, the incidents do not have the universal appeal of some of the Arthur legends, for example, or the Roland tales. Huon's struggles against the Saracens, his meetings with Oberon, his many battles lack a vigor in the telling, a lustre of vivid characterization, which may have been lost in the original translation. However, as a curiosity and as a supplement to the study of legend, this undoubtedly has value, although a weak competitor to other tales of knightly adventure. Attractive traditional illustrations and decorations by Joe Krush.

Spencer G. Shaw

SOURCE: A review of *Huon of the Horn,* in *The New York Times Book Review,* November 11, 1951, p. 26.

The romance of knighthood in the Charlemagne Saga dramatizes the struggles of men to uphold high moral codes. Huon, young Duke of Bordeaux, unknowingly slays Charlemagne's son while avenging an unprovoked attack upon his brother's life. Banished from the kingdom, he is sent on a dangerous mission to Babylon—on which Huon succeeds with the help of Oberon, King of the Fairies. Then new hazards threaten and Huon embarks upon further strange adventures.

In an engaging style appropriate to the period, André Norton carefully retains the mood of the tale. Lacking the breadth of Howard Pyle's *The Story of King Arthur and His Knights,* this adaptation suffers from an overabundance of incident. Black and white line drawings

add to the spirit of the text, adapted from the English translation of Lord Berners.

STAR MAN'S SON, 2250 A.D. (1952; published as *Daybreak, 2250 A.D.,* 1954)

The Saturday Review

SOURCE: A review of *Star Man's Son,* in *The Saturday Review,* Vol. XXXV, No. 46, November 15, 1952, p. 60.

This is an extraordinary story. It will probably have a strong appeal to the older boys and girls who read science-fiction. André Norton sets it in the year 2250 A.D.—two hundred and fifty years after the civilization of our world has been destroyed by atomic warfare. There is still man on earth, and she pictures them in three groups: the Star Men, who live high in the mountains and are descended from scientists who were protected by the mountains when atomic destruction came; the Plainsmen, who are roving tribes; and the men from the South, who have been driven from their homes by volcanoes and earthquakes. Then there are the Beast Things— horrible creatures who are the result of atomic radiation. Fors, the hero, is of the Star Men, but he is an outcast because his mother was of the Plainsmen. Seeking to redeem himself, he goes on a long quest to the ruined cities in search of knowledge. His companion is a catlike creature who is loyal and faithful. It is a strange picture that André Norton paints of the quest and its dangers and difficulties. Fors meets one of the men from the South and they become comrades. He is captured by the Beast Things and then by the Plainsmen. There is a war, and the Beast Things are conquered. Then the three groups meet and vow that men shall war no more. The Star Men know that men had almost conquered space before the great atomic Great Blowup. They vow to learn again to reach outer space and the stars. An unusual story, it is illustrated with vigorous, original drawings by the winner of the Caldecott Medal for 1951 (Nicholas Mordvinoff).

Margery Fisher

SOURCE: A review of *Star Man's Son,* in *Growing Point,* Vol. 6, No. 9, April, 1968, pp. 1087.

André Norton is also concerned with evolution—but in a social sense. *Star Man's Son* takes us 250 years onwards from the Great Blowup which has pushed North America back to a mediaeval way of life where surviving generations more or less mutated from the pre-blast norm have aligned themselves into potentially aggressive groups. Fors, hero of the story, lives with the Star-men, descendants of a group of scientists artificially isolated in a mountain range, but he is half-Plainsman and as such is denied formal entry into the tribe. The book follows his fortunes as he looks for a niche—with the Plainsmen (the hunters) or with the coloured folk from the south who seek land to cultivate. Joining them against the Beast Things, mutated monstrosities who threaten to put an end to civilisation, Fors illustrates for the author the need for tolerance, integration and goodwill if the world as we know it is to continue. But there is no forced moral; rather, it emerges as the product of Fors's moods, thoughts and reactions as he pursues his dangerous path to maturity.

Norman Culpan

SOURCE: A review of *Star Man's Son,* in *The School Librarian,* Vol. 16, No. 2, July, 1968, p. 218.

A new science fantasy novel by Miss Norton is always to be welcomed, this no less than its predecessors. Most of the usual characteristics of her novels are present: the outcast hero who makes good, aided by an animal with whom he can communicate by telepathy, in desperate travel over weird, hostile terrain against a non-human, wholly evil enemy. In 2250 A.D. atomic war has devastated the earth. Small pockets of survivors, here and there, strive to rediscover the secrets of the 'Old Ones', suspicious of any mutation among themselves, and always threatened by the man-sized, rat-faced bipeds whose hordes lurk in the ruins of the old cities. Cast out by his clan for his silver hair and abnormal night vision, Fors, aided by his animal colleague, Lura, and the dark-skinned human comrade with whom he joins forces, escapes the rat-faced ones and averts war between three rival clans of men. The plea for peace, increasingly common in science fiction, is stronger and more overt than in Miss Norton's previous stories.

The Junior Bookshelf

SOURCE: A review of *Star Man's Son,* in *The Junior Bookshelf,* Vol. 32, No. 4, August, 1968, p. 244.

One of the valid remaining distinguishing tests of science fiction is that of thoroughness, distinction which can raise an exceptional novel above the high level now achieved by most published work in this field. Here Mrs. Norton wins high regard as the mere length of this work shows. Her situation this time is also fraught with novel possibilities since the period of her story, like that of *Things to Come,* is the one which follows a disastrous nuclear war which destroys all sophisticated plant and communications and, as concerns her most in this story, provokes mutations among men and beasts from which completely new relationships and problems arise. To say much more would rob the reader of agreeable reactions of surprise but it must be repeated that Mrs. Norton's treatment is thorough in at least two ways: the implications of the initial situation are fully explored, and the episodes which constitute the plot are developed to the fullest possible extent this side of probability; there is no hint of scrappiness in the writing and this still seems a prerequisite of successful science fiction which aims to emulate the work of the classical masters in this genre. The hero-figure's environment and the characters which oppose or assist him are full of interest in themselves as well as moving the story along very capably.

STAR RANGERS ("Central Control" series, 1953; published as *The Last Planet,* 1955)

H. H. Holmes

SOURCE: A review of *Star Rangers,* in *The New York Herald Tribune Book Review,* August 23, 1953, p. 9.

Earlier this year Miss Norton edited an anthology, *Space Service,* in which her tasteful selections proved that stories of the Space Patrol are not limited to the TV or comicbook level; and now she makes the same point in an imaginative and moving adventure novel. This is a historical novel of the collapse of a decadent Galactic Empire; but it obtains its powerful effect by restricting its action to a small area of the surface of one planet and to the problems of a small group of spacemen abandoned by the empire they had lived only to serve. No cut-and-dried star-hopping here, but oddly all the more impact of the awe and wonder of space—as the ocean may have more meaning to a castaway than to a trans-oceanic plane passenger. The plot involves a surprise that should not be mentioned here—an old theme, but one I've never seen so well handled before. In all, an excellent book for the new science fiction reader, and even for the veteran a refreshingly readable one.

Creighton Peet

SOURCE: A review of *Star Rangers,* in *The New York Times Book Review,* January 10, 1954, p. 24.

When their rocket crashes on a planet in a solar system not on any maps, Ranger Sergeant Kartr and his fellow survivors have a rugged time. In an abandoned city they face a deadly robot watchman; and, in the open, they are confronted by hostile, knife-wielding tribesmen still at the cave-man level.

Star Rangers moves at a good clip and the sky's no limit to Miss Norton's imagination. Like so many space writers she assumes her readers are space wise and know all about Bemmys (the non-human races), reptile-type humans, "mind probes," and "com-techneers."

Earth-bound illiterates occasionally may be confused, but space addicts will recognize Miss Norton as an exciting storyteller who knows that an Arcturian is a native of Arcturus, and a Sensitive one with superior mind-probing powers. And what she doesn't know, she makes up.

Norman Culpan

SOURCE: A review of *Star Rangers,* in *The School Librarian,* Vol. 17, No. 1, March, 1969, p. 92.

Although now available from a British publisher for the first time, this is one of André Norton's earlier science fiction stories, being first copyrighted in 1953. In 8054 A.D. Galactic Rangers and Patrols are wrecked on an earth-like planet: indeed it proves to be Earth itself, on the now almost forgotten edge of the galaxy. They find in it a single city which has been seized by a high-intelligence, telepathic Arcturian pirate. The struggle of Kartr and his fellow Rangers to overcome the jealous distrust of the Patrol men, and to wrest power from the Arcturian so that a decent way of life is possible for all, form the plot. The struggle of the dispossessed for a free, co-operative, peaceful way of life, the importance of comradeship and loyalty, fellowship with beasts, and telepathic power are elements common to her novels. But the eerie menace of underground passages, common to most of them, is here almost absent. Somewhat simpler in plot than her later stories, this novel will suit admirably those who do not already know her works, or who find them interesting, but a little difficult.

THE STARS ARE OURS! ("Astra" series, 1954)

Aileen O'Brien Murphy

SOURCE: A review of *The Stars Are Ours!*, in *The Saturday Review*, Vol. XXXVII, No. 34, August 21, 1954, p. 35.

Wild improbabilities and deeds of fantastic valor are the stock-in-trade of science-fiction authors. Good writing is not so common among them. André Norton employs all three in *The Stars Are Ours*. She tells about a company of scientists and men of good will who escape from an enslaved and hideous Earth to travel a lifetime to a star in another galaxy. They manage to survive the endless journey through the use of a macabre mechanism which deep-freezes the explorers while they are in space, automatically defrosting them when their ship reaches a habitable planet. For boys and girls of ten to fifteen.

Leonard T. Bulman

SOURCE: A review of *The Stars Are Ours!*, in *The New York Times Book Review*, August 29, 1954, p. 18.

The year is 2500 A.D. The planet is Terra, devastated by atomic weapons and ruled by the terrorists called Peacemen. Dard Nordis and his little niece, descendants of the despised Free Scientists, join a conspiracy of the few remaining free people on Terra to escape to another galaxy. With fifty-seven others, Dard and Dessie are placed in a cold sleep on a space ship headed for an unknown world. Three hundred years later they awaken on Astra, a land inhabited by two-horned horses, man-eating lizards, spider plants and duck-dogs.

An excellent fabrication of old and new science-fiction ideas. *The Stars Are Ours!* is based on the theme that man's desire for personal liberty can overcome all adversity. Some readers may feel the ending is incomplete, and that too much happens in too few chapters, but even they will agree that this is a rip-snorting adventure tale.

AT SWORDS' POINTS (Third volume of "Swords" trilogy, 1954)

Virginia Haviland

SOURCE: A review of *At Swords' Points*, in *The Horn Book Magazine*, Vol. XXX, No. 6, December, 1954, p. 436.

Successful again in a young novel of international intrigue. Andre Norton combines, superbly well, underground movements, counterfeiting of art treasures, cryptic letters and murder. The story is placed in Dutch towns whose locale emerges clearly as it furnishes Quinn Anders, a young college graduate, stimulus and clues for the completion of his father's historical research as well as for investigation of his brother's murder. It is all wrapped around the counterfeiting and disappearance of an historic collection of miniature jeweled knights in the recovery of which Quinn plays a creditable and harrowing part. Glimpses of early history, the St. Pietersberg Caverns, and post-war Holland bereft of her East Indies.

PLAGUE SHIP ("Solar Queen" series, written under pseudonym Andrew North, 1956; written under name Andre Norton, 1971)

Margery Fisher

SOURCE: A review of *Plague Ship*, in *Growing Point*, Vol. 9, No. 9, April, 1971, p. 1699.

Someone somewhere coined the phrase 'With-Harry-it-was-the-work-of-a-moment' to designate a certain kind of adventure story. The phrase is usually pejorative but I apply it to *Plague Ship* in admiration. The cliffhanger, to give it a shorter name, depends on perfect timing. André Norton has always known when to suspend her characters in danger and when to move them to safety. *Plague Ship* is new to England but it was published in America as long ago as 1956. It makes a good case for a type of narrative not as popular nowadays as it has been, owning a long and respectable ancestry at least as far back as Defoe's 'real life' crime stories, and maybe further.

Dane Thorson played a leading part in *Sargasso of Space*, as the traditional innocent protected by fortune, and his role in the sequel is much the same. He is supported by the more experienced Rip Shannon, the brilliant Ali and an interestingly under-stated character, a Venusian colonist Jasper Weeks, who works in the engine-room. The way Weeks is brought forward gradually into the action is a lesson in narrative construction in itself. André Norton's object in the book is familiar enough. The mysterious 'plague' gradually removes the men of authority from the scene so that the young and inexperienced—salted by chance against the unidentified illness but not yet salted by life—are left to carry the *Solar Queen* through successive dangers from natural and human enemies.

This is emphatically not a plot to give away in advance. I can say that the story opens where the earlier book left off, with the Captain of the *Solar Queen* opening up trade negotiations on the planet Sargol with the concession they won as a prize for their success in defeating the pirates of Limbo. Diplomacy and luck win over the feline Salariki (one of André Norton's most skilfully invented races) but the traditional rivals of Free Traders, the powerful Inter-Solar company, put an abrupt ending to the ritual of trading of catnip for jewels. And so the adventure begins. An unknown disease, Terra after the Big Bang, the fight against wrongful accusation, kidnapping, the bold capture of hostile men and manned posts—we have had all this before. But not often with such fertile invention of details, such compulsive narration and such expert handling of character. Too much inward communing or minutiae of personality would soon check the pace of this kind of story and deflect its aim, which is to hold the reader in an Ancient Mariner grip. André Norton does not make this mistake but her people speak and act in character, and to a proper degree they *make* the action, with the hero, the fairy tale younger son, always in the forefront.

On the last page of this spanking adventure Cargo-Master Van Rycke remarks ". . . there's practically no trouble we can get into on a safe and sane mail route." Dane Thorson's exploits up to the present encourage me to hope that his creator will one day involve him in unexpected complexities in the space-postal service.

THE CROSSROADS OF TIME ("Time Travel" series, 1956)

Margery Fisher

SOURCE: A review of *The Crossroads of Time,* in *Growing Point,* Vol. 14, No. 8, March, 1976, pp. 2822-23.

Crosstime Agent [*Quest Crosstime*] described the work of Blake Walker in tracing a lost girl and resolving a complex revolutionary situation in a conjectural parallel-present of the American continent. In the earlier *The Crossroads of Time,* now available here, André Norton describes, in suitably rousing terms, how Blake first became a cross-time traveller, after he had saved the life of a man purporting to be a Federal agent. The idea of alternative history has been explored in several of André Norton's space-adventures, but it receives unusually full treatment here. When Saxton and his colleagues have decided for security reasons to take Blake into their group, they reveal themselves as Wardsmen, members of various races in a civilisation which has succeeded in outlawing war; these agents, trained in cross-time movement, are hunting a certain ex-colleague who had used their organisation as a cloak for his enormous ambitions. One of André Norton's most frequently stated morals forms the basis of the story and extends the idea of apprenticeship. Though the Wardsmen have a duty of reconnaissance throughout the galaxy, they are sworn not to interfere with the evolution of other races, and particularly not to forward artificially the development of an aspiring planet and so to weaken it. As an adventure story *The Crossroads of Time* must rank with the best of André Norton's work, with its tremendous variety of landscape and atmosphere and its fast, forceful plot. She has given herself an almost limitless power of narrative as she describes Blake's sojourn on one alternative world after another, and has taken every opportunity to bring colour, action and thought to a multiplicity of scenes. Above all she has knit the practical and the philosophical brilliantly in describing how a courageous but untaught young agent adjusts himself to known and unknown worlds and peoples.

M. Hobbs

SOURCE: A review of *The Crossroads of Time,* in *The Junior Bookshelf,* Vol. 40, No. 3, June, 1976, p. 166.

It would seem that this story was written some twenty years ago and must therefore be an early Andre Norton. Its hero is Blake Walker, a kind of inter-galactic James Bond. He inadvertently gets mixed up with a mission from some other time level and becomes involved in their battle against a nasty number named Pranj. He becomes so involved that he cannot be returned to his own time but has been transported to Vroom where his agent potential will be exploited.

This is the traditional struggle between good and evil, liberally spiced with the sci-fi ingredients of sonic barriers, metal worms and mind probes. The most exciting action takes place in an America exhausted by attack from Nazi Germany which succeeded in its attempt to overrun Europe. This may not be Andre Norton at her best but it is still a readable story.

Aidan Warlow

SOURCE: "Post-Nuclear Perils," in *The Times Literary Supplement,* July 16, 1976, p. 878.

Andre Norton predicts even worse fates for mankind in the post-Nuclear Age, ranging from a Nazi-dominated Europe and robot dragons to total environmental pollution. *The Crossroads of Time* was first published in America twenty years ago and is now appearing in England for the first time. As in all her early novels, the characters are stereotype magazine-heroes with tough names like Blake and Kittson. They are incapable of introspection or complex motives though they do possess mysterious "psi" powers of extrasensory observation.

Miss Norton's most ingenious idea is that of "Successor Worlds" so that we don't just move through time and space but *across* "bands" or "levels" of parallel and mutant existences. The hero's chase to save the world from the clutches of the villainous Pranj takes him to some very nasty levels indeed.

📖 *STAR BORN* ("Astra" series, 1957)

H. H. Holmes

SOURCE: A review of *Star Born,* in *The New York Herald Tribune Book Review,* May 12, 1957, p. 27.

In a sequel to her well-remembered *The Stars Are Ours!* André Norton tells what it is like to be a boy coming of age in a race which is itself adolescent—a star born mutation of humanity striving to cope with its new environment and its new powers. It's a fresh and moving theme; and Miss Norton develops it with her accustomed skill and with plenty of rousing excitement. Nobody today is telling better stories of straightforward interstellar adventure, whether for teenagers or for adults.

Heloise P. Mailloux

SOURCE: A review of *Star Born,* in *The Horn Book Magazine,* Vol. XXXIII, No. 4, August, 1957, p. 299.

Sequel to *The Stars Are Ours!* Dalgard, of Terran descent but Astran birth, and Sssuri, his merman friend, discover that Those Others plan annihilation of peaceful peoples. Meanwhile, a space ship arrives from Terra, with crewmen unaware of intelligent life on Astra. The two plots alternate and finally converge as Dalgard, a Terran, and a tiny army of mermen carry the war to the enemy. Favorite devices of science fiction combine with older devices like underground passages to make exciting reading for older boys and girls.

S. William Alderson

SOURCE: A review of *Star Born,* in *Children's Book Review,* Vol. III, No. 4, September, 1973, p. 113.

Star Born! The title itself is something of a pun on the two groups of the story: those born *on* Astra and those borne *to* Astra.

The events are told from two different viewpoints: on the one hand by a colonist—a descendant of a small group of fugitives from a *1984* life on earth—and on the other, by a member of a party of explorers from the now liberated earth. Andre Norton uses this alternation of narrators to give a broader view of events, but also,

more important, to sustain suspense in a way which could not be done by straightforward narrative.

The story tells what happens when the party of explorers lands on Astra during the culmination of a war between the two native races: the Astrans, belligerent, callous and domineering, the former masters of their world, and the Sea People, a gentle, telepathic race of humanoid amphibians. The Sea People have become friends and allies of the Terran colonists and have passed on to them some of their telepathic gifts.

The Astrans intend to harness the Terran explorers to their own destructive aims, but they are thwarted by the efforts of a colonist and the communication which develops between him and one of the party of explorers.

There is, however, no major climax, only a series of incidents. Although told from both colonists' and explorers' viewpoints, there is an obvious bias towards the colonists and although the device of alternating viewpoints helps to sustain interest, the book falls short of the standard of the author's *Breed to Come* where she has employed a similar device and plot much more successfully.

📖 *STAR GATE* (1958)

Virginia Kirkus' Service

SOURCE: A review of *Star Gate,* in *Virginia Kirkus' Service,* Vol. XXVI, No. 16, August 15, 1958, p. 608.

When Kincar, half Star and half Gorthian, decides to leave Gorth and join the Star lords, he passes through a shimmering gate of time. In this new element he encounters Star warriors, quite different from those who raised the Gorthians from a primitive feudal level, for the lords he now meets are tyrannical and without mercy. As Kincar works out his destiny in this new world of time he simultaneously works out the fate of a magic stone which has been left in his care, and which will burn into his flesh until he finds the person to whom it must be delivered. Andre Norton, whose ability to extend scientific thought to the limit of imagination has won [her] many enthusiasts among science fiction fans, elaborates in *Star Gate* on the possibility of alternate destinies governed by optional changes in time. A fascinating concept, masterfully handled by the author.

Robert Berkvist

SOURCE: A review of *Star Gate,* in *The New York Times Book Review,* December 14, 1958, p. 18.

Time . . . is an important factor in *Star Gate,* in which Miss Norton again demonstrates her superb talent for creating and sustaining a world of foreign moods. Gorth is such a world, peopled by Star Lords and Gorthians, sheltering such creatures as mords, larngs and suards, torn by a struggle between good and evil. Miss Norton has captured the flavor of a Beowulfian folk epic so thoroughly that some readers may find the going a bit thick at first, but when one has learned how to separate the Styrs from the Wurds and mords the story moves briskly along.

H. H. Holmes

SOURCE: "Three, Two, One, Zero and a Space Suit," in *The New York Herald Tribune Book Review,* May 10, 1959, p. 27.

Star Gate may well be André Norton's best book yet. It's a complex tale of adventures on a remote planet in several alternate universes, so that the protagonists find themselves at times battling with their own evil selves-as-they-might-have-been—a concept that sounds confusing, but is crystal clear as Miss Norton sets it forth. Her inimitably vigorous storytelling and sense of high emprise are heightened here by a delicate touch of mysticism—and by the creation, in the hero's pet *mord,* of the most fascinating alien animal since Heinlein's Star Lummox.

Norman Culpan

SOURCE: A review of *Star Gate,* in *The School Librarian,* Vol. 18, No. 2, June, 1970, p. 245.

It is a perpetual and pleasant surprise that Miss Norton maintains such freshness and variety while continuing to work with the same basic ingredients. I see no falling off in her outstanding ability to write absorbing fantasy adventure for nine- to thirteen-year-olds. The action in this story takes place on an imaginary planet, Gorth, and the struggle is between those who are good and those who are evil. More sophisticated, though, and a major motivation, is the responsibility of the god-like 'Star-Lords' towards the primitive 'Gorthians' whom they have begun to civilize. There is one new element—for the protagonists of good escape attack through a time-gate into another Gorth, parallel in time with their own, but in which events have taken a different turn, so that among those they fight are some of their own 'other selves', turned to evil. This may sound complicated, but as presented in the novel it is easy to understand. Space-hoppers and strange beasts of burden, ray-guns and bows and arrows, space-ships and medieval castles convincingly co-exist in this typical Norton story which I, as usual, very much enjoyed.

THE TIME TRADERS ("Time War" series, 1958)

Virginia Kirkus' Service

SOURCE: A review of *The Time Traders,* in *Virginia Kirkus' Service,* Vol. XXVI, No. 17, September 1, 1958, p. 666.

At the end of this century Ross Murdock is given the choice between prison and a dangerous role in a secret mission. Accepting the latter, but determined to escape at the first opportunity, the intelligent young man finds himself involved in a project which demands that he be projected back to various periods in history. For the Americans, aware that the Russians, somewhere in time, have learned the secret of space travel, must for the sake of national safety, obtain the same secret. Hurled back into the earliest ages of man, Ross' volatile intelligence is, for the first time, stimulated as he risks death, posing as a member of prehistoric worlds. By the time the Americans gain control of the secret, Ross is rehabilitated and is a willing participant in the benevolent army of the future. An interesting idea, well handled by Andre Norton, science fiction expert, who projects [her] reader deftly both backwards and forwards in time and injects [her] narrative with considerable and interesting historical information.

Robert Berkvist

SOURCE: A review of *The Time Traders,* in *The New York Times Book Review,* December 14, 1958, p. 18.

The time traders combines some fact with much fantasy to produce a believable result. Time travel is not new in science fiction, nor is the anti-social hero a particularly fresh type, but in Miss Norton's skilled hands the story of Ross Murdock's adventures in the past—where he meets not only some very tough prehistoric men, but also must deal with pugnacious Russians of his own era and a flying saucerful of short-tempered galactic aliens—makes fascinating reading.

GALACTIC DERELICT ("Time War" series, 1958)

Virginia Kirkus' Service

SOURCE: A review of *Galactic Derelict,* in *Virginia Kirkus' Service,* Vol. XXVII, No. 17, September 1, 1959, p. 658.

Andre Norton has no peer in [her] chosen field of science fiction for teen agers. This time [her] story involves an expedition in both time and space, as some young scientists and a chance involved "rider for the Double A", Travis, who had been a student in the field of archaeology, set forth on a journey to repossess a lost space ship. Where their journey takes them provides breathless adventures in other worlds, with other-world creatures. Ingenuity, basic knowledge flexibly applied, and dauntless courage provide the handholds for success and a safe—though somewhat shattered—return. There's a hint of racial antagonism—a chip on the shoulder attitude—at the start, for Travis is an Apache—but it has a negligible part in the story, though Travis' background and training stand him in good stead.

Robert Berkvist

SOURCE: "Probing the Galaxies," in *The New York Times Book Review,* January 31, 1960, p. 32.

Galactic Derelict is Miss Norton's sequel to the time-traveling experiences of Ross Murdock (introduced last year in *The Time Traders*). Ross journeys back to the age of the Folsom man for another try at capturing data left behind by galactic visitors some fifteen thousand years ago. Travis Fox, a modern American Indian, joins the party this trip, mainly as a prop for Miss Norton's anthropological overlay. An unwilling flight aboard an alien space ship with pre-set controls allows the author's fertile imagination full play.

📖 *THE BEAST MASTER* ("Beast Master" series, 1959)

Elaine Simpson

SOURCE: A review of *The Beast Master,* in *Library Journal,* Vol. 84, September 15, 1959, p. 62.

Further adventures of Hosteen Storm and the animals making up his Commando Team, this time on a foray of personal vengeance after the destruction of Earth. As always, Miss Norton writes an exciting story for SF readers. This reviewer was annoyed by the fact that the author has merely rewritten a cowboy-and-Indian story in an alien situation and with the addition of SF terms and trappings: the herds, rustlers, nesters, trail drive, fights in the frontier saloons, plains natives, etc., etc. are all there. However, perhaps this will not bother teen-agers who have not read many westerns. Also, the conclusion is the least convincing of any of this author's books, but even so, this is better than much current SF.

Robert Berkvist

SOURCE: "Probing the Galaxies," in *The New York Times Book Review,* January 31, 1960, p. 32.

André Norton . . . has never spread a forensic fog between her audience and the story she has to tell. *The Beast Master* might easily have been just another Western played in futuristic terms. Miss Norton, however, endows the story of a homeless, revenge-driven man with her own inimitable touch, blending an acute sense of primitive mystery with still another of her well-conceived foreign worlds. The result is a compelling and compassionate tale.

The Junior Bookshelf

SOURCE: A review of *The Beast Master,* in *The Junior Bookshelf,* Vol. 30, No. 3, June, 1966, p. 186.

It was bound to happen, one supposes, and here it seems to be: a Space Western. Hosteen Storm, whose home planet, Terra, has been destroyed, seeks a new life on the planet Arzor, first of all as a herd-rider, dealing first with horses and intending later to have a go at herding the Arzorian equivalent of beef cattle. He is temporarily side-tracked into acting as scout to a party seeking important archaeological remains. This leads to further side-tracking whose details must not be revealed, except to say that horses are never entirely out of the picture. Storm adds to the "Western" atmosphere in his capacity as "beast master," accompanied as he is by three specially trained wild animals and an eagle, with all of whom he has a telepathic bond. In addition, there are a few, but not too many of the stock-in-trade gimmicks of established space-fiction writers to lend conviction to a strange territory and an unpredictable era. Excellent entertainment.

Norman Culpan

SOURCE: A review of *The Beast Master,* in *The School Librarian,* Vol. 14, No. 2, July, 1966, p. 203.

Andre Norton shows again in this book the qualities that have made her the best writer of juvenile S.F. Her 'people', whether human or humanoid, are the most real I know in the genre, while her power of manipulating plot and maintaining suspense, and her sheer invention of setting, situation and incident are second to none. Her values are unobtrusive but sound. In this, her fourth story to be published in this country, the hero, a Galactic commando working with a team of eagle, dune cat and a pair of meercats, helps to clean up a tangle of feuds among humans and humanoids on the planet Arzor. There are echoes of *Catseye* in Storm's relationship with animals, and of *Night of Masks* in the storm, flooding and underground chambers; but in this story there is more daylight and open country. It could be regarded as a very good Western streamlined into S.F. terms. The spelling is American.

📖 *STORM OVER WARLOCK* ("Planet Warlock" series, 1960)

Virginia Kirkus' Service

SOURCE: A review of *Storm over Warlock,* in *Virginia Kirkus' Service,* Vol. XXVIII, No. 4, February 15, 1960, p. 152.

Fleeing from Throg invaders, Shann Lantree and Ragnar Thorwald enter the world of beautiful women. Immensely powerful as they are lovely, these witches control men by thought domination. Shann's victory over the beetle-like Throg and his civilized alliance with the women is told here with that sweep of imagination and brilliance of detail which render Andre Norton a primary talent among writers of science fiction. A boy's story, packed with adventure and fancy.

Elaine Simpson

SOURCE: A review of *Storm over Warlock,* in *Library Journal,* Vol. 85, April 15, 1960, p. 1709.

Another of Norton's stories of Terran conflict with the Throgs, insect-derived, merciless, extraterrestrial predators, and of the mutant animals bred to aid man in his explorations of space, in this case a pair of wolverines. Young Lantee, the wolverines, and a space-shipwrecked Scout officer have many adventures on the strange planet of Warlock after the Throgs destroy the survey camp and team. Good, exciting SF, up to Norton's best standards and, therefore, above the general run of SF for young readers. Recommended.

RIDE PROUD, REBEL! (1961)

Virginia Kirkus' Service

SOURCE: A review of *Ride Proud, Rebel!* in *Virginia Kirkus' Service,* Vol. XXIX, No. 5, March 1, 1961, p. 223.

Andre Norton—in a new role—weaves a substantial and dramatic narrative with the Civil War as its focus. Drew Rennie was a rebel in political allegiance and in spirit alike. The outbreak of the war climaxed the feud between himself and his grandfather who resented his very existence because of his Texan father. In hurt and anger Drew joins Morgan's Raiders and despite Morgan's defeat at Cynthiana, he continues the arduous trek with his friends, Anse and Boyd, to join Forrest's troops. Harassed by dwindling supplies, poor weapons and Union soldiers they reach their destination only to retreat further with the southern forces to a final surrender. The army is vanquished, but its pride is not. Knowing how the years have rendered a return to his former life impossible, Drew sets out for the West, perhaps to find his father, surely to find a new and fresh life. A moving and suspenseful tale which carries a conviction of reality.

Marion West Stoer

SOURCE: "In the Days of the Civil War," in *The Christian Science Monitor,* May 11, 1961, p. 5B.

Andre Norton again proves she can look backward in time as effectively as she can "prowl among the stars" picturing intergalactic voyages of the future. Her present book is a timely view of the Civil War, but it contains the same elements which have characterized her other work: taut action, hearty characters, sound motivation, and a knack for vivid description which makes the reader feel that he is not only witnessing a scene but participating in it. The rebel protagonist here is 19-year-old Drew Rennie, a scout with Morgan's raiders, who subsequently joins Forrest's cavalry in the same capacity. There is much bloodshed, certainly, but no more than

may be expected in a retelling of these crucial events. Drew, sobered by his experiences in a score of battles, at one point advises his impetuous young cousin Boyd to "take it slow and ride easy." Boyd's answer explains the significance of the punctuation in the book's title: "You don't ride easy with the General. . . . You ride tall and you ride proud!" This general was, of course, Bedford Forrest. Probably no other officer was ever more loved and respected by his men than this Tennessee cavalry commander.

Margaret Warren Brown

SOURCE: A review of *Ride Proud, Rebel!* in *The Horn Book Magazine,* Vol. XXXVII, No. 4, August, 1961, p. 347.

In this long and absorbing novel of the Civil War, the hero is a young scout for the daring raiders of John Hunt Morgan, a band of Confederate volunteers who swept across Kentucky and Tennesee, burning bridges, raiding public property, and capturing horses and military supplies from Union forces. Characters and action are completely believable, and the account of the impact of war's grim realities on a romantic boy as his cause becomes increasingly more hopeless is admirably convincing.

CATSEYE (1961)

Margery Fisher

SOURCE: A review of *Catseye,* in *Growing Point,* Vol. 1, No. 7, January, 1963, p. 97.

Like most science-fiction, *Catseye* has the outward form of the classic adventure story, using all the devices of split-second timing, suspense, surprise and speed to give the very movement of danger. Indeed, this book would deserve high praise if it were only an adventure story, for it is exceptionally exciting and well devised. The time is very much in the future, the place the planet Korwar, where a young man, Troy Horan, has been domiciled after his own planet has been evacuated in a Galactic war. Troy is a third-class citizen in a society so strictly graded that it is only by fantastic luck that he is assigned a job with Kyger the animal dealer. And here his adventures begin, when chance involves him in a cold war between the ruling Council and the rebel Confederation. In this war of plot and counter-plot, the Confederation has an unusual code for its spies, for, by thought-transference, certain men can communicate with animals imported from Terra, and these are used as messengers (though we doubt from the start whether these intelligent creatures are really under orders).

Troy had been a range-rider on his own planet, and he finds that he too can tune in to the animals. Indeed, five of them (cats, foxes and a kinkajou) become his companions when his innocent eavesdropping is discovered and he flees the city in a space-ship, making a forced landing near the dread ruins of Ruhkarv and taking refuge underground.

Troy's danger is as real to the reader as his ultimate salvation when he joins the Clans (country-dwellers who stand for the natural world against the machine-made). A youth has tested his courage and endurance and has proved worthy. How does the author give fresh life to this theme? First, by the intricate, logical and fascinating detail of the space-world. Its government, its social customs, its dwellings, transport and weather, are very naturally described. So far so good—but this imaginative world has to have a purpose. To put it another way, we have still to ask why the author chose to set his adventure in space.

As I suppose, space-stories give some relief to the half-formed fears that beset us, adults and children alike (and here I must say that this book is not really written 'for children' though its strength and maturity will suit them well in their early teens). As Andre Norton sees it, man does not only fear his fellows. In this story, though the galactic war is over, there is still a struggle for power, but the deepest fear is the fear of Nature as a whole. The story is not based on technological but on biological speculation. To communicate with animals is a future just as possible as to live by machines of the type of Blish's City Fathers, and Andre Norton suggests another danger than that of bombs—the danger of other forms of life evolving to rival our own.

Science-fiction starts with the forms of body, speech and thought we already know. An imaginative writer can make the reader forget these limitations, and Andre Norton has done just this.

LORD OF THUNDER ("Beast Master" series, 1962)

The Junior Bookshelf

SOURCE: A review of *Lord of Thunder,* in *The Junior Bookshelf,* Vol. 30, No. 5, October, 1966, p. 315.

Lord of Thunder takes place on the same planet as an earlier story of Hosteen Storm, the Terran relocated to Arzor, which in these pages was compared with space "western." Although this begins and to a limited extent continues in a similar vein, it diverges fairly soon into complicated scientific ramifications incorporating a system of "translation" of the human body from one location to another by instantaneous means. This is never explained but it accounts for almost half the suspense of the plot. The scientific background to these "translations" is an essential element of the plot also, as it is the overt evidence of a plan to overthrow the political system of Arzor with its duality of social groups and the complications of prejudice among the Terrans against the "natives." It does not give the impression of being

so completely successful a book as *The Beast Master* but it is still a good yarn.

Margery Fisher

SOURCE: A review of *Lord of Thunder,* in *Growing Point,* Vol. 5, No. 7, January, 1967, p. 840.

Now André Norton is not a simple writer but she does know how to simplify. The ideas behind the linked novels (*Catseye, The Beast Master* and now *Lord of Thunder*) belong to real people we can recognise even if they belong to other races than our own. Hosteen Storm, citizen of Arzor, is a Beast-master—which means that he draws his strength, his intuition from Nature: his antagonist is warped by technology. Stated in general terms the opposing ideas may sound naïve but they need to be simplified for a novel where they must rise out of action as well as causing it. Like *The Beast Master,* this book has its roots in Red Indian tradition. In a tremendous climax, crazy Logan's mechanical Thunder is overpowered by an unexplained, almost Titanic cataclysm. There is mystery in the book in plenty, as well as tough, fast action, but it is the mystery of a strong imagination, not the mystery of a plot inadequately exploited.

JUDGMENT ON JANUS ("Janus" series, 1963)

The Junior Bookshelf

SOURCE: A review of *Judgment on Janus,* in *The Junior Bookshelf,* Vol. 28, No. 5, November, 1964, p. 317.

This, the cover tells us, is "a science fiction novel," but in spite of its considerable flights of imagination, the flights into space are a less important part of it, and one feels that it scarcely gets into that category. It is an American story of uneven quality which improves in the second half of the book. In the earlier part the conversation belongs much more to the Wild West, and it is indeed a relief when the author drops it later and words and spelling return to normal—albeit American normal. It is the story of Naill (not Niall as the blurb says) Renfro who arrives on the planet Janus and because he covets treasure is banished and affected by the Green Sick, which changes his appearance and memory. Miss Norton does not quite succeed with this novel, but deserves credit for some very good writing in the second half of it.

NIGHT OF MASKS (1964)

Norman Culpan

SOURCE: A review of *Night of Masks,* in *The School Librarian,* Vol. 14, No. 1, March, 1966, pp. 89-90.

Although *Night of Masks* has been preceded only by *Catseye* and *Judgment on Janus*, Miss Norton already has my unhesitating vote as the best contemporary writer of juvenile science fiction, if within that designation are admitted those stories which move beyond the bounds of the foreseeably probable into the realms which some prefer to call fantasy. There is high technical competence in the speed and suspense of narrative of *Night of Masks*, and real imaginative power in the projection of a world of darkness full of lurking menace. These are obvious, and will be experienced and enjoyed by competent readers as young as eleven. Only more mature readers will notice how Nik grows in moral, as well as in practical judgment, and how young Vendy grows out of (as distinct from merely being free from) the fantasy world into which his long imprisonment has driven him to take refuge. Beside this book most adult S.F. looks thin.

THE X FACTOR (1965)

Dorothy S. Jones

SOURCE: A review of *The X Factor*, in *Library Journal*, Vol. 90, July, 1965, pp. 3134-35.

Diskan Fentress, clumsy and inept on his native world, escapes to an unsettled planet where, in spite of a crashed ship, harsh environment, and pirates, he survives. Increasing mental powers and empathy with the native animals give him courage to desert the only civilization he knows when he learns that he as the X-factor can restore the fabulous city of Xcothal. For established rather than new SF fans. Not as good as earlier Nortons or the juvenile Heinleins but better than the last Norton (*Night of Masks*).

Norman Culpan

SOURCE: A review of *The X Factor*, in *The School Librarian*, Vol. 15, No. 2, July, 1967, p. 226.

Diskan Fentress, ungainly mutant among a kindly and gracious people of the future, is driven by his sense of inadequacy to leave their planet. On a dangerous alien world he wins friends and happiness through endurance, courage and resource. This theme, of the lonely, underprivileged hero who makes good through qualities of character is recurrent in Miss Norton's novels. Recurrent, too, are nightmare trekking through labyrinthine underground passages, and the hero's ability to communicate with animals by telepathy—a gift here made particularly convincing by its slow growth through painful effort. Although at the crux of the story the presentation of a past world in shadowy co-existence with the present makes some demands of the reader, the plot itself is straightforward, and probably the easiest of her plots to follow. As always in her novels the pace is very fast, with the imagination and the sympathies of the reader

wholly engrossed. *The X Factor*, in short, is well up to this author's very high standard.

QUEST CROSSTIME ("Time Travel" series, 1965; published in England as *Crosstime Agent*, 1975)

Jane Manthorne

SOURCE: A review of *Quest Crosstime*, in *The Horn Book Magazine*, Vol. XLI, No. 6, December, 1965, p. 636.

In her latest two S-F concoctions the author shows the varied possibilities of inventiveness within her genre. This title is a political, villains-and-good-guys adventure, earthbound, with ingenious development of time-travel. Characters move in shuttles from one coded point and place to another, level-hopping through successor worlds or crash-landing in dangerous uncoded levels. Particularly imaginative are the pictures of worlds, like E625, in which crucial alterations of events change the future altogether, so that the United States never comes into being, pre-empted by a part-Mayan, part-English civilization. This intriguing adventure will lure girls into S-F fandom since the lead characters are mind-linked twin girls, Marva and Marfy.

Margery Fisher

SOURCE: A review of *Crosstime Agent*, in *Growing Point*, Vol. 13, No. 8, March, 1975, p. 2571.

Crosstime Agent is space-opera rather than space-fiction, in that the story matters most and the undertones of social comment are subdued. In this book André Norton uses one of her favourite devices—the idea of cross-time travel by which the people from one planet system can move not only to another system but to a co-existent time-dimension. To this is added an intriguing historical speculation. What if the Aztecs had not been defeated by Spain in the fifteenth century and if Richard III had not been defeated at Bosworth Field? Crossing from the planet Vroom to the world named E625, in search of kidnapped Marva, her twin sister Marfy and the ferry-pilot Blake Walker find themselves in a South American Empire which allows trade facilities, under rigid controls, to a North America still British, organised on a simple mercantile pattern. In a forceful, romantic narrative, the political intrigues of E625 move in parallel with the contest, on Vroom, between the forward-looking pioneers of cross-time travel and a fascistic body of Limiters who seek to apply every kind of political and racial sanction to the planet. The variety of time and space gives André Norton a chance to extend her fine powers of description even further than usual; the book is full of brilliantly coloured, closely detailed settings which lend reality to men of various types, races and outlooks. This is adventure at its most exotic.

D. A. Young

SOURCE: A review of *Crosstime Agent,* in *The Junior Bookshelf,* Vol. 39, No. 3, June, 1975, p. 201.

One cannot but admire the fertility of Mrs. Norton's invention and the consistency of her imagined worlds. The logic of her technology is so beautifully developed, and her characters are just human enough to enable some identification on the part of the reader to take place. There is little room for romance but we are sustained by the old-fashioned virtues of courage, ingenuity and loyalty which were the mainstay of the stories in the old Boys' Own Paper.

The inhabitants of Vroom are able to visit any planet at any time and have developed their own civilisation by sneaky trips of plunder. They are strictly controlled so that history is not disturbed. The multitude of worlds has enabled alternative cultures to prosper so that the Aztecs, not the Spaniards, inherited the world in which Marva and Marfy (twins of course and super-telepathic into the bargain) come to grips with a plot to take over Vroom. Blake Walker is the linkman who holds together all those masterminding the opposition, and a very attractive hero he makes. On balance it is the human interest which dominates the story despite the ingenious scientific milieu.

STEEL MAGIC (1965; published as *Gray Magic,* 1967)

Priscilla L. Moulton

SOURCE: A review of *Steel Magic,* in *The Horn Book Magazine,* Vol. XLI, No. 6, December, 1965, p. 629.

Off for a picnic and a day of exploration, the three Lowry children discover a miniature castle and, entering through the "Gate of the Fox," find themselves in legendary Avalon. Huon of the Horn tells them how "powers of darkness" are enveloping the land and beseeches them to search for the lost talismans whose powers can hold back and overcome evil—Arthur's sword, Huon's horn, and Merlin's ring. Reluctant, at first, each child surrenders to an irresistible force and follows apprehensively but willingly wherever it leads. In their separate journeys they encounter dangers and obstacles representing their deepest fears. Steel cutlery and sandwiches from their picnic basket provide strength and sustenance and their only tie with the world of reality. The adventures of normal, modern children in a long-ago land are told with a verve and pace to engage any reader with a taste for fantasy. Spirited illustrations capture atmosphere and feeling, and extend an invitation to join the quest. Read aloud, the story can be enjoyed for itself or for whatever overtones the listener hears resounding in the "iron of spirit, the iron of courage."

Zena Sutherland

SOURCE: A review of *Steel Magic,* in *Bulletin for the Center of Children's Books,* Vol. 19, No. 9, May, 1966, pp. 151-52.

A fantasy about three children of today and their adventures in a world of Arthurian legendry. Sara and her two brothers go on a picnic and find a small, deserted castle in the middle of a lake; entering it, they pass into Avalon and find that there is a connection between the triumph of good over evil in Avalon that has a corresponding fluctuation in the affairs of men. Each child, separately, braves danger with the help of a steel implement, since the forces of evil are powerless against cold iron. The writing style is good, but the construction of the plot is just enough too ornate and complicated to read smoothly.

The Junior Bookshelf

SOURCE: A review of *Steel Magic,* in *The Junior Bookshelf,* Vol. 31, No. 3, June, 1967, p. 172.

After the initial shock of finding Arthur and Merlin transported to America, this story can be enjoyed thoroughly.

Three children find their way through a deserted garden into the land of Avalon, from whence they cannot return until they free the land from the powers of evil. They are the only ones who can handle iron and steel without harm, and armed with the cutlery from their picnic basket they set out to recover the three magic talismans that have fallen into the hands of the evil powers. Mrs. Norton does not have William Mayne's masterly touch when it comes to transporting her characters to and from present day reality, but she does handle this difficult journey far better than many, and she tells a very good tale. She knows children and answers many of the small details that puzzle them, such as how Sara feels when she is turned into a cat for a short time. How her paws scrabble at wet rocks, and how uncomfortable wet fur is.

It is good to see such a well illustrated book at such a low cost. Good clear illustrations set off the text, and really add to the story.

David Churchill

SOURCE: A review of *Steel Magic,* in *The School Librarian,* Vol. 15, No. 2, July, 1967, p. 226.

A secret doorway in a ruined castle admits two boys and a girl into a fantasy world of Merlin and Arthur where good and evil continually do battle and where the vital symbols of power can only be won back from the enemy by the children carrying iron weapons—the utensils from their picnic basket. The adventures of the children are traced separately and interest is fully gripped by the three threads of the story. These contain attacks by evil spiders, crossing dark waters, hostile birds, shape changing and still more that is reminiscent of the Hobbit world rather than Narnia, although possibly owing much to both. Of importance is the fact that juniors and less fluent seniors who may never tackle Tolkien will be able to read the controlled, though by no means limited, prose in which this story is so well written. The occasional American spellings could, perhaps, have been avoided, but will hardly create difficulties. The exciting story, clear, large, dramatic illustrations and evocative fantasy make this a book of considerable worth.

VICTORY ON JANUS ("Janus" series, 1966)

Virginia Kirkus' Service

SOURCE: A review of *Victory on Janus,* in *Virginia Kirkus' Service,* Vol. XXXV, No. 16, August 15, 1966, p. 840.

In a follow-up to **Judgment on Janus,** this is one of the most illusory, other-dimensional stories from this excellent science fiction writer. It all concerns the Ifts—plant spirits reincarnated from various exterior sources—aroused from their nirvana-ish state by an attack on their planet from a hostile force (THAT or IT) and from the human off-worlders under IT's control. The battle between good and evil involves an extended, treacherous pilgrimage and occurs more on a psychic than a physical plane. The long complex story is only for Miss Norton's most enthusiastic fans. The writing is in her most involved style and you practically need a machete to break through the underbrush of the Ifts' green, spiritual world.

R. W. Doost

SOURCE: A review of *Victory on Janus,* in *Children's Book News,* Vol. 3, No. 1, January-February, 1968, p. 26.

The magic of Miss Norton's **Judgment on Janus** is back in full in this superb sequel to her earlier book. The mysterious Iftin civilization of planet Janus in its fight against the offworld settlers finds itself under threat of total extinction from a third force, referred to only as IT in the book, which has the power to control men's minds and to animate non-living objects. The struggle of the Iftin race against IT has a positively epic character, but the strangely evocative alien setting of Janus gives the book an atmosphere all of its own—not quite creepy or frightening, but nonetheless completely alien. One really feels present as part of the action of the book, and it is a tribute to the author's skill that I could not put the book down until I reached the end of it—at one o'clock in the morning!

The Junior Bookshelf

SOURCE: A review of *Victory on Janus,* in *The Junior Bookshelf,* Vol. 32, No. 1, February, 1968, p. 52.

This sequel to **Judgment on Janus** reveals that THAT, the mysterious evil power on the planet was not destroyed by the Power of Thanth, the equally mysterious life-force which uses as its channel the green race of Ifts, original dwellers on the planet. Unluckily, the need to explain not only this, but the dual nature of these creatures, originally men who through finding Ift treasure assumed the shape and personalities of centuries-dead Iftin and retain snatches of memory from both existences, makes the beginning obscure. Thereafter the fascination of Miss Norton's well-established space world, with its own natural and sociological history, exerts its usual spell, as the heroic Iftin-few struggle against THAT's new weapons. Yet the book is not successful—the apparently supernatural struggle between good and evil, which occasioned comparisons of the first book with Tolkien, fizzles out with a purely mechanical explanation of THAT's power. The style too is pretentious, though it achieves a certain spell: it reads exactly like the older prose translations of Homer. It is manifestly false in constantly recurring phrases such as "like unto" or inverted classical sentence constructions. "My journey that!" rubs shoulders oddly with colloquial American.

Norman Culpan

SOURCE: A review of *Victory on Janus,* in *The School Librarian,* Vol. 16, No. 1, March, 1968, pp. 89-90.

André Norton's book is up to her usual standard, which is recommendation enough; but I do feel that most readers will find the first chapter, even the whole book, more satisfying if they have first read its predecessor, **Judgment on Janus.** The Ifts, changeling men, waking prematurely from their winter hibernation, find that the evil force they had thought overwhelmed is once more stirring, with even greater power. The novel is concerned with its tracking down and destruction by a small devoted band of Ifts, who fight robots and other strange creatures, real and imaginary, and pass through forests, wastes and subterranean passages to do so. Miss Norton's evocative power is remarkable, and one of her greatest achievements is the avoidance of any sense of deflation in the reader when the nameless Evil, which has brooded so balefully through the action of two novels, is finally confronted.

OPERATION TIME SEARCH (1967)

Kirkus Service

SOURCE: A review of *Operation Time Search,* in *Kirkus Service,* Vol. XXXV, No. 37, July 1, 1967, p. 747.

Ray Osbourne, photographer, was poking around a government secret project when he was accidentally projected into the past (or was it an alternate world?). Anyway in this one Atlantis is up and darkly thriving. The Atlanteans are sons of the shadow, worshippers at the altar of "Ba-Al" and they are about to launch a war against the "Sun-born" who worship light and are (naturally) the good guys. The "Murians" (Sun-Born) are in an uproar. They are telepaths and the Atlanteans have been causing some mysterious interference on their mental wavelengths. It turns out that the only one who can combat this is our hero. He is sent to Atlantis as a spy where he learns that the Atlanteans have a strange, ghastly something called "The Loving One" that they are using as a potent weapon in the war. Outside of some horrendous scenes as the forces of good and evil clash, this is more energetic than original. Miss Norton has done better.

Margaret A. Dorsey

SOURCE: A review of *Operation Time Search*, in *School Library Journal*, Vol. 14, No. 1, September, 1967, p. 134.

With Miss Norton's usual skilled writing, solid construction and sympathetic characters, this book is a pleasure to read and to recommend. It begins when a government project's attempt to break through to an alternate world accidentally projects photographer Ray Osborne thousands of years back in time. In this distant era, Atlantis is a powerful but evil nation, now at war with Mu, whose people worship the purity of the Flame. Osborne is captured by an Atlantean hunting party, then rescued by the gentle Murians, skilled in occult and telepathic arts, for whom he becomes a valuable spy, venturing finally into the heart of Atlantis. There is little here of the provocative speculation, insight or satire which characterizes the best adult science fiction, just a good moralistic adventure story (with a slightly surprising end) in which the righteous Murians are pitted against the evil rulers of Atlantis.

Paul Heins

SOURCE: A review of *Operation Time Search*, in *The Horn Book Magazine*, Vol. XLIII, No. 6, December, 1967, p. 760.

Sent to photograph an Indian mound in Ohio, Ray Osborne is so much affected by the operation of a time machine, which scientists are using to locate the world of Atlantis in time and space, that he is plunged back to an era when the Middle West bordered on a large inland sea and was overrun by a thick forest. Captured by a band of primitive hunters, he is turned over to the crew of an Atlantean ship, where from the other prisoners he learns of the great conflict in progress between the corrupt inhabitants of Atlantis and the inhabitants of Mu, a continent located in what is now the center of the Pacific Ocean. Ultimately, Roy casts his lot with the Murians because he believes in the justice of their cause, and when he is given an opportunity to return to twentieth-century America, he decides against it. The unusual decision of the protagonist gives an added dimension to a story that is noteworthy for its skillful combination of scientific and legendary elements.

OCTAGON MAGIC (1967)

Margery Fisher

SOURCE: A review of *Octagon Magic*, in *Growing Point*, Vol. 7, No. 3, September, 1968, p. 1176.

André Norton's domestic fantasies resemble her space operas in their arresting details and in the multi-patterned light of mystery which shines through them. *Octagon Magic* is a time-fantasy set in a small American town where a Canadian girl is finding it hard to make friends in a strange district. Curiosity leads her to trespass in the garden of the strangely-shaped house which contains its exact replica; here, through the agency of an old rocking-horse and its owner, Lorrie is shown, piecemeal, the past history of the octagonal house. At the same time she and her mother are involved with the troubles of the owner, old Miss Ashemeade, and the acquaintance deepens Lorrie's understanding of grown-ups and of her contemporaries as well.

B. W. Alderson

SOURCE: A review of *Octagon Magic*, in *Children's Book News*, Vol. 3, No. 5, September-October, 1968, p. 264.

Miss Norton is something of a Janus creature herself, with one visage peering ahead to the horrors of the Dipple and the times beyond the great Blow-Up, and the other looking backward to the events of the past and their meaning for the present. *Octagon Magic* is a book in this second category—a fantasy of feminine (but not effeminate) delicacy compared with the starkness of her tracts for the future. The story of Lorrie Mallard's visits to Octagon House present and Octagon Dolls' House past gives the author an opportunity to develop side by side themes about a child's personal development and a society's attitude to its people and its history. The attention to themes perhaps gets in the way of really strong characterization (Lorrie's feud with her classmates is a particularly weak spot), but middle-school girls will probably find the same sort of attractions in the book as (at a different level of fantasy) there are in *Tom's Midnight Garden*. Faith Jaques' painting for the book's wrapper is the only illustration, but its quality makes one wish that it had gained a more permanent place as a frontispiece.

THE ZERO STONE ("Zero Stone" series, 1968)

Kirkus Service

SOURCE: A review of *The Zero Stone*, in *Kirkus Service*, Vol. XXXVI, No. 12, February 15, 1968, p. 191.

Murdock Jern is the adopted son of a man who spent a

lifetime, sometimes on the wrong side of the law, collecting and examining . . . trading . . . the treasures of the universe. He taught Murdock the intricacies of gem evaluation and left him a special legacy . . . a mysterious, curiously lifeless alien ring which he dubbed the Zero Stone. But apparently others are anxious to claim it. Murdock's father died a brutal death and now Murdock finds himself pursued by the notorious "Thieves' Guild" as well as the Space Patrol. Fortunately he has found an ally in the odd little mutant Eet, a mind reader with an assortment of unusual talents. Miss Norton's extraordinary imagination is again at work as she reels her hero from a city where they choose sacrificial victims by lottery to a ship where he is condemned as a plague victim through space sans ship where the "Zero stone" acts as a strange propellant to a planet with hidden tombs bearing the bodies of the "Forerunner races," creatures of legend. Good sustaining action in what could be the start of a very nice series.

Peter J. Henniker-Heaton

SOURCE: Identity Crisis—Sci-Fi Style," in *The Christian Science Monitor,* May 2, 1968, p. B8.

Andre Norton is the American Express and Thomas Cook of time-travel. She has convoyed her readers through more past and future centuries in more galaxies than can be kept track of. Now again **The Zero Stone** parades the familiar props—derelicts of space, pirates, Galactic Patrolmen, and unexpected aliens. Eet, for instance, with a near-catlike body and the intelligence of seven men of more than average smartness; he's going to give the reader a difficult job of self-identification. But the presence of Eet succeeds in making the familiar props fresh and unfamiliar. He even makes the zero stone believable.

R. Baines

SOURCE: A review of *The Zero Stone,* in *The Junior Bookshelf,* Vol. 38, No. 3, June, 1974, p. 170.

Families are compelled to foster embryos, to ensure a properly balanced population, and one of the offspring produced by this process is the hero of this book: his companion is a creature with extrasensory perception born of a cat which swallows a mysterious stone on an alien planet.

In the past it has seemed strange that the science-fiction offered for the adolescent market by Andre Norton was frequently harder to follow than the work of several highly regarded writers for adults, but this story benefits from her use of a simpler format. Murdoc Jern searches through space to discover the significance of an abnormal jewel which he possesses, and in his journeyings he comes into conflict with a variety of other living beings. The first person narration is realistic and convincing, ensuring the involvement of the reader.

DARK PIPER (1968)

Kirkus Service

SOURCE: A review of *Dark Piper,* in *Kirkus Service,* Vol. XXXVI, No. 20, June 15, 1968, p. 650.

Beltane: neutral, pacifistic . . . a planet removed from the inter-galactic war; a place peacefully devoted to biological experimentation. Hardly a community prepared to listen to the warnings of returning veteran Griss Lugard who predicts a post-war scavenger hunt . . . with peaceful planets prime pickings. Lugard becomes the Dark Piper who takes the colony's ten children underground just before his prophecy comes true. The story is told by one of the children, Vere, now recording it on tape for posterity—Griss dies leaving the children to survive in a subterranean world also inhabited by the species monsterosi Miss Norton is so good at bringing to life. Then there's the coming out to find the parents destroyed by a virus plague and the experimental mutants taking over. A taut story line, many tense moments . . . the space age coordinates read—thrill/chill.

Zena Sutherland

SOURCE: A review of *Dark Piper,* in *Bulletin of the Center for Children's Books,* Vol. 22, No. 7, March, 1969, p. 116.

Of all the Scorpio Sector planets, only Beltane had been set aside as a biological experimental station, and its peaceful citizens could not believe that refugees from another planet would harm them. Ten young people were trapped underground when the refugee attack wiped out the population; primarily this is the story of their fight for survival. There are pace and suspense up to the point where the youngsters discover that all their people are dead and that their real enemies are the mutant animals; the brief survey of several years of coexistence ends the book anticlimactically. The characters are good, the action sustained; the writing is weakened slightly by the author's persistent and not always relevant references to plants and animals with exotic names, a device that reminds one jarringly that this is science fiction.

FUR MAGIC (1968)

Kirkus' Service

SOURCE: A review of *Fur Magic,* in *Kirkus' Service,* Vol. XXXVI, No. 28, October 15, 1968, p. 1164.

Had the Changer, the Indian spirit, in reshaping Cory Alder as a beaver and testing his belief in a greater power, really transformed him into a stronger person? What is clearly a rhetorical question to the author demands a credulity of the reader that the story is not strong enough to evoke: Cory as a boy afraid of the slightest movement on his Indian foster uncle's ranch seems a sissy since there's no motivation for his fears; and his extended adventures as Yellow Shell, a beaver-who-is-not-a-beaver, involving animals alternately scrambling about and acting sententious, often seem silly. Especially as expressed in mock-Indian language and phrasing. The climactic contest between the Changer, part-coyote; part-man, who would enslave all creatures, and Thunderbird, the spirit of the White Eagle, who opposes him, and who, with Cory's aid, disarms him, is undeniably exciting but the greater part of the book is shallow realism and fuzzy fantasy.

Peter J. Henniker-Heaton

SOURCE: "The Nice Robot," in *The Christian Science Monitor,* May 1, 1969, p. B5.

Andre Norton never fails to tell a good yarn. Her spaceships and time-machines have over the years ranged through most of known space and time; also through a good section of unknown space and time. On this occasion she does something rather different.

In *Fur Magic* a town-type youngster visits his uncle on the Great Plains, and there in Indian country he finds himself and learns to face the world. His lessons are somewhat like those of Arthur under the wizard Merlin in *The Once and Future King.* Under the tutorship of an old Indian he takes the form of an animal, mixing with other animal denizens of the region and learning from them.

The story is built around ancient Indian legends and the significant part played by animals in these legends. Is this book history or magic or science fiction, or just a boy's dream on a hot day?

Robert Bell

SOURCE: A review of *Fur Magic,* in *The School Librarian,* Vol. 17, No. 4, December, 1969, p. 401.

The author draws on North American Indian legend for the plot of this story, which is as strange and fascinating as her previous *Steel Magic* and *Octagon Magic.*

Cory Alder, staying on the ranch of Uncle Jasper in the far west of America, becomes involved in the powerful 'medicine' of the old Indian Black Elk and is transported back in time to the days before the coming of man. He becomes a beaver named Yellow Shell, and the adventures and perils of his life in this form give full play to André Norton's genius at totally involving her readers in the impossible yet strangely credible situations she creates so well. Cory finally confronts the sinister and powerful 'Changer' and, by the aid of the 'Thunderbird', the messenger of the 'Great Spirit', succeeds in thwarting his evil design and returning to his human form and the present time.

The author's own magic has lost none of its potency, and it is to be hoped that there will be more of her spell-weaving to come; there can never be too much junior fiction of this quality.

📖   *UNCHARTED STARS* ("Zero Stone" series, 1969)

Kirkus Reviews

SOURCE: A review of *Uncharted Stars,* in *Kirkus Reviews,* Vol. XXXVII, No. 36, February 15, 1969, p. 186.

A predicted sequel to *The Zero Stone* which again features jewel merchant Vondar and his unusual alien companion, Eet. Here they are still tracking down the origin of the zero stones (that give off an uncanny power) and the search lands them in the den of the Thieves' Guild. Vondar must pose as his own father (a gem appraiser) to keep them alive and as he is tested he discovers a second zero stone among the Thieves' treasure along with an unusual star map that may hold the key to a lost Forerunner civilization. The author's version of hallucinatory and telepathic effects is excellent and the Vondar/Eet duo is inspired. Perhaps they will continue charting stars even after Eet undergoes a final, surprising transfiguration. So far, two of the author's best.

The Booklist and Subscription Books Bulletin

SOURCE: A review of *Uncharted Stars,* in *The Booklist and Subscription Books Bulletin,* Vol. 65, No. 18, May 15, 1969, p. 1078.

In a sequel to *The Zero Stone* Murdoc Jern and his mutant partner Eet continue their search for the source of the mysterious zero stone. The key to the secret of the stone is a star map that was pillaged from the tomb of a long-dead civilization and taken to Waystar, the hidden and supposedly impregnable asteroid stronghold of the criminal element. Another well-written, first-person science-fiction story with imaginative use of telepathic detail, an extended series of adventures, and a surprising climax.

📖   *POSTMARKED THE STARS* ("Solar Queen" series, 1969)

Kirkus Reviews

SOURCE: A review of *Postmarked the Stars,* in *Kirkus Reviews,* Vol. XXXVII, No. 49, September 15, 1969, p. 1010.

In the beginning Dane Thorson wakes up with the headache the reader will have by the close. This is one of the author's uninhibited efforts where the plot gives up and anything goes. With more "monsters," "oozings" and "blobs" than you can shake a stun gun at. It's all part of Dane's problem. He's the cargo master on the Solar Queen, a free trader with a shipment of "Brachs" and tiny dragonesque creatures. Somehow, someone plants a weird radiation box on board and under its influence the Brachs retrogress. Which means in this case that they get smarter, reverting to an earlier, ancestral life form. The dragons retrogress also . . . with disastrous consequences, and there are all manner of nasty surprises when they finally reach their destination. Like "monsters," "oozings" and "blobs" and a universal conspiracy. This time Miss Norton's energy is enervating.

Margaret A. Dorsey

SOURCE: A review of *Postmarked the Stars,* in *School Library Journal,* Vol. 16, No. 10, May 15, 1970, p. 77.

After several gripping opening pages in which Dane Thorson, assistant cargo master of a free trader spaceship, awakes from attempted poisoning in unknown surroundings, this latest Norton sci-fi novel lapses into standard cosmic cops and robbers. It soon becomes obvious that something is amiss with the cargo of the *Solar Queen.* The crew land in the wilderness of their destination planet to gain time to find out why the cargo of embryos have regressed under mysterious radiation to monstrous forms. A series of encounters with other monsters on the planet and with the men responsible for their presence finally disclose a large and complex criminal operation. There's less to the plot than meets the eye, as the last half of the book consists mainly of repetitive captures and escapes; also, the characterizations, dull and two-dimensional, do not live up to the standards of Miss Norton's other books. This book is not likely to win her new readers, and will only disappoint her many fans.

A. R. Williams

SOURCE: A review of *Postmarked the Stars,* in *The Junior Bookshelf,* Vol. 35, No. 3, October, 1971, p. 321.

In some ways Mrs. Norton's latest novel is a complicated game of hide-and-seek in outer space, first on board the free-trading spaceship, Solar Queen, eventually on Trewsworld, a planet whose constitutional and industrial status is being undermined by a corrupt scientific organisation. A frenzied search takes place on the ship for a mysterious something which is playing genetic havoc with certified livestock on board. On Trewsworld an exhilarating sequence of discoveries and escapes keeps the reader on tenterhooks for what seems a very long time. Mrs. Norton's detail is, as always, convincing, and her extension of the possibilities of mutation in animal strains carries fascinating but forbidding implications for the human race.

Hugh Crago

SOURCE: A review of *Postmarked the Stars,* in *Children's Book Review,* Vol. I, No. 6, December, 1971, pp. 194-95.

Postmarked the Stars—an uninspired title for an uninspired book—is so prototypically Andre Norton that one is prompted to use it to demonstrate what is the matter with the writer whose performance has rarely matched her reputation. Basically, the problem is that too few ideas have been spread over too many novels. *Catseye* and *Judgment on Janus* explored telepathy and alien cultures fully and sympathetically, but *Postmarked the Stars,* a 1969 sequel to *Plague Ship* and *Sargasso of Space,* uses telepathy and regressive mutation simply as counters in a cops and robbers plot. When the restricted corridors of the space ship give way to the more elemental problems of cold, hunger and enemy blasters under the skies of planet Trewsworld, one senses a reluctance to develop suggestive hints to the full, a sketchiness in the background, a reliance on 'nameless horrors' to provide suspense: '. . . the very outlines suggested that it was a nightmare creature, while the stench of it made him sick'. Though readable, and thus superior to *Ice Crown,* this novel irritates by its failure to be more than one-dimensional.

BERTIE AND MAY (with Bertha Stemm Norton, 1969)

Margery Fisher

SOURCE: A review of *Bertie and May,* in *Growing Point,* Vol. 10, No. 4, October, 1971, p. 1799.

Bertie and May takes us back to the 1870s and '80s in rural Ohio. 'Bertie's' daughter André Norton has composed the book from certain written reminiscences of her mother's and from memories of stories told to children, grandchildren and great-grandchildren. It is a surprise to find that the book is not written in the historic present, it is so wonderfully vivid and immediate. The two little sisters, happily barefoot, eagerly await the train bringing Uncle Harris for a visit, they take flour browned with salt to school for a mid-morning treat, watch the auctioning of pies at a local charity fair, make dolls' furniture and cookies for their own private sale, contrive Christmas presents. There is a feeling of family affection transcending domestic difficulties that recalls the books of Laura Ingalls Wilder. Pa's old-fashioned mill is threatened by mechanised rivals in the town and he is forced to sell out and work for the 'roller mill' but matters are explained to the girls and after they have lived in town for a time they are consulted in all seriousness about whether the family stays there or returns to the country. A liberal atmosphere and a tremendous zest for life make this a fascinating book which calls across the years.

DREAD COMPANION (1970)

Diane Farrell

SOURCE: A review of *Dread Companion,* in *The Horn Book Magazine,* Vol. XLVI, No. 5, October, 1970, pp. 483-84.

A skillful intertwining of unlikely elements—folklore and spacelore, sorcery and science—generates an engrossing adventure that begins in the year 2422. Kilda c'Rhyn, the child of a planet cross-marriage, has been raised in a crèche of Service children. Her only chance of independence is to get off-world, perhaps to a frontier planet. One of her teachers helps her to get a job as a house aide caring for the children of the emigrating Zobak family. The girl Bartare is a strange, self-contained little creature, who seems to have extrasensory powers. She communicates with an invisible woman, "the Lady," and dominates her younger brother Oomark. Eventually, Bartare and Oomark—with Kilda in pursuit—penetrate another space-time continuum, an alien world where perspective is distorted, populated by the Folk, the Dark Ones, and the Between. To eat or drink here is to change, to become part of this world with no going back. Oomark stuffs himself with bright fruits and berries and turns into a little hairy animal with hoofs and horns. Kilda struggles to stay "Between," to rescue Bartare from the Folk who are trying to steal the child, to elude the dark monsters who bear the stench of death, to find the gate back to their own world. She has an ally, Jorth, a Survey Scout, who has blundered into this world and become One Between, part beast. Magic helps, too—the magic of the Folk that Jorth has spied out and the magic of the notus, a silver tree with cold, fragrant cream-white flowers, full of power and feared by the Folk. Despite its elaborate setting, this science-fiction fantasy boils down to a suspenseful and satisfying teenage romance; for, of course, when all the spells have been broken, Jorth turns into a handsome red-headed young man.

Elizabeth Haynes

SOURCE: A review of *Dread Companion,* in *School Library Journal,* Vol. 17, No. 4, December, 1970, p. 66.

Miss Norton's contributions have ranged from virtually pure SF to almost equally pure fantasy. This latest volume leans heavily toward the latter and is somewhat below her usual high standard. Kilda c'Rhyn, in order to escape a life of boredom, signs on as house aide to a family bound for the colonial planet of Dylan. Her task is to care for and tutor the two children, and she soon discovers that the older girl is smart, difficult, and far too knowing about matters that should not concern her. Despite her suspicions, Kilda is trapped and drawn through a time gate to another, completely alien world. The book concerns her struggles to return to Dylan, and is replete with strange monsters and fantastical events. Miss Norton's skill at style and characterization give the

book readability and interest, but the plot has a murky vagueness at times. However, female protagonists are rare in juvenile SF, and even a below-average Norton is better than much of the SF/fantasy floating around today.

The Times Literary Supplement

SOURCE: "Nightmare Landscapes," in *The Times Literary Supplement,* No. 3661, April 28, 1972, p. 484.

Andre Norton's *Dread Companion* is as compulsive and relentless as a nightmare—a hideous nightmare to which the reader would not return if the author once allowed him to wake up; but Andre Norton binds her spell tight. Bartare, a planetary child, is possessed by an evil power and leads her reluctant brother and the older woman, in whose care the children have been placed, into a land of monsters and mirages where touch, smell and taste of the indigenous vegetation affect vision and dimension, where age and time take on new and terrifying meanings.

David L. Rees

SOURCE: A review of *Dread Companion,* in *Children's Book Review,* Vol. II, No. 3, June, 1972, pp. 78-9.

'I am one of those planted among human kind to learn their ways and draw with me into this world some of their stock,' says Bartare.

That certainly explains a lot. Sixteen-year-old Kilda has been looking after two children on the planet Chalox and becomes increasingly perturbed about the girl who all too often acts as one possessed. Emigration to the planet Dylan brings the crisis to a head with main characters and reader sent reeling into a world of nightmare where evil forces do all they can to seize and destroy. Nothing is as it seems and the eye dare not trust. Escape leads to further confusion. . . .

The reader has to keep his wits about him or all is lost. He is in the hands of a writer who knows well her craft and who makes no concessions. Absorbing fare for the determined.

EXILES OF THE STARS ("Moon Magic" series, 1971)

Kirkus Reviews

SOURCE: A review of *Exiles of the Stars,* in *Kirkus Reviews,* Vol. XXXIX, No. 5, March 1, 1971, p. 243.

This sequel to *Moon of Three Rings* (1966) again features Krip Vorlund, Free Trader, and the beautiful Maelen. Krip's personality has been transported into the body of a "Thassa" which offers him additional psychic powers, while Maelen is currently residing in the body of a small animal. Their Free Trader ship is caught up in a Civil War on the planet Thoth and the Thothian priests demand that they transport valuable Forerunner treasure to another planet for safekeeping. But they are forced down on an uninhabited world (sabotage?) where they find that they are about to become victims of a totally alien army which has for untold millennia been held in "stass-freeze" (suspended animation). The aliens have totems remarkably similar to ancient Egyptian Gods . . . they also possess remarkable, malignant powers and the secret of personality transference. The author provides her usual dashes of daring and dollops of intrigue in a labyrinthian plot designed to hold the reader in suspended admiration.

Sheryl B. Andrews

SOURCE: A review of *Exiles of the Stars,* in *The Horn Book Magazine,* Vol. XLVII, No. 4, August, 1971, pp. 389-40.

In the sequel to *Moon of Three Rings,* the popular and prolific writer of science-fantasy for young people continues with the story of Krip Vorlund, a Free Trader in some future eon, who through shape-changing entered into the body of a wild animal and then, being unable ever again to regain his original form, was forced to claim as his own the body of a Thassa named Maquad. As in the first book, the Thassa Moon Singer Maelen is integrally bound to Krip although she no longer wears the guise of a woman, having been condemned by her people to take the body of her animal-friend Vors when her own body was broken and dying. Now in the form of a glassia of Yiktor, Maelen uses her advanced esper talents in the service of the crew of the Free Trader ship *Lydis.* And just how important these talents will become is unreckonable when the crew of the *Lydis* first agree to transport the sacred relics of Thoth to a place of safety during a religious uprising on that planet. After sabotage in midspace via esper powers, the crew's encounter with malevolent wills clothed in the humanoid bodies of a race dating back before the pyramids of Egypt eventually forces Maelen, who is dying, to leave the relative safety of stass-freeze and call upon her Thassa gifts. Thus she is able to liberate key crew members of the *Lydis* from body changes not of their choice and to battle for a final chance for herself against the being wearing the diadem of the cat-headed goddess Sekhmet. The story is told in the first person by Maelen and Krip in alternating though not ordered sequential chapters; and though the final explanations for the motivations of the four ancient crowned beings who seek to control the life force of the *Lydis'* crew remain a bit nebulous, the fast pace of the story and the development of the two major characters carries even the literal-minded reader past the stage of mundane questioning to enjoyment.

Norman Culpan

SOURCE: A review of *Exiles of the Stars,* in *The School Librarian,* Vol. 20, No. 3, September, 1972, p. 260.

On beginning to read *Exiles of the Stars* my first reaction was to think: André Norton has now moved away from her vividly imagined pictures of alien planets, from her presentations of self-discovery, and in a new preoccupation with inter-stellar flight machinery and the more mundane conflicts of goodies and baddies has degenerated into a competent but relatively banal purveyor of 'S.F. for boys'. I do not think that her recent novels for children have the imaginative pressure of the first half-dozen or so she wrote; but her effective use of man-animal relationships and description of subterranean passages are here again, her plot skill is undiminished, and her solution of the need for an acceptable man-woman relationship is ingenious. Above all—despite an occasional archaic inversion and the pseudo-poetical use of such words as 'save', 'like', and 'unto', she has a skill, probably unrivalled among S.F. writers, in conveying wonder. I still recommend her, more strongly than any other S.F. writer, for the 10-13 age-range.

ANDROID AT ARMS (1971)

C. S. Hannabuss

SOURCE: A review of *Android at Arms,* in *Children's Book Review,* Vol. II, No. 5, October, 1972, pp. 150-51.

Readers have rightly come to expect excitement in science fantasy of the 'sword and sorcery' type, and from this book they will not come away unfed. Andre Norton's hero, Andras Kastor, is snatched off into mind lock while his android double takes his place as heir to the kingdom of Inyanga. Time has passed on his secret return, and he has to skulk in the threatening darkness of the tunnels which thread their way behind the palace walls. For, through the android usurper, evil rules in the land, negating all, like the Narnian White Torch or Tolkien's Sauron. With a purloined fatal ring, Andras pursues this evil through a time gate into a future Inyanga, where the struggle must be resolved.

Yet readers have come to expect structural efficiency in Andre Norton's science fantasy, and from this book they will come away confused. The plot poses two questions: 'Will Andras win back his throne in the *real* Inyaga?' and 'Is he android?' In the effort to answer the second, the first is rather forgotten. The first 150 pages, obediently developing the title, continuously revolve around question one. But Andras's journey into the future is one-way, so that the climax exists exclusively in the future Inyanga: it is preoccupied with working out question two, leaving the android double untouched upon the throne. Perhaps he/it disintegrates in the general overthrow of evil—if not, much remains to be done. There are two halves of two good books here.

J. Murphey

SOURCE: A review of *Android at Arms,* in *The Junior Bookshelf,* Vol. 36, No. 6, December, 1972, pp. 407-08.

Andre Norton is among the best and most imaginative present day writers of science fiction. This latest fantasy is well up to her high standards. It is a mixture of the future in the past. The empire that Andas Kastor claims could well have been that of the Incas. His problem is, is he the rightful heir or is he an android? He has been imprisoned on an alien planet for an unexplained period and when he returns he brings with him Yolyos, a strange creature from another world who was a fellow prisoner. Together they experience in a haunted palace the future in the past and Andas is so sickened by what he knows will be, he determines at all cost to defeat his rival and enemy. How he does so is powerfully described.

The readership is again hard to define, it is definitely for the older addict of SF, that is the twelve to sixteen-year-old boy or girl—but many adults will also be fascinated by it.

DRAGON MAGIC (1972)

Kirkus Reviews

SOURCE: A review of *Dragon Magic*, in *Kirkus Reviews*, Vol. XL, No. 8, April 15, 1972, p. 485.

Four boys find a magic jigsaw puzzle in a deserted house, and as each completes one of the four pictured dragons he is propelled into a mythological fantasy neatly tailored to his cultural background and personal hangups. Sig Dortmund finds himself transmogrified into Sig Clawhand, a witness to the killing of Fafnir; Ras becomes a Nubian slave who helps Daniel kill the dragon Sirrush-Lau and then escapes from Babylonian captivity; Artie is changed into a loyal retainer who is present at the death of Artos Pendragon; and Kim Stevens sees how the Chinese general known as the Slumbering Dragon became great by accepting responsibility for his failures. The legends (particularly the Arthurian material) are cleverly reworked, but the strict parallels of the plot admit little suspense and restrict the fantasies' appeal by making them patly didactic. As always, however, Andre Norton can be relied upon to convert her magic formulas into adroit entertainment.

Zena Sutherland

SOURCE: A review of *Dragon Magic*, in *Bulletin of the Center for Children's Books,* Vol. 25, No. 10, June, 1972, pp. 160-61.

Four stories that are fanciful occur as episodes lived by each of four boys, the whole set within a realistic framework. In a dusty abandoned house Sig finds a box that has on its cover four dragons, each in a different color. One by one, he and the other three put together the pieces, each working separately and with a different color, and each boy slips back in time to an adventure: Sig, who is of German descent, lives an episode in ancient times and fights the dragon Fafnir, a black boy

becomes a Nubian slave of princely blood in Babylon, a boy of Chinese descent goes back in time to China; Artie Jones becomes Artos Pendragon. When the four boys meet and talk about their experiences, they become friends. The framework is not quite substantial enough to compete with the four fanciful episodes, and is subordinate to them; they are imaginative and wholly-conceived, but written in rather ornate style.

Beryl Robinson

SOURCE: A review of *Dragon Magic,* in *The Horn Book Magazine,* Vol. XLVIII, No. 4, August, 1972, p. 373.

Four boys experience individual adventures in space and time when they explore a deserted old house. Attracted to a jigsaw puzzle lying on a dust-covered table, each boy obeys an irresistible urge to put the puzzle together. As the last piece goes into place and completes one of the four dragons pictured on the cover, each boy is suddenly transported to another time and place, where he bears a different name and identity, and becomes deeply involved in a dangerous adventure. Of different ethnic heritage, each boy's adventure occurs in the past history of his own ancestors, where he lives events that later developed into legends. Fafnir, the terrible dragon of Germanic lore; Sirrush-Lau, the Nubian dragon that Daniel slew at the court of Nebuchadnezzar; Artos Pendragon's struggles to unify Britain after the withdrawal of the Roman Legions; and the "Slumbering Dragon" of an ancient Chinese war come to life: Legend, fantasy, and historical and contemporary situations are interwoven in an absorbing story. Despite the wealth and range of dragon lore and legendry, the story has clarity and immediacy; and the values of courage, loyalty, and strength met in the past help each boy meet problems of the present. Those who read this book may well find themselves seeking eagerly—as did the four adventurers—the hero tales and legends in the library.

THE CRYSTAL GRYPHON ("Witch World" series, first volume in "Gryphon" trilogy, 1972)

Norman Culpan

SOURCE: A review of *The Crystal Gryphon,* in *The School Librarian,* Vol. 21, No. 4, December, 1973, p. 372.

In an indeterminate time and place, Lord Kerovan and Lady Joisan, betrothed when he is ten and she is eight, do not meet until ten years later, when their nuptials are delayed by a savage invasion which involves both their kingdoms. The state of civilization seems to be roughly that of Norman times, complicated by relics of an earlier civilization of high technical achievement, and by magic. This time animals are simply animals, and there are no subterranean labyrinths. Alternate chapters are related in the first person by Kerovan and Joisan: this, I found, brought a brief lapse of imaginative tension at the end of each chapter, though I see the gain in presenting the misunderstandings of the two protagonists. The style, too, with its frequent pseudo-archaisms—I felt forced into using the word 'nuptials', earlier—jarred me somewhat. Despite all this Miss Norton, as usual, retained my interest, and I recommend the book for younger secondary children and some of the older primary ones.

Jessica Kemball-Cook

SOURCE: A review of *The Crystal Gryphon,* in *Children's Book Review,* Vol. III, No. 6, December, 1973, p. 179.

Andre Norton's latest book is an outright tale of sword-and-sorcery. Kerovan of Ulmsdale differs from other men, having hooves instead of feet, and although he is heir to his father's estates, he is kept in isolation and married by proxy to Joisan of Ithkrypt. She likewise stands apart from other girls, being heir to her uncle, and of a serious and resourceful nature. Both also share a desire to know more about the Old Ones who inhabited their world before them, and left not only deserted buildings, but also strange powers and talismans to those who could use them. The Crystal Gryphon is one such, and Kerovan and Joisan use it to bring them closer together (they do not meet until near the end of the book), and to help them when their lands are invaded. The story is told by each in alternate chapters, a device to make us more aware of the bond between the two.

To tell this story the author has plunged fully into the epic world of Tolkien and Morris, of archaisms and Teutonic phrasing, of birthings, healcraft, wife-right, ensorcelling and signs of the Power. It is a world where chance and coincidence operate on the hero's side, so that miraculous escapes and helpful finds are designed to show that fate rather than luck is at work. Rewards come to those who use what they are born with; goodness and humanity come from within rather than from any pleasing outward appearances; Kerovan and Joisan earn their happy ending because they keep faith with one another, even though they have never met. This is an outstanding fantasy of the kind which works on symbolic as well as narrative levels, and one of the most carefully and consistently presented works this author has given us in recent years.

FORERUNNER FORAY (1973)

M. H. Miller

SOURCE: A review of *Forerunner Foray,* in *The Junior Bookshelf,* Vol. 38, No. 3, June, 1974, p. 169.

A million years from now, some "sensitives" have highly developed psychic powers, which can even move physical objects. One Ziantha has to travel back to two previous civilisations in search of a stone loaded with psychic energy. There are fascinating possibilities here: the emotions and relationships of a sensitive; involvement in three distant civilisations. Regrettably, all we are offered is a quasi-exciting psychic adventure story. The characters are puppets, with no development, no genuine emotion; the three civilisations are only sketchily outlined. The dialogue is humourless and hilarious; occasional archaisms—"aught", "bethink you"—indicate the passing of a million years. The plotting is shoddy, with numerous false leads and loose ends. This, plus hundreds of invented names of increasing risibility (Wamage, Sxark, a city called Singakok), makes the story very difficult to follow. The succession of impossible achievements and narrow escapes are straight out of Biggles. There are nine linguistic ineptitudes, including four clichés, in the first eighteen lines, and the standard of the writing is around that level throughout the book. Even science-fantasy addicts will only get a bad trip.

Jessica Kemball-Cook

SOURCE: A review of *Forerunner Foray,* in *Children's Book Review,* Vol. IV, No. 2, Summer, 1974, p. 66.

Ziantha, a highly-trained telepath, makes a 'foray' or mind-search into the times of the Forerunners, an ancient race which predates her own era. While spying for the Thieves' Guild, an interplanetary organisation, she comes across a mysterious stone which magnifies her mental powers and drags her into the personalities of two Forerunner females, each facing a great crisis in their own time. By great mental effort she frees herself not only from the long-dead personalities, but also the slavery of the Thieves' Guild.

With its casual references to terms like 'sight distort', 'nightsight', 'psychic energy', 'chewing gratz' and 'veeps', this book certainly assumes an acquaintance with SF conventions, and takes for granted that we understand what Ziantha is about with her mind-searching. The scene is the galactic empire, peopled with humanoids and 'X-Tee' aliens, long after Man left Terra of Sol to colonise the planets. There he found other races, and relics of extinct peoples, and this book examines the use of 'psychometry', a kind of clairvoyance, in archaeological quests of the future. The story has a more general application, however, as it deals with the right of the individual to determine his own future and go his own way apart from those who have trained him. One can also find kinship with the physically dissimilar: Ziantha's best friend is a telepathic bird-like creature; and her own lack of beauty is compensated for by her amazing mental powers.

With its carefully constructed plot and choice of suitable language this book stands above much by inferior writers; yet the pace is slow and sometimes wearying, so that I would only recommend it to Norton fans and SF addicts, who would best appreciate its quality of elegance blended with intellectual argument.

IRON CAGE (1974)

Kirkus Reviews

SOURCE: A review of *Iron Cage,* in *Kirkus Reviews,* Vol. XLII, No. 13, July 1, 1974, p. 688.

The People are the umpteenth race of highly evolved (dog/cat/bear-like) animals to populate Norton's fictional planets, and when Jony, of human stock himself, realizes that his friends are about to be captured and exploited by the inhabitants of a visiting starship (also human) he fights to defend them. Jony himself started life as a caged specimen in the laboratories of a superhuman race he knew only as the Big Ones, and—lest anyone miss the point—Norton begins and closes with a flashback to a mistreated mother cat on earth, suggesting that man's cruelty to the animal world will trigger cosmic revenge in the form of slavery to another order of Big Ones. Jony's defense of his adopted kin is accomplished with a whole range of weapons from the aliens' own stun guns and lasers to his special ESP powers, and the primitive, communal culture is depicted in careful detail. The premise is hardly new, especially to loyal Norton fans; however, in contrast to her other exotic future worlds, this latest presents a bleaker and more chilling prospect.

Publishers Weekly

SOURCE: A review of *Iron Cage,* in *Publishers Weekly,* Vol. 206, No. 23, December 2, 1974, p. 62.

In this slightly precious story, set a thousand years in the future, the author attempts to stress an obvious yet nonetheless valid moral. The story is a fantasy about one species being imprisoned and exploited by another. Jony, the young hero who liberates the downtrodden, is wise and a railer against injustice. The parallel with animals in our present world is pointed out in a mini-saga at the beginning and end as we learn of a pregnant cat dumped in a trash heap by departing vacationers.

Sarah Hayes

SOURCE: "Far Flung Worlds," in *The Times Literary Supplement,* No. 3836, September 19, 1975, p. 1052.

Mind reading and mind control appear not as a defensive technique but as a dangerous weapon in **Iron Cage,** a more traditional science fiction which again deals in a palatable way with serious issues. Jony and his younger half-brother and sister are discovered and reared by a tribe of primitive vegetarian bear-like creatures whose simple language and gentle tradition they absorb and accept until Jony discovers the ruins of man, a city, a stock of laser-like weapons and an ancient wall painting, which shows the creatures chained and subdued to the will of the more intelligent man. Now stained by his evil forebears, Jony is ostracized by the tribe and forced to

wear a symbolic iron collar. When a human spaceship lands, some of the tribe-creatures are caged for experimentation. While Jony's brother is seduced from the tribe's ways by machines and power, Jony redeems himself by destroying the weapons that make men omnipotent. Life continues with all animals living in peaceful coexistence, united against natural perils and the obscenity of enslavement.

Beginning and ending with the image of a pet cat dumped on a rubbish heap in a cardboard carton, this strong and vivid novel asks important questions about our interaction with the animals we so mindlessly dominate.

Norman Culpan

SOURCE: A review of *Iron Cage,* in *The School Librarian,* Vol. 24, No. 1, March, 1976, p. 52.

All André Norton's old skills are here, but they are here used to make explicit a theme, the important potential of animals, which has been implicit in many of her books from the beginning. Jony, of human origin, who has been nurtured on an alien planet by creatures of about stone-age intelligence who have developed from bears, throws in his lot with them and defeats the attempts of visiting men to colonise what has become to him his home planet. Some adult readers will share—and perhaps be surprised to share—my shock at a human being's choosing to bring disaster on an expedition of morally quite normal men; but few will deplore a plea for greater concern for and understanding of animals.

Young readers will need a certain amount of sophistication to link satisfactorily the Prologue and Epilogue in which a cat is dumped in a cardboard box to die and later rescued, with the imprisonment of the young Jony and his mother in cages by alien invaders, their escape, and their safe-keeping by the indigenous bear-like creatures. The publishers suggest a reading age of twelve and over, which is probably about right.

LAVENDER-GREEN MAGIC (1974)

Kirkus Reviews

SOURCE: A review of *Lavender-Green Magic,* in *Kirkus Reviews,* Vol. XLII, No. 13, July 1, 1974, pp. 681-82.

Set somewhere in the rural South of both the present and colonial days and rooted in old time herb lore, this is one of Andre Norton's more mundane and unassuming fantasies. Three children, Judy, Crock and Holly, are sent to live with their grandparents who are caretakers of the abandoned Dimsdale mansion and of the local junkyard, which seems to be a steady source of restorable antiques. One of the first old treasures Holly discovers, an embroidered herb pillow, has the power to transport the children through the old, overgrown maze garden and back several centuries where they become embroiled in the competition between two sister witches—the virtuous Tamar and the scheming Hagar. As always, Norton weaves an ingenious plot; only one witch is remembered in the local legend and the discovery of the dual witches is made the direct outgrowth of Holly's own two-sided nature which vacillates between spitefulness and generosity. And the herbal magic and country crafts, though by now ubiquitous accessories to juvenile fiction, are satisfactorily substantial. One aspect of the story is, however, awkward and unconvincing: Judy, Crock and Holly are supposed to be black children, but this is somehow difficult to believe. Their schoolmates apparently are totally without prejudice and Holly's defensiveness (she is afraid someone will call her "black") is presented as unfounded in fact and wins her little sympathy, even among her family. If, unlike Holly, one doesn't mistrust the continually insisted upon prevailing colorblindness, then the rest is easy—and the directions for lavender fans, rose beads and fuzzie-muzzies will make everyone want to turn herbalist.

Virginia Haviland

SOURCE: A review of *Lavender-Green Magic,* in *The Horn Book Magazine,* Vol. L, No. 5, October, 1974, pp. 137-38.

A family of black children is drawn from a here-and-now situation in "Sussex," a community obviously north of Boston, into a mysterious colonial past connected with the Dimsdale estate. Judy and Crock, fifth-grade twins, and Holly, who is a year older, come to stay with their grandparents after their mother has received a report that their father is "missing in action" in Vietnam. The Wades live and work in an old barn converted into a house on the Dimsdale land, which, since the death of the last Dimsdale and the burning of the house, has become the town dump. Their earnings derive from the repair and sale of scavenged castoffs and the harvesting of herbs. Herbs account for many threads in the plot: For the children who take turns sleeping on it, an herbal pillow becomes the means of transport to early Dimsdale; they learn more of the curse put upon the Dimsdales after finding—in the center of an herb-garden maze—the house where two sisters used to mix their herbal brews. The witchlore and herbcraft, superimposed on a family situation, is skillfully worked into the plot, although there is a certain amount of light moralizing. The author succeeds particularly well in creating child personalities; Holly is a prickly heroine—her own worst enemy.

Publishers Weekly

SOURCE: A review of *Lavender-Green Magic,* in *Publishers Weekly,* Vol. 206, No. 23, December 2, 1974, p. 62.

Holly, her twin brother Crock and a sister, Judy, move from Boston to a tiny rural community. Near their grandparents' home is an overgrown maze. The day after Judy sleeps on a balsam pillow, she leads the other children confidently through the huge growth, to the colonial cottage of a good witch, Tamar. Consumed by jealousy of Judy and insecure at school, Holly plots to get the pillow for herself. But when she takes the others through the maze, she encounters Hagar, a malevolent witch who wants to use Holly for her own evil ends. The three children are black, and a subplot about Holly's attitude toward her schoolmates fits rather awkwardly into the whole. The Norton skill shows in a fine climax, however, though even that has been signaled a little too obviously.

THE JARGOON PARD ("Witch World" series, 1974)

Kirkus Reviews

SOURCE: A review of *The Jargoon Pard,* in *Kirkus Reviews,* Vol. XLII, No. 15, August 1, 1974, p. 810.

If "jargoon pard" sounds like either an obscure spoonerism or an anagram, put yourself in a properly somber fantasy-receptive frame of mind and be advised that a jargoon is a semiprecious stone and a jargoon pard is thus a (leo)pard skin belt of magical werepeople properties with the power to turn young Kethan into a snarling pard beast. Announced as a "companion piece" to *The Crystal Gryphon,* this is not a sequel, but a second chance for Andre Norton to expand on the Welsh accented neverland setting and the potential of half man/half animal natures. Expand she does with more gravely archaic dialogue, a full tarot reading for Kethan, an evil sorceress Ursilla heading up a cast of villains working at unfathomable cross purposes, and a full spectrum of magic, Green, Yellow and Red. All a bit overdressed for our taste, although anyone so inclined may immerse himself in a dazzling variety of supernatural spells, purple flames, moonflower wands, moly charms, Star Towers, snow cats, Arvon powers and so on . . . even a parting promise that "the whyfor will come to be discovered in time." Perhaps.

Paul Heins

SOURCE: A review of *The Jargoon Pard,* in *The Horn Book Magazine,* Vol. LI, No. 2, April, 1975, p. 153.

In the ancient land of Arvon, a leader could not be succeeded by his own son if his sister had a son. When the Lady Heroise of the House of Car Do Prawn gave birth to a girl, the Wise Woman Ursilla substituted a new-born baby boy, and the two power-mad women hoped to rule their dominion by controlling the boy as he grew into manhood. The boy Kethan tells the story, the events of which were finally made clear to him at the conclusion of his strange experiences. For the mother of the Lady Heroise gave him a belt of golden fur—the clasp of which was a jargoon, a yellow-brown gem, made in the form of a cat's head. In spite of himself, Kethan was attracted by the belt; and when he wore it at full moon, he turned into a leopard and roamed the countryside. But Ursilla stole his belt; he could not resume his human form; and she did her utmost to maintain control over him. The narrative of Kethan's adventures is heightened by the first-person telling since the youth is aware of the duality of his nature. Not only is he conscious of his animal and his human powers at the same time, but in the process of discovering his identity, he learns to make choices and to adjust to the disparate elements of his personality. The fantasy is powerfully concluded in a subterranean scene: Ursilla, having gathered all of the characters of the story before a group of monolithic, faceless figures, is finally defeated by the Lady Heroise's long-forgotten daughter; and justice is meted out to all.

Margery Fisher

SOURCE: A review of *The Jargoon Pard,* in *Growing Point,* Vol. 14, No. 4, October, 1975, pp. 2709-10.

The Jargoon Pard belongs to that section of André Norton's writing which she calls "sword and sorcery". There is a somewhat intricate explanation of the reasons why Kethan is to be regarded as the hero and his "cousin" Maughas the villain of the story, which shows the final stage of a struggle for dominance in an unspecified World where a certain period of chaos in the past has left the kingdom of Arvon uneasily quiescent, always under threat from alien lands and peoples, some even with the power to open "Gates" to other dimensions. Kethan, as son to the Lady Heroise, is by ancient custom heir to the throne of Arvon when his grandmother dies; the discovery that he is a shape-changer, becoming through a certain fur belt a night-prowling leopard, involves him not only with the rival faction at the court but also the Wereman of the Star Tower and his powerful companions, who enable Kethan to discover his true identity and win his proper place in the world. André Norton has always adopted a consciously archaic, literary style for this kind of story and in this one she has I think overdone it; inversions, archaisms, tortuous formality hold up even the highly dramatic opening scene and make the complex plot unnecessarily hard to follow. The chivalric note, the idea of personal honour is strong in the book but over and above this element there is something that seems still more important, the idea that man is distancing himself from the animal kingdom in which so much of his ancestry and aptitude rests. Kethan's changes from man to beast and back to man are far more than a device to hold the attention and further the plot. At one point in the story it becomes necessary for him to learn to control the warring elements in himself without the agency of the belt and its jewel the jargoon:

> How could I seek it within myself? Might I reverse the process—let the pard mind search for me, as an animal noses out the trail of a quarry? But that I did

not know how to do. What I had found within the beast—the vigorous energy, the patience of the feline hunter, the will to defend threatened territory—the instincts of life—they all added up to a force as strong as a man's will—if I could draw upon them without releasing the pard identity.

This seems far more climactic in the book than the sensational confrontation of the evil witch Ursilla and the wise Gillan which finally decides Kethan's fate in this highly coloured adventure. . . .

The Junior Bookshelf

SOURCE: A review of *The Jargoon Pard,* in *The Junior Bookshelf,* Vol. 40, No. 1, February, 1976, p. 52.

The final chapter of this fantasy is headed 'Of Sorcery Wrought and Unwrought and How We Learn our Destiny': it could serve as a fitting subtitle for an engrossing tale of witchcraft and spells, magic and mystery.

Kethan, hated by horse and hound and by his cousin, Maughus, is given a belt of pard skin with a jargoon stone clasp. He changes from man to leopard; pursued by hounds, attacked by a hawk which seizes the belt, Kethan shares completely in the feelings of a hunted animal. Moly provides only a temporary respite from the curse; Kethan's destiny is fraught with danger until he breaks through the force barrier and learns his destiny.

There is considerable tension throughout the story, particularly in the scenes where the man-beast has to use every device he can to keep alive and in the later part of the story when the beast-man is apparently trapped. The world of the Wise-Woman, the circle of Green Magic, the Moon Witch and the Star Tower is created with conviction, a world of the imagination that never leaves the realm of fantasy but hides human danger and daring, suspense and suspicion. The eternal battle between good and evil gives a coherence and significance to a sci-fi yarn that makes definite demands on the reader, particularly if the undertones are to be recognised. The pseudo-archaic style succeeds and keeps well on the right side of gadzookery.

OUTSIDE (1975)

Kirkus Reviews

SOURCE: A review of *Outside,* in *Kirkus Reviews,* Vol. XLIII, No. 6, March 15, 1975, p. 308.

Child survivors of some ecological disaster who live inside a sealed off dome city where the life support machinery is running down. . . . Andre Norton takes this premise, surely as old as sci fi itself, and finds a new solution aptly suited to the child readers this is intended for. Kristie, no longer one of the really little kids, but still young enough to be attached to her pet fox, is one of the young ones lured away by a Pied Piper known as Rhyming Man. And, following his trail of nursery rhymes and his motto, "Believing's Seeing," she finds herself led to the world outside the dome, now livable again. She also discovers that she has acquired the power of telepathy, and sets out to communicate the secret of escape to her big brother Lew. Anyone who knows his way around the genre will find this thin stuff, but the Rhyming Man is clever enough to lure those on the cusp between fairytales and sci fi.

Publishers Weekly

SOURCE: A review of *Outside,* in *Publishers Weekly,* Vol. 207, No. 20, May 19, 1975, p. 176.

A biographical note says that the author now devotes full time to writing. Who could doubt it, knowing that the ubiquitous Ms. Norton has produced more than 70 books? This is an unusual thriller, set in a future when humans must live together in a sealed enclosure, with "breathers" furnishing air and deserted stores providing preserved foods. Kristie is a "Little" and knows better than even to think of "Outside," which has been poisoned. But, looking at tapes in the learning center, the child is enchanted by pictures of grass, trees and animals. When the Rhyming Man (a sort of Pied Piper) comes by, Kristie can't resist following him to the dreaded, deserted world. A sustained mood of tensions and fears is enhanced by Bernard Colonna's mysterious illustrations.

J. Russell

SOURCE: A review of *Outside,* in *The Junior Bookshelf,* Vol. 40, No. 6, December, 1976, p. 327.

Older children have long been fascinated by the marvellous science fiction stories written by the American Andre Norton. It is particularly welcoming then to see this author writing for younger children of eight to ten. Kristie and her brother Lew are among the survivors of a polluted earth who live in the ruins of a concrete city sealed off from the outside by a giant dome. When food is becoming scarce and the "breathers" begin to fail, Kristie becomes convinced that the solution to their problems lies in the world outside the dome. She faces many hazards before meeting the Rhyming Man, a pied-piper figure who lures children to have the courage to break-out of the concrete city and taste the restored green and fertile land outside. When at last Kristie has the courage to break-through she joins the other children who are each concentrating on the mind of one other person inside, willing them to break-out. This taut, highly imaginative story has instant appeal, and the many illustrations and big print will make it popular with younger children. It is a perfect introduction to the exciting world of science fiction.

Norman Culpan

SOURCE: A review of *Outside,* in *The School Librarian,* Vol. 24, No. 4, December, 1976, pp. 324-25.

Kristie, aged nine, has lived all her life in a running-down city, completely domed and wholly shut off from the 'Outside', presumably long past devastated and rendered uninhabitable by nuclear war. She is obsessed with a desire to see the 'Outside', and when she gets there, with the aid of a mysterious Pied Piper, finds all is fresh and well again, with a small group of people planning a new and better world. There is a good relationship between her and her eighteen-year-old brother, and she herself is quite well realised.

Miss Norton has suitably simplified her vocabulary, sentence structure and plot for younger readers than she usually writes for, but in doing so loses some of her considerable power of imaginative evocation. The book is nicely produced, with large type and margins, suited, it seemed to me, to eight-year-olds; but the story itself demands readers of nine or ten. The illustrations are of people, mildly stylised, but at least do not attempt to pre-empt the work the words should do.

📖 *NO NIGHT WITHOUT STARS* (1975)

Kirkus Reviews

SOURCE: A review of *No Night Without Stars,* in *Kirkus Reviews,* Vol. XLIII, No. 19, October 1, 1975, p. 1139.

Another account of simple people coping in a world with only Rememberers to relate sketchy details of the Before Time (before tidal waves and other natural catastrophes destroyed civilization as it once was); in this case it's Sander, a fledgling metalsmith, and Fanyi, a shaman, along with their companions, his a horse-sized coyote and hers two giant otters ("fishers"). Marauders and mutants must be eluded as the two search for a citadel of Before Time Knowledge, each for a personal purpose; when they find it, of course, it's not the fount of wisdom they sought but rather one more evil to overcome before discounting the past and looking forward to a future forged by their own hands. *Deja vu.*

Gerald Jonas

SOURCE: A review of *No Night Without Stars,* in *The New York Times Book Review,* January 25, 1976, p. 12.

Andre Norton's style is not to everyone's taste. She writes sentences like "Hunger was a discomfort within Sander" and "The creatures hopped rather than walked as might men, yet they were not slow." But she is a superb storyteller with a narrative pace all her own. Here she tells the tale of Sander and Fanyi, a young man and woman in a post-nuclear-holocaust world, who team up to seek the dangerous knowledge of the Before People.

Unlike some writers of S.F. juveniles, who pile sensation on sensation for fear of losing their audience, Norton slowly unfolds a succession of images that first intrigue and finally engulf the reader. To reach their destination, Sander and Fanyi must travel across a dry sea-bed where they discover not only those mutated hopping horrors but also the rusting hull of an ancient submarine and some even more ancient stone ruins—the remains of a great civilization that perished in an earlier eon, long before the Before People existed. With this evocative image of oceans periodically sweeping over the earth and then retreating, like a vast slow tide, the author places the quest of her hero and heroine against the grandest possible background. And even when that quest brings Sander and Fanyi into the conventionally sinister clutches of a mad computer and its mechanized minions, Norton never lets the reader lose sight of the larger framework she has so carefully created.

Peter Hunt

SOURCE: "World Weary," in *The Times Literary Supplement,* No. 3890, October 1, 1976, p. 242.

In *No Night Without Stars,* Andre Norton does a professional job on well-worn material. The visions, of whole cities washed up by tidal waves, of submarines rusting in salt deserts, and of the homicidal megalomaniac computer which is all that is left of technological man, are vivid and pointed. And Miss Norton moves the action smoothly enough as Sander the Smith searches for the secrets of metalworking, and Fanyi the Shaman for more mystic knowledge. What is less satisfactory is the desultory attitude to detail. Fantasy—and perhaps especially fantasy for children—needs a solid basis of consistency to sustain credibility. Thus when Sanders' dart-thrower casually becomes a bolt-thrower for a few chapters, it is just as distracting as finding the computer guarded by a mechanical monster straight out of Jules Verne—and about as unlikely to convince a modern child. Similarly, the curious "tushery" of the dialogue tends to spill over into the narrative prose.

Margery Fisher

SOURCE: A review of *No Night Without Stars,* in *Growing Point,* Vol. 15, No. 6, December, 1976, p. 3013.

André Norton's theme, found in many of her space-adventures, is the need for Man to achieve a status by his own efforts and not by power gained from technology imperfectly understood and inadequately controlled. The theme is hardly original but it gains force from the brilliance of her imagination. She has drawn a world (recognisable as an American seaboard) in which after natural cataclysm men have sorted themselves into small, sometimes mutated groups surviving with difficulty in a

semi-barren world, a world where Traders bring news of distant places, where the Remembrancers of each tribe offer vague and much altered descriptions of lost mechanical inventions. André Norton makes us see certain objects—a torch, a submarine, computers—in the way the central characters see them as they wander on their quest for knowledge. Sander the smith hopes to find the secret of certain alloys and so win back his rightful place in his community: Fanyi, whom he meets at the outset of his wandering, looks for the intuitive knowledge which she had sensed but not understood in her mysterious father. The two are complementary not only as man and woman but also as practical and visionary temperaments. As the story proceeds it is enriched as we watch first one character and then the other contending with physical danger—from amphibians, simian forest folk, hostile Traders—and with the unseen, unnerving power of the computers (programmed by and programming degenerate intellects) which give them their ultimate test. Exciting as a story, the book has an idealistic climax, as Sander proclaims his power as a tool-wielding man against abstract evil; as a plea for honesty and individual freedom the book has considerable force.

KNAVE OF DREAMS (1975)

Booklist

SOURCE: A review of *Knave of Dreams,* in *Booklist,* Vol. 72, No. 4, October 15, 1975, p. 294.

Norton weaves her usual spell in a science fiction tale set in an alternate post-holocaust world where feudal societies retain much of the prewar technology and an awesome group of persons—the Enlightened Ones—with great mental powers advise for the good of the land but do not act, leaving the choice to the individuals. Into this world comes young American Ramsay Kimble, transported via a machine that puts his personality into the body of his alternate-world counterpart, Kaskar, heir to the throne of Ulad. Thrust into the intrigue surrounding the throne, Ramsay finds himself fighting for his life without knowing whom he can trust. Learning eventually from the Enlightened Ones that he is the foretold Knave of Dreams destined to alter the pattern set for Ulad, Ramsay takes hold of himself and the throne, defeating those who would use power for evil. A fast-paced adventure yarn for readers of science fiction.

Zena Sutherland

SOURCE: A review of *Knave of Dreams,* in *Bulletin of the Center for Children's Books,* Vol. 29, No. 7, March, 1976, p. 116.

A science fantasy that has plenty of action, a soupçon of romance, a traditional confrontation between good and evil, and some well-conceived details of another world and time, is burdened by a plot that never deviates in its intensity. There are few moments of quiet to balance the persistent clamor of pitched battles, narrow escapes, and perilous masquerades. Ramsay, a denizen of our own world, wakes to find that he is in the body of Prince Kaskar, heir to the throne and dupe of an evil counselor, Ochall. He is in constant danger as he threads his way through the intricate intrigues and counter-intrigues of royalty, seers, soldiers, and experimenters in parapsychology. Dubbed the Knave of Dreams, Ramsay finally accepts the fact that he is Kaskar and fights for the throne and a beautiful bride.

R. Baines

SOURCE: A review of *Knave of Dreams,* in *The Junior Bookshelf,* Vol. 41, No. 1, February, 1977, p. 51.

After a series of dream tormented nights a young American sets out on a supernaturally guided drive through stormy darkness. Awaking after the accident, he discovers that he is lying in state as the honoured but dead Prince Kaskar, his double in another world, in another galaxy.

The theme of this book is Ramsay Kimble's gradual acceptance of the status quo. At first his sole ambition is to return to present day earth, but as time passes he learns a new language (with surprising ease), meets new rulers, fights in a battle and eventually assumes the status of the true Kaskar and falls in love.

The book is largely concerned with politics, a subject which does not automatically increase in interest because the protagonists are fictional. Miss Norton's talent for creating credible new civilisations is impressively abundant, but I prefer it displayed on a smaller stage.

WRAITHS OF TIME (1976)

Kirkus Reviews

SOURCE: A review of *Wraiths of Time,* in *Kirkus Reviews,* Vol. XLIV, No. 13, July 1, 1976, p. 740.

Ashake, a Nubian princess of the blood, knows that she had a prior existence as black archaeologist Tallahassee Mitford before being pulled bodily through a time warp and into the ancient kingdom of Meroe as it is—or was—in some other continuum. Ashake/Tallahassee's mission is the defeat of Khasti, also a time-space interloper whose science is pitted against the ancestral magic of the ruling Candace Naldamak, and the battle is joined largely in contests of will power—as our heroine resists the mental assaults of Khasti and jousts with wraithlike spirits of unknown provenance. The combination of a with-it young scientist and evocative Egyptian talismans—and the omission of feline beings—get this off to a promising start. However, the plot is opaque even by Andre Norton standards and Tallahassee's willingness to remain permanently in Ashake's body where she feels "real" and "welcomed" carries escapism farther than most will care to follow. Save this for those time-space pockets in which the Norton name itself is a powerful fetish.

G. L. Hughes

SOURCE: A review of *Wraiths of Time,* in *The Junior Bookshelf,* Vol. 41, No. 3, June, 1977, p. 182.

Andre Norton is one of those writers who has the happy knack of writing for children and yet ensuring that her stories will be read just as eagerly by adults. There are no juvenile characters in this book, and the story deals with difficult concepts like doorways through time, transferring a memory from a dead person to a live one, half-invisible wraiths who are lost in time, visitors from another planet and, of course, there is the usual fight of good against evil. The story combines all that is best in science fiction with all that is best in juvenile literature resulting in a book to be enjoyed by all ages.

F. J. Molson

SOURCE: A review of *Wraiths of Time,* in *World of Children's Books,* Vol. II, No. 2, Fall, 1977, pp. 56-7.

Andre Norton is a prolific writer. This means, among other things, that in spite of a formidable reputation as a successful writer of fantasy and sf for both adults and children, she sometimes produces less than effective narratives. *Wraiths of Time,* her most recent juvenile space fantasy, is one of these.

Tallahassee Mitford, a young black archeologist who works in the African section of the local museum, is called in to examine an ancient ivory box emanating an unknown form of radiation. She sees that the box's provenance involves the ancient Nubian kingdom of Meroë. Also she senses danger. The box, when opened, reveals an ankh, the key to life revered by ancient Egyptians. Suddenly, Tallahassee is violently drawn back by the power of the ankh into a land similar to old Meroë but different—there are flying machines and stunners, for instance—where she is taken for the Princess Ashake, her look-alike, who has died attempting to retrieve the ankh. Tallahassee is called upon to assist in frustrating a plot by the evil alien, Khasti, to wrest the kingdom from the Candace, the chief ruler and practitioner of the Greater Knowledge, a form of ESP. Through the help of the wraiths, individuals trapped in time, Tallahassee-Ashake and her allies overcome Khasti. Tallahassee, forgoing any attempt to return to her time, decides to remain Ashake.

As the summarized plot should indicate, *Wraiths of Time* has much going for it—an attractive protagonist, young, black and female; Egyptian archeology, history and religion as subject matter and ancient Meroë as specific locale; parallel universes, time jumps, ESP and alien visitors as the chief sf elements. All in all, *Wraiths of Time* is a novel that is contemporary without being faddish or pandering to the current vogue for things "King Tuttish." (There is also only the briefest mention of cats—a surprising feature in a Norton narrative!) Unfortunately, what flaws the novel is the intricacy of its plotting. It is hard to believe that a young reader will have the patience to sort out and follow the various characters, the many incidents and the intrigue. Also disquieting is the relative ease with which both Tallahassee bids goodby to her original identity and her own times, and the author ignores the question more than one young reader is going to ask: what did her friends and associates think happened to the young woman?

Norman Culpan

SOURCE: A review of *Wraiths of Time,* in *The School Librarian,* Vol. 25, No. 4, December, 1977, pp. 361-62.

Tallahasee Mitford, an African archaeologist, is rapt away into a parallel time path to inhabit the newly dead body of Princess Ashake in the ancient Nubian kingdom of Meroe; impersonating the Princess, she aids the priestesses in their fight against the evil Khasti. The usual interests of Miss Norton, such as underground labyrinths and psychic battles, are present, and her usual skills employed. There is an echo of the theme of *Knave of Dreams,* but no sense of repetition in the story. Those who enjoy Norton, from upper sixth to fourteen or younger, will find no falling off.

📖 *RED HART MAGIC* (1976)

Kirkus Reviews

SOURCE: A review of *Red Hart Magic,* in *Kirkus Reviews,* Vol. XLIV, No. 17, September 1, 1976, p. 974.

When Nan's mother marries Chris' father the two resentful children are dumped on an aunt while the parents travel, and soon their mutual hostility is eroded by shared dreams (real ones, not daydreams) of historical adventure, all set centuries back in an old English inn of which Chris has just bought an "antique" model. Whether the dreamed episodes ever really occurred or those "other" Nans or Chrises existed is wondered only in passing; what seems to matter is that, inspired by their bravery in these crises, Nan stands up to real-life shoplifting classmates at her new school and Chris to cheating bullies at his. Otherwise there's not much connection between the night battles (with King Jamie's men, smuggling vigilantes or the local squire) and the present, city apartment reality—and not much point to any of it.

Zena Sutherland

SOURCE: A review of *Red Hart Magic,* in *Bulletin of the Center for Children's Books,* Vol. 30, No. 7, March, 1977, pp. 110-11.

Chris and Nan are staying with his aunt while their newly wed parents (his father and her mother) are in Mexico. They don't like each other—but both are intrigued when they find they have the same dreams, dreams evoked by the model of an old English inn. Each of the dreams is set in the past but takes place in the Red Hart Inn, and a different Chris and Nan have roles in each dream. With this bond and the memories they share of dangers met and conquered with courage, the real Chris and Nan draw closer, so that when Chris is accused of stealing and selling an exam question, Nan is outraged and sympathetic. If not brother and sister, they have become friends. The writing is competent, the contemporary sequences convincing, and the stories-within-the-story, the dreamed adventures, colorful. But the fact that each dream sequence is in a different period and that Nan and Chris play different roles in each makes the story diffuse.

A. R. Williams

SOURCE: A review of *Red Hart Magic,* in *The Junior Bookshelf,* Vol. 42, No. 2, April, 1978, p. 107.

The Red Hart of the title was an Inn of that name, a model of which Chris Fitton discovered to have the magical if sometimes uncomfortable quality of taking both Chris and his stepsister, Nan, back in time in shared dreams. The flashbacks involve them in trying situations, each of which forms a sort of short story within the continuing narrative. Their dilemmas occur in three separate centuries or historical periods although none of these is too explicitly identified except that persecution of one sort or another is common to all, and Chris and Nan in their previous existences are responsible in part for the rescue of the oppressed. The treatment is dignified without being staid, the work of a deliberate mind. Donna Diamond's illustrations are suitably shadowy as though seen through the veil of time.

📖 *THE OPAL-EYED FAN* (1977)

Kirkus' Reviews

SOURCE: A review of *The Opal-Eyed Fan,* in *Kirkus' Reviews,* Vol. XLV, No. 18, September 15, 1977, p. 1008.

Scenic "Lost Lady Key," first the haunt of a vanished Indian tribe, the Old Ones (all have vanished but one, Askra, an old witch), and then of the Spanish (who left a ghost behind to remember them by) is fuller of spirits than cypresses. Persis Rooke, who is shipwrecked there circa 1800, can hardly take a walk without running into a ghost, particularly after she finds the buried opal-eyed fan that conceals a dagger—or does it find her? Fortunately, the ghosts and the dagger inspire her with enough gumption to save her man and her fortune from the unskillful plots of pirate Ralph Grillon and his Lydia. Good thing, too, because Persis is a complete wimp without a supernatural assist. Norton, so good at tales of aliens, smart animals, and the brotherhood of all species, is a washout at romantic leads. One cannot believe that any Gothic passions beat under these starched frocks; and no trace of characterization enlivens these waxen features.

Booklist

SOURCE: A review of *The Opal-Eyed Fan,* in *Booklist,* Vol. 74, No. 4, October 15, 1977, p. 368.

In another departure from her usual science fiction, Norton spins an involving nineteenth-century occult-tinged Gothic tale in the same vein as her **The White Jade Fox.** When her elderly uncle and guardian dies after their ship is wrecked off Lost Lady Key, Persis Rooke is left to her own resources in claiming an inheritance in the Bahamas. But Persis finds herself drawn into the key's dark past through a tenuous link with the island's Spanish lady, whose ghost restlessly walks the area. This link enables her to save her host's life when, betrayed by his sister, he is left to die in the caves beneath the house.

📖 *QUAG KEEP* (1978)

Chuck Schacht

SOURCE: A review of *Quag Keep,* in *School Library Journal,* Vol. 24, No. 7, March, 1978, p. 139.

In Norton's latest sword and sorcery epic, seven fantastic companions, including an elf warrior, a were-boar, and a lizard man, find themselves spell-bound on a quest which none of them understand but all feel compelled to pursue. Whatever their preferred brand of sound and fury, fantasy buffs are almost sure to find it here—it seems, in fact, what with druids, dragons, orcs, amazons, swordsmen, wizards and all, as though the author was afraid to leave anything out. The main characters, more closely akin to Conan the Barbarian than to Bilbo Baggins, are insufficiently developed and in general too cold and competent to invite empathy. Norton, with the deft touch of a master, puts them all through their paces in exciting action scenes set in vividly evoked alien atmospheres—until she gets them to where they've been headed all along; but then she has a hard time explaining satisfactorily what it's all been about.

Publishers Weekly

SOURCE: A review of *Quag Keep,* in *Publishers Weekly,* Vol. 213, No. 18, May 1, 1978, p. 85.

The enormously popular and prolific author of fantasy tales comes through with an arresting novel about people confused in time and identities. A master of war games in this century sets out playing pieces and Martin Jefferson becomes mesmerized by the figure of a swordsman.

Picking it up, Martin becomes Milo Jagon in Greyhawk, an open city where the forces of Chaos and Law coexist. Milo is a swordsman who joins Naile Fangtooth—a berserker—a girl warrior and others in a fight for life and freedom. Each of the company has to battle horrors imposed on them by rolls of the dice in another time. Their thralldom is caused by an evil genius trying to meld two worlds, and Norton keeps the readers nearly as entranced as the actors are, in her expertly realized drama.

Charlotte W. Draper

SOURCE: A review of *Quag Keep,* in *The Horn Book Magazine,* Vol. LIV, No. 3, June, 1978, pp. 285-86.

The author acknowledges that she has used the war game *Dungeons and Dragons* as the context for the science fiction fantasy. Seven wayfarers haunted by the memory of another world, are bound by a "geas"—an uncanny compulsion to seek out an alien force which menaces the precarious balance between Law and Chaos in their own world. The travelers wear bracelets of dice which warn them of new skirmishes with the agents of Chaos. When the companions arrive at Quag Keep, stronghold of the summoning power, they recognize the source of the spell: "[Y]ou aren't real, don't you understand that? I'm the game master." Chance is double-edged, however, and the Seven exert their own power over him. The landscape and its creatures—including some familiar inhabitants of Tolkien's Middle Earth—are cleverly devised and integrated. Skillful exposition in the first two chapters hints at previous incarnation for the Seven, but the reader remains as mystified as the actors in the drama, not understanding until the end why their behavior appears to be preordained. The characterizations derive from the magical or physical power of each player to oppose his or her adversary, and the plot structure is an analogue of the geometric pattern of a game board. The game seems deadly serious and involves a restructuring of the identity not only of the players—but ultimately of the game master himself.

📖 *GRYPHON IN GLORY* ("Witch World" series, second volume in "Gryphon" trilogy, 1981)

Publishers Weekly

SOURCE: A review of *Gryphon in Glory,* in *Publishers Weekly,* Vol. 219, No. 11, March 13, 1981, p. 89.

Among the most popular authors of SF for adults as well as young readers, Norton has written a sequel to **The Crystal Gryphon,** which readers of all ages will welcome. Kervan, convinced that his cursed birth means he is unworthy of his bride Joisan, leaves her in the Dales and the protection of the magic gryphon on the necklace, his gift to her. Kervan is off fighting the despotic enemies of the Dale people, and Joisan, determined that her future is entwined with her husband's, goes in search of him. Since the author alternates chapters narrated by Kervan and Joisan, readers are filled in on all the fraught events leading up to their meeting. Here, they come to grips once more with the Dark Power when the gryphon's secret is revealed, in a clash of wills more hair-raising than what has gone before.

Margaret L. Chatham

SOURCE: A review of *Gryphon in Glory,* in *School Library Journal,* Vol. 27, No. 8, April, 1981, p. 142.

Kerovan, whose cloven hoofs in place of feet have made him an object of fear and scorn among men all his life, renounces his wife Joisan and sets off into the Waste, where many forms of non-human intelligence dwell, to seek the other side of his mixed heritage. Joisan, who is wholly human but loves and believes in him, follows. Their quests are told in chapters alternating between their two viewpoints until, in a confrontation between the exponents of Dark and Light, Kerovan learns to trust himself enough to accept Joisan's love and, incidentally, the forces that were causing war in their land are removed. This is a sequel to *The Crystal Gryphon,* and although not specifically stated, the setting bears a strong resemblance to Norton's Witch World. As always, Norton catches the reader up in a consistent if not completely explained fantasy world and supplies plenty of satisfying action, both physical and magical.

📖 *HORN CROWN* ("Witch World" series, 1981)

Publishers Weekly

SOURCE: A review of *Horn Crown,* in *Publishers Weekly,* Vol. 219, No. 23, June 5, 1981, p. 80.

Elron of the House of Garn espies Garn's daughter Iynne visiting the forbidden Moon Shrine, and is remiss in not reporting this to the clan's heads. When she disappears and Elron confesses his negligence, he is held responsible, and is cast out of the clan. In a society where a person's primary identification is with the clan, Elron is as good as dead. If nothing else, he seeks to salvage his honor by finding Iynne and bringing her back. He journeys to the magic land beyond the shrine's portals, accompanied by the girl Gathea, an acolyte of the Moon Shrine goddess. A number of adventures befall them, bringing them to maturity and a kind of grace. Although somewhat slow at first, this latest novel in the Witch World series develops into a charming tale of enchantment and adventure.

Roland Green

SOURCE: A review of *Horn Crown,* in *Booklist,* Vol. 78, No. 1, September 1, 1981, p. 29.

The latest novel in Andre Norton's deservedly popular Witch World series tells of the coming of the ancestors of the Dalesmen to what becomes High Hallack in later novels. It is also the story of the reluctant allies, Elron the Clanless, who seeks to rescue his kinsmen, and Gathea the Wise Woman, who seeks knowledge concerning the use of her magical powers. Like most Norton novels, *Horn Crown* meets all the requirements of the well-told tale and makes exceptionally effective use of the myth of the horned god and the great goddess, a popular but often abused theme in contemporary fantasy. Highly recommended for any fantasy collection.

George M. A. Cumming, Jr.

SOURCE: A review of *Horn Crown,* in *School Library Journal,* Vol. 28, No. 4, December, 1981, p. 88.

The performance of any world-class athlete is very deceptive. It looks so easy. That is, until you try it yourself. Andre Norton's books are like that. In each novel the story effortlessly and convincingly spins itself out. You may not remember any particular book, but you'll always remember that Andre Norton never failed to entertain you. *Horn Crown* chronicles the first establishment of human beings on Witch World, the scene of many previous Norton novels. It is also the tale of two outsiders thrown together on a strange quest. Elron, a young warrior, and Gathea, a novice witch, discover much of the true nature of Witch World and themselves. *Horn Crown* is fine entertainment, and Witch World is a great place to visit on a rainy afternoon.

📖 *'WARE HAWK* ("Witch World" series, 1983)

Sally Estes

SOURCE: A review of *'Ware Hawk,* in *Booklist,* Vol. 80, No. 1, September 1, 1983, p. 75.

A recurring vision-dream summons Tirtha, the last of the House of Hawkholme, to the ruins of the long-abandoned family holding. She hires a Falconer, exiled from his kind and without a falcon, as guide and fellow-fighter for the arduous, danger-laden journey through the mountains, and they soon come to realize that he, too, has been called to play a role in the latest struggle between the forces of the Dark and the Light. With her customary flair, Norton spins a gripping adventure tale, and if her narrative seems florid at times, it is entirely suited to the vividly projected medievalistic ambience, aura of magic, and sense of morality. Unlike *Crystal Gryphon* and its sequel *Gryphon Glory,* which are almost borderline in the Witch World series, this is set squarely within that series and will be best appreciated by Norton fans already familiar with her alternate universe. A compact prologue sets the scene by scanning the Witch World's history and placing the story within its context.

Ann A. Flowers

SOURCE: A review of 'Ware Hawk, in The Horn Book Magazine, Vol. LIX, No. 5, October, 1983, p. 585.

The author's many books about the Witch World vary in quality; this one is certainly among the best. The story tells of Tirtha, the last of the line of Hawkholme, who is forced by a "geas"—an obligation that one is psychologically driven to fulfill—to return to her long-destroyed family hold. There she is to rescue a casket she has seen only in her dreams. The way is perilous, and she hires a mercenary warrior to assist her on the journey. Nirel, the warrior, is a Falconer, one of a group that traditionally despises women; he proves, however, to be a faithful, valorous companion, and his falcon is a useful addition to the party. Between them, they rescue a boy with extraordinary supernatural abilities, and they defeat, against all odds, the forces of the Dark and deliver the casket to one of the Great Powers. Although the Witch World background seems blurry and the language sometimes a trifle stiff and archaic, sensible Tirtha is an attractive heroine, and Nirel mysterious and romantic. Deeply enmeshed in sorcery and magic, the story is taut with conflict and suspense.

Jack Forman

SOURCE: A review of 'Ware Hawk, in School Library Journal, Vol. 30, No. 5, January, 1984, p. 87.

Born with superhuman abilities to heal, to interpret dreams and other mind powers, Tirtha follows the mysterious dictates of a dream and finds herself on a dangerous journey to recapture Hawkholme—her ancestral home—from the powers of The Dark. Tirtha is helped by a Falconer and his falcon—and later by Alon, a 12-year-old boy they rescue from the enemy. As they get closer to their destination, the dangers increase, and Tirtha unsuccessfully tries to convince the other two not to accompany her. They are attacked and near death when their mind powers, their courage and loyalty to each other and the power of destiny save them. Not only do they rid Hawkholme of the evil which had overtaken the land, but also a love bond between Tirtha and the Falconer is created. In this 15th book of Norton's famous "Witch World" series, the author tells a rich and sophisticated tale of bravery and fidelity. Elaborate descriptive passages often cut into the story's flow and the purposely stylized dialogue adds distance between the characters and readers. Nonetheless, advanced readers and devoted science-fiction buffs will find this an exciting and fulfilling adventure with a very satisfying denouement.

📖 THE MONSTER'S LEGACY (1996)

Sally Estes

SOURCE: A review of The Monster's Legacy, in Booklist, Vol. 92, No. 15, April 1, 1996, p. 1356.

The intent of Dragonflight, a generally fine fantasy series that began with Robert Silverberg's Letters from Atlantis (1990) and includes Tanith Lee's Black Unicorn (1991) and Gold Unicorn (1994), Brad Strickland's Dragon's Plunder (1993), and Esther M. Friesner's Wishing Season (1993), is to provide YAs with novels by leading genre authors, with illustrations by noted sf/fantasy artists. The latest in the series, by one of the masters in the field, will not disappoint fans. Gentle Sarita, apprentice embroiderer, flees into the wilds with Earl Florian's very young son when the earl's holding is invaded and all within are murdered. Luckily, she encounters Rhys, one of the earl's huntsmen, who had been wounded but escaped by playing dead. The three manage to evade pursuers and make their way to the mountains said to be inhabited by the dreaded Loden, a monster who preys on humans. The quest here is for safety, both for the three who flee and for the kingdom; the talisman is a silver awl that had belonged to Sarita's mother; and the talents involve the ability to foresee. Mix in fast-paced adventure, a sense of constant danger, and a mystery about long-gone dragons and their legacy—and you have a very satisfying tale.

Steven Engelfried

SOURCE: A review of The Monster's Legacy, in School Library Journal, Vol. 42, No. 6, June, 1996, p. 154.

A fierce and mysterious attack on an absent Earl's holdings leaves only three survivors: Sarita, a talented embroideress; Rhys, a skilled woodsman who befriends her; and Valoris, the Earl's two-year-old son. The two young adults soon discover they share a common talent: both can sense the future, but in different ways. Together they hide from pursuers and protect the young heir until they can warn the returning Earl. Their flight leads them to the lair of the Loden, a legendary monster. The creature has long ago departed, but they use what it has left behind (its skin and an egg) to help them in their quest. After the violent attack described in the first two chapters, most of the action focuses on the ways in which Sarita and Rhys explore their emerging mental powers. The mystery and importance of the Loden gradually unfold through Norton's smooth, well-paced narrative. The characters are generally appealing, but largely because of their shared predicament and the ways in which they respond to it. Their individual personalities and the interactions between them are not particularly memorable. Many fantasy readers will enjoy Norton's latest. . . .

📖 THE WARDING OF WITCH WORLD ("Witch World" series, 1996)

Publishers Weekly

SOURCE: A review of The Warding of Witch World, in Publishers Weekly, Vol. 243, No. 38, September 16, 1996, p. 75.

Though Norton, born in 1912, often writes with a collaborator now, she flies solo in what's billed as the final entry in her most popular and acclaimed series, which began 33 years ago with the novel *Witch World*. When Alizondern nobles throw open the Gates to other worlds, allowing evil free access to the four corners of the Witch World globe, it is only through the combined heroic actions of all of the planet's disparate and uneasily allied forces of Light that its inhabitants may manage to save themselves. The novel ties together stories from the lives of many previously established characters, including Simon Tregarth, Destree, Jaelithe, the Keplian Mares, the Falconers and the Lady Frost. It also introduces a host of newcomers, such as Liara of Alizondern, who strives to right the tragedy her people have set in motion; Gruck, an otherworldly guardian from beyond the Gates who becomes companion to Destree; and Audha, a talented Sulcar girl who holds the key to Witch World's continued survival. The narrative interweaves various magical battles with a passionate striving for morality and good. Though the patchwork nature of the writing makes for an uneven read, readers already invested in this fabulous world and its enchanted characters should relish this last act in one of fantasy's most enduring spectacles.

Kathleen Marszycki

SOURCE: A review of *The Warding of Witch World,* in *Voice of Youth Advocates,* Vol. 19, No. 6, February, 1997, p. 339.

In the last in this extensive series, Norton writes of the impending doom of Witch World caused by the closing of one of the ancient gates of power, thus unleashing chaotic, evil forces. The witches of Estcarp embark on a race against time to seal up the breach and restore order. Explorations of uncharted territories, devastated lands, battles with demons, furies, and shapechangers are all part of this mythical landscape.

Norton has made a career from this series alone and nothing is lacking—but that is part of the problem. There is so much thrown at the reader, for each page, each paragraph is tightly packed with characters whose names are almost hieroglyphic and difficult to pronounce, and with information that obviously refers back to previous novels. Readers attempting to read Norton for the first time will find too much going over their heads because there are entire histories and genealogies involved with the eighteen novels which comprise the Witch World series. Another concern is the writing style—Norton relies heavily on narrative movement and each paragraph is brief—often only two or three sentences. The resulting feel is jumpy, leaving one wishing for something more substantial to dwell on before the next catastrophe or new character is introduced.

Norton has won several prestigious awards during her career, and she has been recognized as a serious writer who deals with the weighty issues of power and aggression, of cooperation and balance. I would recommend this novel for only those readers who are devoted fans of Norton and the Witch World series.

Additional coverage of Norton's life and career is contained in the following sources published by Gale Research: *Authors and Artists for Young Adults,* Vol. 14; *Contemporary Authors New Revision Series,* Vol. 31; *Dictionary of Literary Biography,* Vol. 52; *Junior DISCovering Authors, Major Authors and Illustrators for Children and Young Adults;* and *Something About the Author,* Vol. 91.

Katherine (Womeldorf) Paterson

1932-

American author of fiction.

Major works include *The Master Puppeteer* (1975), *Bridge to Terabithia* (1977), *The Great Gilly Hopkins* (1978), *Jacob Have I Loved* (1980), *The King's Equal* (1992), *Jip: His Story* (1996).

For more information on Paterson's career prior to 1984, please see *CLR*, Vol. 7.

INTRODUCTION

The recipient of almost every significant award for children's literature, Paterson is universally regarded as a master craftsman with an artistic vision in her fiction that extends to all of humankind. While many of her best-known writings are novels for young adults, she also writes for children from the primary grades through middle school. Paterson's trademark is a tightly knit story in which all of its elements—language, setting, characters, symbols—are distinctively true to the world of that story, a world that "readers see, taste, smell, feel, and hear." Vibrant language and natural dialogue are the hallmarks of her concise, understated writing style. Beyond her elegant craftsmanship, critics applaud the honesty and passion that characterize her work. Firmly grounded in her own Christian convictions, Paterson takes her readers deep into the thoughts and feelings of the characters in her stories. She explores serious, universal moral themes with subtle dramatization and character development, never becoming didactic. The protagonists of Paterson's stories are typically outsiders—often an orphan or an abandoned child—who face a crisis that tests their courage and allows them to achieve an acceptance of themselves and the confidence to look forward hopefully to the future. Whether the setting is medieval Japan or contemporary America, her theme is often the child's quest for a father or mother, bound up with a search for self, and ultimately, with the attempt to understand a human being's relationship with God. Her stories often present several layers of meaning. Even though the deepest level may be more readily accessible to her more sophisticated readers, the outer layers are fully rewarding for all readers. Paterson has enriched children's literature with intelligent, beautifully crafted stories that convey her sense of awe at the world as she finds it and her sense of hope in "an ultimate vision of a world where truth and justice and peace do prevail."

Biographical Information

Born in China of American missionary parents, Paterson and her family lived there for five years before they

twice became refugees—first in 1937 when war between China and Japan forced their return to the United States for a year, and again in 1940 when World War II forced them out of China permanently. Her experience as being "different" from her American classmates would be a foundation for many of her later stories. Her family moved frequently while she was growing up, living in fifteen houses during thirteen years. During these years, reading and writing stories were among her pleasant childhood remembrances. "We didn't have many books when I was little," she recalled. "There were no libraries or bookstores with English books in Hwaianfu, China. But the books we had, my mother read to us over and over." In 1954, Paterson later graduated summa cum laude with a B.A. in English literature from King College in Bristol, Tennessee, and in 1957, received an M.A. in English Bible from Presbyterian School of Christian Education in Richmond, Virginia. She served as missionary in Japan for four years—an experience that had a profound effect on her writing. (She uses Japan as the setting for her first three novels.) She received an M.R.E. in 1962 from Union Theological Seminary, in New York City. In that same year, she met and married John Barstow Paterson, a Presbyterian minister. The couple settled in Takoma, Maryland, and Paterson worked as a teacher until her children were born. Her family later grew to include two sons and two adopted daughters—one born in Hong Kong, the other on an Apache Indian reservation. In 1964, Paterson began her professional writing career formulating curricula for school systems. She eventually turned to fiction, and nine years later, Paterson published her first novel, *The Sign of the Chrysanthemum.* "Although I became a writer for children more or less accidentally," she commented, "I soon learned that I had stumbled into what was for me the world's best job—perhaps, as I say to my husband, the only job I will ever be able to keep."

Major Works

Paterson's deep appreciation for the culture of Japan is well-demonstrated in *The Master Puppeteer.* The story is set in Osaka during a time of famine and chaos, when feudalism was nearing its end in Japan. Saburo, a Robin Hood-type bandit, has a mysterious connection with the puppet theater Hanaza. Thirteen-year-old Jiro, an apprentice puppeteer, is determined to solve the mystery even though it could put him in danger. Meanwhile, Jiro must learn the exacting art of the puppeteer, with the help of Kinshi, the son of the master puppeteer. The two boys, both feeling unloved by demanding fathers, form a deep bond of friendship. In the climax of the story, the sheltered and orderly life in the theater suddenly collides with the chaos of the streets. Paterson takes up a realistic, contemporary story of rural Virginia in *Bridge to Terabithia.* Ten-year-old Jesse Aarons—a quiet, introspective farm boy—befriends his new classmate Leslie Burke, a spirited, imaginative girl who opens up for him the worlds of the imagination and learning. They share a secret meeting place, called Terabithia, which they reach by swinging across a creek on a rope tied to a tree. Tragically, when Leslie attempts to reach Terabithia alone during a flooding rain, she is accidentally killed. Jesse is devastated by guilt and sorrow, but eventually he recognizes that he must reciprocate for the vision and strength that Leslie gave him. He builds a plank bridge and leads someone else to the secret land.

The title character in another realistic, comic story, *The Great Gilly Hopkins,* is a smart, tough, and independent eleven-year-old girl who resists getting softened up by her foster mother, Maime Trotter, and the people around her. While scheming against everyone who tries to be friendly, Gilly cherishes a romantic vision of her biological mother Courtney, a 1960s flower child. In the end, Gilly is briefly reunited with Courtney—only to have her dream of a beautiful and loving mother shattered. With Maime's help, Gilly comes to realize that she has the strength to take up a new life with her newly-met grandmother who wants to make a home for her. In *Jacob Have I Loved,* Louise Bradshaw tells her story of growing up on an island in the Chesapeake Bay during World War II. Envious of her twin sister Caroline's talent and charm, Louise struggles for years with a self-pity that intrudes on her relationships with everyone around her. After Louise finds the courage to leave the island and make a life of her own, the story comes full-circle. Louise—now in her twenties and serving as a midwife at the birth of twins—finds herself drawn to the weaker, younger infant, and her life-long resentment begins to fade.

Paterson admirably demonstrates her ability to tell a story in the style of a fairy tale for younger readers in *The King's Equal.* On his deathbed, a wise old king decrees that his vain and arrogant son Raphael will not wear the king's crown until he marries a woman who is his equal in beauty, intelligence, and wealth. The angry prince abuses his people and searches in vain for a princess that excels in all three qualities. Then he meets Rosamund, a farmer's daughter whose mother's blessing is that she would be a king's equal. Raphael is charmed by her wisdom and compassion, but Rosamund proves to Raphael that he is not her equal, because he is lonely and still wants things, while she is content with what she has. Rosamund refuses to marry Raphael until he spends a year in her mountain hut, where the animals help him to learn humility, grace, and cooperation. When the prince returns a changed man, they are finally married as equals. *Jip: His Story,* set in the nineteenth century, tells the story of Jip (short for Gypsy) who has lived on a village "poor farm" in Vermont ever since he tumbled off a wagon as a toddler and remained unclaimed by family or friends. As he approaches his teens, Jip learns that sinister people have been looking for him because he is the son of an escaped slave and her white master—and therefore a slave himself. Jip learns to stand up to the threat of enslavement and, with the help of his loyal friends, finally makes his escape to Canada.

Awards

The Master Puppeteer won the National Book Award in 1977. *Bridge to Terabithia*, winner of the Newbery Medal and the Lewis Carroll Shelf Award in 1978, also won the Janusz Korczak Medal (Poland) in 1981 and Le Grand Prix des Jeunes Lecteurs (France) in 1986. *The Great Gilly Hopkins* received the Christopher Award in 1978; the National Book Award and a Newbery Honor Book citation, both in 1979; and the William Allen White Children's Book Award in 1981. *The Crane Wife* was honored as an ALA Notable Book, a New York Times Notable Book, and a New York Times Best Illustrated Book, all in 1981. *Jacob Have I Loved*, winner of the Newbery Medal in 1981, was also named an ALA Notable Book and a New York Times Outstanding Book, both in 1980. *Rebels of the Heavenly Kingdom* garnered a Parents' Choice Award in 1983. *Come Sing, Jimmy Jo* was named a New York Times Notable Book in 1985. *The Tale of the Mandarin Ducks* was named a New York Time Best Illustrated Book in 1990 and won a Boston Globe Horn Book Award in 1991. *The King's Equal* earned the Irma S. and James H. Black Award in 1992.

Paterson has been honored for her body of work with the Kerlan Award in 1983, the University of Southern

Mississippi Silver Medallion in 1983, the ALAN Award in 1987 from the Adolescent Literature Assembly Award from the National Council of Teachers of English, the Regina Medal in 1988 from the Catholic Library Association, and the Hans Christian Andersen Award in 1998 from the International Board on Books for Young People.

AUTHOR'S COMMENTARY

Katherine Paterson

SOURCE: "Where Is Terabithia?" in *Children's Literature Association Quarterly,* Vol. 9, No. 4, Winter, 1984-85, pp. 153-57.

A writer friend once complained to me that a certain editor had asked her to make the setting of a story more explicit. "I don't know where your story is taking place," the editor had said. "But," said my friend, "it didn't matter where that story was taking place. It could have taken place anywhere." I have to argue with that point of view. A fairy tale might take place anywhere, but a novel has to take place somewhere, and, usually, the more definite the setting, the more convincing the novel.

Of course that definite world of the novel is not necessarily an actual spot on the map. Nowadays people in my part of the country will sidle up to me and say, "Will you settle an argument for us? Is Rass Island really Smith or Tangier?" naming two islands in the Chesapeake Bay. But Rass is deliberately a fictitious island. I chose to do it that way because Chesapeake Islanders are notoriously protective of their privacy, and I didn't want anyone to feel that I had intruded. Besides, if I created a fictitious island, I did not have to be limited to the specific history or geography of an existing island. I did, in one sense, create my own Chesapeake world, but in another sense, I was strictly bound to the world that actually exists. I couldn't, for example, send Truitt Bradshaw out to crab in the winter months. If Rass had been a Virginia Island, rather than a Maryland one, he might have dredged for crab in winter, but in Maryland, because it is cooler, it would be impractical. It is also, incidentally, against the law in Maryland. I wanted people who knew the Bay to see Rass as a true place, if not an actual one.

It is vital that the place in which the story takes place be a true one. Because the place will shape the story, just as place shapes lives in the actual world. Louise Bradshaw never became flesh, indeed, the poor girl didn't even have a name, until I found out where she lived. When I discovered Rass, I discovered who Louise was and what would happen to her.

Place provides so many wonderful surprises for a writer. It almost seems sometimes that geography and history exist for the writer's benefit—so that she can write

this particular book. Can you imagine the excitement that went through me the day I came upon that scrap of information telling me that the Bay watermen believed you should sing to oysters? I nearly wept for the joy of it—the taciturn Mr. Bradshaw sprang to life. Picture this man, out on the Bay in the freezing air of a Maryland winter, bent to the most exhausting physical tasks left in this modern world, his voice going out over the lonely water in a song for the oysters. If such an image had just come to me out of the blue, I'm not sure I would have had the courage to use it, but it was true—one of the glorious eccentricities of these stubbornly independent, literally red-necked men, who in so many other ways reminded me of my strong, inarticulate uncles who farmed the limestone hills in the Shenandoah Valley. And it makes me wonder, now that it's too late to ask, if they, too, had secret songs that none of us ever heard.

I look back on the books I have written, almost as though someone else had written them. There are things I love in them for which I take no credit. The waterman singing to the oysters is one of the nourishing images of my books—and it was the place of the novel that gave it to me, not I that gave it to the place.

Of course place will limit as well as enlarge. In *Rebels of the Heavenly Kingdom,* it takes the entire book for Wang Lee to begin to grow beyond the prejudices of a nineteenth century Chinese peasant. When he first meets Mei Lin, he cannot help but despise her unbound feet. As silly as it seems to us from our vantage point, everything in his nature demands that he think himself superior to her. He may be poor and illiterate, but he is, after all, the first son of an old family who own their own land. She is a former slave girl with big feet. You cannot write a book about nineteenth century China and force the characters to think or behave as you would like them to. If you are not willing to let them act out of the context of their own place and time, then you are honor bound to leave them alone and devote yourself to a more congenial setting.

This means that the writer of historical fiction would be both dishonest and stupid to write what I've called at various times "bathrobe" fiction. Remember those Christmas pageants we used to do in Sunday School years ago, where all the characters wore bathrobes instead of costumes? Well, some people write historical fiction that way. They simply dress up modern characters in pseudoancient dress. Since the characters are therefore tamer and more like ourselves than the historical characters would have been, we, as readers, should be able to identify with them more readily. Right? Wrong. We're no more convinced and moved by this kind of writing than we were by the sixth-grade cut-up wearing his father's bathrobe and trying to look holy like Joseph. The truer a fictional character is to the time in which he or she lives, the more we are convinced by the reality of the character and the more we may be able to see ourselves in that character. The world of the book must be as accurate as the writer can make it, not only because the writer owes this much to history, but because she also owes this much to fiction. (At precisely this point on the rough draft of this speech is penciled, in my husband's handwriting, "and to the reader." Yes, John, and, of course, it is not only to history and to fiction that the debt is owed, but to the reader, perhaps, most of all.)

When I was writing *Of Nightingales That Weep,* in which Goro is a potter, I had to find out what kind of pottery wheel, if any, would have been used by a potter in twelfth-century Japan. I spent hours, days, as I remember it, researching this single detail without coming up with an absolute answer. Finally, I did some educated guessing, based on how long it seemed to take innovations from Chinese pottery and Korean pottery to get to Japan, and decided that the pottery wheel used by Goro was not a treadle wheel, but one in which a stick is inserted in the wheel to make it spin. The fact that the wheel is marvellously balanced makes it possible to throw a pot on it. At that time at Crowell there was a very picky copyeditor who wrote me a letter asking me if I were *sure* that that was the kind of wheel Goro would have used. Wouldn't treadle wheels have been in use in Japan by this time? Alas, of course, I wasn't sure. So I gathered my courage and called the Freer Gallery of Oriental Art in Washington. I explained my problem to the pleasant secretary who answered the phone. Was there any one at the gallery who could help answer my question? She told me that everyone was out to lunch, but when they returned she would ask one of the curators and call me back. About two hours later the phone rang. It was my friend the secretary, who told me that Dr. So and So and Dr. So and So had leaned across her desk at each other and argued for nearly an hour as to what kind of wheel Goro would have used. And the conclusion was that, although it was *possible* that he might have had a treadle wheel, it was more *likely* that he would have used the wheel I had described. You can imagine my delight when I called the copy editor to say that the experts at the Freer Gallery said that "although it was *possible* for Goro to have used a treadle wheel, it was more *likely*. . . ."

At first I was very shy about asking experts for help, but my courage grew as I realized how useful they could be and how important it was to get the details right. I have a friend in the Oriental section at the Library of Congress whom I call to check things for me. I remember when I was writing *The Master Puppeteer,* I was having the characters walk into an eighteenth century public bath, and I realized that I didn't know whether they would be carrying soap or not. It was suddenly vital that I know whether they had soap or something else to scrub with. It took two days for Mr. Ohta to get back to me to say that it was probably a pumice stone and not a piece of soap. Two days seemed a long time to wait while the bath water cooled, but that scrap of information made the scene more real to me, and, therefore, I think, I was able to picture it more effectively to the reader.

The writer of historical fiction loves these bits of detail, not because she is a teacher of facts, but because she is responsible for creating a world into which the reader is invited to enter. And that world must be rendered true with bits of pumice stone.

Not only must the physical details of that world be as accurate as possible, the sensibilities of that world must ring true. As you know, my parents were missionaries and then my father worked for many years as a Presbyterian pastor in this country. My mother was always trying to push my books and would send them to many of her friends. I still am a bit surprised that my books sell without my mother here to advertise them. Anyhow, she had sent my first two books to friends who were also former missionaries, expecting them to rave. Instead, they told my mother they were very disappointed to find that I had not mentioned the name of Christ in either book. The fact that the books were set in twelfth century Japan where, as far as anyone knows, the name of Christ had never been heard, was beside the point. If Katherine were truly Christian, she would have found some way to work it in.

Other critics are a bit more subtle. For example, they decry the fact that my Oriental women of the twelfth, eighteenth, and nineteenth centuries are not true feminists. But I am not writing a tract advising girls of twentieth century America how they ought to act. I am writing a story set in a different world, and the girls of that story are bound by the world in which they live. They are not totally bound, it's true. The characters from history or fiction that we remember are those who kicked against the walls of their societies. But the writer cannot pretend for the sake of her own prejudices that those walls were so flimsy that a character could demolish them with a single dramatic gesture. She cannot even assume that her character would see all of those walls as evil. A woman in another century, living in another culture, will not look at her world from a twentieth century American feminist viewpoint.

A basic task of any novelist is to create a world. For the historical novelist, the task is to re-create a world. The temptation is to throw so much information at the reader that the reader is overwhelmed by how much the writer seems to know. But the reader is in no way transported into the world of the book by multiplicity of detail. What the writer must do is select the details that will reveal—the details that make the reader experience this world for himself and forget all about the writer. . . .

About ten years ago when my family was on vacation, we stopped at a roadside table for lunch. . . . It wasn't long before some one of the four had disappeared. When you have four children one is always disappearing. The rest of us went to the woods to find him, and stumbled into a cathedral of pines. The trees were so tall that you could hardly see the sky and the ground was a carpet of brown needles. All the running and yelling stopped. It was obviously a sacred place. For a while we stood silently in the cool shadows of the trees, and then in a whisper signaled to each other that it was time to resume our trip.

Several years later when I was writing *Bridge to Terabithia* I put this pine grove into my story. It seemed to belong there, even though the actual grove was many miles away from the scene in my book. Not until I was in the final revisions of *Bridge* did it dawn on me that I had cheated. Maybe such a landscape would not occur in Virginia. With a sickening heart I sought out a botanist. Was the scene I'd described possible? Next to an ordinary Virginia woods, I had planted a pine grove. Was that possible? Yes, my expert said. There were certainly pine groves in Virginia. With cutting and regrowth it was possible that one might grow adjacent to a mixed woods—not usual, but certainly possible. Possible was all I needed. And now when people ask me as they often do if Terabithia is a real place, I say "yes," as it seems rather complicated to explain that actually it is composed of at least three places, as that "ordinary Virginia woods" looks suspiciously like the ordinary North Carolina woods behind the house we lived in in 1946.

But when people ask me "Where is Terabithia?" I don't think this is what they mean. They never ask me where Lark Creek, Virginia is located—only Terabithia. I think it is the idea of the place that haunts them, not the place itself. I say this because the twin question is nearly always: "Where did you get the name, 'Terabithia?'" As though, if the name were understood, the place could be found.

I thought I'd made up the name. I wasn't trying in the least to hide a philosophical secret in it. I was looking for a polysyllabic, rather romantic-sounding word that gave the same feel the name of a country might. The word "Terabithia" occurred to me. I played around with the spelling. I know at one point it was spelled "Tere-bithia." I chose the "a" spelling because I was trying to make it as easy to pronounce as I could. I'm sure no one believes me, but I spend a lot of time trying not to cause my readers undue trouble with pronunciation. Well, at about the time I was to check the final galleys for the book, I happened to re-read *The Voyage of the Dawn Treader* in C. S. Lewis's *Chronicles of Narnia*. As you all know, there is an island in *The Voyage of the Dawn Treader* named "Terebinthia." I was appalled. I had pinched my word right out of Narnia. At first I thought I would have to change it. I didn't want everyone complaining that I was hanging on to Lewis's coattails. But the thought of finding a word of exactly that length and going through the galleys and making all those corrections spurred me to seek another solution. And my kindly brain supplied the needed justification. Leslie Burke had read the Narnia books, too. She would very probably come up with a name for her kingdom that closely resembled something she had seen in *The Chronicles of Narnia* and thought she had made it up out of the blue. Besides, Lewis obviously got the name for his island from the terebinth tree in the Old Testament. It wasn't really original with Lewis, either.

However, to find the true ancestry of Terabithia, I think you have to look elsewhere. To *The Secret Garden*, perhaps, or even to Eden. Or better yet, to the enchanted places of childhood to the secret places of the heart. . . .

When children ask me now, "Where is Terabithia?," I try to explain that for most of us it starts out as a place outside ourselves—a tree, a hideout in the woods, a corner of our backyards, the springhouse on our uncle's farm. As we grow older, however, it becomes a place inside ourselves into which we may go. But the change from an outside Terabithia to an inner one doesn't happen accidentally, I remind them. If you want an inner Terabithia when you are fifty, you must begin to build it now. Some of them smile and nod. They know exactly what I mean. . . .

Fiction . . . is an incarnational art. The word must become flesh. The idea must find shape in a physical form. The Sino-Japanese character for "idea" is made up of two other characters—the character for "sound" written above the character for "heart." An idea is a sound in the heart. And fiction does not only grow out of place, it grows out of passion. If I am to write books for those who weep for falling leaves, not knowing why—whose hearts have not yet grown cold—I must write out of the heat of my own deepest feelings—the sounds of my own heart. I must struggle to capture in a story, as Hopkins said, "what heart heard of" and, at ten, or twelve, or fourteen, neither mouth nor mind could express.

It never fails to amaze me that when I do—when I listen to the sounds of my own heart, my own fears and desires and jealousies and angers and secret joys, the very things in my ordinary life that on social occasions I take care not to expose—when I write a novel out of these, I somehow am able to connect deeply with my readers.

I am often urged to set an example for my readers, or taken to task because I have *not* set a proper example, but, with all due respect, I don't believe that is what I am called to do. I am called to listen to the sound of my own heart—to write the story within myself that demands to be told at that particular point in my life.

And, if I do this faithfully, clothing that idea in the flesh of human experience and setting it in a true place, the sound from my heart will resound in the reader's heart.

Not in every reader's heart, of course. I haven't the power to deeply engage everyone, and if I try, I will fail utterly. A novel designed to please everyone all the time will, in the end, affect no one very deeply. And when a child, sometimes one of my own four, is brave enough to say, "I didn't like that book so much," I try to comfort myself with the hope that my reluctant reader will give my book a second chance some other time. As readers, we all can remember a book which, when we first tried to read it, took us nowhere, but then, coming to that same book at a different juncture of our lives, it became a cloud and fiery pillar leading us through some particular wilderness. I can always hope the same thing will happen to a book I wrote. But as writers we must be content to let our readers come to our books from where they are at that moment in their lives and take from our books what they will. If we have listened to the sounds in our own hearts and served the work those sounds have called into being as faithfully and carefully as we know how—then that is all we can do. The rest is not in our hands.

Katherine Paterson

SOURCE: "Hope Is More Than Happiness," in *The New York Times Book Review,* December 25, 1988, p. 19.

Not long ago a child asked me. "Why are your endings all so sad?" The question threw me a bit. I know sad things happen in my books, but I certainly don't perceive them as all having sad endings. It forced me to take another took at my work, or at least at the endings of my novels, and I must confess that none of them have what might be conventionally called happy endings. But does that make them sad? Or, as one troubled mother complained to me about *Gilly Hopkins,* "totally without hope"?

Now the child who asked about my sad endings was asking for more than I could give her. I think she was expressing a wistful yearning we all share for "happily ever after."

Nothing less than happily ever after will satisfy children who see themselves helpless and hedged in by huge and powerful adults. They need the hope that fairy tales provide. Realistic stories can't give a child this same assurance because, as Bruno Bettelheim reminds us: "His unrealistic fears require unrealistic hopes. By comparison with the child's wishes, realistic and limited promises are experienced as deep disappointment, not as consolation. But they are all that a relatively realistic story can offer."

I think there is a great deal of truth in this view of both realistic fiction and fairy stories. But if I say that Mr. Bettelheim is right, then don't I have to stop writing? How can I justify my realistic novels with their less-than-happy endings?

Recently our public television station broadcast the musical *Oliver!* Dickens's novel *Oliver Twist* is a good example of peripeteia or reversal of fortune, which is as popular a theme in fairy tales as it is in Greek drama, and a favorite plot with Dickens. I first saw the film years ago, and I'd forgotten how it ended. What would the writer do with this devastated child, who has seen his beloved Nancy savagely murdered, and who has then been taken hostage by the killer and dragged through the slums of London, only to end up high above the narrow street on a scaffold, rocking back and forth as the heavy body of Bill Sykes swings below in a grotesque parody of a public hanging?

Dickens himself had no trouble turning Oliver's trauma into a happy ending. It takes three chapters and 28 closely printed pages to do it, but, as always, Dickens manages to tie every stray thread into a splendiferous macrame of justice and joy. The evil are punished, the good are bountifully rewarded, and those in the middle repent and reap such benefits as befit their middling estate. The ending of *Oliver Twist* is a dramatic example of what travesties can befall a good writer with a bad editor, or, as I darkly suspect, no editor at all.

But would the writer of a modern musical film handle the ending any better? Would he insist on a reprise of "Who Will Buy?" with all the people of London singing lustily while clicking their heels in the dazzling sunlight, which would come as a blinding surprise to anyone who has ever lived in that city?

No. The screenwriter turned away both from the excesses of Dickens and from the conventions of the musical comedy form. As you may remember, the carriage draws up in front of the house of Mr. Brownlow, Oliver's benefactor. Mr. Brownlow and an exhausted Oliver get out and walk up the front steps. The kindly housekeeper comes out to greet them and, without a word spoken, much less sung, Oliver puts his arms around her and weeps.

What a lovely ending. I wish Dicken could have seen it. No singing, no dancing, no words. Any of them would have diminished Oliver's pain. We know from the way Mr. Brownlow puts his arm lightly across the boy's shoulder as they walk up the steps, and from the way the housekeeper's warm arms enfold him, that Oliver will be cared for. But his pain is not trivialized, much less erased. He will grow up to be a wise and compassionate gentleman, but deep in his heart he will bear the hunger of the workhouse and the grief of the Jacob's Island slums to his grave.

This, I maintain, is a proper ending. At least, it is a proper ending for me, although not, strictly speaking, a happy ending. It is certainly not happily ever after. But it is a positive demonstration of what I mean when I speak of hope in stories for children.

To make this clearer, think back to the Bible—to the calling of Moses. God first speaks to Moses from a burning bush on the mountainside. Now the reason Moses is wandering around that mountain in the first place is because he's a fugitive from justice. He killed a man and had to run before the law got him. He's living in the desert, under an assumed name most likely, working as a shepherd, when God speaks to him out of a burning bush and tells him to do something totally crazy. Go back to Egypt where your picture is on all the post-office wanted posters, go straight to Pharaoh's palace and tell him you've come to organize all that free labor he has slaving away on those treasure cities he's building. Pharaoh's workers are going to stage a permanent walkout because I've chosen you to march this unruly mob across the trackless desert to the country your ancestors left 400 years ago, which is now inhabited by fierce nations who live in walled cities.

Moses is understandably reluctant. He offers a number of objections. Nothing much has been heard from God in recent centuries. God isn't exactly in the forefront of everybody's mind these days. If Moses starts talking to the average Israelite about God, he's likely to reply: "God who?" So Moses says, "If I come to the people of Israel and say to them 'The God of your fathers has sent me to you,' and they ask me 'What is his name?' what shall I say to them?"

We know enough about ancient thought to know the power of the name. If the people of Israel know God's true name, they will, in a sense, have power over God. But at this point, something wonderful happens. God does indeed give Moses a name, but it turns out to be unpronounceable, and a verb to boot.

"Say this to the people of Israel," God says, "I am who I am, and I will be who I will be has sent me to you." Here is a God of the present time—of the world as it is and also the God of what will be. Nothing will ever be the same again. Being human, we will have to pronounce something to take the place of the name of this reality. We will assign nouns and pronouns, but we won't have hold of God thereby. The One whose true name is a verb is the one in whom we live and move and have our being. It is this One who has hold of us. The story also assures us that the One who is and will be hears the cries of those in distress and acts to deliver them.

As a spiritual descendant of Moses, and the prophets and apostles who followed him, I have to think of hope in this context. We are not really optimists as the common definition goes, because we, like Moses, must be realistic about the world in which we find ourselves. And this world looked at squarely does not allow optimism to flourish. Hope for us cannot simply be wishful thinking, nor can it be only the desire to grow up and take control over our own lives. Hope is a yearning, rooted in reality, that pulls us toward the radical biblical vision of a world where truth and justice and peace do prevail, a time in which the knowledge of God will cover the earth as the waters cover the sea, a scene which finds humanity living in harmony with nature, all nations beating their swords into plowshares and walking together by the light of God's glory. Now there's a happy ending for you. The only purely happy ending I know of.

I am sure that this sort of story does not satisfy children in the sense that "Cinderella" or "Jack the Giant Killer" will satisfy them. I know children need and deserve the kind of satisfaction they may get only from the old fairy tales. For children who are still hungry for happily ever after, my endings will be invariably disappointing. Children need all kinds of stories. Other people will write theirs, and I will write the ones I can.

As a writer I have a responsibility always to come humbly and childlike to the empty page—a responsibility always to be ready to be surprised by truth, ready to be taught, even to be changed. It is a joy to write for the young, for most often they will come to my story eager to be surprised, to be taught, to be changed, and to give their unique vision to the filling out of my imperfect one. And in this exchange of life and vision, of heart and mind, we come to know that we belong to one another.

One such reader wrote me about *Bridge to Terabithia*. "I really respected this book," she said. "You stuck to reality, and you also stuck to a dream." There. That is what hope is in my books. And, come to think of it, isn't it, as well, what we're celebrating when we sing of the babe "all meanly wrapped in swathing bands, and in a manger laid?" Aren't we saying that in this lowly birth the One who is and will be, the author of our creation, stuck to reality and also to a dream?

Katherine Paterson

SOURCE: "What Writing Has Taught Me—Three Lessons," in *The Writer*, Vol. 103, No. 8, August, 1990, pp. 9-10.

Somewhere in the middle of writing my tenth novel, it occurred to me that I had been at this business for twenty-five years. Since the book was moving along about as rapidly as a centipede with corns, I was not in the mood to celebrate the silver anniversary of my life as writer—not published writer, mind you, just writer. The silver anniversary of publication will be a few more years coming. But now the book is in the mail at last, and I am wracking my brain for lessons gleaned along the quarter-century journey. They seem pitifully few, but here they are:

1. *One idea doth not a novel make.* In answer to the often-asked question, Where did you get the idea for this book? I have at long last come to realize that a novel is not born of a single idea. The stories I've tried to write from one idea, no matter how terrific an idea, have sputtered out and died by chapter three. For me, novels have invariably come from a complex of ideas that in the beginning seemed to bear no relation to each other, but in the unconscious began mysteriously to merge and grow. Ideas for a novel are like the strong guy lines of a spider web. Without them the silken web cannot be spun.

The ideas that came together for *Park's Quest* were a long time in process. I had wanted for years to set a story on the Virginia farm where my father grew up and where I had spent many summers of my childhood. Once I even tried setting a short story there which never quite jelled. In one of those flashes that writers are prone to, I saw a scrawny Oriental-looking girl standing in the dark hall of that farmhouse. It was a child I didn't know, and I had no idea what she was doing there, so I tucked her away until I had the other strands for her story.

The second came when my husband and I happened to

visit old friends the day after they returned from the dedication of the Viet Nam memorial. Their eldest son had been killed during the war, and it was evident that the memorial and the services surrounding its dedication had been a time of real healing for their whole family. I went to visit the memorial myself soon afterwards and felt something of that power that all its visitors seem to experience. But still I was not ready to begin a novel.

The final strand began as an almost off-hand remark made by a speaker at the National Women's Conference to Prevent Nuclear War in 1984. She warned those of us concerned about the nuclear threat that we could not simply frighten our friends and neighbors into responsibility: People who are frightened tend simply to deny the fact that any danger exists. "I think what we must do," she said, "is to ask the question of Parzival."

A shiver went through my body. I didn't know what the question of Parzival was, but I knew I had to find out. And, of course, when I found Wolfram's medieval romance, which climaxes in Parzival's powerful question, "Dear Uncle, what aileth thee?" I found why my story would tie together our ancestral farm and the Viet Nam War. For surely for all Americans, not just for those who went to war, that conflict is "the wound that will not heal" and will never heal until we ask ourselves Parzival's question.

2. *My target audience is me.* Since I write primarily for children, people often ask me for what age child a book is intended. I have trouble answering the question, partly because I know very little about developmental psychology, but mostly because I know that people, even people of the same age, vary enormously in their interests and abilities. To try to "target an audience," as we writers for children are urged to do, would be impossible for me. I decided years ago it was not my job to decide who could or would read my books. If the publisher needs to suggest age or grade level designations in the catalogue, fine, but I will simply try to tell a story as well and as truly as I can. It would then be up to each reader to decide if my story was for him or her.

I suppose this truth came home to me after **Bridge to Terabithia** was published. I had written the book after a year during which I had had surgery for cancer and our youngest son's best friend had been killed by lightning. I wrote the book because I could neither bring back the little girl my son had loved nor could I seem to comfort him. In order to keep going, I needed, somehow, to make sense for myself of senseless tragedy. I truly thought that no one whose name was not Paterson would understand the book. I was very much in doubt that my editor would even want to publish it. Over the years the book has not only sold millions of copies and been published in at least seventeen languages, it is the book that prompts readers of all ages to write me and pour out the pain of their own lives. I keep learning that if I am willing to go deep into my own heart, I am able, miraculously, to touch other people at the core.

But that is because I do have a reader I must try to satisfy—that is the reader I am and the reader I was as a child. I know this reader in a way that I can never know a generic target out there somewhere. This reader demands honesty and emotional depth. She yearns for clear, rhythmically pleasing language. She wants a world she can see, taste, smell, feel, and hear. And above all she wants characters who will make her laugh and cry and bind her to themselves in a fierce friendship, as together they move through a story that pulls her powerfully from the first word to the last.

O.K. So she's a fussy reader. I've never fully satisfied her, but I would love to spend the next twenty-five years trying.

3. *A novel can be finished.* Some years ago I was having lunch in a crowded restaurant with a writer friend who has been at this business a lot longer than I. I was moaning that I was stuck—that this book I had poured two years of my life into was going nowhere. "This is my seventh novel! All these years and I haven't learned anything!" I cried out, eliciting a few stares from the diners at the next table.

"Yes, you have," my friend said. "You've learned one thing. You've learned that a novel *can* be finished." I cling to that knowledge every time I hit the invariable stone wall in the middle of a novel. I have finished nine of them now. I can finish another. And when it is done, given time and several sturdy guy lines, I may even be able to begin weaving yet another. There is always the hope that within the next twenty-five years I will be able to fully please my reader.

Katherine Paterson

SOURCE: "Heart in Hiding," in *Worlds of Childhood: The Art and Craft of Writing for Children,* Houghton Mifflin Company, 1990, pp. 145-77.

What I think I'm doing when I write for the young is to articulate the glorious but fragile human condition for those whose hearts have heard but whose mouths, at the age of five or ten or fourteen, can't yet express. But the truth is that I can't really express it either. So what happens is a reciprocal gift between writer and reader: one heart in hiding reaching out to another. We are trying to communicate that which lies in our deepest heart, which has no words, which can only be hinted at through the means of a story. And somehow, miraculously, a story that comes from deep in my heart calls from a reader that which is deepest in his or her heart, and together from our secret hidden selves we create a story that neither of us could have told alone.

When we think of the world of childhood, our first thought is how exposed it is. Children are constantly being stripped and bathed, commanded to eat when they aren't hungry, asked about their most private feelings or told they shouldn't feel the way they do. They are kissed and squeezed by strangers who claim some mysterious right of kinship or friendship. They hear themselves and their bloodlines discussed as if they were livestock in an agricultural show. And I'm only talking about children who are loved and cared for. The exposure of the despised or neglected child is too painful to imagine.

As adults we often assume that we have the authority to tell our children what to do and what to be and how to feel. How dare we? It follows, therefore, that parents and teachers think that people who write books for children ought to be on the adults' side. The question I get most often from people who know I write for children but who have never read my books is: What message are you trying to teach children through your books? Or, if they're a bit more sophisticated: What moral values do your books impart to young readers? I try not to get testy. After all, I don't like it when people who *have* read my books complain that I'm corrupting the morals of the young or, conversely, when critics say that my books are too didactic and moralistic. What I think I'm doing when I write a book for the young is to connect with the part of the child that's hidden. I'm trying to write a story. . . .

I like to think that when we write for children we are working with the basic stuff of life. . . . I'd suggest that the basic stuff of life is love and beauty. In this argument I have on my side, surprisingly, the evidence of modern science. Unlike the scientific materialism of a past generation, modern neuroscience believes in what we call mind: a human intellect and will, a *kokoro* [from the mind and heart] that can't be reduced to brain matter. In fact, modern physics contends that the universe posits mind—intellect and will—that can't be reduced to the elements of matter. Physicists have theorized, and observation seems to bear out, that matter is finite, that the universe had a beginning, has a middle and will have an end. But around and beyond the finite universe, as a growing number of scientists affirm, there is an eternal intellect and will—a mind that existed before the Big Bang, a mind that created all matter out of nothing. . . .

What are the properties of beauty to a physicist? There are three: simplicity, harmony and brilliance. Most discussions of physics mystify me. But beauty is a quality I know something about. A few summers ago I was lying on the couch at our summer house reading a new book. When I finished I said to my husband, "This is a beautiful book."

"What's it about?" he asked.

Instead of answering, I burst into tears. I was amazed at the power of my reaction, but those of you who have read *Sarah, Plain and Tall,* by Patricia MacLachlan, will understand. It *is* a beautiful book, and tears are an appropriate response to beauty.

But for a moment let's apply the scientist's test of beauty. Simplicity? Yes, the book is complete in itself—

direct and without superfluous words. Harmony? You'd have to look far to find a book in which the parts—character, setting and plot—so gracefully conform to one another and to the language of the whole. Brilliance? Here, like the scientist, we aren't talking about intellectual cleverness but about clarity—about the light that the book sheds not only on itself but beyond itself, to other stories and other lives. Don't you keep thinking of it? Don't you compare other books to it? Don't you know the prairie better now? And what it means to care about another person?

Beauty, so defined, is a good test to apply to art of any kind—perhaps particularly to the art of children's books. For the stories that have endured, the stories to which we turn as we seek to shape our lives, are all beautiful in this sense.

The stories that have shaped me most are the stories of the Bible. I know this is true, but I often try to figure out *how* those stories have shaped me. How has the Bible made me the writer I am?

For most of us the image of history or of chronological time is a line. Whenever I see a straight line drawn on a piece of paper or on a blackboard I will, in my head, draw a perpendicular line at either end. In my mind and my psyche, time has both a beginning and an end. At the beginning of the line I mentally write CREATION and at the end write ESCHATON, the end of history. Surrounding this bounded finite line is the great expanse of unmarked paper or blackboard representing unmarked, unbounded eternity. But there is another perpendicular line that bisects my finite line. It's there somewhere between the beginning and the end, always much nearer the right-hand end of the line than the left. This line differs from the other two because it's in the form of a cross.

If you grew up in the religious tradition that I did, after you have located those three basic marks on the line, you add others. One, toward the beginning, is labeled "the call of Abraham." Another is labeled "the exodus," another "the reign of David," another "the fall of Jerusalem. . . . "

What those three primary marks and the secondary marks on the line say to me is something that I find remarkably echoed in my reading of modern physics, which is that time is finite. Within the infinite expanse of eternity, time as we know it on our small planet moves purposefully from beginning to end. Beyond this exciting hypothesis I also see in the Bible the affirmation that, at certain critical points in human history, time is invaded in a special way by the eternal.

By now you've caught on that my view of time is not really Einstein's view, or Newton's, or even the view that most of us have when we set our alarm clocks or consult our daily calendar. My view of time has been shaped by a distinctly biblical view, which is largely ignorant of most scientific or philosophical arguments about the nature of time but which is still a very helpful model for someone who wants to write fiction.

Eudora Welty once said that "Southerners do have, they've inherited, a narrative sense of human destiny." And this "narrative sense of human destiny" is closely related to that time line on the blackboard. Of course that's why the South is known as the Bible Belt. We in the South were raised on this book that has a beginning, a middle and an end—a coherent plot, with wonderful, richly human characters, a vivid setting and a powerful theme. . . .

Every society, as Joseph Campbell has demonstrated, has its myths by which it finds meaning for life, and those myths have certain similarities. For example, the story of the hero who sets out into a realm of supernatural wonder, meets and conquers fabulous foes and returns again to bestow boons on his fellows—this is a story that occurs over and over in the mythologies and folk and fairy tales of the world. But even as I consider the paradigm of the universal story of the hero, I flesh it out with Abraham and Jacob and Moses and Jesus and see evidence throughout of the good will of the Creator toward creation—the Holy Ghost brooding like a mother bird on her nest over the bent world. It's not that I don't know other stories; it's just that Bible stories have had the most influence over me.

That's why I become uncomfortable when people ask me about the morals of my stories or the values I'm trying to impart. Moral judgment is not my prerogative. Of course, I'll make moral judgments for myself, and as a parent I'll try to teach my children what I believe to be right and good and what I see as evil and wrong. I'll also do whatever I can to work for peace and justice, which I believe to be good and right, and to combat war and oppression, which I believe to be evil. But when it comes to passing judgment on other people, even my own children, I have to tread carefully. Moral judgment is the prerogative of the Creator, and if the Bible is to be believed, when the Creator makes a moral judgment it breaks His heart.

So when I write a story for children it's not to make moral judgments, though the story may portray the observed human truth that behavior has consequences. I'm seeking to tell a story from my heart—my *kokoro*—with the hope that it will speak to another heart. I'll try to make the story as good as I can—good in the sense of beautiful. And, again, I define that beauty by the qualities of simplicity, harmony and brilliance.

Simplicity. This is the quality I have the least trouble with. E. B. White said somewhere that he thought he was ideally suited to writing for children because he didn't have a very big vocabulary. I think we'd all agree that Mr. White had a vocabulary equal to whatever need arose. But I understand what he was saying. I think I'm ideally suited to writing for children because I have a simple mind. I don't catch on to things quickly; I have to struggle with questions the way a dog worries a bone.

I prefer the concrete to the abstract. I'm forever trying to reduce everything troublesome or mysterious to a story, or at least to a simile or a metaphor. So, for example, when my eight-year-old son's best friend is killed during the same period when I must struggle with the fact that I've had cancer and am frighteningly mortal, I don't turn to philosophy or theology; I write a story. By writing fiction, which must have a beginning, a middle and an end, I give shape to what seems chaotic and unmanageable in my life. Writing stories is much cheaper than psychotherapy—and far more satisfying.

Harmony is a quality I have more trouble with, certainly if you listen to some of my critics. A book of mine that has garnered considerable abuse is *Jacob Have I Loved,* which many critics felt was out of balance, out of harmony. I often don't know what I'm doing when I write, but in the case of the ending of *Jacob* I was wide awake. I made a deliberate decision to compress Louise's college years to a very few pages, and I jumped from Rass Island to Truitt Valley, with hardly a stepping-stone in between, because I wasn't interested in the academic curriculum of either the University of Maryland or the University of Kentucky. It seemed to me that Louise's higher education had very little to do with what Jill Paton Walsh calls the "trajectory" of the story. In her essay "The Lords of Time," she says: "The trajectory of a book is the route chosen by the author through his material. It is the action of a book, considered not as the movement of paraphrasable events in that book but as the movement of the author's exposition and the reader's experience of it. And a good trajectory is the optimum, the most emotionally loaded flight path across the subject to the projected end."

Every book has its unique trajectory, although the genre will lead you to expect a certain kind. If you're reading a love story, as Jill Paton Walsh says, and the hero is about to kiss the heroine, you become annoyed if the author suddenly decides to insert a police chase. Whereas if you're reading what's meant to be a detective story and the author freezes the chase and pans to a tender love scene just when the murderer is about to be apprehended, you may well skip the romantic scene to get on with the chase. Readers do tend to sense what does or doesn't belong on the trajectory of a particular story. Some years ago I was reading a powerful novel and in the middle of it the writer supplied the recipe for a favorite food. It was a good recipe; I may have even made it for my own family. But as a reader I was jarred.

I used to think that children hated descriptions. But they only hate descriptions that are stuck in for effect, that don't belong on the trajectory. You could no more have *The Secret Garden* without lengthy descriptions of the garden than you could have *Charlotte's Web* without paying tribute to the changing seasons. Though neither element actually furthers the plot, both of them are on the trajectory. They are vital to the harmony of the book.

When you think of harmony you have to consider every

element that has gone into a book. When I was writing *Jacob* I tried to write it in third person, simply because I don't like writing in first person; it seems to me an arrogant and limiting point of view. But I found to my unhappiness that the book was refusing to be told in any voice but Louise's. Now, many years later, I can say, "Well, of course. How obvious. Jealousy can only speak in the first person. It can't imagine another point of view." To maintain the harmony of the book, the point of view had to be first person singular. Think about the play *Amadeus*. A great deal of its power derives from the voice of Salieri telling the tale.

Finally, brilliance. I once said to my editor, Virginia Buckley, when we were struggling with a passage in one of my books, that a suggestion by the copy editor would ruin the rhythm of a particular sentence. "Rhythm," I intoned solemnly, "is everything." Then I heard myself add, "But clarity is more." I rewrote the passage. . . .

Perhaps the basic test for beauty in a book—simplicity, harmony and brilliance (or clarity)—is to read the whole story aloud, preferably at one sitting. In fact, I don't think this is a test only for children's books; I'm suspicious of any book that can't be read aloud. But for a children's writer there is hardly any exercise more helpful. I was very troubled about *Park's Quest* until, by chance, I was asked to read it aloud to a blind friend, and when it worked out loud I knew it was all right. It would do.

The problem with the book, though, was that it was in the shadow of the powerful legend of Parsifal, and I could only compare my feeble words on the page with that immortal story. Usually the specific myth or legend or folktale behind a book is more or less subconscious. I certainly didn't know—as someone later explained to me—that *Gilly Hopkins* was a retelling of *Pilgrim's Progress;* I had thought it was the Prodigal Son. But with *Park's Quest* I knew from the beginning, even before I knew where the story would be set or who its characters would be, that its overriding shape would be that of the Parsifal legend as retold by the German romantic poet Wolfram in the early thirteenth century.

This was the only time I've seen quite so clearly the legend behind the story I was trying to tell. Certainly the story of Jacob and Esau is background to *Jacob Have I Loved,* but in a less direct way. But now, after nine novels, I can see that the overarching theme of them all is the biblical theme of divine good will. The more common word for good will in the Old Testament is loving-kindness. In the New Testament it's called grace. Like God, good will can't be defined. We are always reduced to simile, to metaphor, to once-upon-a-time.

I fell in love with the story of Parsifal before I had ever really heard it, before I knew what a powerful story of good will it was. I fell in love with it when I heard a speaker at the National Women's Conference to Prevent Nuclear War say: "We cannot frighten people into responsibility. People are so frightened now that they have to deny that there is a nuclear threat. I think what we must do is ask the question of Parsifal."

A shiver went through my body. I didn't know what the question of Parsifal was. But I knew I had to find out.

In the legend as Wolfram tells it, Parsifal, the Grail Knight, is brought by enchantment to the castle of the Grail King. The king is suffering from a wound that will not heal, and he will only be healed on the day the Grail Knight appears and asks the question. The young Parsifal, however, is the prototype of the innocent fool. He has no idea that he is the Grail Knight. When he finds himself in the mysterious castle of the Grail he's not about to ask any questions, because he has been told by those wiser than he that a man who keeps asking questions appears to be even more of a fool than he is.

So he doesn't ask the question. The king is not healed. And Parsifal is thrown out of the castle on his ear. In his subsequent wanderings our innocent fool becomes sadder and, if not wiser, certainly less gullible and increasingly world-weary. Try as he will, he can't find his way back to the Grail Castle. He refuses to return to Camelot, convinced that he is no longer worthy to take his seat at the Round Table. Eventually he loses all track of space and time until finally he loses his faith as well.

Then one day in the forest he comes upon a family of pilgrims. They are amazed to see a knight armed and in armor, for it is Good Friday. They speak to the despairing Parsifal, and he takes heart. Perhaps, he thinks, the One mighty enough to bring the world into being would have the power to bring comfort to his lost and despairing soul. Parsifal seeks out a hermit, who tells him again the gospel story, hears his confession and sends him once more on his quest. At last Parsifal comes a second time to the Grail Castle, and this time he asks the suffering king the question. "Dear Uncle," Parsifal asks, "what aileth thee?" Upon hearing these compassionate words the king is healed. And so is Parsifal himself.

In my book *Park's Quest,* Parkington Waddell Broughton V is also the innocent fool, unaware that he is the Grail Knight entrusted with the compassionate question, and so he fails his quest and loses his way in the wilderness. Now, as I've explained, I believe that there is an eternal mind who created from nothing a universe of beauty and whose posture toward all is that of loving-kindness, grace, good will. Thus you will suspect that in the world as I know it—and therefore in all my books—even in the darkest wilderness, there are angels, and a knight, no matter how lost and despairing, will always be given another chance to fulfill his quest.

Katherine Paterson

SOURCE: "*The Tale of the Mandarin Ducks:* Beauty and the Beast," in *The Horn Book Magazine,* Vol. LXVIII, No. 1, January-February, 1992, pp. 32-4.

[The following is Paterson's acceptance speech for the Boston Globe-Horn Book *Award for* Tale of the Mandarin Ducks, *which she delivered in Hyannis, MA, on September 30, 1991, at the annual meeting of the New England Library Association.]*

When I was trying to retrace my journey to this place, my first thought was that it was all my father's fault. Yes, my parents had a long marriage with much trouble and happiness shared, but it wasn't their marriage that led to my writing **The Tale of the Mandarin Ducks**.

My mother died in 1979 and then, four years later, my father. The inheritance they left behind was immense, but hardly any of it was in negotiable currency. There was, however, just the right amount. Not enough money to make me feel nervous and prudent, but just enough to make me feel I should blow it all rather than put it into the family purse, where it would turn inevitably into milk and beans.

I decided to buy a computer. Now, I had been writing on a manual typewriter since high school. I had been writing professionally for nineteen years on the same gray Smith-Corona Classic 12 portable. I'd tried an electric typewriter once or twice, and it had driven me crazy, humming and throwing in stray *k*s and *l*s whenever I paused to think. Why I thought I could learn to write on a computer when I couldn't even manage an IBM Selectric is beyond me. But I reckoned it was now or never. I'd never, I thought, have again that much money in my hands that was not already earmarked for somebody's college education.

In my naiveté, I had thought that when you plunked down that many dollars for something, they would send someone over from the store to set it up and get you going. Ha! It took me hours just to find the on/off switch.

It was summertime and hot in Norfolk. Every morning I would go up to begin the fight again, and when I reappeared hours later, I would be bathed in sweat and thinking language I did not want my children to hear from my lips. "How's it going, Mom?" they'd ask cheerily. It was all I could do to keep from snarling. Why couldn't they be like normal children? Oh, yes, they might be cheerful, bright, artistic—that was all very well—but there wasn't a computer whiz in the lot. I was a techno-peasant surrounded by techno-peasants.

"I'm struggling with the beast in its den!" I'd cry, for the monster had totally taken over my tiny study and made it a habitation of horrors. Finally, after what I remember as weeks, but may have been only one or two, I decided that the problem was in my attitude. I refused to be intimidated by an insentient assemblage of wires and microchips any longer.

I named the beast "Caliban." Its only function was to do my bidding. I was Prospero who knew (or would soon learn) the magic incantations that would turn the beast into my slave.

I decided then that the way to learn the magic spells was to do exercises that would call on the same skills that writing a book would demand. As usual, I didn't have an idea in my head, but I remembered a story about mandarin ducks that I'd read in a book I'd picked up off a remainder table some time before—*Japanese Mythology,* by Juliet Piggott.

I knew nothing of the rules of telling or retelling folk tales, so I changed and embellished to a fare-thee-well. My ending was a total gloss. Miss Piggott had said: "The servants naturally never returned to their master, but took employment in another district, where they married." Well, pooh, I thought, I can do better than that, and ended with a tribute to my husband and a mixed salute to our many children.

But however I mangled the tale, my goal was, at least, partially accomplished. I had learned by the end of the exercise not only where the on/off switch was but how to double space, format, erase, edit, save, and print.

My kindly ducks were laid aside, soon forgotten, while Caliban and I, truce attained, went on to other things. About two years later, I came across an uncut length of computer paper. My mother always said that no one who was literate should try to clean house. But, being literate, I had to read before I threw away. I recognized my early computer exercise. It didn't sound too bad. Actually, it sounded pretty good. I revised it and gave it to my husband for an anniversary present that summer. Then, true to all my crass breed, I got to thinking, Maybe those ducks could turn into something publishable.

Well, there was only one way of finding out, my husband said—send it to Virginia Buckley. To my delighted surprise, Virginia thought it might be publishable—with a bit of work, of course. And then, not long after, she called to say that she and Riki Levinson had decided to ask the Dillons to illustrate it.

Remembering all too well the humble origins of my story, I felt the way the Beast must have when he asked Beauty to marry him. But that is nothing to the humility that engulfed me when this exquisite book was finally put into my hands.

So today I have many people to thank: my father for leaving me just the right amount of money; Juliet Piggott for relating the folk tale in her book on Japanese mythology; her publisher—I guess—for remaindering her book so that it caught my eye; my husband for helping me to know the joy of a mandarin-duck sort of marriage; our children for ensuring that it remained quite human; Virginia and Riki for asking the Dillons to work their magic; and, most of all, the Dillons themselves.

I read the story aloud last spring to a second-grade class in a Boston school. A little girl sitting by my side jammed her small body against mine, the better to see every picture. When I turned to the page where Yasuko is carrying the drake out of the kitchen garden to set him free, she leaned across my lap to stroke the silky page. "This is *so* beautiful," she whispered.

"Yes," I whispered back. "I think so, too."

GENERAL COMMENTARY

Katherine Paterson with Laura Harris

SOURCE: An interview in *Reading Time,* Vol. 37, No. 2, May, 1993, pp. 11-12.

Do you have a store of ideas waiting to become books?

After I finish a book I feel washed-up and used up and I figure that's the end of my career. Every time! (laughs) I think I'll never have another idea worth writing about. Real writers have drawers full of ideas and they'll never live long enough to write all the books. But people like me . . . that can barely make it from one to the next! In fairness to myself I really feel a responsibility not to waste a lot of trees and a lot of my life on something that's not important enough to deal with. So therefore that does narrow down what I'm willing to do, and spend my life doing. So I really have to care about it before I'm going to impose it on someone else.

Lyddie has just been published here in paperback. It's a courageous story set in the textile mills of Massachusetts in the 19th century where child labour was employed. Where did the idea for Lyddie start?

I know exactly where that novel started. Usually I don't know *exactly* but with *Lyddie* I do. I'd finished *Park's Quest* and I didn't have another book to write. I saw a notice in the paper about the Vermont Women's History Project day seminar to celebrate women's history in Vermont. I went to one of the seminars called "Primary Sources" and a woman read letters that had been written by young farm girls who'd gone to the factories to work. Chills went up and down my spine when I heard those stories. The spellings were absolutely amazing and there was homesickness for the farm, asking about every person and a lot about death and religion. But also wonderful descriptions of the factories, the excitement of being in a big city, how hard they were working and how noisy those machines were. And that sent me on a quest to find out more about these young women. It's interesting how a lot of things are a flip of the coin, or lucky and afterwards there seems to be a great design in them but at the time you don't think of it that way.

Lyddie asks herself why she is so happy one day and then remembers that she is going to be read to. It becomes her comfort—as do many of your books for children.

Wouldn't it be wonderful to think that? I love that idea.

Because books have certainly done that for me. There was a child sitting in the front row in Melbourne and she raised her hand for a question. I called on her and she said, "How do you feel when people tell you that your books have really helped them. I read **Bridge to Terabithia** when I was very sick and it was such a help to me." Nothing can mean more to a writer than having a reader respond that way. It's hard to even say how you feel because it's overwhelming to think something you've done means that much to someone else—that you can make this sort of connection, where mostly in the world you're just missing people. Through something that's come out of your insides you've made a connection with another human being. It's rare and I'm very grateful.

In **Jacob Have I Loved,** *Louise says "Life begins to turn upside down when you're thirteen". Are those upside down times you write about things that you remember?*

What I often say when asked if I write about true life or do I make it up, is that the problem with true life is that you can't put it into a book because nobody believes it. Books have to be more believable than life is. Life doesn't make sense, but books *have* to make sense which is one of the things that makes them so satisfying. They can shape this life of ours that is not shapeable. I *can* say, no, I was not a twin, no, I did not live on an island, but I can't write about jealousy unless I've been jealous. When you come to feelings they're always autobiographical. That's where you're opening yourself up—you're running around naked! Feelings are much more revealing than events. You can't deny the feelings your characters have. You couldn't write about them with any power unless you have had those feelings. People think that intense feelings are too much for children but they often have more intense feelings because they don't have any context. Children *do* feel deeply and if we deny that then we are closing ourselves off from them.

Many of your characters feel a little weird and alone. But the reader always comes to care for them. Do they linger with you always?

Oh yes, because I care about them. They haunt me. They stay with me always. I never forget them, but I forget little events and it can be so embarrassing. I was at a school and they had all read the **The Master Puppeteer** and someone asked me a question. I began talking about one of the characters dying in a famine and this boy in the front was saying under his breath, "Plague". I said, "What", and he said, "Plague—he died in the plague", trying to cue me in so I wouldn't embarrass myself. He was really trying to do it so only I'd hear. I started laughing and he was totally right and I'd forgotten.

You're a passionate reader. Do you derive as much pleasure from writing?

I used to say, if I had to choose there would be no contest—forget the writing! But it's not that simple. Over the last year for a period of a couple of months I was totally tied up with some of my family and it was my first priority and that's what I wanted to do, but I began to feel this longing to get back to the story. I really miss it when I can't do it, but I didn't know that I would because I still don't think of myself as a real writer.

Does writing get easier the more books you have published?

No, it gets harder. My standards get higher and higher. I don't want to write something that's not really good. I'll go ahead and write, but I don't want to publish anything I can't be really proud of. So it slows me down. I used to be naive and I was just doing the best I could and that was OK. But now I've read too much, I know too much, I want it to be worthy. But of course the minute you want it to be worthy, you've hexed yourself! (laughs)

Recently you've worked on two picture books, **The Tale of the Mandarin Ducks,** *illustrated by Leo and Diane Dillon, and* **The King's Equal,** *illustrated by Vladmir Vagin (not yet released in Australia). How did that book come about?*

I went to the Soviet Union in 1987 for a symposium with Soviet authors and illustrators and I met Vladmir on that trip. We became quite good friends and it was suggested I write a story for him to illustrate. I had seen what he did and he has this lush style which had won him prizes for illustrating fairytales. I said I couldn't because I didn't write fairytales, and the editor who made the suggestion originally said, "Well, just think about it!" I *didn't* think about it because I was working on *Park's Quest* at the time and I have a one track mind, I only work on one book at a time. Then at Christmas time, when it's general chaos at our house and everything's a wreck, everybody went off to ski and I had the place to myself. I thought I better clean up but I decided to take a shower instead. When I got into the shower I didn't have any thought other than being house wife and mother and when I got out, I had an entire story in my head. I rushed down to my desk and wrote as fast as I could in long hand on a yellow pad to get the whole story down. I do tell children I put on my bathrobe first! I didn't have a chance to look at it again until everybody left and then I went back to it and thought, "Mmm not bad!" So I revised and sent it off to the editor and I thought she's going to say, "Katherine, this sounds like a story written in the shower!" We did a little tinkering with it but essentially it's the same story. It's a lot of fun—it's a subversive fairytale. I kept taking showers religiously hoping for another revelation!

Children are often very open when asking questions of their favourite authors. I've often heard children ask authors how much money they make. What questions do children ask you?

Teachers tend to weed out a lot of questions so I haven't had the money question for years. They want to know about you, your children and things like that. Children are more sophisticated than they used to be. Now they're much more focussed on the books themselves. I've had wonderful exchanges with children. I've been working with inner-city children in Boston for three years now, partly because the teachers are so wonderful—such heroes to me, and I go into schools that look like jails with children half asleep because they've been kept awake all night by gunfire and you walk in there and you suddenly realise these are children who have been given books—who love books and who ask wonderful questions. I'm just staggered that I'm getting that from children the rest of society just count as refuse. It's so thrilling. Any time they ask me, I go. For one thing I think those teachers doing that kind of work should be supported. There's wonderful teaching going on in terrible situations.

And your books are being used in that wonderful teaching.

It's thrilling to me to know my books can. Initially my books were said to be only for the special child, for good readers. I see kids there who are struggling because they want to read my books. They want to know what happens, and I think, "These are my people".

Nancy Huse

SOURCE: "Katherine Paterson's Ultimate Realism," in *Children's Literature Association Quarterly,* Vol. 9, No. 3, Fall, 1984, pp. 99-101.

In a profile in *Language Arts,* Katherine Paterson speaks of writing about "the ultimate things," teaching children "the end of the game." The idealism suggested in such phrases seems odd in a writer who chooses realistic forms like historical fiction and the contemporary problem novels. The assumption that Paterson is a realist, rather than a romanticist who reconciles good and evil, led to the writing of this article, but the term "realism" is not easily applied to writers like Paterson. How shall such children's writers be placed within literary tradition?

Because Paterson conveys the kind of meaning often associated in English-language children's literature with works of high fantasy, she has been called a didactic writer. At least in terms of our current use of such words, being called didactic does not help the critical reputation of children's authors. Paterson herself speaks of such descriptions a little defensively: "I don't even really mind being called a didactic writer because I think teaching is a wonderful thing." The awards Paterson has won suggest that readers don't mind her didacticism either. Her novels seem to win emotional involvement and praise from my students and other child and adult readers to a degree that few other works of "realism" for children and adolescents evoke.

In fact, Paterson's novels are difficult to describe, and important to appreciate, because they combine the accuracy and literal truthfulness expected of realism with another kind of power usually associated with ethics and religion. This combination is not especially easy to explore within the boundaries of our most widely circulated understandings of realism as a literary form. . . .

I believe that . . . Paterson has touched on some deep contemporary need for truth that depicts the simultaneity of alienation and integration in our relationship to the facts of existence and the social order. Telling the truth in terms of her *zeit* as well as in reference to her private beliefs, Paterson writes stories of children who move from a state of flawed and bitter experience to one of coherence and insight about the ultimate nature of human life. Her work is not less truthful because it affirms values as well as offering verifiable historical and social details.

A literary theorist who has discussed realism in ways that can be of real assistance for adults working with children's books like Paterson's is the late Hungarian, George Lukács, whose complete aesthetic commentary is still not available in English. His early book, *Theory of the Novel,* and other volumes on realism and on the historical novel are available, however, and have often been used by contemporary critics of literature.

Lukács may have been the first critic to identify the novel as a genre ordered by time, focusing on the change and development of its subject within the flux of external events. Rather than a primarily reportorial form, realism in Lukács' terms has an overtly interpretive character. The novel is a search for meaning, rather than a representation or parody of meaninglessness, and it links inner and outer worlds by offering descriptive details that are at once private and social, individual and typical. A realistic novelist thus deals with the metaphoric or universal significance of the individual life and event. Paterson's handling of subjects like random death, desertion by a natural mother, and a difficult sexual maturation fuses them into ongoing stories much more important than the discrete incidents themselves.

The assumption of pattern and meaning in events must be accompanied, according to Lukács, by a recognition of the separation of the individual from social laws and customs. The outcome of a realistic novel is the hero's experiential perception of meaning. The "affirmation of a dissonance" between the hero and the world is, for Lukács, the very form of the novel. Unlike other forms, the novel has the ethical intention—the assessment of values—as an effective structural element. It is engaged in the "self-correction of the world's fragility" because it raises the individual to the level of creating and maintaining a world of equilibrium rather than being engulfed by meaninglessness. Given this focus of the novel, its hero takes on the role of "signifier"; by the very act of seeing what the world is actually like, he or she becomes a model for human conduct. The hero's ability to understand the contradictions in experience becomes our ability to withstand them. The novel is perceived as the modern equivalent of the epic, more song than science,

even though it recognizes the loss of oneness with others which consciousness brings. Alan Friedman, too, has discussed the importance of meaning to form in the modern novel, asserting that novels today can "take on the impact and authority of mythic information."

The world of the realistic novel is, then, one whose very purpose is the taking on of order through the hero's changing powers. Paterson's novels, especially the later ones, seem to be resolved in ways that are simultaneously painful and yet more affirmative than their subject matter would allow. As a focus for discussing the novels, I want to suggest that her debatably happy endings provide a means to observe her developing powers as a realist. "The affirmation of a dissonance"—Lukács' way of describing the hero's condition in relation to experience at the resolution of a novel—is present in all of her novels. The adolescent book (*Jacob*) demonstrates its clear difference from the children's books by confronting the hero, Louise, with a much more complex range of details to sort out in a much more isolated condition.

The first book, ***The Sign of the Chrysanthemum,*** allows the Japanese serf Muna to purge himself, through suffering, of his attachment to the rogue samurai he hopes and fears is his natural father. The ending, in which the youth has unequivocally achieved self-definition as well as found an appropriate adoptive father, is the only one of the novels which resolves the conflict so tidily. We feel as little regret as Muna that things turn out the way they do. The nearly "closed" ending completes the book that has the least philosophical depth and psychological realism of the six novels.

In ***Of Nightingales that Weep,*** a samurai's daughter finds her identify at the too-great price of her mother's death. The marriage to her stepfather and their renewal of society are a triumph to the few with spiritual vision, the ability to perceive the hidden design of the "ill-made cup." A bleakness pervades the scarred world Takiko helps to renew, though the consistent character of the stepfather-husband does provide some possibility for doing that.

In the first two novels, Paterson seems to have been searching for ways to avoid too-bitter or too-happy endings. The final Japanese novel, ***The Master Puppeteer,*** moves beyond these resolutions to the kind of unbalanced closing the later novels refine. The boy "finds" his mother only because he loses his father as moral ideal. Even though his needs for social context have been met, Jiro must live in a world where one morally admirable choice seems to necessitate a second dishonorable one: his father's participation in a Robin Hood band left his mother to starve. The problematic nature of our bonds with one another, especially within the family, emerges here as the true subject of Paterson's work.

I emphasize the endings not only in line with critical practice of a formal nature, but because they are what my students want to talk about when we discuss her mature novels in class: how Jesse goes on without Leslie, how Gilly has to separate from Trotter, how Louise uses the baptismal moment to alter the ongoing cycle of human relations for herself and the twins she has midwived. Combining debatably happy endings in the last three novels is a much more focused point of view. In her Newbery acceptance speech, Paterson tells how her editor, Virginia Buckley, urged the writer to give Jesse the mind of an artist, in order to dramatize his sensitivity and the concomitant power to create new meanings out of his play with Leslie. Much of Jesse's ability to deal with the death comes from his linguistic and visual creativity; he is able to recognize and affirm his own separateness, yet create new peers—just as he and Leslie had created each other. Paterson has become skilled at third person limited perspectives. Jesse, Gilly, and Louise each demonstrate well how the hero's mind becomes the meaning-maker in realism.

Bridge to Terabithia opens with the hero, "Jesse Oliver Aarons, Jr.," alienated from his situation as the only boy in a family of girls, a family squeezed by poverty and an ugliness Lukács would see as emblematic of a reified capitalism and which Paterson herself seems to attribute to a lost continuity with spiritual and cultural values now preserved only in religion and the intellectual life. Prizing the idea of gaining his father's recognition by surpassing others in the physical contest of running, Jesse views nearly all contacts with his family as intrusions. Only May Belle, one of two little sisters who share a room with him, seems to have a sympathetic bond with Jesse at this time in his pre-adolescence. She brings him news that a family is moving in at the neighboring farm. "He thought later how peculiar it was that here was probably the biggest thing in his life, and he had shrugged it off as nothing." In response, Jesse tells May Belle to get him his T-shirt. "The flies were more important than any U-Haul": mired in the particularities of his situation, Jesse is reacting normally to the presence of flies, and yet displaying the narrow limits of his imagination and ability to order his own experience.

The final chapter, "Building the Bridge," depicts the change in Jesse since his creative play and friendship with Leslie, and also since his reincorporation as a son into the family his father is now willing and able to guide. Paterson depicts Jesse healed, but his healing has depended to a great extent on the revelation that his parents have the emotional and social resources to deal with the most significant event he has confronted. His father, especially, has known what to do in the face of death, what to say—"Hell, ain't it?"—and "God ain't gonna send any little girls to hell." Now Jesse copes with, and enhances, the physical details of his world, finding an alternate way to the magic of Terabithia, risking his safety to help May Belle, and affirming their right to be afraid of the creek which Leslie had defied. A resonant line, "It's like the smarter you are, the more things can scare you," suggests a mind wary of the world and of life, yet knowing its own power to order the chaos. The key event of the novel, Leslie's death,

thus becomes part of the order of things. The accident calls into its wake the numerous foreshadowings that suggested Jesse's practical wisdom and at-homeness with things that made him more fit for life than the fleet-footed goddess-child who had seemed above nature. While there is no way to become fully reconciled to the harshly unnecessary death, Jesse's statement does convey that "affirmation of a dissonance" that Lukács thinks "the very form of the novel." Taken out of context, the idea that Jesse sees he is smarter than Leslie is painful; the hero must depart from accepted norms of politeness and altruism in affirming his separateness. The tension between the necessity for the hero to perceive a small degree of meaning in even this experience, and the impossibility of the death's being actually meaningful contrasts with the expansive abilities Jesse has developed to participate in the rest of his experience—the "funeral procession" in Terabithia, the welcoming of May Belle to the secret world.

The Great Gilly Hopkins, too, shows a mind in the process of gaining the strength to be both reconciled to the order of things and yet somehow superior to it. At the opening of the novel, Gilly's alienation is depicted as the result of her being shifted through a string of foster homes. The link with her birth mother, the crux of the novel in its illusory promise and undeniable reality, is only hinted at with the reference to Gilly's mother-given name, Galadriel, and her blindly prophetic insistence that this name defines her in relationships with others. The "bale of blubber" who would become Gilly's "true" mother, and the small face jutting "out from behind Mrs Trotter's mammoth hip" which would become—pow!—the face of a brother, remain to be tested by the "barricuda smile" Gilly flashes at her departing social worker. In a contest of will, Gilly is certain, she is "well on the way" to being in charge.

The final chapter, "Homecoming," shows Gilly living out the results of her long idealization of her natural mother and the hasty, untrue letter she had written to her soon after coming to live with Trotter. Again, a pain which seems as if it should have been avoidable becomes the focus for the protagonist's "affirmation of a dissonance." Gilly cannot live with Trotter; this is unthinkable, yet it is irrefutable and—because Gilly does belong with her grandmother and even with Courtney—somehow all right. Her quest for her mother's falsely idealized love gives backbone to this tough little girl, and yet—as Trotter must teach her even on the last page of the novel—the secret of life is not a happy ending, but the living out of what is. Gilly has actually come to share this view with Trotter through experience; the Thanksgiving siege of illness in her foster family, for example, revealed her understanding of the goodness of life and the acceptance of the ordinary. That Gilly's "old" self remains, and yet is bonded to Trotter is shown by one of her good-byes, the playful yet sorrowful "Go to hell, Trotter." This is the Trotter-transformed remnant of the battered foster child in the realist who is also able to say "I love you." As Jesse incorporates Leslie into his personality, [Gilly] takes on the steady and large-souled attitude of Trotter so that she can be at home in a world of unpromising blandness and ugly contradictions.

The child protagonists' dependence on others for their ability to order meaning differentiates these novels from many adult books, but it is clear that both Jesse and [Gilly] will continue to recognize the artificiality of laws and customs which violate the imagination and the heart. Jesse, more than Gilly, has power over his life. In *Jacob Have I Loved,* the female hero is caught far more intricately in a web of circumstances than Jesse or Gilly, with no one figure to assist her in ordering them. Paterson's sixth novel, set in a harsh environment, has a more conventionally realistic form, yet the ability of the protagonist to understand her experience thus becomes a larger triumph.

For Sara Louise, the dissonant fact lacks even the contingency of a sudden accident or desertion by a selfish mother. Her actual birth, as the stronger firstborn in a set of twins, torments her, and forms the basis of her quest for equilibrium. While her delicate and musically gifted twin sister seems able to command the love and admiration of every person meaningful to Louise, she fears for herself a lonely, even crazed future. Returning to historical research after basing the two previous novels more directly on personal experience, Paterson takes on here the task of the regional writer. The opening chapter, a precise and detailed description of Rass Island, reflects the now-mature narrator's no-nonsense understanding of the conditions which shaped her childhood, a set of clipped words to describe the landscape— *faded, unpainted, wearily, primly, fierce, narrow*—is succeeded by a gentler set when she recounts the crabbing on the island and her childhood relationship to nature: *soft, distinctive, small, warm;* and a number of balanced contrasts: *jagged* and *rough, faint* and *brackish.* Her love for the island has come late to her understanding, but the fact that she and her sister, by their very natures, could not be sustained by the old and dying culture of the island is one she accepts, despite the "pure sorrow" evoked by the knowledge that she must live separately from the ways that were enough for her parents and gave her life. The opening section, prelude to the story of her adolescence, makes no allusion to the powerful motif "Jacob have I loved" which the girls' island-confined grandmother repeated at painful times in Louise's development. But the adjectives describing the terrain have caught the tone of the rigid, tormented, and immature woman's ugly but truthful insight into the girl's heart. Seemingly forgotten in the opening account, the grandmother—for whom the girl is named—becomes in her way as much a mythic and shaping force in the story as Mrs. Trotter in Gilly's.

An example of stunted growth and an unacceptable ending to a life, the grandmother is the catalyst for Louise to separate from the island and thus grow; the bitter old woman, however, cannot provide the final, freeing confidence. That comes only when, drawn into tender proximity with her quiet, bright, but too submissive mother because of the grandmother's rage, Louise finally reveals enough of her own feelings to elicit the one directly preferential statement the mother has ever made to either of the twins. She and the father will miss Louise "more" than they miss Caroline (who is studying to be an opera singer).

To speak of the freeing encounter with Louise's mother, however, is not to suggest that she "heals" Louise in the sense that Jesse's father or Gilly's foster mother assisted them. Too much else has gone on in Louise's development to focus on one dramatic event as an almost single explanation. Louise's growth is very much the result of a long and complex experience with the sea, with an old man who unwittingly awakens her sexuality along with her separate identity as someone who was "never meant to be a woman on this island," and with the model of male strength and ingenuity provided by the girls' father.

Compared with the affirmation of Jesse's rural religious background and of Trotter's earth-mother Christian spirit, the religious theme in *Jacob* is depicted as a rather amoral force which can be shaped by human choices. Inferring that it is god who has "hated" her, Louise becomes an outsider to religion until the final scene of the book. In an ending saved from overcoincidence by its complex implications for the story, Louise exhibits the behavior of maturity by reinterpreting the letter of religious dogma to coincide with her perceptions of human need. In order to "self-correct the world's fragility" (Lukács), she assigns the new babies' grandmother to baptize the stronger twin because the father of the children had insisted she baptize the twin in danger of death, in accordance with Church law for Catholics. Louise thus attempts belatedly to guarantee the stronger twin the birth-tradition she had lacked. Her own family were unable to recall what her first hours of life were like, although they remembered vividly their struggle to keep Caroline alive. Entering wholly into communion with the fragile life that needs her desperately, she feeds "my baby" with milk from the breast ready for her own newborn son. Nonetheless, as she leaves the scene of the birth and hears the clear, Caroline-haunted lines of "I wonder as I wander" sung nearby, the reader knows that even in reconciliation and integration Louise will struggle not to repeat the unfairness of things she has come to understand. The device of telling the story as the recollection of Louise emphasizes the limitations on our ability to overcome sorrow, yet shows how she values her hard-won maturity.

This unusually thorough treatment of a girl's coming-of-age places her story in the context of mother and grandmother as comparative figures defined by their eras. Louise, too, is defined by hers—she is first denied and then forfeits the opportunity to be a doctor; she needs her female sexual identity. The novel exemplifies Paterson's power as a realist who can use descriptive details and the specific life events of a clearly defined individual to create a metaphoric realism with powerful contemporary meanings. We are left with the partial realization of Louise's dreams, yet the suggestion that things do and must change. Paterson says she "believes in stories" ("Profile") and it is easy to see why. *Jacob,* seen both as an example of Paterson's growing strength and commitment as a writer, and as a book which may suggest a delineation between children's novels and works directed to a teen-age audience because of its emphasis on the hero's lonely world-making, is a provocative example of realism dealing with ultimate values. How many examples of such realism do we have in adolescent literature? The "hero as signifier" who makes a painful and precarious order of the flux of mortal experience: how many have we imagined for the young?

Joel D. Chaston

SOURCE: "The Other Deaths in *Bridge to Terabithia,*" in *Children's Literature Association Quarterly,* Vol. 16, No. 4, Winter, 1991-92, pp. 238-41.

In writing about Katherine Paterson's *Bridge to Terabithia,* Alleen Pace Nilsen and Kenneth L. Donelson claim that "Paterson's novel set impossibly high standards that no other such book about the death of a friend has equalled" . . . Certainly, it has been one of the most honored children's books about death published in the last two decades. Besides the 1978 Newbery Medal, it has received the Lewis Carroll Shelf Award, the Januscz Korcazk Medal, the Le Grand Prix des Jeunes Lecteurs, and the Colorado Blue Spruce Young Adult Book Award.

Not surprisingly, *Bridge to Terabithia* now occupies a prominent position on a number of bibliographies about death. Masha Kabakow Rudman's *Children's Literature: An Issues Approach* discusses the novel as an example of one of many books whose "characters do not respond heroically or admirably to death." It is a useful book, she implies, because it depicts a child who "passes through all of the stages of mourning. . . . " In her chapter on realistic fiction in *Literature and the Child,* Bernice Cullinan devotes most of a section called "On Death" to *Bridge to Terabithia.* She discusses three fifth-grade girls who feel that the novel "showed them that one could, and should get over the death of a friend and that Jess was a good model of how they might react if they were in similar circumstances." John Stewig's *Children and Literature* also places the novel in a section on death and aging, discussing it along with books like Sharon Bell Mathis's *The Hundred Penny Box* and Lois Lowry's *A Summer to Die,* works published around the same time.

Paterson, however, is bothered by the inclusion of *Bridge to Terabithia* on "death lists." While not entirely opposed to recommending a book to readers with special problems, she is wary of bibliotherapy. She writes [in *The Spying Heart*]:

> The first time I was told that *Bridge to Terabithia* was "on our death list," I was a bit shaken up. There

follows, you see, the feeling that if a child has a problem, a book that deals with that problem can be given to the child and the problem will be cured. As Jill Paton Walsh points out, only children's books are used this way. "One does not," she says, "rush to give *Anna Karenina* to friends who are committing adultery, or minister to distressed old age with copies of *King Lear.*" Still, if we look at life as a series of problems needing solving, it is hard not to offer nicely packaged, portable solutions, preferably paperback. I know. No one has given out more copies of *Ramona the Brave* to first graders in distress than I have.

Paterson goes on to address what she sees as shallowness in "problem novels" for children, arguing that the best a writer can do is to "share with children works of the imagination, those sounds deepest in the human heart, often couched in symbol and metaphor." These works, she continues, don't give children ready-made answers, but invite them "to go within themselves to listen to the sounds of their own hearts." In other words, books like *Bridge to Terabithia* should not be used as a cure for or fast solution to the problems children face. It is only when literature stimulates readers to look within themselves and search their hearts for their own solutions to problems that it is effective.

A close reading of *Bridge to Terabithia* reveals that these same ideas are present in the novel itself. This book, which is so often featured on "death lists," can be read as an argument against attempting to solve children's problems through literature. According to the novel, stories, whether written or oral, are no substitute for real experience; no amount of literary exposure to death, for example, can prepare Jess for Leslie Burke's death. When such works help readers "listen to the sounds of their own hearts," however, they are valuable indeed. At the same time, through its allusions to other death stories, *Bridge to Terabithia* shows how its own treatment of the subject is distinctive, suggesting a movement towards a new kind of death literature.

Many discussions of *Bridge to Terabithia* have rightfully focused on Leslie Burke's death and its impact on Jess Aarons. It is, after all, at the heart of the book, which grew out of real events involving Paterson's son and one of his friends. In her "Newbery Award Acceptance," Paterson describes how her son's best friend was struck by lightning, launching her child into "all the classical stages of grief, inventing a few the experts have yet to catalogue." Encouraged by Ann Durrell, an editor at Dutton, she decided to write the story, but not without feeling that she could not do it, that she was too close to it.

Somewhere along the way, however, the novel expanded beyond a simple account of Leslie's death and Jess's reaction to it. Indeed, as Paterson explains in an essay, "The Aim of the Writer Who Writes for Children," the book is not even really about death, but friendship. She goes on to argue that while "all mortal friendships come to a close, death is not always the most painful ending."

Even so, death permeates the novel and, upon close analysis, Leslie's death is only one of many within the novel—the books and stories Jess and Leslie share are also concerned with death. In fact, Jess and Leslie can be seen as subjects of a type of bibliotherapy before either of them has to cope with death; their own list of death books and stories would seem to be preparing them for what eventually happens to Leslie. These works also suggest a variety of attitudes towards death. The children read and hear stories in which death is an obsession, death comes as a result of revenge, death is caused by suicide, and death is chosen to save others or to further a social, political, or religious cause. The stories they encounter do not, however, treat purposeless, accidental death, the kind that comes when least expected.

It is through his friendship with Leslie that Jess becomes acquainted with these death stories as they are creating Terabithia. Since Jess is deprived of some of the imaginative sources Leslie has to draw on, she lends him "all of her books about Narnia, so he would know how things went in a magic kingdom—how the animals and the trees must be protected and how a ruler must behave." While the two children do not discuss it directly, C. S. Lewis's *The Chronicles of Narnia,* the very series which helps them create their magical kingdom, frequently portrays death. . . .

That death can be noble, even wonderful, is reiterated when Leslie accompanies Jess to church on Easter Sunday. There, apparently for the first time, Leslie is introduced to the story of the crucifixion of Jesus. For her, it is "better than a movie." She explains to Jess, "It's really kind of a beautiful story—like Abraham Lincoln or Socrates—or Aslan." To Jess and May Belle, the story is scary and frightening, but for Leslie, it is beautiful, despite the fact that no one has ever forced her to believe it. Both *The Chronicles of Narnia* and the New Testament make sacrificial death beautiful and noble. In these stories, as well as those detailing the lives of Lincoln and Socrates, death is put in a larger context. . . .

Of course, these are not the only sorts of death stories that Leslie and Jess share. When they are in Terabithia, Leslie also introduces Jess to *Moby Dick* and *Hamlet.* "Say, did you ever hear the story about Moby Dick?" she asks Jess on one occasion. Jess, of course, has never heard of Herman Melville or of Captain Ahab's obsession with the great white whale. Leslie, however, matter-of-factly tells him "a wonderful story about a whale and a crazy sea captain who was bent on killing it." The story is powerful enough that his fingers itch to draw it. "There ought to be a way," he muses "of making the whale shimmering white against the dark water." . . .

Unlike Aslan's sacrifice in *The Lion, the Witch, and the Wardrobe,* Ahab's death is less than heroic—it is the result of his obsession with the whale, the natural consequence of earlier events in the novel. Instead of saving those around him, his death destroys them.

It is while Jess and Leslie are planning their own revenge against Janice Avery that yet another death story captures their attention. "Jess Aarons, I'm going to kill you," Leslie says when he accuses her of having a secret love back in Arlington. When Jess responds that she can't kill a king, Leslie mentions "regicide" and then tells him about *Hamlet.* As she speaks, Jess mentally draws a picture of a "shadowy castle with the tortured prince pacing the parapets." Once again, he hears a story full of death, including the murder of a monarch because of a desire for revenge. At the end of the play, the stage is strewn with the corpses of Hamlet, Gertrude, Claudius, and Laertes. Several other characters have met their deaths earlier, including Ophelia, Polonius, Rosencrantz, Guildenstern, and Hamlet's father.

Like *King Lear,* which Paterson suggests should not be prescribed to solve the problems of the aging, *Hamlet* is no cure for those dealing with death. Indeed, the deaths in the play have little in common with Leslie's. While Ophelia, Hamlet's intended, drowns in a river, too, her death is the result of madness. Leslie, on the other hand, is quite sane, a good swimmer, and, as someone who loves to go down into the water, a very unlikely candidate for drowning.

Although many characters die in *The Chronicles of Narnia, Moby Dick,* and *Hamlet,* these tales do not provide Jess with much insight into death—he savors them as stories which he would like to draw or as inspiration for Terabithia; but after Leslie's death, they cannot wipe away his grief. They are not, however, his only chance to become vicariously acquainted with death. When his classmates write about their favorite hobbies, Jess, through Leslie's essay on scuba diving, feels what it is like to drown. When Mrs. Myers reads it aloud, Jess feels drawn into the water—what he hears causes him to choke and sweat, giving him the sensation of drowning.

During his visit to the Smithsonian with Miss Edmunds, Jess is affected by yet another death story, dramatized by a diorama of "Indians disguised in buffalo skins scaring a herd of buffalo into stampeding over a cliff to their death with more Indians waiting below to butcher and skin them." He feels "a frightening sense of kinship" with the display and can barely tear himself away from it. Both Leslie's essay and the buffalo diorama have a strong emotional impact on Jess, fascinating him, giving him a sense of the violence of death. In the end, however, like the other death stories, they do not console him after Leslie's death.

When the rope across the river breaks and Leslie falls into the water and drowns, her death is as unreal as an earlier image Jess has had of her "flattened straight out like the coyote on *Road Runner,*" easily repaired and able to fight again another day. Jess's first response to Leslie's death is that his family has told him a lie. Even when he and his parents visit the Burke family, Jess finds the grief of Leslie's grandmother incomprehensible—it is "as if the lady who talked about Polident on TV had suddenly burst into tears. It didn't fit."

At this point, one final story does have a sort of "therapeutic" effect on Jess. It differs sharply from Leslie's novels and the essay she has written because it validates his own experience and does not try to erase his feelings. Ironically, it is Mrs. Myers, the teacher he and Leslie have openly despised, who begins to make him feel better. "When my husband died," she explains to Jess, "people kept telling me not to cry, kept trying to make me forget." She tells him, however, that she did not want to forget. Jess is surprised by the image of a loving, caring Mrs. Myers, but recognizes that she "had helped him already by understanding that he would never forget Leslie." It is important to Jess that Mrs. Myers does not diminish the importance of his experience or make him deny that it has affected him.

Even though Jess has been fascinated by earlier encounters with death stories, they cannot alter what has happened to Leslie, nor can they provide the "portable solutions, preferably paperback" that Paterson cautions against [in *the Spying Heart*]. Paterson carefully refrains from turning Jess's own story into a prepackaged set of solutions that would try to cure the problems of yet another grieving child. Yet, as Rudman has suggested, Jess does pass through typical stages of mourning such as anger, denial, and acceptance. Paterson, however, respects his personal response to Leslie's death, making it clear that Jess's grief is genuine and should not be lightly dismissed.

While Paterson suggests that the stories of Aslan and Jesus, Captain Ahab and Hamlet are powerful, even beautiful, her own book treats death differently. Leslie's death is never glorified. Unlike the works the children have read, *Bridge to Terabithia* does not imply that her death is noble, nor is it anyone's fault. Leslie has not been urged to stampede off a cliff nor has she brought about her own death by a desire for revenge. Her death is immediate, unalterable, and accidental. Paterson has created a book which, like Mrs. Myers' story, does not ask the reader to dismiss the pain of death or to forget about it. Instead, she asks her readers to "go within themselves to listen to the sounds of their own hearts."

While Paterson questions the validity of bibliotherapy, she also feels that books can provide readers with strength, sustenance, and hope. Certainly, the books Leslie shares with Jess accomplish this. But they provide no quick cure—reading needs to be a cooperative effort between the writer and the reader. In *Gates of Excellence,* Paterson maintains, "I have no more right to tell my readers how to respond to what I have written than they have to tell me how to write it." In another essay [in *The Spying Heart*], she writes that it is "only when the deepest sound going forth from my heart meets the deepest sound coming forth from yours—it is only in this encounter that the true music begins."

Paterson has written the kind of book Jess would have appreciated reading, though it is clear that it would not have provided him with pat solutions or wiped away his grief. In the end, Jess must resolve his feelings through his own actions, building a bridge into Terabithia, sharing with May Belle what he has learned from Leslie. Ultimately, the stories Jess has heard, as well as his friendship with Leslie, help him to "push back the walls of his mind and . . . see beyond to the shining world— huge and terrible and beautiful and very fragile," but it is up to him to stand up to his fears and create his own story.

Joel D. Chaston

SOURCE: "Flute Solos and Songs That Make You Shatter: Simple Melodies in *Jacob Have I Loved* and *Come Sing, Jimmy Jo,*" in *The Lion and the Unicorn*, Vol. 16, No. 2, December, 1992, pp. 215-22

In Katherine Paterson's first collection of essays, *Gates of Excellence,* she compares writing fiction for children to playing a musical instrument. She feels that one of the few limitations of her choice of audience has to do with the intricacy, density, and design of what she writes. She compares great novels for adults, such as Mary Lee Settle's *Blood Tie,* Anne Tyler's *Celestial Navigation,* and John Fowles's *Daniel Martin,* to "a symphony orchestra." On the other hand, she calls her own *Bridge to Terabithia* "a flute solo, unaccompanied." Even when she is dealing with complicated situations, "through all the storm and clamor" of her books, she hears "a rather simple melody."

The notion that her books are "simple melodies" is also an important concern of several essays in *The Spying Heart.* In her first essay, **"The Story of My Lives,"** Paterson concedes that she has a "limited gift" when it comes to writing fiction, one which prevents her from exploring other genres. She goes on to admit that, as she tells one of her editors, there is a sameness about her books; they all have kinship with Joseph Campbell's monomyth in which a "hero ventures forth from the ordinary world into a realm of wonders. There he is met by a supernatural guide who aids him as he confronts and defeats fabulous forces and returns a victor, able to bestow boons on his fellows."

Both in the collection's title essay and in **"Sounds of the Heart,"** Paterson confesses that she often revises her simple melodies to obscurity, at least in part due to the adage that "what is left out of a work of art is as important as . . . what is left in" and because of her love of form. She feels, however, that her stories, like the old, traditional tales, take us back to basic archetypal images, providing "no one has scrubbed them up. . . ." In **"Stories,"** she further makes her case for "simple melodies," once again resorting to musical images. She discusses a lunch she had with the composer Alice Parker, who "loves melody—the more primitive the better." Parker condemns music which has become "intellectualized" and both composers and novelists who despise "story." "These are the writers," she contends, "who spend their time performing intellectual tricks. . . ."

In these and other essays, Paterson is careful to make the point that she does not write down to her readers, that simplicity is not a matter of readability. She also maintains that simple melodies can strongly affect the listener and reader, once again using music to talk about literature. It requires, however, some effort on the part of the audience. [In *The Spying Heart*] She quotes Frances Clarke Sayers, who talks of "the shattering and gracious encounter that art affords." But, Paterson goes on to explain, it is "only when the deepest sound going forth from my heart meets the deepest sound coming forth from yours—it is only in this encounter that the true music begins." Continuing with her musical imagery, Paterson explains that she wants to be one of the "scarlet tanagers, who . . . rise up, sing, and fly free."

Critics of Paterson's work have often commented on the "simplicity" of her books and her interest in form. [In *Books and Bookmen*] Patricia Craig maintains that her second novel, *Of Nightingales that Weep*, "has something of the formality and simplicity of a retold folk tale." Writing about *Jacob Have I Loved* [in *Children's literature in education*], Sarah Smedman argues that it is a "tightly woven novel; each character, each episode, each speech, each image helps to incarnate what the author is imagining."

Since Paterson views herself as a musician, a flute soloist who provides "shattering encounters" for her readers, it should not be surprising that her fiction is filled with descriptions of powerful, yet simple songs. For example, Okada, the blind writer of puppet plays in *The Master Puppeteer,* is said to sing his plays to those who transcribe them. In *The Sign of the Chrysanthemum, Of Nightingales that Weep,* and *Rebels of the Heavenly Kingdom,* music helps to heal or restore the listener. At the end of *The Sign of the Chrysanthemum,* Fukuji sings of the cycle of life, his voice shimmering "in the night air—the voice bright above the zither's chords like raindrops on a spider web." The young emperor in *Of Nightingales that Weep* discovers a healing power in Takiko's songs of the Dragon King and longs to learn how to play the flute so he too can make music. Mei Lin and Chu of *Rebels* try to convert Wang Lee to their faith through the hymns they sing, songs which make Mei Lin's face "come alive," causing Wang Lee to forget that she is "ugly and unwomanly."

Music also helps the characters of *Bridge to Terabithia, The Great Gilly Hopkins,* and *Angels and Other Strangers* to communicate with one another. It is while singing "Free to Be You and Me" that Jess Aarons resolves that he might as well make friends with Leslie Burke, while Gilly Hopkins tries to attract her foster brother's attention by humming the theme songs of the television shows he watches. Similarly, in the story "Guests," from *Angels and Other Strangers,* the carol "Joy to World" helps create a bond between a Japanese minister, the policemen who wanted to arrest him, and a Korean child.

Paterson's most developed use of music, however, occurs in *Jacob Have I Loved* and *Come Sing, Jimmy Jo.*

In these works, she once again celebrates the power of simple music and its effect on both the listener and the performer. A close reading of these novels, however, reveals that, as in her essays, Paterson uses music as a metaphor through which she defends her own writing, both what she sees as its basic simplicity, as well as her decision to write for children and young adults.

In *Jacob Have I Loved,* Louise Bradshaw's jealousy of her sister, Caroline, centers, at least in part, on her musical ability. All of the children of Rass Island, under the guidance of Mr. Rice, sing every day because there is little to entertain them. They perform "surprisingly well," Louise explains, "for children who had known little music in their lives." Caroline, however, has a "gift," and picks out tunes on the piano by ear, making up songs for herself. Her music is so entrancing that "people would stand outside the house just to listen while she practiced." Among the listeners is Auntie Braxton, who drinks in Caroline's piano playing "as though it were heavenly nourishment."

The power of simple, unaffected music becomes apparent during the school's annual Christmas concert. As always, Caroline sings a solo, but unlike the year before, she is not asked to sing "O Holy Night," which Louise feels is "showy." Instead, Mr. Rice asks her to sing a "simple" song, "I Wonder as I Wander." To Louise, Caroline's unaccompanied song is "a lonely, lonely sound" which is "so clear, so beautiful," that she has to tighten her arms to "keep from shaking, perhaps shattering." Leaving the gymnasium, Louise is caught up in the song and in the stars overhead that pull her like a magnet. The song continues in her head as she presses up "against the bosom of heaven, dizzied by the waking brilliance of the night." To Louise, the simple tune is affecting, even more powerful than the more showy one. In fact, Caroline ridicules Betty Jean Boyd's rendition of "O Holy Night."

Louise, however, becomes jealous of the attention lauded on Caroline because of her gift. When Caroline goes off to school, however, she is able to rediscover the power of music. The happiest days of Louise's life occur when she has the chance to go oystering with her father. One of her big surprises is that he sings to the oysters. "It was a wonderful sound," she explains, "deep and pure. He knew the Methodist hymnbook by heart." There is a contentment that comes from being with her father, a man who seems to communicate with nature through music. Later, Louise is attracted to her future husband because he looks like "the kind of man who would sing to oysters."

Interestingly, Louise reacts to Caroline's and her father's songs much as she does the books she reads. When Louise feels unhappy because she thinks she has become merely a minor character in her sister's life, the only thing she can lose her "miserable self in" is books. She reads Scott, Dickens, and Cooper, pulling back the black air raid curtains so she can "read on and on," huddled close to her bedroom lamp. She imagines she is

Uncas from *The Last of the Mohicans*, "standing ready to die before the Delaware, when an enemy warrior tears off his hunting shirt revealing the bright blue tortoise tattooed on Uncas's breast."

Louise eats, drinks, and sleeps books, drawing strength from them to keep on living. Besides nineteenth-century novels, she read magazines, poetry, and "a delicious scary" book "about some children who had been captured by a bunch of pirates in the West Indies." This book, with a "picture of a great sailing vessel on the front," fuels her passion for the sea, as well as her impatience. She does not want to spend her life "passively waiting," like the other women she knows. Her reading also seems to strengthen her desire to become someone important, someone unique, as in her desire for a blue tortoise tattoo like that of Cooper's Uncas. Not unlike Jess and Leslie of *Bridge to Terabithia*, who create an imaginary world from their reading of *The Chronicles of Narnia, Hamlet*, and *Moby Dick*, Louise develops a rich imaginative life. It is often the simplest stories, however, such as the tale of Jacob and Esau and the story of her own birth which affect her most deeply, nearly trapping her into self-destruction.

Along the way, Louise learns that the most sentimental, complicated and overwrought writing is often ineffective. She decides to become a song lyricist, at least in part because of an advertisement in a Captain Marvel comic book. She uses as a model "The White Cliffs of Dover," which to her has all the requisite elements, "romance, sadness, an allusion to the war, and faithful love." She fancies herself "the perfect lyricist—romantic, yet knowledgeable." Her friend Call, however, sees her song for what it is. "I call it dumb," he says simply. When Louise receives a letter from Lyrics Unlimited, she learns she has bought into a scam. The company apparently only wants to make money from would-be writers. Angry, she rips "the letter down to its last exclamation point," flinging "it like confetti out into the water."

In the end, Louise learns the power of both simple music and stories. She comes to understand the story of her own life much better when she finally becomes independent of Caroline by moving to the mountains. There she relives her own birth when she is forced to deliver another set of twins. Now, Louise is ready to let her sister's music back into her life. The novel ends with Caroline's rendition of "I Wonder as I Wander" once more haunting Louise, this time giving her strength. Louise concludes her narrative, saying, "Hours later walking home, my boots crunching on the snow, I bent my head backward to drink in the crystal stars. And clearly, as though the voice came from just behind me, I heard a melody so sweet and pure that I had to hold myself to keep from shattering . . . "

Like *Jacob Have I Loved*, music is also central to *Come Sing, Jimmy Jo*, although it focuses more directly on those who perform the songs. Once again, Paterson argues both for simple music and for books of the "flute solo" variety. The Johnsons are a family of country music singers who have begun to be successful, mainly because of their affecting renditions of simple ballads and folksongs. As they gain fame, however, they are all tempted to change themselves and their music to become more marketable. James, the protagonist, becomes "Jimmy Jo," while his mother, Olive, changes her name to "Keri Su." They soon desert their roots, moving to the city, eliminating first James's grandmother and then his grandfather from the group, opting for more professional backup music.

As the family changes, so does their music. When Keri Su and Earl "steal" James's song, "Broken Bird," their successful recording has "a brassy, synthesized sound, and . . . rhythm souped up with a heavy donk-donk beat." The family's music loses it purity. Both Jimmy Lee and James remark that the sound just isn't the same, not what it used to be. It has changed—the electronic bass is no replacement for the sound of Grandpa Johnson's standing bass. Ultimately, Mr. Wallace, of the television show *Countrytime*, forces the family to realize what they have lost, telling them to return to their original sound. "Now that slick, new Nashville sound is awright for a club," Wallace tells them, "but it don't go over so well here on *Countrytime*, now do it?"

James, however, needs no convincing. He instinctively understands the power of the music he sings, as well as his responsibility to use his gift. During his second appearance on *Countrytime*, James learns to sing to a specific person, in this case, his grandmother:

> With his voice he did what his body could not—he put his arms around his grandma's old body and told her how beautiful she was to him. Maybe through the air waves she could see and hear, could tell that he was still James, that he hadn't forgotten her, that he would never slip up again in a way that would make people sneer at her.
>
> He poured everything into the song—all the pain of the day, all the homesickness of the weeks. When it was over the tears were rolling down his cheeks.

Like Paterson herself, James has learned to send out "the deepest sound from his heart" to create the "true music."

On his next appearance, James is convinced to sing, "My Mama Is a Angel." This time, he sings to both his grandparents, performing "right at the camera to make sure they'd know he was singing for them. He was so full of love that it oozed out his pores, making everyone in the audience think he was in love with them." The song is so powerful, in fact, that afterwards, James is "knocked off his feet by people shoving up, trying to stick autograph books under his nose. . . . "

Like Caroline Bradshaw, James's gift becomes the object of others' jealousy. His mother claims he is trying to upstage her; his uncle Earl constantly disparages him. In the end, after learning that Jimmy Lee is not his real father, James and his family come together again when they sing "Let the Circle Be Unbroken." He realizes both his need to sing and that his audience needs him. Looking out at the crowd, he realizes, for the first time, that it is composed of distinct individuals; they are "so full of love, looking up at him." They are "like little children on Christmas morning—waiting all full of hope for a present." The novel concludes, "And he had the gift."

Of course, early in the novel, his grandmother has already taught him that his gift must be shared. "The Lord don't give private presents," she has told him. She carefully explains, "If he give you somethin', it's only because he thinks you got the sense to share it or give it away. You try to keep the gift to yourself, it's liable to rot. Remember how the Lord give the manna to those Hebrew children? They had to use it or pretty soon it start to crawl with the maggots."

As in *Jacob Have I Loved,* the power of James's music closely resembles that of the books he reads. Chapter 13 of the novel centers on a book report which James has to write and, at first, seems to have little to do with the rest of the novel. In it, James writes an essay on an adult romance which he plucks from his mother's bookshelf at the last minute. He is pleased with the book report he writes; he is convinced Mr. Dolman, his teacher, will give it an "A." James never really connects with the book, *Follow the Wild Wind,* despite the fact that it deals with the question of true parentage, a problem he also faces. His report, recorded in full, indirectly points out the book's overly complicated plot and its unreality.

After condemning the report, Mr. Dolman sees that James finds a "suitable" book so he can write a "suitable" book report. Thus, he sends James to the school librarian, Mrs. Sheldon:

> [At first, James is] insulted by what Mrs. Sheldon thought was suitable for an eleven-year-old boy in the sixth grade who could read a three hundred eighty-four page book—well, almost all the pages—in one night. The book she had given him was far skinnier, with pictures and large print. And it was all about a girl. In the first grade. The longer he read, however, the more he loved the crazy kid. Boy, would Ramona have ever run Mr. Dolman wild.

Paterson herself admits to often recommending Beverly Cleary's *Ramona the Brave* to children with problems and allows James to discover it as well. This simple, skinny "flute solo" of a book strongly affects James who rereads several chapters when he wants to calm down before he performs. Like Louise Bradshaw, James discovers the value of simple stories which, like his own simple music, have great power, despite their lack of "density, intricacy, design."

Ultimately, both *Jacob Have I Loved* and *Come Sing, Jimmy Jo* argue for the affective power of music and literature, as well as the need for flute solos and sym-

phony orchestras. Those who can sing to the oysters, performing carols that almost make the listener shatter, as well as those who can bring to life an Uncas or Ramona, a Louise Bradshaw or James Johnson, create the true music. For Paterson, any act of creation is musical. After all, in *Of Nightingales that Weep,* when Takiko has a baby she is described as "the *koto* of a god whose powerful hand struck a chord so fierce that for a moment she became the storm music of the sea." In her mind, she sings, "I am music and storm and creation." Certainly in her own work, Paterson makes a strong case for her own "music and storm and creation," for flute solos and songs that make you shatter.

Gary D. Schmidt

SOURCE: Preface to *Katherine Paterson,* Twayne Publishers, 1994, pp. vii-ix.

Paterson's novels typically bring characters along the road that Christian trod. They move through various distressing valleys, both of humiliation and of the shadow of death. They search for fathers, for families, for love and acceptance, for themselves. They recall the characters of Flannery O'Connor, who also find themselves caught in moments of distress and then find, like Paterson's characters, moments of grace. That moment may come in the building of a bridge, or in beginning to understand the implications of a carol or poem, or in resolving to live a life of burdens shared. For a Paterson book to work—for it to be effective for a child reader, or any reader—the reader must come to know the feeling.

Gary D. Schmidt

SOURCE: "Conclusion: With the Child's Cooperation," in *Katherine Paterson,* Twayne Publishers, 1994, pp. 135-38.

In her essay **"A Song of Innocence and Experience"** [in *Gates of Excellence*] Katherine Paterson addresses the question of whether she should be considered a didactic writer.

> When I write for the reader whose life I want to change, I am not writing for one of the beautiful people, but for one of the terrified—one of the "tired, the poor, the huddled masses, yearning to breathe free." If you must call me a didactic writer, go ahead. I do believe that those of us who have grown up have something of value to offer the young. And if that is didacticism, well, I have to live with it. But when I write a story, it is not an attempt to make children good or wise—nobody but God can do that, and even God doesn't do it without the child's cooperation. I am trying in a book to give children a place where they may find rest for their weary souls.

Here is a passage that will send up all sorts of flags to moderns; it all sounds positively Victorian. Should a writer be about the business of changing lives? Should a writer be didactic? Aren't children, in all of their spontaneity and innocence, able to teach us adults? Isn't it the adults who have the weary souls and children who are as fresh as a spring of heather? Shouldn't the proper adult role be one of nurturing the child along routes that the child is inclined to rather than plopping down knowledge and wisdom from on high?

To all of this Paterson seems impenitent. If one is to be a spy for hope, as she suggests in her novels, one brings to bear all of the experience that leads one to conclude that life must be lived in the context of hope. This does not mean, her novels assert, that life is easy; life is, in Trotter's word, "tough." It does not mean that life is a desert; it does mean, though, that life is rich. And [as she wrote in her article **"Living in a Peaceful World"** in *The Horn Book Magazine*] Paterson feels very keenly that her role as a novelist for the child reader is to show the child that life is rich:

> We are not living in Nazi Germany, nor in a totalitarian state of the left or of the right. Not yet. But children have only so much time; the world has only so much time. We can't stop children from wasting time, but we don't have to abet it. We can, as far as it lies in our power to do so, offer them books which will nourish them in freedom, justice, and harmony; which will speak to their fears and widen their vision.

In this sense the work of Katherine Paterson is indeed didactic. But what lends Paterson's work its power—in addition to its language, imagery, and deft characterization—is the fusion of story with teaching. The two are woven together in such a way as to make the story predominant, but the story carries with it the teaching—like Yohei's white and glowing cloth marked by a single blood-red line through it. Nancy Huse [in her *Children's Literature Association Quarterly* essay "Katherine Paterson's Ultimate Realism"] sees Paterson's work as being dominated by such a fusion: "Telling the truth in terms of her *zeit* as well as in reference to her private beliefs, Paterson writes stories of children who move from a state of flawed and bitter experience to one of coherence and insight about the ultimate nature of human life." She concludes from this that it is difficult to place Paterson simply in the genre of realistic fiction—a difficulty that may seem specious at first glance. Certainly everything that happens in her novels is within the realm of the possible, therefore she must be seen as a realist. And yet, as Huse suggests, Paterson's goal of "telling the truth," of moving to "ultimate things," makes this categorization an uneasy one.

Paterson is uneasy with categorizations, though she feels comfortable with the label of children's writer. She has frequently been labeled a Christian writer, but there she feels less comfortable, preferring instead to be seen as a writer who is a Christian. Certainly one cannot read her essays in *Gates of Excellence* or *The Spying Heart* for very long without realizing that the Bible and her Christian, specifically Calvinist heritage strongly influences her notion of what humanity is all about. Her

works vibrate to the Calvinist rhythms of fall and redemption, and the hope that she holds out to her child readers is quite distinctly a Christian hope [from Paterson's **"Hope Is More Than Happiness,"** published in the *The New York Times Book Review*]:

> As a spiritual descendant of Moses, and the prophets and apostles who followed him, I have to think of hope in this context. We are not really optimists as the common definition goes, because we, like Moses, must be realistic about the world in which we find ourselves. And this world looked at squarely does not allow optimism to flourish. Hope for us cannot simply be wishful thinking, nor can it be only the desire to grow up and take control over our own lives. Hope is a yearning, rooted in reality, that pulls us toward the radical biblical vision of a world where truth and justice and peace do prevail, a time in which the knowledge of God will cover the earth as the waters cover the sea, a scene which finds humanity living in harmony with nature, all nations beating their swords into plowshares and walking together by the light of God's glory. Now there's a happy ending for you. The only purely happy ending I know of.

It is hard to imagine other children's authors who are or have been so explicit about faith commitments. Perhaps only C. S. Lewis or Madeleine L'Engle come to mind. Certainly it is the case that if one is to understand the hope Paterson examines through her novels, and the hope that Paterson holds out to her readers, one must understand her biblical, Calvinist perspective.

Perhaps it is ironic that when Paterson's novels are attacked, they are more often than not attacked by Christian groups. *The Great Gilly Hopkins* has been attacked for its profanity, *Of Nightingales That Weep* for the marriage of a stepdaughter and stepfather, and *Bridge to Terabithia* for the crush that Jess has on Miss Edmunds and the scene in which Jess prays to spirits. Paterson seems aware of the possibility for offense as she describes some of her early novels [in *Gates of Excellence*]:

> In the first, the hero is a bastard, and the chief female character ends up in a brothel. In the second, the heroine has an illicit love affair, her mother dies in a plague, and most of her companions commit suicide. In the third, which is full of riots in the streets, the hero's best friend is permanently maimed. In the fourth, a central child character dies in an accident. In the fifth, turning away from the mayhem in the first four, I wrote what I refer to as my "funny book." In it the heroine merely fights, lies, steals, cusses, bullies an emotionally disturbed child, and acts out her racial bigotry in a particularly vicious manner.

Stated baldly, this does seem to be a line of novels filled with distress, anguish, and viciousness. But in fact each of these elements is placed in the context of hope. The bastard hero finds a true father, the heroine who finds illicit love also finds true love, the maiming of a protagonist's friend leads to the healing of two parent/child relationships, the death of one child leads to new life for another and others after him, and the stealing and cussing of Gilly give way to clouds of glory. Hope is a yearning rooted in reality, looking forward toward joy.

Paterson will be remembered for her powerful plots, but she will also be remembered for telling the truth about universal things. Her work is, as I suggested in the preface, story woven with truth, so that the reader will know the place and the feeling. It is a bridge lovingly and expertly built, girded by the reality of a fallen world, and arching gracefully toward the Promised Land, for which she is a spy.

TITLE COMMENTARY

JACOB HAVE I LOVED (1980)

Caroline R. Goforth

SOURCE: "The Role of the Island in *Jacob Have I Loved*," in *Children's Literature Association Quarterly*, Vol. 9, No. 4, Winter, 1984-85, pp. 176-78, 198.

John Donne may have thought "no man is an island," but he never knew Louise Bradshaw. The prickly heroine of Katherine Paterson's *Jacob Have I Loved* certainly lives in the right place. As Paterson herself pointed out in her Newbery Medal acceptance, the Chesapeake Bay setting of the novel reflects Louise's feelings of isolation. And Rass Island is charged with other associations essential to understanding Louise's character. Stark and treeless, with graves in its front yards, the island is as much a desert as Louise's resentful, angry self. At the same time, the tightly organized social structure of the island provides a refuge for the inhabitants, just as Louise's withdrawal from others contributes to her developing self-reliance.

As an image, the island is particularly rich because of its complex associations. Carl Jung notes its multifaceted nature as refuge, as limitation, and as region of danger. In his essay on transference he uses the island as an image for the consciousness of a patient who is hesitating to confront the contents of the unconscious. Though the island is a necessary refuge against the unconscious the person fears, Jung points out in *The Practice of Psychotherapy* that the doctor "knows that the island is a bit cramped and that life on it is pretty meagre and plagued with all sorts of imaginary wants because too much life has been left outside. . . . " Louise spends her adolescence in just such a state, desperately clinging to a stagnant, shrinking self, afraid to make the human connections that would open her to love and to a new range of experience and awareness. In *Psychology and Alchemy* Jung identifies the island with the "region of danger" to which the hero of a myth must descend to find the treasure. The treasure Louise seeks is release from the "hate and guilt and damnation" she

associates with the island. Paradoxically, attaining redemption means learning to love her island self, embracing the very region of danger she fears.

Because the island setting reflects Louise's personality and because her activities on and in reference to the island parallel her progress toward self-acceptance and toward loving relationships with others, the influence of place on character and theme can be explored by examining Rass Island in light of Jung's associations—as refuge, as limitation, and as region of danger.

As refuge, Rass Island provides a quiet, isolated environment for a population that lives close to nature. The social structure provides a well-ordered support system with its own set of values and its own socio-economic hierarchy. Though culturally separate from the mainland, the Rass Islanders are not cut off from the outside world. For example, medical care must be obtained on the mainland. Islanders who view Rass primarily as a refuge are Louise's mother, Susan Bradshaw, and Captain Hiram Wallace. Susan came to the island because "it seemed romantic" and she hoped to find herself. When Louise presses her to justify the use she has made of her life, she admits that she "found nothing much to find" in herself. The natural cycle of life with her waterman husband Truitt, her vitriolic mother-in-law, and her twin daughters has satisfied her because she has lived in love. Captain Wallace, on the other hand, fled the island in disgrace after revealing himself as a coward when he chopped down the mast of his father's boat during a storm. When he comes back nearly fifty years later, he has apparently made peace with his alienated island self and has returned to the physical refuge that represents the core of himself.

Louise also finds refuge on the physical island and in her island self. Whenever she needs refuge for consolation of for solitude, she goes to a driftwood stump at the south end of Rass. On one occasion soon after Pearl Harbor, she melodramatically proposes to her teacher and classmates that they "cancel Christmas". She is humiliated by her teacher's lack of support and by her classmates' ridicule. As soon as school is dismissed, she races to the driftwood stump and spends the afternoon there, leaving reluctantly only after her despised twin sister Caroline comes looking for her.

Louise's island self is the refuge she seeks when she withdraws from relationships with others, and she relies heavily on that self, rarely asking any kind of help from anybody. Instead, the money she earns supplements the family's income, paying for Caroline's voice and piano lessons. When she convinces herself that escape from Rass to boarding school will release her from her hatred of Caroline and from her guilt, she doubles her crabbing efforts and even tries writing song lyrics. Hoping for physical rescue from the island, she takes her letter from Lyrics Unlimited to the driftwood stump. But the letter is a mimeographed form, offering encouragement only at a price and personalized only by her name, which is misspelled. While the mainland seems to welcome Caroline with open arms, Louise is rejected in her first attempt at joining the outside world, and the driftwood stump, an island on an island, seems the appropriate place for her as she slips further into herself.

Perhaps Louise's most significant period of refuge is what she calls her "time of hibernation," when she withdraws from everyone but her parents, quits school and church, and goes to work full time with her father. . . .

To seek refuge is often to accept limitation, for shutting out requires keeping in. The people of Rass are limited by their isolation. Most have only a minimal education, and their Methodism is a narrow, severe version of Christianity. That their social contacts are painfully restricted is evident in the lives of Grandma Bradshaw and Trudy Braxton, both of whom loved Captain Wallace in their youth. Few islanders marry mainlanders, and Louise mentions that her family lived on Rass Island for two hundred years, an indication that the population is inbred. Because the island is so small, families bury their dead in their front yards, a visible reminder of the cramped, tradition-bound society.

Louise's character is shaped by the limitations of her environment. She rarely leaves the island, usually staying behind with Grandma while her mother and sister go to the mainland for groceries and music lessons. Though she tells herself she wants to go to boarding school and even implements plans for earning extra money, she refuses to go when her parents offer her the chance. Her physical isolation reflects her self-obsession and her failure to establish relationships with others. She is disgusted by Caroline's public displays of affection and jealous of her sister's ability to make friends. She looks so intently inward, however, that she is not sensitive to others. She ignores her friend Call Purnell's feelings, yet is enraged when he asks Caroline to marry him. When she flings her arms around the Captain in a burst of sympathy after his home is destroyed, she immediately supplants warmth with self-absorbed eroticism. When Trudy dies, Caroline takes his hand at the funeral while Louise cringes from him in sudden realization of his age. As Rass Island can not touch another land mass, neither can Louise touch others physically or emotionally. Caroline, however, has no trouble expressing affection. It is no surprise that she moves freely back and forth from island to mainland.

The physical limitations of Rass Island, especially its size, also make it a region of danger. Storms are a matter of course. Preparing for them is as much a part of the island's order as Wednesday night prayer meeting, and cleaning up after them is just another chore. But their threat to life is real, and their gradual gnawing away at the island will eventually end the watermen's way of life. During the storm that destroys the Captain's house, the sea gobbles up the south marsh and puts Louise's driftwood stump out of reach.

The danger is internal, too. Just as the island is shrink-

ing, so Louise is withdrawing further into her isolation. She becomes more jealous of her sister when Caroline establishes friendships with Call and the Captain. . . .

Between this time and the winter she goes to work on the *Portia Sue,* Louise risks losing herself on the island of hate and jealousy and fear she has become. At the same time she can not abandon her shrunken self-concept, for she must build a stronger self from it. If she fails, she will grow into the likeness of the woman for whom she is named—Grandma Louise Bradshaw.

Grandma is Louise's ever-present reminder that the island of self-obsession is a region dangerous to the point of destruction. "I hate the water," says Grandma constantly. What she really means is that she hates anything beyond the island, that she hates anything beyond her desert island self. Grandma's total self-absorption is represented by her refusal ever to leave the house. She has become an island that has lost its identity to resentment and bitterness.

In addition to its role as setting for most of Louise's story, the island functions as a point away from which most of the characters act. Only Grandma never leaves the island. Even Trudy Braxton is moved to the mainland to be healed physically at the hospital and emotionally by her marriage to the Captain.

Louise's spiritual progress is also mirrored in her painfully slow physical departure from the island. The deadly desertness of Rass Island is concentrated in Grandma's character. Every member of the family must deal with her empty hatred, through escape or through acceptance. Even in the beginning of the novel, Louise is straining to rid herself of the dark, isolated chaos Grandma represents, and her effort is paralleled by her active outdoor life with Call. The island marsh is a morass that symbolizes Louise's inner stagnation; and her dredging and probing of the marsh parallel her inner struggle to find a way out of her anger and frustration. Her decision to work with her father on the *Portia Sue,* as well as her attitude toward this time in her life, is a significant advancement in her development. She leaves the island, if only to explore a narrow band of water around it. Her father, who has always avoided the limitations of the island by following the water, guides her physically and psychically, giving her the space she needs to move outward. Both he and Louise's mother are sensitive to her needs, neither pushing her to fulfill their expectations nor blocking her withdrawal from society in the form of church and school. With Caroline gone, with increased confidence in herself as a productive member of the family, Louise is eventually able to accept the fact that her parents and the Captain love her and view her as a strong individual capable of planning and directing a future away from the island. Her entrance into the human fellowship is predictably accompanied by physically breaking outside the island's circle, to attend college and to settle in the mountains she has dreamed of for so many years.

Louise does find her redemption and her connection with others—in her marriage, in her work as a nurse-midwife, and in her reconciliation with her sister. But why does she trade one island for another? She describes Truitt, the Appalachian community where she chooses to live, as "a mountain-locked valley . . . more like an island than anything else I know." Throughout the story, setting has reflected Louise's mental state. Assuming the correspondence continues, how can she be a strong, loving person and still live in a place that she herself sees as an island?

The answer may lie in the character of the island. For Louise, Rass Island, as well as her stunted, hating island self, served during her adolescence as refuge, limitation, and region of danger. All these elements remain in her adult life in Truitt, but they are set within a context of island as home, as center. As long as Louise's attention is directed inward, her self has no room to grow, and the concern of those who love her cannot penetrate. But when she reaches out to the people of Truitt and through them to her sister, she opens herself to the potential of love. In "The Aim of the Writer Who Writes for Children," Paterson points out that the novel is not a quest for self knowledge but a story of reconciliation. She emphasizes the focal point of Louise's experience in delivering the mountain girl's twins as her recognition that she has loved Caroline. As she turns her attention outward, her island self becomes an island home from which she can move outward and into which she can invite the people she loves.

John Donne notwithstanding, every man and every woman must exist as an island, but love realizes the potential of bridging gulfs to touch one another. When Louise finally turns outward, she does not begin to love Caroline; instead, she discovers that she *has loved* her sister. From earliest childhood she has thought of Caroline in images of light, and she has admired Caroline's talent. Her resentment and jealousy have always been perverted love. Her hatred has been for herself, the twin she has always linked to shadow images. Through selfless love Louise finally discovers self love. There is room for the old Louise on the island home.

The adult Louise's acceptance of herself is mirrored in her warm description of Rass Island in the first chapter of the novel. She introduces herself as a character "straining for the first sight of *my* island" (italics mine). With this use of "my" she embraces the island that symbolizes her isolated, eroding, adolescent self; and just before she begins the flashback that is her story, she sets it in the context of its end. "I love Rass Island," she says, "although for much of my life, I did not think I did. . . . "

Patricia A. Liddie

SOURCE: "Vision of Self in Katherine Paterson's *Jacob Have I Loved*," in *The ALAN Review,* Vol. 21, No. 3, Spring, 1994, pp. 51-2.

Set almost entirely on a fictional Chesapeake Bay island in the mid-to-late 1940s, *Jacob Have I Loved* chronicles one person's search for and acceptance of self. Although intended for an audience of young adult readers, Katherine Paterson's portrayal of this personal journey is so real that it has achieved universal appeal. The beauty of teaching this Newbery Award-winning classic, then, is that the work is as meaningful to teacher as it is to student, to forty-year old as it is to fourteen-year-old.

Jacob Have I Loved takes its title from the Biblical story about Jacob and Esau, the twin sons of Isaac and Rebecca. The relationship between the sons is one of jealousy bordering on violence. Esau, the first born, foolishly gives up his birthright out of physical hunger and later loses his rightful blessing as a result of the deceit of his mother and brother. Even God turns against Esau. In Romans 9:13, God says, "Jacob I loved and Esau I hated." Thus Esau is an extremely bitter person who feels so victimized, so angry, that he is believed capable of murder. Jacob, afraid of his brother, leaves, only to return years later to a reconciliation with Esau, who has remained at home assuming all of the responsibilities that would have been his anyway had he received the blessing he deserved.

In *Jacob Have I Loved,* the parallels to the Jacob-and-Esau story are clear. This is the story of Sara Louise Bradshaw and her twin sister, Caroline. Sara Louise, born first, is healthy and strong whereas Caroline is weak and near death, thus becoming the focus of concern and attention from the start.

> I was the elder by a few minutes. I always treasured the thought of those minutes. They represented the only time in my life when I was the center of everyone's attention. From the moment Caroline was born, she snatched it all for herself.

> I felt cold all over, as though I was the newborn infant a second time, cast aside and forgotten.

> The story always left the other twin, the stronger twin, washed and dressed and lying in a basket. Clean and cold and motherless.

These feelings of resentment, having had their inception at birth, continue throughout Sara Louise's youth. She is in a futile situation as she strives to define herself in terms of her sister. Even in their teenage years, Sara Louise feels robbed, victimized, and completely unappreciated. Caroline, on the other hand, with her operatic voice and golden good looks, is smiled on by all, and "Caroline is the kind of person other people sacrifice for as a matter of course."

And sacrifice they do, not only Sara Louise and her parents, but also an island friend who gives Caroline money in order that she may leave the island and attend music school. Thus, Sara Louise, the "Esau figure," is left behind on the island. Caroline's leaving is just as well, because, like the elder twin in the Biblical story, Sara Louise finds herself entertaining thoughts of her sibling's death. . . .

It is only with Caroline's departure from Rass Island that Sara Louise can even begin her search for self. That search must begin at home, for thus far in her life she has seen herself in the role of sacrificer. Although bordering on martyrdom, she does truly feel that her father Truitt, a fisherman, needs her help to make up for the absence of young men during this time of war. There is more to her problem than her need to help her father, however. Sara Louise is almost incapable of moving on towards another phase in her life. Indeed, her vision of herself at this point in her life is tied as inextricably to her vision of her surroundings as it is to her vision of Caroline as the favored child. The island of Rass has come to reflect the island that is her soul. Throughout the course of the novel, we see Sara Louise becoming more and more island-like in her relationship to those around her. Ironically, as she sacrifices for others, she withdraws from them. As she attempts to increase their need of her (thus gaining their attention), she more and more tries to deny her need of them. Needing them, she pushes them away, fortifying her walls of defense. "I was a good oyster in those days. Not even the presence at Christmastime of a radiant, grown-up Caroline could get under my shell."

Having spent a year with her father, Truitt, helping him support the family, Sara Louise, an Esau-hunter figure fishing the waters of the Chesapeake, is ultimately liberated, not by her Isaac-like father but, rather, by her unRebecca-like mother, Susan. No woman of deceit, this mother shares with her daughter her own youthful journey toward and realization of self, and, in so doing, opens her daughter's eyes to her own choices and potential actions.

> And, oh my blessed, she was right. All my dreams of leaving, but neath them I was afraid to go. I had clung to them, to Rass, yes, even to my grandmother, afraid that if I loosened my fingers an iota, I would find myself once more cold and clean in a forgotten basket.

> "I chose the island," she said. "I chose to leave my own people and build a life for myself somewhere else. I certainly wouldn't deny you that same choice. But," and her eyes held me if her arms did not, "oh, Louise, we will miss you, your father and I."

> I wanted so to believe her. "Will you really?" I asked. "As much as you miss Caroline?"

> "More," she said, reaching up and ever so lightly smoothing my hair with her fingertips.

> I did not press her to explain. I was too grateful for that one word that allowed me at last to leave the island and begin to build myself as a soul, separate from the long, long shadow of my twin.

And so Sara Louise's journey toward enlightenment, toward an understanding of others and an understanding of self, truly begins. Before the novel ends, she has gone through college, graduating as a nurse-midwife. In that capacity, she moves to a poverty-stricken Appalachian mountain town, chosen because its name is Truitt, the same as her father's. Never far from her past, she has moved from one island existence (Rass) to another (Truitt). Sara Louise herself observes that "A mountain-locked valley is more like an island than anything else I know." It is here in Truitt that she meets and marries her husband and bears her son whom she names Truitt. Thus, as Paterson moves toward the resolution of the Jacob-and-Esau conflict, she introduces the image of the Holy Trinity as a guiding factor in Sara Louise's life at this point.

As readers, we are certainly aware of her father as Truitt and her son as Truitt; but, if they are to be considered the first two parts of the Trinity, then the town of Truitt must be considered the last, that of the Holy Spirit. An examination of the concept of the Holy Spirit and the novel's final scenes explains all. The Holy Spirit is that part of the Trinity that is active and enabling: it enables us to see; it causes change and it enlightens; it moves a person from where she is to where she needs to be. The Holy Spirit is responsible for knowledge and wisdom. And it is in the town of Truitt that Sara Louise is enlightened, able to see and finally understand self. It is here that she recognizes, becomes, and accepts self, something that could only happen as a result of understanding her own haunting birth.

Paterson develops this understanding by Sara Louise in the novel's final chapter, in which she is called to help in the delivery of twins born to a young and impoverished woman named Essie. As the delivery begins, we are reminded of the story of the birth of Caroline and Sara Louise. The circumstances are parallel:

> The first twin, a nearly six-pound boy, came fairly easily, despite Essie's slender frame, but the second did not follow as I thought it should. . . . Before I even cut the cord, I put my mouth down and breathed into her tiny one.

And so in the case of her own birth, the healthier first-born is placed in a basket and given to the grandmother for safekeeping, seemingly forgotten. The weaker of the two, the "Caroline twin," receives all of Sara Louise's attention. Warming the baby by the kitchen oven door, Sara Louise is approached by the babies' father who asks that the weak one be baptized in the event of her death. Sara Louise consents, even though, "I wanted to be left in peace to guard my baby." (Note the use of the possessive pronoun.) She baptizes the child Essie Susan, giving her an identity " . . . in the name of the Father and of the Son and of the Holy Ghost. Amen." She then proceeds to feed this Essie Susan, this Caroline, with her own breast milk. "I took my baby out of the oven and held her mouth to catch the milk, which began to flow of its own accord."

Embodied in this weaker twin, then, are Caroline, the babies' mother (Susan), and Sara Louise (Essie-Esau) herself. Through the act of breathing life into the child ("breath" being "spirit") and then feeding her, Sara Louise does what she has always done for Caroline: she takes part in her nurturing. Even more, however, she is also forgiving her mother. She does this by feeding the child as her mother fed Caroline, thus finally exhibiting an understanding of and acceptance of her mother's actions during that other delivery so many years before. Of course, most important of all, Sara Louise nourishes self, for the Trinity is complete. She has acquired knowledge and understanding of her own birth and, therefore, reborn, nurtures her new self, that self which not only hears but now can welcome the line of the hymn that Caroline had sung so many years before: "I wonder as I wander out under the sky. . . ."

Jacob Have I Loved, like so many of Katherine Paterson's works, confirms the importance of the individual as set against the backdrop of all humanity. To her youthful audience, the author declares her belief in the one and in the whole and, in so doing, reminds them of their role in the larger scheme of things. This novel is indeed a classic, and the beauty of it is that it's so readable for and appropriate to the older junior-high student. At a time when vision of self is all-important, ninth graders are relieved to discover that most of us take years to find self and to accept the self that we find, that such acceptance is not an easy passage, and that, very often, the self we find is not the one we expected.

Janice Mori Gallagher

SOURCE: "Pairing Adolescent Fiction with Books from the Canon," in *Journal of Adolescent & Adult Literacy,* Vol. 39, No. 1, September, 1995, pp. 8-14.

In the push to integrate the curriculum, pairing of books surfaces as yet another way to make learning meaningful. Pairing books allows both "teachers and students to feel a sense of progression" [according to K. Donelson and A. Nilsen in *Literature for Today's Young Adults*]. Pairing an adolescent novel with a more difficult novel requires two steps. First the teacher selects an adolescent novel to use as a springboard to the adult novel. The idea is that the teacher hooks the young readers with a manageable adolescent novel. The second step comes once the readers have tasted success with the adolescent novel and have experienced the joys that reading can bring. The teacher encourages the readers to move from adolescent fiction to the successful reading of a classic or an advanced novel.

By connecting an adolescent novel to a more advanced novel, the students learn another important lesson. Themes weave the tapestry of the written word and of life itself. By understanding the connections and by being able to relate theme to theme and book to book, the students learn to make associations and connections.

As Donelson and Nilsen state, "the long-term benefit for young readers is that they are more likely to make the connection between adolescent literature and its adult counterpart (and then go on to become lifelong readers)." Perhaps an even deeper and more lasting long-term effect exists. Learning to find the connections and to make the associations from theme to theme and book to book is good practice for finding connections throughout life. This finding of connections is one important way for a person to feel an integral part of total living. Making connections fosters a concern for the world and empathy for fellow human beings. . . .

[In *Jacob Have I Loved,* twins] Caroline and Louise, growing up in the Chesapeake Bay area in the early 1940s, present the struggle of siblings vying for their parents' attention and love. Louise, the elder twin, feels that, like the biblical Esau, she is the despised daughter. She believes that Caroline has robbed her of any hopes for advanced education. In addition, Louise blames Caroline for robbing her of her mother's attention, her friends, and even her name (which Caroline has shortened to "Wheeze").

Young readers, both male and female, will have little difficulty associating with the problems these two sisters face. Learning to live with a sibling who is weaker or smarter or better looking is nothing new to any adolescent. Readers may identify with Caroline, who is gifted musically and knows exactly what she wants to do with her life. They may identify with Louise whose life in Caroline's shadow adds to the confusion she feels about the direction she wants her life to take. Only when Louise stops focusing on Caroline and begins to focus on herself do things begin to change for her.

King Lear [by William Shakespeare] presents readers with siblings, also sisters, who compete for their father's love. Before King Lear divides his property among his three daughters, he wants them to come before him to tell him how much they love him. Regan and Goneril pour forth the words they know their father wants to hear. Cordelia, on the other hand, claims that it is her nature to show her love for her father—not to talk about it. Angered, King Lear divides his kingdom between Regan and Goneril, leaving the honest Cordelia nothing. Regan and Goneril prove to be greedy and cruel. Neither daughter shows real love or compassion for their father. Too late, King Lear realizes his mistake, and knows that it is Cordelia alone who really loves him.

These two works can be paired to enhance a discussion of sibling rivalry, family relationships, and the different ways that people show their love for each other. Students can also discuss the various roles each person plays within a family unit. They can compare the sisters or the plot development found in these two works. Students can also discuss the difference it makes in a piece of literature when an ending is happy as in the case of *Jacob Have I Loved* or tragic as in *King Lear*.

📖 *COME SING, JIMMY JO* (1985)

Cathryn A. Camper

SOURCE: A review of *Come Sing, Jimmy Jo,* in *School Library Journal,* Vol. 31, No. 8, April, 1985, p. 91.

Paterson's talent for storytelling truly shines in this book. Music has always been the center of James' life. His parents and his uncle sing in the family bluegrass band. While the family is away performing, James stays in the country with his grandmother, who was also part of the band before she grew too old to travel with them. All this changes when the family decides to include James in the singing group. James is forced to move with his family to the city, away from his grandmother, so the group can be closer to the television studios where they perform. Now James is known as Jimmy Jo, the star singer on the *Countrytime* TV show. With fame comes new problems: fans hound him, and he must adjust to a new school. James' mother becomes jealous of his stardom and treats him coldly, and he learns that Jerry Lee is not his biological father. At first, he hates his new life and wants only to go back home. But gradually, James comes to terms with both the joys and heartbreaks of his musical talent—what his grandmother calls a "gift." Paterson captures the subtleties of childhood friendships in James' relationships with his classmates and records family interaction with a sensitive ear. The book expresses a deep appreciation for the tribulations of a child growing up gifted and reflects the heartfelt energy of the Appalachian music and people it describes. Like James' songs, this book is a gift to its audience, a special gift, that should not be passed by.

Kirkus Reviews

SOURCE: A review of *Come Sing, Jimmy Jo,* in *Kirkus Reviews,* Vol. LIII, No. 5, May 15, 1985, p. J-43.

His name is James, but the Johnson Family's new agent changes it to Jimmy Jo when the 11-year-old joins the adults in their country music group. So shy at the start that he will sing only for his beloved Grandma, James finds himself on stage "so anxious to sing and pick that he never once thought about being scared." A sweet singer with what Grandma calls "the Gift," he pours all his love for her into his delivery, and the crowd goes wild. Soon, he is singing just as sincerely out of love for the audience.

Trouble is, his uncle Earl (Daddy Jerry Lee's brother) doesn't want James butting in, and his mother Keri Su feels eclipsed by his success. So Keri Su and Earl go their own way with a flashier sound; and when their new slickness doesn't go over on the family TV show, the two split for Nashville and cut a record—of the song Daddy wrote for James! Worse, it seems there's more than music between the two. Why won't Daddy stand up to them? Then, to James' grief, he discovers that Jerry

Lee is not his father. Upset with all the Johnsons, he refuses to join them onstage.

There is more to James' story: his whole other, uncomfortable life at school adds flesh and texture, as well as urgency, for James and some humorous relief for readers. Paterson is so good at making readers feel for and with her child character that any question of manipulation is bound to appear unseemly. And if the more resistant will wince at the family's last-page reunion onstage, most readers will have already given their hearts to Jimmy Jo.

Campbell Geeslin

SOURCE: A review of *Come Sing, Jimmy Jo,* in *The New York Times Book Review,* May 26, 1985, p. 26.

During the late 1930's, the best thing about a family visit to my cousin Mary Louise's house in Goldthwaite, Tex., was her mother's poems. Aunt Virginie grew up in West Virginia and had memorized old rhyming stories. One was about a little boy whose father died. The boy wrote him a letter in care of heaven, put a stamp on it, ran out to mail it and was hit by a carriage and killed. The poem concluded, amid a heavy flow of tears from little listeners, that the letter was getting special delivery.

Katherine Paterson's new novel has that same kind of direct, no-nonsense approach to grabbing a reader's emotions and wringing out the tears. Her subject is a family of country singers, and the quality of the prose in this story is much like the lyrics of their songs. These include such numbers as "My Momma Is a Angel Up in Heaven" and "In the Sweet Bye and Bye."

Eleven-year-old James lives with his beloved Grandma on a farm in the West Virginia mountains. The rest of the Johnson family—Grandpa, Uncle Earl, Jerry Lee and Olive (the last two are James's parents)—are on the road most of the time, singing gospel and country music at fairs and church meetings. Grandma's singing voice has gone, but she has taught James all the family's songs. James plays a guitar named Chester and wears glasses like John Denver, who sings "too much folk and pop to be genuine country."

Hoping to move into the big time, the family hires an agent. He comes to the house, overhears James singing and, with the boy as part of their act, gets the family a contract to do a weekly television show in Tidewater, VA, James's simple life at home with Grandma is over. His name is changed to Jimmy Jo, and his mother, Olive, becomes Keri Su. He has to go to a city school where the students are all colors and he is an outsider, longing desperately to get by unnoticed.

As a performer, James's shyness works in his favor. But he is not prepared for his fans. After the first television show, women from the audience rush to the stage. "One of them poked her face right down into James's. 'You so sweet, I could eat you right up,' she said, grinning as though she just might."

His daddy, Jerry Lee, writes a sad song about a little bird just for James to sing, and when his mother and Uncle Earl sneak off to Nashville and record it as a duet, "Broken Bird" becomes a hit. Then a strange man begins turning up, even on the school grounds, wanting to talk to James; his Grandma goes to the hospital with a heart ailment, his mother is acting funny, and James's problems begin to seem overwhelming.

Mrs. Paterson, a National Book Award and two-time Newbery Medal winner, has written a novel about China in the 1850's (*Rebels of the Heavenly Kingdom*), translated a Japanese folk tale (*The Crane Wife*), solved a "forgotten twin" problem in a story set on a Chesapeake Bay island (*Jacob Have I Loved*), confronted racism in an urban school (*The Great Gilly Hopkins*) and created an imaginative, surprisingly upbeat story of death (*Bridge to Terabithia*). Her range in both subject matter and settings is amazing.

In *Come Sing, Jimmy Jo,* Mrs. Paterson provides an engaging fantasy about what it might be like to become famous. Young people, who see so much about celebrities on television, will surely be fascinated. With touching seriousness, James finally succeeds in handling life's complexities. And through the character of the wonderfully funny and wise Grandma, Mrs. Paterson provides something more than entertainment. When James asks why his own mother seems jealous of him, Grandma says: "Nothin's ever pure, James. Joy and pain always show up in the same wrapper." Sounds just like the lyrics of a country music hit, doesn't it?

Zena Sutherland

SOURCE: A review of *Come Sing, Jimmy Jo,* in *Bulletin of the Center for Children's Books,* Vol. 38, No. 10, June, 1985, pp. 191-92.

This is a story of country music, of family bonding and friction, and above all of the realignment of perspectives for eleven-year-old Jimmy Jo. His real name is James, and he is uncomfortable with the "Jimmy Jo" his mother (who has also decided she'll be known as Keri Su rather than Olive) has decided should be his professional name. He joins the family singing group, and his sweet singing brings them more fame than they've ever had. It also brings publicity, and with his new prominence James is a target for fans, and for a man who insists he's James' real father. What James learns to accept is the fact that the man's telling the truth and that the loving man he's always called his father is still the one he loves. He even understands why Olive never told him, understands why the family circle must hold fast. This is a tender, touching story of familial love that prevails over the petty jealousies and abrasions of family life and the tensions of professional differences. Paterson creates strong characters and convincing dialogue, so that her story is ef-

fective even to those to whom the heavy emphasis on country music strikes no sympathetic chord.

Ethel L. Heins

SOURCE: A review of *Come Sing, Jimmy Jo,* in *The Horn Book Magazine,* Vol. LXI, No. 4, July-August, 1985, p. 456.

Having written historical fiction about Japan and China as well as American regional novels, the versatile author turns to another setting she knows well—Appalachia. The Johnsons are a country music family, but now Grandma's voice is old and cracked; so, while the others travel about as singers and "string pickers," Grandma is content to stay at home with eleven-year-old James— small for his age, bespectacled, and timid. But she knows that the boy, with his sweet, pure voice, is the most gifted of them all. When the family takes on a professional manager, James is pushed into joining the group. Now life for him is full of terrifying changes: It is decided to give him a stage personality and call him Jimmy Jo, while the flashy, ambitious Olive, his mother, becomes Keri-Su—which to James "sounded more like a Barbie doll than a mother." Worst of all, the boy has to wrench himself away from his adored grandmother and the serenity of his West Virginia mountain home. Feeling like a hillbilly stranger in his city school, James also finds little peace with the family. His mother seems actually jealous of the instant popularity he wins from his "whooping and hollering" fans, and even the boy's patient, forgiving father appears unable to prevent a family split when James's mother, together with his uncle, threatens to desert their old-time country sound for "what Grandma would call Nashville honky-tonk." Katherine Paterson has said, "When I look at the books I have written, the first thing I see is the outcast child searching for a place to stand." James may well be distantly related to Jesse in *Bridge to Terabithia*, and although the two books are vastly different, they share an essential theme. Adjusting her storytelling to its context, the author writes without a trace of self-consciousness in a fluent, effortless, supple style. And what might have become a sentimental melodrama is peppered with native humor as she looks with clear-eyed compassion and emotional honesty at her characters and their circumscribed lives.

CONSIDER THE LILIES: PLANTS OF THE BIBLE (with husband John Paterson, 1986)

Pat Pearl

SOURCE: A review of *Consider the Lilies: Plants of the Bible,* in *School Library Journal,* Vol. 33, No. 2, October, 1986, p. 181.

Handsomely presented material on 45 shrubs, crops, trees, weeds, fruits, and flowers mentioned in the Old and New Testaments with emphasis on the rich symbolic values of each. Divided into three groups—plants of Revelation, Necessity, and Celebration—each plant is cited in a Bible story or passage (quoted from the King James, New English, or Revised Standard versions of the Bible or paraphrased with graceful dignity). Plants of Revelation include the apple in the Garden of Eden, Jeremiah's Balm of Gilead, the mustard seed, etc. Plants of Necessity are foods such as Esau's lentils and Ruth's barley. Solomon's lily, the oils of anointment, and palm branches represent some of the plants of Celebration. Sometimes the categories overlap, as with the olive and the grape, which fit into all three, but the groupings help give order to the work. Most of the plants are shown, alone or in groups, in meticulous and elegant color illustrations [by Anne Ophelia Dowden] painted from living specimens and shown two-thirds of their actual size. Botanic names are given. Each is accompanied by a lengthy caption discussing the Biblical history, usages, and symbolic meanings. Added beauty is given by an attractive variety of clear type-faces. Carol Lerner's *A Biblical Garden* is also a fine book on this subject, but it covers only half as many plants and uses only citations from the Old Testament.

Betsy Hearne

SOURCE: A review of *Consider the Lilies: Plants of the Bible,* in *Bulletin of the Center for Children's Books,* Vol. 40, No. 3, November, 1986, pp. 55-6.

The Patersons have selected verses from various translations of the Bible, with a few adaptations of their own, centering on plants important for symbolic, cultural, or material reasons: the lily, the laurel, and the lentil represent a cross-section. [Anne Ophelia] Dowden's botanical drawing is, as usual, meticulously detailed and colored. The problem here is a format that sometimes causes organizational confusion. The layout follows a pattern of Bible passage(s), plant picture, and information; but these pages are sometimes staggered rather than sequential, as in the case of barley and corn poppies, a double-page informational spread that falls in the middle of the story of Ruth. There is also an occasional confusion in the factual references: anemones are illustrated on page 6 but not mentioned until page 74; laurel is illustrated beside a section that does not mention it; the first illustration is not labeled at all; the date looks to be part of the fig foliage, while the date palm is shown in a later section. Although these are quibbles, they may trip the untutored. On the other hand, the quality of the art and intelligent explanations coupled with carefully selected examples from both Old and New Testaments will make the book prime read-aloud material for family sharing, Sunday School classes, and religious reports.

Ethel L. Heins

SOURCE: A review of *Consider the Lilies: Plants of the Bible,* in *The Horn Book Magazine,* Vol. LXIII, No. 2, March-April, 1987, pp. 224-25.

A Presbyterian pastor and a much-honored writer have collaborated with a distinguished botanical painter to produce a volume gracefully written, elegantly designed, and exquisitely illustrated in full color. In an unusual approach to an understanding of the Bible, the authors examine the symbolism as well as the scientific, historical, and contextual aspects of numerous trees and plants, fruits and flowers referred to in the Old Testament and the New. Making use of modern scholarship in the translation of ancient Hebrew and Greek texts and in the study of Palestinian botany, they divide the book into three sections—Revelation, Necessity, and Celebration—and point out that functions may overlap and that a plant may belong in more than one section. Botanical names are given, along with common English nomenclature. In some cases Biblical passages are paraphrased and narratives retold, while some excerpts are quoted directly, chiefly from the Revised Standard Version. The illustrator, [Anne Ophelia Dowden] known for her astonishing detail and precision, works slowly and painstakingly, first doing elaborate research and then using as models nothing but living, often fragile, specimens—many of which she cultivates herself. The illustrated plants are exactly two-thirds of their natural size. In beauty, scope, and abundance of information, the unique book surpasses Carol Lerner's *A Biblical Garden,* which includes only Old Testament material. List of scriptural references and index of plants.

PARK'S QUEST (1988)

Kirkus Reviews

SOURCE: A review of *Park's Quest,* in *Kirkus Reviews,* Vol. LVI, No. 5, March 1, 1988, p. 368.

In a multilayered novel filled with themes of reconciliation and renewal, the two-time Newbery winner draws parallels between a boy's quest for the family of his father, killed in Vietnam, and the Arthurian legends.

Park's pretty mother, grieving and withdrawn, has told Park nothing of his origins, so, when Park is 11 and the Vietnam War Memorial is being dedicated in Washington, his need to know increases and he convinces his mother to let him visit his paternal grandfather on a Virginia farm. There Park discovers the existence of his Uncle Frank, Frank's Vietnamese wife and stepdaughter (Thanh, six months younger than Park)—plus an inarticulate grandfather, paralyzed by strokes. Thanh is "sassy" and competitive, full of life and mischief, and at first has no use for Park; but she is also wise and generous at heart; when she and Park discover that they are half-brother and sister, it advances their growing friendship.

Park has long had the habit of imagining himself a knight errant or long-lost heir; in truth, he is finally both, but not in the conventional terms of his fantasies. Using elegantly chosen symbols, Paterson entwines noble legend with contemporary realism; and the two worlds merge when the pure springhouse water Thanh defends so fiercely when she first meets interlope Park is shared by the two and their grandfather. Park's quest is a fine journey of discovery, and the characters he meets are uniquely memorable.

Marcia Hupp

SOURCE: A review of *Park's Quest,* in *School Library Journal,* Vol. 35, No. 8, May, 1988, p. 111.

Like the heroes of his Arthurian fantasies, Park has a quest. Kept in the dark by a mother whose memories are too painful for her to face, Park knows nothing of his father, who was killed in Vietnam. The dedication of the Vietnam War Memorial arouses his need to know, and Park sets out to find the man who was his father from the family he left behind. What he finds is not at all what he expected: an invalid grandfather, an uncle his mother never mentioned, a truculent Vietnamese girl, and a host of unpleasant surprises. If the characters in this novel seem incomplete—and they do—it may be because all are victims of the war, their lives stalled mid-course, their chance to right a wrong denied them by the finality of death. Only Park's uncle has been able to pick up the pieces of his life (and his brother's) and go on. But Paterson suggests that the others, together, may yet do the same. What young readers will make of this remains to be seen. Much reading between the lines is necessary to discern characters' motivations; careful attention is required to follow quick transitions of plot and a confusing timetable of events. Puzzling questions and loose ends remain. In grappling with large issues, Paterson seems to have lost control of small details. Still, she gives readers much to ponder at all levels and a sufficiently engaging plot to draw them on. Margaret Rostkowsky's *After the Dancing Days* deals with similar issues (albeit an earlier war) in a more tightly structured framework. Thoughtful readers will gain from reading both titles.

Alice McDermott

SOURCE: "Brought Together by Thanh," in *The New York Times Book Review,* May 8, 1988, p. 25.

In *Park's Quest,* the highly praised author of *Bridge to Terabithia* and *The Great Gilly Hopkins,* among other novels, offers her young readers a glimpse of the Vietnam War from what might be considered their own perspective: that of the next generation, the children of veterans, those for whom Vietnam is a vague historical event that has nevertheless somehow changed their lives.

Parkington Waddell Broughton 5th; Park to himself and his friends, is just such a child. Eleven years old and pudgy, with glasses and a long-running imaginary life as a kinght of the Round Table, Park knows his father only as a smiling photograph, a collection of unopened books and a name, "Parkington Waddell Broughton, IV, deceased." "On legal papers the *deceased* was always tacked on just like the Roman numeral." His mother refuses to speak about him, except to say that he did see Park once, when Park was only 3 months old, before he returned to Vietnam for a second tour. There is no other relative in his native Washington whom Park can question.

But with the dedication of the Vietnam Veterans Memorial, his curiosity about his father reaches a new height. On a secret excursion to the wall, Park touches his father's name engraved there and sees that his quest to know him is as noble, and as important, as was the knights' quest for the Holy Grail. Reluctantly, his mother arranges for Park to spend two summer weeks in southern Virginia, at the home of his grandfather, the Colonel, Parkington Waddell Broughton 3d.

The adventure perfectly suits Park's romantic imagination, and he dreams of a wise, white-bearded grandsire who will embrace him, his namesake, as his true heir. But at the bus depot Park is met by his uncle Frank, his father's younger brother, and told that the Colonel, the victim of two debilitating strokes, had been too upset by the news of his arrival to see him.

Left on his own, Park wanders the manure-laden fields and chokes down the overcooked meals provided by Mrs. Davenport, his grandfather's nurse and housekeeper. His idle disappointment is soon made all the more trying by Thanh, a fiery, pestering girl, the child of Frank's Vietnamese wife. She soon becomes both the bane of Park's visit ("geek" he calls her to himself, with great satisfaction) and his only real companion. She too has seen what Park, horrified, glimpses late one night—his grandfather, alone in his room, crying out in a terrible, stifled voice. Indeed, she seems to be the only person willing to speak freely about the old man, or to remember he may require something more than mashed vegetables and a warm afghan.

Over the course of his visit, Park's quest for knowledge about his father changes to one for forgiveness. The knowledge itself comes to him inadvertently, when he finds a photograph of a smiling American airman in Thanh's room and his uncle Frank mentions that Park's parents had divorced before his father returned to Vietnam. But the forgiveness, for himself and his mother, for his suffering grandfather, comes only when he and the old man, through Thanh's manipulations, recognize their shared sense of guilt, and their grief, and join Thanh in a gentle communion.

No story of the Vietnam War, even one meant for children, can be made as simple and as noble as the war stories of old, or as the story of the quest for the Holy Grail. Katherine Paterson clearly acknowledges this and in *Park's Quest* she confronts the complexity, the ambiguity, of the war and the emotions of those it involved with an honesty that young readers are sure to recognize and appreciate. But what is even more remarkable is that she has fashioned from this complexity a story for young adults that does not offer an antidote, or even a resolution, for the irreversible damages of this war but that speaks instead of the opportunity for healing; the possibility, despite the damage, of sharing the grief without ever shedding it, and going on.

THE TALE OF THE MANDARIN DUCKS (1990)

Carolyn Phelan

SOURCE: A review of *The Tale of the Mandarin Ducks,* in *Booklist,* Vol. 87, No. 1, September 1, 1990, p. 59.

A Japanese fairy tale, in picture-book format, about a Mandarin duck caught and caged at the whim of a wealthy Japanese lord. Separated from his mate, the bird languishes in captivity until a compassionate servant girl sets him free. The lord sentences the girl and her beloved to death, but they in turn are freed and rewarded with happiness. In the best fairytale tradition, their rescuers, ostensibly servants of the Emperor, turn out to be the grateful drake and his mate. The unity, simplicity, and grace of Paterson's writing find apt expression in the Dillons' [Diane and Leo] watercolor and pastel illustrations. Resembling traditional Japanese prints in their strong, expressive lines, the horizontal pictures feature muted colors with warm undertones. The artwork, like the text, uses repeated patterns and motifs to good effect. The occasional positioning of a small, bordered picture within the larger double-page spread enables the viewer to see in two places at once, for example, the palace where the caged drake sits and the nest where his mare awaits him. A good choice to read aloud, this picture book offers children an appealing folktale expressed with quiet dignity.

Kay E. Vandergrift

SOURCE: A review of *The Tale of the Mandarin Ducks,* in *School Library Journal,* Vol. 36, No. 10, October, 1990, p. 111.

There is a quiet subtlety of tone in both text and illustration that perfectly captures the spirit of this Japanese folktale. Paterson's economical use of language conveys the pure essence of a story that needs no verbal embellishment. A mandarin drake is separated from his mate by a cruel lord who covets beautiful things, only for the honor they bring him as their possessor. When the drake's magnificently colored plumage fades, he is banished to a far corner of the kitchen where Yasuko, the kitchen maid, frees him. The lord blames Shozo, the one-eyed chief steward who had once been a powerful samurai, beats him, strips him of his rank, and forces him to haul waste and scrub toilets. When Yasuko and Shozo fall in love, the lord sentences them to death; they are saved, however, by two messengers announcing that the emperor has abolished capital punishment. The Dillons' watercolor and pastel paintings have the appearance of woodcuts with a luminous quality, conveying both the gentleness and the strength of the characters and of the bond of love between the two couples, human and duck. The illustrations are simultaneously powerful and ethereal with bold lines and fine details which, nonetheless, are more suggestive than definitive. This visual understatement is seen most clearly in the depiction of nature. Each tree, flower, or blade of grass hints of more behind. There is a grace in the flowing lines of the kimonos and beauty in the muted autumn/winter palette, giving a golden, blue-gray, or mauve glow to the various scenes. Although the obvious message of this tale is that of kindness rewarded, there is a more subtle message brought home in the final words, "trouble can always be borne when it is shared."

Jan Susina

SOURCE: "'Tell Him about Vietnam': Vietnamese-Americans in Contemporary American Children's Literature," in *Children's Literature Association Quarterly,* Vol. 16, No. 2, Summer, 1991, pp. 58-63.

While the central focus of Katherine Paterson's *Park's Quest* is the search of the twelve-year-old Park Broughton for an understanding of his father who was killed eleven years ago in the Vietnam War, it also touches on the issue of the integration of Vietnamese-Americans into the U.S. A bookish boy, Park too often sees the world in terms of an Arthurian romance. As the novel's title suggests, he sets out to recover his father's past, which his mother refuses to discuss. On a visit to his grandfather's farm in Strathaven, Virginia, Park learns from the housekeeper, Mrs. Davenport, that Uncle Frank, his father's brother, has recently married a Vietnamese woman with an eleven-year-old daughter. Mrs. Davenport recounts that Frank's marriage did not meet with the approval of the local community:

> That was a set-to in this county, let me tell you. A Broughton marrying one of them. Broughton has always been a big name around here. You got to admire the man. Loses his tenants, his daddy has a stroke, the neighbors won't hardly speak, but he goes right ahead and gets married.

Park develops an immediate antagonism towards the confrontational daughter Thanh. In an interesting role reversal of *Angel Child,* it is the Vietnamese girl who taunts the American boy and makes him feel the outsider and unwelcome in his new environment, the farm. Park is quick to reduce Thanh from a person into a stereotype:

> There were lots of Orientals in his school, mostly refugees. Vietnamese, he decided, or Cambodian. They all looked alike to him—the people who had killed his father.

Uncle Frank inadvertently informs Park that the boy's mother and father divorced before the father's second tour of duty. This revelation, coupled with a photograph that Thanh owns, confirms what Park suspects: that he and Thanh share the same father, and that they are half-brother and half-sister. The biological recognition completely erases any previous hostility and competitiveness between the two characters, which seems odd coming from the author whose *Jacob Have I Loved* is a much more believable study of the tensions and jealousy between two sisters. Paterson's solution to the cross-cultural conflicts stemming from the Vietnam War seems to be glibly resolved to the tune of Walt Disney's "It's A Small World After All."

Eric Kimmel has called *Park's Quest* "the most consciously mythic of Paterson's novels, pointing out that it is a reworking of Wolfram von Eschenbach's *Parsifal*. Like Parsifal, the young Park is raised by a loving mother, who has kept him ignorant of the ways of his soldier father. He begins his quest uncertain what he may discover. The family farm becomes the Grail Castle for the boy, and his wheel chair-bound grandfather is Fisher King. The taunting Thanh, like Sigûne, forces him on in his quest, not with answers but with questions. Yet, at the same time that she is Park's opponent, she is also his guide and shows him how to bring the joy of life back to his sickly grandfather. Kimmel's tracing out the pattern of the grail myth in the novel is brief, but convincing.

It also helps to explain why *Park's Quest* is the least convincing of these novels which deal with the cross-cultural conflicts of Vietnamese-Americans, because its primary function is not so much to be a realistic presentation of contemporary social issues, but a reworking of the hero's journey. In this modern version of *Parsifal*, the combat is limited to verbal exchanges and the racially-mixed offspring of the wandering soldier are half-brother and half-sister. The aggressive and constant taunting by Thanh of Park makes sense as part of the testing of the grail knight figure, but is completely out of character with the other Vietnamese-Americans presented in the other books.

LYDDIE (1991)

Kathleen Odean

SOURCE: A review of *Lyddie,* in *School Library Journal,* Vol. 37, No. 2, February, 1991, p. 82.

In this superb novel, Paterson deftly depicts a Lowell, Massachusetts fabric mill in the 1840s and a factory girl whose life is changed by her experiences there. Readers first meet 13-year-old Lyddie Worthen staring down a bear on her family's debt-ridden farm in the Vermont mountains. With her fierce spirit, she stares down a series of metaphorical bears in her year as a servant girl at an inn and then in her months under grueling conditions as a factory worker. Lyddie is far from perfect, "close with her money and her friendships," but she is always trying. She suffers from loneliness, illness, and loss at too early an age, but she survives and grows. An encounter with a runaway slave brings out her generosity and starts her wondering about slavery and inequality. Try as she might to focus on making money to save the farm, Lyddie cannot ignore the issues around her, including the inequality of women. One of her roommates in the company boarding house awakens Lyddie to the wonder of books. This dignity brought by literacy is movingly conveyed as she improves her reading and then helps an Irish fellow worker learn to read. The importance of reading is just one of the threads in this tightly woven story in which each word serves a purpose and each figure of speech, drawn from the farm or the factory, adds to the picture. Paterson has brought a troubling time and place vividly to life, but she has also given readers great hope in the spirited person of Lyddie Worthen.

Mary L. Adams

SOURCE: A review of *Lyddie,* in *Voice of Youth Advocates,* Vol. 14, No. 1, April, 1991, p. 34.

Lyddie and Charles are abandoned in their log cabin in rural Vermont by their mentally ill mother during the 1840s. Their father had deserted them earlier. Lyddie and Charles make it through a winter of near starvation only to find their mother has indentured them to pay her debts. Charles is sent to a miller's where he is accepted as their own son. Lyddie goes to stay with an innkeeper and is treated like a slave. She escapes to become a mill girl in one of the weaving factories in Lowell, MA. Lyddie's life in the girl's dormitory, sharing a small room with three girls; the daily toll of hard labor at the factory on 12 to 16 year old girls; and the infant stirring of organized labor are pulled together in this fascinating, moving account of Lyddie's life during one hard year of adolescence during the 1840s.

Paterson has looked in a new direction for her setting and story. According to the jacket, this book came out of Paterson's participation in the Women's History Project celebrating Vermont's bicentennial in 1991. This gripping story set in the Northeast's budding weaving industry, using the factory girls and showing evolving labor legislation, is accurately depicted. Paterson alludes to outside readers with expertise in the field, and to extensive research. Her use of *Oliver Twist* as Lyddie's primer and favorite book inserts another layer of continuing social commentary. While the setting is interesting and authentic, the story and characterizations are Paterson at her best. Readers will carry the image of Lyddie with them for many years.

Natalie Babbitt

SOURCE: "Working Girl," in *The New York Times Book Review,* May 19, 1991, p. 24.

Katherine Paterson's novels are all, in one way or another, celebrations of the resilience of the human spirit at war with adversity. *Lyddie* has for its battleground the American Industrial Revolution, specifically the mills of Lowell, Mass., in the mid-1840's.

The courage of boys in the working world has been dealt with often, most memorably, of course, by Charles Dickens. But novels of this kind about girls are rare. Books like *Julie of the Wolves* deal with characters isolated from human contact, and the demon to be conquered is nature itself, á la *Robinson Crusoe.*

People in real life rarely find themselves in that kind of position. Since the Industrial Revolution began, the demon has tended to be the machine, and the setting has been a mill, a factory, a sweatshop. We often forget that there were places where girls were the preferred laborers, if we ever knew it in the first place. The mills of Lowell wove thread into fabric on huge, mechanized looms, and weaving has traditionally been women's work.

So, while this novel pays tribute to the triumph of the spirit, as do Ms. Paterson's other novels including *Bridge to Terabithia* and *The Great Gilly Hopkins,* and although she has often chosen heroines over heroes for central characters, *Lyddie* is outstanding because of the nature of its setting. The author did a lot of research as part of the Women's History Project of this year's Vermont bicentennial—research that, combined with her great skill as a writer, has given us a work place that can be heard, tasted, smelled, seen, all clearly: a roaring, merciless work place where the air is full of lint and a 13-hour workday is the norm.

The story does not begin in the mill, however. It begins at Lyddie's family farm in rural Vermont and it begins with the creation—for Lyddie and the reader—of a metaphor. Into the Worthens' shabby farmhouse comes a huge black bear. He is after the pot of oatmeal Lyddie is stirring on the stove. She and her mother and brother and sisters escape up a ladder to the loft and the bear manages to upend the steaming oatmeal kettle onto his head. Thus capped, he runs howling away into the woods and the family is spared. But the bear comes to symbolize for Lyddie the demon to be faced in the trials ahead.

This encounter with the bear marks the end of farm life and the beginning of the breakup of Lyddie's family. Her father has already gone West to seek "vain riches," and her mother, who has become "somewhat queer in the head," believes that the appearance of the bear signifies the coming of the end of the world. She takes the two little girls, Rachel and Agnes, and goes to live with a sister while Lyddie, age 13, and her brother, Charlie, 10, stay behind to tend the farm. But soon a letter from their mother informs them that she has let the farm to a neighbor to repay a debt, and tells Lyddie, "Meentime I hav hire you out to M. Cutler at the tavern and fer yr. brother to Bakers mill."

This is a rich story packed with a great variety of characters. It would be pointless to try to tell about them all or to detail the complexities of the plot. Suffice it to say that Lyddie, after a winter in the kitchen of Cutler's tavern, finds her way to Lowell and a job in the mills. Her goal is to earn enough money to rescue the farm and reassemble her scattered family. It is not to be, however. First Agnes dies, and Mrs. Worthen is confined to an insane asylum where she, too, dies. Then Rachel and Charlie are adopted by the family with whom Charlie has been living.

Lyddie works mightily at the mill, enduring dreadful conditions, sharing a room in a boardinghouse with three other mill girls and saving as much of her earnings as she can. She also saves herself from the sexual advances of the mill overseer. But in saving another girl from the same man, she gets herself dismissed. What will she do? There is no family left to work for. Well, then, she will take the money she has saved and go to Ohio to Oberlin College, "a college . . . that will take a woman just like a man." This she tells the man whom we expect she will one day marry. But first she will "stare down all the bears!"

Lyddie is in many ways larger than life. To endure what she endures (the loss of her father, then her mother and sisters, and finally her cherished brother); to lose her home and go out alone among strangers to make her own way in a job and in a place next to impossible to survive; to be virtually without education; to be, as she describes herself, ugly (though the painting for the jacket, an especially beautiful one by Deborah Chabrain, shows her to be handsome indeed)—how can the reader identify with such strengths, such goodness, such unquenchable hope?

Oliver Twist, read aloud to Lyddie by one of her boardinghouse roommates, provides her with a pattern, and the likenesses are clear. But Dickens relied on *deus ex machina* justice and alternation between comedy and tragedy to give his novels their depth. Katherine Paterson does not engage in Dickensian caricature, and though her hand is never heavy, comedy is not her forte. Still, *Lyddie* works as a novel. If its heroine sometimes seems superhuman, so be it; the reader identifies with her anyway. And *Lyddie* is full of life, full of *lives,* full of reality.

Elizabeth S. Watson

SOURCE: A review of *Lyddie,* in *The Horn Book Magazine,* Vol. LXVII, No. 3, May-June, 1991, pp. 338-39.

Rich in historical detail, with characters who emerge to become real people, this story encompasses three years in the life of Lyddie Worthen. At the onset, the author establishes the bleak conditions faced by a fatherless family on a poor hill farm in mid-nineteenth-century Vermont. Forced to leave her beloved home when her mother hires her out to pay her absent father's debts, Lyddie regretfully takes her place as the new girl at a tavern, where the guests bring glimpses of other places—sometimes of cities as far off as Boston but more often of the commercial center of Lowell, Massachusetts. Lyddie's single-minded determination to earn money to reclaim the farm, which her mother has leased to a neighbor, leads her to brave the unknown and set out for Lowell. Her life as a factory worker in the mills is thoroughly explored. As Lyddie sorts out her values and develops a personal philosophy, she faces questions about the rights of workers and the ethics of slavery in various forms. Not only does the book contain a riveting plot, engaging characters, and a splendid setting, but the language—graceful, evocative, and rhythmic—incorporates the rural speech patterns of Lyddie's folk, the simple Quaker expressions of the farm neighbors, and the lilt of fellow mill girl Bridget's Irish brogue. Metaphors are consistently worked out—"the sky had turned into the underside of a thick quilt" is followed a few pages later by "a tracery of snow lay on the fields. . . . In a week or so, everything would be sleeping under a thick comforter"—and the real bear that drives Lyddie's mother from the farm becomes a sustained allusion throughout. A superb story of grit, determination, and personal growth.

THE SMALLEST COW IN THE WORLD (1991)

Hazel Rochman

SOURCE: A review of *The Smallest Cow in the World,* in *Booklist,* Vol. 88, No. 2, September 15, 1991, p. 169.

Plain words and lively, cartoon-style color illustrations tell a heartfelt story of a small boy's insecurity about moving. Marvin loves the cow Rosie, even though everyone thinks she's mean. His older sister tells him that he knows nothing: "You don't feed her. You don't wash her. You don't milk her. You don't shovel her manure." When the family is forced to move to another farm, Marvin misses Rosie and cries all the time in the family's new trailer home. Then he imagines a tiny Rosie who's with him all the time, even at school. His family enters into his play and reassures him that they will always be together, even if they have to move again. Based on a version that Newbery-winner Paterson originally wrote for the Vermont Migrant Education Program, this is simply told, with quiet surprises in story, character, and language. [Jane Clark] Brown's illustrations set Marvin's drama against the daily farmchores, from milking to apple picking. An I Can Read Book.

Nancy Vasilakis

SOURCE: A review of *The Smallest Cow in the World,* in *The Horn Book Magazine,* Vol. LXVII, No. 5, September-October, 1991, pp. 593-94.

Using simple sentence structure and an easy vocabulary, the author tells a remarkably shrewd and touching story about a boy who overcomes the trauma of moving and the loss of a favorite pet with the help of his understanding family. When they leave their Vermont farm, Marvin is saddest at losing Rosie. Heartily disliked by others because of such nasty habits as butting and stepping on people's feet, Rosie the cow is, to Marvin, beautiful. He mopes around for a while in his new surroundings and then one day happily announces that Rosie has been transformed by a witch into a tiny cow visible only to him. She begins living up to her reputation as the meanest cow in the world by pulling up the flowers from Mother's garden and tearing up older sister May's books. Rosie only does this, Marvin insists, because she didn't want to move. A valuable lesson on parenting can be gleaned from his family's reactions to this minor domestic crisis. Marvin's father makes a miniature barn for the cow, and Marvin, entranced, plays happily with his new toy. When school begins and he insists on taking his invisible pet along with him, however, he is subjected to ridicule by the other children. Wise by now to the powers of imagination, May informs her younger brother that Rosie is about to have a calf and needs to stay home with her young one. Seeing life replayed in miniature, Marvin finally asks the all-important question: Will Rosie always be taken care of and never be abandoned? Reassured, he is reconciled to the move at last. As always, Katherine Paterson gets to the very heart of what matters most to children. This time around she has written a beginning reader that offers much food for thought to adults.

Betsy Hearne

SOURCE: A review of *The Smallest Cow in the World,* in *Bulletin of the Center for Children's Books,* Vol. 45, No. 5, January, 1992, p. 136.

In her first easy-to-read book, Paterson has proved once again that a good writer can filter simplified vocabulary through a rich imaginative process. This is the story of Marvin, who loves the meanest cow in the world, loses her when the farm his Dad works on is sold, and deals with the loss and the move in the most ingenious way possible. After discovering meanness doesn't work, Marvin fantasizes a miniature version of the cow to keep him company. What makes the story more than just adjustment-to-change bibliotherapy are the authentic conversations between Marvin and his sister ("'You are the dumbest boy in the world,' May said") and the quirky details enlivening the classic dynamics that Marvin's family use to support him through a crisis. Kids will get so involved they'll forget all about decoding—and read the book. [Jane Clark] Brown's literal crayon-and-watercolor illustrations have a homely humor that brightens the scenes without overwhelming them.

THE KING'S EQUAL (1992)

Hazel Rochman

SOURCE: A review of *The King's Equal,* in *Booklist,* Vol. 88, No. 21, July, 1992, p. 1944.

Paterson collaborates with acclaimed Russian illustrator Vagin in a long, magical story that revitalizes many folk traditions. It's a story not simply of virtue rewarded, but of virtue so clever and strong it can change the world. A greedy and arrogant young king can't wear his crown until he finds a woman who's his equal. He exploits his people and lays waste the land, sneering at all the prospective brides his counselors parade before him, though the women are the most beautiful, wise, and wealthy in the kingdom. Rosamund's a poor goatherd. She befriends a hungry wolf, who transforms her into the bride the king wants—except she won't have the king. She shows the ruler that he's beneath her and sends him away to be a goatherd. He learns humility and also to sing and play and make his daily bread. Then, he's her equal. Occasionally the message is spelled out ("Isn't it better to share . . ."), but the prince is a great villain and his comeuppance is wonderfully satisfying. The paintings are lush and romantic, with richly colored, elaborately detailed costumes and interiors in an old-fashioned style. Each frame of the court is set within a larger painting of the kingdom bathed in bright blue light. The story is told in chapters, with rhythm, repetition, and immediacy, and with dramatic confrontations and reversals that make it great for reading aloud.

Martha Rosen

SOURCE: A review of *The King's Equal,* in *School Library Journal,* Vol. 38, No. 9, September, 1992, p. 255.

Finding a princess who is the "king's equal" in comeliness, intelligence, and wealth is an order that confounds the wisest, most loyal councilors in this distant realm. Finding a book equal in quality and brilliance to this one is an even more formidable task. Paterson weaves her story within the structure of familiar fairy tales; she includes romance, repetition of language, the number three, and a moral of goodness and love triumphing over selfishness and greed. Her careful attention to the beauty and variety of descriptive language is evident on every page. The story gains dimension with the inclusion of "the Wolf." At first glimpse, he seems a menacing, negative force, but he is revealed ultimately to be the purveyor of magic, and even the perfect matchmaker. He never intrudes upon court life in the capital city, but remains in his remote mountain lair, an enigmatic character to ponder at the story's end. Vagin's illustrations are exquisite, luminous in color, clarity, and precision. Readers are drawn into the courtly world of a wealthy kingdom through details of costume, architecture, furniture, and decorations. Because there are six chapters, the book is a lengthy read-aloud. This is, however, no drawback; young listeners will be a spellbound and appreciative audience, and should want to return to the book again and again.

Maeve Visser Knoth

SOURCE: A review of *The King's Equal,* in *The Horn Book Magazine,* Vol. LXVIII, No. 5, September-October, 1992, pp. 583-84.

When the wise old king dies, leaving an arrogant son to rule his country, he declares that the son may not become king until he finds a wife who is "the king's equal." The wicked son, of course, cannot find any woman good enough to marry until he meets the generous, clever Rosamund. Rosamund tells the prince that he must live in a hut in the woods and learn to care for himself before she will marry him. Willing to do anything to wear the crown, Raphael agrees. His year living with goats and a magical wolf transforms the young prince into a generous, humble man who is finally "equal" to the job of ruling a kingdom. Paterson's original fairy tale is remarkable for its carefully crafted language and important theme. She develops, in a short space, vivid three-dimensional characters. Vagin's formal, detailed illustrations depict court scenes filled with pompous, coiffed royalty, and his pastoral paintings are equally elaborate. Frames serve to contain the scenes and lend additional formality to the tone. Readers will not be disappointed by Katherine Paterson's newest tale.

📖 *FLIP-FLOP GIRL* (1994)

Kirkus Reviews

SOURCE: A review of *Flip-Flop Girl,* in *Kirkus Reviews,* Vol. LXI, No. 24, December 15, 1993, p. 1596.

Paterson writes of today's gritty reality in an easily read story about a fourth grader whose father's death has thrown her family out of balance. Momma has moved them to backwater Virginia to live with Daddy's stepmother ("Nurses can always get jobs. They just can't get a lot of money"); Vinnie has lost her home, a best friend, and—because 5-year-old brother Mason hasn't spoken since the funeral—Momma's attention. Grandma, too, is a trial; she buys Vinnie ugly clothes at the Salvation Army and insists on making her teacher an embarrassing Christmas present. Mr. Clayton is Vinnie's one comfort, sensitive to his pupils' troubles and source of unobtrusive gifts—barrettes to hold Vinnie's hair out of her eyes; shoes for Lupe, who only has flip-flops and whose troubles are greater than Vinnie's: her father's in prison for killing her mother (Lupe is sure he's not guilty). Mr. Clayton marries; affection-starved Vinnie feels so betrayed that she slashes his car with her barrette and—in an agony of guilt when Lupe is blamed—lashes out at Mason, who runs away. Repentant, Vinnie goes to look for him, willingly aided by Lupe, whose generosity and plucky survival in the face of local prejudice subtly contrast with Vinnie's unreasoned, more childlike response to her losses. Once again, Paterson sets characters drawn with extraordinary empathy in a story distinguished by its overarching theme. Vinnie is ordinary, fallible; but with the help of Lupe's quietly courageous model of grace—plus the values enduring in her own family—she reclaims her equilibrium. Touching, engrossing, beautifully wrought.

Ellen Fader

SOURCE: A review of *Flip-Flop Girl,* in *The Horn Book Magazine,* Vol. LXX, No. 2, March-April, 1994, pp. 200-01.

Katherine Paterson's respect for young readers permeates every word of this remarkable novel. As she explores the universal themes of grief and healing, jealousy and forgiveness, readers will find themselves immersed in an intellectually accessible but emotionally challenging reading experience. The Matthews family has recently moved to Virginia to live with the children's grandmother, and both children are having difficulty adjusting to the continual changes in their lives. Vinnie believes that her five-year-old brother Mason stopped talking nearly three months ago when their father died because of a cruel comment she made to him at their father's funeral. Vinnie's fascination with classmate Lupe Mahoney, a tall girl "with skin the color of Ovaltine" who comes to school every day wearing rubber flip-flops with bright orange thongs, quickly turns to rivalry when a series of incidents leads Vinnie to believe that their teacher, Mr. Clayton, favors Lupe over herself. Vinnie's emotions become uncontrollable, and she lashes out at Mr. Clayton, Mason, and herself. In the end, Vinnie finally achieves some insight into, and control over, the feelings that have been flip-flopping out of control since her father's death. This novel resembles some of Paterson's most honored and affecting books, such as *Bridge to Terabithia* and *The Great Gilly Hopkins,* in that it showcases the author's uncanny ability to craft stories that penetrate and examine the elemental nature of human behavior. All children will discover parts of themselves in Vinnie, and, like Vinnie, will know more about themselves when they get to the conclusion of this powerful story.

Susan Oliver

SOURCE: A review of *Flip-Flop Girl,* in *School Library Journal,* Vol. 40, No. 5, May, 1994, pp. 117-18.

Sorrow and loneliness sweep over Vinnie and her little brother, Mason, after their father dies and their mother moves them to a small town to live with their grandmother. Mason has been mute since the funeral, and Vinnie's mother, overwhelmed with worry about him and her struggle to support the family, seems to have nothing left to give her daughter. Thrust into a new school, without friends or the right clothes, and with rumors about her troubled brother wafting around her, Vinnie is drawn to a very tall, very odd girl who wears long dresses and orange flip-flops. Lupe is more of an outcast than she, and has suffered tragedy and rumor as well. But Lupe is strong, confident, and intuitive, and is able to offer support to Vinnie and her brother when it's needed, to stand back when it's not, and to accept whatever befalls her with grace. It's Lupe and a gentle, generous teacher who help the girl through her grief and her guilt and give her back her family. Life has been

reckless with the children in this book, but Paterson has not—she's given them complex problems and personalities, compassionate adults, and a compelling story that is as strong as the power of redemptive love that prevails in this thoughtful tale.

Jane Resh Thomas

SOURCE: "Nobody Understands Vinnie," in *The New York Times Book Review,* May 22, 1994, p. 20.

Katherine Paterson, twice the winner of the Newbery Medal for her novels **Bridge to Terabithia** and **Jacob Have I Loved,** has typically drawn characters wounded by death or other terrible trouble. Her characters, unable to escape their circumstances, must confront themselves and transcend their own pain in order to be free.

Ms. Paterson's books are not, however, the formulaic "problem novels" that proliferated when taboos about unpleasant realities fell in the 1960's. She is more interested in the transfiguration of the human spirit than in the problems that bring about that change. She takes her readers to the nadir, the dead of winter, when it seems that almost all is lost, and then propels them up into springtime. While her situations sometimes border on melodrama, her quiet voice, merely stating the facts, sounds so sensible that one accepts her stories as hard truths.

Lavinia (Vinnie) Matthews, the 9-year-old protagonist of Ms. Paterson's new novel, **Flip-Flop Girl,** is just such a character. Vinnie's father is in the grave, recently dead of cancer, at the story's beginning. Before the funeral, Vinnie's 5-year-old brother, Mason, announced that he was glad that Daddy had died, because he smelled bad. Vinnie snapped that Daddy died to get away from a bad son who could say such things; Mason has been mute ever since.

Vinnie's life is in tatters. Unable to afford rent on nurse's pay, Momma moves the family from Washington to Grandma's house in southern Virginia. Nobody understands Vinnie or cherishes her as her kindly father did. Mason's affliction occupies Momma, and Grandma is obtuse. In the new school, Vinnie's classmates ostracize her, except Maria Guadalupe Mahoney, a long rail of a girl known as Lupe. Her straits are worse than Vinnie's. Her father having been imprisoned for the murder of her mother, Lupe now lives in her grandmother's shack amid a field of pumpkins.

Lupe makes a few aborted overtures to Vinnie, who sees her as a competitor for the affection of their teacher, Mr. Clayton, a model of kindness. Vinnie envies his compassion, having decided to marry him when she grows up, and the sudden announcement of his wedding stuns her. In a trance of anguish, she takes revenge on him. Lupe serenely accepts the blame. Mason wanders away, looking for Daddy. And the two girls who have circled each other in distrust team up to do what they can, despite being caught in the gears of grim daily circumstance.

The narrative is as steady as Lupe's demeanor. The viewpoint from Vinnie's perspective never wavers. A reader therefore feels the world as she does, hating pumpkin pie's squashy taste that cinnamon can't mask; furious at Mason, whose muteness draws their mother's concern from Vinnie's needs; disgusted at her clownishly rouged grandmother whose gifts are worn toys from the thrift shop; jealous of others' good fortune.

While Katherine Paterson's characters are troubled, she focuses on them rather than their problems. She resists casting even devastated children as victims, nor does she shrink from their capacity for nastiness. They have the power to transform themselves, she suggests, and thus to alter the *effects* of their circumstances. Her clear vision of humanity's mixed character and her hope despite that knowledge give realism a good name.

📖 *A MIDNIGHT CLEAR: STORIES FOR THE CHRISTMAS SEASON* (1995)

Hazel Rochman

SOURCE: A review of *A Midnight Clear: Stories for the Christmas Season,* in *Booklist,* Vol. 92, No. 2, September 15, 1995, p. 171.

Like Paterson's *Angels and Other Strangers,* this collection of stories reveals the spirit of Christmas in contemporary life. A few are sentimental with contrived parallels and saintly characters; a few may be too adult in viewpoint to appeal to young readers. But the best of the stories reveal hope and light in a dark, uncertain world. Paterson writes with simple immediacy about outcasts: strangers on the street and at your door, runaways, failures, and illegal immigrants—people who can find no room at the inn. The endings offer no easy resolution, only an opening out of possibilities. One exquisite story about a teenage runaway in the empty night celebrates the song of "stubborn sweetness" that persists despite our turning away from it again and again.

Jane Marino

SOURCE: A review of *A Midnight Clear: Stories for the Christmas Season,* in *School Library Journal,* Vol. 41, No. 10, October, 1995, p. 40.

A collection of 12 stories that center on the meaning of Christmas. In each of the strikingly original plots, the crisis that the characters face teaches them about a strength they didn't know they had, the power of giving, or the value of family. A homeless woman is befriended by a scared, lonely teenager; a haughty but lonely retiree is mistaken by a poor neighborhood kid as being in need of his help; a young husband is stranded in the

middle of nowhere with his wife about to give birth; a little girl is sent to live with her gruff maiden aunt; and a minister's daughter wants mothering more than the lead in the Christmas pageant. But Paterson never preaches; instead, she lets her characters show readers their ordeals and how they deal with them. In many cases, the line between humor and poignancy becomes blurred, as in "Merit Badges," when Kate gets "bushwacked" into visiting a resident of a nursing home. Others are wrenchingly sad, like "In the Desert, a Highway" the story of suffering in the name of freedom by Chinese victims of Communism. Although Paterson originally wrote these for her husband, a minister, to use as sermons for Christmas, they are for everybody to read and enjoy throughout many holiday seasons to come.

Nancy Vasilakis

SOURCE: A review of *A Midnight Clear: Stories for the Christmas Season,* in *The Horn Book Magazine,* Vol. LXXI, No. 6, November-December, 1995, pp. 729-30.

These stories were originally written for the author's husband, a pastor, to read to his congregation on Christmas Eve. Among them are the story of a man on his way to his dying father's bedside who picks up a troubled young hitchhiker; a Girl Scout and an eccentric old woman in a nursing home who form an unlikely friendship; and a minister's daughter who plays the coveted part of Mary in the Sunday School pageant despite a series of humorous mishaps in previous years. While the collection as a whole is uneven, these stories celebrate the human spirit and will make good family fare.

📖 *THE ANGEL AND THE DONKEY* (1996)

Publishers Weekly

SOURCE: A review of *The Angel and the Donkey,* in *Publishers Weekly,* Vol. 243, No. 7, February 12, 1996, p. 71.

In her informative afterword to this sprightly retelling of a story from the Book of Numbers, two-time Newbery Medalist Paterson explains that the tale is notable in that it is one of two in the Bible that concerns a talking animal; and that, unlike most Old Testament entries, it is not told from the perspective of the Jews. The author keeps her fluid, narrative tone appealingly lighthearted as she relays the frustration of Balak, king of Moab, who calls on the soothsayer Balaam to lay a curse on Moses and the Israelites who, under his leadership, are seeking to cross Moab on their way out of Egypt. Seduced by the promised reward of riches, Balaam ignores an angel's command not to curse the Israelites "for the Lord has blessed them." But the greedy soothsayer soon recognizes the error of his ways. Rendered in watercolor, tempera and gouache, [Alexander] Koshkin's dramatic, vibrantly hued paintings feature an intriguing range of ancient symbols and motifs. Kids will be especially charmed by Balak's talking donkey, who emerges a hero while many of the human characters are decidedly asinine.

Patricia (Dooley) Lothrop Green

SOURCE: A review of *The Angel and the Donkey,* in *School Library Journal,* Vol. 42, No. 3, March, 1996, p. 213.

The prophet Balaam, ordered by the King of Moab to curse the invading Israelites, is visited by an angel who warns him that the Lord has blessed those very people. Tempted by a rich reward, he sets out anyway on his faithful donkey, who unaccountably balks and bumps, causing the man to beat him. Finally the beast halts and speaks reproachfully. Thereupon Balaam sees again the angel, now with a flaming sword, who tells him to go on to Moab, but to speak God's words. Balaam then enrages the king by blessing the Israelites, as God inspires him to do. This faithful, graceful retelling is embellished with many equally graceful watercolor, tempera, and gouache paintings executed in a detailed and realistic manner. Winged lions, hawk-headed gods, hoofed firepots, and elaborate ornaments and dress exhibit Egyptian and Assyrian motifs. Rich colors and exotic settings emphasize the antiquity of the story (though Balaam's venality makes it timeless), while the androgynous angel, with wings, sandaled feet, halo, and sword, still meets conventional expectations. This beautiful book merits a place on Bible-story shelves.

Ilene Cooper

SOURCE: A review of *The Angel and the Donkey,* in *Booklist,* Vol. 92, No. 13, March 1, 1996, p. 1189.

Paterson takes her story from an incident reported in the Hebrew Bible, Numbers 22-24. In the city of Pethor, a powerful soothsayer named Balaam rides on his faithful donkey to bless the worthy or curse the unworthy, all for a proper fee. When the king of Moab learns that Moses and the Israelites are defeating nearby neighbors, the king sends for Balaam to curse the Israelites. Balaam is willing until an angel of God warns him off, but when offered a house full of gold and silver, Balaam reconsiders. Only the intervention of his loyal donkey saves Balaam from the angel's wrath, and when God puts blessings for the Israelites into Balaam's mouth, the king knows he is doomed. The telling is lengthy, but Paterson has done a fine job of shaping the story so that its most appealing elements are in the forefront for a juvenile audience. Illustrator [Alexander] Koshkin has used traditional Assyrian, Israelite, and Egyptian motifs to excellent effect, though several of the pictures are repetitious. Executed in watercolor, tempera, and gouache, the artwork is almost incandescent, reflecting the mood of the story. Paterson's author's note will be extremely useful to adults and can serve as an introduction to biblical writings.

JIP: HIS STORY (1996)

Hazel Rochman

SOURCE: A review of *Jip: His Story,* in *Booklist,* Vol. 93, No. 1, September 1, 1996, p. 127.

What a story. It's not often that the revelations of the plot are so astonishing—and yet so inevitable—that they make you shout and think and shiver and cry. Paterson has taken the old orphan foundling tale, set it in Vermont in the 1850s, and made it new. Jip (as in "Gypsy") doesn't know where he came from; they say he fell off the back of a wagon and was found on the road somewhere when he was about two years old. Now, as a young boy, he lives and works on the town poor farm with the other paupers and strays. He just about runs the farm, cares for the plants and animals, and helps ease the pain and sorrow of those around him. His closest bond is with Put, an old man who must spend much of his life in a cage because of the raging madness that comes over him at times. People are scared of the lunatic, but Jip loves Put and comforts him ("he belonged to Jip in a way no one else ever had"). The real danger is from a menacing stranger who is watching Jip. What does the stalker want? At school, Teacher reads aloud from *Oliver Twist,* and Jip wonders, as he always has, whether he might have a loving parent far away somewhere. Is Jip somebody's lost boy? The answer is devastating. There are some problems with this book. Jip is idealized, too saintly to be true; in fact, as in Dickens, most of the characters are either totally good or totally bad. But the time and the place are drawn with powerful realism. Paterson's simple sentences lay bare the dark historical truth and the transforming light of love.

Ellen Fader

SOURCE: A review of *Jip: His Story,* in *School Library Journal,* Vol. 42, No. 10, October, 1996, p. 124.

Paterson's companion novel to *Lyddie* rewards readers with memorable characters and a gripping plot. Jip has been told that he tumbled off the back of a wagon when he was a toddler in 1847. He has been raised on a poor farm in a Vermont town, where he is an indispensable asset to the lazy manager and his equally lazy wife. The boy befriends the newly arrived "lunatic" Put, who is kept imprisoned in a cage because he is subject to violent, self-destructive episodes. Jip's life is quietly circumscribed—until a stranger plants the idea that his father might be searching for him. Although he has long fantasized that a loving parent awaits him, he sees the stranger as an unlikely messenger. His instincts prove correct when the man is revealed to be a slave catcher. Then Jip learns the truth about his past: his mother was a runaway slave. With the help of his teacher, Lyddie Worthen, and her sweetheart, Quaker neighbor Luke Stevens, Jip escapes to Canada, where he is welcomed as a free man into the home of a former slave whom Lyddie helped shelter in the earlier book. Paterson's story resonates with respect for the Vermont landscape and its mid-19th-century residents, with the drama of life during a dark period in our nation's history, and with the human quest for freedom. Fans of the previous book will relish meeting up with Lyddie and Luke again at a somewhat later period in their lives. Readers will be talking and thinking about this book long after they finish the last chapter.

Kelleher Jewett

SOURCE: "The People Nobody Wants," in *The New York Times Book Review,* November 10, 1996, p. 50.

The words of the old Sam Cooke song, "Don't know much about history," may turn out to be our national epitaph. When I tell people that's what I teach, they often explain apologetically that it was their least favorite subject—"all those names and dates." It's not that hard to cover the facts when you teach history, the challenge (and the fun) is to get students to feel what it would have been like to live in another time and place, to understand the ideas and forces that made people tick. Textbooks rarely do that, but novels can and do. Katherine Paterson's *Jip: His Story* is just such a work of fiction; issues that too often remain abstract in a textbook come to life through the story of a young boy living on a town "poor farm" in Vermont in 1855.

The book portrays the friendship between an orphan called Jip ("on account of I fell off the back of a wagon and some says it was a gypsy wagon") and an old man named Putnam who is subject to periods of insanity. Because they have neither money nor family, Jip and Put (Putnam, the old man says, is "too grand a name for the likes of me") live at the 19th-century version of a homeless shelter, a place to house the poor, the insane and the retarded so they will "not offend the eyes and nostrils of God-fearing citizens, nor strain their purse strings overmuch." When Put arrives at the farm, Jip (who is about 11, though no one knows for sure how old he was when he was discovered in the road) is the only one who is not afraid of the unkempt man who's locked in a cage like a wild beast. Jip's ability to see past his frightening appearance restores Put's dignity and allows "the raving lunatic" to become a part of the makeshift family of the farm: a widow and her three children, cast on the town's charity by the death of their drunken father, a simple young man named Sheldon and an assortment of elderly people who have outlived whatever means of support they once had. Jip struggles to save Put from his illness, to watch out for Sheldon, to improve the living conditions at the poor farm and to free his friend Lucy from the shame of her father's death. His heroic efforts underscore the casual brutality and inhuman neglect faced by many outsiders in 19th-century America.

This portrait of poverty and mistreatment gains a deeper historical resonance when Jip discovers that his mother was a runaway slave. The boy's fate becomes tied up with the great crisis of the century: the struggle between the abolitionists and the slaveholders, between the men and women of the underground railroad and those who combed the free states looking for fugitive slaves. Jip finds allies in a young woman who teaches school and a Quaker family whose house is a stop on the underground railroad, and the final chapters of the novel pit him and his friends against the Legree-like slave catcher. The most painful elements of the story are handled with considerable delicacy, but Ms. Paterson, whose well-loved novels include *The Great Gilly Hopkins* and *Lyddie,* does not shrink from bitter truths. Jip understands "the shame of how he had been conceived" and begins to learn the lessons of racism, when Lucy warns him that her mother, a woman he had trusted and helped, now hates him for "making out like you was white as us."

Jip probably won't find many fans among the people who want our children to learn a sanitized version of American history—the kind, as Arthur Schlesinger Jr. has said, that extols "patriotism, religion. Ozzie and Harriet . . . and, in general, the superior virtues of unregulated capitalism." It's a history that doesn't allow much room for the Jips of our past. Poverty, child abuse, slavery, racism, rape, insanity and death may not be what you expect to find in a novel for young readers, but Katherine Paterson is consciously writing in the great tradition of *Oliver Twist* and *Uncle Tom's Cabin.* She allows her readers to face some disturbing parts of our history, but she also gives them a hero to admire and emulate; she teaches that every life has value and that loyalty and courage matter more than power and money.

Jip may lead thoughtful young readers to think about the present as well as the past, to question what they hear on the news and to wonder why there are still so many children who are victims simply because they are poor or because their parents are immigrants. Be prepared for some interesting dinner-table conversations.

Mary M. Burns

SOURCE: A review of *Jip: His Story,* in *The Horn Book Magazine,* Vol. LXXII, No. 6, November-December, 1996, pp. 739-40.

A brief prologue and a short epilogue written in the first person frame an intense, third-person novel that maintains its riveting pace from the opening chapter to the final moment when the protagonist triumphs over adversity. Set in Vermont in the years 1855-1856, the book evokes the attitudes and social conditions of the times in lucent prose, enhanced by imagery drawn from the realities of farm life. The central character is Jip, thought to be a gypsy, who, eight years before the story opens, fell from a wagon on a hilly road, leaving no clue to his origins. Without kin or means of support, he becomes a resident of the town's poor farm and seems likely to spend his days in permanent servitude—until an elderly man, subject to intermittent fits of violence, is sent there for safe-keeping and confined in a wooden cage. Sympathy for the man impels Jip to befriend him, releasing emotions never previously acknowledged as he becomes more aware of the wretched conditions under which the paupers live. This awareness, combined with the concern of a new teacher and the ominous presence of a curious stranger, foreshadows the outcome and propels the plot to a startling revelation about Jip's origins (as well as a surprising identification of the teacher). Descriptions of the poor farm are Dickensian in their evocation of poverty and despair; it is perhaps no accident that Teacher chooses to read *Oliver Twist* to her students, offering a glimmer of hope and momentary escape from squalor. Because style and story are so closely welded, the narrative flows effortlessly. Only retrospective analysis reveals how carefully each element—from the naming of the characters to the final scene—has been considered and joined to the whole.

PARZIVAL: THE QUEST OF THE GRAIL KNIGHT (adapted by Paterson, 1998)

Kirkus Reviews

SOURCE: A review of *Parzival: The Quest of the Grail Knight,* in *Kirkus Reviews,* Vol. LXVI, No. 1, January 1, 1998, pp. 60-1.

Written in high-toned but not ornately formal language, this abridged rendition of a 13th-century, pre-Galahad Arthurian legend highlights the Grail Knight's spiritual growth.

Having had all knowledge of his family, the world at large, even his name, kept from him since birth, Parzival sets out for King Arthur's court a complete innocent. Several ritualistic knightly adventures later, taking some bad advice not to seem foolish by asking questions, he sees the Grail, but by remaining silent, leaves its keeper Anfortas with a wound that will not heal. Condemned by all for his inaction, Parzival angrily blames God for allowing so much misfortune. Although fond of jousting, Parzival nearly always spares his opponents' lives, and the tally of his deeds is illuminated both by flashes of humor—he's forever having to wash off the rust when he doffs his armor—and the exotic names of those he encounters, from his wife Condwiramurs to his half-Moorish half-brother Feirefiz. After years of searching, Parzival repents with the help of a holy hermit, and not only finds the Grail again, but becomes its keeper. Paterson never explains the Grail's origin, which has the effect, for readers who don't already know, of making it a less specifically Christian talisman; she analyzes the story's metaphorical underpinnings, discusses her rendition, and introduces the author, Wolfram von Eschenbach, in a closing note.

CUMULATIVE INDEXES

How to Use This Index

CUMULATIVE INDEX TO AUTHORS

MacLachlan, Patricia 1938-.................. **14**
See also AAYA 18; CA 118; 136; JRDA;
MAICYA; SATA 62; SATA-Brief 42

Maddison, Angela Mary 1923-
See Banner, Angela
See also CA 53-56; SATA 10

Maestro, Betsy C(rippen) 1944-............. **45**
See also CA 61-64; CANR 8, 23, 37; MAICYA;
SATA 59; SATA-Brief 30

Maestro, Giulio 1942- **45**
See also CA 57-60; CANR 8, 23, 37; MAICYA;
SATA 8, 59

Mahy, Margaret 1936-.......................... **7**
See also AAYA 8; CA 69-72; CANR 13, 30, 38;
JRDA; MAICYA; SATA 14, 69

Major, Kevin (Gerald) 1949- **11**
See also AAYA 16; CA 97-100; CANR 21, 38;
CLC 26; DAC; DLB 60; INT CANR-21;
JRDA; MAICYA; SATA 32, 82

Manley, Seon 1921- **3**
See also CA 85-88; SAAS 2; SATA 15

March, Carl
See Fleischman, (Albert) Sid(ney)

Mark, Jan(et Marjorie) 1943-................ **11**
See also CA 93-96; CANR 17, 42; MAICYA;
SATA 22, 69

Markoosie **23**
See also Markoosie, Patsauq
See also DAM MULT; NNAL

Markoosie, Patsauq 1942-
See Markoosie
See also CA 101

Marks, J
See Highwater, Jamake (Mamake)

Marks-Highwater, J
See Highwater, Jamake (Mamake)

Marsden, John 1950- **34**
See also AAYA 20; CA 135; SAAS 22; SATA 66, 97

Marshall, Edward
See Marshall, James (Edward)

Marshall, James (Edward) 1942-1992 ..... **21**
See also CA 41-44R; 139; CANR 38; DLB 61;
MAICYA; SATA 6, 51, 75

Martin, Ann M(atthews) 1955- **32**
See also AAYA 6; CA 111; CANR 32; INT CANR-
32; JRDA; MAICYA; SATA 44, 70; SATA-
Brief 41

Martin, Fredric
See Christopher, Matt(hew Frederick)

Maruki, Toshi 1912- **19**

Mathis, Sharon Bell 1937-..................... **3**
See also AAYA 12; BW 2; CA 41-44R; DLB 33;
JRDA; MAICYA; SAAS 3; SATA 7, 58

Mattingley, Christobel (Rosemary) 1931- . **24**
See also CA 97-100; CANR 20, 47; MAICYA;
SAAS 18; SATA 37, 85

Mayer, Mercer 1943- **11**
See also CA 85-88; CANR 38; DLB 61;
MAICYA; SATA 16, 32, 73

Mayne, William (James Carter) 1928- **25**
See also AAYA 20; CA 9-12R; CANR 37; CLC
12; JRDA; MAICYA; SAAS 11; SATA 6, 68

Mazer, Harry 1925-............................. **16**
See also AAYA 5; CA 97-100; CANR 32; INT 97-
100; JRDA; MAICYA; SAAS 11; SATA 31, 67

Mazer, Norma Fox 1931- **23**
See also AAYA 5; CA 69-72; CANR 12, 32, 66;
CLC 26; JRDA; MAICYA; SAAS 1; SATA
24, 67

McBratney, Sam 1943- **44**
See also CA 155; SATA 89

McCaffrey, Anne (Inez) 1926-............... **49**
See also AAYA 6; AITN 2; BEST 89:2; CA 25-
28R; CANR 15, 35, 55; CLC 17; DAM NOV,
POP; DLB 8; JRDA; MAICYA; MTCW;
SAAS 11; SATA 8, 70

McCaughrean, Geraldine 1951- **38**
See also AAYA 23; CA 117; CANR 52; SATA 87

McCloskey, (John) Robert 1914-.............. **7**
See also CA 9-12R; CANR 47; DLB 22;
MAICYA; SATA 2, 39

McClung, Robert M(arshall) 1916- **11**
See also AITN 2; CA 13-16R; CANR 6, 21, 46;
MAICYA; SAAS 15; SATA 2, 68

McCord, David (Thompson Watson) 1897-
1997 .... **9**
See also CA 73-76; 157; CANR 38; DLB 61;
MAICYA; SATA 18; SATA-Obit 96

McCulloch, Sarah
See Ure, Jean

McCully, Emily Arnold **46**
See also Arnold, Emily
See also SAAS 7; SATA 5

McDermott, Gerald 1941-...................... **9**
See also AITN 2; CA 85-88; MAICYA; SATA
16, 74

McFadden, Kevin Christopher 1961(?)- .. **29**
See also AAYA 13; CA 136; CANR 66; JRDA;
SATA 68

McGovern (Scheiner), Ann 1930- **50**
See also CA 49-52; CANR 2, 44; MAICYA; SAAS
17; SATA 8, 69, 70

McHargue, Georgess 1941- **2**
See also CA 25-28R; CANR 24; JRDA; SAAS 5;
SATA 4, 77

McIlwraith, Maureen Mollie Hunter
See Hunter, Mollie
See also SATA 2

McKee, David (John) 1935- **38**
See also CA 137; MAICYA; SATA 70

McKinley, (Jennifer Carolyn) Robin
1952- **10**
See also AAYA 4; CA 107; CANR 31, 64; DLB 52;
JRDA; MAICYA; SATA 50, 89; SATA-Brief 32

McKissack, Patricia (L'Ann) C(arwell)
1944-...**23**
See also BW 2; CA 118; CANR 38; JRDA;
MAICYA; SATA 51, 73

McMillan, Bruce 1947- **47**
See also CA 73-76; CANR 13, 35; MAICYA;
SATA 22, 70

McMillan, Naomi
See Grimes, Nikki

Meaker, Marijane (Agnes) 1927-
See Kerr, M. E.
See also CA 107; CANR 37, 63; INT 107; JRDA;
MAICYA; MTCW; SATA 20, 61

Meltzer, Milton 1915-.......................... **13**
See also AAYA 8; CA 13-16R; CANR 38; CLC
26; DLB 61; JRDA; MAICYA; SAAS 1; SATA
1, 50, 80

Merriam, Eve 1916-1992 .... **14**
See also CA 5-8R; 137; CANR 29; DLB 61;
MAICYA; SATA 3, 40, 73

Metcalf, Suzanne
See Baum, L(yman) Frank

Meyer, June
See Jordan, June

Milne, A(lan) A(lexander) 1882-1956 ... **1, 26**
See also CA 104; 133; DAB; DAC; DAM MST;
DLB 10, 77, 100, 160; MAICYA; MTCW;
TCLC 6; YABC 1

Milne, Lorus J. **22**
See also CA 33-36R; CANR 14; SAAS 18; SATA 5

Milne, Margery **22**
See also CA 33-36R; CANR 14; SAAS 18; SATA 5

Minarik, Else Holmelund 1920- **33**
See also CA 73-76; CANR 48; MAICYA; SATA 15

Mohr, Nicholasa 1938- **22**
See also AAYA 8; CA 49-52; CANR 1, 32, 64;
CLC 12; DAM MULT; DLB 145; HLC; HW;
JRDA; SAAS 8; SATA 8, 97

Molin, Charles
See Mayne, William (James Carter)

Monjo, F(erdinand) N(icholas III) 1924-1978 ... **2**
See also CA 81-84; CANR 37; MAICYA; SATA 16

Montgomery, L(ucy) M(aud) 1874-1942 .... **8**
See also AAYA 12; CA 108; 137; DAC; DAM
MST; DLB 92; DLBD 14; JRDA; MAICYA;
TCLC 51; YABC 1

Moore, Lilian 1909-........................... **15**
See also CA 103; CANR 38; MAICYA; SATA 52

Moser, Barry 1940- **49**
See also MAICYA; SAAS 15; SATA 56, 79

Mowat, Farley (McGill) 1921- **20**
See also AAYA 1; CA 1-4R; CANR 4, 24, 42,
68; CLC 26; DAC; DAM MST; DLB 68; INT
CANAR-24; JRDA; MAICYA; MTCW; SATA
3, 55

Mude, O.
See Gorey, Edward (St. John)

Author Index

Author Index

CUMULATIVE INDEX TO NATIONALITIES

Nationality Index

CUMULATIVE INDEX TO TITLES

Title Index

Title Index

Title Index

Title Index

Title Index

Title Index

Title Index

Striding Slippers (Ginsburg) **45**:12
Strike! (Corcoran) **50**:31
A String in the Harp (Bond) **11**:26
A String of Chances (Naylor) **17**:57
Strings: A Gathering of Family Poems (Janeczko) **47**:102
Stripe: The Story of a Chipmunk (McClung) **11**:179
A Striving after Wind (St. John) **46**:103
The Strongest One of All: A Caucasian Folktale (Ginsburg) **45**:11
The Stronghold (Hunter) **25**:84
Stuart Little (White) **1**:195
Studenplan: Roman (Noestlinger) **12**:187
The Stupids Die (Marshall) **21**:175
The Stupids Have a Ball (Marshall) **21**:172
The Stupids Step Out (Marshall) **21**:170
The Submarine Bird (Scott) **20**:198
The Submarine Pitch (Christopher) **33**:51
Such Nice Kids (Bunting) **28**:64
A Sudden Puff of Glittering Smoke (Fine) **25**:24
A Sudden Silence (Bunting) **28**:62
A Sudden Swirl of Icy Wind (Fine) **25**:25
Suds: A New Daytime Drama (Gaberman) **33**:10
The Sugar Disease: Diabetes (Silverstein and Silverstein) **25**:218
Sugar Ray Leonard (Haskins) **39**:41
Sugaring Time (Lasky) **11**:117
Suicide: The Hidden Epidemic (Hyde) **23**:164
Sukey and the Mermaid (San Souci) **43**:186
The Sultan's Perfect Tree (Yolen) **4**:263
Sumi and the Goat and the Tokyo Express (Uchida) **6**:256
Sumi's Prize (Uchida) **6**:253
Sumi's Special Happening (Uchida) **6**:254
The Summer after the Funeral (Gardam) **12**:166
A Summer at Sea (Allan) **43**:13
The Summer Birds (Farmer) **8**:76
The Summer Book (Jansson) **2**:95
Summer Fun (Haywood) **22**:105
Summer Girls, Love Boys, and Other Short Stories (Mazer) **23**:228
Summer Ice: Life Along the Antarctic Peninsula (McMillan) **47**:188
The Summer In Between (Spence) **26**:191
A Summer in Brittany (Estoril) **43**:8
A Summer in Provence (Pilgrim) **43**:10
A Summer in the South (Marshall) **21**:172
Summer Is for Growing (Clark) **16**:82
A Summer Life (Soto) **38**:192
The Summer Night (Zolotow) **2**:237
The Summer Noisy Book (Brown) **10**:60
Summer of Decision (Allan) **43**:6
Summer of Fear (Duncan) **29**:70
Summer of Little Rain (Fisher) **49**:36
The Summer of My German Soldier (Greene) **2**:86
The Summer of the Falcon (George) **1**:93
The Summer of the Swans (Byars) **1**:37
The Summer People (Townsend) **2**:174
Summer Rules (Lipsyte) **23**:208
Summer Story (Barklem) **31**:2
Summer Switch (Rodgers) **20**:191
A Summer to Die (Lowry) **6**:192
The Summer with Spike (Willard) **2**:223
The Summerboy (Lipsyte) **23**:209
The Summer-House Loon (Fine) **25**:17
Summers of the Wild Rose (Harris) **30**:124
The Sun (Zim) **2**:231
The Sun and Its Family (Adler) **27**:9
Sun and Moon (Pfister) **42**:134
The Sun, Dancing: Christian Verse (Causley) **30**:41

Sun Dogs and Shooting Stars: A Skywatcher's Calendar (Branley) **13**:45
Sun Flight (McDermott) **9**:118
Sun God, Moon Witch (Katz) **45**:32
The Sun He Dies: A Novel about the End of the Aztec World (Highwater) **17**:29
Sun Horse, Moon Horse (Sutcliff) **37**:167
The Sun Looks Down (Schlein) **41**:177
The Sun: Our Nearest Star (Branley) **13**:30
The Sun: Star Number One (Branley) **13**:31
The Sun, the Wind, the Sea and the Rain (Schlein) **41**:183
Sun Up (Tresselt) **30**:203
Sun Up, Sun Down (Gibbons) **8**:97
Sunburn (Stine) **37**:122
Sunday Morning (Viorst) **3**:209
The Sunday Outing (Pinkney) **43**:172
The Sun-Egg (Beskow) **17**:18
The Sun's Asleep Behind the Hill (Ginsburg) **45**:16
Sunshine (Bemelmans) **6**:68
Sunshine (Klein) **19**:88
Sunshine (Ormerod) **20**:174
Sunshine Makes the Seasons (Branley) **13**:40
The Sunshine Years (Klein) **19**:89
Super People: Who Will They Be? (Bendick) **5**:50
Super, Super, Superwords (McMillan) **47**:172
Superbowl Upset (Gaberman) **33**:17
Supercharged Infield (Christopher) **33**:57
Supercomputers (Carter) **22**;18
Superfudge (Blume) **15**:77
Supergirl (Mazer) **23**:230
Superhare (Heine) **18**:146
The Supermarket Mystery (Scarry) **41**:164
Supermouse (Ure) **34**:175
The Supernatural: From ESP to UFOs (Berger) **32**:18
Superpuppy: How to Choose, Raise, and Train the Best Possible Dog for You (Pinkwater) **4**:167
Supersuits (Cobb) **2**:67
Suppose You Met a Witch (Serraillier) **2**:142
The Supreme, Superb, Exalted and Delightful, One and Only Magic Building (Kotzwinkle) **6**:182
Surprise for Davy (Lenski) **26**:113
The Surprise Mouse (Mattingley) **24**:124
The Surprise Party (Hutchins) **20**:144
The Surprise Picnic (Goodall) **25**:48
Surprises: An I Can Read Book of Poems (Hopkins) **44**:93
Surrender (White) **3**:222
Surrogate Sister (Bunting) **28**:58
Survival Camp! (Bunting) **28**:47
The Survivor (White) **3**:223
The Survivors (Hunter) **3**:101
The Survivors: Enduring Animals of North America (Scott) **20**:194
Susan (Smucker) **10**:189
Susanna B. and William C. (Field) **21**:78
Suzuki Goodbye (McBratney) **44**:130
Swallowdale (Ransome) **8**:174
Swallows and Amazons (Ransome) **8**:171
The Swallow's Song (St. John) **46**:106
Swampy Alligator (Gantos) **18**:142
Swan Sky (Tejima) **20**:205
Swans (Scott) **20**:201
Sweeney's Ghost (Fisher) **18**:125
Sweet Baby Coming (Greenfield) **38**:96
Sweet Bells Jangled out of Tune (Brancato) **32**:73
Sweet Dreams, Spot (Hill) **13**:95
Sweet Friday Island (Taylor) **30**:193
Sweet Illusions (Myers) **16**:143
The Sweet Patootie Doll (Calhoun) **42**:5
Sweet Pea: A Black Girl Growing Up in the Rural South (Krementz) **5**:150

Sweet Whispers, Brother Rush (Hamilton) **11**:84
Sweetgrass (Hudson) **40**:94
Sweetwater (Yep) **3**:238
The Swift Deer (McClung) **11**:184
A Swiftly Tilting Planet (L'Engle) **14**:150
Swimathon! (Cross) **28**:91
Swimming with Sea Lions and Other Adventures in the Galapagos Islands (McGovern) **50**:126
Swimmy (Lionni) **7**:129
The Swineherd (Zwerger) **46**:190
The Swing in the Summerhouse (Langton) **33**:109
Swings and Roundabouts (Ure) **34**:181
Swiss Holiday (Allan) **43**:5
Switch On, Switch Off (Berger) **32**:41
Switcharound (Lowry) **46**:32
The Switherby Pilgrims (Spence) **26**:193
The Swoose (King-Smith) **40**:168
The Sword and the Circle: King Arthur and the Knights of the Round Table (Sutcliff) **37**:173
The Sword and the Scythe (Williams) **8**:221
Sword at Sunset (Sutcliff) **37**:156
The Sword is Drawn (Norton) **50**:132
The Sword of Esau (Southall) **2**:156
The Sword of King Arthur (Williams) **8**:229
The Sword of the Spirits (Christopher) **2**:42
Sword of the Wilderness (Coatsworth) **2**:62
Swords from the North (Treece) **2**:189
Sylvester and the Magic Pebble (Steig) **2**:161
The Sylvia Game (Alcock) **26**:3
Sylvie and Bruno (Carroll) **2**:36
Symbiosis: A Book of Unusual Friendships (Aruego) **5**:28
Symbol Art: Thirteen Squares, Circles, Triangles from Around the World (Fisher) **18**:136
Symbols: A Silent Language (Adkins) **7**:24
Tabi No Ehon (Anno) **14**:33
Tabi No Ehon II (Anno) **14**:37
Tabi No Ehon III (Anno) **14**:39
Tabi No Ehon IV (Anno) **14**:41
The Table, the Donkey, and the Stick: Adapted from a Retelling by the Brothers Grimm (Galdone) **16**:102
Tackle without a Team (Christopher) **33**:60
Taffy and Melissa Molasses (Haywood) **22**:100
The Tail of the Trinosaur (Causley) **30**:35
The Tailor and the Giant (Kruss) **9**:88
The Tailor of Gloucester (Potter) **1**:153
Takao and Grandfather's Sword (Uchida) **6**:252
Take a Look at Snakes (Betsy and Giulio Maestro) **45**:86
Take a Number (Bendick) **5**:39
Take Another Look (Hoban) **13**:105
Take Joy! The Tasha Tudor Christmas Book (Tudor) **13**:198
Take Me Out to the Ballgame (Kovalski) **34**:119
Take My Word For It (Marsden) **34**:150
Take Sky: More Rhymes of the Never Was and Always Is (McCord) **9**:99
Take This Hammer (Epstein and Epstein) **26**:62
Take Two and...Rolling! (Pfeffer) **11**:205
Take Wing (Little) **4**:148
The Take-along Dog (McCully) **46**:64
Takedown (Christopher) **33**:61
Taking a Stand Against Racism and Racial Discrimination (McKissack) **23**:242
Taking Care of Carruthers (Marshall) **21**:176
Taking Care of Terrific (Lowry) **6**:197
The Taking of Mariasburg (Thompson) **24**:231
Taking Root: Jewish Immigrants in America (Meltzer) **13**:138
Taking Sides (Klein) **2**:100
Taking Sides (Soto) **38**:194
Taking Terri Mueller (Mazer) **23**:227

Title Index

Title Index

Title Index

Title Index

ISBN 0-7876-2078-5

9 780787 620783

90000